# MACROECONOMICS

# MACROECONOMICS

## THE MEASUREMENT, ANALYSIS, AND CONTROL
## OF AGGREGATE ECONOMIC ACTIVITY

### FIFTH EDITION

**THOMAS F. DERNBURG**
American University

**DUNCAN M. McDOUGALL**
Queen's University, Canada
and University of Kansas

McGRAW-HILL BOOK COMPANY
New York   St. Louis   San Francisco   Auckland
Düsseldorf   Johannesburg   Kuala Lumpur   London
Mexico   Montreal   New Delhi   Panama   Paris
São Paulo   Singapore   Sydney   Tokyo   Toronto

# MACROECONOMICS

## The Measurement, Analysis, and Control of Aggregate Economic Activity

234567890   VHVH   79876

This book was set in Optima by Progressive Typographers.
The editors were J. S. Dietrich and Michael Weber;
the designer was Nicholas Krenitsky;
the production supervisor was Leroy A. Young.
The drawings were done by J & R Services, Inc.
Von Hoffmann Press, Inc., was printer and binder.

**Library of Congress Cataloging in Publication Data**

Dernburg, Thomas Frederick.

    Macroeconomics: the measurement, analysis, and
control of aggregate economic activity.

    1. National income—Accounting.  2. Macroeconom-
ics.  I. McDougall, Duncan M., joint author.
II. Title.
HB601.D45 1976      339.2      75-23242
ISBN 0-07-016526-2

# CONTENTS

# PREFACE

A decade ago, just prior to the escalation of the war in Vietnam, some of our more optimistic colleagues were asking us what we were planning to do now that obsolescence had overtaken us. The new economics had triumphed; the macroeconomic problem had been solved; and technological unemployment was to be the fate of the macroeconomist.

In view of the indisputable fact that in early 1975 the United States was in the worst recession since the great depression of the 1930s, it is not unreasonable to suggest that the singing of such a requiem was a bit premature if not also somewhat naïve. The fact remains that macroeconomics continues to be one of the most important fields of economics as well as its most challenging, bewildering, and fascinating. The 1974–1975 recession was accompanied by a rate of inflation that, until a few years ago, would have been regarded as intolerable even under boom conditions. The new malady of stagflation, or inflationary recession as it is sometimes called, was not even viewed as conceivable ten years ago, yet it has plagued us much of the time during the first half of the 1970s.

Conditions are vastly different now from what they were in the past, yet in many ways they are much the same, which merely confirms the wisdom of the Frenchman who said that the more things change the more they remain the same. We are, in a sense, back to square one. Aside from the novelty of stagflation and the impact of flexible exchange rates, the main difference between today's economic situation and that of two generations ago is that previously economic misfortune tended to happen automatically, whereas today considerable effort is expended in bringing it about.

Given the conditions of the United States economy in 1975, as well as the chaos that characterizes the economy of the entire planet, it seems self-evident that macroeconomics is an extremely important subject. In this new edition we have attempted to deal with some of the momentous changes that continue to make it so. For example, we have added an entirely new chapter on inflationary recession which takes the view that when unemployment and prices are both going up, something is very likely to be wrong with the mix of policy. Also, we have attempted to call attention to the revolutionary changes that a transition to a flexible exchange rate system has brought about, and we have added an entirely new chapter on international monetary problems.

Beyond a general tidying up and updating of the entire book, other significant changes include elimination of some of the material on national income accounting in Part 1, the restructuring of the chapter on employment and the price level in terms of aggregate demand and aggregate supply functions, and the use of these tools to present a completely revised and updated treatment of inflation.

The basic structure of the book appears, by all accounts, to have been sound and we have therefore not tampered with it. Part 1 introduces the reader to the problems of the measurement of economic activity. Part 2 builds up the basic macrostatic model, beginning in Chapters 4 through 6 to develop the analysis of the market for goods and services, then adding monetary considerations in Chapters 7 through 9, the factor market in Chapter 10, and finally, the foreign sector in Chapter 11. In previous editions this latter chapter contained considerable policy analysis. However, such material was, quite correctly we think, viewed as inappropriate at that stage of the discussion by the majority of the persons who were kind enough to suggest improvements, and it has therefore been reserved, in greatly expanded form, for treatment in a subsequent chapter on international economic policy.

Part 3 takes up a number of dynamic problems: stability of equilibrium, growth, cycles, and inflation. The subject of inflation now serves as a bridge between Parts 3 and 4, the last chapter of Part 3 surveying the traditional materials, with the first chapter of Part 4 moving into the perplexing land of inflationary recession. Part 4, as usual, deals with policy problems.

Over the years this book has benefited from valuable comments from countless persons—students, teachers, friendly critics—so that it is no longer possible to give thanks to individual persons. The contributors know who they are, and we thank them most sincerely for their help.

As usual it is appropriate to say that we have only ourselves to blame for errors, omissions, and other deficiencies.

Thomas F. Dernburg
Duncan M. McDougall

# MACROECONOMICS

# 1

# THE MEASUREMENT OF ECONOMIC ACTIVITY

# INTRODUCTION TO THE MACROECONOMY

## MACROECONOMICS AND THE MACROECONOMIC PROBLEM

Macroeconomics is a subject of the utmost importance. Because it attempts to analyze the causes of unemployment, the causes of inflation, and the causes of sluggish growth of income and employment, and because it attempts to find remedies to cure these diseases, it is a subject that vitally affects the lives and interests of people everywhere.

It would be pleasant if we could report that the macroeconomic problem has been solved, as was thought by some to be the case ten years ago. At that time politicians in the United States were finally persuaded to adopt the teachings of John Maynard Keynes by legislating a tax reduction that, because it stimulated the economy, resulted in the resumption of economic growth and a subsequent return to full employment. However, following that success came an unending series of disasters, many of them caused by misguided government policies. At this moment in early 1975 we find ourselves in the throes of the worst recession the United States has experienced since the great depression of the 1930s and, because the economy has been so twisted out of shape as a result of past blunders, we are simultaneously suffering from a rapid rise in the cost of living. As a result of this combination, we are experiencing a double dilemma in the form of an inflationary recession of a kind that would have been regarded as inconceivable only a few years ago, and of a kind that economists still have very little idea how to deal with.

Malfunctioning of the macroeconomy creates very serious difficulties for members of society. The business executive faced with demands for higher wages to keep up with the cost of living, the retired person trying to live on a fixed income, and the homemaker who struggles to put food on the family table in a period of rising prices need hardly be told that inflation is a serious problem. Similarly, the unemployed worker, the graduating senior who has difficulty finding a job, and the businessperson who finds orders declining and profits shrinking are all too familiar with the evil of recession. Economic ailments affect us individually and collectively. They create psychological as well as material hardship, and they can severely strain the social and political order.

It may seem curious that an understanding of what is perfectly obvious to those suffering the consequences of an economic disease should require elaborate economic analysis. One reason is that personal experience is often a poor guide to generalization. An automobile worker may be laid off because of a recession. But it might also be the case that he has been working on an assembly line which produces large automobiles in the medium price range. Then, along comes a doubling of the price of gasoline so that car buyers want to switch to smaller autos. The misfortune of the worker who gets laid off is not necessarily a sign of general economic decline requiring an overall (macroeconomic) policy change. In this example the market system is giving signals to the auto companies that different kinds of cars should be produced. But if the layoff of auto workers spreads because consumers become uncertain about the future, or because the cost of consumer credit rises to intolerable levels, then a recession, which is a distinctly macroeconomic problem, is at the root of the difficulty.

The first thing we have to do is to find a way of getting an overall picture of the level and rate of change of the nation's economic activity. We want to be able to tell what the resources of the economy are producing and the uses to which this output is being put. This is the function of the national income and product accounts that we shall study in the first part of the book. These accounts will tell us the level of performance of the economy in an aggregate sense and allow us to compare that performance with the past. In addition, we shall need a theoretical superstructure within which to analyze the picture presented by the accounts. The mass of numbers that compose a complete national account would be of use only in a limited measurement sense if there were no theory available through which the record of the past could be used as a basis for predicting the future. The development of such a theory forms the second part of the book. Finally, the combination of the statistical measures and the theoretical structure forms the basis for a discussion of questions of policy making with which the book concludes. It is at this final level that the previous two stages really come together in a way that provides the policy maker with the capability of assisting the economy to operate at the level providing the maximum welfare for its citizens.

There are two basic categories of economics: microeconomics and macroeconomics. Formally, they are distinguished from each other by degree of aggregation. However, there is more to the distinction than this. As the examples above have illustrated, what is valid in a specific instance may not be true for the sum total. If we could simply analyze the operation of a single business firm and then assume that the economy as a whole were really only one big firm, the study of microeconomics (the study of single economic units such as the household or the firm) would be sufficient. But macroeconomics (the study of the operation of the whole economy) is set apart as a separate discipline with its own rules because aggregate economic behavior does not correspond to the summation of individual activities. For example, a firm may find that when wages fall, the resulting reduction in costs would make it profitable to expand its production and therefore hire more workers. However, for the economy as a whole a widespread reduction in wages may cause consumers to conserve their income by buying less, and this would then result in a reduction in production for at least some firms. Similarly, when one individual borrows from another, he or she receives money which represents a claim on goods and services and which must be paid back at some future time by giving up a claim on resources. But the community as a whole cannot borrow resources from itself in one year for repayment at some future time. Resources and labor effort that are used to produce goods and services cannot be transferred through time. One needs therefore to maintain a careful distinction between the debt of individuals and the public debt of society as a whole.

As a final example of the danger of reasoning from the specific to the general, consider the effect of an increase in the desire of individuals to save a larger fraction of their income. If single individuals wish to increase their savings, they need merely exercise the proper degree of self-control. But if all individuals in the economy make such an effort, the reduction in the total purchases of goods and services may lead to such a shrinkage in total income that total saving may decline even though the fraction of income saved may have increased.

Many similar examples could be given. Most of these apparently paradoxical cases stem from the fact that what is true for an individual firm or consumer is true only if other things remain equal. This *ceteris paribus* assumption is legitimate only in microeconomics where the individual decision-making unit being examined is so small that its actions can be assumed not to affect other units. But in macroeconomics, which is concerned with the study of aggregate units such as all consumers and all business firms, this *ceteris paribus* assumption must be dropped. It is this, more than anything else, that sets macroeconomics apart as a wholly separate field. It is, moreover, the understandable tendency to confuse the whole with the part that has given rise to some of the most fundamental errors of macroeconomic theory and policy.

By way of conclusion, it is perhaps well to point out that the neat distinction between the two main branches of economics is not always as easy to maintain as it may first appear. For example, consider the many roles played in the economy by the government sector. In some circumstances the government is expected to behave as a profit-maximizing business firm. At other times it is asked to forget narrow economic goals and to express the social conscience of the community as a whole. When government allocates resources for slum clearance and the provision of subsidized housing for low-income families, it obviously is not acting as a profit-maximizing business firm. Or when it cuts taxes to restore full employment, it acts in the interest of the total economy, but it deliberately incurs a deficit in a way that no private industry would ever contemplate.

## 1–2
## THE HISTORICAL RECORD

To become more specific, we now turn to a description of the behavior of the American economy since 1929. We do this within the context of national accounting concepts since it is important for subsequent analysis that we become familiar with these concepts. Although the exact definitions of the statistics are somewhat complex, their essential characteristics are easy enough to describe and grasp.

We begin with the concept of gross national product, or, more familiarly, GNP. GNP is a measure of the market value of the output of final goods and services produced by a nation's economic resources during a specified period of time, usually a year. In this definition, final production means the production of goods and services that are not resold during the accounting period. When a consumer buys a new stove or visits the doctor he or she is purchasing a part of final output. However, when the steel is purchased to produce the stove, the steel itself is not part of final output because its value will appear again when the stove is sold. Anything used as part of the production of something else is termed an intermediate product, and to add its value to GNP as well as the value of the good produced would result in double counting.

The national accountant must classify output into useful subcategories. It would be of little use, for example, simply to list all the final goods produced because the resulting reams of paper could never be read. At the other extreme, a single number representing GNP would hide a great deal of useful information. The problem, then, is to aggregate the data into a limited number of meaningful subtotals. Of the very many possible aggregation schemes, it is now generally agreed that it is most useful to divide final output into that purchased by consumers, by businesses (investment goods), by government, and by foreigners. Because GNP is a measure of goods produced but not resold, it includes goods added to inventory; since such goods are held within the business sector, they are considered to be purchased by business. If goods added to inventory were not included, the GNP would measure current sales rather than production. Also, because of trade between nations, a nation might use more output than it produced if imports exceeded exports. Or if exports exceed imports, the nation would be producing more output than it was using. Thus the GNP, which is a measure of total *national* production, should include an adjusting item called "net exports of goods and services," which is simply the difference between the value of the nation's exports and the value of its imports.

The United States economy produces a tremendous variety of final goods and services during a year. The national income accountant is therefore faced with the need for a common measure to aggregate these diverse goods and services. The most convenient procedure is to assume that value is reflected by market price and to sum up the market values of the things produced. While such a procedure is certainly convenient, it does introduce an obvious difficulty since prices fluctuate from year to year. Because of this, an increase in the value of GNP need not reflect an increase in the volume of physical output; it can, instead, reflect merely an increase in prices. To avoid this difficulty, a measure of "real" GNP and its components is calculated by valuing the output of any given year in terms of the prices that prevailed in a selected base year. The resulting "real" or "constant dollar" GNP then reflects only changes in the physical output of the economy.

What do these real magnitudes look like over a period of time? In Figure 1–1 we have plotted GNP and its major components (personal consumption expenditure, gross private domestic investment, and government purchases of goods and services) valued in terms of the prices of the base year 1958. The net export of goods and services, a relatively tiny component, is omitted. The first thing to notice about GNP is that it grows. During 1929, generally regarded as a full-employment year, GNP was $204 billion. By 1969, again a year of full employment, GNP had grown to $727 billion.[1] The second thing to notice is that this growth does not take place smoothly. Thus GNP declined after 1929, falling to a low of $142 billion in 1933. A slow recovery began in 1934 and continued until 1938 when it was interrupted by what could be called at the time a mild setback. With the coming of the war, GNP jumped precipitously and continued to climb until 1946, when a large reduction in government purchases produced a decline. The decade following the fairly short period of postwar adjustment was marked by relatively even advance. A mild slump developed in 1949 but was soon followed by recovery and, subsequently, by the expansion associated with the Korean war. Another moderate slump occurred in 1954, but the economy recovered with little difficulty. Between 1957 and 1964, however, the economy was beset by a period of continuing unsatisfactory performance. The unemployment rate was high, and while the value of output grew in real terms in each year except 1958, the rate of growth of the economy was so disappointing that the period was one of stagnation and mounting unemployment. It was not until the federal tax reduction of 1964 took effect that the economy again performed satisfactorily. The subsequent behavior of the economy was dominated by the im-

---

[1] The reason for beginning the comparison with the year 1929, the last year before the descent into the great depression, is simply that the official national accounts begin with that year.

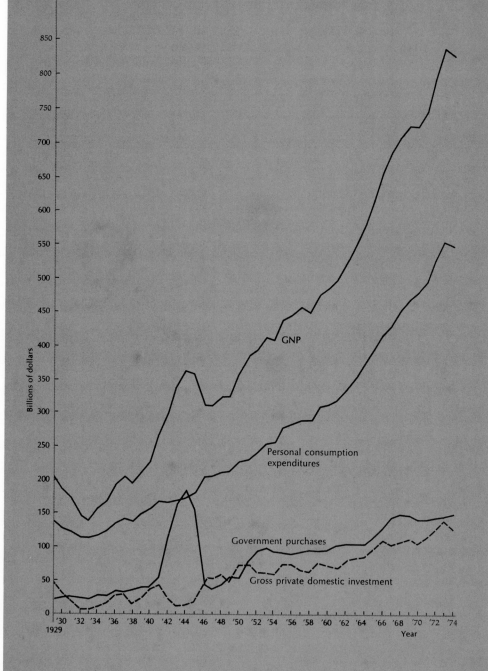

pact of the growing American involvement in Southeast Asia. The result of the attempt to provide the means to fight the war in Vietnam without reducing the flow of goods and services to the domestic economy was an excess of total demand over available output. Thus, inflation returned as a major problem during the last half of the 1960s.

Even with the cessation of direct American involvement in Vietnam, prices continued to rise even through periods of wage and price controls administered from Washington. The persistence of price increases may ultimately be attributed to what can be called an inflationary psychology among the American people. The widespread expectation that prices will rise persuades people to act in ways that increase upward pressure on prices. The expectational psychology was not confined to the United States but became a widespread symptom throughout the whole industrial world. In 1972, just at the time there was a hope that the inflationary spiral could be halted, poor crops in many parts of the world pushed up sharply the prices of internationally traded agricultural commodities, particularly grains. This had its inevitable effect on world food prices. Then, in 1973, oil-exporting countries raised the price of crude oil. This action threw shock waves across the entire world economy, causing sharp price increases in almost all categories of goods and services. Given the uncertainty and the fear of inflation that already existed, the result, instead of being a one-step upward adjustment of prices, added to a continuing spiral of inflation.

Meanwhile, in an attempt to slow the "double digit" inflation, economic policy in the United States became sharply restrictive in 1973. Government expenditure was deliberately held down by executive action, taxes were permitted to rise as rising money wages pushed taxpayers into higher brackets, and the supply of money and credit was severely curtailed by the actions of the Federal Reserve System. The result, for reasons that it is the job of this book to explain, was to curtail the boom of 1972–1973 and to replace it with the very deep and harsh recession of 1974–1975.

In the past, war and preparation for war often affected the economy's performance. Periods of high employment and recovery from recession have often been associated with an increase in federal government expenditure for armaments. Some have concluded from this circumstance that the economy

**FIGURE 1–1**
**Gross national product and the expenditure components, 1929–1974, (1958 prices).**
(*Source:* 1925–1965, U.S. Department of Commerce, *The National Income and Product Accounts for the United States, 1929–1965,* Government Printing Office, Washington, 1966; 1966–1973, U.S. Department of Commerce, *Survey of Current Business,* July 1974, Government Printing Office, Washington, 1974; preliminary 1974, Ibid., January 1975)

is a war economy in the sense that it will operate at full employment only during a war. This belief, which is often associated with Marxist thinking, is viewed as fallacious by most liberal economists. Two points should be made with respect to it. First, the official data are available only for a period that has been dominated by international conflict. Data for earlier periods of international tranquillity give examples of very rapid economic advance in which defense expenditures played no part whatever. Second, the belief that America has a war economy fails to recognize that there are alternative ways of generating the expenditures that are necessary to provide full employment. Prosperity can be generated from spending on armaments and war making, but expenditures can also be raised for schools, hospitals, and slum clearance programs. If it is decided not to do any of these things, it is still possible to generate additional expenditures by reducing taxes and thereby providing households and businesses with the wherewithal to increase their consumption and investment spending, respectively. Peaceful progress toward full employment during the first half of the 1960s proved that the economy could be made to prosper by constructive policies of the kind described above. Indeed, it was the rapid escalation of the war in Vietnam, during and after 1965, that is at the root of our present economic difficulties. War is certainly not a necessary condition of prosperity.

## 1-3
## THE TARGETS OF ECONOMIC ACTIVITY

Thus far we have attempted to familiarize the reader with some of the basic measures of macroeconomics, and we have attempted to describe how these statistical aggregates have behaved over time. A real appreciation of the past cannot, however, be gained only from description. To gauge performance, we must somehow specify some goals, or targets, of economic activity, and we must then assess actual performance in terms of how closely this performance succeeds in achieving our targets. The macroeconomic goals of the economy are generally considered to be full employment, full production, price stability, and rapid growth. Economists are fairly well agreed that the United States economy is operating at a satisfactory level of performance when 4.0 percent of the labor force is unemployed, when the productive facilities of the economy are fully utilized, and when there is reasonable stability of the general price level.

As we have already seen, the economy fell disastrously short of these goals in the decade of the 1930s. During five of the ten years of that decade, more than 20 percent of the civilian labor force was unemployed. The waste of that era was truly monumental. Its repercussions, moreover, have echoed through time. The economy fell so far short of its potential during the 1930s that to talk of carefully defined goals is not very relevant. In other words, when 20 percent of the labor force is unemployed, it is hardly worth worrying whether the target rate of unemployment should be 3.5 or 4.0 percent. Discussion of goals becomes much more appropriate during a period such as 1957 to 1964 when the economy is operating in the region of its goals, but its performance is nonetheless unsatisfactory. Let us, therefore, turn to an examination of the American economy's performance as contrasted with its potential in this more recent context.

In Figure 1–2 we present three measures of the performance of the economy. The chart shows the rate of unemployment of the civilian labor force and the consumer price index. It also shows the path of real GNP and contrasts this with a measure of "potential" GNP as calculated by the Council of Economic Advisers. The difference between potential GNP and actual GNP has been called the "GNP gap." It measures the output that the economy lost because of its failure to achieve a 4 percent rate of unemployment.

Once at full employment, the economy must continue to grow in order to remain at full employment. This situation is caused by labor force growth and increases in "productivity," that is, output per hour of work. The latter occurs because of improvements in the skill and training of the labor force, because of improved management and technology, and because of the enlarged quantity and higher quality of the stock of capital. Estimates of productivity growth suggest that output per hour of work tends to grow at a rate of about 2.5 percent a year. Between 1960 and 1970 the labor force grew at a rate of about 1.75 percent a year; however, because of shorter hours and longer vacations, average hours worked per year have declined about 0.25 percent. Adding all these growth rates together, we can easily see that potential output tends to grow at a rate of about 4.0 percent a year.[1]

The statistics on the labor force and unemployment are obtained by the Census Bureau through a monthly sample survey of approximately 47,000 households. Persons are asked if they were employed during the census week. If they answer in the affirmative, they are automatically recorded as employed and in the labor force. If the answer is negative, an attempt is made to ascertain if they were actively seeking work. Only if they were actively looking for work are they classed as unemployed and as members of the labor force. If they are not active job seekers, it is assumed that they are not labor force participants and that their unemployment is voluntary and therefore not to be counted. It is clear from the chart that even periods of high-level prosperity are characterized by the presence of some unemployment. Economists attribute some of this to the circumstance that at any point in time there are workers in transit between jobs, that information as to job opportunities is imperfect, and that labor mobility is sluggish. Such factors are said to be responsible for "frictional" unemployment.

Economists seem to be agreed that it would be virtually impossible, except at the cost of severe inflation, to lower the unemployment rate below 3 percent in peacetime. However, as recent experience shows, even 3 percent may be too ambitious a target. When unemployment gets very low, labor scarcities

---

[1] Although it is difficult to discern in Figure 1–2, it should be noted that the line of potential output is not a straight line. Growth of potential output is estimated at 3.5 percent from mid-1955 to the end of 1962. From there to the end of 1965 it was raised to 3.75 percent, and for 1966 it was raised to 4 percent. These different rates of growth of potential GNP primarily reflect differences in the rate of labor force growth that characterized the periods.

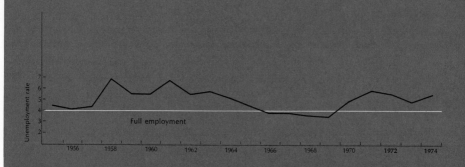

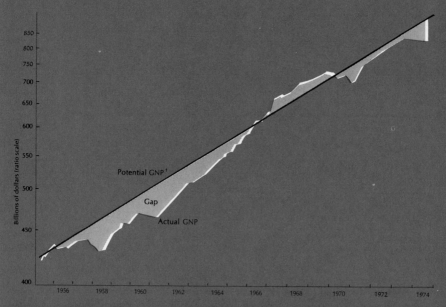

Potential GNP[1]

Gap

Actual GNP

[1]Trend line of 3½ percent through middle of 1955 to 1962 iv, 3¾ percent from
1962 iv to 1965 iv, and 4 percent from 1965 iv to 1973 iv.

develop, and wages therefore tend to rise more rapidly. The result, then, is that costs increase and prices rise. Unemployment averaged 3.6 percent in 1968 and 3.5 percent in 1969. Unhappily, it was not possible to combine this good performance with price stability. The consumer price index, for example, rose 4.2 percent and 5.4 percent in the two years, respectively. In addition it has been noted that the composition of the labor force has gradually shifted, increasing the relative proportion of women and teenagers who have higher average unemployment rates, and reducing the relative size of the central-aged male group that has lower average unemployment rates. Some infer from this that we will henceforth have to accept 4.5 percent rather than 4.0 percent unemployment as a realistic noninflationary target.

A further note on the concept of potential output is in order. We have seen that potential output grows as the labor force, the stock of capital, and the productivity of capital and labor expand through time. But the line of potential output should not be interpreted as a line of maximum possible growth. It represents only what is feasible at any time with the existing stock of resources. During periods when the economy experiences high rates of unemployment, investment will be depressed and the stock of productive capacity will therefore not grow as rapidly as would otherwise have been the case. Idleness due to unemployment, moreover, tends to reduce the quality and therefore the productivity of the labor force. It is possible, finally, that some of the workers who are discouraged and withdraw from the labor force during periods of high unemployment never return, and that the resources that industry normally devotes to worker training are reduced. The measure of potential output treats such bygones as bygones, and it therefore does not represent the path of output that the economy could have achieved had full employment been maintained continuously.

The third measure presented in Figure 1-2 is the annual percentage change in the consumer price index, CPI. The CPI is an index number that attempts to measure the extent to which prices paid by typical city wage earners and clerical workers for a typical bundle of commodities bought by such workers have changed in comparison with some arbitrary base period. Thus, it is a very special index that is not necessarily representative of overall price changes in the economy.[1] Nevertheless, the CPI is the index that is most

---

[1] A better measure of the overall price level is the so-called implicit price deflator for GNP published by the Department of Commerce.

**FIGURE 1-2**
**Measures of macroeconomic performance**
(*Source:* Council of Economic Advisers, *Annual Report,* 1974, Government Printing Office, Washington, 1974, and earlier *Reports;* preliminary 1974 data from *Survey of Current Business*)

commonly referred to in discussions°of price stability, and it is for this reason that we refer to it here.

Price stability is the most difficult of all the targets to define, and we will have much more to say about the matter later. For the moment it is sufficient to note a fact of life. As Figure 1–2 makes clear, consumer prices have not fallen in a single year covered in the chart. Indeed, consumer prices tend to continue rising even during years of high unemployment when total demand in the economy could by no stretch of the imagination be regarded as excessive. When output and employment fall, one would expect an accompanying fall in prices, and indeed, this did occur during the 1930s. However, during the recession of 1958 real GNP fell, but the CPI continued to rise. Similarly, although the unemployment rate jumped from 3.8 percent in October 1969 to 5.6 percent a year later, no discernible headway was made against inflation during this period.

Without, for the moment, delving into the reason why prices keep rising even during periods of recession, it is clear that if we were to insist on absolute price stability, we would have to pursue such restrictive policies that we would fall far short of our other goals of full employment and full production. Clearly, we must relax our goal and in some periods be prepared to tolerate a certain degree of creeping inflation. Hopefully, this inflation would not exceed 3 percent a year in a smoothly growing, full-employment economy. Certainly the 6.2 and 11.0 percent rates that characterized the economy in 1973 and 1974, respectively, are cause for serious alarm.

## 1–4
## A MACROECONOMIC MODEL

We have seen that the American economy has not always been successful in achieving its targets. It is the purpose of macroeconomic analysis to diagnose the reason for such failure and to point the way toward better performance in the future. An understanding of the way the economy operates cannot be attained solely by an examination of the past statistical record. What is also needed is a systematic guide that permits the complexities of the real world to be understood and interpreted. This systematic guide is macroeconomic theory. The first step in constructing such theory is the development of a model which, because it is a simplifying device, paves the way to clear thinking about macroeconomic problems.

An economic model is a simplification of reality. It deliberately submerges detail so as to highlight those processes and relationships that are of greatest importance for the problem at hand. As we shall see subsequently, macroeconomists frequently attempt to describe the complicated behavior of the economy by means of a few simple relationships that show how the major aggregate variables are related to each other. These models may consist of mathematical equations; they may be a set of diagrams; or they may take the form of a schema such as the flow chart of the computer programmer or the electrical engineer.

The example of a road map is an instructive way to illustrate the purpose of a model. If a person wishes to drive from Columbus, Ohio, to Kansas City, Missouri, it is not necessary for him or her to know all the details of the terrain that lies between or all the available alternative routes. In fact, all that one needs to know is that by following Interstate Highway 70 west from Columbus one will arrive at the destination. This simple bit of information constitutes the model that is sufficient for the purpose. It provides a minimum of detail while incorporating all the needed information. Presumably, the traveler would not complain about the lack of detail or realism of the model since added realism would contribute nothing to the solution of the problem at hand. Nevertheless, macroeconomic models are often criticized for lack of realism. However, as the road map example makes clear, such criticism merely discloses that the critic fails to understand the purpose of a model. The road map that gets the traveler from Columbus to Kansas City with a minimum of fuss can be judged to be a good map. The economic model that describes those aspects of the economy that we want to consider, and that does so with a minimum of distractions, is a good model.

Let us begin with a very simple hypothetical economy in which there are only two kinds of agents: producers and consumers. Producers are those who produce output for sale, and we shall lump them all into one sector known as the "business sector." The other sector consists of the consumers who purchase the output of business. We shall call this the "household sector." In this model the household sector is assumed to own all the factors of production (land, labor, and capital), and household income is derived from the sale of the services of these factors to the business sector.

The present model is represented pictorially in Figure 1–3. As shown in the figure, it is assumed that the household sector earns $10,000 from the sale of factor services to business, and that business uses these services to produce output worth the same $10,000. We assume next that consumers use their entire income to buy the output of the business sector. As long as the income payments by business for factor services are returned to business to purchase output, the circular flow of income and product tends to perpetuate itself. Production and sales are equal—output equals demand—and there will be a tendency to continue operating at this same level. It is such a situation that we describe as "macroeconomic equilibrium."

The macroeconomy is not a closed system as depicted above. It resembles, rather, a hydraulic system in which the water level tends to fall because there are several sources of drainage. Besides, the tub is characterized by several spigots that provide a fresh inflow, or "injection," to offset the "leakages." One leakage results because households in the aggregate tend to save a fraction of their income. Therefore, imagine that households wish to save $1,000 out of their income of $10,000; as a consequence, consumption spending equals $9,000. But if business produces $10,000 worth of goods, there would be unsold output, and unwanted inventories would accumulate; since business would not continue to produce $10,000 worth of output indefinitely

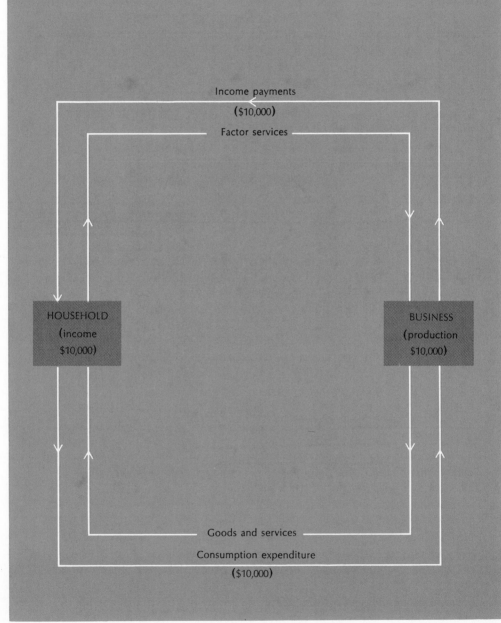

Income payments
($10,000)

Factor services

HOUSEHOLD
(income
$10,000)

BUSINESS
(production
$10,000)

Goods and services

Consumption expenditure
($10,000)

when all that can be sold is $9,000, production would be cut back, and this would, in turn, reduce the flow of income to households. Clearly, a leakage from the income stream due to saving tends to reduce production and income.

All is not lost, however. If business itself wishes to buy the leftover output of $1,000, either because it wishes to add to its stock of productive facilities or to its inventories, total spending can remain equal to output despite the saving leakage. Indeed, it is the willingness of households to save that releases resources for capital expansion. Thus, if intended or desired business investment equals saving, equilibrium will be maintained at the original level of output and income. This situation is illustrated in Figure 1–4, where the household sector is shown saving $1,000 and spending $9,000 for consumption, and where the business sector is shown purchasing $1,000 for its own use. The total demand for output is equal to output produced, and the circular flow remains in equilibrium.

The foregoing discussion suggests that macroeconomic equilibrium requires that the leakage into saving be balanced by an equivalent injection in the form of intended investment. Figure 1–4 shows a capital market between the saving and investment flows. In older (often called "classical") economic theory it was assumed that the capital market acted in such a way that saving would automatically be matched by investment. Modern macroeconomic theory stresses the fact that the decisions to save and invest are made by different people and for quite different reasons. Moreover, modern theory suggests that there is no automatic capital market mechanism that necessarily makes saving and investment equal. This suggests that there is room for an outside force that will influence the market in such a way as to equate saving and investment at a satisfactory level of output and income. This outside force is monetary policy which, accordingly, is included in our diagram to indicate that money and credit policies can help to stimulate or retard investment spending. A sizable portion of this book is devoted to discussing how monetary policy works.

We can now take another important step by adding a government sector to our model. Here again we simplify the analysis by combining all the many different kinds and levels of government into one big sector which we will assume collects taxes from the household sector and purchases some part of the output of business. If the government collects $1,000 of the household sector's income in the form of taxes, this will tend to reduce both household consumption and saving. Since consumption will fall, business sales and income will shrink. However, here again there is a new source of injection available to offset the tax leakage. If the government makes purchases from the business sector equal to the amount by which its taxes reduce consump-

**FIGURE 1–3**
The circular flow of income
and expenditure

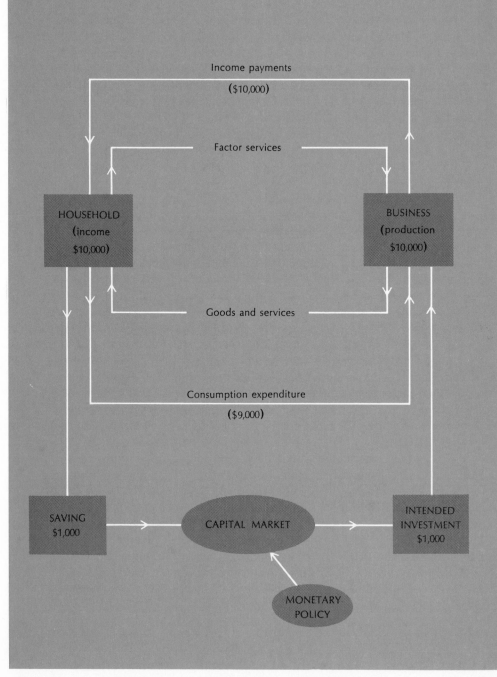

tion, total business sales will again equal production, and the circular flow will remain in equilibrium. Such a situation is illustrated in Figure 1–5. Here total output of $10,000 results in income before taxes of $10,000. The government now takes $1,000 in taxes from the household sector so that household income after taxes (disposable income) is $9,000. We assume that this fall in disposable income causes households to reduce consumption by $900 and saving by $100. Consequently, the new level of saving is $900, and the level of consumption is $8,100. If intended investment remains the same as before, total consumer and investment demand will be $9,100, and therefore the government must purchase $900 worth of goods and services in order to bring total demand back to $10,000.

Now notice that we have not made government purchases equal to taxes, that saving no longer equals intended investment, and that macroeconomic equilibrium obtains nevertheless. The only thing that is important is that total expenditure equals total output, and this is equivalent to saying that total leakages must equal total injections. In the present example, taxes and saving have reduced consumption to $8,100. What is needed is some source of demand for the remaining $1,900 of output. This could be in the form of intended investment, it could be in the form of government purchases, or it could be any combination of the two that adds up to $1,900. If investment falls short of saving, government should compensate by spending more than it taxes. Or if investment is buoyant and tends to exceed saving, aggregate demand will exceed output unless government adjusts its expenditure and revenue policies in such a way as to offset discrepancies between saving and investment. In either case, we say that it is engaged in "compensatory fiscal policy."

Our pictorial representation of the economy can be expanded still further by including foreign trade in the model. When the household sector purchases goods abroad and imports them into the economy, the expenditure represents a leakage from the circular flow. Offsetting this leakage are foreigners who buy domestic goods (exports) and produce an injection into the domestic circular flow. If these flows were added to our diagram, we would show imports as leakages and exports as injections. These flows would be shown passing through a sector called the "balance of payments," which could be influenced by foreign trade policies of various kinds. The equilibrium condition would still be that total leakages must equal total injections. However, now leakages would consist of imports in addition to saving and taxes, and injections would consist of exports in addition to investment and government purchases.

As a transitional step to subsequent work, it is now appropriate to spend a moment to express our model in symbolic form. Let us begin by denoting the

**FIGURE 1–4**
The circular flow including saving
and investment

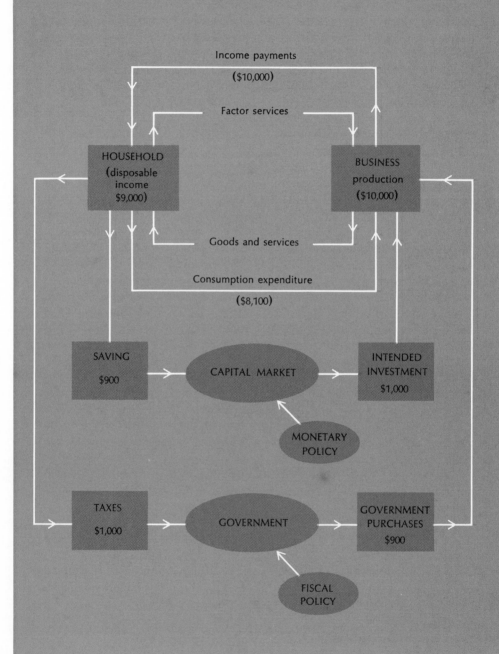

Income payments
($10,000)

Factor services

HOUSEHOLD
(disposable
income
$9,000)

BUSINESS
production
($10,000)

Goods and services

Consumption expenditure
($8,100)

SAVING
$900

CAPITAL MARKET

INTENDED
INVESTMENT
$1,000

MONETARY
POLICY

TAXES
$1,000

GOVERNMENT

GOVERNMENT
PURCHASES
$900

FISCAL
POLICY

production of goods and services as $Y$, consumption expenditure including imports as $C$, intended investment as $I$, government purchases as $G$, exports as $X$, and imports as $Z$. The supply of output available to the economy consists of its domestic production $Y$ plus the level of imports $Z$. In equilibrium this supply must exactly equal the sum of the demands of the household, business, government, and foreign sectors. Accordingly, we can write the equilibrium condition as

$$Z + Y = C + I + G + X$$

or on rearranging terms

$$Y = C + I + G + (X - Z) \tag{1-1}$$

where the term $(X - Z)$ represents the net export of goods and services which we sometimes refer to as the "trade balance."

Next denote saving as $S$, taxes as $T$, and disposable income of the household sector as $Y_d$. Since income receipts are divided between the household and the government sector we may write

$$Y = Y_d + T$$

but since disposable income can be either spent on consumption or saved, we obtain

$$Y = C + S + T \tag{1-2}$$

Finally, when we equate Eqs. (1–1) and (1–2), we observe that $C$ can be netted from both sides, so that we then obtain the condition

$$I + G + X = S + T + Z$$

according to which injections must equal leakages under conditions of macroeconomic equilibrium.

Despite its crudeness and simplicity, the present model helps us to understand the behavior of the "real world" economy. We can well imagine how the large increase in government purchases after 1940 led to dramatic increases in GNP. And we can also begin to appreciate how excessive or deficient demand might cause the economy to fall short of the targets we discussed previously, and how policy might help to move the economy toward these targets.

## 1-5
## A PREVIEW

One of the things we did in this chapter was to present a picture of the aggregate behavior of the American economy since 1929 by using a simpli-

**FIGURE 1-5**

The circular flow including government
purchases and taxes

fied statistical framework. We now turn to a more detailed and rigorous examination of this framework, looking closely at the assumption used by the national income record keeper in deriving the estimates upon which so many important policy decisions are made. Great masses of data are published by the United States government. Unfortunately, these data can be badly misused if the user does not know how to interpret the figures properly. A discussion of the nature of national income and product data and how the estimates are arrived at takes up the remainder of Part 1.

In Part 2 we will examine in much greater detail the model of the economy introduced in skeleton form in this chapter. We will attempt to convert the model from an impressionistic flow chart into a rigorous predictive model that will permit us to analyze how the equilibrium levels of income and employment are determined and how these levels can be influenced by public policy.

In Part 3 we shall turn our attention to so-called dynamic problems, including the analysis of the growth process, the problem of inflation, and the cause of the business cycle. Part 4, finally, completes the book. Here we will try to pull together our accumulated knowledge and look at the practical problems of policy making.

# INTRODUCTION TO THE NATIONAL ACCOUNTS

## INTRODUCTION

As we saw in the previous chapter, the aggregate economic system can be represented by a system of flows of income and product that circulate among a limited number of sectors. The national income and product accounts that we shall now examine represent the accounting framework that measures the values of these various flows.

When we divided the economy into the four sectors, personal, business, government, and foreign, we did so to simplify the complexity of the real world. Aggregating all consumers into a single sector, even though we know that they differ wildly in tastes, attitudes, and economic circumstances, permits us to build a model with comprehensible components. For the model to be useful, we also have to be able to assume that, in the aggregate, consumers can be expected to behave in a predictable way with respect to changing economic events. For example, we shall soon introduce the fundamental hypothesis that the personal sector's consumption spending is determined primarily by its disposable income. Happily the national income accounting framework of the United States has been so designed that the categories lend themselves to treatment as variables that can be functionally and statistically related in a manner that permits analysis of cause and effect to be performed.

The process of aggregation permits simplification. It also, however, involves a cost in terms of detailed information that may be lost from view. When we lump all income together, we no longer have information on the way income is distributed. Similarly, when we aggregate all business firms into a single sector, we lose information about the distribution by size of firms within industries. Any accounting framework necessarily risks loss of information as the price for presenting a simple and comprehensive picture. This is true whether the accounts are the summary statement of an individual firm or whether they are the summary statements for the economy as a whole. Like the circular flow model of the preceding chapter, what we ask of the accounts is that they provide the information needed to fill the boxes of our theoretical model.

The GNP accounts for the economy are very similar to the kinds of business accounting used by firms to measure their performance over an arbitrarily defined accounting period. Business firms draw up accounts of their operation because they need to know how their receipts stack up against the various items of cost that were incurred in generating the goods and services they produce. It is useful, in studying the national accounts, to begin with the example of an individual firm.

## 2-2
## AN ACCOUNTING STATEMENT FOR A HYPOTHETICAL FIRM

A business firm that is interested in measuring its progress during a year and in establishing a basis for controlling costs will ask an accountant to present a statement summarizing the multitude of daily transactions into a comprehensive summary statement. To illustrate such a statement we shall consider a hypothetical firm that, with characteristic imagination, we shall call the X Corporation. The statement is shown in Table 2–1.

The right side of the statement for the X Corporation shows the sources of the cash receipts of the firm during the year plus any additions made to its stock of inventory. The corporation is assumed to have received a total of $2 million from its sales and at the same time to have increased the value of its stock of inventory by $100,000. Consequently, the total value of its current production is $2.1 million. Notice that this firm has made sales primarily to other firms. Only $125,000 of total sales are assumed to be made to non-business customers such as consumers or government.

The left side of Table 2–1 presents an allocation of the costs of production for the corporation and a profit item which is the residual difference between the value of production and the cost of production. The first cost item is purchases from other firms of $820,000. It is important to note that this total will appear on the right side of the accounts of other firms. The next set of items represents the cost to the firm of hiring the services of the factors of production. The corporation paid wages and salaries of $846,000, and it paid $27,000 into the social security fund on behalf of its employees. In addition, the firm paid rent for land and buildings of $12,000, and it made a net

**TABLE 2-1**
Production statement for the X Corporation for the period January 1, 1976 to
December 31, 1976 (thousands of dollars)

| Allocations | | | Receipts | |
|---|---|---|---|---|
| Purchases from other firms | | $  820 | Sales to: | |
| Wages and salaries | | 846 | Company A | $  810 |
| Social security contributions | | 27 | Company B | 240 |
| Rent | | 12 | Company C | 650 |
| Net interest | | 8 | Company D | 175 |
| Depreciation | | 60 | Other sales | 125 |
| Indirect business taxes | | 30 | Inventory increase | 100 |
| Corporate profits before tax | | 297 | | |
|    Corporate profits tax | $155 | | | |
|    Dividends paid | 100 | | | |
|    Undistributed profits | 42 | | | |
| Total charges against | | ——— | | ——— |
|    current production | | $2,100 | Total production | $2,100 |

payment for borrowed capital of $8,000.[1] The next two items represent so-
called nonfactor costs of production. The corporation charged $60,000
against its current receipts as an allowance for the wear, tear, and obsolescence of its capital equipment. Indirect taxes, such as property and excise
taxes, added $30,000 to total cost.

The deduction of these factor and nonfactor costs from the total value of
goods produced leaves a profit residual of $297,000. On this profit the cor-
poration paid corporate income taxes of $155,000, and it paid $100,000
to its shareholders in the form of dividends. This left a residual of $42,000
known as "undistributed profits."

The two sides of the income statement must balance. The right side shows
the total receipts of the corporation; the left side shows the way that these
receipts were allocated among the various items of cost and profit. Profits, the
balancing item, may of course be positive, negative, or zero, depending upon
the relative magnitudes of receipts and expenses.

Although the X Corporation produced goods valued at $2.1 million during
the accounting period, its contribution to the final output of the economy was
considerably less than that. The corporation purchased raw materials and
partly finished goods from other firms, increased the value of these inputs by
further processing, and either sold the resulting product or added to its inventory. The materials purchased from other firms are known as "intermediate
product." The amount by which the corporation increased the value of the
goods and materials received from other firms is shown by the difference
between the total value of production and the cost of materials purchased.

[1] This $8,000 is the net sum of interest paid minus interest received. Many firms are borrowers of
long-term funds. However, at the same time they often seize the opportunity of converting temporarily excessive cash holdings into interest-bearing short-term assets.

This difference is called the "net value added," and in the present example it amounted to $1.18 million ($2.1 − $0.82 million). It is the net value added that is the contribution of the X Corporation to the total national product. To include the whole $2.1 million in national product would involve counting the value of the goods the corporation had purchased from other firms at least a second time in the national total because they would also have been counted when they were originally produced by other firms.

An illustration will help to make this point clear. Take, for example, a loaf of bread purchased by a consumer. Assume that four productive units contributed to making and distributing the bread. Suppose that the value of the grain produced by the farmer was 5 cents; that the miller sold the flour to the baker for 12 cents; that the baker sold the bread to the grocer for 20 cents; finally, that the grocer sold the bread to the consumer for 25 cents. To add together the value of production of each of the four units would give a total value of production of 62 cents. The consumer, however, paid only 25 cents for the loaf of bread, and it is this amount that should be entered as national product. The correct answer of 25 cents is derived from the production statements of each of the separate units by adding together the net value added by each of them. The net value added by the farmer (assuming he purchased no goods or materials from others) is 5 cents. The net value added by the miller is 7 cents; that is, the 12 cents which is the value of production minus the 5 cents worth of grain purchased from the farmer. Similarly, the value added by the baker is 8 cents, and by the grocer it is 5 cents. The sum of all these net-value-added figures is then equal to 25 cents. The 62-cent figure resulted from counting the 5 cents of value added by the farmer four times, the 7 cents of value added by the miller three times, the 8 cents of value added by the baker twice, and the 5 cents added by the grocer once.

As the previous example has attempted to show, the national product is the sum of the value added by firms at all stages of production. The value-added principle is extremely important because it assists the accountant to determine whether the loaf of bread is final product (as would be the case if it were sold to a homemaker) or whether it is intermediate product (as would be the case if it were sold to a restaurant). Another very important reason for toting up value added instead of trying to identify the value of final output is that production and sales do not take place instantaneously. The consequence of this is that the value added in producing commodities often overlaps accounting periods. To illustrate, suppose an automobile is produced and sold to a dealer for $4,000 in 1975. The auto is then sold to a consumer in 1976 for $4,500. What, then, is the contribution of the auto to national product in the respective years? The value-added principle provides the answer. The sum of value added in 1975 is $4,000; in 1976 it is $500. These, then, are the amounts that are recorded as contributions to national product in the respective years.

Returning to Table 2–1, note that the net value added of the X Corporation is exactly equal to the costs other than those incurred by the corporation for purchases from other firms. If intermediate costs are deducted from both sides of a production statement, the balance will not be altered. The value added through production will then appear on the right side; the left side will show total current factor and nonfactor costs incurred in production plus the profit (or loss) residual.

## 2-3
## THE GROSS NATIONAL PRODUCT ACCOUNT

In Table 2–2 we show a GNP account for the American economy for the year 1973. The table is based on data published by the Department of Commerce. The general framework of the account is very similar to that of the production statement for the individual firm. The right side shows how the total value of final goods and services was distributed according to the sector which purchased them. The four-sector classification introduced earlier is retained. The account shows, in addition to the value of the goods purchased by each sector, some minimum detail on the kinds of goods that are involved. The left side shows the total factor and nonfactor costs of producing the current output. This shows the way the various charges against the total value of the flow of product were allocated to the various items of cost and to profit. Note that the right side measures expenditures for goods and services by the four final demand sectors, whereas the left side shows the costs associated with current production. The difference between expenditure for output and pro-

## TABLE 2-2
**National income and product account, 1973 (billions of dollars)**

| | | | | |
|---|---|---|---|---|
| Compensation of employees | | $ 786 | Personal consumption expenditure | $ 805 |
| Wages and salaries | $692 | | Durables $130 | |
| Social security payments | | | Nondurables 338 | |
| (employer) | 48 | | Services 337 | |
| Supplements and other | 46 | | Gross private domestic investment | 209 |
| Proprietors' income | | 96 | Residential construction $ 57 | |
| Rental income of persons | | 26 | Business fixed investment 137 | |
| Net interest | | 52 | Net change in inventory 15 | |
| Corporate profits | | | Net export of goods and services | 4 |
| (and inventory valuation adjustment) | | 105 | Exports $100 | |
| Profits tax liability | 50 | | Imports −96 | |
| Dividends (domestic) | 26 | | Government purchases of goods and | |
| Dividends (foreign) | 4 | | services | 277 |
| Undistributed profits | 39 | | Federal $107 | |
| Foreign branch profits | 4 | | State and local 170 | |
| Inventory valuation adjustment | −18 | | | |
| National income | | $1,065 | | |
| Business transfer payments | | 5 | | |
| Indirect business taxes | | 119 | | |
| Charges against net national product | | $1,189 | | |
| Depreciation | | 111 | | |
| Statistical discrepancy | | −5 | | |
| Charges against gross national product | | $1,295 | Gross national product | $1,295 |

*Source:* U.S. Department of Commerce, *Survey of Current Business, July 1974,* Government Printing Office, Washington, 1974.

duction of output is the net change in inventory component of business investment.

Let us examine the right side more closely. The first item shown is the consumption expenditure of the personal sector. This flow of goods and services purchased by consumers is subdivided into three categories on the basis of durability. Goods that generally last more than a year are classed as durables; those that are generally consumed within a year are classified as nondurables; those that are consumed at the moment of purchase are classed as services.[1]

Gross private domestic investment is the value of output retained by the business sector. It includes additions to the stock of plant and equipment, the stock of residential housing, and the net change in business inventories. In discussing the X Corporation, we saw that sales of goods to other firms represented intermediate rather than final product. However, the purchases of plant and equipment, and the accumulation of inventories by the business sector as a whole, represents additions to the nation's stock of capital, and they are regarded as different from intermediate product inasmuch as they continue to be used in production over a period of years.

That part of the current production of capital goods that replaces capital worn out in production is not a net addition to total output. Nevertheless, it is included in the investment total and is balanced by the inclusion of the depreciation expense item on the left side of the accounts. The word "gross" is then used in describing the investment item to denote the fact that not all investment represents a net addition to the capital stock. The net change in inventory is included under investment because goods added to inventory are part of current production and must therefore be included to balance the flow of production costs that are associated with them and included on the opposite side of the account.

Residential construction, which is the value of currently produced housing for private use, is included as part of the flow of investment. The alternative would be to include the cost of new housing purchased by private owners under personal consumption expenditure. However, to do so would imply that the whole house was consumed during the year of purchase. Thus this procedure would ignore the substantial flow of services provided by the stock of housing over time. To treat homebuilding as current consumption would clearly be inappropriate; consequently, additions to the stock of housing are treated by the Commerce Department as part of the flow of investment. The consumption part of housing is then estimated as the annual rental value that would occur if all housing (including owner occupied) were rented.[2]

---

[1] Clearly, the classification is arbitrary. Clothing is classified as nondurable. In the case of fashion-conscious, affluent women, clothing should clearly be viewed as nondurable. On the other hand, the typical impoverished college professor would not deign to buy a suit that was not expected to last at least five years.

[2] Note that a similar argument could be made with respect to consumer durable goods. Indeed, some economists argue that purchases of consumer durables should be treated as investment, and that annual depreciation should then be regarded as the consumption expenditure component attributable to these goods.

The net export of goods and services is the net difference between the value of currently produced goods and services that were exported during the year and the value of currently produced foreign goods and services that were imported. When goods are produced in foreign countries, there is no equivalent flow of factor and nonfactor costs on the left side of the United States GNP account. Consequently, imports should not appear as part of *national* product. They do appear on the right side with a negative sign because other components of expenditure include imported goods; for example, consumption expenditure includes total expenditures for goods and services including those imported. By subtracting imports from the right side, the flow of national output balances the flow of national income.

The final component of expenditure is the purchases of goods and services by governments at all levels. Customarily, these purchases are divided into those made by the federal government and those made by state and local governments. As is always the case in a national product statement, the expenditures that are entered include only government expenditures for currently produced goods and services. Included are such things as typewriters and paper clips, the pay of government employees, expenditures by the Department of Defense, and the like. Included also are expenditures for construction and for equipment items of a sort that would be counted as investment if they had been purchased by business.[1]

Most of the items on the left side of Table 2–2 are already familiar from our discussion of the X Corporation. There are, however, some new items. The first new item is proprietors' income. This item represents the net income of the various unincorporated business enterprises. These include self-employed persons such as doctors, lawyers, farmers, and storekeepers who, for accounting purposes, are considered part of the business sector. If these enterprises were treated in the same manner as corporations, their profits, wages (paid partly to themselves), and interest on capital investment (also paid partly to themselves) would have to be separated and included under the appropriate items in the account. However, most such enterprises are not legally obliged to distinguish between these income categories, nor are they subject to corporate income taxation. Rather than attempt an arbitrary separation of these income flows, an aggregate net income figure that lumps together all proprietors' income is entered as a separate item on the left side.

Another item that requires comment is the inventory valuation adjustment. (IVA) This adjustment, which is included as part of corporate profits, is inserted to account for the fact that gains (or losses) result when a corporation sells goods out of inventory during periods of rising (or falling) prices. Inventory profits due to rising prices do not result from current productive activity; rather, they are more in the nature of windfall returns. They should therefore be excluded from national product. On the other side of the account, the net change in

---

One can claim that public construction ought be treated as investment, and that the stock of publicly owned highways, buildings, and the like should be recorded as part of the nation's stock of capital.

inventory is valued in terms of current prices. The inventory valuation adjustment therefore ensures that the two sides will balance.

Rental income of persons differs from rent paid by the X Corporation. The payment that the X Corporation makes to the real estate corporation that owns the building which houses X's offices is a rental payment as far as X itself is concerned. But when all businesses are aggregated together into the business sector, the payment disappears as an intermediate transaction. Rental income of persons originates from the fact that residential construction is treated as investment. As a consequence, homeowners are thought of as owning their own homes as businesses and then as renting the homes from themselves. In this manner the annual flow of services to the community from the stock of housing is included on the right side of the accounts as a portion of personal consumption expenditure, and this is balanced on the left side by rental income of persons. We should note also that the rental income of persons is a rather small item. It is small because the equity of individuals and families in their homes is rather small on the average. Rental income of persons, finally, also includes a small amount of rental payments received by persons who are not primarily engaged in the real estate business. The entry therefore includes such items as rental payments received by persons who rent rooms to students. Finally, royalties received by persons from ownership of property rights in patents, copyrights, and rights to natural resources are also included here.

When the factor costs on the left side of Table 2–2 are added together, we get the national income total of $1,065 billion. Thus, national income is the sum of the total payments of wages, rent, interest, and profit received by the factors of production. When business transfer payments of $5 billion and indirect business taxes of $119 billion are added to this total, the resulting figure of $1,189 billion is the net national product. Finally, when we add depreciation charges of $111 billion, we get the total estimated charges against GNP, but the two sides of the account do not yet balance. The difference of $5 billion is the statistical discrepancy.

These last nonfactor costs require some explanation. Business transfer payments are made up principally of two factors: charitable contributions by corporate enterprises to nonprofit organizations and consumer bad debts. Both are charges against business revenue but because the payments are not associated with a current factor service they cannot be included in the national income. Indirect business taxes, such as property, sales, and excise taxes, are charged by business against their current operations. They are therefore part of the sale price of the final product and appear on the right side of the account. However, because such taxes are not associated with the employment of factors of production, they cannot appear as part of national income. Therefore they must be added to national income if the two sides are to balance.[1] Depreciation must be added to the left side to balance the gross

---

[1] Taxes paid by corporations on their profits and by persons on their incomes are related to current productive activity and thus are a part of national income.

flow of investment goods on the right side. Finally, when all the independently derived estimates that make up the national accounts are put together, it is in the nature of things that the two sides will not quite balance. A "statistical discrepancy" is then added to ensure balance. It is a tribute to the practicing national income accountants of the Department of Commerce that the discrepancy is usually so very small.

## 2–4
## MEASURES OF AGGREGATE INCOME

A complete representation of receipts and expenditures in the economy would require us to develop complete accounts for each of the sectors that we have been discussing. Detailed development of such sector accounts can usefully be postponed to Chapter 3. In completing this chapter, we intend to provide such supplementary materials as are necessary to complement our subsequent analysis. Thus, we shall look at the derivation of the four major measures of production and income flows, the federal budget, and the balance of payments of the United States.

Income payments can be viewed as accruing to different factors of production. However, income receipts can also be classified according to the sector that ends up with the income. Such a statement begins with the total GNP and then makes various deductions and additions in order to derive the income that is finally available to the personal sector to spend or save as it chooses.

It will be useful to resort to a pictorial representation in the form of the bar chart shown as Figure 2–1. The chart begins on the left with the value of the current production of final goods and services (GNP) divided in exactly the same way as it was in Table 2–2. From this total we subtract the nonfactor costs: statistical discrepancy, depreciation, indirect business taxes, and business transfer payments. This, as we saw before, leaves national income which represents the income earned by the factors of production. While this total of $1,065 billion represents the earnings of the personal sector, not all of it is in fact received by this sector. Profits taxes paid by business and earnings retained within business must be deducted. In fact, the only part of corporate profits that accrues to the personal sector is dividend payments. The contributions by business to the social security fund on behalf of their employees represent taxes and must also be deducted, as must the social security taxes paid by employees themselves. On the other hand, some receipts accrue to the personal sector that are not part of national income because they were not earned in the current period. National income includes only the flow of income and product associated with current productive activity. But people do receive some part of their total income in the form of what are called "transfer payments," largely from the different levels of government; examples include unemployment compensation, veterans benefits, social security benefits, and the like. Because these receipts were not earned currently, they are not included in national income. However, they clearly are part of

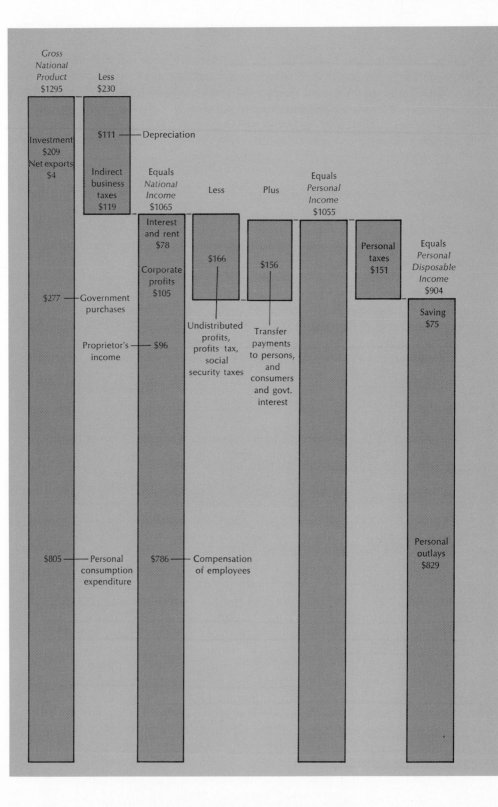

the income of the personal sector, and they must be added in deriving personal income.

Once these deductions and additions have been made, we arrive at the income of the personal sector *prior* to the deduction of personal income taxes. The resulting figure of $1,055 billion is known as "personal income." If we then deduct the personal income tax payments of $151 billion made to governments at all levels, the result is a "personal disposable income" total of $904 billion. This is the amount that the personal sector finally has at its disposal to spend or save as it sees fit. In 1973 the personal sector spent $829 billion on consumption; this left a residual of personal saving of $75 billion.

Notice that the difference between disposable income and net national product (NNP) is the amount withheld by the business and the government sectors. The business deduction is retained earnings, all other business receipts being paid either to the government or to the personal sector. The government deduction consists of *all* taxes net of government transfer payments. Thus we can write

$$Y = Y_d + T + S_c$$   $Y = $ disposable income $+$ taxes $+$ corp. savings

where $Y_d$ stands for disposable income, $T$ (net taxes) stands for all taxes minus government transfer payments, $S_c$ stands for net corporate saving (retained earnings), and $Y$ stands for net national product. This is a fundamental definition that is of great importance for subsequent analysis.

## 2-5
## THE FEDERAL BUDGET

Much of this book is concerned with fiscal policy. As we saw in Chapter 1, the term "fiscal policy" means the adjustment of government expenditures and revenues in such a way as to maintain equilibrium in the circular flow at the full-employment level of output. In Chapter 3 we will present income and product accounts for all sectors of the economy including a consolidated income and product account for all levels of government: federal, state, and local. However, since fiscal policy is essentially the province of the federal government, special interest attaches to the federal budget, and it is therefore important to take a look at the federal budget and to discuss the various concepts of federal surplus and deficit. Before we do this we need to make some general points about government receipts and expenditures.

The receipts and expenditures for the government sector cannot be derived directly from the GNP account of Table 2–2 because of transfer items that are

**FIGURE 2–1**
The relation between the four major measures of national income, 1973 (billions of dollars) (*Source:* U.S. Department of Commerce, *Survey of Current Business,* July 1974, Government Printing Office, Washington, 1974)

not a part of GNP but that nevertheless play an important part in determining GNP because of their influence on the various components of expenditure. For 1973 the GNP account shows that government purchases of goods and services totaled $277 billion. In addition, government transfer payments to other sectors totaled $112 billion. Of great importance, also, are the substantial intergovernmental transfer payments. Transfer payments to other sectors are not a part of GNP since they are not a payment for currently produced goods and services. On the other hand, there are various tax and nontax payments to social security and other welfare funds that are a part of GNP. The result is that if the government receipts and expenditures were derived from the GNP account, expenditures would be understated, and the government surplus would be overstated by the amount of the transfer payments made out of social insurance funds.

The government budget on the national income accounts (NIA) basis includes all receipts and expenditures of government units. In addition, the federal NIA budget includes the grants-in-aid to state and local governments as an expenditure, and these grants show up in the budget of state and local governments as receipts. In a consolidated government statement, these intergovernmental transfers would, of course, be netted out in the process of aggregation. The NIA budget for the federal government is shown for selected years in Table 2–3.

Consider first the expenditure side. In 1973 the federal government made purchases of goods and services of $106.6 billion of which $74.4 billion represented defense purchases. This $106.6 billion is the federal part of the government purchase item of Table 2–2. In addition, the federal government made transfer payments to persons totaling $95.5 billion. Grants-in-aid to state and local governments came to $40.5 billion. Next, interest on the federal debt, classified as a transfer payment, came to $16.3 billion. Subsidies less current surplus of government expenses, mainly representing the postal deficit, came to $5.3 billion. Adding these components together, we obtain a federal expenditure total of $264.2 billion. Note that only $106.6 billion actually represented purchases of goods and services.

On the receipts side, the federal government received $114.1 billion in personal income taxes and $43.7 billion in corporate profits taxes. Federal excises, customs, and other indirect business taxes yielded $21.2 billion, and social security taxes (contributions for social insurance) came to $79.5 billion. Since total receipts came to $258.5 billion while expenditures totaled $264.2 billion, there was a federal deficit on NIA account of $5.7 billion.

It is important to emphasize once again that, although federal expenditures totaled $264.2 billion in 1973, only $106.6 billion actually represented a purchase of goods and services and was recorded as a portion of GNP. Nevertheless, the other items are important because their magnitudes influence the level of expenditures of other sectors, and they therefore indirectly affect GNP. Federal grants-in-aid will ultimately result in state and local purchases. Increased taxes will reduce disposable income and corporate profits after tax,

**TABLE 2–3**
Receipts and expenditures of the federal government sector, 1929–1973
(billions of dollars)

| | 1929 | 1940 | 1944 | 1950 | 1960 | 1970 | 1973 |
|---|---|---|---|---|---|---|---|
| **Receipts** | | | | | | | |
| Personal tax and nontax receipts | 1.3 | 1.4 | 17.5 | 18.1 | 43.6 | 92.2 | 114.1 |
| Corporate profits tax accruals | 1.2 | 2.6 | 12.5 | 17.0 | 21.7 | 30.6 | 43.7 |
| Indirect business taxes and nontax accruals | 1.2 | 2.7 | 6.2 | 8.9 | 13.5 | 19.6 | 21.2 |
| Contributions for social insurance | 0.1 | 2.0 | 4.8 | 5.9 | 17.7 | 49.3 | 79.5 |
| Total | 3.8 | 8.7 | 41.0 | 49.9 | 96.5 | 191.7 | 258.5 |
| **Expenditures** | | | | | | | |
| Purchases of goods and services | 1.3 | 6.0 | 89.0 | 18.4 | 53.5 | 97.2 | 106.6 |
| Defense | | 2.2 | 87.4 | 14.1 | 44.9 | 75.4 | 74.4 |
| Other | | 3.8 | 1.6 | 4.3 | 8.6 | 21.9 | 32.2 |
| Transfer payments | 0.7 | 1.5 | 1.8 | 14.4 | 23.4 | 63.4 | 95.5 |
| Grants-in-aid to state and local governments | 0.1 | 0.9 | 0.9 | 2.3 | 6.5 | 24.4 | 40.5 |
| Net interest paid | 0.4 | 0.7 | 2.4 | 4.5 | 7.1 | 14.6 | 16.3 |
| Subsidies less current surplus of government enterprises | 0.1 | 0.9 | 1.4 | 1.2 | 2.5 | 5.5 | 5.3 |
| Total | 2.6 | 10.0 | 95.5 | 40.8 | 93.0 | 205.1 | 264.2 |
| Surplus (+) or deficit (−) | +1.2 | −1.3 | −54.5 | +9.1 | +3.5 | −13.4 | −5.7 |
| Addendum: total federal government expenditures as a percent of GNP | 2.5 | 10.0 | 45.5 | 14.3 | 18.5 | 21.1 | 20.0 |

Source: 1929–1960: U.S. Department of Commerce, The National Income and Product Accounts of the United States, 1929–1965, Government Printing Office, Washington, 1966. 1970 and 1973: U.S. Department of Commerce, Survey of Current Business, July 1974, Government Printing Office, Washington, 1974, Table 3.1.

and this will affect consumption and investment spending. Increased transfer payments will raise disposable income and consumption.

Table 2–3 provides a picture of the federal NIA budget as it has changed through time. To keep the numbers in perspective, an addendum has been inserted at the bottom of the table which shows total federal expenditures as a percentage of GNP. This line provides a very rough indication of the importance of federal activities relative to the level of overall economic activity. We wish to emphasize once more, however, that all federal expenditures are not a part of GNP.

It is clear from the table that the federal budget played very little part in the predepression economy of 1929. With a GNP in current dollar values of

$103.1 billion, federal receipts totaled only $3.8 billion and expenditures totaled $2.6 billion. The ratio of total expenditures to GNP was therefore only
2.5 percent. Clearly, cutting taxes to stimulate the economy after 1929 would
have had very little effect because there was very little in the way of available
taxes to cut.

By 1940 the ratio of expenditures to GNP had risen to 10 percent; federal
purchases increased as the result of the New Deal programs, and some small
preparation for World War II was also under way. Transfer payments increased as a result of the establishment of the social security system in the
1930s, and this is also reflected by a jump in social security taxes on the
receipts side.

During the war year of 1944, federal defense purchases totaled $87.4
billion. This alone represented 42 percent of GNP. Although taxes were
raised during the war, this was not nearly enough to cover the expenditure
increases, with the result that a massive deficit of $54.5 billion was recorded
in 1944.

As measured by the accounts for 1950, the relative level of federal activity
declined sharply from its World War II proportion. Tax rates were cut after the
war, but since the economy expanded rapidly, receipts continued to increase.

The 1950s, which we usually think of as a decade of conservatism, re-
trenchment, and reduction in government participation in economic life, nevertheless witnessed a remarkable increase in the relative importance of government activity. Federal expenditures as a ratio to GNP increased 4.2
percentage points from 14.3 percent to 18.5 percent. This contrasts sharply
with the subsequent decade which was presided over by the activist Presi-
dents Kennedy and Johnson. Between 1960 and 1970 the increase was held
to 2.6 percentage points, rising from 18.5 percent to 21.1 percent. The subsequent Nixon administration did manage to reduce the proportion slightly to
one-fifth of GNP.

The primary cause of the increased federal activity during the 1950s was
the mounting defense budget in response to the Korean war and the subsequent intensification of the cold war. Defense purchases more than tripled.
However, despite the conservatism of the decade and the administration
which represented it, other expenditure components rose sharply. Transfer
payments increased $9.0 billion, and grants-in-aid more than doubled. Fur-
ther historians may indeed mark down the 1950s as the time when big federal
government became an essential fact of economic life.

As we have seen, federal activity, by relative standards, grew less during
the 1960s than it did in the 1950s. And this appears to have been the case
despite the War on Poverty and despite the war in Vietnam. Notice that
between 1960 and 1970 the absolute level of total expenditures and receipts
more than doubled. Defense purchases increased under the impact of the
Vietnam war and the space program. The war itself has been estimated as
costing close to $30 billion a year at its peak. Rising social security benefits
and medicare are reflected in the huge rise in transfers. Grants to state and

local governments, finally, more than doubled. Yet for all this mass of activity, federal expenditures as a ratio to GNP came to only 21.1 percent; this was not much higher than the 1960 proportion of 18.5 percent, and it represented a far smaller relative increase than during the preceding decade.

The reasons for this startling set of circumstances are several. First, the war in Vietnam was quantitatively a much smaller operation relative to total GNP than was the war in Korea. Second, the 1950s were a period of economic stagnation, whereas the 1960s were marked by spectacular and sustained expansion. Because GNP grew so rapidly during the 1960s, it was possible to expand federal expenditure programs enormously without this expansion having much effect on the relative share of federal government activity. All components of GNP expanded rapidly, and the relative increase in the federal share was as a consequence quite modest.

In the period since the end of the direct American involvement in Vietnam, the most impressive change in the federal budget has been in the area of social insurance. To be sure, the inflation had its impact in raising all aspects of the budget, but the really dramatic increases between 1970 and 1973 were in social insurance taxes and in federal government transfers to persons, either directly or in the form of grants to state governments.

On the receipts side, it is evident that personal and corporate tax yield increased greatly. This occurred despite a major reduction in personal and corporate tax rates in 1964. However, the growing economy yielded such enlarged incomes that the Treasury's receipts more than doubled despite lower rates on personal and corporate income.

There is one tax that continues to increase more rapidly than the others: the social security tax, which came close to tripling between 1960 and 1970 and then jumped a fantastic 60 percent in the next three years. Amazingly enough, it now exceeds the yield from the federal corporate profits tax and indirect business taxes combined, and it has increased so much that it has far more than offset the reduction in tax rates legislated in 1964. In 1963 the sum of federal personal income taxes plus social security taxes came to 16.0 percent of personal income. This ratio dropped to 15.1 percent in 1964 but then rose to 17.6 percent by 1970. By 1973 it had risen again to 18.3 percent.

Our purpose here has been to give the reader some indication of the relative importance of federal government economic activity. In closing this section, it is appropriate to discuss the numerous concepts of federal budget and especially how this translates into a federal deficit or a surplus.

The various federal expenditure and revenue concepts have traditionally been so different that it has been necessary to distinguish between three different federal budget concepts. First, there is the federal NIA budget that we have been discussing; second, there is the "administrative" budget; a third budget is the "cash" budget; and a few years ago, a presidential commission recommended a consolidation of concepts into a single "unified" budget. Despite attempts at unification, each form of budget does have its special advantages for different purposes, and each will continue to receive attention.

The federal cash budget records the moneys paid and received by the United States Treasury. It differs from the NIA budget in that the NIA budget operates on an accrual basis. By an accrual basis we mean that taxes are recorded at the time the obligation is incurred even though no actual cash payment may as yet have been made. The NIA budget records corporate taxes at the time the liability is incurred; the cash budget records the tax at the time it is actually received by the Treasury. Thus, the main difference between the cash and the NIA budget is a matter of timing. The administrative budget records the moneys allocated to federal government departments and agencies, whether or not they are for spending in the current year. And it includes committed expenditures, whether they have actually been made or not. It excludes such items as payments into and disbursements from trust funds such as the social security system. Since social security taxes have typically been in excess of disbursements, the administrative budget has tended to show a much larger deficit than either the NIA or the cash budget. From the economist's point of view, the administrative budget is the least useful. Social security taxes and benefits both affect disposable income and therefore total spending in the economy, and it is therefore necessary to include these items in order to measure the fiscal impact of the federal government.

## 2-6
## THE BALANCE OF PAYMENTS

During much of the past two decades, the United States has had a deficit in its balance of payments. As we shall see later, balance of payments deficits have serious impacts on economies primarily because they tend to interfere with attempts to achieve domestic macroeconomic goals. In view of the importance of the balance of payments, it is appropriate that we inquire into the meaning of the concept of a deficit or surplus in the balance of payments; in order to do this we must extend our accounting framework to include international transactions.

When Americans import goods from Britain, they may pay for the goods with dollars, or they may first purchase British pounds from their own banks. If British exporters accept dollars in payment, they may then convert these dollars into pounds at their local banks. The local bank in Britain may then take the dollars and convert them into pounds at the Bank of England. The Bank of England, finally, may then send the dollars to the United States Treasury which, until very recently, committed itself to buy the dollars in exchange for pounds or gold at a fixed price. The Treasury's holdings of pounds and other foreign currencies—its "foreign exchange holdings" as this is known—plus its holdings of gold constitute the "official reserves" of the United States. Any transaction that tends to add to our foreign exchange and gold reserves is denoted as a credit in the balance of payments account; any transaction that tends to reduce these reserves is called a debit. The net change, over an accounting period, is the balance of payments deficit or surplus on an official reserves basis.

**TABLE 2-4**

Summary balance of payments account, United States, 1935–1973 (billions of dollars)

| (Credits +; Debits −) | 1935 | 1939 | 1946 | 1950 | 1958 | 1965 | 1968 | 1970 | 1973 |
|---|---|---|---|---|---|---|---|---|---|
| **Current Account** | | | | | | | | | |
| Exports | 3.3 | 4.4 | 14.9 | 14.4 | 25.5 | 41.0 | 51.4 | 62.9 | 101.0 |
| Imports | −3.1 | −3.4 | −7.0 | −12.0 | −20.9 | −32.3 | −48.1 | −59.3 | −96.6 |
| Balance | 0.2 | 1.0 | 7.9 | 2.4 | 4.6 | 8.7 | 3.3 | 3.6 | 4.4 |
| **Capital Account** | | | | | | | | | |
| U.S. private capital | . . . | . . . | −0.6 | −1.3 | −2.9 | −3.8 | −5.2 | −6.9 | −14.1 |
| Foreign capital | . . . | . . . | −1.0 | 1.9 | 1.3 | 0.4 | 9.4 | 5.8 | 18.7 |
| Balance | 1.5 | 1.5 | −1.6 | 0.6 | −1.6 | −3.4 | 4.2 | −1.1 | 4.6 |
| **Unilateral Transfers** | | | | | | | | | |
| Private | . . . | . . . | −0.7 | −0.5 | −0.6 | −0.6 | −0.7 | −0.9 | −1.3 |
| U.S. government (net) | . . . | . . . | −5.3 | −4.2 | −5.0 | −5.4 | −5.2 | −2.2 | −2.6 |
| Balance | −0.2 | −0.2 | −6.0 | −4.7 | −5.6 | −6.0 | −5.9 | −3.1 | −3.9 |
| Errors and omissions | 0.4 | 0.8 | 0.2 | −0.2 | 0.4 | −0.6 | −0.7 | −1.9 | −2.6 |
| U.S. official reserves (increase −) | −1.9 | −3.1 | −0.5 | 1.9 | 2.2 | 1.3 | −0.9 | 2.5 | −2.5 |

*Source:* 1935–1939: U.S. Bureau of the Census, *Historical Statistics of the United States, Colonial Times to 1957,* Government Printing Office, Washington, 1960, Series U182–192. 1946–1970: U.S. Department of Commerce, *Survey of Current Business, June 1974,* Government Printing Office, Washington, 1974, Table 2.

A balance of payments account generally includes three major categories of transactions. First, there are so-called current transactions. These include exports and imports of merchandise, payments for services such as shipping, insurance, and tourist expenditures, and income payments such as interest and dividends. When an American buys a foreign car, flies on a foreign airline, or visits Paris, such expenditures are recorded as imports into the United States. These current transactions appear in Table 2–4 with a minus sign to indicate that they are debits which have resulted in an outflow of dollars and/or foreign exchange. Conversely, when foreigners buy goods or visit the United States, the transactions are recorded as credits since these transactions earn foreign exchange. The net difference between these flows make up the "net export" of goods and services. Since these transactions represent flows of current income and product, they are a part of GNP, and they may therefore also be located in the GNP account of Table 2–2.[1]

The second major category of transactions is the capital transactions. Americans build plants in foreign countries, they purchase shares in foreign companies, and they buy foreign bonds. All these transactions result in an outflow of United States dollars, and they are therefore recorded as a debit

[1] The difference between the $4 billion shown in Table 2–2 and the $4.4 billion of Table 2–4 for 1973 is produced by rounding errors in the earlier table.

under "U.S. private capital" in the balance of payments account. However, since none of these transactions reflect current income and product flows, they are not recorded in the GNP accounts. Similarly, when foreigners purchase American assets, there is an inflow of capital. Such inflows are recorded as credits in the United States balance of payments account.

The third major category of transactions is the international flow of transfer payments. This flow represents gifts and grants between individuals and governments; they are transfer payments in the same sense as in GNP accounting, and they are therefore not associated with current economic activity. An American resident might remit money to his family abroad; and the United States government remits substantial sums to foreign governments in the form of economic aid and military assistance. Intergovernmental loans are also recorded under unilateral transfers. Although these are not strictly transfers since promissory notes are received in exchange, they tend to take place outside the free market, and thus they can reasonably be regarded as transfers. The net flow of transfers and loans is shown as a single item in Table 2–4. As is evident in the table, unilateral transfers has consistently been a debit item in the United States balance of payments.

Measuring the values of all the transactions that should be entered in the balance of payments is a very difficult task. Many of the flows are not directly reported at all and must therefore be estimated in fairly roundabout ways. The value of tourist expenditure, for example, cannot be directly measured. Consequently, there are various errors hidden in the several components of the account that can be taken care of in an accounting sense only by including the offsetting "errors and omissions" item.

The last item in the table balances the account in such a way as to make the column total add to zero. This balancing entry is the change in the official reserves of the United States that resulted from the various inflows and outflows that occurred during the year. If the United States had a credit balance on its combined trade, capital, and transfer accounts, its foreign exchange reserves would, in principle, increase by the amount of the credit balance. Traditionally, official reserves were held in the form of gold; thus, a net credit balance in the trade, capital, and transfer accounts was reflected in an increase in the gold stock. However, since 1947 official reserves have also included United States gold held by the International Monetary Fund. Since 1961, reserves have included holdings of convertible foreign currencies. And the international currency known as "special drawing rights" is now also included. Despite these complications, it is still true that a net surplus on current, capital, and transfer account implies an increase in total official reserves. Notice that such an accumulation of reserves is shown with a *minus* sign at the bottom of Table 2–4. As a result of this procedure, the columns total to zero. Thus, the balance of payments must balance even though substantial deficits may be run in the several individual accounts.

Now that we are familiar with the meaning of the items in Table 2–4, we can use the table to trace changes in the balance of payments of the United

States as they have developed over the years. As shown in the table, we have had a persistent excess of exports over imports. This competitive strength became eroded during the inflation of the last several years, with the result that the trade balance turned negative in 1971, the first time that had happened since 1900. In 1972 there began a series of devaluations of the dollar relative to other currencies. As can be seen by comparing the export figures for 1973 with those for 1970, this greatly improved our competitive position and caused a trade surplus to be recorded in 1973. The figures for 1974, however, again moved into deficit because of the sharp rise in the price of imported oil.

The record in the capital account has not been as consistent. During the 1930s there was a substantial and persistent capital inflow. Some of this was no doubt due to the deteriorating political situation in Europe which caused foreign capital to seek a "haven" in the United States. Between 1934, when the United States raised the price of gold to $35 per ounce, and 1940, the value of the gold stock held by the Treasury more than doubled.

The balance of payments was severely distorted by World War II. There were very large exports of goods to allied governments and very large unilateral transfers to aid these governments to purchase the goods. By the end of the war, the domestic gold stock had fallen by about 10 percent to a value of about $20 billion.

The years from the end of the war to 1957 were marked by a much larger volume of both exports and imports than during the prewar period. Again each year showed a positive balance on current account. American private capital going abroad remained fairly small and below foreign investment in the United States, and the capital account therefore showed a surplus. The most notable change from the prewar situation occurred in the unilateral transfer account which showed a substantial jump in outflows from the United States. This change was attributable to the large-scale United States aid programs, such as the Marshall Plan. Subsequent to the economic recovery of Europe, some aid from the United States flowed to the underdeveloped countries, and, in combination with our military commitments, caused unilateral transfers to continue to be a significant debit item in the balance of payments. Over the period 1946 to 1957 United States official reserves increased in seven years and decreased in four. The cumulative result was to increase reserves by about 10 percent.

From 1958 to 1967 the United States experienced ten consecutive years during which there was a decrease in her official reserves. The turnabout to a consistent deficit position as compared with the previous period was associated with a growing and persistent outflow of capital. Although the current account surplus remained strong until 1968, this was overshadowed by the combination of private capital and government transfer outflows. There was, as a consequence, a persistent balance of payments deficit and a steady outflow of gold during this period. Since then the position of American official reserves has fluctuated. The trend is somewhat difficult to determine, largely because there has developed an enormous difference between the free market and the official value of United States gold holdings.

It is tempting to conclude from a hasty inspection of the data for a year such as 1965 that the balance of payments deficit suffered by the United States has been due to our government's foreign commitments and to the desire of Americans to invest abroad. Our large exports surplus, moreover, suggests that our deficit was not due to any deterioration in our competitive position. Such conclusions, however, require qualification. If American firms found it increasingly profitable to establish overseas subsidiaries rather than to produce goods for export at home, this most certainly suggests that our competitive position was deteriorating. The fact that we had a sizable trade surplus was therefore only a partial clue to our competitive position. Similarly, if we had reduced our foreign aid, this ought to have reduced our deficit. But such a reduction in aid would also have reduced our exports, and there might, therefore, have been little gain in the overall balance of payments. Finally, if we had limited foreign investment, we would sooner or later have reduced our dividend and interest income. The fact is that the various components of the balance of payments are closely linked to each other. One cannot simply say that a particular item is out of line and responsible for a deficit.

As shown in Table 2–4, official reserves increased during 1968. They also increased in 1969. In both years, although imports increased very rapidly due to the demands created by a booming economy, this was offset by massive inflows of foreign capital. This circumstance reflected the fact that interest rates in the United States rose to levels that made it very attractive for foreigners to invest their funds here. Such short-term capital flows react very quickly to international interest rate differentials, and they form a very volatile element in the balance of payments. With the decline in interest rate differentials that occurred in 1970, capital once again flowed out, and the balance of payments registered a deficit of $2.5 billion.

## 2–7
### SUMMARY

In this chapter we have presented a brief look at three of the aggregate accounts that are central to the study of macroeconomic theory and to the formulation of policy. The three accounts are only a small part of a broad accounting framework that includes a nation's current income and product flows, its asset or "wealth" position, and its relations with other countries. We cannot take time to discuss all the elements of such an interconnected tableau in this book. However, it is important to provide greater detail with respect to the current relations between the several sectors of the economy. Chapter 3 attempts to provide such detail.

# 3

# THE SECTOR
# ACCOUNTS

## INTRODUCTION

In Chapter 2 we described the construction of a GNP account based on the flows of currently produced final output and the equivalent flows of factor and nonfactor income generated in producing that output. We noted that because the account deals only with flows generated through current production, there is no explicit reference to saving by the personal and government sectors or in the foreign sector. Also, the GNP account does not include nonbusiness transfer payments between sectors because such flows do not result from current productive activity. Such concepts did make their appearance in Figure 2–1, which describes the relation between the four major measures of production and income flows, and it is important to explore the relations between expenditures and income more carefully; this is the purpose of the sector accounts.

The macroeconomic models that form the content of Part 2 of this book are based on assumptions about the economic behavior of the aggregate sectors of the economy. For example, we will be describing the expenditure decisions of the personal sector because consumption expenditure is an important part of the aggregate demand for current output and thus an important determinant of the current level of income. It is clear that the income consumers earn currently is an important factor in determining how much of current output they are prepared to buy. But it is also true that other flows of income they receive, such as transfer payments, are also a factor in determining their expenditures. Thus from the point of view of the following theoretical part of the book, the GNP account does not present all the information about the economy that we need. Therefore, in this chapter we present complete current accounts for the four sectors into which we have divided the economy. These accounts detail all the income flows in the usual sense of the word as opposed to just those originating in current production, and they show the disposition of these income flows between expenditures for current output and saving. Note that these accounts are still income statements because they deal with flows that occur during the accounting period. They do not, like a balance sheet, deal with changes in the values of stocks of asset holdings.

An understanding of the difference between a stock magnitude and a flow magnitude is crucial for an understanding of macroeconomic theory. It is therefore appropriate that we digress for a moment to clarify this distinction. In general a flow magnitude is meaningful only if it is specified over what period of time the flow takes place. If a person's income is said to be $10,000, this conveys no information at all since it has not been said over what period of time this income is earned. If it is $10,000 a week, she is on the way to becoming a millionaire, but if it is $10,000 over a decade, she is probably on the way to the poorhouse. In the case of a stock magnitude it is not necessary or meaningful to add a time dimension. If one has $1,000 cash in the bank, or if one owes $1,000 to someone, time is not involved.

The distinction between stocks and flows arises most clearly in business accounting. The balance sheet or "position statement" records the assets and liabilities of the firm at an instant of time. A moment's reflection shows that all the items recorded there are stock magnitudes. On the other hand, the income (or profit and loss) statement records the receipts and expenses incurred over a period of time. These items are all flows.

To the mathematician a flow would be the rate of change, per unit time, of a stock magnitude. Thus, net investment is the flow which represents the change in the stock of capital. Inventory investment, similarly, represents the change in the stock of inventories.

## 3–2
## SECTOR ACCOUNTS

The sectors to be discussed in this chapter are the same as those introduced in Chapter 1: business, personal, government, and foreign. As we have noted before, that particular division of the economy is most useful for the analysis that will follow in this book and the one that has been found best adapted for the presentation of aggregate data to the policy maker. However, for other purposes, other forms of presentation might be found more appropriate. The point to remember is that a GNP account and its particular form are matters to be decided by the national income accountant in consultation with those who will use the data. We turn now to an examination of the accounts for each of the sectors.

## The Business Sector

The business sector is defined to include in addition to corporate enterprises all organizations producing goods and services at a price intended to cover at least the costs of production. This definition is broad enough to include such government business enterprises as the Tennessee Valley Authority. Also included are unincorporated business enterprises such as family businesses, farm operators, independent professional practitioners, and lessors of real property. Finally, it includes financial intermediaries such as banks, insurance companies, and other financial institutions.

The income and product account for the business sector is given in Table 3–1. Because the business sector has been defined to include only enterprises engaged in productive activity, the table shows all the flows into and out of the business sector during the year. Because the business sector is the major source of product and income in the economy, Table 3–1 looks very much the same as the GNP account of Table 2–2. On the left side of the two accounts, proprietors' income, rental income of persons, and net interest are identical because these income payments originate only in the business sector. Wages and corporate profits differ because wages are also paid by the personal, government, and foreign sectors, and profits that are earned by American enterprises operating abroad are included in GNP as an income originating in the foreign sector. The combination of the current factor payments by business is a measure of the income originating from current productive activity in the business sector of the economy. This flow is analogous to national income in Table 2–2.

The nonfactor costs, indirect business taxes, business transfer payments,

## TABLE 3–1
**Consolidated business income and product account, 1973 (billions of dollars)**

| | | | | | |
|---|---|---|---|---|---|
| 1. Compensation of employees | | $ 598 | 20. Sales to personal, government, | | |
| 2.   Wages and salaries | $518 (2.11) | | and foreign sectors | | $ 890 |
| 3.   Social security payments | | | 21. Sales of investment goods and | | |
| (employer) | 34 (3.17) | | residential construction | | 194 (5.2) |
| 4.   Supplements and other | 46 (2.11) | | 22. Net change in inventory | | 15 (5.3) |
| 5. Proprietors' income | | 96 (2.15) | | | |
| 6. Rental income of persons | | 26 (2.16) | | | |
| 7. Net interest | | 52 (2.21) | | | |
| 8. Corporate profits | | | | | |
| (and inventory valuation adjustment) | | 97 | | | |
| 9.   Profits tax liability | $ 50 (3.14) | | | | |
| 10.   Dividends (domestic) | 26 (2.18) | | | | |
| 11.   Undistributed profits | 39 (5.8) | | | | |
| 12.   Inventory valuation adjustment | −18 (5.10) | | | | |
| 13. Income originating | | $ 869 | | | |
| 14. Business transfer payments | | 5 (2.26) | | | |
| 15. Indirect business taxes | | 119 (3.15) | | | |
| 16. Charges against business net product | | $ 993 | | | |
| 17. Depreciation | | 111 (5.11) | | | |
| 18. Statistical discrepancy | | −5 (5.13) | | | |
| 19. Charges against business gross product | | $1,099 | 23. Business gross product | | $1,099 |

*Source:* See table 2–2. The code numbers used in this table refer to entries in tables 3–2 to 3–5.

depreciation, and the statistical discrepancy, are the same in the two accounts because no other sector has such costs. The addition of indirect business taxes and business transfer payments to income originating in the business sector gives a measure of the net product originating, and the addition then of depreciation and the statistical discrepancy gives a measure of gross product originating which is equal to the total on the right side of the account. On the right side of the account, it can be seen that the gross product originating in the business sector is less than the GNP total of Table 2–2. This, of course, is another reflection of the fact that not all current production originates in the business sector.

These sector accounts are constructed so that it is possible to see the complete transactions between the sectors; that is, wages paid by the business sector will appear as a payment by the business sector and again as a receipt of the personal sector. In order to follow through these flows, a set of code numbers is appended to the entries in the various tables. Thus, item 2 of Table 3–1, "wages and salaries," is followed by the code (2.11) to indicate that it appears as item 11 of Table 3–2. Similarly, when it appears in Table 3–2, it carries the code (1.2).

### The Personal Sector

The personal sector is defined to include, in addition to households and individuals, all institutions of a nonbusiness (roughly nonprofit) character such as universities, charitable organizations, and the like. Even though such institutions are nonprofit, they do pay wages and salaries and other items of current income. Such items must appear on the flow of income (left) side of the GNP account, and if the account is to balance, there must be an equivalent flow of product on the right side of the account. Here we run into the problem that nonbusiness organizations do not produce a product that is sold on the open market at a price intended to cover the costs of production. How do you value the product of the schoolteacher or professor? Because there is no physical product associated with the service performed, it must be assumed that the value of that service is equal to the wage and salary received. Thus, in the GNP account the wage payment appears on the left side, and an equal amount appears under consumption expenditure on the right side.

In 1973 the productive activity of the personal sector, as measured by the wages, salaries, and supplements paid from the sector, amounted to $41 billion. This $41 billion is equivalent in meaning to the measure of the income and product originating in the business sector as shown in Table 3–1. Because there are no indirect business taxes or depreciation allowances for the personal sector, the $41 billion is a measure of income originating in the sector, and it is also both the net and gross product (output) of the sector. Thus, in Table 3–2 the $41 billion appears on both sides of the income and product account, once as an outlay and again as a receipt.

The largest source of receipts of the personal sector is wages, salaries, and supplements which is shown in the table with the sector of origin. It is clear

## TABLE 3-2
**Personal income and outlay account, 1973 (billions of dollars)**

| | | | | | |
|---|---|---|---|---|---|
| 1. Personal taxes | | $ 151 (3.13) | 10. Wages, salaries, supplements | | $ 738 |
| 2. Personal outlays | | 829 | 11. Business | $564 (1.2) + (1.4) | |
| 3. Wages, salaries, supplements | $ 41 (2.13) | | 12. Government | 133 (3.2) | |
| 4. Social security payments (employer) | * (3.19) | | 13. Personal | 41 (2.3) | |
| 5. To business sector and imports | 764 | | 14. Foreign | * (4.2) | |
| 6. Interest paid by consumers | 23 (2.23) | | 15. Proprietors' income | | 96 (1.5) |
| 7. Transfers to foreigners | 1 (4.10) | | 16. Rental income of persons | | 26 (1.6) |
| 8. Personal saving | | 75 (5.6) | 17. Dividends | | 30 |
| | | | 18. Domestic $26 (1.10) | | |
| | | | 19. Foreign 4 (4.4) | | |
| | | | 20. Personal interest income | | 90 |
| | | | 21. Business $52 (1.7) | | |
| | | | 22. Government 15 (3.8) | | |
| | | | 23. Personal 23 (2.6) | | |
| | | | 24. Foreign * (4.3) | | |
| | | | 25. Transfer payments | | 118 |
| | | | 26. Business $ 5 (1.14) | | |
| | | | 27. Government 113 (3.6) | | |
| | | | 28. Minus: employee social security tax | | −43 (3.20) |
| 9. Personal taxes, outlays, and saving | | $1,055 | 29. Personal income | | $1,055 |

* Less than $0.5 billion.

*Source:* See table 2–2. The code numbers used in this table refer to entries in tables 3–1 to 3–5.

that most people earn their living through current earnings, and that the business sector is by far the largest source of labor income. Proprietors' income (plus inventory valuation adjustment) is also included as part of the receipts of the personal sector and represents the net income of unincorporated businesses, an aggregate total that includes salaries and interest payments to the owners as well as profit in the economic sense. In the case of corporate income where a proper allocation of costs is made, only dividends accrue to persons, and therefore dividends are the only part of corporate profits included in the receipts of the personal sector.

As we have noted above, the treatment of interest payments in the accounts depends upon the sector from which they originate. In the GNP account of Chapter 2, net interest payments are shown as $52 billion which is the sum of the interest payments by the business ($52 billion) and foreign (less than $0.5 billion) sectors. In Table 3–2 the interest receipts of the personal sector are shown as $90 billion. The $38 billion difference between the two figures is made up of interest payments by the personal sector ($23 billion) and net interest payments of the government sector ($15 billion), both of which are considered transfer payments and thus not part of GNP. The remaining item of personal receipts includes all other transfer payments which are shown here to originate in the business and the government sectors. Social security contributions which are a personal expense are nevertheless shown on the receipts side of Table 3–2 with a negative sign. This procedure is followed to give some idea of the net flow from the social security accounts. The picture is, of course, incomplete because employers also contribute to the social security fund on behalf of employees as shown in Table 3–3.

The first expense shown on the left side for the personal sector is income taxes paid to all levels of government. Sales and excise taxes paid by consumers are not shown separately here but are included as part of consumer expenditure. They do appear as indirect taxes paid by the business sector. The various social insurance contributions made by the personal sector are not shown as taxes, but as noted above they are listed as negative receipts. Many people consider these as insurance premiums rather than taxes which is perhaps another reason for listing them separately.

The second expense category is shown as personal outlays, the direct purchases of goods and services by the personal sector. The wages, salaries, and supplements item is composed primarily of the payments to employees of the nonprofit institutions that are included in the personal sector. Direct employment by households of servants, cleaners, etc., is also included, but it is a small amount. The total of $41 billion will be recognized as the income originating and the net and gross product of the sector. The social security payments by the personal sector on behalf of its employees are relatively small, and no figure is given for them. As social security coverage is extended to more and more employees and as the rates rise over time, this situation will presumably change. The next outlay is by far the largest. It is the total value of household purchases from the business and foreign sectors. The sum of all the items under personal outlays, excluding interest paid by consumers, represents the total consumption expenditures of the personal sector ($805 billion) included in the GNP account. The final outlay item is the interest paid by consumers which used to be included as part of total consumption expenditure but is now considered a transfer payment within the personal sector. It therefore appears on both sides of the personal sector account.

Because Table 3–2 shows the income and outlays of the personal sector, there is a residual item called "personal saving" which balances receipts and expenditures. Saving is the total left over after the sector has made its expenditures, and it can be positive, negative, or zero. It is at this point that the current flows as shown in the table intersect the accounts showing changes in stocks of assets that we do not discuss here. A positive level of saving would mean that the assets of the personal sector had been increased over the year because the sector has received more income than it has spent. Remember that this is but one of the ways in which asset values for the sector can change. Captial gains and losses are an example of another.

### The Government Sector

The three levels of government, federal, state, and local, form the government sector of the economy. In the case of this sector, as in the case of the personal sector, there is a problem of measuring the value of productive activity. Here again, the value of product is measured by income paid although in the case of the government sector there is the added complication that the services

## TABLE 3–3
**Government receipts and expenditures account, 1973 (billions of dollars)**

| | | | | | |
|---|---|---|---|---|---|
| 1. Government outlays | | $276 | 13. Personal taxes | | $151 (2.1) |
| 2. Wages, salaries, supplements | $133 (2.12) | | 14. Profits tax liability | | 50 (1.9) |
| 3. Social security payments (employer) | 14 (3.18) | | 15. Indirect business taxes | | 119 (1.15) |
| 4. Net purchases from business and | | | 16. Social security receipts from: | | 91 |
| foreign sectors | 129 | | 17. Business | $34 (1.3) | |
| 5. Transfer payments to: | | 116 | 18. Government | 14 (3.3) | |
| 6. Persons | 113 (2.27) | | 19. Personal | * (2.4) | |
| 7. Foreigners | 3 (4.9) | | 20. Employees | 43 (2.28) | |
| 8. Net interest paid | | 15 (2.22) | | | |
| 9. Surplus or deficit (−) | | 4 (5.12) | | | |
| 10. Federal | −6 | | | | |
| 11. State and local | 10 | | | | |
| 12. Government expenditures and surplus | | $411 | 21. Government receipts | | $411 |

* Less than $0.5 billion.
*Source:* See table 2–2. The code numbers used in this table refer to entries in tables 3–1 to 3–5.

produced are not paid for voluntarily but rather through obligatory tax payments. It might be argued that the willingness of people to tax themselves to pay for government services is a measure of the value they place on those services. But then the accountant is faced with the fact that the government frequently runs deficits or surpluses, and there would then be the question of interpreting the value of government services under those conditions. The solution therefore has been to value the activities of the government sector by the wage and salary costs of government.

In 1973 all levels of government paid $133 billion in wages and salaries and $14 billion in social security contributions on behalf of their employees. Thus, the income originating and net and gross product of the sector was $147 billion. This total also includes an imputed value of food and personal issue of the armed forces, as well as wages and salaries paid to government employees in positions requiring them to live abroad.

The government sector borrows substantial amounts of capital from other sectors in order to buy equipment and structures and to finance its operations. Nevertheless, the interest payments by government are not considered a cost associated with the current production of government services, and they do not appear on the left side of the account for the government sector. The justification for this is that while some borrowing by government was used to finance productive facilities such as roads and airports, most of it was incurred during recession and for defense and has left no discernible productive residual. If no current production is associated with the borrowing, then there can be no current income generated. The argument is similar to the argument given above concerning the interest payments of the personal sector.

Note that there is no rent item under government outlays. If the government were to rent all the land and buildings it uses, the rent payments would be part of the income paid by government, and the equivalent amount would be considered the value of the production of the real estate industry. But governments own the bulk of the real estate and buildings they use, and rent payments to other sectors are relatively minor. The accountant could, of course, add in an imputed rent to both sides of the account. However, the severe valuation problems associated with deciding the "rent," in the sense of the current productive use of the Capitol building, persuaded the Department of Commerce to ignore rental imputations in the case of government. Furthermore, if rent were to be imputed, government construction and other "investment" expenditure would have to be shown as a capital item rather than as a current expense as is presently the case. The final type of factor cost, profit, is defined out of the government account because the government is not considered to make a profit on its general operations. Government business enterprises are considered to be part of the business sector. As far as the nonfactor costs are concerned, government does not pay indirect business taxes, and since it has no capital stock, it cannot charge depreciation.

The government receipts and expenditure account, like the personal sector account, records total receipts and expenditures, not just those that originate in current economic activity. By far the largest share of the receipts of the government comes from taxes. The personal sector contributed $151 billion in 1973. The business sector contributed a total of $169 billion in corporate profit and indirect business taxes. The remaining receipt items are the employer and employee contributions to the various social insurance funds. The employer contributions are shown in Table 3–3 by sector of origin.

On the expenditure side of the account, the first two items of government outlay are the wage and social security cost of purchasing labor services. This total of $147 billion is also the measure of the income originating and net and gross product of the government sector. In the account of the personal sector, income originating appears as both an expense and a receipt. This does not occur in the government sector account, where only social security payments by government on behalf of their employees appear on both sides of the account. The wages, salaries, and supplements which are the other part of government product are an expense of government and a receipt of the personal sector.

In addition to purchasing labor services, the government sector purchased goods and services from the business and foreign sectors totaling $129 billion. The total is shown in the account as net purchases. The use of the word "net" is not to be confused with the concept of "net value added," for the government is considered a final consumer; that is, it purchases no intermediate product. The word net is entered because government sells goods to the business and foreign sectors.[1] The receipts from such sales could go on the receipts side of the account. However, because the government sector is not primarily in the business of selling things, such receipts are subtracted from government purchases, and the total is then shown as "net purchases from business and abroad."

---

[1] Such sales generally involve surplus goods. Sales by government business enterprises such as TVA are included in the account of the business sector.

The final two expenditure items are transfer payments (foreign and domestic) and net interest paid by government. Domestic transfer payments are primarily payments out of the various social insurance funds. Interest payments are shown as "net" because the government does receive interest, although largely from itself. Social insurance funds, as well as the Federal Reserve System and other government institutions, are large holders of government securities, and they receive interest payments on these holdings. Rather than show such intragovernmental receipts and expenditures separately, a net figure representing interest payments only to other sectors is given. Businesses also hold substantial quantities of government securities. However, the total net interest payments of $15 billion appears only as a receipt of the personal sector (Table 3–2, item 22). The reason is that the government does not know who actually holds the government debt, and it is therefore impossible to segregate government interest payments by the sector that receives them. The Department of Commerce assumes that all net government interest payments really accrue to the personal sector even though they may actually be paid to an insurance company or to a manufacturing corporation. By making this assumption, personal sector receipts are larger and business sector receipts are smaller than they might in fact be.

The residual item that balances the account is the surplus or deficit which in 1973 amounted to a surplus of $4 billion. The federal government showed a deficit of $6 billion, but this was more than offset by a surplus of $10 billion at the state and local levels. The size of this surplus is not affected by the fact that "net" purchases and "net" interest are shown on the expenditure side of the account because the "net" refers in each case to intragovernmental transactions. It should be remembered, as we noted in Chapter 2, that the government surplus or deficit on a national accounts basis differs from the surplus or deficit shown in the government's administrative and cash budgets. The latter include items that are on a different conceptual basis than the national accounts.

## The Foreign Sector

As we saw in discussing the balance of payments account, some of the income originating in current production in the United States accrues to foreigners who control factors of production situated in this country. For example, when a German automobile company establishes an American subsidiary, wages are paid to German nationals working here, and the profits from the operation belong to the German owners. Similarly, American oil companies operating in the Middle East pay Americans working there and in addition bring profits home. The national accounts measure the income and product of the nation's resources wherever located, and they exclude the income and product of the resources of other countries.

The account shown in Table 3–4 measures the net movement of factor payments to American residents, that is, wages paid to Americans working abroad minus wages paid to foreign nationals working in the United States.

**TABLE 3–4**
**Foreign transactions account, 1973 (billions of dollars)**

| | | | | | |
|---|---|--:|---|---|--:|
| 1. Net income payments to the United States | | $ 8 | 8. Transfers to foreigners from: | | $ 4 |
| 2. Wages, salaries, supplements | $* (2.14) | | 9. United States | | |
| 3. Interest | * (2.24) | | government | $3 (3.6) | |
| 4. Dividends | 4 (2.19) | | 10. United States | | |
| 5. Branch profits | 4 (5.9) | | individuals | 1 (2.7) | |
| 6. Exports of goods | | 92 | 11. Imports of goods | | 95 |
| 7. Receipts from foreigners | | $100 | 12. Net foreign investment | | 1 (5.4) |
| | | | 13. Payments to foreigners | | $100 |

* Less than $0.5 billion.
*Source:* See table 2–2. The code numbers used in this table refer to entries in tables 3–2 to 3–5.

Similar treatment is accorded to the other factor payments, interest, dividends, and the profits of foreign branches. Thus, the total income originating can be negative if the factor income originating in the United States and accruing to foreigners is greater than the reverse. Whatever the sign, the equivalent total represents the measure of the (net) value of the production by national resources located abroad in the same way as factor payments are taken to measure the value of the output of the personal and government sectors. In 1973 the United States earned a net total of $8 billion on income transactions.

There is no real need for a separate measure of the international flows of income. The income earned by American residents located abroad could be added to the appropriate heading of the business sector account. For example, profits of American branch plants located abroad could be consolidated with domestic corporate profits. But particular interest attaches to these current flows originating in the rest of the world, and the Department of Commerce therefore includes a separate account for such transactions.

The left side of Table 3–4 shows that during 1973 the United States exported goods worth $92 billion. The receipts from the foreign sector accruing to the United States thus totaled $100 billion.

The right side of Table 3–4 shows what can be thought of as the expenditures to the foreign sector by the United States in a manner analogous to the other sector accounts. The largest expenditure in 1973 was the $95 billion paid to foreigners for goods and services purchased by Americans. In addition, there were transfer payments to foreigners by the United States government and by individuals of $4 billion. The final item is the balancing item, which in this account is called "net foreign investment." In 1973 it amounted to $1 billion, which means that as a result of current economic activity, the credit position of the United States abroad was increased by $1 billion. This balancing item could, of course, have been negative or zero. As we pointed out in Chapter 2, this $1 billion does not represent the total investment position of the United States with respect to the foreign sector during 1973. When all transactions with the foreign sector are considered, specifically the capital transactions in addition to the current transactions included in Table 3–4, the United States comes out as a net debtor in the amount of $2.5 billion as shown in Table 2–4. It must be remembered that the GNP account and the sector accounts we are now examining do not deal with capital transactions. We now turn to this point explicitly.

## The Saving and Investment Account

This final account, shown in Table 3–5, does not record the transactions of a separate sector but instead ties together the loose ends of the sector accounts. Each sector account has a balancing item, representing some form of saving, that appears only once in the sector accounts; every other item appears twice, once as a receipt and again as an expenditure. The saving items appear only once because they are transactions on capital rather than on current accounts. For example, personal saving is, by definition, income that is not spent by the personal sector for the purchase of a currently produced good or service (or for some form of tax), and therefore there is no current income flow associated with the saving. It shows that the personal sector took $75 billion out of the current flow of income by not returning it in the form of an expenditure that would generate further income.

The flow of saving in the economy is made up of personal saving, the government surplus or deficit, and gross corporate saving. The latter includes the undistributed earnings of domestic corporations, the depreciation allowance, the corporate inventory valuation adjustment, and the net flow of foreign branch profits. This last item is included because we are dealing with national accounts and are therefore concerned with the activity of resources owned by Americans, wherever these resources are located. The flow of investment goods on the other side of the account records the share of the flow of current output that is not considered to be consumed by the final user in the national economy within the accounting period (net investment), plus the change in inventory, plus depreciation. The inclusion of depreciation means that the flow of saving includes gross corporate saving, and that the flow of investment includes gross business purchases on capital account. As we explained

**TABLE 3–5**
**Gross saving and investment account, 1973 (billions of dollars)**

| | | | | | |
|---|---|---|---|---|---|
| 1. Gross private domestic investment | | $209 | 6. Personal saving | | $ 75 (2.8) |
| 2. Construction and | | | 7. Gross corporate saving | | 136 |
| equipment | $194 (1.21) | | 8. Undistributed profits | | 38 (1.11) |
| 3. Change in inventory | 15 (1.22) | | 9. Foreign branch profits | | 4 (4.5) |
| 4. Net foreign investment | | 1 (4.12) | 10. Inventory valuation adjustment | | −18 (1.12) |
| | | | 11. Depreciation | | 111 (1.17) |
| | | | 12. Government surplus or deficit (−) | | 4 (3.9) |
| | | | 13. Statistical discrepancy | | −5 (1.18) |
| 5. Gross investment | | $210 | 14. Gross saving | | $210 |

*Source:* See table 2–2. The code numbers used in this table refer to entries in tables 3–1 to 3–4.

in the previous chapter, the Department of Commerce has not been successful in deriving an adequate net investment total because it has proved impossible to derive a reliable estimate of the current value of the depreciation of the capital stock. Thus, gross business saving includes the business accounting estimate of depreciation to balance the gross flow of additions to the capital stock.

It is important to realize that the two sides of Table 3–5 must balance because of the definitions that are used even though the items do not appear twice under the same name within the sector accounts. Consider the total flow of goods and services produced and the equivalent flow of income generated in production. When a sector saves part of its income, it is, by definition, not buying part of the current flow of product. That part of current production that is not currently consumed is called "investment," and it can take the form either of capital goods produced for the business sector or of net changes in the stock of inventory. Thus, what is not currently consumed has been defined to be both saving and investment, depending on which side of the circular flow is being examined, and the two amounts must be equal.

We have now finished the presentation of the sector accounts, which with the GNP account presented in Chapter 2, present a fairly detailed picture of the flows of income and product associated with current economic activity plus various current transfers of income and transactions with capital accounts. To consider only the GNP account alone is to lose a great deal of information that is important for macroeconomic analysis.

### The National Income and Product Account

We can now complete the system we have been presenting by deriving from the sector accounts the GNP for the economy. In the discussion of each sector account presented above we noted that there was an element measuring the income originating and net and gross product of the sector. We have been emphasizing that a system of national accounting is based on measures of the flows of income generated by current economic activity and the flow of product that is produced by the activity. In Table 3–6 we present a GNP account based on this conception of the economy. It will be noted that this account is logically consistent with the concept of the circular flow of income and product in a way that the GNP account is not. In the GNP account, the two sides are separate in the sense that there is no way to compare the figures on one side with those on the other. Consumption expenditure, for example, includes the value of imported goods, and it is not possible to determine the income flows that were associated with the production of consumption goods by domestic resources. The GNP account is in fact a compromise reflecting the data needs of users. The flow of product side is taken from one double-entry account which shows the flow of product and the equivalent income generated by that production. The flow of income side, on the other hand, is taken from another double-entry account which shows the flow of income by type and the equivalent flow of product. It cannot be said, of course,

**TABLE 3–6**

National income and product account by sector of origin, 1973 (billions of dollars)

| Income originating in: | | Net product originating in: | |
|---|---|---|---|
| Business sector | $ 869 | Business sector | $ 993 |
| Personal sector | 41 | Personal sector | 41 |
| Government sector | 147 | Government sector | 147 |
| Foreign sector | 8 | Foreign sector | 8 |
| National income | $1,065 | Depreciation | 111 |
| Business transfer payments | 5 | Statistical discrepancy | −5 |
| Indirect business taxes | 119 | | |
| Charges against net national product | $1,189 | | |
| Depreciation | 111 | | |
| Statistical discrepancy | −5 | | |
| Charges against gross national product | $1,295 | Gross national product | $1,295 |

Source: tables 3–1 to 3–4.

that the GNP account as presented by the Department of Commerce is wrong in any sense. The only point is that different sectoring devices have been used in presenting the two sides of the account, and it is therefore not possible to relate one directly to the other.

The right side of Table 3–6 lists the values of the products produced by each of the sectors, and the left side gives the factor and nonfactor costs of production; or in other words, the income paid to the factors that produced the output. The sum of factor costs of $1,065 billion is the national income. It represents the total income received by American factors from participation in the current productive process. The addition of indirect taxes and transfer payments to national income yields $1,189 billion, the total charges against net national product. Finally, the addition of depreciation charges and the statistical discrepancy yields $1,295 billion which accounts for the total value of the final goods and services currently produced, that is, GNP.

Table 3–6 presents the GNP account in a form which is logically consistent with the concept of the aggregate economic system as a circular flow of income and product. It shows what kinds of income originated in each sector and the value of the goods and services produced by that sector. Such an account shows the relative size of the sectors into which the economy has been divided, and, more importantly, it represents the conceptual basis from which other formulations of the accounts are derived.

## 3–3
## A SYSTEM OF ECONOMIC ACCOUNTS

Before closing this brief discussion of production accounting, some remarks should be made about modern developments in economic accounting. The GNP account of production forms the basis of the economic accounts of all nations. However, under the stimulus of the statistical section of the United

Nations, many countries are now moving toward the presentation of much more complete sets of data on economic performance.[1]

The earliest extension of the production account was in the direction of making detailed estimates of the transactions in intermediate flows between productive sectors that are consolidated in the GNP accounts. The input-output matrix is the name given to the presentation of these data. What the matrix does is to show the source and destination of all current productive activity by industrial sectors, whether it is immediately destined for final use or not. Thus the economy is divided not only into sectors of final demand but also into the productive sectors that produce goods and services. Suppose, for example, that agriculture is separated as an individual sector. Like the GNP account, the input-output matrix shows the income payments to factors of production by the sector and the distribution of final product to consumers, such as retained home production. In addition, the matrix records the value of the industry's purchases of products from other sectors (such as fertilizer from the chemical industry) and its sale of products to nonfinal users (such as raw cotton to the textile industry). The construction of such a matrix of both final and intermediate flows permits economists to examine the whole complex of productive economic activity. It also allows them, under certain assumptions, to examine a host of problems dealing with such things as the impact on the industrial structure of changes in final demand or its components. For example, the matrix permits one to examine the total induced effect, through all productive sectors of the economy, of an increase in the government's demand for final product. Alternatively, one can examine the impact of a change in the input requirements of a sector and the impact of that change on all other sectors.

The next development of economic accounting arose out of the saving-investment account described above. For the economy as a whole, the two sides of the saving-investment account always balance as a matter of definition. Income that is not spent for current production is saved, and current production that is not purchased for current use is investment. But this matter of overall balance is achieved within the economy by the transfer of funds between sectors. Some sectors are net savers (households) and some sectors are net borrowers (business), and during the course of a year there will be a transfer of funds between them. If, in addition to the four sectors distinguished in the GNP accounts, the various financial intermediaries such as banks, savings and loans, and insurance companies are distinguished, then an accounting of the flow of funds can be generated that will trace the movement of financial resources from savers to borrowers, and the financial institutions through which the transfer takes place. Each sector then will contain an

---

[1] United Nations, Department of Economic and Social Affairs, *A System of National Accounts, Studies in Methods*, Sec. F, No. 2, Rev. 3, New York, 1968. See also R. Ruggles and N. Ruggles, *The Design of Economic Accounts*, National Bureau of Economic Research, New York, 1970; and J. W. Kendrick, *Economic Accounts and Their Uses*, McGraw-Hill Book Company, New York, 1972.

accounting of the sources of funds available to it and the uses to which the funds are put. The household sector, for example, generates a flow of saving from current economic activity and at the same time it purchases capital goods such as houses. In general, the household sector can be expected to have a positive balance on such activity, that is, its saving will exceed its capital expenditures, and the difference measures the resources available for financial investment in the business, government, finance, or foreign sectors. The unique aspect of this accounting of the flow of funds is that it shows in detail the distribution of these available funds by sectors. Thus the household sector may accumulate assets in financial institutions (time deposits, insurance reserves) or claims against other sectors (corporate shares, government bonds). The accounts of these other sectors will then show such transactions as sources of funds and will similarly detail the uses to which the funds are put.

All the accounts that have been discussed to this point have concerned flows. But once a set of accounts is available that includes both current productive and financial activity, it is a natural step to a national wealth balance sheet. Such an account would show the total stock of assets, liabilities, and net worth for each sector of the economy at any one time. As a result of current productive activity, sectors accumulate saving out of which they acquire capital assets which are added to their existing stock of assets. If saving exceeds investment, surplus financial assets are available for lending to other sectors for which claims against the other sectors are received in exchange. At the same time, parts of a net saving sector may be financing asset accumulation by borrowing from other sectors (mortgages to build houses), thus accumulating financial liabilities. Thus the balance sheet permits an examination of the structure of the capital resources of the individual sectors of the economy.

Although sectoral balance sheets or wealth statements are not produced on a regular basis in any country at the present time, balance-sheet items form an important element in modern macroeconomic analysis. As subsequent discussion will show, wealth is an important determinant of the flow of consumption and investment expenditure. Wealth and consumption expenditure are positively related, households with a large stock of assets tend to spend a larger proportion of their income than those without assets, and a business firm's decision about whether to invest in further productive capacity is influenced in part by its existing capital structure. Furthermore, the capital stock plays a significant role in the determination of the level of potential GNP and in the production function approach to the analysis of the growth of the economy over time.

One of the most exciting developments in modern economic accounting has arisen from the question of the definition of capital in national wealth, particularly as it affects the problem of economic growth. The point at issue is essentially how wide the definition of capital should be cast. Production accounting as it is currently practiced defines capital narrowly to include tangible nonhuman assets (plant, equipment, and inventories). But increasing interest has been expressed in the position that human capital formation ought realistically to be considered a part of national wealth. Expenditures on human health, education, and training ought to be considered just as much a part of a nation's assets as a machine. Analogously, the depreciation of human capital ought to be considered as a charge against the current formation of wealth.

At some time, a complete set of economic accounts will become available for one or more countries, and the result will be a tremendous extension of the field of macroeconomic analysis. Until such time, the rather limited GNP and sector accounts will form the empirical basis of macroeconomics.

## 3–4
### SUMMARY

In this first part of the book we have presented a fairly detailed picture of the national income and product accounts as developed by the Department of Commerce. At various stages in the discussion we pointed out that in some details the accounts are, for practical reasons, not always consistent. At the same time, there is an underlying rationale to the accounts that overrides the practical difficulties of estimation. The underlying rationale derives from the attempt to measure the annual flows of income and final product in the economy as a basis for evaluating the economy's utilization of its economic resources. In presenting figures, the Department of Commerce tries at the same time to give those that will fit into the body of economic theory from which evaluation and predictions can arise.

As the discussion in Chapter 1 indicated, the annual volume of output is determined by the expenditures for final goods and services, which, in turn, are related in part to the incomes received by the units making expenditure decisions. Therefore, the GNP account is broken down by the Department of Commerce in terms of income receipts by economic units and expenditures by the same units.

In Part 2 we shall examine the factors underlying the expenditure decisions of the economic units and the effects of these decisions upon the volume of final output. From such a study, and with the picture of the economy derived from the national accounts in mind, we shall be in a position to understand what determines the level of national output and to suggest measures that may be employed to affect that level.

# 2

# THE
# LEVEL OF
# ECONOMIC
# ACTIVITY

# CONSUMPTION, SAVING, AND INCOME DETERMINATION

## THE CONSUMPTION FUNCTION

One of the central propositions of national income analysis is that aggregate real consumption expenditures of the economy are determined primarily by the level of real disposable income. The relationship between consumption and disposable income is usually called the "consumption function," although it is occasionally referred to as the "propensity to consume."

A consumption function for a hypothetical economy is shown in Figure 4–1. Real disposable income is measured on the horizontal axis, and real consumption expenditure is measured on the vertical axis. The 45-degree line is a guideline which denotes that any point on the line is equidistant from the two axes. This means that the distance from the origin to some point on the horizontal axis will be the same as the vertical distance from that point on the horizontal axis to the 45-degree line. The level of disposable income can therefore be measured either vertically to the 45-degree line or along the horizontal axis.

The consumption function is drawn as a straight line with a slope of less than one. Although no one would seriously argue that the straight-line as-

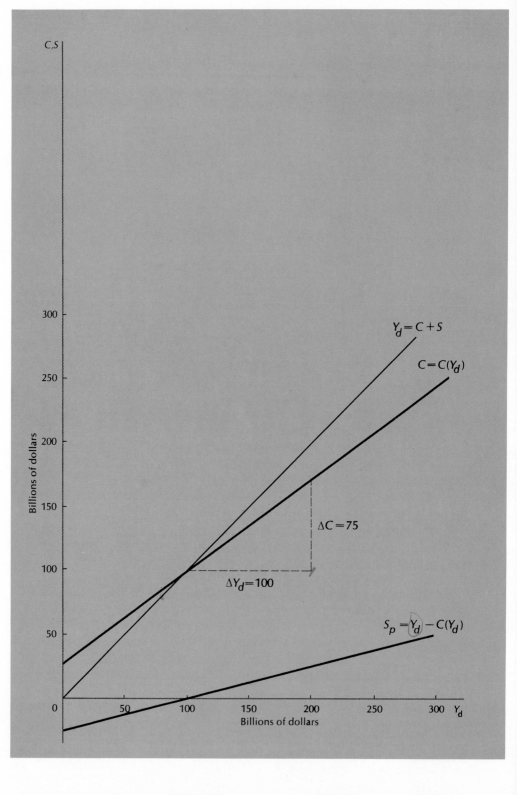

sumption is not an oversimplification, it is not enough of a distortion to justify the added complication of introducing a nonlinear schedule. The slope of the consumption function, or "marginal propensity to consume," measures the fraction of each additional dollar of disposable income that will be consumed. Both theory and evidence suggest that the marginal propensity to consume is less than unity. Consequently, out of each additional dollar of disposable income received the community will increase its consumption by a fraction of the additional dollar and will save the remainder.

An additional assumption of our example is that there is some level of disposable income ($100 billion in Figure 4–1) at which all disposable income is consumed. Below this disposable income level (often called the "point of zero saving") consumers will make expenditures in excess of their disposable income even though this means dissaving, i.e., dipping into past saving or going into debt.

The marginal propensity to consume is, in the example of Figure 4–1, assumed to be 0.75. The point of zero saving is assumed to occur when disposable income is $100 billion. But as disposable income rises to $200 billion, consumption rises by only 0.75 × 100, which means that saving must rise by 0.25 × 100. When disposable income is $200 billion, consumption expenditure must therefore be $175 billion, and saving must be $25 billion. At disposable income levels below $100 billion the community is so poor that it prefers to go into debt rather than spend only its current disposable income on consumption. If it were possible to reduce disposable income to zero dollars, consumption would fall to $25 billion. Personal saving would therefore be − $25 billion.

In addition to the consumption function, Figure 4–1 also includes the schedule of intended personal saving $S_p$. This schedule is simply the difference between the consumption function and the 45-degree line. The slope of the saving schedule, called the "marginal propensity to save," is always one minus the marginal propensity to consume. In the present example, the marginal propensity to consume is 0.75. The marginal propensity to save is therefore 0.25 because any addition to disposable income that is not spent must, by definition, be saved.[1]

---

[1] Algebraically we may summarize what has been said thus far as follows: The hypothesis that consumption is a function of disposable income can be written

$$C = C(Y_d)$$

where $C$ stands for aggregate real consumption and $Y_d$ represents aggregate real disposable income. In the event that the consumption function is linear,

$$C = a + bY_d$$

**FIGURE 4–1**
**The consumption and saving functions (all values in real terms)**

## 4-2
## SIMPLE INCOME DETERMINATION

As a means of getting the analysis off the ground in an uncomplicated manner, let us visualize an economy in which there is no government, in which corporations retain no earnings, in which there is no foreign trade, and in which the level of net intended investment is geared to long-term expectations and is therefore independent of the level of current income. Let us agree, also, to think of all magnitudes in real terms. Without any government or retained earnings, disposable income and NNP (Y) are identical. The national income accountant's framework in this economy is

$$Y \equiv C + I_r \tag{4-1}$$

where $C$ is consumption and $I_r$ is net realized investment. By "realized investment" we mean all net investment regardless of whether it is intentional or unintentional. All income becomes disposable income under present assumptions, so that

$$Y \equiv C + S_p \tag{4-2}$$

By assumption, there is no corporate saving, and so net private saving $S$ becomes identical with net personal saving $S_p$. By equating (4-1) with (4-2) and substituting $S$ for $S_p$, we note that

$$I_r \equiv S \tag{4-3}$$

which becomes the fundamental accounting identity in this simplified economy.

Now consider Figure 4-2. The consumption function is the same as in Figure 4-1, but it is now assumed that producers desire to spend $20 billion on investment goods (net of depreciation) at all levels of income.[1] Let us see what the equilibrium level of income will be under these circumstances.

---

where $b$ is the marginal propensity to consume and $a$ is the level of consumption at zero disposable income. In the present example $b = 0.75$. Therefore,

$C = a + 0.75Y_d$

From Figure 4-1 it is evident that at an income level of $100 billion, savings are zero. Consumption is therefore equal to disposable income at this point. Accordingly,

$100 = a + 0.75 \times 100$

so that

$a = 25$

The equation for the schedule of intended consumption therefore becomes

$C = 25 + 0.75Y_d$

Because personal saving is simply the difference between consumption and disposable income,

$S_p = Y_d - C = Y_d - (25 + 0.75Y_d) = -25 + 0.25Y_d$

is the equation for the saving function.

[1] Note that we now have $Y$ instead of $Y_d$ on the horizontal axis.

One way to determine the equilibrium level of income is to add the schedule of intended investment to the consumption schedule and to observe at what points this "aggregate demand" function $C + I$ intersects the 45-degree line.[1] Another way of finding equilibrium is to find the point where the schedule of intended investment cuts the saving schedule. In both cases equilibrium is at $180 billion.

What is the logic behind the equilibrium solution? Suppose that producers believe they will be able to sell $220 billion worth of goods. With production at $220 billion, disposable income will be $220 billion. The consumption function indicates that at an income level of $220 billion consumers will spend $190 billion on consumption goods and save $30 billion. (Observe the situation at an income of $220 billion in Figure 4–2.) The intended investment schedule shows that businesspersons wish to purchase $20 billion worth of investment goods. The total demand for goods and services (aggregate demand) at an income level of $220 billion is therefore $210 billion. But since production is greater than sales by $10 billion, the extra $10 billion worth of goods will be accumulated by businesses in the form of unintended investment in inventories $I_u$. If businesses continue to produce $220 billion worth of goods, inventories will continue to pile up at the rate of $10 billion per year. There will thus be a tendency for business to cut back production.

At the $220 billion income level the level of saving is $30 billion, intended investment $I$ is $20 billion, and unintended investment $I_u$ is $10 billion. Consequently the national income accountant will note that realized investment ($I_r$ = intended + unintended investment) is exactly equal to the level of realized saving. It must always be true that

$$I + I_u = I_r = S$$

but only in equilibrium will it be true that intended investment equals saving, or

$$I = S$$

because the existence of unintended inventory investment or disinvestment indicates that production and sales are not synchronized.

Again, consider the situation that will arise if businesspersons underestimate the demand for goods and services and therefore produce only $140 billion worth of goods while intended investment remains unchanged at $20 billion (see Figure 4–2 again at $Y = 140$). When $Y = 140$, $C = 130$, with the consequence that aggregate demand $C + I = 150$; thus there will be a $10 billion reduction in inventories not anticipated by businesspersons. Since saving is $10 billion and unintended investment is $-$10 billion,

$$I + I_u = 10 = S$$

---

[1] Algebraically, if $C = 0.75Y + 25$ and if $I = 20$, then by substituting into $Y = C + I$, we have

$$Y = \frac{25 + 20}{1 - 0.75} = 180$$

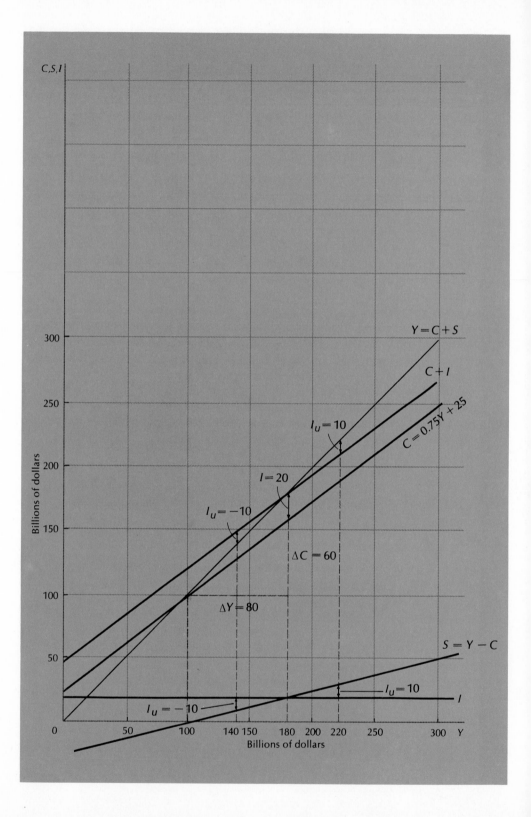

There will now be a tendency for production and income to increase to a level of $180 billion where $C = 160$, $S = 20$, $I = 20$, and $I_u = 0$. The equilibrium level of income, it appears, necessarily requires equality between intended investment and saving.

## 4–3
## THE MULTIPLIER

Suppose that the level of intended investment expenditure is zero. The equilibrium level of income would, in this case, be $100 billion (see Figure 4–2 again). Next pretend that businesspersons suddenly decide to spend $20 billion each year on new plant and equipment. The aggregate demand schedule $C + I$ would therefore shift up by $20 billion. Notice, however, that the level of income rises not by $20 billion but by $80 billion. Observe, finally, that the overall change in income of $80 billion consists of two components: the change in investment expenditure of $20 billion and an additional increase in consumption expenditure of $60 billion. How does this change in consumption of $60 billion come about?

To illustrate this "multiplier" effect let us suppose that changes in expenditure are instantaneously translated into income receipts, but that income recipients do not spend today's income until tomorrow. Suppose next that, instead of a permanent shift in the investment demand schedule, an increase in investment spending of $1 takes place in day 1. This $1 is immediately paid out to the wage earners, stockholders, etc., of the investment goods industry. The marginal propensity to consume $b$ tells us that on day 2, $b$ percent of the additional income earned in day 1 will be spent on consumption goods. Consequently, income originating in consumption goods industries rises by $b$ dollars on day 2, of which $b$ percent, or $b^2$, is spent in day 3, of which $b$ percent, or $b^3$, will be spent in day 4, and so on indefinitely. The day-by-day income changes, in excess of the original equilibrium level, resulting from the $1 increase in investment expenditure in day 1 will therefore be

$$1, b, b^2, b^3, \ldots, b^t$$

Since $b$ is a fraction, the differences between the initial equilibrium income level and the actual income level become successively smaller as time passes. Note that as $t$ becomes very large, $b^t$ becomes very small so that income returns to its initial equilibrium.

The time path of income for a value of $b = 0.75$ is traced in Figure 4–3. In day 1 the $1 increase in spending raises the income level by $1 over the initial value of $Y_0$. In day 2 the amount of $0.75 \times \$1$, or 75 cents, is respent on consumption goods. Income in day 2 is therefore $Y_0 + 75$ cents. In day 3 income will be $0.75 \times 0.75$, or $(0.75)^2 \times \$1$, in excess of the initial level, and

## FIGURE 4–2
Simple income determination (all values in real terms)

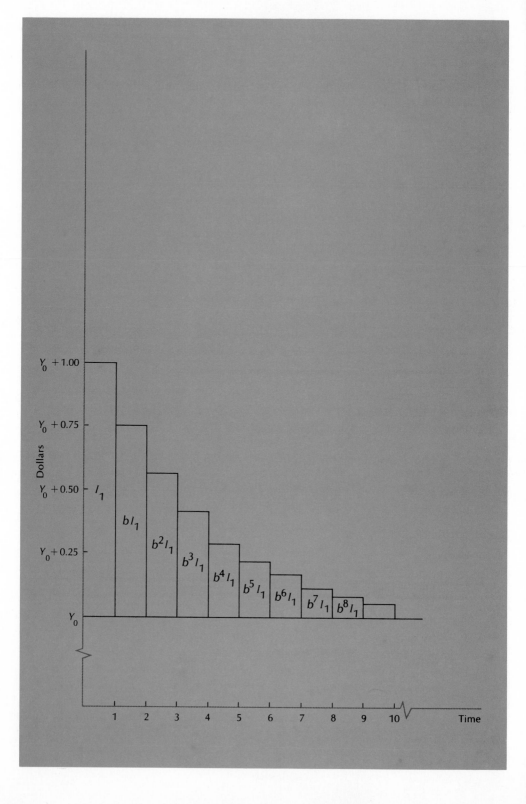

in day $t$ it will be $(0.75)^{t-1} \times \$1$ in excess of the initial level. As $t$ grows very large, the difference between the initial level and the actual level of income approaches zero.

The case just considered may be visualized most easily by imagining an automobile cruising down a level road at a constant speed of 40 miles per hour with the accelerator held steady exactly halfway from the floor of the car. Imagine that the driver pushes the accelerator to the floor but then immediately releases it and holds it steady in its original position. The car will first lurch forward, picking up speed, but will immediately begin to decelerate and gradually approach its previous 40-mile-per-hour speed.

What will happen if the driver pushes the accelerator to the floor and keeps it there? The car will pick up speed and continue to accelerate, but at a decreasing rate, until gradually the speed of the car approaches a new constant velocity. This latter case, in which the accelerator is pressed to the floor and held there, is exactly the kind of thing that happens when investment expenditure is increased by some amount and is then maintained at the new higher level permanently. In other words, an upward shift of the investment demand schedule of $1 implies that there will be a $1 increase in investment spending in period 1; another dollar will be spent in period 2, another dollar in period 3, and so on indefinitely.

How will the level of income change over time under this new set of assumptions? In day 1 the investment schedule shifts up so that on this first day the level of income rises by $1. The level of income in day 1 is therefore

$$Y_1 = Y_0 + 1$$

where $Y_0$ is the initial income level. In day 2 another dollar of investment expenditure is added to the income stream. But in addition to this extra dollar, $b$ percent of the dollar of the investment expenditure of the first day will be spent on consumption. Consequently on day 2 the level of income is

$$Y_2 = Y_0 + 1 + b$$

In day 3, $b$ percent of the income change in day 2 over the initial level, or $b(1 + b) = b + b^2$, will be respent on consumption, in addition to which another dollar of investment expenditure is added to the income stream. Consequently on day 3 the level of income rises to

$$Y_3 = Y_0 + 1 + b + b^2$$

The process repeats itself indefinitely so that in day $t$

$$Y_t = Y_0 + 1 + b + b^2 + b^3 + \cdots + b^{t-1}$$

**FIGURE 4–3**
**The multiplier with a single expenditure (all values in real terms)**

which, as can easily be shown,[1] simplifies to

$$Y_t = Y_0 + \frac{1 - b^t}{1 - b}$$

As $t$ grows very large, $b^t$ becomes very small so that in the limit the new equilibrium value of income $Y_t$ is

$$Y_t = Y_0 + \frac{1}{1 - b}$$

The change in income $Y_t - Y_0$ due to a $1-per-day increase in investment spending therefore is $1/(1 - b)$, which is known as the "multiplier." Remember that $b$ is the marginal propensity to consume and that $1 - b$ is the marginal propensity to save. Consequently, if $b = 0.75$, $1 - b = 0.25$, and the multiplier has a value of 4. Thus a permanent $1 increase in investment spending raises the level of income by $4. If $b = 0.50$, the multiplier is 2. If $b = 0$, the multiplier is 1. In this last case, all additional income that results from the increase in investment will be saved, so that there is no respending on consumption, and consequently the level of income rises only by the amount of the permanent increase in investment expenditure.

A diagram similar to Figure 4–4 may help to illustrate the process of adjustment to the new equilibrium level. Assume that $b = 0.50$ and that each day $1 of new investment expenditure materializes. In the first day the level of income rises by $1. In the second day 0.50 of this is respent, in addition to which another dollar of investment expenditure takes place. In the third day 0.50 of the $1.50 is respent on consumption and added to the $1 of investment spending which materialized on day 3. This gives an increase in income, over the initial level, of $1.75. The successive day-to-day increases over the previous day become smaller and smaller and gradually the level of income approaches its new equilibrium level of $Y_0 + 2$.

[1] Note that

$$Y_t = Y_0 + 1 + b + b^2 + b^3 + \cdots + b^{t-1}$$

is a geometric series. In order to sum such a series, we need merely multiply each term by $b$:

$$bY_t = bY_0 + b + b^2 + b^3 + \cdots + b^{t-1} + b^t$$

and observe that when the second series is subtracted from the first series, all but the first two terms from the right-hand side of the first series drop out, and only the first and last terms of the right-hand side of the second series remain, i.e.,

$$Y_t - bY_t = Y_0 - bY_0 + 1 - b^t$$

which simplifies to

$$Y_t = Y_0 + \frac{1 - b^t}{1 - b}$$

**FIGURE 4–4**
**The multiplier with a continuous injection**
**(all values in real terms)**

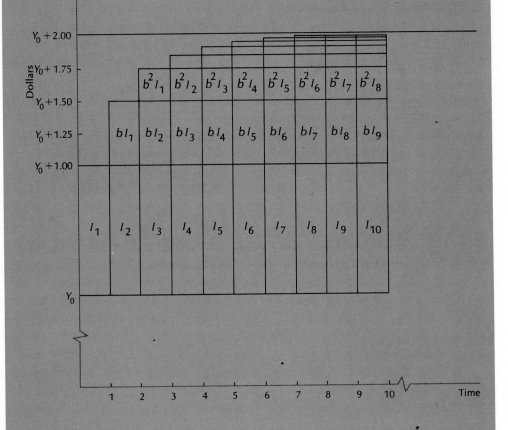

One of the most useful ways to visualize the multiplier is as follows: We know from our previous discussion that income cannot be in equilibrium unless intended investment and saving are equal. If, therefore, we begin in a position of equilibrium and if intended investment now rises permanently by $1, we know from the equilibrium condition that unless saving also rises by $1, equilibrium will not have been restored. Thus all we need to do is ask: By how much must income rise in order that one more dollar of saving be generated? This question is identical to asking what the value of the multiplier is. If the marginal propensity to consume is 0.75, the marginal propensity to save is 0.25. This means that each time income rises by $1, saving rises by 25 cents. But since we require saving to rise by $1, and since a $1 rise in income generates only a 25-cent increase in saving, the necessary income increase must be $1/0.25, or $4. Had the marginal propensity to save been 0.5, an additional dollar of income would generate an additional 50-cent saving so that the multiplier would be $1/0.50 = 2$. In general, if the marginal propensity to save is $1 - b$, an additional dollar of income creates added saving in an amount $1 - b$ so that a $1 increase in saving would be generated by an income increase of $1/(1 - b)$.[1]

## 4-4
## FACTORS AFFECTING THE LEVEL OF AGGREGATE CONSUMPTION

The proposition that aggregate real consumption is a function of the aggregate level of real disposable income stems from the revolutionary work of Lord Keynes.[2] Keynes's theory of the consumption function held out the hope that a firm basis for forecasting consumption expenditure had at last been discovered. However, forecasts of post–World War II consumption were quite far off the mark. Since that time economists have devoted considerable research effort to attempt to isolate the factors which, in addition to real disposable income, determine real consumption expenditure.

It should be obvious to anyone who thinks about his own circumstances that his spending habits are influenced by a large and complicated set of interrelated factors. Demographic characteristics, age, sex, the size of family, etc., do much to determine the fraction of income that is saved. He will realize, also, that he may be able to consume more than a person with the same

---

[1] If $Y = C + I$ and the consumption function is $C = a + bY$, the equilibrium level of income is

$$Y = \frac{a + I}{1 - b}$$

The multiplier can now be calculated directly by differentiating this expression with respect to $I$. The result is

$$\frac{dY}{dI} = \frac{1}{1 - b}$$

[2] J. M. Keynes, *The General Theory of Employment, Interest and Money,* Harcourt, Brace & World, Inc., New York, 1936.

income because he is fortunate to have a larger accumulation of assets, or because he does not have to save toward a target such as a retirement fund or college tuition, or because he is in an occupation in which steady income and employment are assured. In addition to these economic factors, he may find that it is necessary to spend less to "keep up with the Joneses" than a person with the same income who lives elsewhere. Finally, it will have occurred to him that his current income is often subject to various windfalls, and that his consumption pattern is probably more closely geared to his long-range circumstances (for example, an average of expected incomes) than it is to current income. In this event, the person may find that it would be appropriate to redefine the whole concept of income for purposes of predicting consumption and saving behavior.

As the above paragraph has attempted to suggest, the study of consumer behavior is a vast and complex field. We cannot hope to survey all the possibilities, although we will try to indicate the main directions economic research has taken since Keynes first introduced what has come to be called the "absolute income" hypothesis.[1]

In searching out additional economic variables that help, along with aggregate income, to explain the level of consumption, economists have focused attention upon such variables as wealth, the rate of interest, and the distribution of income. The proposition that consumption is a function of the level of wealth rests on a solid empirical foundation and, as will be seen from a later stage of our discussion, is of great significance from both a theoretical and a policy point of view. For two persons with equal current incomes, the one with a higher net worth, that is, the difference between the various assets owned and the debts (liabilities) owed, will consume a larger fraction of that person's income. Had statistical consumption functions taken account of the large accumulation of government bonds by households during World War II, their postwar consumption forecasts would have been considerably more accurate.[2]

---

[1] For a careful and comprehensive survey of the material discussed in this section see R. Ferber, "Research in Household Behavior," *American Economic Review*, 52:19–63, 1962.

[2] The idea that wealth influences consumption is anything but new. Some important theoretical discussions are A. C. Pigou, "The Classical Stationary State," *Economic Journal*, 53:343–351, 1943; A. C. Pigou, "Economic Progress in a Stable Environment," *Economica*, New Series, 14:180–188, 1951; A. P. Lerner, "Functional Finance and the Federal Debt," *Social Research*, 10:38–51, 1943; G. Ackley, "The Wealth-Saving Relationship," *Journal of Political Economy*, 59:154–161, 1951. Important empirical studies are those of J. Tobin, "Relative Income, Absolute Income, and Savings," in *Money, Trade, and Economic Growth: Essays in Honor of John H. Williams*, The Macmillan Company, New York, 1951; W. Hamburger, "The Relation of Consumption to Wealth and the Wage Rate," *Econometrica*, 23:1–17, 1955; J. N. Morgan, "Factors Relating to Consumer Saving When It Is Defined as a Net Worth Concept," in L. R. Klein, ed., *Contributions of Survey Methods to Economics*, Columbia University Press, New York, 1954; L. R. Klein, "Estimating Patterns of Savings Behavior for Sample Survey Data," *Econometrica*, 19:438–454, 1951; L. R. Klein, "Assets, Debts, and Economic Behavior," in National Bureau of Economic Research, *Studies in Income and Wealth*, Vol. 14, Columbia University Press, New York, 1951, pp. 195–227; and A. Zellner, "The Short-Run Consumption Function," *Econometrica*, 25:552–567, 1957.

A time-honored proposition of economic theory is that an increase in the rate of interest will induce consumers to forgo some additional present consumption in order to take advantage of the better earnings opportunities that additional saving affords. Statistical evidence generally fails to support this hypothesis. Perhaps this is because a good deal of saving aims at a specific target, for example, a definite sum by a certain future date to finance a child's college expenses, or a specific nest egg to be available at the time of retirement. For such "target savers," an increase in interest rates reduces the annual amount to be saved to reach the objective. Thus, to some people higher interest rates are an incentive to save more, whereas to others they are an opportunity to save less.[1]

It was Keynes's belief that the marginal propensity to consume of low-income groups would be higher than the marginal propensity to consume of high-income groups. This belief suggested that aggregate demand might be raised by a policy of income redistribution. If the marginal propensity to consume of a rich person is 0.60 whereas it is 0.90 for the poor person, a redistribution of $1 from the rich person to the poor person would raise aggregate consumption by 30 cents. If a redistribution of a given level of disposable income would change the level of consumption, the consumption function for the community as a whole would have to be treated as a function of both the level of disposable income and the way in which disposable income was distributed.

The evidence on the effect of income redistribution is somewhat mixed.[2] Investigations using American cross-section data fail to disclose any dramatic relationship between the distribution of income and aggregate consumption. Perhaps this is because there is no necessary reason why the marginal propensity to consume of the poor person should be higher than that of a rich person. Superficially, it would appear that because rich people save while poor people dissave, a redistribution that favored the poor would raise consumption. However, the crucial issue is whether their marginal propensities to consume differ. While poor people may desperately need to increase their consumption, they may just as avidly desire to escape debt. Thus it would be entirely reasonable to expect them to save a sizable fraction of any additional income they obtain. Although greater income equality has much to commend it, one must nevertheless recognize that greater equality would probably have little effect on total consumption.

Statistical studies have shown that the shape of the consumption function

[1] There is, however, some evidence that consumer demand for durable goods is influenced by interest rates. See M. J. Hamburger, "Interest Rates and the Demand for Durable Goods," *American Economic Review*, 62:1131–1153, 1967.

[2] H. Staehle, "Short Period Variations in the Distribution of Incomes," *Review of Economic Statistics*, 19:133–143, 1937; and H. Lubell, "Effects of Income Redistribution on Consumers' Expenditures," *American Economic Review*, 37:157–170, 1947. See also J. Marschak's classic paper, "Personal and Collective Budget Functions," *Review of Economic Statistics*, 21:161–170, 1939.

differs radically depending upon the type of data used to plot the function. When aggregate consumption expenditures are plotted against disposable income for different years, the consumption function appears as a line ($C_L$ in Figure 4–5) emanating from the origin with a slope of approximately 0.9. But when consumption expenditures are plotted for a cross section of family-income groups at one point in time, the shape is more in line with the consumption function plotted in Figure 4–1 and corresponds to the functions $C_{S_0}$, $C_{S_1}$, $C_{S_2}$ of Figure 4–5. The poorest families do indeed dissave in the short run, and, as became evident in 1932, the community as a whole may dissave for a time under the pressure of a drastic income shrinkage.

How can these differently shaped consumption schedules be reconciled? One possible approach is to suppose that the observed community consumption level for a period of time is but one point on an existing schedule of intentions and that the short-run schedules drift upward over time. In Figure 4–5 points $(C_0, Y_0)$, $(C_1, Y_1)$, and $(C_2, Y_2)$ are observed points in the years 0, 1, and 2. The schedules $C_{S_0}$, $C_{S_1}$, and $C_{S_2}$ are the schedules that reflect the true propensity to consume in years 0, 1, and 2. If a hypothesis can be introduced that explains why the short-run consumption function drifts upward over time, the cross-section and time-series observations can be reconciled.

One possible explanation for the secular upward drift of the consumption function is Duesenberry's "relative income" hypothesis.[1] Duesenberry observed that a nonwhite family with an income of $8,000 saves more than a white family with a comparable level of income. Since the nonwhite family is likely to reside in a lower rent district than the white family and since a nonwhite with an $8,000 income is likely to be on a higher point in the distribution of income in the neighborhood, Duesenberry concluded that the difference in consumption behavior could be explained by differences in the level of relative income, i.e., income in relation to what one is accustomed to. These observations then led Duesenberry to formulate the following hypothesis with respect to aggregate consumption behavior. Referring to Figure 4–5 suppose the community's level of income is $Y_0$. A fall in income from $Y_0$ causes consumers, accustomed to this standard of living, to defend their living standards by maintaining their consumption expenditures. They therefore move backward along the function $C_{S_0}$, reducing saving sharply while maintaining consumption at close to its $Y_0$ level. Should income rise back toward $Y_0$, consumption rises by only a little because consumers attempt to recover the preceding peak level of saving. This implies that as income rises the community moves upward along the $C_{S_0}$ schedule. But when $Y_0$ is reached, the previous highest standard of consumption and saving to which the community is accustomed is restored. Further increases in income then cause a sharp rise in the marginal propensity to consume. Additions to in-

[1] J. S. Duesenberry, *Income, Saving, and the Theory of Consumer Behavior,* Harvard University Press, Cambridge, Mass., 1949. F. Modigliani, "Fluctuations in the Savings–Income Ratio: A Problem in Economic Forecasting," in *Studies in Income and Wealth,* Vol. 11, National Bureau of Economic Research, Inc., New York, 1949.

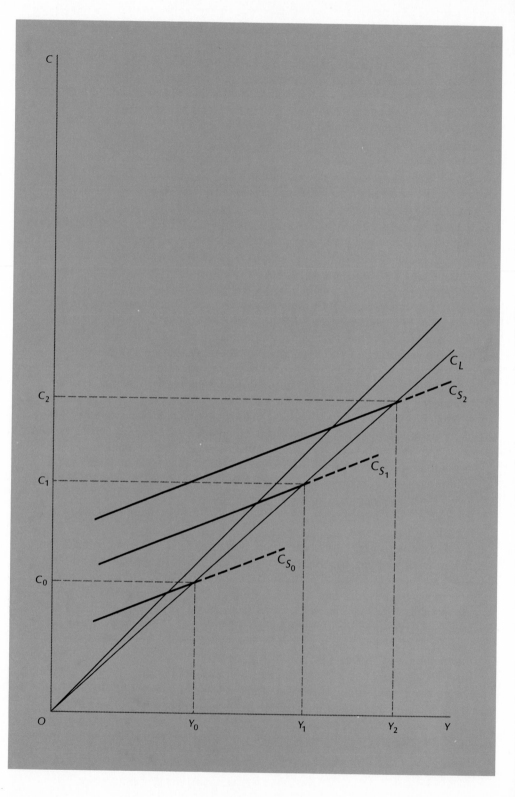

come are then split so as to maintain a constant consumption-income ratio. When income is above the highest past peak, the community moves along $C_L$. If income reaches $Y_1$ but subsequently falls, the community repeats its attempt to preserve its newly acquired higher living standard and moves backward along $C_{S_1}$.

While Duesenberry's hypothesis explains the secular upward drift of the consumption function, his "relative income" hypothesis is by no means the only explanation. Tobin,[1] for example, showed that the difference in the saving habits between nonwhite and white families could be explained by the fact that although a nonwhite and a white family might have the same current income, the white family is likely to be wealthier and more secure and will therefore tend to save less.

Most modern theories of consumption are more comfortable with the empirical finding that consumption, over the years, has been proportional to disposable income than with the cross-section finding that the ratio of consumption to income falls as income rises. Unlike the hypothesis of Duesenberry, who took the statistical results at face value and attempted to reconcile them, more recent hypotheses suggest that the cross-section results are systematically biased and that if such bias were removed the consumption-income ratio would be found to be constant. The first important finding which supports this conclusion is that consumption cross sections give different results depending upon the time period over which the flows of consumption and income are measured. Specifically, if the value of family consumption for a six-month period is plotted against family disposable income for the same six-month period, the resulting consumption function will exhibit a substantially lower slope than if a full year is chosen as the time period over which the variables are measured. Indeed, the longer the chosen time period, the steeper the observed consumption function becomes. The presumption is that lengthening the period over which the flow of income and consumption are measured tends to eliminate the effects of short-run variations in income and of lags in the adjustment of consumption to changes in income. It has been shown[2] that if families are divided according to income class, the higher-income groups will contain a larger proportion of people whose incomes have recently risen, or whose incomes are temporarily higher than normal, whereas the lower-income groups will contain a larger proportion of people whose incomes have recently fallen or are temporarily below normal.

[1] Tobin, op. cit.

[2] R. P. Mack, "The Direction of Change in Income and the Consumption Function," *Review of Economics and Statistics*, 30:239–258, 1948.

FIGURE 4-5
Long-run and short-run consumption functions (all values in real terms)

Professor Friedman's theory of consumption suggests that consumption will not change at all under the impact of temporary income changes.[1] And even if the changes are permanent, it will take time to adjust consumption expenditures to the change in income. For both these reasons the measured consumption levels of the higher-income groups will be lower than would be true in the long run, whereas the measured consumption levels of the lower-income groups will be higher than would be true in the long run. Therefore, a cross-section consumption function of consumption plotted against income over some fairly short period of time will tend to make the observed consumption function a good deal flatter than the "true" propensity to consume.

Studies of consumption patterns of individuals over their lifetimes support the tendency of cross-section data to give biased results. These studies suggest that young families who tend to have low incomes also tend to save little or even to dissave. As they grow older and their incomes rise, their saving also rises substantially in order to pay back past debts and to accumulate wealth in anticipation of retirement, at which time saving again becomes negative and income declines. This "life-cycle" pattern means that from any representative cross section of the population high income will be associated with high saving, and low income with low or negative saving. But this says nothing about the effect on consumption and saving that would be caused by a change in disposable income.[2]

These findings suggest that perhaps consumption ought to be related to some longer-run measure of income or wealth than current income. Indeed, attempts to derive the consumption function from the basic microeconomic theory of consumer utility maximization suggest that rational consumers will make their current consumption a function of their "normal" rather than their actual income. Actual income is subject to temporary windfall gains and losses and should therefore be broken down into a "permanent" and a "transitory" component. In principle, consumption should also be broken down in this way, and one should then relate permanent consumption to permanent income.

If consumption is a function of permanent income, a rise in actual income would be expected to affect consumption only insofar as the rise in income raises the consumer's permanent income. Since the direct effect of a change in current income on permanent income is small, one would expect a low marginal propensity to consume current income, and changes in income would be reflected primarily in fluctuations in the level of saving. On the

---

[1] M. Friedman, *A Theory of the Consumption Function*, National Bureau of Economic Research, Inc., New York, 1955. A similar hypothesis is advanced by F. Modigliani and R. Brumberg, "Utility Analysis and the Consumption Function: An Interpretation of Cross-Section Data," in K. K. Kurihara, ed., *Post-Keynesian Economics*, Rutgers University Press, New Brunswick, N.J., 1954. See also R. Brumberg, "An Approximation to the Aggregate Savings Function," *Economic Journal*, 66:66–72, 1956.

[2] A. Ando and F. Modigliani, "The 'Life Cycle' Hypothesis of Saving: Aggregate Implications and Tests," *American Economic Review*, 53:55–84, 1963; and M. J. Farrell, "The New Theories of the Consumption Function," *Economic Journal*, 69:678–696, 1959.

other hand, an increase in income may give rise to the expectation that permanent income will be greater than it was originally thought to be, and if this is the case, the marginal propensity to consume may be quite high. Thus the new theories suggest that because it is difficult to estimate the effect of a change in actual income on permanent income, it will be difficult to predict its effect on consumption. The marginal propensity to consume may therefore be very unstable and unpredictable. In any case the simple rule that a given change in income will always produce a given predictable change in consumption cannot be relied upon.

What is meant by permanent income? Imagine a consumer who contemplates the sale of all her expected future earnings for a lump-sum payment to be made immediately. Add to this the value of her accumulated wealth, and then imagine that she purchases a perpetual annuity with the entire sum. The annuity payments that would continue over time, while leaving wealth intact, are what we call the individual's permanent income.

Measuring permanent income is difficult because the concept involves anticipated future receipts and can therefore not be calculated from existing data. However, insofar as the past record of earnings is indicative of future earnings, a proxy for permanent income can be obtained from a suitably weighted average of past earnings. Viewed in this light, actual data sometimes have a curious way of being consistent with competing theories. For example, when quarterly data are used to estimate a purely Keynesian consumption function such as

$$C(t) = a + bY_d(t)$$

where $C(t)$ and $Y_d(t)$ are current quarter consumption and disposable income, respectively, the results are unsatisfactory with respect to both statistical criteria and predictive power. However, when lagged consumption is added as an explanatory variable and the equation becomes

$$C(t) = a + bY_d(t) + cC(t-1) \qquad (4-4)$$

both the statistical fit and the forecasting power of the equation improve dramatically. The lagged consumption term could be interpreted on relative income grounds as a stabilizing force that imposes past standards on current consumption spending. It can also be interpreted as providing a compromise between the absolute and permanent income concepts.

To see why this is the case, note that if Eq. (4–4) holds, it must also be true that

$$C(t-1) = a + bY_d(t-1) + cC(t-2)$$
$$C(t-2) = a + bY_d(t-2) + cC(t-3)$$

and so on. Using the first of these expressions to eliminate $C(t-1)$ in Eq. (4–4) we get

$$C(t) = a(1+c) + bY_d(t) + cbY_d(t-1) + c^2C(t-2)$$

We next eliminate $C(t-2)$ in the same way, and by keeping this procedure up long enough note that an alternative way of writing Eq. (4–4) is

$$C(t) = a/(1 - c) + bY_d(t) + cbY_d(t - 1) + c^2bY_d(t - 2)$$
$$+ c^3bY_d(t - 3) + \cdots + c^nbY_d(t - n)*$$

Thus, we now see that a consumption function such as Eq. (4–4) may be interpreted to imply that consumption is a function of all past income levels with weights that diminish geometrically as we recede into the past attached to the influence of past incomes. Such an equation clearly represents a suitable compromise between absolute and permanent income hypotheses and, happily for the forecaster, works fairly well much of the time.

If it is true that consumers gear their consumption expenditures to their lifetime earning prospects rather than to their current incomes, one ought to be able to find an association between consumption and the age of individuals. Young families, for example, will have a low current income but a high permanent income, and they are therefore likely to consume a larger fraction of their income than older families whose actual incomes may be higher than their permanent incomes. These and other presumptions are confirmed by numerous studies. One of the most interesting is the study by Watts.[1] He proposes the hypothesis that current consumption spending is primarily a matter of expected income, where expected income $E$ is, in principle, very similar to permanent income as we previously described it. A high $E$ implies a high level of current consumption, whereas a low $E$ implies the opposite. Among the factors affecting $E$, Watts finds age, education, occupation, race, and location to be significant. Spending units with younger heads who have a college education save the least because their expected income is greatest. Professional and business people have a higher expected income and therefore save a smaller part of their income than unskilled workers. Opportunities for high future income are presumably greater in urban areas, and in areas of high population density there are likely to be stronger imitative effects. Urban households therefore generally save less than rural households with the same income. Spending units close to retirement save more than younger units because their expected income and their current income are tending to equality. However, the age group that is currently putting its children through college saves less than the other older age groups.

In order to construct the foundations of macroeconomic analysis in as simple a manner as possible, we shall return, throughout the next few chapters, to the simple hypothesis that consumption is a function of current disposable income. But it should be borne in mind, as the foregoing discussion has suggested, that the determination of aggregate consumption expenditure is no simple matter.

* The parameter $c^2$ is of course, a positive fraction. Consequently, the series $a(1 + c + c^2 + c^3 + \cdots + c^n)$ sums to a value $a/(1 - c)$; while the weights attached to past income levels diminish geometrically.

[1] H. Watts, "Long-Run Income Expectations and Consumer Savings," in T. F. Dernburg and others, *Studies in Household Economic Behavior*, Yale University Press, New Haven, Conn., 1958.

# FISCAL POLICY AND INCOME DETERMINATION

## GOVERNMENT PURCHASES, TAXES, AND THE EQUILIBRIUM CONDITION

In this chapter we turn our attention to the effect of government purchases and taxation on the level of income. The assumptions that corporate saving is negligible and that the economy does not engage in foreign trade are retained. Under these conditions real net national product $Y$ is the sum of personal consumption expenditure, net private domestic investment, and government purchases of goods and services, or

$$Y \equiv C + I_r + G$$

The level of income is divided between the government sector (net taxes) and the household sector (disposable income).[1] Hence

$$Y = Y_d + T \tag{5–1}$$

and since households are free either to spend or to save their disposable income,

$$Y = C + S + T$$

---

[1] We assume that there is only one government unit and that the household sector is made up only of consumers.

When government purchases and taxes are introduced, the equilibrium condition is that intended investment plus government purchases must equal saving plus taxes. That this must be true can easily be seen by introducing the notions of an income leakage and an injection. In the simplified model of Chapter 4, where government did not enter the picture, a portion of the current income stream was spent on consumption and therefore reentered the flow of spending. A portion, however, "leaked" into saving. It was noted that if an amount of intended investment just sufficient to balance the saving took place, the level of income would remain unchanged because production and sales plus intended changes in inventories would then be synchronized. But this is the same as saying that investment expenditure is just sufficient to make up for the leakage, due to saving, from the spending stream. If the level of saving is greater than the level of intended investment, more will leak out of the spending stream than is pumped in via intended investment. Taxes, like saving, are income leakages, whereas government purchases, like intended investment, are injections. If the sum of taxes and saving is greater than the sum of government purchases and intended investment, more will have been produced than sold or intentionally accumulated because insufficient expenditures will have been made to compensate for the leakages.

To summarize: By the definition of the national accounts it must always be true that

$$Y \equiv C + I_r + G$$

and

$$I_r + G \equiv S + T \quad \text{Leakages}$$

Injections

but only in equilibrium is it true that the level of output equals the level of aggregate demand so that

$$Y = C + I + G$$

and that total injections equal total leakages so that

$$I + G = S + T \tag{5–2}$$

## 5–2
## GAP ANALYSIS AND THE EFFECT OF CHANGES
## IN THE LEVEL OF GOVERNMENT PURCHASES

Throughout the analysis of this chapter it will be useful to follow the procedure of the previous chapter and to imagine a hypothetical economy in which consumption is a linear function of disposable income and in which the level of investment is independent of the level of income. It should be borne in mind that our assumed numerical values bear no relation whatever to reality and are picked in order to facilitate the exposition and to assist the reader to grasp the fundamentals. Our purpose here is to understand the mechanics of fiscal policy. The practical difficulties of implementation will be considered in Part 4.

Consider the situation depicted in Figure 5–1. The consumption function is linear, and the marginal propensity to consume is assumed to have a value of $2/3$. We assume also that the point of zero saving is at an income level of $75 billion. Consequently, the level of consumption associated with $Y = 0$ is $25 billion, and when $Y = 375$, $C = 275$.*

The level of intended investment is assumed to be $25 billion at all levels of income. Thus the intersection of the aggregate demand schedule with the 45-degree line is at an income level of $150 billion. Inspection of the diagram also confirms that $150 billion is the income level at which intended investment equals saving.

This situation, which we shall call state I, is the basic starting point against which we intend to compare the effects of various fiscal policies. To summarize the situation we have

*State I*

$Y = 150 = Y_d$

$C = 125$

$I = S = 25$

$G = T = 0$

Economists have found the concept of an inflationary or a deflationary gap useful in conducting national income analysis. To illustrate this concept, let us imagine that the resources available to the economy are such as to enable it to produce a level of real output equal to $375 billion. This $375 billion income level is denoted the "full-employment level of income," and the gap is then defined as the difference between the actual level of aggregate demand at the *full-employment level of income* and the amount of aggregate demand that would be needed to attain full employment. If we erect a vertical line at the full-employment level of income, we see that full employment would require the aggregate demand schedule to cut the 45-degree line where it intersects the full-employment vertical line. In other words, aggregate demand would have to be $375 billion at the full-employment level of income. In the present example, however, we see that, at the full-employment level of income, consumption would be $275 billion and investment would be $25 billion. Consequently, aggregate demand at full employment would be $300 billion, and therefore there is a deflationary gap of $75 billion. Had the aggregate demand schedule cut the vertical line at full employment above the intersection of the vertical with the 45-degree line, aggregate demand would have been in excess of what is required for full employment, and we should then say that an inflationary gap was present. For example, if aggregate demand at full employment is $400 billion and the full-employment level of income is $375 billion, the inflationary gap would be $25 billion.

* The equation for the consumption function is

$C = a + bY_d = 25 + 2/3\, Y_d$

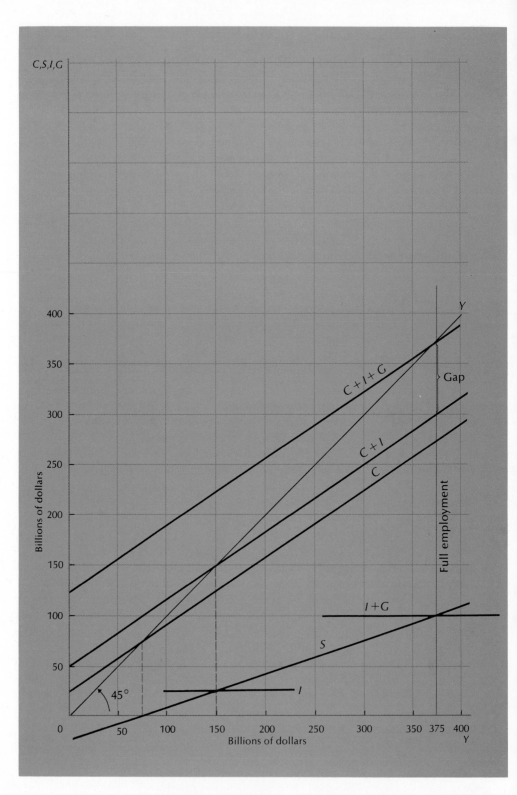

Knowledge of the magnitude of the gap and the value of the multiplier provides yet another way of locating the equilibrium level of income. Imagine that the economy is at full employment and that a gap of $75 billion develops because of a downward shift of the investment function. The level of income would fall by the amount of this decline in aggregate demand times the multiplier. Because the marginal propensity to consume in this hypothetical economy is ⅔, the multiplier has a value of 3, and this means that a fall in aggregate demand of $75 billion would cause income to fall by $225 billion to a level of $150 billion. Thus the presence of a deflationary gap of $75 billion implies that the level of income falls short of the full-employment level by an amount equal to the magnitude of the gap times the multiplier. We may therefore state quite generally that the equilibrium level of income may be calculated by the formula

$$Y = Y^* - (\text{gap} \times \text{multiplier}) \tag{5–3}$$

where $Y^*$ is the full-employment level of income. Using the numerical values of our example, we have

$$Y = 375 - (75 \times 3) = 150$$

The magnitude of the deflationary gap is equivalent to the amount by which aggregate demand must be raised in order to lift income to the full-employment level. In the present example the deflationary gap is $75 billion, and this means that aggregate demand must *shift up* by $75 billion. If such a shift materializes, the level of income would rise by the amount of the increase in aggregate demand times the multiplier. Let the level of aggregate demand be denoted by the symbol $D$. We can then state a general multiplier formula

$$\frac{\Delta Y}{\Delta D} = \frac{1}{1 - b} \tag{5–4}$$

where $\Delta Y$ is the change in income and $\Delta D$ is the change (vertical shift) in the aggregate demand schedule.

As far as its effect on the level of income is concerned, the source of an increase in aggregate demand is irrelevant. Aggregate demand could rise because consumer tastes change or because consumers have more disposable income as the result of a tax cut. Aggregate demand could rise because of an increase in the desire of business to invest or, finally, because of an increase in government purchases. Regardless of the source, an upward shift in the aggregate demand schedule will raise the equilibrium level of income by the amount of the shift in aggregate demand times the multiplier. In the present

**FIGURE 5–1**
The deflationary gap and the effect of government purchases on the level of income (all values in real terms)

example, this would mean that for every $1 billion increase in aggregate demand, the equilibrium level of income would rise by $3 billion.

Suppose now that we return to the situation of state I. The equilibrium level of income is $150 billion, the full-employment level of income is $375 billion, and the economy finds itself suffering from a deflationary gap of $75 billion. Assume next that it is decided to close the gap by raising the level of government purchases by $75 billion.[1] As a consequence, the aggregate demand schedule shifts up by $75 billion, i.e., the $C + I + G$ schedule is now the relevant aggregate demand schedule, and the equilibrium level of income rises by $225 billion to the full-employment level of $375 billion.

The new situation is depicted in Figure 5–1. The aggregate demand schedule, $C + I + G$, cuts the 45-degree line at an income level of $375 billion, and this income level is where total injections $I + G$ now equal $100 billion. Since the level of saving is $100 billion, these injections are balanced by an equal amount of leakages. Call this new situation state II and observe that

*State II*

| | |
|---|---|
| $Y = 375$ | $G = 75$ |
| $C = 275$ | $S = 100$ |
| $I = 25$ | $T = 0$ |

Therefore,

$$I + G = S + T$$
$$25 + 75 = 100 + 0$$

In summary: (1) An increase in the level of aggregate demand will raise the equilibrium level of income by the amount of the increase in aggregate demand times the multiplier regardless of the source of the increase in demand; (2) the deflationary gap is a measure of the deficiency of aggregate demand at full employment; (3) one way to close the gap is to raise the level of government purchases by an amount equal to the size of the gap.

### 5–3
### LUMP-SUM TAXATION AND THE
### BALANCED BUDGET MULTIPLIER

In this and the next section we will examine the effects of taxation on the level of income. There is, of course, a vast array of different taxes that the government can impose. Economists have tended to classify these taxes into two broad categories, "direct" taxes and "indirect" taxes. Direct taxes such as personal income and corporate income taxes are, as the name implies, levied directly on taxpayers. Indirect taxes, such as sales taxes, excise taxes, and customs duties are paid indirectly by taxpayers as part of the price they

---

[1] Here again we should remind ourselves that we are not concerned with the practical difficulties of putting such an enormous increase in $G$ into effect.

pay for the goods and services that they purchase. It should be borne in mind that our present discussion is confined to direct taxes and that we further restrict our discussion to taxes on persons.

Inasmuch as the analysis of the effect of taxes on the level of income is somewhat more complicated than the analysis of the effect of government purchases, we will begin with the simplest case of lump-sum taxation. By a lump-sum (or "head" or "poll") tax we mean that each taxpayer must pay a sum which is independent of his or her economic circumstances. In the next section we shall extend the analysis to cover the case of proportional income taxation.

Consider Figure 5–2, where the consumption function of Figure 5–1 is reproduced as the function $C_0$, and assume that the economy is presently in state II. With government purchases at a level of $75 billion and with no tax collection, there is an annual budgetary deficit of $75 billion. Let us assume that Congress legislates a lump-sum tax, the yield (i.e., the value of collections) of which is $75 billion. The tax reduces disposable income at all income levels by $75 billion. Since the marginal propensity to consume is $2/3$, the loss of disposable income causes consumers to reduce consumption spending by $50 billion, that is, $2/3 \times $75$ billion, and saving by $25 billion. Consequently, the consumption function shifts down by $50 billion at all levels of income.

The new consumption function is the function $C_1$ in Figure 5–2. The vertical distance between $C_1$ and $C_0$ is $50 billion, which equals the amount of the change in tax yield multiplied by the marginal propensity to consume. The horizontal distance between the two functions is equal to the amount of the change in tax yield. The important fact to bear in mind is that whereas the relationship between consumption and disposable income remains unaffected by a change in taxes, the change in taxes changes the level of disposable income associated with a particular level of national product, so that the level of consumption associated with that level of national product also changes.[1]

We saw in the preceding section that an increase in government purchases of $1 would shift the aggregate demand schedule up by $1. We now discover, however, that a similar rule does not apply to taxation. Because a frac-

---

[1] Analytically, consumption is a function of disposable income. Consequently,

$$C = a + bY_d$$

However, disposable income is given by

$$Y_d = Y - T$$

and the consumption function may therefore be written

$$C = a + b(Y - T)$$

At a given level of income, the change in consumption associated with a change in $T$ is

$$\Delta C = -b \, \Delta T$$

which, since we have fixed the level of income, represents the magnitude of the vertical shift in the consumption function.

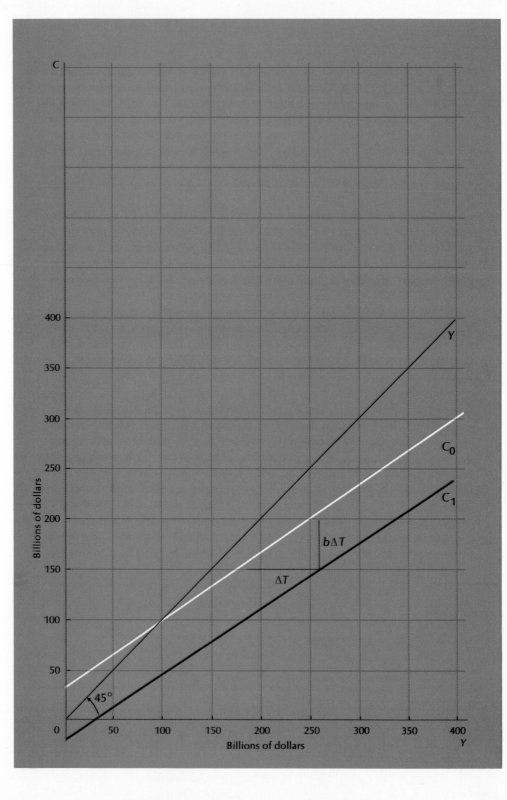

tion of the increase in tax yield comes out of income that would have been saved anyway, the shift in the consumption function and therefore the aggregate demand schedule is not equal to $1. It is, rather, equal to the change in tax yield times the marginal propensity to consume.

Since the initial change in aggregate demand due to the increase in taxes is

$$\Delta D = \Delta C = -b\,\Delta T$$

we may substitute this change into Eq. (5–4) to calculate the multiplier with respect to tax changes. This substitution yields

$$\frac{\Delta Y}{\Delta T} = \frac{-b}{1-b} = \frac{-\frac{2}{3}}{1-\frac{2}{3}} = -2$$

and we therefore see that the multiplier with respect to taxation is exactly 1 less than the multiplier with respect to a change in government purchases. Thus, for each $1 of increased tax yield, we expect the level of income to decline by $2, and if the total increase in taxes is $75 billion, the equilibrium level of income ought to drop by $150 to a new equilibrium level of $225.

Figure 5–3 confirms this result. Let $C_0$ be the original consumption function, and let $C_0 + I + G$ be the aggregate demand function of state II. Imposition of the tax causes the consumption function to shift down by $50 billion to $C_1$, and this causes the entire aggregate demand schedule to shift down to where it is represented by $C_1 + I + G$. The downward shift of $50 billion produces a deflationary gap of $50 billion, and given a multiplier with respect to aggregate demand of 3, the level of income ought to drop by $150 billion to a new level of $225 billion. Figure 5–3 does, in fact, show that the new aggregate demand schedule cuts the 45-degree line at an income level of $225 billion. To check whether the result is correct, we calculate the equilibrium magnitudes of our variables in this new situation and note that with $Y = 225$ and $T = 75$, $Y_d = 150$. But with disposable income at $150 billion, consumption is $125 billion, and the level of saving is therefore $25 billion. Thus we see that government purchases of $75 billion plus investment of $25 billion are exactly balanced by $25 billion worth of saving and $75 billion of tax collections.

To summarize this new situation which we describe as state III, we see that

*State III*

$Y = 225$

$Y_d = Y - T = 225 - 75 = 150$

$C = 25 + \frac{2}{3}Y_d = 25 + \frac{2}{3}(Y - T) = 25 + \frac{2}{3}(150) = 125$

**FIGURE 5–2**
**Effect of a lump-sum tax on the consumption function (all values in real terms)**

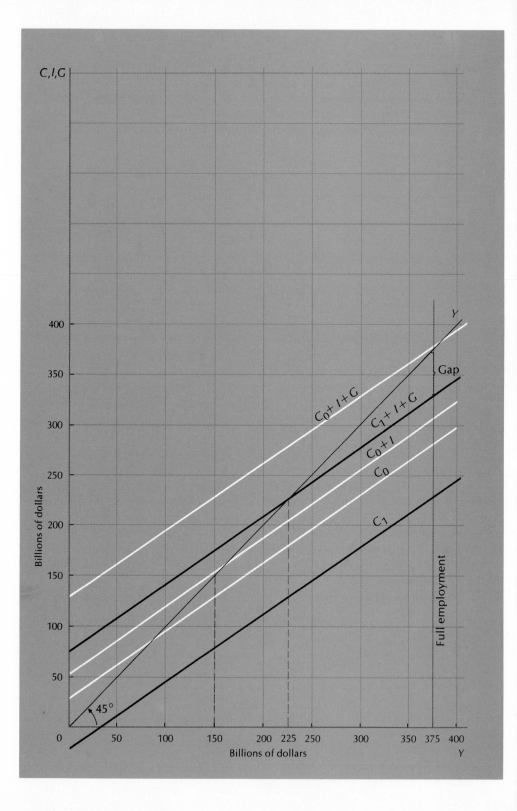

$$S = Y_d - C = 150 - 125 = 25$$
$$I = 25$$
$$G = 75$$

Therefore,

$$I + G = S + T$$
$$25 + 75 = 25 + 75$$

Let us take another look at this result. We have seen that if we begin in state I with the level of income at $150 billion and with government purchases and taxes both at levels of zero, an increase in government purchases balanced by an equal increase in tax collections will not leave the level of income unaffected. The simultaneous effect of such a "balanced budget" policy is, in fact, to raise the level of income by exactly the amount of the increase in government purchases and taxes. And it therefore appears that the multiplier for such a simultaneous equal increase in $G$ and $T$ is exactly equal to 1. This result is no accident. It would occur regardless of the value of the marginal propensity to consume. To see why this is the case, note that the multiplier for an increase in government purchases is

$$\frac{\Delta Y}{\Delta G} = \frac{1}{1 - b}$$

and the multiplier for a change in taxes is

$$\frac{\Delta Y}{\Delta T} = \frac{-b}{1 - b}$$

When we add the two together, we have

$$\frac{\Delta Y}{\Delta G} + \frac{\Delta Y}{\Delta T} = \frac{1}{1 - b} - \frac{b}{1 - b} = \frac{1 - b}{1 - b} = 1$$

To make absolutely sure that we understand this result, let us look at it purely from the point of view of the effect of the policies on the deflationary gap. Starting with state I, we have a deflationary gap of $75. When we increase government purchases by $75, we eliminate the gap; however, when we raise taxes by $75 billion, the consumption function and therefore the aggregate demand function shift down by $50 billion. Thus, in combination, the two policies cause the aggregate demand schedule to shift up by $25 billion (compare $C_0 + I$ of state I with $C_1 + I + G$ of state III). Since the net change in aggregate demand is $25 billion, we apply our multiplier formula to this change and see that the net change in income must be $3 \times 25 = 75$.

**FIGURE 5–3**
The balanced budget multiplier (all values in real terms)

To see why the result is independent of the value of the marginal propensity to consume, imagine that the marginal propensity to consume has a value of $4/5$. The multiplier with respect to aggregate demand would, in this case, have a value of 5. If the level of government purchases rises by $1, the aggregate demand schedule would shift up by $1. If this is balanced by an increase in tax yield of $1 the consumption function would shift down by 80 cents. Consequently, the net change in aggregate demand would be 20 cents, so that when we apply our multiplier of 5 to this change in aggregate demand, we find that income again changes by exactly the amount of the simultaneous increase in $G$ and $T$.

In summary: The result that we have been discussing is known as the "balanced budget" or "unit" multiplier theorem. It states that equal increases in the level of government purchases and taxes will raise the level of income by exactly the amount of the increase in $G$ and $T$. It implies that government purchases and equivalent changes in taxes do not exactly offset one another and that therefore it is incorrect to say that government has no effect on the level of income if the budget is balanced. Budgetary balance is not enough; it is important also to consider the level at which the budget is balanced.

## 5–4
## INCOME TAXATION AND AUTOMATIC STABILITY

We now propose to take a step in the direction of reality by replacing the lump-sum tax with a proportional 25 percent income tax. Thus the tax function can be written

$$T = tY = 0.25Y$$

where $t$ is the tax rate.[1]

Consider first the effect of the income tax on the consumption function. We saw earlier that a lump-sum tax produces a parallel downward shift of the consumption function. The effect of a proportional income tax, on the other hand, is to rotate the function. The situation is illustrated in Figure 5–4, where $C_0$ is the original consumption function and $C_2$ is the consumption function after the imposition of the tax.

The reason for the rotation is not difficult to grasp. The magnitude of the yield from the tax is proportional to the level of income. Consequently, the magnitude of the associated change in disposable income and consumption

---

[1] It is customary to distinguish between a marginal and an average tax rate. The former is the increase in taxes per dollar income increase $\Delta T/\Delta Y$; the latter is the percent of income that is taxed $T/Y$. Under proportional taxation, as in the present example, the two are the same.

**FIGURE 5–4**
Effect of proportional income taxation on
the consumption function (all values in real
terms)

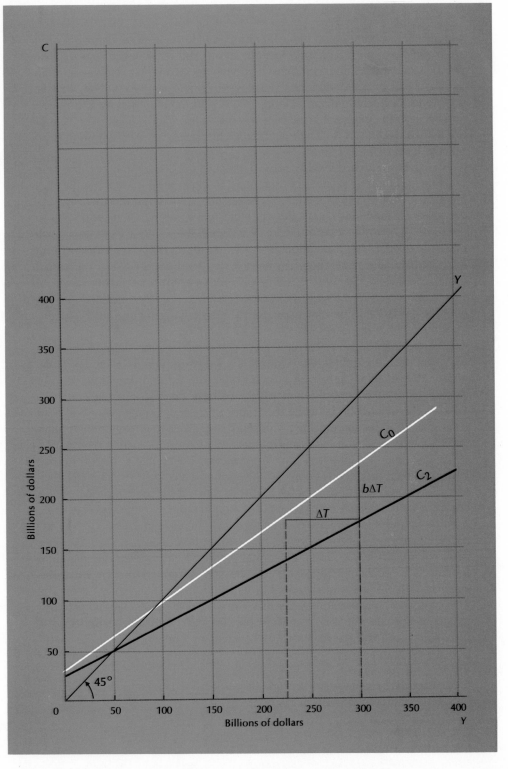

will also be proportional to the level of income. If the level of income is zero, an income tax will produce no revenue at all, and the level of consumption will be exactly the same as if there had been no income tax. However, at an income level of $300 billion, the tax yield would be $75 billion, that is, $0.25 \times \$300$. Because disposable income would therefore fall by $75 billion and because the marginal propensity to consume is $2/3$, the level of consumption would decline by $50 billion. Thus $C_2$ lies below $C_0$ by $50 billion at an income level of $300 billion.

As we have seen, the proportional income tax rotates the consumption function and thereby reduces consumption in direct proportion to the level of income. As in the case of the lump-sum tax, the vertical distance between the consumption functions equals the tax yield times the marginal propensity to consume. As can be seen in Figure 5–4, when the level of income is $300 billion, the level of consumption after the imposition of the tax is $50 billion less than it would have been had the tax not been imposed. The horizontal distance between the two consumption functions from an income level of $300 billion measures the tax yield of $75 billion. Thus the intersection of $C_0$ with the horizontal line that connects the two consumption functions identifies the level of disposable income of $225 billion.

It is important to note that income taxation reduces the slope of the consumption function and therefore lowers the value of the multiplier. The slope of $C_0$ is the marginal propensity to consume, the value of which we earlier represented by the symbol $b$ and which we have here assumed to equal $2/3$. To keep the distinction between the slopes of $C_0$ and $C_2$ clear, we shall now call $b$ the "marginal propensity to consume disposable income," and we shall call the slope of $C_2$ the "marginal propensity to consume national product."

To calculate the slope of $C_2$, we need merely notice that if the level of income (national product) rises by $1, this will raise tax yield by 25 cents. Disposable income therefore rises by 75 cents. Since the marginal propensity to consume disposable income is $2/3$, consumption will rise by 50 cents, that is, $2/3 \times 0.75$, and it is therefore evident that a $1 increase in income is now associated with a 50-cent increase in consumption. Thus we see that the marginal propensity to consume national product is $1/2$, whereas the marginal propensity to consume disposable income is $2/3$. Figure 5–4 shows that the slope of $C_2$ is, in fact, exactly equal to $1/2$.

As a general matter we may say that if the tax rate is $t$ percent, an increase in income of $\Delta Y$ will raise tax yield by $\Delta T = t\Delta Y$, and the change in disposable income will therefore be

$$\Delta Y_d = \Delta Y - \Delta T = (1 - t)\,\Delta Y$$

If the marginal propensity to consume disposable income has a value of $b$, the change in consumption will be

$$\Delta C = b\,\Delta Y_d = b(1 - t)\,\Delta Y$$

from which it follows that the slope of the consumption function $\Delta C/\Delta Y$ is

$b(1-t)$. Thus the marginal propensity to consume national product is $b(1-t)$, which in our numerical example is $\frac{2}{3}(1-\frac{1}{4})=\frac{1}{2}$.

The circumstance that income taxation causes the marginal propensity to consume national product to decline is an extremely important one because it means that income taxation reduces the value of the multiplier. From the equilibrium condition it follows that if injections increase by some amount, the level of leakages must rise by exactly the same amount if equilibrium is to be restored. Therefore, suppose that government purchases rise by $1, and consider by how much income must rise in order to generate an additional $1 of saving and taxes. If income rises by $1, tax yield rises by 25 cents:

$$\Delta T = t\,\Delta Y = 0.25$$

Disposable income rises by 75 cents:

$$\Delta Y_d = (1-t)\,\Delta Y = 0.75$$

and consumption rises by 50 cents:

$$\Delta C = b\,\Delta Y_d = b(1-t)\,\Delta Y = 0.50$$

This means that saving rises by 25 cents:

$$\Delta S = \Delta Y_d - \Delta C = (1-b)(1-t)\,\Delta Y = 0.25$$

Consequently, an increase in income of $1 raises taxes by 25 cents and savings by 25 cents. Total leakages therefore increase by 50 cents:

$$\Delta T + \Delta S = t\,\Delta Y + (1-b)(1-t)\,\Delta Y = [1-b(1-t)]\,\Delta Y = 0.50$$

and this implies that if total leakages are to rise by $1, income must rise by $2. It follows that our multiplier formula now becomes

$$\frac{\Delta Y}{\Delta G} = \frac{1}{1-b(1-t)} = \frac{1}{1-\frac{2}{3}(1-\frac{1}{4})} = \frac{1}{\frac{1}{2}} = 2$$

The term $b(1-t)$ is the marginal propensity to consume national product. The term $1-b(1-t)$ measures the fraction of each dollar of additional national product that leaks into saving and taxes. The multiplier is therefore the reciprocal of the sum of these marginal leakage propensities.

Let us make sure we understand these results. When taxation is absent or when taxation is of the lump-sum variety, an increase in government purchases of $1 initially raises disposable income by $1, of which $b$ percent is then respent on consumption. When we sum up the entire respending chain, we get the multiplier

$$\frac{\Delta Y}{\Delta G} = \frac{1}{1-b}$$

However, when taxes become a function of income, an increase in government purchases raises the level of disposable income only by $1-t$ times the increase in income because a proportion $t$ flows right back to the Treasury in the form of tax collections. Since disposable income rises by only $1 - t$ times the increase in government purchases, and since $b$ times the change in disposable income is respent on consumption, the proportion $b(1 - t)$, instead of $b$ percent, will be respent on consumption. Thus the marginal propensity to consume national product is reduced, and the multiplier takes on the lower value, given by the formula

$$\frac{\Delta Y}{\Delta G} = \frac{1}{1 - b(1 - t)}$$

This analysis illustrates an important point that is frequently overlooked in discussions of economic policy. An increase in government purchases of X dollars will not necessarily create a budgetary deficit of X dollars because part of the increase in income that results from the increase in government purchases flows right back to the Treasury in the form of taxes. This analysis also suggests that efforts to balance the budget by means of tax rate increases may, to some extent, defeat themselves because the tax rate increases lower the level of disposable income, and tax collections may therefore not increase by as much as anticipated. In our present hypothetical economy, an increase in government purchases of $1 would raise the level of income by $2. Consequently, tax collections would rise by 50 cents, and this means that a $1 increase in government purchases will produce a net addition to the deficit of only 50 cents.

Another important concept illustrated by our present model is the idea of built-in or automatic stability. By reducing the marginal propensity to consume national product, the income tax reduces the value of the multiplier and therefore makes the economy less sensitive to changes in aggregate demand. The automatic stabilizing effect becomes even more pronounced when the income tax is progressive, which means that the marginal tax rate rises as taxable income rises. Thus the tax system takes a larger fraction of higher incomes than it does of lower incomes. In practice, progressivity in the personal income tax is attained by dividing income into successive brackets, or slices, and applying increasingly higher statutory marginal rates to the incomes falling in the successively higher brackets. This ensures that the tax paid on any individual dollar of income is higher than was paid on average on preceding income, so that the proportion of total income paid in taxes rises as total nominal income rises. The effect of progressivity is to cause tax revenues to rise more rapidly than taxable income and by the same token to cause yield to fall disproportionately as income shrinks.

An automatic stabilizer may be thought of as a mechanism that is built into the economy and that produces an automatic Treasury deficit (and corresponding increase in disposable income) whenever national product falls. The consequence of such automatically induced deficits is that disposable income and consumption are kept from falling by as much as would otherwise be the case. The personal and corporate income taxes are important sources of built-in stability. Also of importance are unemployment compensation programs which bolster the disposable incomes of laid-off workers. Farm price support programs prevent farm prices and incomes from falling during recession. Finally, the social security program helps stabilize disposable income because social security tax collections decline during recessions.

To complete the analysis, let us now consider the effect of the imposition of the 25 percent income tax on the level of income and from there move on to see whether the balanced budget multiplier theorem remains valid under conditions of income taxation. We assume, at the outset, that the economy is in state II. Thus the equilibrium level of income is at the full-employment level of $375 billion, and the aggregate demand function is the function $C_0 + I + G$ of Figure 5–1. This function is redrawn in Figure 5–5 and labeled $C_0 + I + G_0$. At an income level of $375 billion, $C = 275$, $I = 25$, and $G = 75$. In state II there are no taxes. The level of disposable income is therefore $375 billion, the level of saving is $100 billion, and the budgetary deficit is $75 billion.

Given this situation, we now impose the 25 percent income tax. The tax causes the consumption function to rotate downward from $C_0$ to $C_2$, and the entire aggregate demand schedule therefore rotates downward and becomes the schedule $C_2 + I + G_0$. At the full-employment level of income of $375 billion, a 25 percent tax implies a tax yield of $93.75 billion and a reduction in disposable income of the same amount. Given a marginal propensity to consume disposable income of $\frac{2}{3}$, this means that consumption declines by $62.50 billion. Aggregate demand at the full-employment level of income therefore declines by $62.50 billion as a result of the income tax, and a deflationary gap in this amount therefore develops.

With a deflationary gap of $62.50 billion and a new multiplier with respect to aggregate demand of 2, we expect the level of income to drop by $125 billion, that is, $2 \times \$62.50$, from the full-employment level ($375 billion) of state II. Thus the equilibrium level of income should turn out to be $250 billion, and this is where the new aggregate demand schedule $C_2 + I + G_0$ cuts the 45-degree line.

This new situation is state IV. To check the results, we again inquire whether the equilibrium condition is met and note that

*State IV*

$Y = 250$

$I = 25$

$G = 75$

$T = 0.25(250) = 62.5$

$Y_d = Y - T = 250 - 62.5 = 187.5$

$C = 25 + \frac{2}{3} Y_d = 150$

$S = Y_d - C = 37.5$

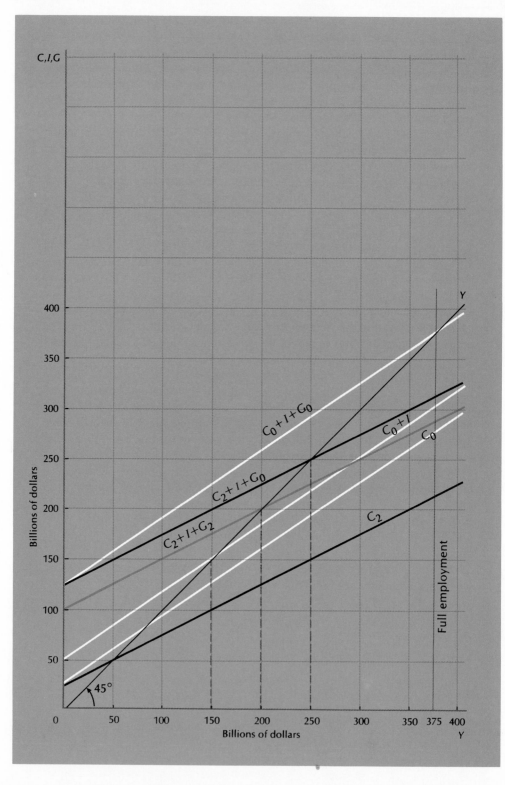

Therefore,

$$S + T = I + G$$
$$37.5 + 62.5 = 25 + 75$$

and the deficit

$$G - T = 75 - 62.5 = 12.5$$

To summarize this result: The change in the equilibrium level of income that results from a change in the rate of income taxation can be derived by calculating the magnitude of the deflationary gap the tax creates and by multiplying this gap by the new multiplier with respect to changes in aggregate demand that applies *after* the imposition of the tax. In the present example, a 25 percent tax reduces the multiplier to a value of 2. The tax creates a deflationary gap of $62.5 billion. The level of income therefore drops by $125 billion to a level of $250 billion.

State IV finds the economy with a level of government purchases of $75 billion and a tax yield of $62.5 billion. There is therefore a budgetary deficit of $12.5 billion. Imagine as state V that government purchases are adjusted in such a way as to eliminate the deficit.

A reduction in government purchases of $1 lowers income by $2 and therefore induces a fall in tax yield of 50 cents. Consequently, those who believe that the deficit will decline by the full amount of the decline in the value of government purchases will be disappointed. What they will discover is that for each dollar by which G is reduced T will also fall by 50 cents and that the deficit will therefore decline by only 50 cents. From this reasoning, it follows that if the deficit of $12.5 billion is to be eliminated, the level of government purchases will have to be cut by $25 billion, that is, 12.5/0.5.

If G is cut by $25 billion, the level of income will drop by $50 billion to a new level of $200 billion. Figure 5–5 confirms that the new aggregate demand schedule $(C_2 + I + G_2)$ cuts the 45-degree line at an income level of $200. This situation is state V, where we again see that injections equal leakages because

*State V*

$Y = 200$

$I = 25$

$G = 50$

$T = 0.25(200) = 50$

**FIGURE 5–5**
**The balanced budget multiplier under income taxation (all values in real terms)**

$$Y_d = Y - T = 150$$
$$C = 25 + \tfrac{2}{3}\, Y_d = 125$$
$$S = Y_d - C = 25$$

Therefore,

$$S + T = I + G$$
$$25 + 50 = 25 + 50$$

and

$$T = 50 = G$$

Notice now that when we started in state I with $G = T = 0$, the equilibrium level of income was $150 billion. In state V we find the equilibrium level of income to be $200 billion and the levels of $G$ and $T$ to be balanced at values of $50 billion. Observe also that this $50 billion turns out to be the difference between the income levels of states I and V. We conclude from this result that the balanced budget multiplier theorem holds under conditions of income taxation just as it held in the lump-sum tax economy. The proposition may be put as follows: Given any income tax rate, the level of government purchases that balances the budget will result in a new equilibrium income level that will exceed the level that would be attained if $G = T = 0$ by exactly the amount of the balanced budget. Or, to turn the proposition around, if for any level of government purchases one can find a tax rate that balances the budget, the resulting equilibrium level of income will exceed the level at which the economy would be if $G$ and $T$ were both zero by the amount of the level of $G$ and $T$.[1]

## 5-5
### SUMMARY AND FINAL NOTES

In this chapter we have focused upon the purely mechanical aspects of fiscal policy. We have seen that government purchases have a more high-powered effect on the level of income that an equivalent level of tax yield. This implies that the full impact of fiscal policy on the level of income cannot be measured purely by the size of the budgetary deficit. We saw also that income taxation reduces the size of the multiplier and therefore introduces an automatically stabilizing element.

Although the analysis has emphasized the mechanical aspects of fiscal policy, it nevertheless provides us with some useful and important insights regarding practical policy problems. For example, if the economy were to enter a slump, one form of appropriate action would be a reduction in taxes.

---

[1] These propositions are proved in the appendix to this chapter. The interested reader should also consult Richard A. Musgrave, *The Theory of Public Finance*, Chap. 18, McGraw-Hill Book Company, 1959; and William A. Salant, "Taxes, Income Determination, and the Balanced Budget Theorem," *Review of Economics and Statistics*, 39:152–161, 1957.

However, standing in the way of such a cut is the fact that when income falls, tax collections automatically fall, and thus there will already be a budgetary deficit. Because many people think that a time of budgetary deficit is a poor time to cut taxes, there is danger that tax cuts will arouse opposition just at the time when they are most needed.

Political capital is often made because of the widespread lack of sophistication in matters having to do with taxes and government spending. It is common practice for politicans to attract votes during a period of recession by claiming that the party in power not only cannot maintain prosperity but runs a slovenly fiscal system as well. The logic of the argument has considerable surface appeal because a recession is always accompanied by a budgetary deficit. However, if it is borne in mind that government revenues automatically fall as recession develops, and that a budgetary deficit is therefore practically inevitable, we would soon learn to ignore such specious arguments.

To avert fiscal confusion of the kind described above, and to gain public acceptance for policies designed to restore full employment, the Council of Economic Advisers long ago attempted to popularize the concept of the full-employment budget surplus. In 1961, for example, the actual budgetary deficit was in excess of $4 billion; however, the economy was far from full employment. Had income increased by an amount sufficient to restore full employment, additional tax revenues would have been generated so that if expenditure programs had remained unchanged, the actual deficit would have been converted into a surplus of $10 billion. This full-employment surplus suggested quite clearly that the federal budget was oppressively deflationary, for it implied that a surplus of investment over saving of the amount of the full-employment surplus would have been required to achieve full employment in the face of the extremely restrictive budget. Thus even though the actual budget registered a deficit, and therefore gave the appearance of being expansionary, it was in fact quite the opposite.

The fact that revenues and some expenditures are functions of the level of income suggests that the distinction should always be kept in mind between those budgetary deficits that are *passively* encountered due to income shrinkage and those deficits that are *actively* incurred in an effort to stimulate the economy. The concept of the full-employment surplus attempts to eliminate the misleading signals produced by the passive deficits and to isolate and measure the degree to which the federal budget falls short of or exceeds full-employment requirements.

In Chapter 18 we will discuss practical problems of fiscal policy implementation, and we will review the developments of fiscal thinking that have taken place over the years. Central to these developments and to the formulation of rational fiscal policy are the simple concepts set forth in this chapter.

# 6

# THE LEVEL
# OF INVESTMENT

## INTRODUCTION

In the two preceding chapters we found it convenient to simplify our analysis by assuming that investment is a constant. It is now time to drop this assumption and to turn to an examination of the determinants of investment spending. In studying the behavior of investment, GNP analysts very quickly come to recognize that gross private domestic investment must be divided into three distinct components, business fixed investment, residential construction, and the net change in business inventories, because each of these components appears to be influenced by substantially different sets of factors. In this chapter we confine ourselves to the analysis of investment by business in capital goods. Inventory investment and residential building will receive attention at a later stage of our discussion.

In considering how to arrange a portfolio intelligently, a holder of wealth must remember that different assets yield different returns and have different risks attached to them. One must, for example, decide whether the disutility of the risk of holding an equity as opposed to a bond is balanced by the utility of the higher earnings on the equity. The wealth holder must decide whether, and in what proportion, to hold long-term bonds, short-term bonds, equities, and other types of asset. A businessman must decide whether it is more profitable to use his funds for capital expansion or for the purchase of some existing asset, say an equity in another company. Similarly, he must decide whether the cost of borrowing for purposes of capital expansion is more than compensated for by the expected return on the new investment. The problem of determining the demand for new investment goods may therefore be looked at as a problem in portfolio management, because the decision to invest depends on the profitability of the new investment as opposed to the profitability of holding existing earning assets. If, for example, an investor is able to earn 8 percent on a government bond and can expect to earn only 7 percent on the purchase of a new machine, he will certainly not buy the machine, unless the bond is a far more risky venture than the machine. If, furthermore, the monetary authority would like to see him purchase the machine because that will raise the level of income, it must somehow contrive to change his asset preference in such a way that the machine becomes a more appealing alternative than other earning assets. The first step that needs to be taken if we are to understand this relationship between different types of assets is to inquire into the relationship between the market value of an asset and the rate of return, or yield, of the asset.

## 6–2
### DISCOUNTING AND THE PRESENT VALUE OF AN ASSET

Suppose that the rate of interest is 5 percent. If today an individual lends $100, he will at the end of one year get back the original $100 plus the original sum multiplied by the rate of interest. Arithmetically,

$$100 + 100 \times 0.05 = 100(1 + 0.05) = \$105$$

In general, if the interest rate is denoted by $i$ and the sum lent is denoted by $P_0$, the individual will get back at the end of one year

$$P_1 = P_0(1 + i) \tag{6-1}$$

If he lends the whole sum $P_1$ for a second year, he will receive

$$P_2 = P_1(1 + i)$$

But since $P_1 = P_0(1 + i)$,

$$P_2 = P_0(1 + i)(1 + i) = P_0(1 + i)^2$$

If he lends $P_0$ for three years, he will get back

$$P_3 = P_0(1 + i)^3$$

from which we may infer that a sum $P_0$ lent at interest for $t$ years will pay back at the end of $t$ years[1]

---

[1] In Eq. (6–2) it is assumed that interest is compounded once a year. Often, however, interest is compounded semiannually. In the latter case interest for the first six months is figured on $P_0$. But since only a half year's interest is earned, the effective rate on $P_0$ is not $i$ but $i/2$. This means that the value of the claim at the end of six months is $P_0(1 + i/2)$, which becomes the principal on which interest for the next six months is figured. At the end of the year

$$P_1 = P_0\left(1 + \frac{i}{2}\right)\left(1 + \frac{i}{2}\right) = P_0\left(1 + \frac{i}{2}\right)^2$$

$$P_t = P_0(1 + i)^t \tag{6-2}$$

The next step is to turn the original question around and ask: If an individual gets back $P_1$ dollars in one year, what is today's value of that claim? The answer can be found by solving for $P_0$ in Eq. (6–1). This yields

$$P_0 = \frac{P_1}{1 + i}$$

which indicates that a claim worth $105 in one year, with the current market rate of interest at 5 percent, has a value today of $100. If the owner tried to sell this future claim for anything more than $100, it would not be possible to find a buyer because with an outlay of $100 today the potential buyer can get back $105 in a year and therefore would be foolish to give more than $100 for this claim. Similarly, the owner would be unwise to sell his future claim for anything less than $100. If he sells the claim for less than $100 and reinvests the proceeds, he would end up with less than $105 at the end of the year, assuming a market rate of 5 percent. The only possible value that the $105 future claim can therefore have is $100. Notice that if the market rate of interest falls to 2 percent, the present value of the claim which pays $105 would increase to $102.94 because this is the amount that would have to be

---

from which we may infer that

$$P_t = P_0\left(1 + \frac{i}{2}\right)^{2t}$$

If interest is compounded g times a year, we have

$$P_t = P_0\left(1 + \frac{i}{g}\right)^{gt}$$

For some purposes it is useful to know $P_t$ if compounding takes place instantaneously. Rewrite the above equation as

$$P_t = P_0\left[\left(1 + \frac{i}{g}\right)^{g/i}\right]^{it}$$

The term $(1 + i/g)^{g/i}$ approaches the number 2.7183 when g grows very large. This number is often referred to as e and forms the base of the natural logarithmic system just as 10 forms the base of the common logarithmic system. Hence we have

$$P_t = P_0 e^{it} = P_0(2.7183)^{it}$$

Notice that

$$\log_e P_t = \log_e P_0 + it \log_e e$$

But since $\log_e e = 1$, we have the straight-line function

$$\log_e P_t = \log_e P_0 + it$$

To give some concrete meaning to e, imagine that interest is compounded instantaneously at a rate of 100 percent. If $1 is lent for one year, its value will build up to

$$\$1(2.7183)^1 = \$2.72$$

by the end of the year. This contrasts with the $2.00 that would be received on a one-year loan of $1 with interest at 100 percent compounded only once.

lent at the new rate of interest in order to get back $105 at the end of one year.

A sum $P_0$ lent today will be worth $P_2 = P_0(1 + i)^2$ at the end of two years. Such a claim could today be sold for $P_0$. Anyone foolish enough to give more than $P_0$ for the claim would, at the market rate, have been able to earn more than $P_2$ in two years with the sum he has paid. On the other hand, if the owner were foolish enough to sell the claim for less than $P_0$, he could not get back as much as $P_2$ in two years by lending the amount he sold the claim for. In general, if in $t$ years a claim for $P_t$ is collectible, the present value of that claim is

$$P_0 = \frac{P_t}{(1 + i)^t} \tag{6-3}$$

A claim that is not collectible until far in the future must have very little present value, as compared with the collection sum. Although the Indians who sold Manhattan Island for $24 in wampum in 1624 are now derided for having made a foolish bargain, they could theoretically, by lending the $24 out at interest and waiting to the present, have earned a sum which might compare favorably with what Manhattan Island could be sold for today.

Consider next the determination of the present value of a bond. Instead of one claim collectible at a certain future date, a bond represents a series of claims collectible at different times in the future. Suppose that each year a coupon can be clipped from the bond and cashed in for a fixed sum $R$. When there are no more coupons left, the bond reaches maturity and is cashed in for its par value $P$. Today's value of the bond must be the present value of the sum of all the discounted future returns plus the discounted value of the maturity value. The coupon that is to be clipped in one year and that will have a value of $R$ could be sold today for $R/(1 + i)$; the coupon which is to be clipped two years from now could be sold today for $R/(1 + i)^2$; the last coupon to be clipped could be sold for $R/(1 + i)^n$, where $n$ is the number of years from the present to maturity; and the claim over the maturity value can be sold for $P/(1 + i)^n$. Consequently the present value of the bond is

$$V = \frac{R}{1 + i} + \frac{R}{(1 + i)^2} + \cdots + \frac{R}{(1 + i)^n} + \frac{P}{(1 + i)^n}$$

which, by summing this geometric series (just as we summed the multiplier chain in Chapter 4), reduces to[1]

$$V = \frac{R}{i}\left[1 - \frac{1}{(1 + i)^n}\right] + \frac{P}{(1 + i)^n} \tag{6-4}$$

---

[1] Note that when the market rate of interest just equals the rate earned on the par value of the bond, $R = iP$, so that

$$V = \frac{iP}{i}\left[1 - \frac{1}{(1 + i)^n}\right] + \frac{P}{(1 + i)^n} = P$$

Notice that when the maturity date is far off in the future (when a bond has no maturity date it is called a "consol"), n becomes very large so that

$$V = \frac{R}{i} \qquad\qquad (6-5)$$

Equation (6–5) says that if a consol earns $50 each year and if the market rate of interest is 5 percent, the value of the bond must be $1,000. Even if the owner is not familiar with the mathematics of compound interest, he will soon find through painful experience that there can be only one price for the bond. If the owner tries to sell the bond for more than $1,000, prospective buyers will scoff because they could earn $50 by lending $1,000 on the market; since that is all the bond will yield, it would be quite senseless to pay more than $1,000 for it. If the owner were foolish enough to accept $900 for the bond, he would discover to his dismay that when he lent the $900 for one year, he would get only $45 in return; if he had kept the bond, he would have received $50 at the end of the year.

Equations (6–4) and (6–5) show that there is an inverse relationship between bond prices and interest rates. Suppose that the interest rate falls to 2 percent. The value of the consol that previously sold for $1,000, to yield 5 percent or $50 per year, now increases in value to $2,500. The reason for this is that with an interest rate of 2 percent a potential buyer would have to put up $2,500 to earn $50 per year, whereas at the 5 percent rate he has to put up only $1,000. Again the owner would be foolish to sell the bond for $2,000 because if he lent this sum he would earn only $40 in interest, whereas if he keeps the bond he can earn $50.

The value of a very long term bond can be approximated by Eq. (6–5). If, on the other hand, the bond is practically ready to be cashed in for its maturity value, n will be very small and when $n = 0$, Eq. (6–4) reduces to

$$V = P$$

This result, of course, is just what we expect. A bond that is on the verge of maturity can hardly have a market value that differs from the par value.

From the foregoing analysis we can infer that the longer the date from present to maturity, the more important the market rate of interest in determining the value of the bond and the less important the par value. Similarly, the closer to maturity, the less important the market rate of interest and the more important the par value.

## 6–3
## THE DECISION TO INVEST

Whether or not to invest in new physical capital, such as machinery, equipment, factories, stores, and warehouses, depends on whether the expected rate of profit on the new investment is greater or less than the interest rate that must be paid on the funds that need to be borrowed to acquire these assets. Even if the funds were readily at hand, a decision would have to be made between the alternative of using the funds to purchase the new physical asset or of lending the funds to someone else at the existing market rate of interest, perhaps by purchasing a bond. A moment's reflection confirms the fact that these two decisions are one and the same. Whether the funds are available or must be borrowed makes no difference; the asset should be bought if its expected rate of return exceeds the market rate of interest.

Portfolio management decisions always involve comparisons of alternative rates of return. In the case of the bond the annual dollar (nominal) return is the same each year, and, apart from the possibility of default, it is a certain return. With a new investment in physical capital there are two differences. First, the expected returns from year to year may vary over the life of the asset. Second, the returns are only best guess expectations at the time the investment decision is made. Nevertheless, despite the fact that allowance must be made for variable returns and for uncertainty, the calculations involved in finding the rate of return on a new investment are quite similar to ordinary compound interest calculations.

Before attempting to make such calculations we should agree on terminology. Let the market rate of interest, or yield on existing assets, be denoted by the symbol $i$. This is both the cost of borrowing and the return from lending at interest. The rate of return on new investment, which we denote as $r$, is generally known as the "marginal efficiency of capital" (MEC) and sometimes as the "expected rate of return over cost" on the new investment. The crucial matter for our purposes is to maintain a clear distinction between the rate of return on existing assets $i$ and the expected rate of return over cost on new physical capital $r$. Or one could perhaps keep the distinction in mind by thinking of $r$ as an internal rate of return to the firm, whereas $i$ is the external rate of return.

To make matters as simple as possible, imagine that we are trying to decide whether to install a machine that lasts exactly one year and that has no scrap value at the time. Suppose also that after deducting labor, material, and all other costs except interest and the cost of the machine, there is a profit of $1,200 left at the end of the year. Out of this *gross* profit $1,000 goes to defray the cost of the machine. The remaining $200 represents a $200 earning for one year on an investment of $1,000. In this case, therefore, the rate of return over cost is 20 percent. Obviously, the way we arrived at this result was to equate the cost of the machine, $C$, with the gross return on the machine, $R$, discounted by the rate of return $r$. Symbolically,

$$C = \frac{R}{1+r} \qquad \text{or} \qquad \$1,000 = \frac{\$1,200}{1+r}$$

so that $r = 0.20$ or 20 percent. Consequently, we see that if we know the original cost of the machine and if we have an estimate of the expected gross profit, we can compute the rate of return over cost on the machine.

Matters become somewhat more complicated when we attempt to take into account the fact that the machine's earnings are distributed over several years, and when we recognize that it may also have some scrap value at the end of its useful life. However, here again the analogy with the value of a bond helps us to understand the problem. Let $R_1, R_2, \ldots, R_n$ be the gross profits on a new capital asset in years $1, 2, \ldots, n$, respectively; let $J$ be the scrap value of the machine at the end of $n$ years; and let $C$ be the machine's original cost.[1] If we now equate the cost of the machine with the sum of the gross returns plus the scrap value all discounted by the rate of return on the machine, we have

$$C = \frac{R_1}{1+r} + \frac{R_2}{(1+r)^2} + \cdots + \frac{R_n}{(1+r)^n} + \frac{J}{(1+r)^n} \qquad (6\text{--}6)$$

Evidently, if $C$, $J$, and the $R$'s are estimated, the marginal efficiency of capital $r$ can be calculated. The decision whether or not to make the investment then involves a comparison of the marginal efficiency of capital with the market rate of interest. If the MEC is 10 percent and the market rate of interest is 5 percent, it clearly pays to purchase the machine.

Unfortunately, there is no simple algebraic trick that permits $r$ to be calculated easily because the terms in the numerator of Eq. (6–6) are not equal. As a consequence, an alternative, though similar, way of deciding whether to buy the machine is sometimes employed. If we take the right-hand terms of Eq. (6–6) and replace $r$ by the market rate of interest $i$, the result of summing this series is the present value of the machine's stream of future earnings. If this present value exceeds the cost of purchasing the machine, the machine is worth buying, and it follows also that $r$ must exceed $i$. Similarly, if the present value of the machine falls short of its cost, $r$ must be less than $i$, and it therefore pays to purchase a bond rather than the machine or to refrain from borrowing in order to buy it.

Figure 6–1 depicts a situation for a hypothetical firm. The firm's most profitable opportunity is the purchase of a machine costing $10,000 with an MEC of 10 percent. Its next most profitable possibility is a new truck that costs $5,000 and is expected to yield a return of 8 percent. The firm could also spend $15,000 on expanding its warehouse capacity to gain an expected return of 6 percent. And, finally, $10,000 could be invested in the installation of air conditioning which, by improving morale and worker productivity, is expected to yield 4 percent.

These prospective projects are ranked in order of decreasing profitability in Figure 6–1. The solid line thus traced out may be thought of as the firm's investment demand schedule. If the rate of interest is 5 percent, the firm will forget the air conditioners and spend $30,000 on capital expansion. However, if the rate of interest is 7 percent, the warehouse project will be dropped, and the firm's investment outlays will be reduced to $15,000. Thus for any individual firm it appears clear that its investment expenditures will be higher, the lower is the rate of interest.

[1] The $R$'s are again calculated without deducting interest or the cost of the machine. Since the cost is distributed over the life of the asset, we now speak of each $R$ as including an annual depreciation charge. The sum of these depreciation charges plus scrap value equals the cost of the asset.

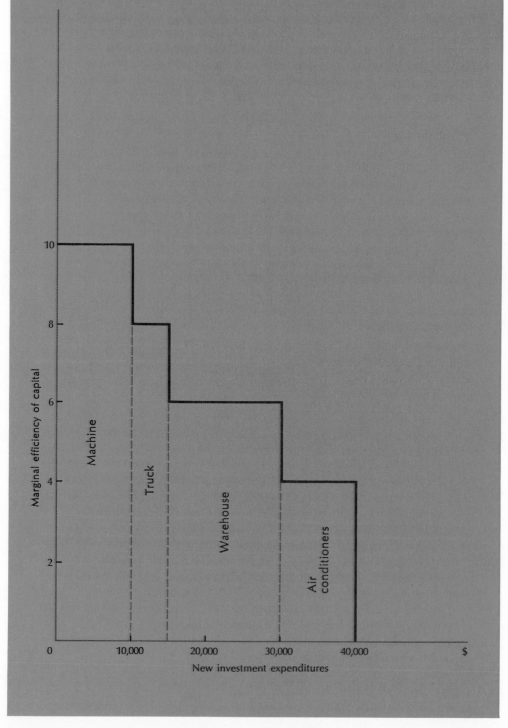

The individual firm's MEC schedule moves along in steps as in the illustration of Figure 6–1. If the MEC schedules for all firms in the economy were added together horizontally, we would get a downward sloping aggregate MEC schedule which would be a continuous curve because the bumps would be ironed out in the aggregation process.

It is tempting to jump to the conclusion that such an aggregation of MEC schedules represents the investment demand schedule for the economy as a whole. However, such a schedule might greatly exaggerate the volume of additional investment that a fall in the rate of interest would bring about. The problem is that if the interest rate falls and all firms therefore attempt to expand their capacity, the result will be to raise the cost of capital goods and therefore to lower the MEC's on all investment projects for all firms. It is for this reason that some economists[1] have insisted on distinguishing between the marginal efficiency of capital MEC and the "marginal efficiency of investment" MEI. The latter concept differs from the MEC in that it shows the relationship between the rate of interest and the economy's level of investment when changes in capital goods prices are taken into account.

The distinction is illustrated in Figure 6–2. Suppose that an interest rate of 10 percent exactly justifies the replacement of worn-out capacity, but that it does not justify any net investment, and that, finally, the resultant demands on the capital goods industries are such as to keep capital goods prices from changing. Then the MEC and MEI schedules intersect at a 10 percent rate of interest. Now suppose that the rate of interest falls to 5 percent. Given the existing capital goods prices, all firms taken together, but each planning as if no one else wished to add to capacity, wish to spend $I_0$ on new investment goods. However, the quantity of capital goods demanded increases, the cost of the goods also increases, and the MEC's of firms decline for all their projects. Thus the actual result may be to limit the level of investment to $I_1$. It is this circumstance that the MEI schedule attempts to incorporate.

Clearly, it is the MEI schedule that represents the relevant investment demand schedule for the economy as a whole. The curve is obviously negatively sloped. The level of investment can therefore be thought of as a decreasing function of the rate of interest, and it is for this reason that economists frequently write the investment demand function as

$$I = I(i) \tag{6-7}$$

In Figure 6–2 an interest rate of 5 percent is associated with investment of $I_1$. A fall in the rate of interest to 3 percent then causes investment to rise to $I_2$.

[1] For a very careful discussion of this problem the reader should consult G. Ackley, *Macroeconomic Theory*, Chap. 17, The Macmillan Company, New York, 1961.

**FIGURE 6–1**
**Investment opportunities for a hypothetical firm**

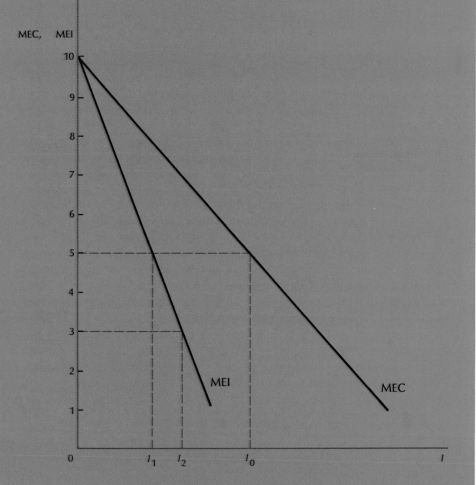

**6-4**

## INVESTMENT AND THE STOCK OF CAPITAL

If told the level of disposable income, an amateur economist could probably do a fair job of forecasting the level of consumption. If told the value of the rate of interest, the economist probably would not have the faintest idea what level of investment this would imply. Indeed, our foregoing discussion has only suggested that there ought to be some inverse association between investment and the rate of interest. It has not told us anything about the position of the investment demand schedule or about the forces that cause this schedule to shift. Clearly, there is much more to be considered.

The level of output that the economy is capable of producing at one time depends upon its available stock of productive facilities, what economists call its "capital stock," and its available supply of workers. Abstracting from complications introduced by the possibility that a given output could be produced with different combinations of productive factors, we may imagine as a rough-and-ready first approximation that the stock of capital which business in the aggregate desires to have is proportional to the level of output it desires to produce. Symbolically we could write

$$K_d(t) = \alpha Y(t) \tag{6-8}$$

where $K_d(t)$ is the desired stock of capital at time $t$ and $\alpha$ is the capital-output ratio that relates the desired stock of capital to the level of output.

Gross investment consists of two components. The first component is the replacement investment required to keep the stock of capital intact. The second component is net investment, which represents investment for the purpose of enlarging the capital stock. Economists have found it useful to think of the decision to undertake net investment as a response by businesspersons designed to rectify a discrepancy between the actual capital stock and the desired capital stock. A glance at Eq. (6-8) shows at once that if the level of output remains the same, the desired stock of capital would also remain the same so that if the actual capital stock equals the desired capital stock, there would be no need for any net investment. Clearly, a steady and rising level of net investment cannot occur without actual capacity constantly lagging behind desired capacity, and this could happen only if output were steadily growing. The *level* of investment therefore is a function of *changes* in output. Economists call this idea the "acceleration principle."[1]

[1] There is a vast amount of literature on the acceleration principle. A well-known early exposition is J. M. Clark, "Business Acceleration and the Law of Demand," *Journal of Political Economy*, 25:217–235, 1917. The principle has played an important role in the business cycle literature. In this area some of the more well-known works are P. A. Samuelson, "Interactions between the

**FIGURE 6-2**
The aggregate marginal efficiency of capital
and investment schedules

To illustrate the principle in somewhat more detail, suppose there is a lag in creating new capital such that the actual capital stock in the current period is equal to the stock which was desired in the preceding period. We then have $K(t) = K_d(t - 1)$ so that from Eq. (6–8) we have

$$K(t) = \alpha Y(t - 1) \tag{6-9}$$

However, net investment in the current period will be undertaken to bring actual capacity up to desired capacity. Therefore when we combine Eqs. (6–8) and (6–9) we get the investment function

$$I(t) = K_d(t) - K(t) = \alpha [Y(t) - Y(t - 1)] \tag{6-10}$$

Inspection of the investment function confirms again that the level of investment is a function of the *change* in output, and the absence of output growth implies zero net investment.[1]

The rate of interest appears now to have dropped out of sight. However, other things being equal, a fall in the rate of interest would make it profitable to produce a given level of output with more capital than before and with less labor and other factors than before. Thus a fall in the rate of interest would raise the desired ratio of capital to output so that this fall would be reflected in a rise in $\alpha$. Quite generally one might write the investment function as

$$I = I(i, \Delta Y)$$

to reflect the hypothesis that the level of investment depends upon both the rate of interest and upon changes in the level of output.

In the short run there are many reasons why investment may not conform to the rigid proportionality implied by the acceleration principle. The most obvious reason is that the adjustment of actual desired capacity is asymmetric with respect to positive and negative output changes. When the economy expands and actual capacity lags behind desired capacity, business firms

---

Multiplier Analysis and the Principle of Acceleration," *Review of Economics and Statistics,* 21:78–88, 1939; J. R. Hicks, *A Contribution to the Theory of the Trade Cycle,* Oxford University Press, London, 1950; and R. M. Goodwin, "The Nonlinear Accelerator and the Persistence of Business Cycles," *Econometrica,* 19:1–17, 1951. For empirical evidence on the acceleration principle see J. R. Meyer and E. Kuh, *The Investment Decision,* Harvard University Press, Cambridge, Mass., 1957; and R. Eisner, "Investment: Fact and Fancy," *American Economic Review,* 53:237–246, 1963.

[1] A proportional relation between the stock of capital and the level of output also implies a proportional relation between the fraction of output invested and the rate of growth of output. Take the investment function of Eq. (6–10) and divide both sides by the level of output. This gives

$$\frac{I(t)}{Y(t)} = \frac{\alpha [Y(t) - Y(t - 1)]}{Y(t)}$$

and shows that a steady percentage rate of growth will tend to generate a level of investment that is a constant fraction of the level of output. In the United States economy the ratio of business fixed investment to GNP tends to average slightly over 10 percent. A ratio substantially in excess of this proportion suggests to GNP analysts that excess capacity is accumulating and that a slump in investment spending can be anticipated in the near future.

place orders to build their stock of facilities in proportion to the growth of sales. On the other hand, no firm would deliberately destroy enough of its machines to bring actual capacity into line with desired levels when the economy enters a slump and demand declines. Owners of the equipment are stuck with the equipment and the fixed charges that are tied up in it. The rate at which actual capacity can be economically reduced is therefore limited to the rate of depreciation. Thus when output drops, excess capacity accumulates, and the ratio of capital to output rises above the desired level. The accelerator clearly works only when output is expanding.

We must now attempt to explain why positive net investment occurs even during periods of economic slack when output either declines or fails to rise, and when crude capital to output comparisons imply the presence of excess capacity. One explanation for this paradox lies in the advance of technology. To see the impact that new technology might have, consider the following two examples. First, imagine an industry in which no new technology is developed that would lead either to a reduction in costs, an improvement in products, or to the introduction of new products. In such a stagnant industry, there would never be any reason to invest except if demand were expected to increase. The size of the investment expenditures in this industry would depend on the size of the expected increase in demand. All net investment here involves the installation of more equipment of a kind that duplicates existing facilities, and the acceleration principle would therefore tend to describe investment behavior very adequately. Alternatively, consider an industry in which entrepreneurs propose to put cost-saving innovations into practice, or propose to manufacture new products, or propose to improve existing products. Under these conditions the size of the investment expenditures that will be undertaken depends not so much on how much demand is expected to increase as upon the absolute size of expected markets. The entrepreneurs, moreover, would be likely to invest even if demand were expected to be stationary, or even to decline slightly, although the size of projected expenditures might be reduced in the face of a decline in the level of economic activity.

Considerations such as these explain why investment takes place even during periods of slack demand and idle capacity, and they also suggest that the level of investment is to a large extent a function of the *level* of income as opposed to the accelerator hypothesis that investment is a function of changes in income. Formally, we could write

$$I = I(i,Y) \tag{6-11}$$

as our aggregate investment demand function.

Studies have shown that firms have a strong aversion to financing capital outlays by resort to borrowing or equity issue, and that they appear to prefer to limit their investment expenditures to the funds that can be generated internally. These "residual funds" consist of depreciation allowances and retained earnings. Such funds are highly correlated with the level of profits, and because the level of profits, in turn, is highly correlated with the level of in-

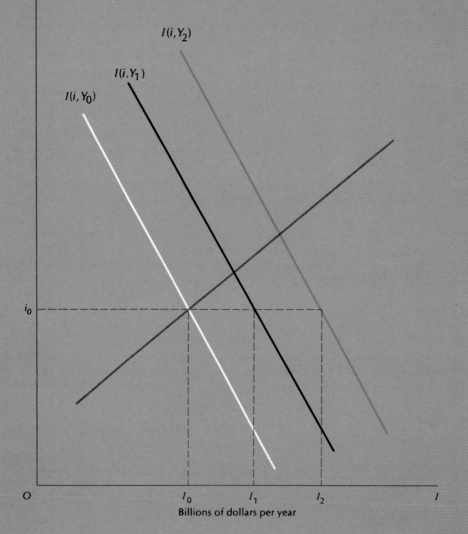

come, we have yet another reason for expecting investment to be an increasing function of the level of income.[1]

If investment is a function both of the rate of interest and the level of income, there will be not one but rather a whole family of investment demand schedules each one of which is associated with a particular level of income. In Figure 6–3 if the rate of interest is $i_0$ and the level of income is $Y_0$, the level of investment will be $I_0$. If income rises to $Y_1$, investment rises to $I_1$, and when income rises to $Y_2$, investment rises to $I_2$. The hypothesis that investment is a function both of the rate of interest and of the level of income explains the circumstance that investment and interest rates are positively correlated during the course of a business cycle. If the investment demand schedule were always fixed at $I(i, Y_0)$, investment could not rise without a decline in the rate of interest. However, if a rise in income causes the investment demand schedule to shift to the right, it can easily be seen by drawing a positively sloped line through the investment demand schedules of Figure 6–3 that the level of investment and the rate of interest may move in the same direction.

To conclude: We have encountered several hypotheses concerning investment behavior. For the purpose of short-run analysis the most important of these is the possible link between investment and the rate of interest. Therefore, let us agree, as we did at the end of our chapter on consumption, to keep the model simple. To this end, the short-run analysis of Part 2 proceeds on the basis of the hypothesis that investment is a decreasing function of the rate of interest. When we get to the dynamic problems discussed in Part 3, we will want to reintroduce both the acceleration principle and the hypothesis that investment increases as the level of income increases.

[1] The study of Meyer and Kuh, op. cit., suggests that the acceleration principle does well as a predictor of investment spending during periods of expansion and high-capacity utilization. On the other hand, periods of slack find the accelerator doing poorly, while the size of the internal funds that are generated becomes an important explanatory variable. The Meyer-Kuh ideas and findings are known as the "accelerator–residual funds hypothesis." A useful and lucid discussion of theoretical and empirical work is J. R. Meyer and R. R. Glauber, *Investment Decisions, Economic Forecasting, and Economic Policy*, Harvard Business School, Division of Research, Boston, 1964. Another excellent summary is E. Kuh, "Theory and Institutions in the Study of Investment Behavior," *American Economic Review*, 52:260–268, 1963. The impact of financial variables on investment decisions has been carefully analyzed by W. H. L. Anderson, *Corporate Finance and Fixed Investment*, Harvard Graduate School of Business Administration, Boston, 1964. J. S. Duesenberry, *Business Cycles and Economic Growth*, McGraw-Hill Book Company, New York, 1958, is a seminal work on the subject.

**FIGURE 6–3**
Investment as a function of the rate of interest and the level of income (all values in real terms)

# THE DEMAND AND SUPPLY OF MONEY

## INTRODUCTION

Money consists of currency and "demand" deposits held by the nonbank private sector. In this chapter we are concerned with such questions as why people hold money when they could instead be holding stocks and bonds that yield a return, what determines the size of the stock of money that exists at any moment of time, and how can the size of this stock of money be changed? These questions are important because the answers to them also supply the answer to the question of how the rate of interest is determined. Since the rate of interest is the cost of borrowing money, one looks for the factors that determine this particular price by looking at the factors that determine the demand for and supply of money.

In the preceding chapter we noted that there was an inverse association between bond prices and interest rates. Indeed, if bond prices are in equilibrium, this would mean that the rate of interest was also in equilibrium..Yet now we are suggesting that the equilibrium rate of interest is that price that makes the demand for money balances equal to the supply. There is no problem of reconciliation here since the two conditions really amount to the same thing. This is because the supply of and demand for different types of earning assets (bonds, etc.) will not be in equilibrium unless the supply of and the demand for money are also in equilibrium. Wealth holders who have deposits in their banks and cash in their pockets in excess of the amount they wish to hold for various purposes will try to trade these deposits and cash in return for earning assets. An excess supply of money, other things being equal, implies the presence of excess demand for bonds and other earning assets, and this, in turn, implies that bond prices will be rising and interest rates will be falling. The question of determining equilibrium interest rates may therefore be viewed in terms of the supply of and the demand for bonds, and it may also be viewed as a problem of determining the supply of and the demand for money.

To begin, assume that the financial sector of the economy is competitive and that there is no risk attached to the making of loans. We assume, in other words, that a bank takes no risk of default when it makes a loan; a bondholder encounters no risk of capital loss; and the expected future returns on new investment projects are, in fact, certain returns. Under these conditions the bank lending rate, the interest rate (yield) on bonds, and the internal rate of return on the least profitable (marginal) investment projects undertaken must all tend to equality. If the bond rate is 8 percent, the rate of return on new investment is 15 percent, and banks try to charge 20 percent on their loans, the banks will be unable to find borrowers, while bondholders will sell their bonds and use the proceeds to make loans for new investment projects. They will, to put it differently, trade existing securities for new securities. The effect of these transactions will be to force bond prices down and bond rates up. Meanwhile the banks, in order not to lose business, would be obliged to lower their loan rate. The bond rate and the loan rate must therefore tend to equality. Alternatively, if the bond rate and loan rate are less than the rate of return on the next most suitable investment project, businesspersons will be tempted to purchase additional new machines with borrowed funds and to sell their bondholdings in order to buy machines. The effect of all such transactions will be to bring all the different rates of return into equality.

In reality there are many different bond rates, none of which is likely to correspond to the bank lending rate or to the rate of return on the marginal investment project. This simply follows from the fact that there are different degrees of risk attached to different types of assets; that imperfect knowledge as to the most profitable opportunity for the investment of funds prevails; and that funds, once committed, may be recovered only on pain of capital loss if more profitable opportunities arise in the future. A bank takes a greater risk when it makes a business loan than it does when it buys a government bond. Similarly, the bank probably takes a greater risk by buying a long-term bond than a 60-day Treasury bill. If bond prices fall, holders of short-term bonds need merely hold the bonds to their maturity date (say 60 days) in order to collect the face value. However, if they hold a 20-year bond they may not be so lucky. The price of the bond may not rise in the near future to what they had previously paid for it. They may therefore be "locked in" in the sense that if they want to recover the par value of the bond, they must hold it for 20 years, meanwhile forgoing the possibility of more profitable ways of using their funds. Investors in short-term bonds have a different kind of problem. They are assured of the par value of their investment in a short time, but if interest rates fall and they want to reinvest their funds, the return will be less than before. Investment in capital goods is obviously a risky business because the future returns can only be estimated. Some wealth holders therefore prefer a fairly safe bond on which they earn 6 percent to a share of common stock on which they are likely, but less certain, to earn 12 percent. Similarly, entrepreneurs may be unwilling to risk investment in a new machine unless the expected rate of return over cost is 15 percent even though the cost of borrowing may be only 8 percent.

If one could abstract from differences in risk and from market imperfections, one could then imagine the rate of return on all types of assets tending to equality at the margin. Under such conditions the structure of interest rates could be thought of as one common rate, and we might suppose that there is no difference between the yield on a long-term bond and a short-term bond, and no difference between the yield on a promissory note that a bank gets in return for the loan of funds and the bond which an individual might get from the United States Treasury or from a corporation in return for the loan of his or her funds. Under these circumstances the yield from loaned funds, which is also the cost of borrowing, is simply the rate of return required to induce the public and the banks to part with funds. Because an excess supply of money implies an excess demand for earning assets, with a consequent downward pressure on interest rates, the problem of interest rate determination may be viewed simply as a problem of determining the supply of and the demand for money.

Before proceeding with the analysis of the chapter, we need to be clear about three very important matters. First, for present purposes money is defined as the quantity of currency and demand deposits held by members of the nonbank private sector. Consequently, we exclude time deposits of all kinds, whether they be savings deposits at commercial banks, saving and loan shares, or the like. Since the latter earn interest and are not an efficient medium of exchange, they more closely resemble bond ownership than ownership of money. Because one of our principal concerns will be to understand the factors that govern the choice between money and bond holding, it seems inappropriate to include time deposits in the money supply, as some economists would have us do.

Second, it is important to emphasize again the distinction between money and income that was pointed out in Chapter 3. Income is a *flow* of receipts per unit time, whereas money is a *stock* to which no time dimension is attached. To say that one's income is $1,000 conveys no useful information unless it is specified over what time the $1,000 is earned or received. This is true of all flow concepts such as consumption, saving, investment, etc., whose values have no meaning unless a time dimension is attached. On the other hand, money is a stock of a certain kind of asset. In the case of all stock magnitudes such as money, bonds, promissory notes of all kinds, etc., the magnitudes are timeless. Thus when it is said that one has $5,000 cash, useful information is provided. One can have a large income without having any money, and the opposite could also easily be the case.

Finally, we want to remind the reader that the variables with which we are dealing are assumed to have been deflated for changes in the price level and are therefore expressed in real terms. It is now important to note that a similar deflation procedure will be assumed to have been conducted with respect to the rate of interest, which therefore will also be regarded as being expressed in real terms. The rate of interest is a percentage, and it is perhaps not evident why a change in the price level should affect the rate of interest. Observe, however, that if the price level rises by 5 percent in a year, and if an individual lends money at the beginning of the year at 5 percent, the real return at the end of the year will be zero. Thus we may say, in this case, that the *nominal* rate of interest was 5 percent, but that the *real* rate was 0 percent. In general, we would expect that if lenders are willing to lend at $i$ percent when prices are stable, they will be willing to lend the equivalent amount when the rate of inflation is expected to be $\dot{\Delta}p_e$ only if the nominal rate of interest is $i_n = i + \dot{\Delta}p_e$ since that is what would be required to secure a real rate of $i$.

The distinction between the real and the nominal rate of interest becomes extremely important during periods of rapid inflation. During the recent period of surging inflation, nominal interest rates rose quite substantially, and this caused considerable consternation among borrowers. However, since the rate of inflation rose more rapidly that the nominal rates of interest, the truth of the matter is that the real rate of interest fell, which means that it was the lenders, rather than the borrowers, who were penalized. At any rate, it should not surprise us to find rapid inflation associated with high nominal interest rates. A correctly anticipated 10 percent rate of inflation might well be associated with nominal interest rates of 13 to 15 percent, with real rates therefore coming to only 3 to 5 percent. It is these real rates of interest that we will have in mind throughout our discussion.

## 7-2
### THE DEMAND FOR MONEY

In his *General Theory of Employment, Interest and Money*,[1] Lord Keynes suggested that the demand for money could be divided into three separate demands or "motives." People hold money, according to Keynes, because they need cash balances to make day-to-day transactions, because it is important to have money balances on hand to meet unforeseen contingencies, and because, for various reasons, they prefer to hold money balances as an asset in preference to, or in combination with, other forms of wealth. Thus the demand for money is a combination of the *transactions*, the *precautionary*, and the *speculative* or *liquidity preference* demands. Although modern monetary theory suggests that these distinctions are artificial, they are nevertheless useful for the purpose of organizing our discussion.

[1] J. M. Keynes, *The General Theory of Employment, Interest and Money*, Chap. 13, Harcourt, Brace & World, Inc., New York, 1936.

## The Transactions Demand for Money

Individuals and business enterprises maintain certain average levels of cash and deposits because of the need to make day-to-day transactions. If receipts of income and expenditures were always synchronized perfectly with respect to time, there would be no need for such idle balances. Because typically people are paid once a month or once a week and because they do not make all their disbursements at exactly the time they receive their income, they must maintain some amount of cash for the purpose of meeting their transactions needs.

Consider the hypothetical bank account depicted in Figure 7–1. Time is measured horizontally, and the amount in the bank account at any time is measured vertically. We assume that the individual receives $y$ dollars of income at the beginning of the period (time zero), that the entire amount is spent at a uniform rate throughout the period, and that there is a zero balance at the end of the period (time one). At the beginning of the month the person holds $y$ dollars; at the end he holds no money; and since he spends at a uniform rate throughout the period, the average idle balance is $y/2$ dollars. It is this average idle balance that we call the transactions demand for money.

The size of the transactions demand for money obviously depends upon the magnitude of the individual's money income. If income and expenditures both rise by $\Delta y$ dollars, his average idle bank balance will tend to rise by $\Delta y/2$ dollars. Thus, as a first approximation, we may say that the transactions demand for money is a function of the level of money income.

If our concern is with the long run, we have to take changes in institutional payments practices into account. If individuals begin to receive their paychecks each week instead of each month, they would have to maintain approximately one-fourth of the average balance they had previously maintained. Thus, even though their incomes remain the same, the fact that they are paid more frequently implies that their transactions demand for money falls by roughly three-fourths. Similarly, individuals who pay all their bills at the beginning of the month would have very little need for transactions cash, and individuals who pay their taxes every weekly pay day need not accumulate cash balances for tax purposes, whereas those who settle up on a quarterly basis would need to do so.

Two important contributions to monetary theory that appeared during the 1950s suggest that the transactions demand for money may be a function not only of the level of income but also of the rate of interest.[1] To see why this might be the case, consider the individual whose bank account is plotted in Figure 7–2. Of the $y$ dollars received at the beginning of the period, three-

[1] W. J. Baumol, "The Transactions Demand for Cash: An Inventory Theoretic Approach," *Quarterly Journal of Economics*, 66:545–556, 1952; and J. Tobin, "The Interest Elasticity of the Transactions Demand for Cash," *Review of Economics and Statistics*, 38:241–247, 1956. The present discussion is based on Tobin's analysis.

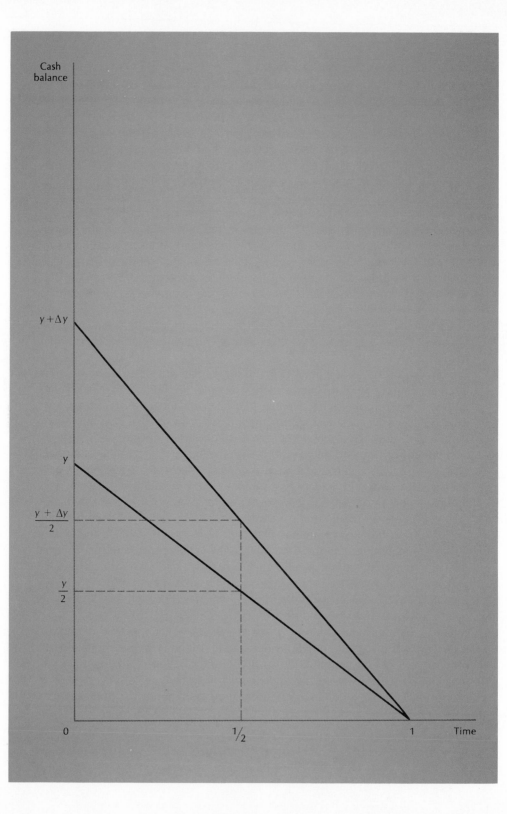

quarters will be idle for one-fourth of the period; one-half of the balance will be idle for half the period; and one-quarter of the balance will be idle for three-fourths of the period. Under these circumstances, it might be profitable for the individual to take some fraction of these idle funds and purchase earning assets which can then be sold when he runs out of cash.

It is evident from inspection of Figure 7–2 that if the individual contemplates one bond purchase and one sale during the period, he will maximize his interest earnings if, at the beginning of the period, he puts exactly one-half of his income into bonds which he then sells when he runs out of cash at $t = \frac{1}{2}$. The shaded rectangle in Figure 7–2 represents the time profile of his bondholdings. The largest such rectangle that can be drawn under the cash balance curve is the one that makes the initial balance equal to $y/2$ and implies sale at $t = \frac{1}{2}$. Any other date of purchase or sale, and any other value for the bond purchase, would be suboptimal.

If the individual wishes to make three transactions, the optimal program is to buy bonds at $t = 0$ with two-thirds of his income. He should then sell one-half of his bondholdings when he runs out of cash at $t = \frac{1}{3}$ and sell the remainder when he again runs out of cash at $t = \frac{2}{3}$. This program is illustrated in Figure 7–3. In the case of four transactions the initial purchases should equal $(\frac{3}{4})y$, which are then sold off in equal amounts of $(\frac{1}{4})y$ at times $\frac{1}{4}$, $\frac{1}{2}$, and $\frac{3}{4}$.

The initial bond purchase for two transactions is $(\frac{1}{2})y$; for three transactions it is $(\frac{2}{3})y$; and for four transactions it is $(\frac{3}{4})y$. From this we can readily infer that if the wealth holder makes $n$ transactions, the value of the individual's initial purchase of bonds should be $[(n-1)/n]y$. Because he begins the period with initial bondholdings of $[(n-1)/n]y$ and ends the period with zero holdings, the average value of his bondholding must be

$$\frac{n-1}{2n} y$$

Consequently, if the interest return is $i$ percent per period, the revenue will be

$$R = \frac{n-1}{2n} iy$$

The revenue function is plotted in Figure 7–4. As can be seen there, revenue rises continuously as the number of transactions rises. The rise proceeds at a diminishing rate, however, and revenue therefore approaches a limiting value of $iy/2$. This maximum revenue is obtained if the bondholder puts his entire initial income into bonds and sells these bonds off continuously in infinitely small amounts as cash is needed. In this case the initial purchase of bonds equals $y$; the average holding is $y/2$; and the revenue therefore is $iy/2$.

**FIGURE 7–1**
**The profile of a hypothetical bank account**

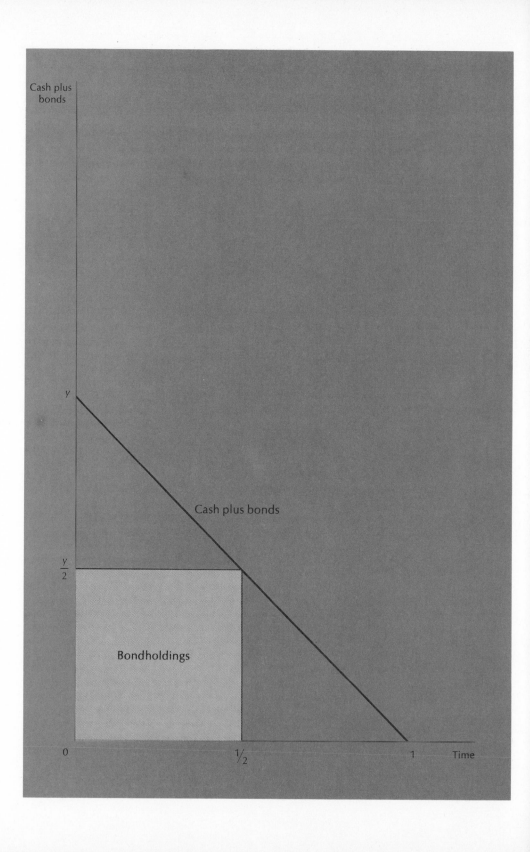

If the wealth holder were to follow this plan, he would never hold any money balances at all and his transactions demand for money would therefore be zero.

The investor is prevented from maximizing his revenue, which could be done by making an infinite number of small transactions, because there are costs associated with each transaction. Such costs tend to have a variable component that is proportional to the value of the transaction and a fixed component that is the same for each transaction regardless of its value. It is this fixed cost that makes small transactions unprofitable and that limits the number of bond purchases and sales that wealth holders will make.

A sophisticated analysis[1] would take into account both the fixed and variable costs. However, for present purposes it is sufficient to assume that transactions costs are exclusively of the fixed variety. Consequently, we assume that for each transaction there is a cost of $a$ dollars and that total transactions costs are therefore given by the function

$$C = na$$

The profit-maximizing investor will pick the number of transactions that maximizes the difference between cost and revenue. As can be seen in Figure 7–4, the maximum point on the profit function $P$, where $P = R - C$, is at a level of $n^*$ transactions.[2] This is the value of $n$ at which the slopes of the $R$ and $C$ functions are equal. This means that the marginal revenue of the next transaction just equals the marginal cost of making the transaction. Profits are therefore at a maximum.

As the reader can easily verify by inspecting Figure 7–4, the optimum number of transactions will increase if income and the rate of interest rise, and it will decrease if the cost per transaction increases. A rise in $i$ or $y$ will rotate the revenue curve counterclockwise about the origin, and the maximum profit will therefore be obtained with a higher volume of transactions. On the other hand, an increase in transaction costs as reflected in a rise in $a$

---

[1] Tobin, ibid., incorporates the effect of both fixed and variable transactions costs into his analysis.

[2] The optimum number of transactions $n^*$ can be calculated by noting that the profit function is

$$p = \frac{n-1}{2n} iy - na$$

by differentiating the function with respect to $n$, and by setting the resulting derivative equal to zero. The result is

$$n^* = \sqrt{\frac{iy}{2a}}$$

The optimum number of transactions therefore increases with increases in $i$ and $y$, and decreases with increases in transactions costs.

**FIGURE 7–2**
**Optimal program for two transactions**

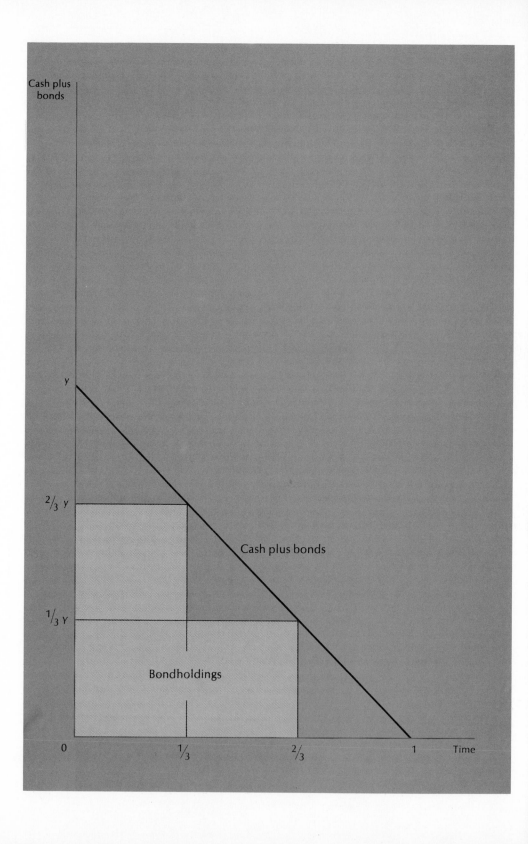

will rotate the cost function counterclockwise, and the optimum number of transactions will therefore decline.

The fact that the optimum number of transactions is influenced by the income of an individual is explained by the presence of the fixed transactions cost. It probably will not pay a person with an initial balance of $1,000, which he will spend in a month, to use a fraction of this balance to purchase bonds because the bonds cannot be held long enough to earn the interest needed to overcome the fixed transactions cost. On the other hand, a large corporation faced with the need to accumulate sizable cash balances in anticipation of a quarterly income tax payment may very well find that it is profitable to invest these funds temporarily in short-term bonds.

The most important result of this analysis is that the transactions demand for money is a decreasing function of the rate of interest. A rise in the rate of interest increases the number of times during the income-expenditure period that bondholders find it worthwhile to enter the bond market. And this implies that a rise in the rate of interest reduces wealth holders' average holding of idle cash balances. If they buy bonds in an amount $[(n-1)/n]y$ at the beginning of the period, they retain $y/n$ dollars of cash. Since they spend all this before replenishing their cash balance, the average holding of money must be $y/2n$ dollars; this clearly implies that the average cash balance is inversely proportional to $n^*$.

To summarize: The traditional theory of the transactions demand for money assumes that this demand is proportional to the level of income. However, because a rise in the rate of interest raises the optimum number of times that wealth holders find it profitable to enter the bond market and because this has the effect of reducing their average level of money holding, it follows that the transactions demand for money is a decreasing function of the rate of interest. The higher the rate of interest, the more costly it is to hold money relative to other assets, and a rise in the rate of interest therefore produces an incentive to economize money balances and to substitute earning assets in their place.

### The Precautionary Demand for Money

A salesman about to embark on a business trip from Chicago to New Orleans will have to take with him a certain amount of (transactions) cash to pay for travel and living expenses. However, if he is a prudent person, he will probably take along more money than the amount he actually plans to spend on the trip. If, for example, his car breaks down and he is unable to pay for the repairs, he may never get to New Orleans to conduct his business. Because of this failure he may miss out on a promotion or he may even lose his job. Because his reputation will be damaged, he may have difficulty finding a new

**FIGURE 7–3**
Optimal program for three transactions

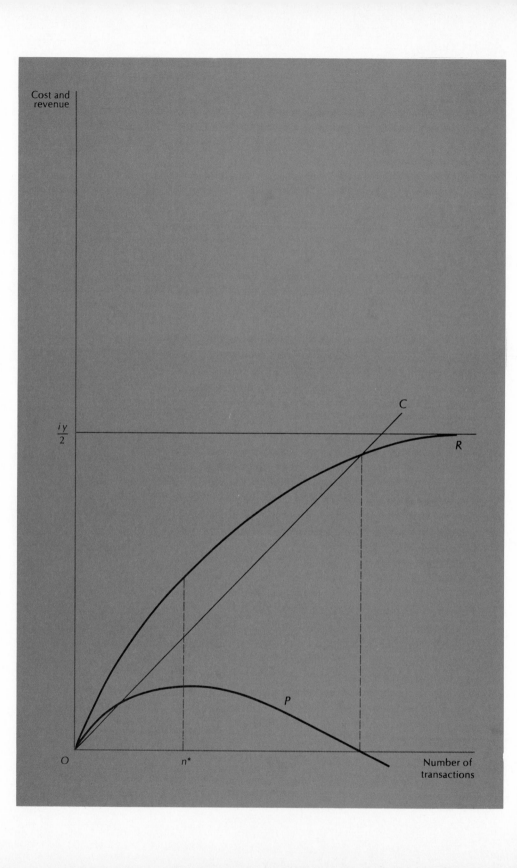

job. All these misfortunes befall him because he has failed to maintain some precautionary balance of money and has therefore fallen prey to what economists describe as the "linkage of risks."

The nominal precautionary demand for money, like the transactions demand, is probably quite closely related to the level of money income. If the cost of automobile repairs rises or if the number of business trips taken each year increases, the salesman's precautionary requirements will probably rise in proportion. However, as in the case of the transactions demand, the precautionary demand may be responsive to changes in the rate of interest. An increase in interest rates may make the purchase of earning assets so tempting that the salesman may be willing to assume a slightly greater risk in the form of a lower precautionary in return for the added interest earnings.

## The Speculative Demand for Money

To hold money balances for reasons unconnected with transactions and precautionary needs appears irrational because money balances that exceed required transactions and precautionary holdings may be exchanged for earning assets. Nonetheless there are grounds for believing that wealth holders do at times include money as one of the assets in their portfolios and that there is therefore an asset, or speculative or liquidity preference as it is often called, demand for money.

When the rate of interest is very low, bond prices are very high. Consequently, a small yield can be earned only at the expense of a relatively large outlay. In such a situation a bond purchase is not an attractive investment. Moreover, if in the past the rate of interest was high but has since fallen to a lower level below which it is not expected to go, the balance of expectations will be in favor of a future rise in the rate. Anyone owning a bond at a time when the rate rises will suffer a capital loss. Consequently, if there is a general expectation that the rate of interest will rise, there will be a preference for liquidity. Since a capital loss cannot be taken on cash (except through a rise in the price level),[1] a situation may arise in which individuals will prefer to hold onto their cash rather than invest in earning assets. They do this in the expectation that interest rates in the future will be higher than at present and that they will therefore be able to strike a better bargain at a subsequent date.

This argument, first presented by Lord Keynes, has been subjected to con-

---

[1] The expectation of a fall in the price level will make money a relatively more attractive way to hold wealth than physical assets. But this is true of any kind of liquid asset whose money value does not vary with the price level. Price expectations help explain relative preferences between physical and liquid assets but do not explain relative preferences among different types of liquid assets.

**FIGURE 7–4**
**Interest revenue and fixed transactions costs**
**as functions of the number of transactions**

siderable criticism. If the interest earnings of a bond are in excess of the expected capital loss, it will pay to invest all one's funds in bonds. If the expected capital loss is greater than the interest earnings, no bonds will be held. Consequently, the minute the critical point is reached where the scales tip in favor of bonds, one would expect a mass exodus from cash into bonds. Keynes's explanation for the fact that this mass exodus does not occur was based on the assumption that different people have different expectations with regard to the future. This view, however, is open to the criticism that if the low rate of interest persists long enough, it will begin to be viewed as permanent so that expectations will converge, the fear of capital loss will disappear, and the speculative demand for money will fade out.

The modern theory of liquidity preference[1] has liberated the concept of a speculative or asset demand for money from reliance upon the expectation that interest rates will rise in the future. Even if no future change in asset prices or yields is expected, wealth holders cannot be certain of what the future will bring. The extent of such *uncertainty* varies with the nature of the asset and tends to run in the same direction as the expected yield of the asset. The expected return on oil exploration and uranium prospecting may be very high; however, the probability that this return will in fact be realized is quite low. The expected return on cash, on the other hand, is zero; and there is no uncertainty about this at all.

Gamblers who enjoy risk will put all their assets into prospective oil wells and uranium mines. However, most investors are "risk averters." Risk averters are characterized by the fact that they will be willing to accept some additional risk only if they expect to receive some additional return, and by the fact that each successive equal increment of risk accepted must bring with it successively greater increases in returns. Given this type of preference, risk averters arrange their portfolios in such a way as to balance, at the margin, the utility of additional return, against the disutility of additional uncertainty. They will, therefore, diversify their portfolios. They will hold some highly speculative stocks on which the expected return and the degree of uncertainty are high; they will hold some blue-chip stocks and bonds that are characterized by lower, but more certain, returns; and they may also hold some cash. Although the cash earns no interest, it has the valuable property of being the most liquid of all assets. This means that one can always convert cash into other assets, but that one might have to wait or to take a lower price if attempting to reverse the process. Individuals who have cash on hand are therefore in a better position to take advantage of the unexpected opportunities that may arise.[2]

---

[1] This discussion follows the line of J. Tobin, "Liquidity Preference as Behavior towards Risk," *Review of Economic Studies,* 25(2):65–86, 1958. The current view seems to have been quite clearly foreshadowed by J. R. Hicks, "A Suggestion for Simplifying the Theory of Money," *Economica,* New Series, 2:1–19, 1935.

[2] In addition to risk lovers and risk averters, Tobin, "Liquidity Preference as Behavior towards Risk," op. cit., delineates a third set of investors known as plungers. Like risk averters, plungers must be compensated for more risk with higher return. However, unlike the case of risk averters,

Now consider the effect that a rise in the general level of yields would have upon the composition of an investor's portfolio. The rise in interest rates causes the potential interest that is forgone by holding cash to increase, and it therefore becomes more expensive to hold cash. Returns being higher, some of the investor's risk aversion will be overcome, and he will tend to substitute some oil-well stocks for blue chips; some blue chips for long-term bonds; some long-term bonds for Treasury bills; and some Treasury bills for cash. The composition of this portfolio will therefore move in the direction of decreased liquidity. On the other hand, if yields generally fall, the return on oil wells no longer compensates for the risk, while the loss of interest due to the holding of cash and the low-yield assets becomes smaller. The investor will therefore tend to adjust his portfolio in the direction of increased liquidity. The investor's preference for liquidity can therefore be seen to increase with a fall in the rate of interest, and his asset demand for money may also be a decreasing function of the rate of interest.

## 7–3
## ALTERNATIVE THEORIES OF THE DEMAND FOR MONEY

One of the major questions that we shall attempt to answer in this book is why some economists have supreme faith in the ability of the competitive market system to bring the economy out of recession and back to full employment automatically, while other economists are skeptical of the ability of the patient to cure himself and believe that the monetary-fiscal doctors must be called upon. A closely related question is the issue of why some economists would put their faith in the effectiveness of monetary policy, while others regard fiscal policy as the salvation. As we shall see in Chapters 9 and 10, both questions hinge, to a considerable extent, on the nature of the demand for money. It is therefore exceedingly important that we take care to classify the assumptions that different groups of economists make about the demand for money.

One of the most familiar expressions in monetary economics is the "quantity equation"

$$MV = pY$$

The equation is a truism which states that the quantity of money $M$ times the velocity of turnover of money in the purchase of newly produced goods and services $V$ must equal the value of money income $pY$, where $p$ is an index of prices and $Y$ is the level of real income measured in base-period prices.

In some interpretations it is assumed that $V$ is a constant. This assumption amounts to saying that the only reason people hold money balances is to

---

the successive returns for each additional unit of risk need not increase. For example, plungers might always be willing to swap risk for return at a fixed rate. In this event, the situation may be too risky for them to hold anything but cash. A reduction in risk relative to yields may then induce them to take the plunge and put all their wealth into earning assets. Thus plungers are either in all the way, or not at all.

finance day-to-day transactions. Any additional money balances are immediately used to purchase earning assets. Under these "classical" assumptions, the quantity equation becomes more than a mere truism: it becomes instead the well-known quantity theory according to which an increase in the money supply must lead either to an increase in real income $Y$, or to an increase in the price level $p$, or to some combination of the two. An increase in the money supply, velocity being fixed, implies that wealth holders will attempt to rid themselves of the idle balances by purchasing earning assets. This means that the prices of earning assets will be bid up, interest rates will fall, and investment and income will increase. If idle resources are available, $Y$ may rise. If, instead, the economy is already at full employment, competition for the available supply of output will raise prices. Since competition for earning assets will continue until all the excess money balances are absorbed into transactions demands, we may infer that, with $V$ fixed, the level of money income will always be proportional to the money supply.

The quantity equation can be written

$$m = \frac{M}{p} = kY$$

where $M/p$ is the real value of the money supply and $k$ is the reciprocal of $V$, and therefore represents the fraction of a time period the average dollar is held between transactions. In this form the equation has been called the "Cambridge quantity equation," and $k$ has been denoted as the "Marshallian $k$ ratio."

By introducing the speculative demand for money, Keynes specifically denied the constant velocity assumption. Like his predecessors, however, Keynes believed that the transactions and precautionary demands were dependent on the level of income and not specifically associated with the rate of interest. The Keynesian variant of the demand for money may therefore be written

$$m = \frac{M}{p} = kY + L(i)$$

where $L(i)$ is the speculative demand for money which varies inversely with the rate of interest and where $k$ must now be interpreted to mean the ratio of transactions balances to the volume of transactions.

An important possibility pointed out by Keynes is that once a critically low rate of interest is reached, increases in the supply of money may not achieve any further reduction in the rate of interest. Such a situation may arise from the fact that at very low rates of interest the yield on earning assets is so low and the risk of holding earning assets is so high that, given the liquidity premium of holding money, wealth holders will be willing to substitute money for earning assets in their portfolios without requiring an inducement in the form of higher bond prices. Thus bonds and money become perfect substitutes, and a change in their relative supplies has no effect on their relative prices and therefore on the rate of interest. An economy in such a situation is said to be in the "liquidity trap" where expansionary monetary policy is powerless to lower the rate of interest.

Another monetary variant, which for lack of a better name we shall arbitrarily call the "modified Keynesian" variant, would include in the transactions and precautionary demands the assumption that these demands are inversely related to the rate of interest. Therefore, this variant may be written

$$m = L_1(i,Y) + L_2(i)$$

where $L_1$ refers to the transactions and precautionary demands and $L_2$ to the speculative demand. Since all the motives for holding money appear to depend on the rate of interest, the modified Keynesian variant implies that the distinction between the various motives is somewhat artificial, so that the above expression may just as well be compressed to

$$m = L(i,Y)$$

Developments in monetary theory of the past two decades place emphasis on the importance of wealth in determining the demand for money. The theory of portfolio balance suggests than an increase in the quantity of money demanded will occur not only if income rises or the rate of interest falls but also if wealth holders become richer. In other words, an increment to wealth causes wealth holders to attempt to distribute this increment over additional holdings of not one but several forms of wealth. For example, in one of his many important contributions Tobin specifies the demand for money as

$$m = L(i,Y,K)$$

where $K$ the capital stock represents the earning power or productive wealth of the economy.[1] Let us denote this form of the demand for money as the "modern Keynesian" variant.

The emphasis on wealth as a determinant of the demand for money becomes most pronounced in the writings of the "Chicago School." Their gospel is the "modern quantity theory" and their high priest is Professor Milton Friedman. The modern quantity theorist views the demand for money as part and parcel of the overall problem of determining the demand for all assets both physical and financial. As we saw in discussing consumption, Friedman views the spending of households as a function of their total resources and not their current income. Presumably then, the transactions balances of households must also be reflections of their overall asset position, so that current income has as little role in explaining the demand for money as it does in determining consumption. In the work of Brunner and Meltzer, for example, the usual Keynesian attempt to relate the demand for money to current income is replaced by relations between money and measures of

[1] J. Tobin, "A Dynamic Aggregative Model," *Journal of Political Economy*, 63:103–115, 1955.

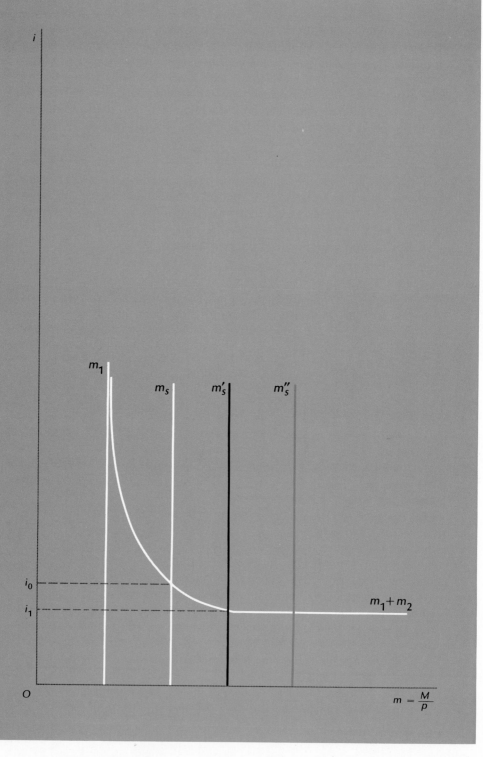

wealth.[1] Friedman himself carries the demotion of Keynesian ideas even further by eliminating both income and the rate of interest and making the demand for money a function of the level of permanent income alone.[2]

To illustrate the determination of the equilibrium rate of interest, let us now diagram the Keynesian variant. In Figure 7–5 the rate of interest is measured on the vertical axis, and the quantity of money is measured on the horizontal axis. The transactions and precautionary demand for money $m_1$ is assumed to be inelastic with respect to the rate of interest. When the speculative demand for money $m_2$ is added, the total demand for money $m_1 + m_2$ is obtained. If the supply of money balances is $m_s$, the demand and supply schedules intersect at interest rate $i_0$. If the money supply increases to $m'_s$, wealth holders will be induced to hold the added balances only if the interest rate falls to $i_1$. At $i_1$ the liquidity trap, where the demand for money is infinitely elastic, is reached. An increase in the supply of money from $m'_s$ to $m''_s$ yields no fall in the rate of interest.

In closing this section, we want the reader to note very carefully that the demand for money is linked only to income transactions and not to financial transactions. The reason for this is that the various equations are equilibrium relations that specify the amount of money that wealth holders would hold for various purposes if their portfolios were in balance. General monetary equilibrium is a situation in which all portfolios are balanced, in which case there are no financial transactions at all.

## 7–4
## THE SUPPLY OF MONEY

The money supply, defined as the total of currency and demand deposits held by the nonbank public, totaled $270.4 billion at the end of 1973 as compared with the level of GNP for the year of $1,295 billion. To determine why and how the money supply got to be exactly this size would require an involved historical, statistical, and theoretical study. It is fortunate for our present purposes that our concern is not with how the money supply got to be what it is, but rather with how the money supply can be changed.

[1] K. Brunner and A. H. Meltzer, "Predicting Velocity: Implications for Theory and Policy," *Journal of Finance,* 18:319–343, 1963; A. H. Meltzer, "The Demand for Money: The Evidence from Time Series," *Journal of Political Economy,* 71:219–246; and K. Brunner and A. H. Meltzer, "Some Further Investigations of Demand and Supply Functions for Money," *Journal of Finance,* 19:240–283, 1964.

[2] M. Friedman, "The Quantity Theory of Money: A Restatement," *Studies in the Quantity Theory of Money,* Chap. 1, The University of Chicago Press, Chicago, 1956; and "The Demand for Money: Some Theoretical and Empirical Results," *Journal of Political Economy,* 67:327–351, 1958.

**FIGURE 7–5**
**Demand and supply for money balances (all values in real terms)**

**TABLE 7–1**

| Federal Reserve Banks | | | |
|---|---|---|---|
| Securities | +1,000 a | Member bank deposits | +1,000 a |
| **Commercial Banks** | | | |
| Loans and securities | + 800 b | Deposits | +1,000 a |
| | + 640 d | | + 800 c |
| Reserves | +1,000 a | | + 640 e |
| | − 800 b | | |
| | + 800 c | | |
| | − 640 d | | |
| | + 640 e | | |
| **Nonbank Private Sector** | | | |
| Deposits | +1,000 a | | |
| | + 800 c | | |
| | + 640 e | | |
| Securities | −1,000 a | | |
| | − 800 b | | |
| | − 640 d | | |

To analyze how the money supply changes, it is useful to draw up some hypothetical balance sheets as in Table 7–1. One such balance sheet represents a consolidation of the assets and liabilities of the nonbank private sector. The second balance sheet records the consolidated assets and liabilities of the commercial banking system. The commercial banks, in turn, are assumed to rely on the Federal Reserve System (Fed), which is the central bank of the United States, for their banking services, and so there is a balance sheet for the Fed. The United States Treasury also gets into the money generating process in various ways, but its balance sheet need not concern us at the moment.

The Fed is legally empowered to purchase and sell government securities from private dealers. Such transactions, known as open market operations, are the most important way in which the Fed can influence the supply of money. To see how this works, suppose that the Fed purchases $1,000 worth of bonds from private persons. The Fed writes a check in return for a bond, and we assume that the recipients then deposit their checks in their bank accounts. The banks, in turn, send the checks back to the Fed in order to receive deposit credit in their accounts with the Fed. The various transactions involved in this exchange are recorded as transactions a in the respective balance sheets. For the nonbank private sector, security holdings diminish, but the loss of this asset is offset by an increase in bank deposits. As far as the commercial banks are concerned, this deposit is a liability since it is something that is owed to depositors, and the deposit is therefore entered on the right side of the balance sheet. However, offsetting this is the fact that when a commercial bank sends the check to the Fed it receives deposit credit in its bank account at the Fed. Thus the left side of the commercial bank's balance sheet shows that *reserves* have increased; this is then also shown on the Fed's books as an increase in member bank deposits. The Fed, finally, acknowledges by its right-side entry that its liabilities to member banks have increased, but by the same token it has gained an asset in the form of a government security.

Summing up: The nonbank private sector has traded securities for deposits, the commercial banks have additional deposit liabilities but also a higher level of reserves, and the Fed has acquired the government security while increasing its indebtedness to member banks. The important thing to note is that this open market purchase by the Fed has increased the money supply as measured by the deposits and currency held by the nonbank private sector.

So far the money supply has increased by $1,000. However, this is not necessarily the end of the story in a "fractional reserve" banking system. Suppose there is a legal minimum reserve requirement of 20 percent. This means that the commercial banks must hold a sum equal to at least 20 percent of their demand deposits idle in the form of a cash reserve in their accounts with the Fed. This amount is called "required reserves" whereas the remaining $800 is called "excess reserves" and may be utilized to make loans and purchase earning assets. Suppose therefore that the bank which receives the $1,000 uses its excess reserves to purchase a bond for $800 from an individual. The bank writes a check which is received in payment for the bond (*b*), but the check is redeposited somewhere in the commercial banking system (*c*). This means that the added reserves due to the open market purchase are still $1,000. But with deposits of $1,800 there are now excess reserves of only $640 because required reserves have increased by $160. If this $640 is used to purchase additional securities (*d*), reserves will first fall (*d*), but when the proceeds are redeposited (*e*), reserves again increase.

Notice that each time excess reserves are used to buy earning assets, the proceeds are redeposited somewhere in the commercial banking system. This means that, after the original $1,000 increase in reserves, which came from outside the commercial banking system, the purchase of earning assets does not change total reserves. But the purchase of earning assets does change required reserves because these purchases cause deposits to increase. Thus, from the fact that the net change in reserves is $1,000, and from the fact that required reserves are 20 percent of demand deposits, we may infer that excess reserves will be exhausted when deposits have risen by $5,000. A five-to-one expansion of deposits will therefore be possible on the basis of the original increase in reserves of $1,000. The final situation is shown in Table 7–2, where it can be seen that after the initial $1,000 increase in deposits and reserves due to the open market purchase (*a*), the nonbank private sector has traded the banking system $4,000 worth of earning assets in return for $4,000

**TABLE 7–2**

| Commercial Banks | | | |
|---|---|---|---|
| Loans and securities | +4,000 b | Deposits | +1,000 a |
| Reserves | +1,000 a | | +4,000 b |
| Nonbank Private Sector | | | |
| Deposits | +1,000 a | | |
| | +4,000 b | | |
| Securities | −1,000 a | | |
| | −4,000 b | | |

of deposits (b). The net effect of the open market purchase on the supply of money is therefore $5,000.[1]

Deposit expansion and money supply creation may proceed whenever additional reserves are placed in the commercial banking system. As discussed subsequently, a government deficit will increase the money supply if it is financed by printing money or borrowing from the Fed. Also a surplus in the country's international balance of payments will raise the money supply. Another source of potential additional reserves is the borrowing privilege that member banks enjoy at the Fed. The Fed sets an interest rate, called the "rediscount rate," at which it will lend to member banks. On the balance sheets a loan of this sort would increase commercial bank reserves on the left side, and there would be a corresponding right-side liability showing indebtedness to the Fed. Thus, member bank borrowing increases excess reserves by the amount of the loan and provides the basis either for deposit expansion or for the prevention of contraction in the event that excess reserves are initially negative.

A decision on the part of the nonbank private sector to hold less currency by swapping currency for deposits provides the basis for multiple expansion of deposits. If firms or individuals decide to reduce their currency holdings by $100 and increase their deposits by this amount, commercial bank balance sheets will be changed according to transaction a of Table 7–3. If the commercial banks, in turn, now decide that their holdings of currency (till cash) are excessive, they may turn this currency over to the Fed in exchange for

---

[1] Whether banks use excess reserves to purchase bonds or whether they use these reserves to lend to their customers directly is irrelevant from the point of view of monetary expansion. In either case the banks are engaged in lending, and the effect on the money supply is the same. The accounting procedures are, however, slightly different. Take the case of a commercial bank in Table 7–1 after it has received an increase in deposits and reserves of $1,000. Instead of going directly to buy an earning asset, the bank now lends $800 directly to a customer. Its procedure is to create a deposit of $800 for the customer and to record his I.O.U. of $800 on the left side of its balance sheet. The customer then withdraws the funds to pay bills (this reduces both the bank's deposit liabilities and its reserves), and the recipient of the check then deposits the funds (which again increases deposits and reserves), thereby leaving the commercial banking system in exactly the situation it would have been in had the $800 been used to buy a bond.

**TABLE 7–3**

| Federal Reserve Banks | | | |
|---|---|---|---|
| | | Federal Reserve Notes outstanding | −100 *b* |
| | | Member bank deposits | +100 *b* |
| **Commercial Banks** | | | |
| Currency | +100 *a* | Deposits | +100 *a* |
| | −100 *b* | | |
| Reserves | +100 *b* | | |

deposit credit. Thus transaction *b* shows a reduction in commercial bank currency holdings offset by an increase in reserves, while the Fed reduces its notes outstanding liability and grants additional deposit credit to the commercial banks.

Currency can be created by reversing the foregoing. If the commercial banks need additional currency they need merely call the Fed to set the printing press in motion. The bookkeeping transactions will be exactly the opposite of those shown in Table 7–3.

We have seen that the decision to reduce the holdings of currency outside the banking system and to swap these for deposits provides the commercial banking system with additional reserves that may then be activated to produce a multiple expansion of deposits and, therefore, the supply of money. Thus total commercial bank reserves plus currency held by the nonbank private sector represents the potential base for deposit expansion and money supply creation. It is for this reason that the sum of these two quantities is known as the monetary base, or sometimes as "high-powered money."

It is clear from what has been said that the money supply depends on various factors such as the level of reserves, the legal minimum reserve requirement, and the private sector's desire to hold currency relative to deposits. We can now formalize these relationships as follows: Define high-powered money $H$ as

$$H = CU + RR + ER$$

where $CU$ is currency held by the nonbank private sector, $RR$ is required reserves, and $ER$ is excess reserves. The nominal stock of money is given by

$$M = CU + D$$

where $D$ stands for demand deposits. The ratio of money supply to high-powered money is obtained by dividing the second equation by the first. Upon doing this, and also dividing numerator and denominator by $D$, we get

$$\frac{M}{H} = \frac{CU/D + 1}{CU/D + RR/D + ER/D} \tag{7-1}$$

The ratio of currency to deposits, $CU/D$, depends on the habits of individuals and business firms and tends, except for systematic seasonal variation, to be fairly stable. The ratio of required reserves to deposits, $RR/D$, is the legal minimum reserve requirement which is subject to variation within limits at the discretion of the Fed. Looking at Eq. (7–1) we can see that when the legal minimum reserve ratio is raised, $M/H$ will have to fall because a larger fraction of any deposit must be held by the commercial banks as required reserves. Notice also that if no one wants to hold currency, and if banks hold no excess reserves, Eq. (7–1) would reduce to

$$\frac{M}{H} = \frac{1}{RR/D}$$

which gives us the $5:1$ theoretical maximum result that we obtained in the numerical example used to discuss the effect of an open market purchase.

The ratio in Eq. (7–1) that is most apt to vary systematically with changes in economic conditions is the ratio of excess reserves to deposits, $ER/D$. Banks are not likely at all times to utilize all their excess reserves to make loans and purchase other earning assets. The typical bank operates under conditions of uncertainty. Whether new deposits in any period will exceed withdrawals is never known for certain. Even if the bank regards the chances that deposits will match withdrawals as even, the penalty attached to being caught short is enough to make it hold excess reserves. There is little reason to suppose, moreover, that banks differ fundamentally from other wealth holders. If it is assumed that their portfolio balance behavior is similar to that of individuals, banks will be likely to hold larger quantities of excess reserves during periods of low interest rates. A rise in bond yields and loan rates will make banks less reluctant to lend and will therefore increase the ratio of earning assets to reserves and also the supply of money. Thus the supply of money, as well as the demand for money, is a function of the rate of interest.

Although the Fed can, through the use of its policy tools, make the level of bank reserves whatever it wants to make them, it has only partial control of the ratio $M/H$, and it cannot therefore always be sure that the money supply will rise in proportion to a change in reserves. In particular it seems likely that the ratio of excess reserves to deposits will rise as the interest rate falls, and we might therefore utilize this likelihood to compress Eq. (7–1) into a money supply function of the form

$$m_s = \phi(h,i)$$

to express the hypothesis that the real value of the money supply will rise as both the real value of high-powered money, $h$, increases and the rate of interest increases.

In summary, the potential size of the money supply depends primarily on the volume of bank reserves. Since the volume of these reserves is almost entirely dependent on Fed-Treasury action, the money supply is often treated as a so-called policy variable; i.e., it is assumed fixed unless changed by government policy. We have already seen that this is an inadequate assumption.

Nevertheless it will not do serious harm if we adopt it for the purposes of the next chapter. And subsequently we will try to reintroduce a more adequate treatment.

## 7–5
## MONETARY EFFECTS OF A FISCAL OPERATION

If we are to gain a clear understanding of the effectiveness of monetary and fiscal policies in changing the level of income, we will first have to understand the monetary effect of a fiscal operation. Some of the controversy over whether monetary or fiscal policy is the most effective tool of stabilization policy has involved a senseless quibble that results from a failure to distinguish one policy from the other in a correct manner. Some fiscal policies affect the money supply and, depending upon the method of finance, others do not. The economic effects of the policies can be expected to be different, and we must therefore be careful to sort out just what is happening.

We define a "pure" fiscal operation as an expenditure or tax change that affects the size of the current income stream but leaves the money supply unaffected. A "pure" monetary policy is defined as an operation that affects the money supply without directly altering the current income stream. A Fed purchase of government bonds from a member of the nonbank private sector alters the money supply but has no direct effect upon the level of current income.[1] On the other hand, an increase in government spending directly increases income, whereas an increase in taxes has the opposite effect.

Insofar as the payment of taxes to the Treasury reduces demand deposits, the fiscal operation will not be "pure" in the sense that there is no effect on the money supply. If we are able to talk about "pure" fiscal policy, we must assume that the tax revenues are utilized to retire debt held by the nonbank private sector, or that government expenditures in an equal amount are made at the same time. In both cases, the monetary effects of the fiscal operation(s) just cancel.

Consider the monetary effects of an increase in government purchases. Suppose that the Treasury makes a payment of $100 to a mail carrier. The $100 is an income payment and therefore constitutes a fiscal operation. But the $100 payment is also an addition to the money supply; if it is not offset by a corresponding reduction, it must be considered a combined monetary-fiscal change. Whether or not such an offset occurs depends on the method of financing the $100 expenditure.

**1** If the Treasury increases tax collections by $100, there will be a reduction in demand deposits of $100. The monetary effects of the expenditure and the tax cancel each other. A tax-financed expenditure can therefore be regarded as a pure fiscal policy.

[1] The Fed purchase may through its effect on interest rates raise the level of investment and income; such an effect we would describe as indirect.

**2**   If the Treasury replenishes its account by selling bonds to the nonbank private sector, the purchasers of the bonds will make payment from their deposits in return for bonds. Again, the monetary effects of the fiscal operation cancel out. A deficit financed by a sale of bonds to the nonbank private sector may therefore be considered a pure fiscal policy. When reference is made to fiscal policy throughout this book it should always be understood that deficits are financed by borrowing from the nonbank private sector, and that surpluses are used to retire some of the public debt held by that sector.

**3**   It is possible for the Treasury to replenish its account by selling bonds to the Fed. In this case, the $100 payment to the mail carrier remains as a net increase in the reserves of the banking system. The government expenditure in this case is a combined monetary-fiscal operation since it both increases income and changes the money supply. By manipulating the various balance sheets, readers should convince themselves that the effects on the money supply would be the same whether the Treasury borrows from the Fed or whether it just prints currency and spends it.

## 7-6
### THE PROGRAM

The discussion of the last four chapters provides the building blocks with which to construct a general equilibrium model of the economic system. We will need to do this since otherwise we will be caught in an endless chain of action and reaction. To illustrate the difficulty, consider Figure 7–5 again and imagine starting at interest rate $i_0$. Now suppose that the money supply is increased to $m_s'$ so that the rate of interest drops to $i_1$. Associated with this lower rate of interest will be a higher level of investment; this, in turn, implies a higher level of income. However, if the level of income rises, the quantity of money needed for transactions purposes rises, and this means that the entire demand for money function of Figure 7–5 will shift to the right. Consequently, the rate of interest which first declined now has a tendency to increase. To avoid going around in circles in this manner, we can construct a model that not only avoids this problem but provides a framework within which a host of macroeconomic problems can be analyzed. Constructing this model is the task of the next chapter. One of the beauties of the model is that it merely juxtaposes the tools that are already at our disposal.

# 8

# GENERAL
# EQUILIBRIUM
# OF THE PRODUCT
# AND MONEY
# MARKETS

## INTRODUCTION

The purpose of the present chapter is to pull together the various strands that have been developed in the last four chapters and to integrate these strands into a coherent model that provides equilibrium solutions for the many macroeconomic variables that have concerned us.[1] Once we construct and understand this model, we shall be in a position to analyze the effectiveness of alternative monetary and fiscal policies, whether or not the economy tends automatically to full employment, and a host of other important and controversial macroeconomic issues. We begin with a model that assumes the absence of government although we shall rectify this situation very shortly. To facilitate our understanding, moreover, we shall follow the procedure of Chapters 4 and 5 and resort to a numerical example that has been cooked up

---

[1] The model to be constructed here was first presented by J. R. Hicks, "Mr. Keynes and the 'Classics': A Suggested Interpretation," *Econometrica*, 5:147–159, 1937.

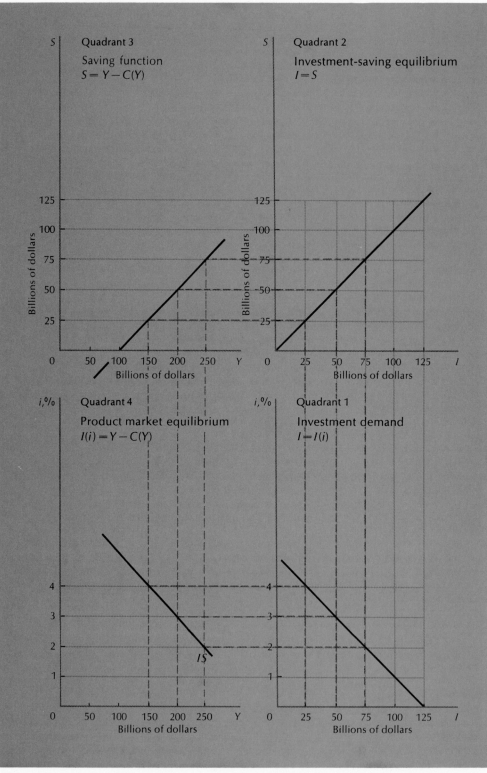

for purposes of illustration. Neither the numerical values nor the shapes of the functions are intended to bear any resemblance to reality.

## 8-2
## GRAPHIC DERIVATION OF JOINT PRODUCT AND MONETARY EQUILIBRIUM

In Chapter 6 we saw that investment demand can be represented as a decreasing function of the rate of interest. We now plot this function in the first quadrant of Figure 8–1. The rate of interest is measured on the vertical axis and the level of investment on the horizontal axis.[1] In quadrant 2 the intended investment-saving equilibrium condition which we discussed in Chapter 5 is represented. This curve must be a straight line rising from the origin at a 45-degree angle because intended investment must equal saving at equilibrium. The familiar saving schedule is plotted with respect to the level of income in quadrant 3. We assume in this case that the level of saving is zero at an income level of $100 billion and that the marginal propensity to save is 0.5.[2]

Starting with an interest rate of 3 percent, we note in quadrant 1 that investment of $50 billion will be undertaken. Moving to quadrant 2, we observe that saving must also be $50 billion. In quadrant 3 the saving function indicates that $50 billion will be saved at an income level of $200 billion. Finally, in quadrant 4 we obtain one point of product market equilibrium; i.e., when the rate of interest is 3 percent, the level of income that will just make intended investment equal saving is $200 billion.

If the rate of interest is raised to 4 percent, the level of investment drops to $25 billion. This means that saving must be $25 billion and therefore that the level of income must be $150 billion. If the rate of interest falls to 2 percent, investment rises to $75 billion, so that the equilibrium level of income must be $250 billion.

If this procedure of selecting arbitrary rates of interest and then finding the level of income that is consistent with each rate of interest is continued, a curve called the "*IS* curve" will be traced out in quadrant 4. This curve is a simple graphic representation of the product market equilibrium condition, and it shows the level of income that will yield equality of intended investment and saving at different possible interest rates.[3] Because a fall in the rate

---

[1] The equation of the assumed investment demand schedule is $I = 125 - 25i$.

[2] The equation of the assumed saving function is $S = -50 + 0.5Y$.

[3] The equation for intended investment is $I = 125 - 25i$, and the saving function is $S = -50 + 0.5Y$. If intended investment is equated with saving, we have

$$125 - 25i = -50 + 0.5Y$$

## FIGURE 8-1
**Product market equilibrium (all values in real terms)**

of interest implies a higher level of investment and therefore a higher level of income, it is evident that the *IS* curve has a negative slope.

The identical procedure as used above may now be applied to the problem of finding monetary equilibrium. In quadrant 1 of Figure 8–2 the speculative demand for money $m_2 = L(i)$ is plotted against the rate of interest. It is assumed that wealth holders balance their portfolios in such a way that when the rate of interest is 3 percent, the speculative demand is $25 billion. At 2 percent it is $50 billion, at 1 percent it is $75 billion, and at 0 percent it is $100 billion or more.

Quadrant 2 shows how the given money supply of $125 billion can be split between transactions and speculative balances. If the transactions demand is $100 billion, then $25 billion will be left over for speculative purposes. If the transactions demand is $75 billion, $50 billion will be left over for speculative balances. In quadrant 3 the transactions demand, assumed to be proportional to the level of income in a 1:2 ratio, is posted. Finally, in quadrant 4 the rate of interest that is consistent with monetary equilibrium is posted against the level of income.

Beginning with an interest rate of 3 percent, we note in quadrant 1 that wealth holders desire to hold $25 billion of idle cash and deposits for speculative purposes. In quadrant 2 we observe that $100 billion will be released for transactions purposes. But quadrant 3 indicates that $100 billion of transactions money is consistent with a level of income of $200 billion. Moving to quadrant 4, we observe that the level of income that yields monetary equilibrium with a money supply of $125 billion and an interest rate of 3 percent is $200 billion.

Now start with an interest rate of 2 percent. At this rate of interest wealth holders will wish to hold idle speculative balances of $50 billion. This means that the amount released for transactions purposes will be $75 billion, which is consistent with a level of income of $150 billion (quadrant 3). Accordingly, we note in quadrant 4 that the level of income that will yield monetary equilibrium at a 2 percent rate of interest is $150 billion.

If this process of selecting arbitrary rates of interest and finding the level of income that is consistent with monetary equilibrium at each rate of interest is continued, a curve known as the "*LM* curve" will be traced out in quadrant

---

so that on rearranging terms we get

$$Y = 350 - 50i$$

This last expression is the equation of the *IS* curve and corresponds to the points plotted in quadrant 4 of Figure 8–1.

**FIGURE 8–2**
**Monetary equilibrium (all values**
**in real terms)**

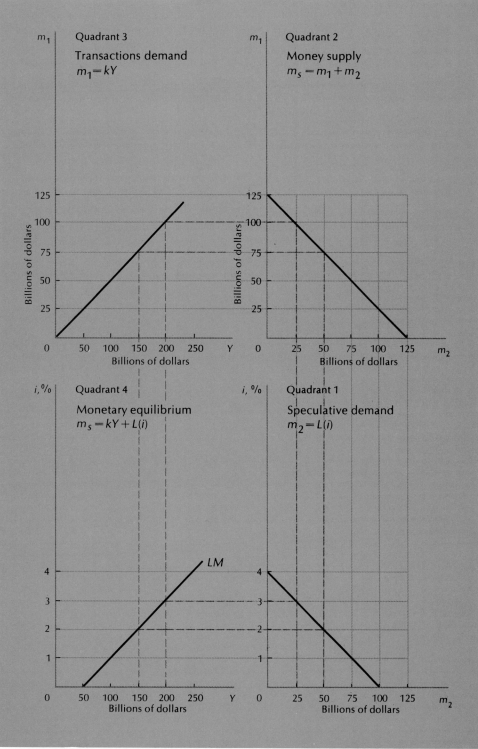

4.[1] This curve is a diagrammatic representation of the monetary equilibrium condition and specifies the level of income which, for different rates of interest, makes the demand for money equal to the supply of money. Since higher rates of interest are associated with a lower demand for idle balances, a given money supply can support a larger volume of transactions, and the LM curve therefore has a positive slope.

Although the LM schedule suggests that several rates of interest are consistent with monetary equilibrium and the IS schedule suggests that several rates are consistent with product market equilibrium, there is only one rate of interest and level of income that is consistent with both. In Figure 8–3 the IS and LM functions of Figures 8–1 and 8–2 are superimposed. The intersection of the two curves is at an income level of $200 billion with an interest rate of 3 percent.[2] Once these equilibrium values have been found, it is easy enough to trace back once again through the product market diagrams and verify that the level of investment is $50 billion and the level of saving is $50 billion. Similarly, if we retrace our steps through the money market, we find that at equilibrium the speculative demand is $25 billion and the transactions demand is $100 billion. General equilibrium prevails: There is no tendency for any magnitude to change.

We can generalize the results of the specific example just presented in the following way. Product market equilibrium requires intended investment to

---

[1] The equation of the assumed speculative demand function is $m_2 = 100 - 25i$. The transactions demand is $m_1 = 0.5Y$, and the money supply is $125 billion. Substituting these expressions into the equilibrium condition $m_s = m_1 + m_2$ we obtain

$$125 = 0.5Y + 100 - 25i$$

which upon rearranging gives the equation for the LM curve $Y = 50 + 50i$.

[2] It is now possible to find the equilibrium values by solving the IS and LM equations simultaneously. The IS function is $Y = 350 - 50i$, and the LM function is $Y = 50 + 50i$. When we equate these two functions, we find that $i = 3$ percent and $Y = $200 billion. Given the solution for the level of income, we can then go to the saving function and note that

$$S = -50 + 0.5Y = -50 + 0.5(200) = 50$$

The equilibrium rate of interest can be substituted into the investment demand function so that

$$I = 125 - 25i = 50$$

and therefore we see that intended investment equals saving.

Similarly, the level of income of $200 billion requires transactions balances of

$$m_1 = 0.5Y = 100$$

Because the money supply is $125 billion, $25 billion is released for speculative purposes. This result is consistent with a 3 percent interest rate because from the speculative demand equation we have

$$m_2 = 100 - 25i = 25$$

**FIGURE 8–3**
**General equilibrium (all values in real terms)**

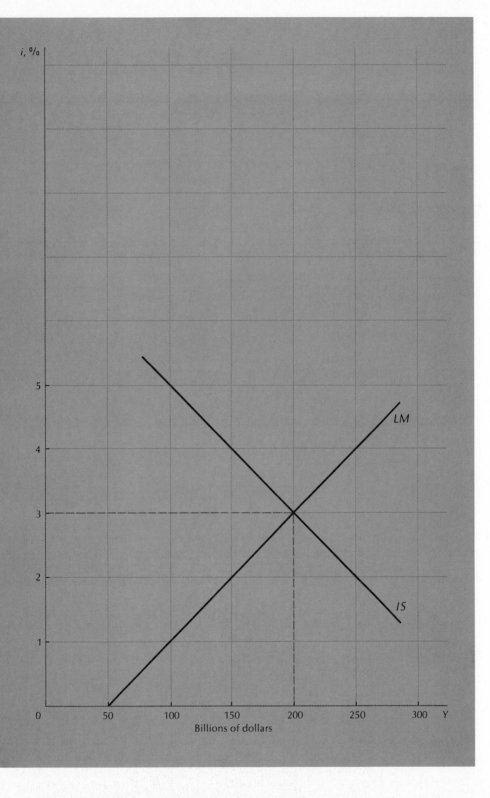

equal saving so that

$$I = S \tag{8-1}$$

which is the condition represented in quadrant 2 of Figure 8-1. Saving is a function of the level of income which in general terms may be written

$$S = Y - C(Y) \tag{8-2}$$

where $C$ is the level of consumption. Intended investment here has been assumed to be a decreasing function of the rate of interest so that

$$I = I(i) \tag{8-3}$$

When Eqs. (8-2) and (8-3) are substituted into Eq. (8-1), we obtain

$$I(i) = Y - C(Y) \tag{8-4}$$

which is the equation of the *IS* curve.

Similarly, monetary equilibrium is represented in quadrant 2 of Figure 8-2 as

$$m_s = m_1 + m_2 \tag{8-5}$$

The transactions demand for money is assumed to be proportional to the level of income and may be described by the equation

$$m_1 = kY \tag{8-6}$$

and the speculative demand for money is a decreasing function of the rate of interest so that

$$m_2 = L(i) \tag{8-7}$$

When these three relations are combined we get

$$m_s = kY + L(i) \tag{8-8}$$

which is the equation of the *LM* curve in quadrant 4 of Figure 8-2.

When we look at the fourth quadrant of both Figures 8-1 and 8-2, we have the situation shown in Figure 8-3 which combines the *IS* and *LM* curves. The equations are

$$I(i) = Y - C(Y) \qquad \text{*IS* curve} \tag{8-4}$$

$$m_s = kY + L(i) \qquad \text{*LM* curve} \tag{8-8}$$

a set of two simultaneous equations in two variables $i$ and $Y$. These two equations can then be solved, and the equilibrium values can be determined.

To make sure that we understand the complete model let us look at a disequilibrium state, that is, a situation in which the level of income and rate of interest are different from the equilibrium values. Focusing on Figure 8-3, suppose that the level of income is $150 billion and that the rate of interest is 2 percent. This puts the economy on the *LM* curve and means that the quantity of money demanded equals the quantity supplied. However, a glance at the *IS* curve shows that it would take a 4 percent rate of interest to equate intended investment with the savings that are generated at the $150 billion income level. Consequently, intended investment exceeds saving and the level of income must therefore rise. As the level of income rises the quantity of money needed for transactions purposes rises, so that in order to acquire these balances, wealth holders sell earning assets. The effect of this is to raise the rate of interest which, in combination with the rise in income, acts to narrow the gap between the rate of interest that equates the demand for and supply of money, with the rate of interest that equates intended investment with saving. The process stops when the rate of interest reaches 3 percent and the level of income reaches $200 billion. At that point intended investment equals saving, and the demand for money equals the supply of money. The original excess of intended investment over saving is eliminated by the rise in the rate of interest that reduces intended investment, and by the rise in the level of income, which raises the level of saving.

In Chapter 13 we will have a careful look at the so-called dynamics of adjustment. However, in the meantime the reader should pick other disequilibrium combinations and trace the adjustment to equilibrium. There are two points that should be borne in mind. First, any combination of income and interest rate that implies a point below the *LM* curve is a point at which the quantity of money demanded exceeds the quantity supplied, whereas any combination that lies above the curve implies excess supply of money. To see this, consider the equilibrium point of Figure 8–3 with the interest rate of 3 percent and the level of income at $200 billion. If the rate of interest is arbitrarily held constant and the level of income is increased to $250 billion, the quantity of speculative balances would remain unchanged, but the quantity of transactions balances demanded would be higher. Since the money supply is fixed, there is excess demand for money at this point, which is to the right of the *LM* curve. As a result of the excess demand, wealth holders will attempt to acquire the needed balances by selling earning assets. The consequence of this is that the prices of earning assets will fall, and the rate of interest will rise. The rate of interest therefore tends to be pulled up towards the *LM* curve.

The second important point is that any combination of *i* and *Y* that lies above the *IS* curve is a point at which intended investment falls short of saving, which means that income tends to decline from such a point. The opposite is the case for points below *IS*. To see this, start at some point of product market equilibrium (for example at $i = 3$ percent, and $Y = \$200$ billion in Figure 8–3). A rise in the rate of interest, income being arbitrarily held fixed for the moment, would lower intended investment relative to saving. This point, which lies above the *IS* curve, cannot be a point of product market equilibrium, because the excess of saving over intended investment will cause the level of income to fall. Or, starting again at the same equilibrium point, if income were arbitrarily lowered to $150 while the rate of interest is held fixed at 3 percent, this lower level of income would mean lower saving, while the fixed interest rate keeps intended investment at its original level. Note that we are now to the left of the *IS* schedule; that intended investment exceeds saving; and that income will therefore tend to rise.

In summary: The dynamics of adjustment can usually be traced without serious difficulty provided we bear in mind that the rate of interest tends to move vertically towards the *LM* curve, whereas the level of income tends to move horizontally gravitating towards the *IS* curve.

## 8-3
## FISCAL POLICY AND PRODUCT MARKET EQUILIBRIUM

As we noted in Chapter 5, the condition that must hold at the equilibrium level of income is that total leakages must equal total injections. Thus intended investment plus government purchases must equal saving plus taxes. This means that the *IS* curve, which represents product market equilibrium, becomes[1]

$$I(i) + G = Y - C(Y - T)$$

In order to observe the effect of fiscal policy, we now take the assumed economy of Section 8-2 and first add \$25 billion of government purchases and then \$25 billion in the form of lump-sum taxes. In Figure 8-4 the *IS* schedule prior to the imposition of government purchases and taxes is $IS_0$.

Government purchases have the same effect on the level of income as investment expenditures. We may therefore add the \$25 billion government purchases to the investment demand schedule in quadrant 1. The combined investment demand schedule and government purchases schedule (what we have been calling injections) is now denoted as $I(i) + G$. Note that if $G$ is added to the investment demand schedule, the horizontal axis of both quadrants 1 and 2 must be changed to $I + G$. The new equilibrium condition is

---

[1] Since we are ignoring all but personal saving, we may write

$$S = Y_d - C$$

Disposable income is defined as

$$Y_d = Y - T$$

and since consumption is a function of disposable income we have

$$C = C(Y - T)$$

Combining these expressions gives us the savings schedule

$$S = Y - T - C(Y - T)$$

so that upon adding $T$ to both sides of the equation, we obtain the total leakages schedule

$$S + T = Y - C(Y - T)$$

**FIGURE 8-4**
Government purchases and taxation
(all values in real terms)

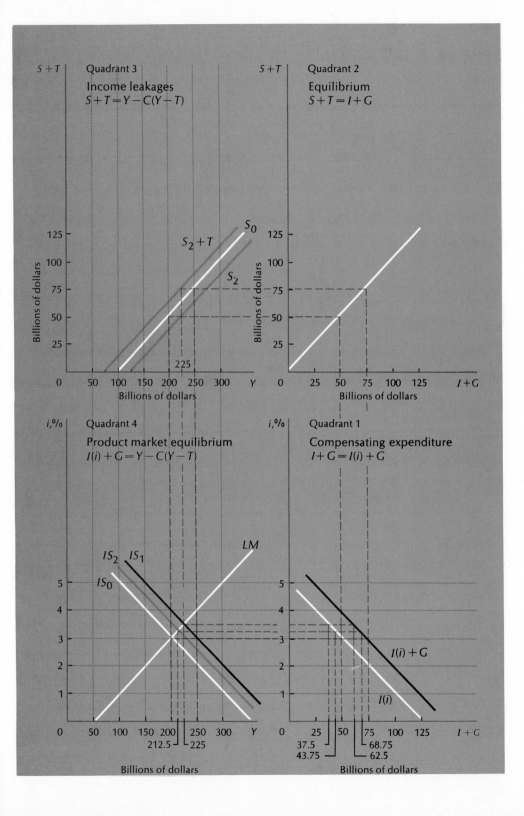

that the injections $I + G$ must be balanced by an equal amount of leakages $S + T$ so that $S + T$ becomes the vertical axis in quadrants 2 and 3.

At a 3 percent rate of interest, an investment expenditure of $50 billion will be undertaken, to which must be added the $25 billion government purchases. This means (quadrant 2) that $75 billion of leakages are now required to match the injections. Observe in quadrant 3 that these leakages are generated at an income level of $250 billion. Dropping a perpendicular into quadrant 4, we note that product market equilibrium at a 3 percent rate of interest, instead of being at an income level of $200 billion, is now at $250 billion. If product market equilibrium is found for a number of other interest rates, it will always be the case that for any rate of interest, product market equilibrium is at an income level $50 billion higher than before the addition of the $25 billion of government purchases. Apparently the IS schedule shifts to the right by $50 billion at all rates of interest. This new schedule is denoted as $IS_1$ in Figure 8–4.

If the $I(i) + G$ schedule of quadrant 1 shifts by $1, the IS schedule of quadrant 4 will shift horizontally by $1 times the multiplier, which in this example is 2. This is so because the increase in investment or government purchases will require an additional dollar of saving to offset it. Income must therefore rise by enough to generate an additional dollar of leakages. Consequently the shift in the IS schedule will always equal the shift in the $I(i) + G$ schedule times the multiplier—a result that would be expected from the analysis of Chapter 5.

Although the IS schedule will shift by the change in investment or government purchases times the multiplier, is it also true that the change in income will be of this magnitude? In Figure 8–4 the $IS_1$ schedule cuts the LM schedule at an income level of $225 billion. Although the multiplier is 2, the level of income rises by only $25 billion. What accounts for this?

Observe first of all that the rate of interest in the new equilibrium position is 3.5 percent. The increase of 0.5 percent over the original level has been caused by the fact that the government cannot borrow $25 billion from the private sector without a higher yield inducement. Given the assumption that the money supply is fixed, the funds borrowed by the government must come from a reduction in speculative balances and/or from a reduction in transactions balances. In any event, if wealth holders are to be persuaded that government securities are more attractive than the other forms in which they have been holding wealth, interest rates must rise. But this in turn implies that the level of investment will fall, and this means that the level of income will fall. The stimulus provided by the fiscal policy is therefore partially offset by a decline in investment spending.

At the new equilibrium rate of interest of 3.5 percent, investment expenditures are only $37.5 billion. Add to this the government purchases of $25 billion and note that total injections in the new equilibrium position are not $75 billion, as originally expected, but only $62.5 billion. Thus the net change in injections is only $12.5 billion (62.5 − 50.0), which means that the change in income will be 2 (the multiplier) times $12.5 billion, or $25 billion.

The *IS-LM* model shows that the crude multipliers of past chapters implicitly assumed that any change in government purchases or taxes would not affect the rate of interest and therefore the level of investment. The present analysis, however, shows that an increase in government purchases could conceivably not raise the level of income at all. If, through monetary repercussions, an increase in government purchases of $1 leads to a fall in investment expenditure of exactly $1, there will have been complete "crowding out," so that income will not change at all. If, on the other hand, the deficit spending can be financed with no change in interest rates, there will be no "crowding out," and a full multiplier effect will be realized. It is evident, then, that the simple multipliers of Chapters 4 and 5 will hold only if the added transactions resulting from an increase in expenditure can be financed without changes in interest rates. Observe that if the *LM* function is a horizontal line, changes in income will equal the shifts in the *IS* schedule.

Next let us impose a tax of $25 billion to match the government purchases and assume, as in the simplest fiscal policy model of Chapter 5, that the tax is independent of the level of income. Previous considerations lead us to suppose that $25 billion of taxes will lower the level of income by $25 billion because, the marginal propensity to save being 0.5, $12.5 billion of the tax will be drawn from saving. Leakages therefore rise by a total of only $12.5 billion so that, given a marginal propensity to save of 0.5, the level of income will have to fall by $25 billion in order to eliminate the leakages in excess of injections. We should therefore expect the *IS* schedule to shift to the left by $25 billion.

In Figure 8–4 we observe that the $25 billion tax shifts the saving schedule down by $12.5 billion from $S_0$ to $S_2$. If we add the tax function to the saving schedule, we obtain the total leakages schedule $S_2 + T$, which is $12.5 billion greater at all levels of income than the $S_0$ schedule. The combined investment and government purchases of $75 billion, which are generated at a 3 percent rate of interest, will now be offset by $75 billion of leakages at an income level of $225 billion instead of an income level of $250 billion, as in the previous example. At all other interest rates the same thing will happen: The level of income that yields product market equilibrium at different rates of interest is always $25 billion less than the level prior to the imposition of the tax. The *IS* schedule therefore shifts to the left by the amount of the change in leakages, $b \, \Delta T$, times the multiplier, or by $b \, \Delta T/(1 − b)$. After the imposition of the tax, the *IS* schedule is $IS_2$ of Figure 8–4.

Although the equilibrium level of income prior to the imposition of the tax was $225 billion and the tax causes a leftward shift in the *IS* schedule of $25 billion, the equilibrium level of income falls to only $212.5 billion. Again, monetary effects have kept the full multiplier from working its way out. If the tax proceeds are used to retire the bonds that were issued to borrow the $25 billion previously spent by the government, there will be no net shrinkage in the money supply, although the reduction in consumption caused by the tax will release some money balances from transactions. If monetary equilibrium is to be established, interest rates must fall, investment will be stimulated, and the level of income will rise. The depressing effect of the tax is therefore partly offset by an increase in investment.

Notice that in the final equilibrium situation, the rate of interest is 3.25 percent. At this rate of interest the level of investment is $43.75 billion, whereas at the previous equilibrium rate of 3.5 percent the level of investment was $37.5 billion. Although the tax would tend to lower the equilibrium level of income by $25 billion, the monetary effects of the tax are such as to raise the level of investment by $6.25 billion (from $37.5 billion to $43.75 billion) and the level of income by $12.5 billion. The net effect, as shown in Figure 8–4, is to lower the equilibrium level of income by $12.5 billion.

## 8–4
### SHIFTS IN THE *IS* AND *LM* FUNCTIONS

In the preceding section it was seen that the addition of $25 billion of government purchases shifted the *IS* schedule to the right by $50 billion because, the marginal propensity to save being 0.5, income would have to rise by $50 billion to generate the additional leakages needed to offset the added $25 billion of government purchases. Similarly, the addition of a $25 billion tax shifted the *IS* schedule to the left by $25 billion because the level of income would have to fall by $25 billion to offset the additional leakages of $12.5 billion caused by the imposition of the tax. These are but two of the ways in which the *IS* schedule may shift. Some other factors that may cause such a shift in the *IS* schedule, as well as some changes that will shift the *LM* schedule, are considered briefly in this section.

A reduction in intended saving (increase in intended consumption) will shift the saving schedule of quadrant 3 down and thereby reduce the leakages generated at all income levels. This means that the *IS* schedule will shift to the right. Such a change in the saving schedule may result from the introduction of a new product which consumers feel they must have even if it is at the expense of saving. The downward shift in the saving schedule may also result from an increase in the community's wealth. A persistent governmental deficit, for example, may result in the accumulation of such a large stock of liquid assets in the hands of individuals that wealth holders no longer feel the necessity of saving at their previous rate. Similarly, the expectation of price increases and shortages of consumer goods may bring about a fall in the saving schedule and lead to a burst of consumer buying.

The *IS* schedule will shift to the right if the investment demand schedule shifts to the right. Such a shift may occur as a result of an innovation, as the result of additional housing requirements brought about by population increases, and as the result of better profit expectations in the future. In all these cases, the *IS* schedule will exhibit a horizontal shift equal to the amount of the shift in the investment demand schedule times the multiplier, or, what amounts to the same thing, the reciprocal of the marginal propensity to save.

Shifts in the *LM* schedule may result from monetary policy, from changes in expectations, and from changes in payments practices. If the Fed decides to pursue an expansionary monetary policy, it will purchase government bonds on the open market. Wealth holders trade part of their stock of government bonds to the Fed in return for bank deposits. This means that the money supply schedule of quadrant 2 of Figure 8–2 shifts to the right, a greater volume of money is available for both transactions and speculative purposes at all rates of interest, and the *LM* curve of quadrant 4 shifts to the right. Consequently, the rate of interest will fall and the levels of investment and income will therefore rise.

Changes in expectations are likely to make their presence felt in the money market by shifts in the speculative demand for money. If, for example, investors become accustomed to a low rate of interest, the fear of capital loss that usually accompanies a low rate may gradually become less powerful. Thus the $m_2$ schedule will shift to the left, and the greater volume of transactions, and therefore income, can be supported at all rates of interest. This means that the *LM* schedule shifts to the right and a new equilibrium will therefore be established at a lower rate of interest and a higher level of income.

Changes in payments practices will change the volume of transactions that a given money supply will support. If individuals are paid twice as often as before, the average idle deposits that must be held for transactions purposes will decline by one-half. This means that the $m_1$ schedule of quadrant 3 of Figure 8–2 will rotate in a clockwise fashion, and so also will the *LM* schedule. The effect of this, of course, is again expansionary, tending to lower the rate of interest and raise the level of income.

Factors that shift the consumption and investment functions, or changes in government expenditure and tax policies, have the effect of shifting the *IS* function and are sometimes referred to as "real" disturbances. On the other hand, changes in the money supply or liquidity preference shift the *LM* curve and may be denoted as "monetary" disturbances. In Figure 8–5(a) it can be seen that an expansionary real disturbance which shifts the *IS* curve from $IS_0$ to $IS_1$ raises both the rate of interest and the level of income. However, as is clear from Figure 8–5(b), an expansionary monetary disturbance which shifts the *LM* curve from $LM_0$ to $LM_1$ is associated with a rise in the level of income but a fall in the rate of interest. Consequently, a real disturbance can be distinguished from a monetary disturbance by noting that in the case of the real disturbance, income and the rate of interest move in the same direction, whereas in the case of a monetary disturbance they move in opposite directions.[1]

---

[1] See J. L. Stein, "A Method of Identifying Disturbances Which Produce Changes in Money National Income," *Journal of Political Economy*, 68:1–16, 1960.

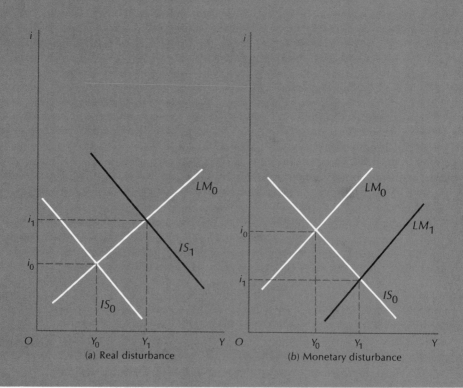

(a) Real disturbance  (b) Monetary disturbance

It is extremely important to bear in mind that expansionary fiscal policy, because it shifts the *IS* curve to the right, tends to raise both the rate of interest and the level of income. On the other hand, expansionary monetary policy shifts the *LM* curve to the right and, because it lowers the rate of interest, tends to raise the level of income. There are, perhaps surprisingly, some extreme cases for which these rules do not hold. Strangely enough, it is these extreme cases that have caused much controversy among economists. In the next chapter we shall examine these extremes and their implications for policy.

**FIGURE 8–5**
Identifying real and monetary disturbances
(all values in real terms)

# 9

# FACTORS GOVERNING THE EFFECTIVENESS OF MONETARY AND FISCAL POLICY

## INTRODUCTION

In this chapter we will employ the model that we have been developing and will focus our attention on the effectiveness of monetary and fiscal policies in changing the level of real income. We will attempt to delineate the conditions that are favorable and those that are unfavorable for the successful operation of the respective policies. We will also resort to the findings of empirical research to see if that body of information sheds any light on the issue of the impacts of the alternative policies. At the outset we will assume that fiscal policy is "pure" in the sense of Chapter 7, which is to say, government deficits are financed by the sale of securities to the nonbank private sector. However, in the last section of the chapter we will examine the differences that are caused by financing a deficit through borrowing from the central bank with concomitant increases in the money supply.

## 9-2
## POLICY EFFECTIVENESS UNDER EXTREME
## MONETARY ASSUMPTIONS

Consider the hypothetical speculative demand function of Figure 9–1. It is assumed that between interest rates of 2 and 6 percent the speculative demand for money is inversely related to the rate of interest. However, when the rate of interest rises to 6 percent the interest loss from holding idle balances becomes so great and the expected risk of capital loss resulting from a further rise in interest rates becomes so small that the speculative demand disappears. On the other hand, once the rate of interest falls to 2 percent, the interest loss is so low and the risk of capital loss so great that investors would just as soon hold idle money balances as earning assets. When increases in the money supply reduce the interest rate to 2 percent, further increases will not affect the rate of interest. The region above 6 percent will be recognized as the region within which the classical quantity theory assumption of no speculative demand holds, while the region of speculative demands of $100 billion or more will be recognized as the Keynesian liquidity trap region.

Given this speculative demand function, let us trace out the LM curve on the assumption that the money supply is $125 billion and the ratio of transactions balances to the level of income is 0.5. For interest rates between 2 and 6 percent the derivation is straightforward, following the lines of the preceding chapter. But what about the classical range? For an interest rate of 7 or 8 percent the same transactions balances are released as for a 6 percent rate. The same level of income is therefore associated with any rate of interest of 6 percent or more. This means that for all interest rates of 6 percent and above the LM curve becomes a vertical line.

Next consider a speculative demand of $125 billion. Evidently this is just as consistent with a 2 percent rate of interest as a speculative demand of $100 billion. In the former case the level of income that could be supported would be zero, whereas in the latter case it would be $50 billion. Thus we observe that monetary equilibrium is consistent with all levels of income between zero and $50 billion at an interest rate of 2 percent. For levels of income between zero and $50 billion the LM function must be a horizontal line.

Now suppose that the money supply is increased by a Fed purchase of government bonds. This purchase will shift the LM function to the right by $50 billion because each dollar added to the money supply will support $2 of added transactions. How will this monetary policy affect the level of income?

1 If the IS schedule (IS₀) cuts the LM schedules in the Keynesian liquidity trap region, the increase in the money supply will not affect the level of in-

**FIGURE 9–1**
**Monetary policy (all values in real terms)**

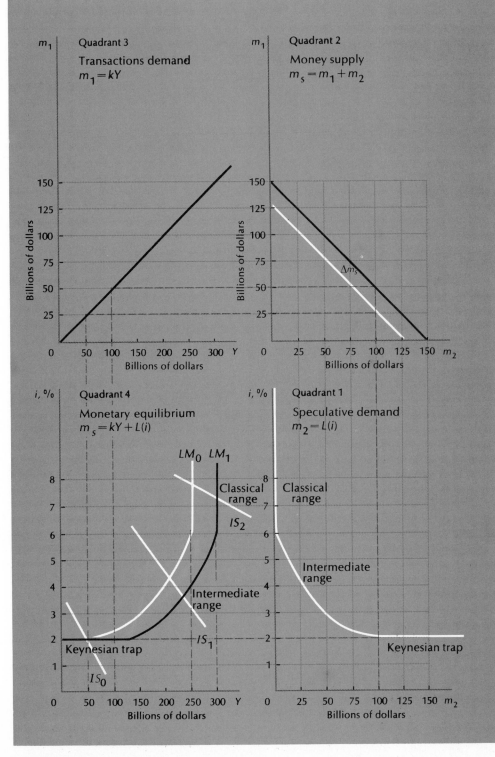

come at all. Any slight fall in the rate of interest produces such a strong preference for liquidity that all the added balances move into idle holdings, and
none move into added transactions balances. In equilibrium the rate of interest therefore remains the same, investment is not stimulated, and the level of
income remains unchanged. If the liquidity trap prevails, monetary policy is
totally ineffective in changing the level of income.

2   If the IS schedule ($IS_2$) cuts the LM schedules in the classical range, quite
the opposite picture emerges. If sellers are to be found for the bonds that the
Fed wishes to buy, the prices of government bonds must be bid up by enough
to persuade wealth holders that other assets are now relatively more attractive
than government bonds. Only under these conditions will they accept money
balances in exchange for the government bonds. There being no speculative
demand for money to hold, wealth holders will take these new money balances and use them to purchase other earning assets. These other assets may
take the form of new capital investment (new securities) or of purchases of
existing securities. New capital investment will raise the level of income and
therefore the quantity of transactions money demanded. However, as long as
some idle money balances in excess of those required for transactions remain,
wealth holders will continue to compete with each other for earning assets.
Hence bond prices continue to rise and interest rates continue to fall until the
point is reached where new investment raises the level of income by exactly
enough to absorb the added money balances into transactions. To repeat, as
long as there are some money balances in excess of those needed for transactions, there will be competition for earning assets. This means that interest
rates will continue to fall and that investment will continue to rise until the
idle balances are absorbed. The equilibrium level of income must therefore
rise by $\Delta m_s/k$, where $\Delta m_s$ is the change in the money supply measured in real
terms.

3   If the IS curve ($IS_1$) cuts the LM functions in the intermediate range, the
increase in the money supply succeeds in increasing the level of income, but
not by as much as in the classical case. In the classical case the rate of interest falls by enough to absorb the whole addition to the supply of money into
transactions demands. In the present case, however, part of the increase will
be absorbed into speculative holdings because the decline in the rate of interest raises the desire of wealth holders to hold speculative balances. Thus investment will not increase by as much as in the classical case, and the level
of income will rise by only a fraction of $\Delta m_s/k$.

The next step is to consider the effectiveness of fiscal policy under our
three alternative assumptions about the demand for money. Consider Figure

**FIGURE 9–2**
Fiscal policy (all values in real terms)

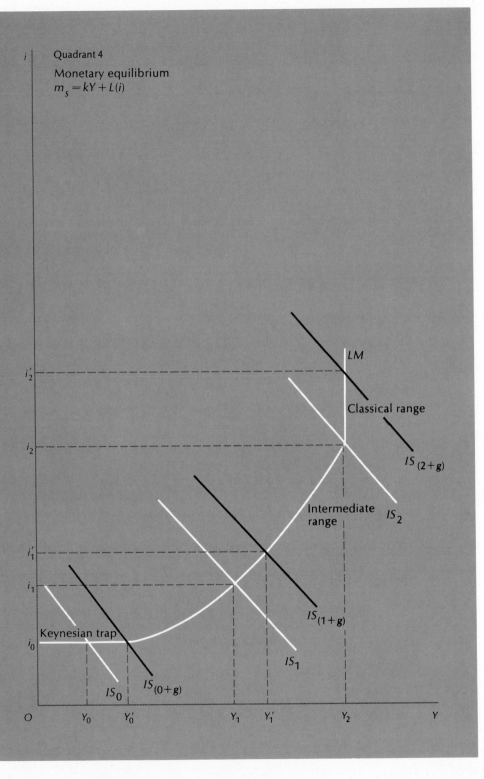

Quadrant 4

Monetary equilibrium
$m_s = kY + L(i)$

$i$

$i'_2$

$LM$

Classical range

$i_2$

$IS_{(2+g)}$

$IS_2$

Intermediate
range

$i'_1$

$i_1$

$IS_{(1+g)}$

Keynesian trap

$i_0$

$IS_1$

$IS_0$

$IS_{(0+g)}$

$O$     $Y_0$   $Y'_0$       $Y_1$   $Y'_1$     $Y_2$      $Y$

9–2 in which the three-range $LM$ function is reproduced together with six $IS$ schedules. $IS_0$, $IS_1$, and $IS_2$ are the same schedules as in Figure 9–1. $IS_{(0+g)}$, $IS_{(1+g)}$, and $IS_{(2+g)}$ are the schedules that emerge after an increase in the level of government purchases of goods and services.

**1**  In the Keynesian region the increase in government purchases causes the level of income to rise by $Y_0' - Y_0$. This amount is equal to the full multiplier times the increase in $G$.[1] Since we have assumed that the increase in $G$ is not tax-financed and since we assume a fixed money supply, the funds are obtained by borrowing from the public. The fiscal policy is therefore a "pure" fiscal policy as described in Chapter 7. Because the interest elasticity of the demand for money is infinite, a small increase in the interest rate due to deficit financing will decrease the quantity of money demanded for liquidity preference purposes, thereby permitting a larger level of transactions to be financed by a fixed money supply. In the new equilibrium the rate of interest will be the same as before. As a result, investment will be the same as before, and the increase in income will therefore equal the full multiplier times the increase in government purchases.

**2**  In the intermediate range the increase in $G$ succeeds in increasing the equilibrium level of income from $Y_1$ to $Y_1'$. However, in this intermediate range the need to finance the increased volume of transactions forces the rate of interest up. Because of this increase in the rate of interest, the level of investment falls, and the expansionary effect of the fiscal policy is therefore dampened.

**3**  In the classical range, the increase in the level of government purchases has no effect on the level of income whatsoever. Because there are no idle money balances available in the private sector of the economy, government can borrow funds from the private sector only by making it worthwhile for the sector to reduce investment spending in direct proportion to the amount borrowed by the government. This means that interest rates must rise by enough to make the return on government bonds greater than the prospective yield on private investment. Any increase in $G$ will therefore be matched by an equal reduction in private investment. It is evident therefore that in the classical case crowding out, as it is called, is complete and fiscal policy has no effect on the level of income whatsoever. Changes in the levels of government purchases and taxes can change the allocation of resources as between consumption, investment, and government, but they cannot change the level of income.

The terms "Keynesian" and "classical" have fallen out of fashion and have been replaced by the terms "fiscalist" and "monetarist." The fiscalist is the

---

[1] Remember from the discussion of the preceding chapter that the horizontal shift in the $IS$ schedule will equal the multiplier times the horizontal shift in the $I + G$ schedule.

modern counterpart of the Keynesian who thinks for various reasons (many of which have not been discussed yet) that the monetary system is so elastic with respect to the rate of interest that it is better to rely on fiscal policy for purposes of income stabilization. The monetarist, of course, takes the opposing view, preferring to place his faith in the efficacy of monetary policy.

## 9–3
## FACTORS INFLUENCING THE EFFECTIVENESS OF MONETARY POLICY

Having considered the extreme cases in some detail, let us now consider the implications of some of the alternative assumptions about the demand for and the supply of money that were discussed in Chapter 7. Let us define as our measure of the "effectiveness" of monetary policy the change in real income that accompanies a change in the money supply of $1 in real terms. As we have seen, the range of effectiveness can vary between an extreme fiscalist value of zero and an extreme monetarist value of $1/k$.

Looking again at Figure 9–1, it is clear that the effectiveness of monetary policy, assuming a given negatively sloped $IS$ curve, depends upon the slope of the $LM$ curve. Although the $LM$ curve always shifted by $\Delta m_s/k$, we found monetary policy to be completely ineffective when the slope of $LM$ was zero, partially effective when it was positive, and completely effective when it was infinite.

The different values of the slope of the $LM$ schedule in the different ranges were the consequence of assumptions about the speculative demand for money. In the absence of a speculative demand, $LM$ was vertical; with speculative demand inversely related to the rate of interest, $LM$ had a positive slope; and with infinitely elastic speculative demand, $LM$ was horizontal. Let us now see what happens to the slope of the $LM$ curve when we assume, first, that the transactions demand for money and, second, that the supply of money are both sensitive to interest rate changes.

Consider first the transactions demand for money. We found in Chapter 7 that it would pay wealth holders to enter the bond market more and more frequently during an income-expenditure period as interest rates rise. This means that, as interest rates rise, average transactions balances fall so that the transactions demand for money is inversely related to the rate of interest.

In Figure 9–3 $LM_0$ is drawn on the assumption that there is no speculative demand for money (hence the blank first quadrant) and that the transactions demand, assumed to be the curve labeled $m_{t4}$, is not sensitive to interest rate changes. As we have seen, these assumptions imply a vertical $LM$ curve. On the other hand, $LM_1$ is drawn on the assumption that at an interest rate of 6 percent, $m_{t6}$, relates the transactions demand to the level of income; $m_{t4}$ relates the transactions demand to the level of income when the rate of interest is 4 percent; $m_{t2}$ is appropriate for a 2 percent rate; and $m_{t8}$ represents the situation for an 8 percent rate. We now have a whole family of transactions demand schedules, each one appropriate to a particular rate of interest. In

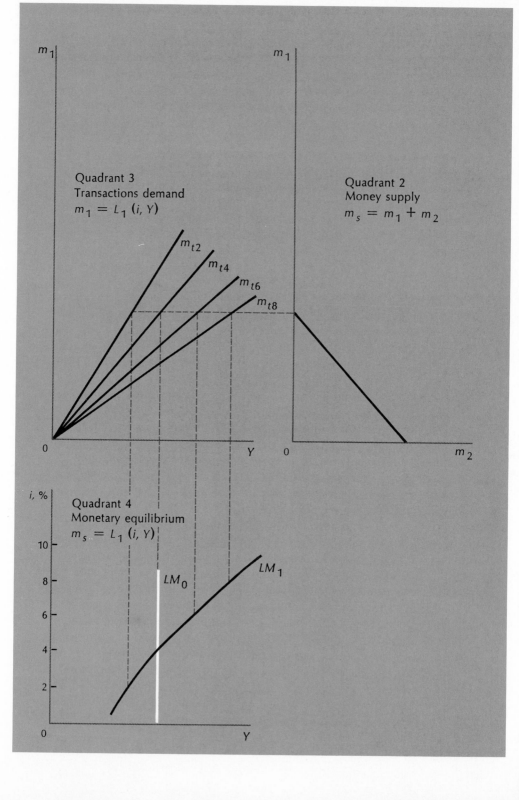

deriving the *LM* curve, therefore, we must trace through quadrants by starting with different interest rates and then picking the appropriate transactions demand curve in quadrant 3. The $LM_1$ curve has a positive slope. There is now no pure classical range because there is no longer a fixed relationship between money balances and the volume of transactions despite the fact that there is no speculative demand. This flattening out of the *LM* schedule implies that the more interest-elastic transactions and precautionary demands become, the less (more) effective does monetary (fiscal) policy become.

Let us consider next the possibility, discussed in Chapter 7, that rising interest rates cause banks to activate excess reserves and thereby increase the money supply. A useful way to approach this problem is to assume again that there is no speculative demand for money and that the transactions demand is insensitive to interest rate changes. In this way the effect of interest elasticity of the money supply can again be compared with the classical *LM* function.

In Figure 9–4 quadrant 1 is left blank to denote the absence of speculative demand, and the absence of interest sensitivity of transactions demand means that there is only one transactions demand function in quadrant 3. Beginning with interest rate $i_0$, we assume that the money supply is $m_{i0}$. Since there is no speculative demand for money, all balances are available for transactions. Consequently, the level of income that can be supported is $Y_0$. If the interest rate rises to $i_1$, banks activate excess reserves so that the money supply now becomes $m_{i1}$, and the income level that can be supported becomes $Y_1$. Similarly, a rise in the interest rate to $i_2$ causes a further increase in the money supply so that income level $Y_2$ yields monetary equilibrium. Without any increase in reserves a time must come when interest rate increases induce no further increases in the supply of money. Consequently, the slope of the *LM* curve becomes steeper as the interest rate rises and eventually becomes vertical as in the classical case.

Notice that our present assumption produces an *LM* curve that takes on a shape similar to that attained when we assumed the existence of a speculative demand. Indeed, it may very well have been the case that, during the great depression of the 1930s, what appeared to have been a liquidity trap caused by a highly elastic demand for money may have been partially caused by a highly interest-elastic supply of money resulting from bank behavior. Certainly banks held large quantities of excess reserves and appeared to make little effort to convert these reserves into earning assets.

The money supply function implicit in this analysis is that of Chapter 7:

$$m_s = \phi(h,i)$$

where $h$ is high-powered money measured in real terms. An increase in bank

**FIGURE 9–3**
**Interest-elastic transactions demand (all values in real terms)**

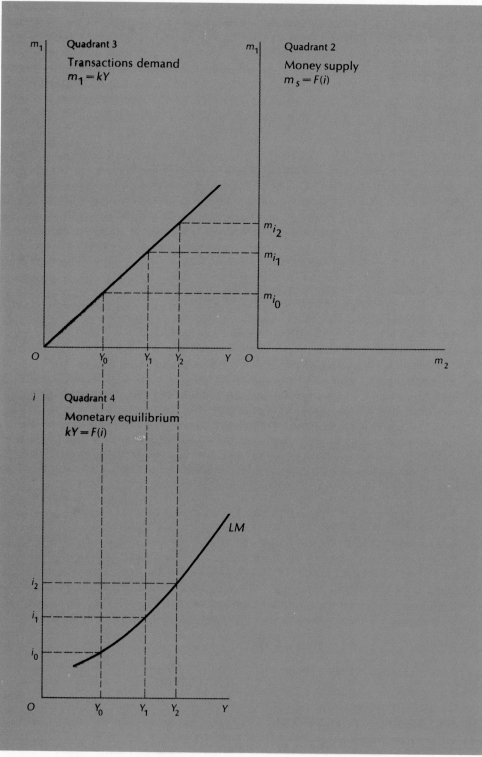

reserves brought about by a Fed purchase of securities from the nonbank private sector automatically increases the money supply by the amount of the value of the purchase and will tend to produce a further multiplied increase in the money supply as banks use their excess reserves to purchase earning assets. But the consequence of this is that interest rates fall, producing reluctance to engage in further expansion. During a deep depression interest rates may already be so low that Fed open market purchases may not induce banks to use their resulting excess reserves at all. As a result, the ratio of a change in the money supply to a change in reserves may be only 1:1, whereas the potential ratio may be as high as 5:1.[1] Thus the Fed's leverage effect on the money supply may, during such periods, be severely reduced. Therefore, at low interest rates it may take a far more sizable Fed open market purchase to shift the *LM* function to the right by some amount than it would take during periods of higher interest rates.

Another reason why monetary policy may yield disappointing results stems from the circumstance that the demand for investment may be insensitive to changes in the interest rate. Some of the evidence that we shall review in the next section suggests that interest rate changes, even if they could be brought about, may not make a significant contribution toward raising the level of investment during periods of slack demand. Keynes himself viewed this circumstance as a distinct possibility. In the extreme case of a vertical investment demand schedule, the *IS* curve will also be vertical (see Figure 9–5), so that even if monetary policy could change interest rates, there would be no effect on the level of income.

In classical monetary assumptions it is implicit that the investment demand schedule is interest-elastic.[2] If the ratio of real cash balances to the level of real income is fixed, an increase in the money supply must find its way into new transactions in the form of either consumption or investment expenditures. If consumption expenditures are insensitive to changes in the interest rate, which nearly everyone assumes to be the case, investment must be interest-elastic; if it is not, existing security prices will be bid up indefinitely, and interest rates will fall indefinitely. If this possibility is ruled out, it must

---

[1] If the Fed purchases the bonds from commercial banks, and the banks then merely hang on to the resulting additional reserves, there will be no change in the money supply at all. However, in general we cannot predict the fraction of a Fed purchase that will come from banks and the fraction that will come from the nonbank private sector, and so we do not wish to make too much of an issue of this distinction.

[2] J. Tobin, "Liquidity Preference and Monetary Policy," *Review of Economics and Statistics*, 29:124–131, 1947.

**FIGURE 9–4**
**Interest-elastic money supply (all values
in real terms)**

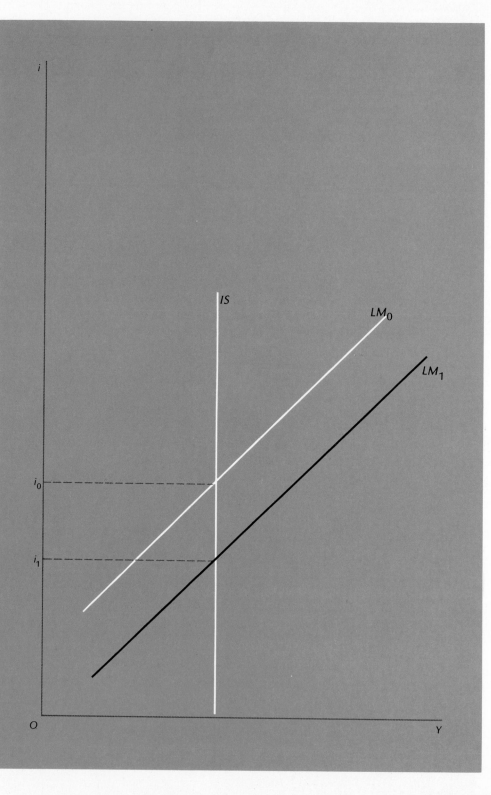

follow that either the investment demand schedule or the demand for money is elastic with respect to the rate of interest.

In conclusion, it appears to be the elasticities of the various functions with respect to the rate of interest that are crucial from the point of view of policy effectiveness. If the rate of interest cannot be made to fall as a result of policy action to increase the supply of money, the shape of the investment demand schedule will be of no importance. If, on the other hand, an increase in the money supply succeeds in reducing the rate of interest, the level of investment must necessarily rise. If it does not, the increase in the supply of money will cause interest rates to continue falling until the liquidity trap is reached.

## 9-4
## SOME EVIDENCE FROM EMPIRICAL RESEARCH

In recent years economists have made great strides in testing their theories against pertinent data and in measuring the parameters of the macroeconomic system. Some of the evidence bears heavily on the issues discussed in this chapter. Indeed, there is a wealth of elegant and careful studies that have attempted to measure the slopes and elasticities with which we have been concerned. Definitive results do not of course exist. There are unfortunately innumerable ingenious ways to make facts fit theories. And the worst problem, perhaps, is that economic data do not originate in laboratories where they can be generated under controlled conditions.

Let us take up first the question of the elasticity of demand for money with respect to the rate of interest.[1] Nearly all studies show a significant inverse relationship between the demand for money and the rate of interest. Earlier studies generally found interest elasticities whose absolute values exceeded 0.5. A notable exception is Professor Friedman who finds no relationship between the demand for money and the rate of interest.[2]

[1] For an excellent discussion of many of the issues raised in attempting to estimate demand and supply functions empirically, as well as a review of the pertinent literature, the reader should consult R. L. Teigen, "The Demand for and Supply of Money," in W. L. Smith and R. L. Teigen, *Readings in Money, National Income, and Stabilization Policy,* Richard D. Irwin, Inc., Homewood, Ill., 1970, pp. 74–111.

[2] Some of the earlier empirical studies are A. J. Brown, "Interest, Prices, and the Demand Schedules for Idle Money," *Oxford Economic Papers,* 2:46–99, 1939; Tobin, op. cit.; A. Kisselgoff, "Liquidity Preference of Large Manufacturing Corporations," *Econometrica,* 23:334–344, 1945; M. Bronfenbrenner and T. Mayer, "Liquidity Functions in the American Economy," *Econometrica,* 28:810–834, 1960; H. A. Latané, "Cash Balances and the Interest Rate: A Pragmatic Approach," *Review of Economics and Statistics,* 36:456–460, 1954; H. A. Latané, "Income Velocity and Interest Rates: A Pragmatic Approach," *Review of Economics and Statistics,* 42:445–449, 1960. Professor Friedman's findings are reported in M. Friedman, "The Demand for Money: Some Theoretical and Empirical Results," *Journal of Political Economy,* 67:327–351, 1959.

## FIGURE 9-5
**Interest-inelastic investment demand**
**(all values in real terms)**

Many of these earlier studies may have exaggerated the interest elasticity of the demand for money because of the difficulty of statistically isolating movements along a function from shifts in the function. Consider Figure 9–6 in which the interest rate and the quantity of money are measured in the usual fashion. Let $m_{d1}$ and $m_{d2}$ be the "true" demand for money functions in two different years, and let $m_{s1}$ and $m_{s2}$ be the "true" money supply functions in the same years. Observed data tell us only that in year 1 the interest rate was $i_1$ and that the quantity of money was $m_1$, and that in year 2 the respective values were $i_2$ and $m_2$. If a statistician were to fit a line through these observed points, he would obtain the flat curve connecting points a and b, and we might then be led to the erroneous conclusion that the demand for money is highly elastic with respect to the rate of interest.

More recent attempts to deal with problems of this nature have shown that the earlier studies did indeed exaggerate the magnitude of the interest elasticity of the demand for money.[1] However, the new measures nevertheless indicate that this elasticity is by no means negligible. In particular, all the studies show that a great deal of substitution takes place between demand and time deposits in response to changes in the rate of interest earned on time deposits.

Professor Friedman's work remains the exception. He finds no statistical association between the rate of interest and the demand for money. His critics claim that he has stacked the deck. Friedman includes time deposits in his definition of money. Because much of the substitution that occurs in response to interest rate changes takes place between demand and saving deposits, the very phenomenon that ought to be measured is simply defined away. The baby may very well have been thrown out with the bath water.

The idea that an increase in the rate of interest causes commercial banks to economize on excess reserves and thus to cause the money supply to increase is well founded in fact and theory. In their study of this question, Polak and White found evidence that member banks tend to increase their borrowings from the Fed and decrease their excess reserves when the return from lending rises relative to the cost of lending.[2] Other studies confirm the fact that the money supply is quite responsive to interest rate changes.[3]

[1] F. de Leeuw, "A Model of Financial Behavior," in J. Duesenberry, G. Fromm, L. R. Klein, and E. Kuh, *The Brookings Quarterly Econometric Model of the United States,* Chap. 13, Rand McNally & Company, Chicago, 1965; S. M. Goldfeld, *Commercial Bank Behavior and Economic Activity,* North-Holland Publishing Company, Amsterdam, 1966; and R. L. Teigen, "Demand and Supply Functions for Money in the United States: Some Structural Estimates," *Econometrica,* 32:476–509, 1964.

[2] J. J. Polak and W. H. White, "The Effect of Income Expansion on the Quantity of Money," *International Monetary Fund Staff Papers,* 4:398–433, 1955.

[3] See the previously cited studies by de Leeuw, Goldfeld, and Teigen.

**FIGURE 9–6**
**Illustration of statistical bias due to shifting functions over time**

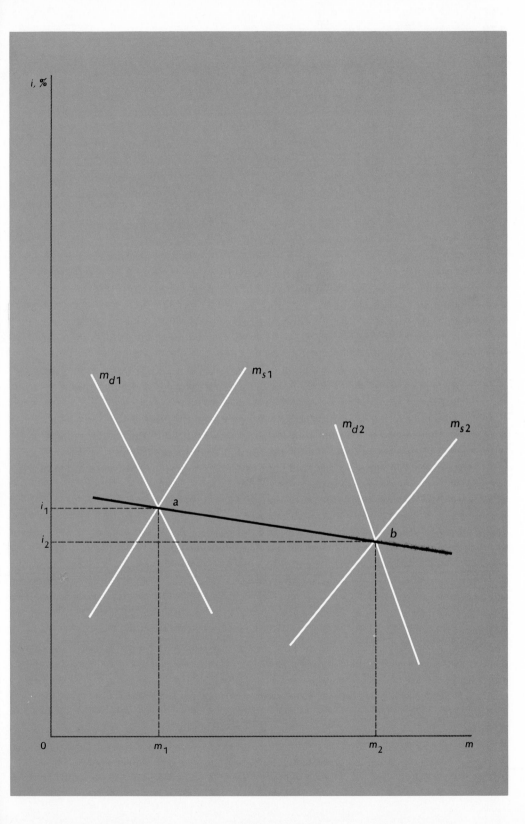

In our discussion in the preceding section, we saw that another potential way in which monetary policy might yield disappointing results is through the failure of interest rate changes to affect the level of investment. Surveys of business executives taken as early as the late 1930s in the United Kingdom seemed to indicate that the cost of credit had little to do with investment decisions.[1] Moreover, the contribution that interest rate changes make to the explanation of investment in statistical functions is unimpressive.[2] A change in the interest rate is certainly not going to have much effect on entrepreneurs who include a large risk premium in their marginal efficiency calculations or on firms that have excess capacity. In addition, interest paid is a tax-deductible expense, so that if the tax rate is 50 percent of corporate profits, a one-percentage-point increase in the rate of interest represents only an effective one-half of one-percentage-point increase to the borrower.

The effect of interest rate changes may be more important in determining categories of spending other than fixed investment. Residential construction is highly sensitive to credit conditions,[3] as are the public projects of state and local governments, the outlays of consumers on durable goods, and possibly inventory investment by business. The "credit crunch" of 1966, when the restrictive money policy of the Fed staggered the home-building industry, would seem to be proof enough that the *IS* curve is at least somewhat interest-elastic and that a stiff monetary policy is quite capable of slowing down the economy.[4]

The bulk of the evidence from the empirical studies shows that most of the time the intersection of the *IS* and *LM* curves lies within the "intermediate" range of the curves. This would suggest that both monetary and fiscal policy have their roles to play in stabilization policy. Most economists would agree

[1] J. E. Meade and P. W. S. Andrews, "Summary of Replies to Questions on the Effects of Interest Rates," *Oxford Economic Papers,* 1:14–31, 1938; R. S. Sayers, "Businessmen and the Terms of Borrowing," *Oxford Economic Papers,* 3:23–31, 1940; P. W. S. Andrews, "A Further Inquiry into the Effects of Rates of Interest," *Oxford Economic Papers,* 3:32–73, 1940; J. F. Ebersole, "The Influence of Interest Rates upon Entrepreneurial Decisions in Business: A Case Study," *Harvard Business Review,* 17:35–43, 1938. For a critical survey of these studies, see W. H. White, "Interest Inelasticity of Investment Demand," *American Economic Review,* 46:565–587, 1956. Results of a more recent survey are reported in J. Crocket, I. Friend, and H. Shavel, "The Impact of Monetary Stringency on Business Investment," U.S. Department of Commerce, *Survey of Current Business, August, 1967,* Government Printing Office, Washington, 1967, pp. 10–27.

[2] For a survey of the impact of monetary variables on spending decisions, see M. J. Hamburger, "The Impact of Monetary Variables: A Survey of Recent Econometric Literature," *Essays in Domestic and International Finance,* Federal Reserve Bank of New York, New York, 1969; reprinted in W. L. Smith and R. L. Teigen, *Readings in Money, National Income, and Stabilization Policy,* Richard D. Irwin, Inc., Homewood, Ill., 1970, pp. 414–432.

[3] The term "credit conditions" is an omnibus term that takes account of the fact that not only the cost of credit but also its availability may be a determinant of borrowing. In the case of home building, the availability of mortgage financing, not its cost, seems to be the important consideration.

[4] Residential construction expenditures in the first quarter of 1966 were at an annual rate of $27.7 billion. Under the impact of monetary stringency, the annual rate slipped to $21.1 billion by the first quarter of 1967, a decline of nearly 23 percent.

that in a deep depression, such as that of the 1930s, fiscal policy must be called on, whereas the inflationary conditions of the 1940s and subsequent periods required help from monetary policy.

Measuring elasticities helps to settle only a very small fraction of monetary controversy. Among the factors that we have not yet considered are the following: First, there may be reasons why a shift in the money supply function may lead to a corresponding shift in the demand for money, so that emphasis on elasticities may by misplaced. Second, there may be lags between the time a policy is introduced and the time its effect is felt. Third, there are institutional and political reasons why one policy may be more reliable than another even though the latter may be preferred on strictly economic grounds. Fourth, a distinction has to be made between effectiveness in controlling inflation and effectiveness in combating recession. Fifth, international considerations may impose constraints on the extent to which any individual policy may be carried out and also govern the extent to which the policies are effective in controlling the domestic economy. Sixth, and perhaps most important, economic policy generally must aim at the attainment of more than one goal. Under such conditions the relevant question is not whether one policy is more effective in attaining a particular goal than another, but rather how the several policies can best be coordinated to achieve the several goals simultaneously.

We will consider most of these issues at the appropriate stage of this book. Meanwhile, we have one piece of unfinished business, which is to consider what happens when a government expenditure is financed by money creation.

## 9-5
## EFFECT OF DEFICIT FINANCE THROUGH
## MONEY CREATION[1]

The assumption that fiscal and monetary policies are "pure" in the sense defined in Chapter 7 permitted us to shift either the *IS* or the *LM* function without simultaneously shifting the other. Recall that pure fiscal policy was considered to be in operation when government purchases or taxes were changed in such a way as to leave the money supply constant. Implicitly, this meant that an increase in government purchases, or the deficit resulting from tax reduction, is financed by government borrowing from the nonbank private sector of the economy.

In practice, there are a number of reasons, for example, the desire to avoid

---

[1] Emphasis on the possibility that expansionary fiscal policy may be accompanied by expansion of the money supply is provided in a number of contemporary works. See in particular C. F. Christ, "A Simple Macroeconomic Model with a Government Budget Restraint," *Journal of Political Economy*, 76:53–67, 1968; C. F. Christ, "A Short-Run Aggregated-Demand Model of the Interdependence and Effects of Monetary and Fiscal Policies with Keynesian and Classical Elasticities," *American Economic Review*, 57:434–443, 1967; B. Hansen, "On the Effects of Fiscal and Monetary Policy: A Taxonomic Discussion," *American Economic Review*, 63:546–571, 1973.

high interest rates and falling government security prices, for government deficits to be financed in whole or in part by resort to borrowing at the central
bank. The United States Treasury, for example, has frequently found it expedi-
tious to sell some of its new securities to the Fed. The result is that there is less
pressure for the value of government securities to drop because the Fed is
"supporting" the bond market. However, the money supply increases as a
result of this method of finance so that what, in fact, results is a combination
of two expansionary policies: expansionary fiscal policy conducted by the
Treasury, along with expansionary monetary policy conducted, perhaps inadvertently, by the Fed.

Figure 9–7 illustrates the situation. Suppose we commence with functions
$IS_0$ and $LM_0$ and with the economy in equilibrium at $i_0$ and $Y_0$. Suppose also,
for reasons that will become clear in a moment, that this is a situation in
which the budget of the government is in balance so there is no net government borrowing. Now let an increase in government purchases move the $IS$
curve to $IS_1$. Under the pure fiscal policy assumptions, the expenditure is
financed by borrowing from the nonbank private sector, so that the money
supply remains unchanged and the new equilibrium interest rate is at $i_1'$ and
the level of income rises to $Y_1'$. However, if part or all of the expenditure is
financed by borrowing from the Fed, the increased expenditure will be accompanied by an increase in the money supply. Suppose that this has the effect of shifting $LM$ to $LM_1$. The result is that the rate of interest rises by less
than would otherwise have been the case, and the level of income rises by
more.

This says no more than that if we want to figure out what is going to
happen we have to keep track of both our monetary and our fiscal policy
variables. However, consider what happens without any further fiscal policy
change. The new situation at $Y_1$ and $i_1$ is associated with a higher level of government expenditure than prior to the change, so that the government deficit
generated by the increase in purchases which caused the $IS$ curve to shift
continues into the next period of time. The money supply therefore again
increases, and the $LM$ curve again shifts, this time to $LM_2$. The rate of interest
drops to $i_2$, and the level of income rises to $Y_2$. Again in the next period, and
even with no change in government expenditure, the deficit continues, so that
the Treasury will borrow from the Fed. This will increase the money supply,
and this will once again shift the $LM$ curve to the right ($LM_3$), lowering the rate
of interest and raising the level of income. The vital point here is that a given
*level* of budget deficit may give rise to perpetual increases in the money

**FIGURE 9–7**
Expansionary fiscal policy financed by borrowing from the central bank (all values in
real terms)

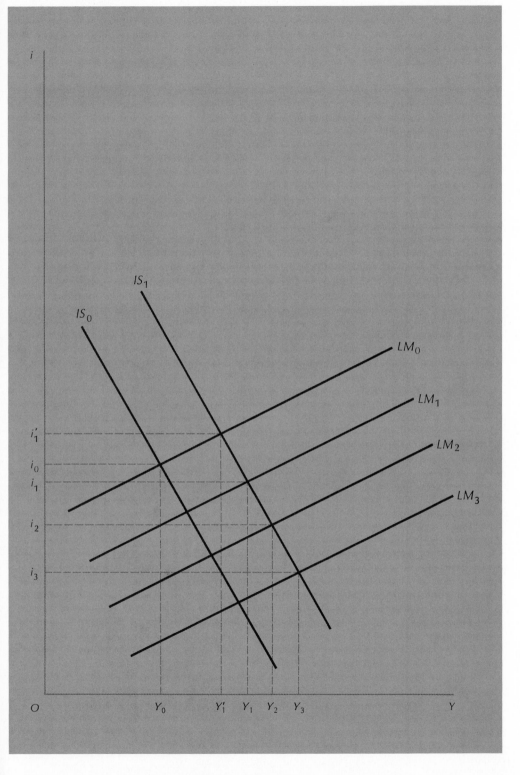

supply, if the deficit is financed by printing money or, what amounts to the same thing, by borrowing from the central bank.

From looking at Figure 9–7 one gets no clear idea of whether, or where, the process of expansion will end. As long as the money supply keeps increasing, the *LM* curve will keep moving to the right and the level of income will keep rising. Is there, then, a place where the system comes to rest? First an obvious answer: The Fed can stop buying government securities and force the Treasury to sell them for what it can get in an unsupported bond market. Second, if taxes are a function of the level of income, the steady expansion of income will gradually raise tax receipts and eventually eliminate the deficit. At that point there will be no further borrowing, and the money supply will stop expanding. This solution implies that income will rise by the amount of government purchases multiplied by the reciprocal of the tax rate. If the marginal tax rate is 20 percent, income would have to rise by $5 to generate additional taxes needed to equal a $1 rise in government purchases. Third, and this is getting ahead of our story, a continued rise in income will bring with it a rise in imports from abroad and this may cause an outflow of money. The point may therefore be reached when the increase in the money supply brought about by a given level of budget deficit is just offset by the same level of balance of payments deficit.

# 10

# EMPLOYMENT AND THE PRICE LEVEL

## INTRODUCTION

In this chapter we will complete the basic macroeconomic model of the economy. In doing this, we shift our attention to the determination of the equilibrium price level and the equilibrium level of employment. In concentrating, as we have thus far, on the level of real income and the rate of interest, we arbitrarily held the price level constant and we assumed that output was perfectly elastic with respect to the price level up to a level of real income that was arbitrarily termed the full-employment level of income. It is now time to discard this assumption and to inquire into the nature of the determinants of the equilibrium level of prices. The meaning of full employment must be explored, and the central question of whether the economy tends to return to full employment automatically following a disturbance or whether it might remain in a state of "underemployment equilibrium" needs to be explored.

To see what we will be driving at, consider the situation of an individual firm. The link between its output and its input of factor services is a technical relationship that specifies the amount of output that will result from the application of different quantities and combinations of quantities of factor inputs. For the economy as a whole, economists visualize an aggregate production function which relates total inputs to total output. Such a function might be written

$$Y = X(N, K^*, T^*)$$

where $N$ is labor input (the level of employment), $K$ is the economy's capital stock (its stock of plant and equipment), and $T$ may be thought of as an index which measures the level of technology, or what might be termed the state of the arts. In a short-run analysis such as we have been undertaking, it is assumed that $K$ and $T$ are fixed (this is denoted by the asterisks), so that output can be changed only by varying the level of employment. It follows therefore that, once the level of output is known, the level of employment must also be directly implied.

Suppose, however, that the level of employment as implied by demand conditions is different from the amount of labor supplied. The *IS-LM* intersection is a position at which the market for goods and services and the money market are simultaneously cleared. But the level of production consistent with the *IS-LM* intersection may require the use of less labor than is willing and able to work at the existing level of wages. If this is the case, equilibrium in the product and money markets will be accompanied by disequilibrium, specifically excess supply, in the market for labor services. The question that we now must ask is whether such a situation can be sustained. Will not excess supply in any market cause prices to fall, and will not this in turn set off forces that disrupt equilibrium in other markets? Finally, will not these price adjustments continue until all markets are cleared? Can we, to put it differently, really talk about an equilibrium level of income that is less than the full-employment level of income?

The variable that becomes all important in the further development of the discussion is the level of prices. To focus attention on this variable, and to extend our macroeconomic model to handle the new problems of employment and price level determination, it is important to develop, with some care, the so-called aggregate demand and aggregate supply functions. We have previously talked about aggregate demand as the level of total spending in real terms $(C + I + G)$ which is associated with different levels of real income. However, the meaning that we will now give to aggregate demand is the level of output (income) demanded at different price levels. Therefore, the aggregate demand function may be thought of as an ordinary schedule of demand for goods and services with respect to price except that it refers to the economy as a whole, rather than to an individual market. Aggregate supply, similarly, is the level of real output (income) that will be supplied to the economy at different price levels. The aggregate demand part traverses familiar territory, and so let us begin there.

## 10–2
## THE AGGREGATE DEMAND FUNCTION

The aggregate demand function can be derived directly from the *IS-LM* product-money market equilibrium model. The *IS* curve specifies the combinations of incomes and interest rates that equate intended investment plus government purchases with savings plus taxes. All the variables including the policy variables $G$ and $T$ that enter into the determination of the *IS* curve are specified in real terms. Consequently, it is assumed that no real magnitude in the product market is influenced by the price level. Implied in this is the as-assumption that if prices double, government purchases in nominal terms are immediately doubled so as to keep the real value of government purchases constant. An equivalent assumption applies to consumption and investment. Such an *IS* curve is depicted as curve $IS_0$ in Figure 10–1.

The *LM* curve in Figure 10–1 equates the demand for real money balances with the real value of the money supply. Now assume, in contrast with the as-sumption about the fiscal variables, that the monetary authority fixes the *nominal* stock of money. Writing the familar equation for the *LM* curve we have

$$\frac{M}{p} = L(Y, i)$$

The equation is identical to a form of the monetary equilibrium condition met earlier, except that the symbol for the real value of the money supply, *m*, is replaced by the equivalent expression $M/p$. *M* is the nominal stock of money, and *p* is the price level.

Consider the two quadrant diagram, Figure 10–1. The upper quadrant shows the familiar *IS-LM* curves where, as usual, the level of real income is measured along the horizontal axis. The lower quadrant once again measures the level of real income on the horizontal axis. The price level is posted on the vertical axis. Now suppose that the initial level of prices is $p_0$ and that the initial *IS* and *LM* curves are $IS_0$ and $LM_0$. Equilibrium then implies interest rate $i_0$ and income $Y_0$, and this income level is associated with price level $p_0$ as shown in the lower quadrant.

Suppose next that the price level falls to $p_1$. Via our assumption that all varia-bles that determine the *IS* curve are in real terms, this change in the price level will have no effect on the *IS* curve. However, this is not true of the *LM* curve since we have assumed that it is the nominal money supply that is held fixed by the monetary authority. Recalling that the real value of the money supply is $m = M/p$, we see that when the price level falls, the real value of the money supply increases just as it would have had the Fed raised the nominal quantity of money with the price level held fixed. The result, therefore, is that the fall in the price level shifts the *LM* curve to the right (to $LM_1$ in Figure 10–1). This creates excess supply of real money balances, which lowers the rate of interest and in turn raises the level of investment and income. The $IS\text{-}LM_1$ intersection implies a new equilibrium rate of interest, $i_1$, and a new equilibrium level of income, $Y_1$. As can be seen in the lower quadrant, the result is to identify a second point on the aggregate demand curve, namely, when the price level is $p_1$, the demand conditions of the economy imply a level of real income $Y_1$.

It is evident that the aggregate demand curve shown in the lower quadrant will normally have a negative slope. A fall in the price level raises the real value of the money supply, lowers the rate of interest, and raises the level of

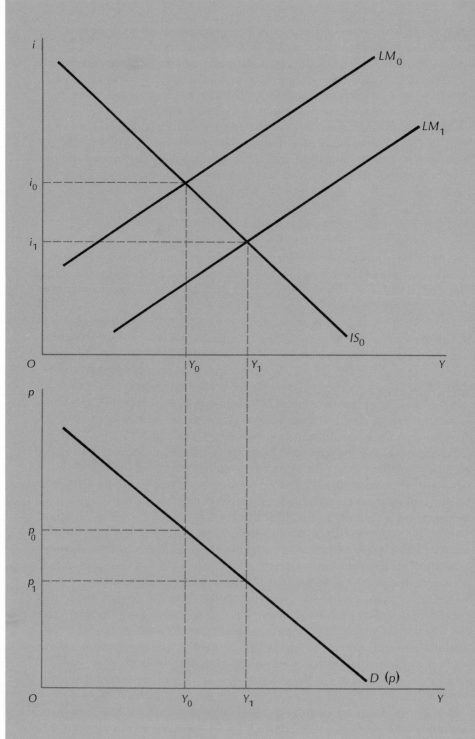

investment and income. Consequently, from the demand point of view, the lower the price level, the higher is the level of real income.

The sources of shifts in the aggregate demand curve can be easily identified. A rise in government purchases or fall in taxes shifts the *IS* curve up and therefore increases the level of aggregate demand associated with a particular price level. Similarly, an increase in the nominal money supply shifts the *LM* curve to the right and raises aggregate demand. Indeed any shift in the *IS-LM* functions that would tend to raise the demand for goods and services at the existing price level has the effect of shifting the aggregate demand function of the lower quadrant to the right.

Before moving to the aggregate supply side, let us briefly consider the special cases that were discussed in Chapter 9. Consider first the case of the liquidity trap which implies a horizontal *LM* curve as illustrated in Figure 9–1. It was just pointed out that a fall in the price level raises the real value of the money supply and shifts the *LM* curve to the right. However, in the liquidity trap this will have no effect on the rate of interest (please refer back to Section 9–2 if the reason for this is not clear), and it therefore does not stimulate investment and raise the level of income. It follows that the change in the price level has no effect on aggregate demand, and the aggregate demand function in this case is therefore a vertical line, as shown in Figure 10–2.

Another important special case arose when the *IS* curve was vertical as a consequence of investment's being completely unresponsive to changes in the rate of interest, as illustrated in Figure 9–5. In this event, a fall in the price level that once again raises the real value of the money supply and lowers the rate of interest has no effect on investment or the level of income. Consequently, we again have a case in which the aggregate demand function is vertical, which is to say, aggregate demand is independent of the level of prices.

Both of these Keynesian cases are described by the vertical aggregate demand function of Figure 10–2. It is important to bear in mind, and better still to understand why, both of the special cases outlined in Chapter 9 that are unfavorable to the effective functioning of monetary policy make for price-inelastic aggregate demand functions.

## 10–3
### THE CLASSICAL THEORY OF THE LABOR MARKET
### AND THE AGGREGATE SUPPLY FUNCTION

To derive the amount of output that will be supplied at different price levels, it is necessary to examine conditions in the labor market since that will determine how much work people are willing to do and how much employment is

**FIGURE 10–1**
Derivation of the aggregate demand function

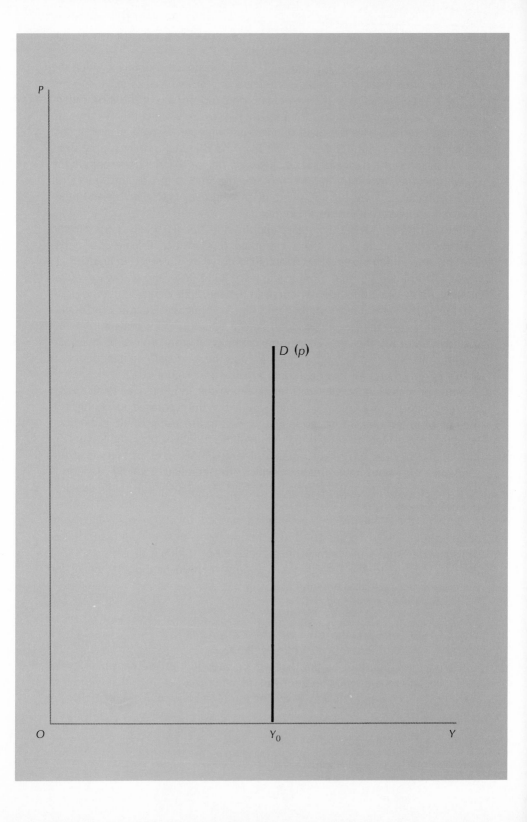

available for them. Given the production function, that, in turn, will determine how much they produce. To understand the demand side of the labor market we have to consider a few elements of the theory of the profit-maximizing business firm.

The contribution that a worker makes to the revenue of a competitive firm equals the additional output that the firm gains by employing the worker, multiplied by the price at which the output can be sold. The additional output attributable to the hiring of one more worker is the "marginal product of labor." When these additional units are multiplied by price, the result is the "value of the marginal product." If the value of the marginal product exceeds the cost of hiring the worker (the wage rate), it pays the firm to hire the worker. Even though it may pay to hire worker $n$, it may not be profitable to hire worker $n + 1$ even if wages and prices remain the same. The reason for this is that, as more workers are applied to a fixed quantity of capital, each worker will have less capital to work with, so that the marginal product of worker $n + 1$ will be less than the marginal product of worker $n$. It follows that the value of the marginal product of worker $n + 1$ will be smaller than the value of the marginal product of worker $n$, and if the value of the marginal product of worker $n + 1$ is below the wage rate he will not be hired. All of this merely states that the theory of the competitive firm implies that the firm will hire workers up to the point where the value of the marginal product equals the wage rate.[1]

[1] Some readers may be more familiar with the profit-maximizing condition that a firm in a competitive industry will produce up to the point where marginal cost equals price. This condition is, in fact, the same as the condition stated in the text that the firm will hire units of labor up to the point where the wage equals the value of the marginal product. The difference between the two conditions is simply that they are stated in different units, the former in terms of units of output, and the latter in terms of units of factor (labor) input. We may write

$$MC = p$$

where $MC$ is marginal cost (the cost of producing one more unit of output) as one way to state the profit-maximizing condition. However, marginal cost equals the cost of hiring one more worker (the wage) divided by the additional units he or she produces. Hence we also have by way of a definition

$$MC = \frac{w}{MP}$$

where $MP$ is the marginal product of labor. Combining the two expressions we get

$$p = \frac{w}{MP}$$

so that on multiplying both sides by the marginal product we get

$$pMP = w$$

where, of course, $pMP$ is the value of the marginal product.

## FIGURE 10–2
**The aggregate demand function under extreme Keynesian assumptions**

The foregoing implies that a profit-maximizing relation for the economy as a whole may be written

$$w = pX_n$$

or

$$\frac{w}{p} = X_n$$

where $w$ is the *nominal* or *money* wage rate, $p$ is the price level, $w/p$ is the *real* wage rate, and $X_n$ is the marginal product of labor. The marginal product is derived from the production function, and it is assumed to be positive but declines as employment increases in accordance with the assumption of diminishing marginal productivity.

A rise in the money wage rate would increase the cost of employing an additional worker over and above the value of his marginal product so that the firm would reduce employment if money wages increase. Similarly, a rise in the price at which output can be sold would raise the value of the marginal product of labor. Thus anything that raises the ratio of wages to prices, as the real wage is known, will tend to reduce employment, whereas anything that reduces the real wage will increase the level of employment. We may summarize this discussion by writing the function

$$N_d = \theta\left(\frac{w}{p}\right)$$

where $N_d$ is the demand for labor, to incorporate the theory that the demand for labor is a decreasing function of the real wage rate.

Much of the controversy in macroeconomic analysis has centered about the supply of labor. The classical economists believed that the supply of labor depends upon the real wage, just as does the demand for labor. Presumably intelligent workers would not imagine themselves to be better off if both wages and prices double. If they do feel better off under such conditions they are viewed as prone to "money illusion." If money illusion is ruled out as irrational, a change in the quantity of labor supplied will take place only if the real wage changes. A higher real wage provides an inducement to greater labor effort and in the short run is apt to increase the quantity of labor supplied.[1] These considerations then suggest a classical labor supply function

---

[1] Students of labor supply note that a rise in real wages increases the price of leisure and that workers will therefore maximize their utility by substituting additional work in place of leisure. On the other hand, the increase in the wage rate increases workers' income, and this will tend to cause them to purchase additional leisure. Thus the net effect of a wage increase on labor effort is not readily predictable, the *substitution* effect making for more work and the *income* effect making for less. Over the long run a rise in real wages has been associated with shorter hours, and persons in poor countries tend to have to work harder than persons in rich countries. However, such evidence is not pertinent to the identification of the short-run labor supply curve in a particular country at a particular time, since such evidence does not control for differences in the level of wealth. In connection with these issues, see Y. Barzel and R. J. McDonald, "Assets, Subsistence, and the Supply Curve of Labor," *American Economic Review*, 63:621–633, 1973.

as

$$N_s = \psi\left(\frac{w}{p}\right)$$

where $N_s$ is the supply of labor, and where it is assumed that $N_s$ is an increasing function of the real wage.

A four-quadrant approach similar to that employed in Chapter 8 to derive the IS and LM curves will help us to understand the relationship between conditions in the labor market and the aggregate supply function. The labor demand and supply functions are shown in quadrant 2 of Figure 10–3. The real wage rate is measured on the horizontal axis, and the quantity of labor is measured on the vertical axis. The demand curve for labor is negatively sloped in line with the assumption of diminishing returns and, in fact, traces the marginal product of labor. The supply curve is positively sloped on the assumption that higher real wage rates will be needed to induce additional workers to take jobs. At real wage rate $(w/p)_1$ the quantity of labor demanded by business is $N_d$. Workers, however, are willing to offer $N_s$ units of labor, which means that there is an excess supply of labor. When more workers are willing to work at the going real wage rate than business is willing to hire, we have "involuntary unemployment." Should the real wage fall to $(w/p)^*$, involuntary unemployment would be eliminated and the economy could then be said to be operating at full employment.

Quadrant 3 of Figure 10–3 shows the aggregate production function which relates output Y to labor input N. The increasing slope of the function reflects the assumption of diminishing returns since the marginal product of labor declines as the quantity of labor input increases. Quadrant 1 is utilized to plot the real wage rate against the price level for different assumed money wage rates. Each of the negatively sloped curves applies to a different money wage rate and shows, for that money wage rate, that a rise in the price level reduces the real wage. Quadrant 4, finally, measures the price level on the vertical axis and the level of real income on the horizontal axis and therefore shows the aggregate supply curve.

Now notice, in the classical case that we are discussing, that the aggregate supply curve is a vertical line. Consequently, there is only one equilibrium level of aggregate output and it is independent of the level of prices. The reasons for this can be easily explained. Assume, to begin, that the economy is in equilibrium at full employment. Thus, referring to Figure 10–3, this implies a cleared labor market so that the real wage must be $(w/p)^*$, and the level of employment must be $N^*$. The production function then implies that the equilibrium level of output is $Y^*$. If the money wage is $w_0$, then quadrant 4 shows that the equilibrium price level must be $p_0$. Now suppose that the price level falls to $p_1$. This raises the real wage to $(w/p)_1$ and, as can be seen in quadrant 2, creates an excess supply of labor. However, the excess supply of labor will now cause workers to compete for jobs, the money wage therefore falls, and this means that the money wage function of quadrant 1 will shift to

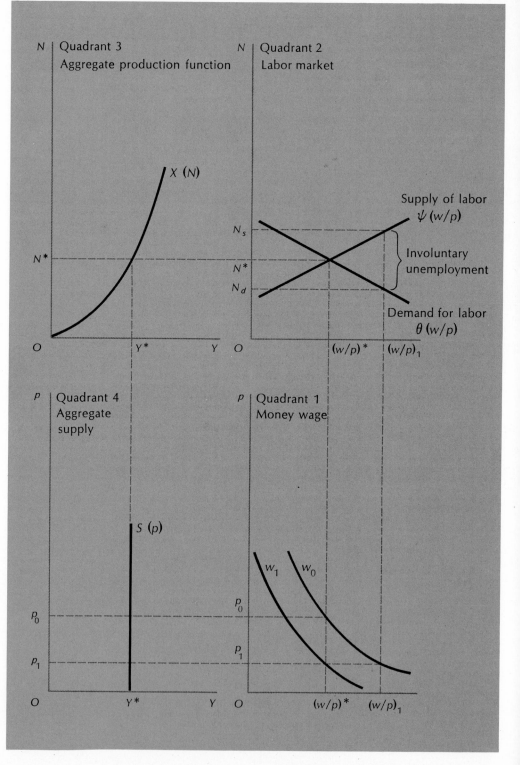

the left. As long as the real wage remains above $(w/p)^*$ this labor market competition will continue; it therefore follows that the money wage must fall in proportion to the fall in the price level. In the new equilibrium the money wage will be $w_1$, the price level will be $p_1$, the real wage returns to its original value $(w/p)^*$, and the levels of employment and output return to their original levels $N^*$ and $Y^*$, respectively. It follows that equilibrium aggregate supply will be the same as before, so that aggregate supply is seen to be independent of the price level. The aggregate supply curve therefore is a vertical line as seen in quadrant 4.

Having constructed the complete classical system, we can now consider how various monetary and fiscal policies affect the equilibrium values of the variables. In Figure 10–4 we retain only quadrant 4 of Figure 10–3, and we now combine this with the aggregate demand side and also show the $IS$ and $LM$ functions in the top portion of the diagram. We assume that the economy is in initial equilibrium at income $Y^*$, interest rate $i_0$, and price level $p_0$. The vertical aggregate supply function $S(p)$ reflects the classical theory of the labor market. Now suppose that this equilibrium is disrupted by an increase in the level of government purchases which shifts the $IS$ curve to $IS_1$. This also has the effect of raising the aggregate demand curve in the lower quadrant from $D(p)_0$ to $D(p)_1$.

As a consequence of the increase in aggregate demand, aggregate demand exceeds aggregate supply at the initial price level $p_0$. This excess demand for goods and services causes the price level to rise, and this has two consequences. First, the rising price level lowers the real wage rate and creates excess demand for labor (check Figure 10–3 to see this), so that money wages rise. Second, the rise in the price level reduces the real value of the money supply, and this means that it causes the $LM$ curve to shift to the left. Since this raises the rate of interest, it reduces investment expenditure. The continuation of these forces will eventually restore equilibrium with the values of the variables equal to $p_1$, $i_1$, and $Y^*$, as shown in Figure 10–4, and the implied associated equilibrium values $N^*$ and $(w/p)^*$ of Figure 10–3. These values have the following properties. The money wage rate must rise in proportion to the change in the price level since that is the only way the labor market clearing real wage $(w/p)^*$ and level of employment $N^*$ can be restored. This implies the same equilibrium level of real income $Y^*$. Since aggregate supply does not change, aggregate real demand in the new equilibrium must be the same as initially. This means that the rise in the government purchases must be offset by a fall in the level of investment; this comes about because the rise in the price level reduces the real value of the money supply and raises the rate of

**FIGURE 10–3**
Derivation of the aggregate supply function:
classical case

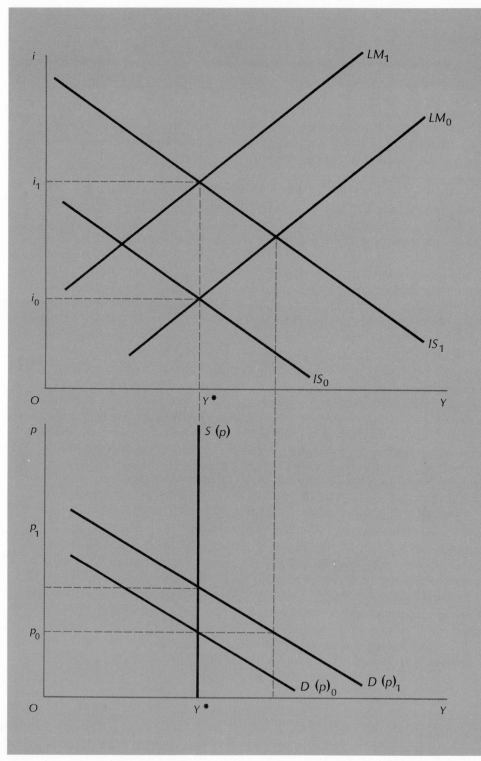

interest. This circumstance is reflected in Figure 10–4 by the shift in the *LM* curve from $LM_0$ to $LM_1$.

Next consider the effect of an increase in taxes. This deflationary policy shifts the *IS* and aggregate demand curves to the left and creates excess aggregate supply at the initial price level. The price level therefore falls, and since this raises the real wage, it produces excess supply of labor. In a competitive labor market this then causes the money wage rate to fall. In addition, the fall in the price level increases the real value of the money supply, lowers the rate of interest, and raises the level of investment. Equilibrium is restored when the same levels of employment $N^*$, income $Y^*$, and real wage $(w/p)^*$ combine with a rate of interest that is sufficiently lower to raise investment by the amount by which the tax increase reduces consumption.

Notice that in the classical system neither a change in government purchases nor taxes has any effect on the level of real income. The policies change the rate of interest and therefore alter the mix among the components of aggregate spending, consumption, investment, and government purchases, and they change the equilibrium price and money wage levels proportionately. But they do not change the equilibrium level of real aggregate economic activity. Except for the results with respect to the money wage rate and the price level, about which nothing was said earlier, these results are the same as the classical case of Chapter 9. However, they no longer rely on the extreme assumption that the demand for money is completely inelastic with respect to the rate of interest. They follow, rather, from the classical theory of labor supply with the price-inelastic aggregate supply function this implies.

It has been said that in the classical system money is a "veil," which is to say, it affects the price level and the money wage rate but does not affect the equilibrium values of any real magnitude of the system. To see the basis for this argument, refer again to Figure 10–4, and imagine starting with $IS_1$ and $LM_1$ and with the system in equilibrium at $Y^*$, $i_1$, and $p_0$. Now suppose the nominal money supply is increased so that the *LM* curve shifts from $LM_1$ to $LM_0$. This raises aggregate demand and shifts the function up from $D(p)_0$ to $D(p)_1$. Excess demand now exists at the existing price level $(p_0)$, and the price level therefore rises in response to competition among buyers for the available output and will continue to rise until excess demand is eliminated. Since aggregate supply is inelastic with respect to changes in the price level, the price level must rise to where the new aggregate demand curve $D(p)_1$ cuts the aggregate supply curve at price level $p_1$. Since this price level must be coincident with equilibrium in the product and money markets, we must assume that the price level rises by enough to shift the *LM* curve back to where it came from, thereby restoring equilibrium at interest rate $i_1$ and income level $Y^*$. This means, to summarize, that the increase in the nominal quantity of

**FIGURE 10–4**
Effects of policy in the classical system

money must raise the price level in exact proportion to the increase in the nominal money stock, and that all other variables—income, employment, consumption, investment, the rate of interest, the real wage—return to their original equilibrium values.

We close this section by consolidating our work with a formal summary of the classical system. The real wage and equilibrium level of employment are determined by equating the demand for labor,

$$N_d = \theta\left(\frac{w}{p}\right)$$

with the supply for labor

$$N_s = \psi\left(\frac{w}{p}\right)$$

With the equilibrium level of employment thus known, the level of real income is implied by the production function

$$Y = X(N, K^*, T^*)$$

Since this fixes aggregate supply, the product market equilibrium equation (*IS*)

$$I(i) + G = Y - C(Y - T)$$

must now adjust to the predetermined level of income, which means that it determines the real rate of interest and the way the full-employment level of real income is distributed among consumption, investment, and government purchases. Finally, since both the equilibrium level of income and the rate of interest are predetermined, the *LM* curve,

$$\frac{M}{p} = L(Y, i)$$

must shift in a way as to be compatible with these predetermined values. This means that the equilibrium price level must be proportional to the nominal quantity of money, and this must also be true of the money wage rate.

## 10–4
## THE KEYNESIAN THEORY OF THE LABOR MARKET
## AND THE UNDEREMPLOYMENT EQUILIBRIUM

The situation that is of concern during recession or depression is a disrupted labor market in which the quantity of labor demanded is substantially below the quantity that workers are willing to offer at the prevailing rate. In Figure 10–3 such a situation exists at real wage $(w/p)_1$ because the amount of labor demanded by firms is only $N_d$ whereas the amount of labor offered by workers is $N_s$. Figure 10–3 also suggests that in the classical framework the existence of involuntary unemployment, which is the gap between $N_s$ and $N_d$, is a reflection of the fact that the real wage rate is too high, and that to eliminate involuntary unemployment and restore equilibrium, the real wage should be reduced to $(w/p)^*$.

The classical theory of the labor market suggests that persistent unemployment must be attributable to imperfections in the labor market that prevent the money wage rate from falling. Presumably, such a reduction in the money wage would lower the real wage and bring the supply of and demand for labor back into equilibrium. In criticizing this line of reasoning, Keynes advanced the proposition that money wages tend to be sticky in the downward direction even when involuntary unemployment exists. This, in itself, is not very startling since it reflects a well-known institutional fact of life. However, he added the very novel and important claim that, even if the money wage could be made to fall, this would not reduce the real wage and it would not, therefore eliminate involuntary unemployment and restore equilibrium at full employment. Let us take up the second proposition first and examine the effect of a reduction in the money wage rate.

A fall in money wages temporarily reduces the real wage rate, and this will cause profit-maximizing firms to increase production and employment at the existing price level. When all firms increase real output, this increase in real income will also increase consumption. However, since the marginal propensity to consume is less than unity, Keynes reasoned that the rise in consumption will be less than the rise in income. Consequently, there will be an excess supply of goods, unintended inventory investment will take place, and there will therefore be downward pressure on the price level. This fall in the price level then tends to offset the reduction in the real wage which was brought about by the initial money wage reduction. Consequently, there will be a tendency for production to be cut back. Indeed, if the price level falls in proportion to the money wage rate, the real wage will return to its initial level; this will imply that output and employment will return to their initial levels, and the fall in money wages will then have accomplished nothing. It is, therefore, not sufficient for the money wage rate to fall, because this does not guarantee that the real wage will also fall.

The argument is crucial to an understanding of the process of macroeconomic adjustment and therefore bears repetition and illustration. Consider Figure 10–5 which is similar to the type of diagram introduced in Chapter 4. The $C + I$ schedule cuts the 45-degree line at income $Y_0$, and the full-employment level of income is assumed to be at $Y^*$. Since the level of income is less than the full-employment level, there must be an excess supply of labor. As a consequence, money wages will fall. Suppose that the fall in money wages causes firms to produce $\Delta Y = Y^* - Y_0$ additional units of output. If there are no taxes, the increased output creates additional disposable income in the same amount. But since the marginal propensity to consume is less than unity, the increase in consumption $\Delta C$ is less than $\Delta Y$, and the difference represents unintended accumulation of inventories, $I_u$. As we saw in Chapter 4, equilibrium will not be restored until unintended investment is eliminated; this means that in a competitive economy prices will fall and output will return to the original level $Y_0$. Because at $Y_0$ the absence of unintended investment implies that firms are again operating at their profit-maximizing output levels, and because the same level of output implies that the same amount of

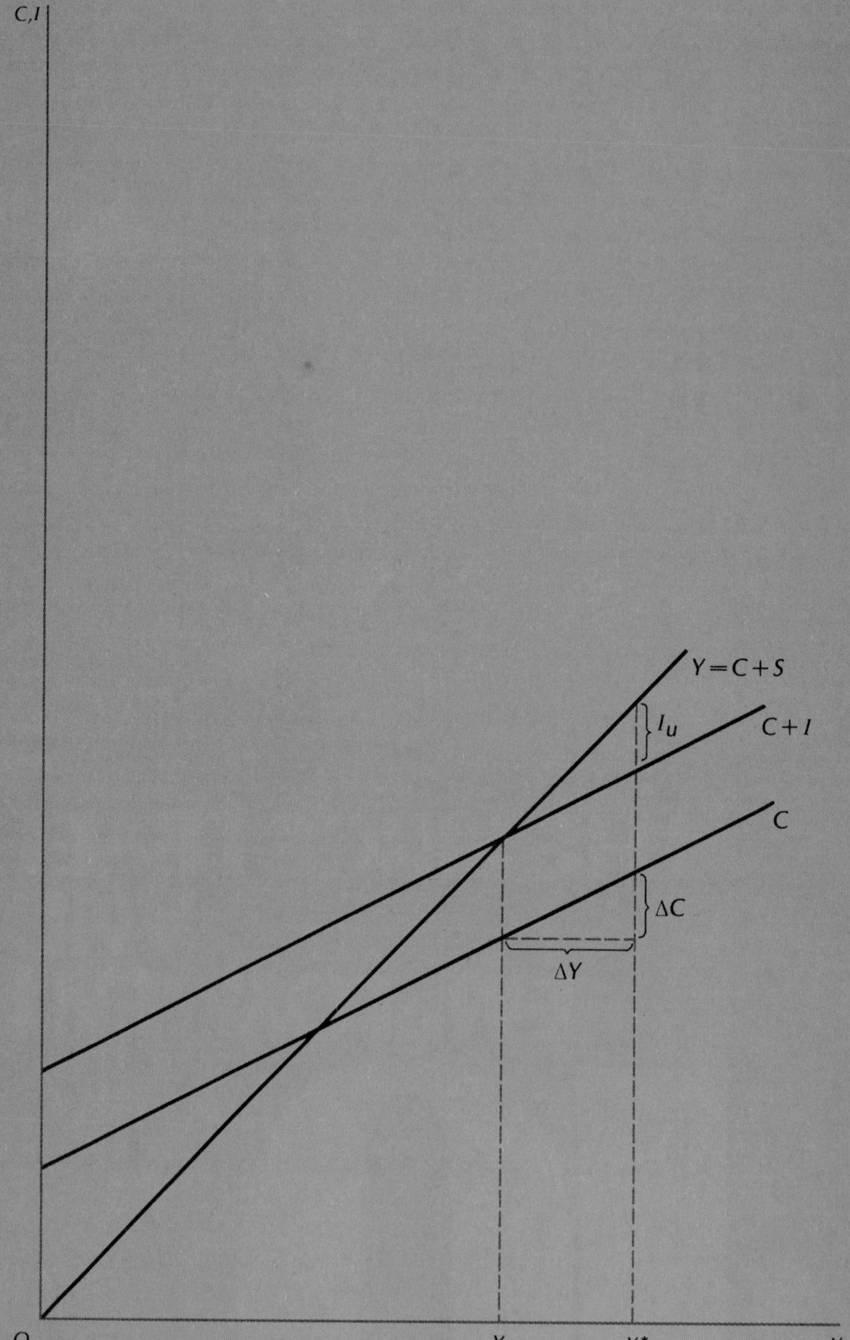
C,I
Y=C+S
$I_u$
C+I
C
ΔC
ΔY
O
$Y_0$
Y*
Y

labor will be hired as before the fall in wages, the fall in prices must have been in exact proportion to the fall in money wages. Real wages remain the same; and there appears then not to be an effective mechanism that clears the labor market.[1]

The foregoing argument would be correct if there were nothing in the nature of the adjustment process that raises the $C + I$ schedule of Figure 10–5. Note, however, that one consequence of the fall in wages is that the price level falls. As a result of this, the real value of the money supply increases. This lowers the rate of interest, raises the level of investment, and increases the level of income and employment. Moreover, assuming a competitive labor market, money wages will continue to fall until this mechanism restores full employment.

The process is illustrated in Figure 10–6. Aggregate supply is at income level $Y^*$, but with the IS and LM curves initially at $IS_0$ and $LM_0$, respectively, aggregate demand is at $Y_0$. This implies price level $p_0$ and a real wage in excess of that which clears the labor market. Money wages then fall and, via the process described above, so do prices. The real value of the money supply therefore increases (shifting the LM curve to the right) so that the rate of interest falls, and the level of investment and income rise. As shown in Figure 10–6, the final equilibrium is established at the full-employment level $Y^*$ and lower price level $p_1$. Looked at from the point of view of Figure 10–5, the fall in the price level continues until the $C + I$ schedule shifts up to where it intersects the full-employment level of income at $Y^*$.

The Keynesian reply to the foregoing argument centered on the liquidity trap and on the empirical judgment that even if the rate of interest could be made to fall, this probably would not raise the level of investment during depressed economic conditions characterized by the presence of excess capacity. The implications of the liquidity trap argument are illustrated in Figure 10–7. In the upper quadrant the $IS_0$ curve cuts the $LM_0$ curve in the liquidity trap at interest rate $i_0$ and income level $Y_0$. Since this is below full employment, the competitive labor market assumption implies that the money wage rate will fall and this, in turn, will induce a fall in the price level. This raises the real value of the money supply, shifting the LM curve to the right to, for example, $LM_1$ in Figure 10–7. However, in the liquidity trap this has no effect on the rate of interest. It therefore fails to raise the level of invest-

[1] For discussions of the effect of money wage reduction on the level of employment see J. M. Keynes, *The General Theory of Employment, Interest and Money,* Chap. 19, Harcourt, Brace & World, Inc., New York, 1936; papers by A. P. Lerner and J. Tobin, in S. E. Harris, ed., *The New Economics,* Chaps. 10 and 40, Alfred A. Knopf, Inc., New York, 1950; W. J. Fellner, *Competition Among the Few,* Alfred A. Knopf, Inc., New York, 1949, pp. 266–272; F. Modigliani, "Liquidity Preference and the Theory of Interest and Money," *Econometrica,* 12:45–88, 1944; T. Wilson, *Fluctuations in Income and Employment,* Chap. 10, Sir Isaac Pitman & Sons, Ltd., London, 1942.

**FIGURE 10–5**
Effect of a fall in wages and prices

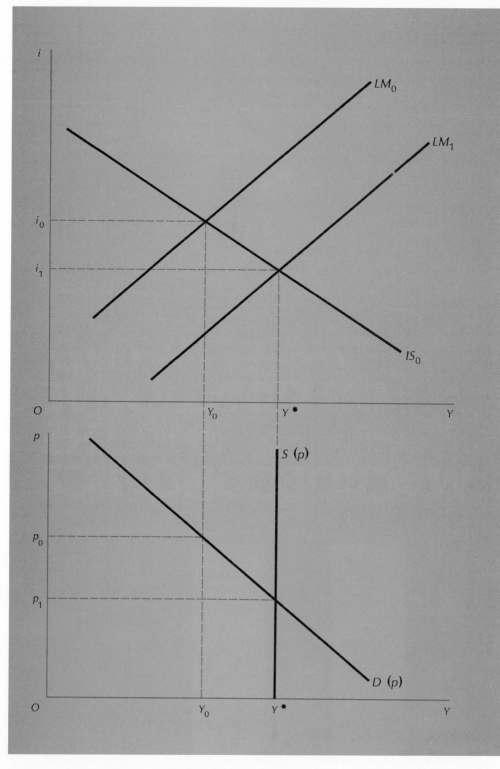

ment or the level of income. Consequently, in this case the fall in the money wage rate is accompanied by a proportional fall in the price level and the level of real income and employment therefore remain unchanged.

It is evident, also, that the same result would occur if investment is not responsive to changes in the rate of interest. Both cases, as shown in the discussion of aggregate demand of Section 10–2, imply vertical aggregate demand curves. The situation is shown in the lower quadrant of Figure 10–7. The classical aggregate supply curve is vertical, but so, under present assumptions, is the aggregate demand function. The system therefore is indeterminate, which is to say, there is no equilibrium solution. If a fall in money wages produces a proportional fall in the price level, leaving the real wage unchanged, the level of employment will not change. Since this means that excess supply in the labor market will continue indefinitely, it implies, as well, that wages and prices will continue to fall indefinitely.

Keynes's reaction to this dilemma was to attack the assumption of downward wage flexibility. In doing this he found support in the institutional facts that wages are not generally downwardly flexible even under conditions of heavy unemployment. However, he averted the charge that his theory differed from standard doctrine only in its reliance on market imperfections by introducing an alternative theory of labor supply. He claimed that the money wage rate would be inflexible downward even without the presence of unions, minimum wage laws, and similar elements that prevent competition in the labor market. Keynes suggested that workers are concerned with their wage relative to other workers. They would not, therefore, accept a fall in money wages relative to their coworkers. However, they would accept a fall in real wages if this were brought about by a rise in the price level, since this would impinge on all workers equally. This does, to be sure, imply money illusion since it suggests that it matters how the fall in real wages is brought about.

At all events, the conventional interpretation of Keynesian doctrine is that the money wage rate is historically determined and fixed in the short run, despite the presence of involuntary unemployment. The implication of this is that the supply of labor is infinitely elastic with respect to the money wage rate. Figure 10–8 illustrates Keynesian labor market assumptions. The historically given money wage rate is $w_0$, and $p_0$ is the existing price level. At money wage $w_0$ workers will offer anywhere between zero and $N^*$ units of labor. Consequently, the labor supply curve is a vertical line at $w_0/p_0$. Although the money wage rate cannot be made to fall, it will rise when all those who are willing to work at $w_0$ are employed and additional workers are desired. Consequently, the labor supply curve bends to the right, once $N^*$ has

**FIGURE 10–6**
Restoration of full employment
by wage flexibility

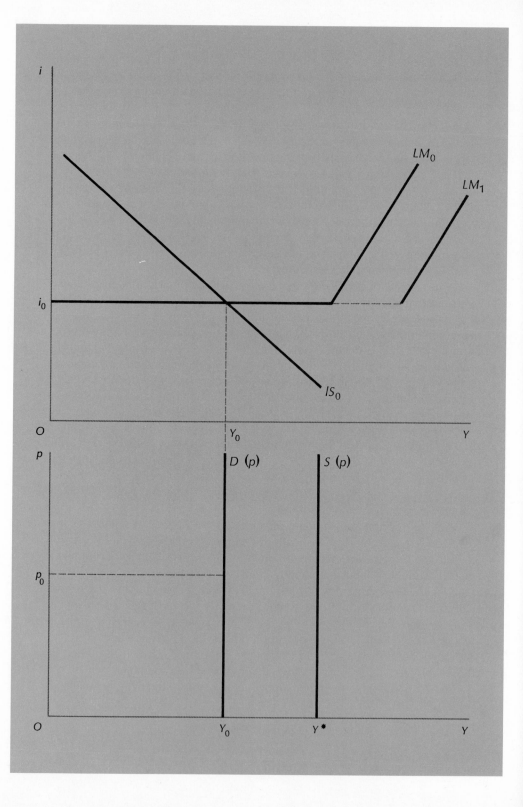

been reached, indicating that beyond the level of employment a rise in the real wage will be needed to call forth additional labor supply. The demand for labor function of Figure 10–8 cuts the supply schedule at $N_0$. Consequently, the distance $N^* - N_0$ measures involuntary unemployment, the amount of labor willing to work at existing wages that cannot find employment.

Since the money wage rate is assumed to be downwardly rigid (and since a fall in wages, even if it could be brought about, would produce a proportional drop in the price level with a vertical aggregate demand curve) the restoration of full employment in the Keynesian system requires that the needed reduction in the real wage rate be brought about by an increase in aggregate demand. This would bring with it a rise in the price level, and this would shift the entire labor supply schedule of Figure 10–8 to the left and in this manner eliminate involuntary unemployment. Thus at real wage $w_0/p_1$ the labor demand schedule cuts the supply schedule at $N^*$, where all who are willing to work at the new real wage are employed. In the Keynesian system aggregate demand determines the condition of the labor market, whereas in the classical system the labor market takes care of itself.

It is not necessary to repeat a four-quadrant representation such as that of Figure 10–3 to derive the aggregate supply curve implied by the Keynesian analysis. The result of such an analysis would be the aggregate supply curve shown in the bottom quadrant of Figure 10–9; it can be explained quite simply if Figure 10–8, which shows the Keynesian labor market, is borne in mind. With the price level at $p_0$, the situation depicted in Figure 10–8 implies the level of employment $N_0$. Via the production function, this implies a particular level of aggregate output which we may denote as $Y_0$. Accordingly, the point $(p_0, Y_0)$ is one point on the aggregate supply curve of Figure 10–9. At the higher price level $p_1$, the level of employment would be the level $N^*$ (of Figure 10–8), which implies output level $Y^*$. Thus the point $(p_1, Y^*)$ is another point on the aggregate supply curve. We therefore have the extremely important result that in the Keynesian model the aggregate supply curve is positively sloped, higher aggregate supply being associated with a higher price level. Beyond employment level $N^*$, however, and as shown in Figure 10–8, labor supply becomes a function of the real wage, so that at this point the aggregate supply curve assumes the vertical shape of the classical model.

General equilibrium in the Keynesian system occurs at the intersection of the aggregate demand and aggregate supply functions. If the aggregate demand function is the curve $D(p)_0$ illustrated in Figure 10–9, the equilibrium level of income will be $Y_0$ which, translated back into labor market terms, implies employment level $N_0$, with involuntary unemployment $N^* - N_0$. If the

**FIGURE 10–7**
Illustration of macroeconomic
indeterminacy

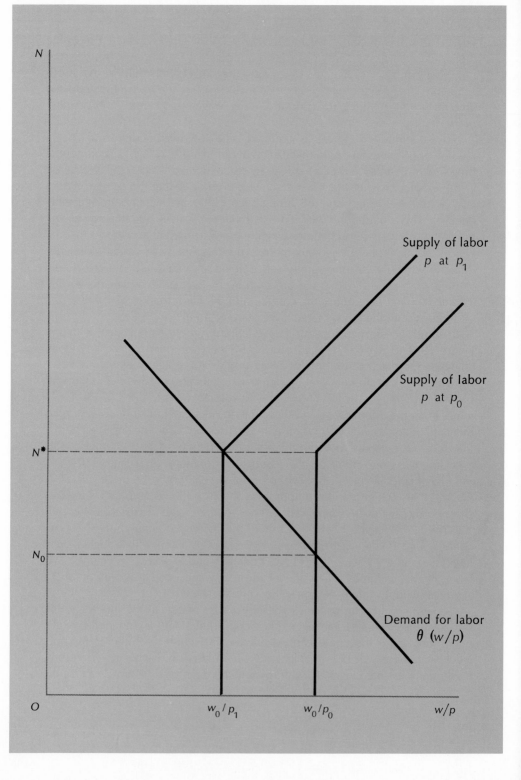

aggregate supply curve shifts to $D(p)_1$, income rises to the full-employment level, and involuntary unemployment is eliminated. Once at full employment, the distinction between the Keynesian and the classical models vanishes.

The increase in expenditures needed to shift the aggregate demand function to $D(p)_1$ can be brought about by any combination of IS and LM curve shifts that causes the two functions to intersect at the vertical line drawn at the full-employment level of income $Y^*$. For example, a rise in government purchases that shifts the IS curve from $IS_0$ to $IS_1$ would restore full employment, as would a shift in the LM curve from $LM_0$ to $LM_1$ brought about by expansionary monetary policy. The rise in spending generated by either of these policies creates excess demand for goods, raises the price level, which, combined with the rigid money wage, lowers the real wage and secures an expansion of production and employment.

We now complete the discussion of the Keynesian system in the same way as we did the classical system by writing the model formally. Product market equilibrium

$$I(i) + G = Y - C(Y - T)$$

and monetary equilibrium

$$\frac{M}{p} = L(Y,i)$$

combine to specify aggregate demand at different price levels,

$$Y_d = D(p)$$

The demand for labor is

$$N_d = \theta\left(\frac{W_0}{p}\right)$$

and since the money wage rate is fixed, this function when combined with the production function

$$Y = X(N,K^*,T^*)$$

implies a positively sloped aggregate supply curve,

$$Y_s = S(p)$$

In the classical system aggregate supply is inelastic with respect to the price level so that aggregate demand must adjust to aggregate supply. By contrast, under the extreme Keynesian liquidity trap assumption, aggregate demand is inelastic with respect to the price level so that aggregate supply adjusts to aggregate demand. Demand basically determines the level of income

**FIGURE 10–8**
Labor market: Keynesian case

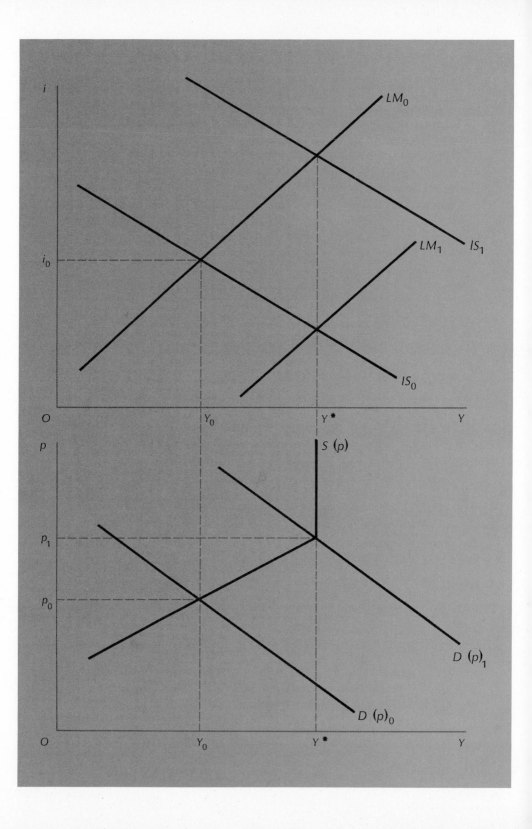

in the Keynesian system, whereas supply determines it under classical assumptions.

## 10–5
## ADDITIONAL NOTES ON MONEY WAGE RATES, MONEY ILLUSION, AND EMPLOYMENT

The analysis of the effect of wage changes on the economy is central to an understanding not only of depression economics but of inflation economics as well, and it is therefore appropriate that we add some further notes to the subject.

The Keynesian argument that the liquidity trap would prevent wage-price flexibility from restoring full employment has not gone unchallenged. The distinguished economist A. C. Pigou argued that, even though the liquidity trap might bar the way to an increase in employment via the path of changes in interest rates and investment, falls in wages and prices would sooner or later restore full employment because a decline in the price level would cause the consumption function to shift up.[1] The mechanism by which the consumption function shifts up, commonly known as the "Pigou effect," has the following rationale: If consumption is an increasing function of the level of wealth, as well as of the level of income, we can presume that if falling wages and prices cause wealth holders to feel wealthier, they will increase their consumption outlays at all levels of income. Why, however, should a fall in the price level cause wealth holders to feel wealthier?

As the level of prices falls, the real value of the assets whose prices are fixed in nominal terms rises. A fall in the price level makes debtors poorer and creditors richer. Because each $1 of debt is matched by $1 of credit, the presence of a Pigou effect would have to depend upon the presence of a difference between the spending behavior of debtors and creditors in response to a change in the price level. The reason for supposing that there is such a difference in the consumption responses to wealth changes is that the government is a large net debtor whereas the private sector, which holds a net balance of government obligations, is a net creditor. If, then, it is assumed that the marginal propensity of the government to spend wealth is zero, while the marginal propensity to consume wealth is positive for the private sector, a transfer of wealth from one sector to the other due to a change in the price level will cause the level of total spending to change.

The operation of the Pigou effect is illustrated in Figure 10–10. The

[1] A. C. Pigou, "The Classical Stationary State," *Economic Journal*, 53:343–351, 1943, and "Economic Progress in a Stable Environment," *Economica*, New Series, 14:180–188, 1947.

**FIGURE 10–9**
Aggregate supply and general equilibrium
in the Keynesian system

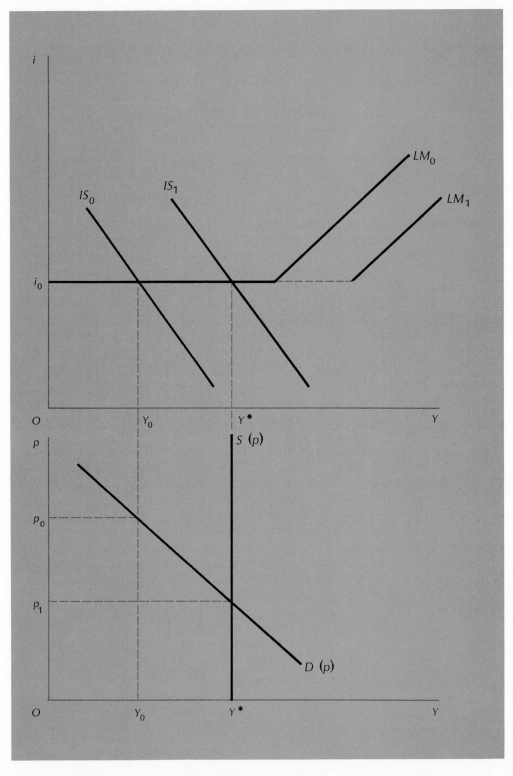

economy is initially mired in the liquidity trap at income level $Y_0$ and interest rate $i_0$. When the price level falls, the $LM$ curve shifts to $LM_1$, but under the liquidity trap assumption the interest rate does not fall and the aggregate demand curve then tends to assume a vertical shape, producing the indeterminacy noted earlier. However, if the fall in the price level raises consumption, the $IS$ curve is no longer independent of the price level and will shift to the right as the price level falls. Thus the Pigou effect restores the negative slope to the aggregate demand curve and thereby also restores determinacy to the system. Final equilibrium is shown in Figure 10–10 at income level $Y^*$ and price level $p_1$.

Money wage cuts may have additional effects on the level of income and employment as suggested below.

1   A fall in wages and prices will make it more attractive to purchase domestically produced goods. This will raise exports and reduce imports, and this will stimulate domestic economic activity. We should keep in mind, however, that recessions tend to coincide internationally. Improvements in domestic income and employment arising from an increase in net exports generally come from the exportation of domestic unemployment to foreign countries rather than from any overall expansion in the level of total world employment. This subject is discussed in more detail in subsequent chapters.

2   A money wage cut represents a redistribution of income from workers to dividend earners. If, as is likely, high-income groups have a lower marginal propensity to consume than low-income groups, each dollar taken from a wage earner and given to a dividend earner will produce a net decline in aggregate consumption expenditure. A money wage cut may therefore cause aggregate consumption to decline, and if this redistributive effect is dominant, a cut in money wages will reduce, rather than raise, the levels of income and employment.

3   It is difficult to believe that money wage reductions could occur in an instantaneous, across-the-board manner. The piecemeal wage reductions that are more likely to be experienced would foster the expectation that further cuts are in the offing. Acting on this expectation, entrepreneurs will cut back production, make sales out of inventory, and postpone new plant and equipment expenditures. Similarly, consumers might well expect the trend of prices to continue downward and therefore postpone consumption expenditures. The adverse expectations induced by the wage cut may therefore defeat its intended effect.

**FIGURE 10–10**
**The Pigou effect combined with wage-price**
**flexibility restores full employment**

**4**   As we have seen, Keynes believed labor to be subject to money illusion. He believed, in other words, that workers were far more conscious of changes in money wage rates than of changes in the price level and that they would therefore be likely to regard an increase in money wages as an increase in real wages even if prices rose in proportion to the wage increase. This implies that if money wages remained unchanged, an increase in the price level would not be noticed by workers, who therefore would offer the same supply of labor even though real wages had fallen.

There is no reason to suppose that money illusion is confined to labor supply. Imagine, for example, the effect of its presence on consumption spending. If money wages and prices fall and consumers notice the fall in money income but not the fall in prices, they will be under the illusion that real income has fallen. However, when real income falls, the percentage of income consumed rises (provided that the consumption function has a positive intercept). Thus, if consumers think their real income has fallen, they will spend a greater percentage of their money income than previously. This means that the consumption function in terms of real disposable income will shift up as a result of the wage cut and that the level of income will rise.

Personal income tax structures are among the greatest sources of money illusion in many economies. Tax rates and brackets are usually based on money rather than real income. If money income and prices both fall, leaving real income unchanged, taxpayers nevertheless shift into lower brackets and the real value of their tax burden declines. Consequently, a proportional fall in wages and prices will raise real disposable income and the level of consumption spending.

As long as we are on the subject of money illusion, we should point out that the existence of money illusion does not necessarily imply irrational behavior on the part of those whose economic behavior is not in strict conformity with the classical "homogeneity postulate."[1] The primary reason for this

---

[1] A fancy way of saying that the supply of labor is a function of the real wage is to say that the function is homogeneous of degree zero. In general we may write

$$N_s = S(w,p)$$

as the labor supply function. In the absence of money illusion a proportional increase in $w$ and $p$ will not affect the amount of labor supplied. To a mathematician this means that the labor supply function has the property of zero degree homogeneity. In general, an $n$th-order homogeneous function has the property that if all the independent variables are multiplied by a constant, the dependent variable will be multiplied by that same constant raised to the power $n$.

Mathematically, if

$$y = f(x,z)$$

then

$$yu^n = f(xu,zu)$$

and if $n = 0$, $u^n = 1$, so that

$$y = f(x,z) = f(xu,zu)$$

is that workers, consumers, and business executives all make long-term contracts that are fixed, not in real, but in money terms. Wage earners, for example, may still have many years of payments to make on the mortgage on their homes. If wages and prices decline in the same proportion, their real wages will be the same. But the real value of their debt burden will increase, and they may therefore be obliged to reduce current consumption expenditures. Although workers appear to be subject to money illusion, their decisions to consume less may be based on a perfectly rational calculation. Since workers tend, in general, to be debtors, a fall in money wages, even though real wages remain the same, will be regarded as a serious real loss.

Money illusion has usually been regarded as a stabilizing force by economists even though there are conspicuous cases where this has not been the case. The personal income tax illustrates both possibilities. Consider first a recession during which both wages and prices are falling at the same rate. Despite the fact that the real wage remains constant under these assumptions, the progressivity of the tax causes tax collections to fall in a greater proportion than the fall in nominal wages. Since this means that real disposable income rises, the effect is stabilizing. Unfortunately, this stabilizing property becomes destabilizing when excessive unemployment coincides not with falling prices, but rather with rising prices. In 1974, for example, real GNP fell steadily as the United States economy fell into a serious recession. Nevertheless, price inflation continued at a rapid rate. As a result of this inflation, nominal personal income continued to increase, and the ratio of income taxes to personal income continued to rise even though real GNP was falling. Consequently, in this instance the money illusion in the tax structure, that is, the fact that tax changes are linked to changes in nominal income rather than to changes in real income, caused the recession to be worse than it otherwise would have been.

Before concluding our discussion of the effect of reductions in money wages, we should note the obvious fact that our present-day institutional environment precludes the implementation of such a policy. But it would be foolish to infer from this that it is pointless to analyze the effects of wage reductions on the level of employment.

---

which means that multiplication of the two independent variables by a constant does not change the value of the dependent variable.

Therefore, in the case of the labor supply function,

$N_s = S(w,p) = S(uw,up)$

and since $u$ is an arbitrary constant, we can let $u = 1/p$ so that

$$N_s = S\left(\frac{w}{p}, 1\right)$$

which is to say that the supply of labor depends only on the ratio of $w$ to $p$, the real wage rate.

If workers are subject to money illusion, the labor supply function will not be homogeneous, and hence it is said that the homogeneity postulate is denied. In this connection see W. W. Leontieff, "Postulates: Keynes' General Theory and the Classicists," in Harris, ed., op. cit., Chap. 10.

First, the analysis brings out the important point that little can be accomplished by wage reduction that cannot be accomplished by monetary policy. Indeed, prior to consideration of the complications introduced in this section, it appeared that wage reduction would be no more and no less effective than a monetary policy that produced an equivalent effect on the real value of the money supply.

Second, an economist who believes that money wage cuts can restore full employment, and who is opposed to remedies that restore full employment by raising the price level, is apt to advocate policies designed to restore wage-price flexibility. While centrally enforced wage cuts are unrealistic, a strong antitrust policy designed to control the monopoly power of unions and enterprises is not beyond the realm of possibility. Because price flexibility is a necessary feature of an automatically regulating economic system, monopoly is anathema to the tradition-minded economist.[1] The Keynesian, less convinced of the importance of wage-price flexibility, is apt to be a less enthusiastic trustbuster than his classical counterpart. At the same time, the realities of the modern economy may, as we shall see later, turn the Keynesian in the direction of wage-price guidelines.

Third, the question of whether money wage cuts will be effective in restoring full employment is really the same as the question of whether or not the economy has an automatic steering wheel. An economist who believes that full employment at stable prices is the norm to which the economy will return after a disturbance from equilibrium will prescribe radically different policies than the economist who believes that full employment is an accidental state that cannot be maintained, or even achieved, without considerable assistance from governmental policy.

Fourth, the discussion of money wage cuts has focused attention on one of the most important differences between Keynes and the traditional economists, namely, the theory of liquidity preference. As we saw in Chapter 9, the existence of a demand for idle balances was one of the vital ingredients of the debate over the relative effectiveness of monetary and fiscal policy. It now appears that this is also one of the vital differences between an automatically adjusting economy and one in which several equilibrium levels of employment are possible.

Finally, although discussion of the effect of money wage reduction may strike us as a bit unreal, discussion of the effect of wage increases most certainly does not, since such analysis is central to an understanding of the process through which inflation is generated. Thus the analysis of this chapter will stand us in good stead when we come to consider the problem of inflation that we shall be tackling a few chapters hence.

---

[1] The view that stabilization policy of any description is doomed without vigorous action to restore competition is expressed most lucidly by Henry Simons, *Economic Policy for a Free Society*, Chap. 5, The University of Chicago Press, Chicago, 1948.

# MACROECONOMICS
# AND THE
# INTERNATIONAL
# ECONOMY

## INTRODUCTION

An economy that functions in isolation is usually denoted a "closed" economy, whereas one that is heavily interdependent with other economies is known as an "open" economy. In this chapter we will attempt to transform the foregoing closed economy analysis into one that takes account of the fact that economies are economically linked in many important ways. Trade dependence implies macroeconomic interdependence; this, in turn, implies that the fiscal and monetary policies of one country will affect the macro-economic variables of the other. Expansion of the money supply in one country will tend to spill over and cause monetary expansion elsewhere, and expansionary fiscal policy will raise the demand for imports and stimulate economic activity abroad. Even a large and relatively self-sufficient economy such as that of the United States finds itself dependent on foreign sources of supply and upon foreign markets. And although we have not always been willing to face up to the fact, the very size of the American economy causes its domestic policies to have a significant impact on the stability of other countries.

In past editions of this book we restricted our discussion of international macro problems to a single chapter. However, international monetary problems have become so important and complex in recent years that a more detailed treatment is now appropriate. We will therefore divide our work as follows: The present chapter attempts to incorporate international economic interdependence into the basic macroeconomic model of the economy. We begin by amending the *IS* curve to include exports and imports, and we then move on to incorporate the effects of balance of payments deficits and surpluses on the money supply and *LM* curve. The major policy issues, how to deal with a deficit in the balance of payments, whether the exchange rate should be fixed or be permitted to fluctuate freely, can be more appropriately dealt with after the theory of economic policy is introduced. We shall, therefore, return to the subject of international monetary problems in Chapter 17.

Let us begin with a short description of the international monetary setting. As is well known, the United States has for many years suffered from a "balance of payments deficit" which has caused a "gold drain" and a "dollar problem." All of this refers to the simple fact that the United States was unable to earn, from its sales of exports, its receipts of interest and dividends from its investment in other countries, and from investments by foreigners in the United States, a quantity of foreign money sufficient to balance the quantity of dollars that the United States spent abroad for imports, foreign investments, economic aid, and military assistance. Consequently, more dollars have steadily flowed out of the United States than foreign moneys have flowed in.

Under the international payments system that prevailed until fairly recently, the procedure for making an international settlement was roughly as follows: If a German exporter earned some dollars, he could convert these dollars into D. marks at his bank. The bank, its supply of domestic money having been depleted, would go to the central bank and convert whatever excess amount of dollars it had into domestic money. Because dollars are an acceptable means of paying bills with third countries, the central bank might decide to hold the dollars as "international reserves." On the other hand, if the central bank decided that its dollar holdings were excessive, it could call upon the United States Treasury to buy back the dollars in exchange for D. marks. Finally, if the Treasury was short of D. marks, or "foreign exchange," as holdings of foreign money are called, it would have to buy the dollars back in exchange for gold. When this happens as a steady process, the United States is said to be suffering from a "gold drain."

To see how the organization of the international monetary system may change, let us repeat the above sequence in reverse order. If the United States Treasury refuses to honor its commitment to buy the dollars back in exchange for gold, this suspension of "gold convertibility" forces upon foreign central banks the necessity of deciding whether or not to accept dollars from their own commercial banks in exchange for domestic money balances. If they decide to continue to purchase dollars at a fixed price, all currencies will then be effectively linked to the dollar, which is why such a situation has been described as a "dollar standard." To maintain the dollar standard, foreign central banks have to be willing to accumulate dollars indefinitely, which means in effect that they are willing to underwrite more or less permanent deficits in the United States balance of payments. It means, also, that their domestic money supplies will increase as long as they continue to buy dollars, because, as they take in the dollars, they feed out domestic money balances in return. Finally, if the foreign central banks refuse to continue such a policy and they stop purchasing dollars, foreign exporters and other holders of dollar balances will then no longer be assured of a fixed price for their dollars in terms of their local currency. If they wish to convert one currency into another, they can no longer go to the central bank but must take what they can get in the "foreign exchange market," where the terms of exchange are established by supply and demand. When currency prices are unsupported by official guarantees to purchase and sell, they are described as "freely floating," or "fluctuating," or "flexible" exchange rates.[1]

Until August 15, 1971, when President Nixon suspended Treasury gold sales to official foreign agencies, the postwar international monetary system was characterized by the presence of officially fixed rates of international currency exchange. The United States fixed the value of gold at $35 per fine ounce, and other countries defined the values of their currencies in terms of dollars. In so doing, each country automatically established a fixed parity with respect to the monetary unit of each other country as well as with gold. It is important to bear in mind that the analysis of international income transmission in the present chapter applies only to conditions of fixed exchange rates. The case for, and the implications of, flexible exchange rates will be examined in Chapter 17.

## 11-2
## INTERNATIONAL INCOME TRANSMISSION:
## DIRECT EFFECTS

In this section we propose to analyze the effects of international trade on national income. Initially, the model is assumed to be free of monetary complications or changes in the price level. Thus, for the moment, we treat investment as exogenous, and we are therefore essentially taking the fiscal policy model of Chapter 5 and adding exports and imports to it.

We begin with the preliminary task of extending the national income equi-

[1] International currency confusion has greatly enriched the vocabulary. Some governments have subscribed to the principle of freely fluctuating exchange rates but have not, in practice, been able to resist the temptation to enter the foreign exchange market in support of their currency. Such a situation has been termed a "dirty" float as opposed, presumably, to a "clean" float.

librium condition. In the closed economy, equilibrium obtains when output $Y$ equals aggregate expenditure $C + I + G$. Thus we have

$$Y = C + I + G$$

and since $Y - C = S + T$ we obtain the familiar condition

$$I + G = S + T$$

In the open economy, imports $Z$ add to the supply of available goods and services, whereas exports $X$ add to the demands on these resources. Consequently, equilibrium now implies

$$Y + Z = C + I + G + X$$

However, in line with the accounting framework of Part 1 it is customary to transfer imports to the right-hand side of the expression so that

$$Y = C + I + G + (X - Z)$$

The difference between exports and imports $(X - Z)$ is sometimes referred to as the "trade balance," sometimes as the "surplus on current account," and sometimes as "net exports."

A positive level of net exports is an addition to national income in the same way as a positive level of inventory investment.[1] Since it must still be true that income is in equilibrium when injections equal leakages, we can write the equilibrium condition as

$$I + G + X = S + T + Z$$

Exports, like investment and government purchases, represent injections into the domestic income stream; imports, like saving and taxes, represent leakages.

Now that we have introduced trade into our model, we require some hypothesis that explains variations in exports and imports. When disposable income and consumption rise, part of the increase in consumption is in the form of imports. Moreover, as income rises, the importation of materials for use in the production of domestic goods also rises. Consequently, we have the hypothesis that the level of imports is a function of the level of income. In linear form we could write

$$Z = u + vY$$

where the parameter $v$ is known as the "marginal propensity to import."

By similar reasoning it would appear that the level of exports is a function of the level of income abroad. Thus domestic income becomes, in part, a function of foreign income; foreign income, in turn, is partly determined by

[1] The analogy between inventory investment and a positive trade balance is particularly appropriate since both represent discrepancies between national output and national expenditure. If inventory investment is positive, the nation's production is in excess of purchases by users of final goods and services. Similarly, if exports exceed imports, the nation produces more than it uses.

domestic income. Models can be constructed, and equilibrium solutions derived, in which the equilibrium income levels at home and abroad become functions of exogenous spending in *both* countries, and multipliers could be calculated that measure the effect of a change in exogenous spending in either country on the income levels of both countries. We shall present such a model in the appendix to this chapter. However, a basic understanding of the factors involved can be obtained just as easily by ignoring the effect of a foreign income change on exports and instead treating exports as exogenous. The model, thus simplified, has often been called the "small-country model" because it implies that the import changes of the country are so small relative to the income level of the rest of the world that they have a negligible effect on the incomes and imports of the rest of the world. Consequently, the exports of the small country would not, subsequently, be affected by its own income changes.

In Figure 11–1 the small-country model is illustrated. Taxes and government purchases are ignored so that injections consist of investment and exports and leakages consist of saving and imports. The equilibrium condition therefore is

$$I + X = S + Z$$

The saving function is plotted as the $S$ curve. Imports are plotted as the $Z$ schedule and are assumed to be proportional to the level of income. The slope of the $Z$ curve is the marginal propensity to import. Total leakages are shown by the $S + Z$ schedule which is a vertical summation of the $S$ and $Z$ curves. The slope of this total leakage function is the sum of the marginal propensity to save $1 - b$ and the marginal propensity to import $v$. Exports and investment are both assumed to be exogenous. Only the export $X$ and the export plus investment $I + X$ schedules are shown in the diagram. Investment can be read as the vertical distance between $X$ and $I + X$.

In this example, total injections equal total leakages at income level $Y_0$. For convenience, the example is constructed in such a way that at this initial equilibrium investment equals saving; exports therefore equal imports, so that net exports equal zero.

Now let us suppose that the injections schedule shifts up because of an increase in intended investment. This new schedule is the $I + X + \Delta I$ schedule. It intersects the $S + Z$ schedule at income level $Y_1$ which, accordingly, is the new equilibrium level of income. The change in income induces a change in saving equal to the marginal propensity to save times the change in income, and it also induces an increase in imports equal to the marginal propensity to import times the change in income, so that total leakages increase by $(1 - b)\Delta Y + v\Delta Y = (1 - b + v)\Delta Y$. Since this increase in leakages must equal the increase in injections, we have

$$\Delta I = (1 - b + v)\Delta Y$$

from which it immediately follows that the multiplier is

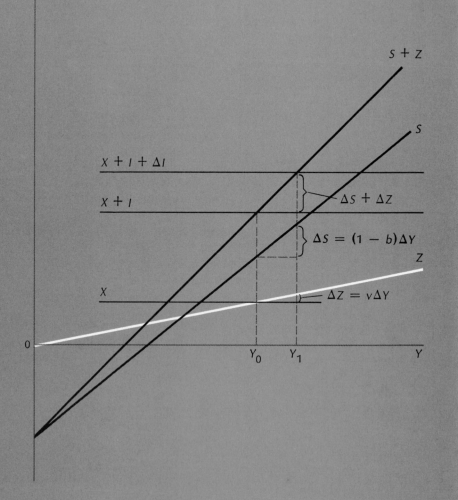

$$\frac{\Delta Y}{\Delta I} = \frac{1}{1 - b + v}$$

If we compare this formula with the formula $1/(1 - b)$ of the closed economy of Chapter 4, we see that the effect of foreign trade is to lower the value of the multiplier. Imports, like saving, are leakages that divert a fraction of additional disposable income away from domestic spending. Although an increase in disposable income of one dollar raises consumption by $b$ dollars, only $b - v$ dollars enter the domestic spending stream.

Now let us see what has happened to the balance of trade. Exports are exogenous and fixed, but imports have increased by $v\Delta Y$. Consequently, we see that net exports have fallen, and we therefore conclude that income expansion brought about by a rise in domestic spending tends to produce a deficit in the trade balance. If foreigners will not extend credit and accept only their own currency (or gold) in payment for the excess of their exports over their imports, our small country will have to dip into its "reserves" of foreign exchange and/or gold to pay for its deficit. If the supply of these resources is limited, the country may have to think twice about the desirability of pursuing policies designed to expand the domestic economy.

Next let us imagine that an equivalent increase in aggregate demand occurs but that it is the result of a change in foreign tastes that causes the export demand schedule to shift up to $X + \Delta X$. Figure 11–2 illustrates this situation. The income change is the same, but this time the export function shifts up. The multiplier, clearly, must be the same as before, namely

$$\frac{\Delta Y}{\Delta X} = \frac{1}{1 - b + v}$$

but the effect on the trade balance will be different. From the equilibrium condition $I + X = S + Z$ we can infer that the change in equilibrium quantities implies that

$$\Delta X_e = \Delta S_i + \Delta Z_i \tag{11-1}$$

where the subscripts $e$ and $i$ stand for exogenous and induced, respectively. The exogenous increase in the small country's exports causes income to rise. This then induces an increase in both its level of saving and its level of imports. Because the sum of these two changes must equal the exogenous change in exports, it must be the case that $\Delta X_e - \Delta Z_i$ will be positive. Consequently, the country will enjoy a trade surplus along with the increase in income. Only in the case where the marginal propensity to save is zero, so that

**FIGURE 11–1**
The effect of an exogenous increase in
investment on the level of income and the
trade balance (all values in real terms)

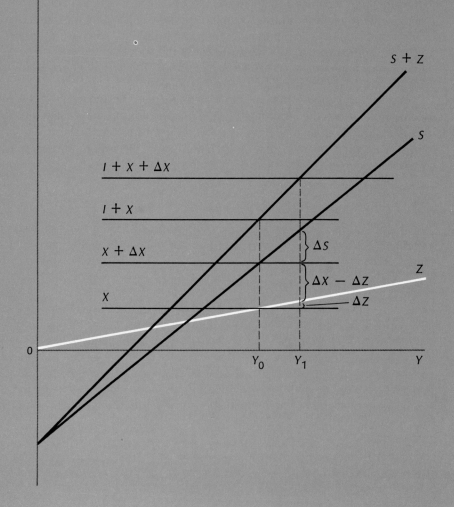

$\Delta S_i$ is zero, is there no improvement in the trade balance. In this case the multiplier reduces to $1/v$ because equilibrium cannot be restored until leakages rise by enough to offset the initial increase in exports completely.

The small-country model is a special case. Nevertheless, the results remain essentially valid when we permit exports to be a function of foreign income. We can, moreover, develop these results without a complicated model by reasoning with our equilibrium conditions. Consider two countries A and B, and imagine that consumer tastes in A shift from domestic to foreign goods. Income in A will fall, and there will therefore be some subsequent induced reduction in imports. Meanwhile, income in B rises, and this induces an increase in its imports (A's exports); so that on both counts A's initial deficit will tend to be offset. Is it, however, possible for this offset to be complete?

If we continue to assume the absence of a government sector and if we again hold investment constant, an autonomous increase in exports of country B of $\Delta X_e$ due to a change in tastes in country A will produce three induced effects in country B. First, the increase in income in B will cause imports to rise by some amount $\Delta Z_i$; second, the increase in income will cause saving to increase by some amount $\Delta S_i$; and third, the fall in income in A due to the original diversion of expenditures from domestic to foreign production will cause a fall in A's imports, and therefore in B's exports, by some quantity $\Delta X_i$. If income in country B is to reach a new equilibrium, the change in injections must equal the change in leakages. Consequently, for country B we can write

$$\Delta X_e - \Delta X_i - \Delta Z_i = \Delta S_i \tag{11-2}$$

where the subscripts $e$ and $i$ again stand for exogenous and induced, respectively.

The left side of the equation is the change in the trade balance which must equal the change in saving. Moreover, since B's export surplus must equal A's import surplus, it follows that saving in A must change by an equal amount, though in the opposite direction, as saving in B.

It is evident that if B's trade balance is not to exhibit any net change, the initial increase in its exports must be exactly offset by the induced increase in its imports and by the induced decrease in exports. Consequently, complete offset for B requires that the change in its level of saving be zero. This could occur either because the level of income in B does not change or because the marginal propensity to save in B is zero.

If the level of income in B does not change, B's imports also will not change. Therefore for country B, Eq. (11-2) reduces to

$$\Delta X_e - \Delta X_i = 0$$

**FIGURE 11-2**
The effect of an exogenous increase in exports on the level of income and the trade balance (all values in real terms)

However, if this happens, then from A's point of view the induced decreases in imports must exactly equal the initial exogenous change in imports. The only way this can occur is if income in A falls sufficiently to reduce A's imports by the amount of the original increase. This means that the marginal propensity to save in A must be zero.

On the other hand, if complete offset in B's trade balance is achieved because the marginal propensity to save in B is zero, the increase in B's income that results from the exogenous increase in its exports must induce an equal increase in its imports from A. In this case Eq. (11–2) becomes

$$\Delta X_e - \Delta Z_i = 0$$

From A's point of view there will be no income change. The expected reduction in its domestic income because of the increase in imports fails to materialize because it is offset by the induced increase in its exports.

In summary: Complete offset in the trade balance can occur only if one of the two countries has a marginal propensity to save equal to zero. In this unlikely event the whole burden of domestic income adjustment will be borne by the country with the zero marginal propensity to save. However, because the marginal propensities to save cannot in general be expected to equal zero, we can conclude that direct income effects will not yield complete adjustment of the trade balance. The country that receives the initial exogenous increase in exports will enjoy an increase in income and an improvement in its trade balance, while the opposite will be the case in the other country.[1]

To parallel the analysis of the small-country case, we wish also to examine the effects of an exogenous increase in internal spending in one of the countries. Therefore, let us assume that the investment demand schedule shifts up in country A. A's income rises and since this increases its imports, B's income also rises. Thus both countries enjoy an increase in income in response to a net increase (as opposed to a transfer) in aggregate demand. The increase in B's income raises its imports, and this helps to moderate the size of A's deficit. However, again adjustment cannot be complete.

As far as country B is concerned, all changes are induced. Its exports increase because A's income increases, and its saving and import levels change as a result of the change in its own income. Thus for country B the changes in equilibrium magnitudes imply

$$\Delta X_i - \Delta Z_i = \Delta S_i \qquad\qquad (11\text{–}3)$$

With positive marginal propensities to save in both countries, it must be the case that B's equilibrium income level rises, that its saving level increases, and that it enjoys an improvement in its trade balance. Had the increase in exports been exactly matched by an induced increase in imports, the level of

---

[1] We should remind readers that these results are given explicit quantitative form in the appendix to this chapter at the end of the book. Those readers who find algebraic treatment instructive may find it useful to examine this appendix before continuing with the text.

income would not have changed, and imports would therefore have remained constant. This, as Eq. (11–3) makes clear, is impossible as long as there is a positive increase in exports. We therefore conclude that the increase in investment in A must, provided this raises A's imports, lead to income expansion in B along with an increase in B's trade surplus. With respect to country A our conclusion is the same as before. Its income expansion, which was brought about by an upward shift in its investment demand schedule, causes its trade balance to deteriorate.

Notice, finally, that for country A the equilibrium condition implies that

$$\Delta I_e - \Delta S_i = \Delta Z_i - \Delta X_i$$

Since we already know that the change in imports exceeds the change in exports, the increase in investment must exceed the magnitude of the increase in saving. This difference between the increase in investment and saving in country A must then exactly equal the increase in saving in country B.

To summarize: Direct income effects will not produce complete offset to exogenous shocks that disturb the trade balance, and there will therefore remain some change in net exports. There are, however, other mechanisms involving monetary flows and price level changes that operate to bring about overall balance of payments equilibrium. In the next section we shall examine these mechanisms.

## 11–3
## MONETARY AND PRICE LEVEL ADJUSTMENTS
## AND THE BALANCE OF PAYMENTS

It is important, at the outset, to be clear about the distinction between the balance of trade and the overall balance of payments. If country A has an excess of exports over imports, its net exports are positive; this is equivalent to saying that it has a trade surplus or a positive trade balance. If nothing else happened, it would experience a net accumulation of the money of country B. If A then converts these currencies into its own money by exchanging currencies at B's central bank, B will find its reserves of foreign exchange dwindling and it will then regard itself as suffering a deficit in its balance of payments. On the other hand, if the accumulation of foreign currencies that results from the positive net exports is voluntarily used by A's citizens to purchase securities in country B, there will be no problem for B's central bank. In that event B has a deficit in its balance of trade, but its overall balance of payments will be in equilibrium, because the trade deficit is offset by a surplus on capital account.

The stage is now set for analysis of balance of payments adjustment within the context of the open economy. Since we will be concerned with monetary effects and with changes in the price level, the IS-LM and aggregate demand-supply diagrams will again be of considerable value. Figure 11–3 shows a single IS curve together with three separate LM curves. Notice that the figure also contains a new function in the form of the positively sloped curve,

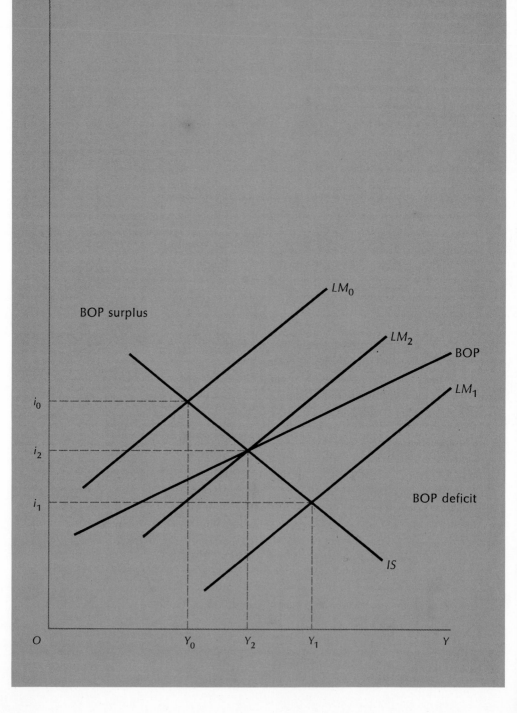

labeled BOP, that traces the combinations of income and interest rate that keep the balance of payments in equilibrium. It is important that we have a clear understanding of this function, and so let us take a careful look at it.

The balance of payments surplus BOP equals the level of net exports plus the surplus on capital account. Accordingly, we may write

$$\text{BOP} = X - Z + K \qquad\qquad (11\text{--}4)$$

where $X$ and $Z$ stand for exports and imports, respectively, and $K$ is the net inflow of capital (including government transfers). Equilibrium in the balance of payments requires that BOP equal zero since otherwise the money supply will be changing. Thus, if equilibrium in the balance of payments is to be attained, positive net exports must be offset by an equivalent net capital outflow, whereas if imports exceed exports there must be an offsetting capital inflow.

Now consider the individual components of the balance of payments. In the small-country case we treated the real value of exports as exogenous since exports depend on developments abroad. However, we should also recognize that if the domestic price level in country A falls relative to foreign price levels, A's domestic goods will gain a competitive edge in foreign markets and exports will therefore increase. Also, if country A raises the official price at which it buys and sells foreign currency in exchange for its own currency, this *devaluation* of its own currency vis-à-vis other currencies will stimulate exports. This is because foreigners will have to give up a smaller quantity of their own currency to purchase a given amount of A's currency, which, in effect, cheapens A's goods to foreign buyers. These considerations suggest that we might write the export function for a small country as

$$X = X(p,\pi)$$

where $p$ is the domestic price level, and $\pi$ is the exchange rate, defined as the price of foreign currency in terms of the domestic currency. A rise in the domestic price level will reduce exports, whereas a rise in the exchange rate will stimulate exports.

In a similar vein, the import function is now written

$$Z = Z(Y,p,\pi)$$

where $Z$, the real value of imports, is assumed to be an increasing function of domestic income and the price level, and a decreasing function of the exchange rate. Clearly if A's price level rises, foreign goods become more at-

**FIGURE 11–3**
Automatic balance of payments adjustment
through international money flows and
changes in real income (all values in real
terms)

tractive so that imports will be stimulated. Similarly, if A's citizens have to give up more domestic money in exchange for foreign money, this has the effect of raising the price of foreign goods to consumers in A, and the tendency, therefore, will be to reduce imports and to substitute domestic goods in their place.

We come, finally, to the capital account. This account reflects so-called exogenous factors such as government aid and various other forms of unilateral transfers; it also reflects the flow of private capital in response to investment opportunities. Thus, not surprisingly, economists often write the net capital inflow as an increasing function of the rate of interest

$$K = K(i)$$

to reflect the hypothesis that if interest rates in country A rise relative to interest rates elsewhere, this interest rate differential will make it profitable for wealth holders elsewhere to cash in their domestic securities and to transfer funds to country A where security prices are lower and yields are higher.

We can now pull all these strands together by substituting the previous three expressions into Eq. (11–4). Upon doing this the BOP equation becomes

$$BOP = X(p,\pi) - Z(Y,p,\pi) + K(i) \tag{11–5}$$

where it is understood that the surplus in the balance of payments will increase if the price level falls, if the exchange rate rises, if the level of income falls, and, finally, if the rate of interest rises.

The *IS* curve is next in line for consideration. The product market equilibrium condition in the open economy is

$$I + G + X = S + T + Z$$

When we gather together the various behavioral relationships from past discussion and substitute them into the equilibrium condition, we get the equation for the *IS* curve:

$$I(i) + G + X(p,\pi) = Y - C(Y - T) + Z(Y,p,\pi) \tag{11–6}$$

Investment is represented by the standard function $I = I(i)$, the level of saving plus taxes is equal to $Y - C(Y - T)$ as shown in Chapter 8, and the export and import functions are as developed in this chapter. As long as the price level and the exchange rate are fixed, Eq. (11–6) implies a straightforward negatively sloped *IS* curve. A rise in income raises the leakages due to saving, taxes, and imports, so that in order to maintain equilibrium the rate of interest must fall to generate additional investment. A rise in the price level would shift the *IS* schedule to the left. This is because imports would rise, while exports would fall, thereby simultaneously causing a given level of income to be associated with higher leakages (imports) and lower injections (exports). The same level of income could, however, be sustained if these changes are compensated by a greater level of investment which implies that the interest rate must be lower.

Let us utilize Figure 11–3 to analyze the simple case in which both the exchange rate and the price level remain fixed. This means that both of these variables can be ignored and the BOP equation may therefore be conveniently reduced to

$$BOP = X - Z(Y) + K(i) \tag{11-7}$$

Under these conditions exports again become exogenous and imports respond only to changes in real income. Balance of payments equilibrium requires that $BOP = 0$. If this condition is imposed on Eq. (11–7) and the resulting equation in the two variables $i$ and $Y$ is plotted, we get a BOP function such as the one shown in Figure 11–3. The function traces the combinations of interest rate and income level that maintain equilibrium in the balance of payments.

The BOP curve will normally have a positive slope. If the balance of payments is in equilibrium and income rises, this will increase imports and therefore reduce the level of net exports. However, this could be offset by a rise in the rate of interest which, because it causes capital to be attracted from abroad, compensates for the fall in net exports by increasing the net inflow of capital. It is very important to understand that any point below the BOP curve implies a deficit in the balance of payments, whereas any point above the curve implies a surplus. For example, if the combination $i_2$ and $Y_2$ in Figure 11–3 implies equilibrium in the balance of payments, then $i_1$ and $Y_1$ must surely imply a deficit, since the lower rate of interest implies a lower net capital inflow, whereas the higher income level implies a higher level of imports and therefore a lower level of net exports.

If the initial $LM$ curve in Figure 11–3 is $LM_0$, the levels of income and rate of interest will initially be $Y_0$ and $i_0$, respectively. This situation, however, will not persist because it is above the BOP curve and therefore implies the presence of a surplus in the balance of payments. Since this causes the nominal money supply to increase as the monetary authority accumulates foreign exchange, the $LM$ curve will shift to the right, and the level of income then expands as the rate of interest falls. Both the rise in the level of income and the fall in the rate of interest reduce the balance of payments surplus, so that the economy tends to come to rest at $Y_2$ and $i_2$, where the $LM_2$ curve cuts the $IS$ and BOP curves at their point of intersection. At that point the balance of payments is in equilibrium, and there is no further tendency for the money supply to change.

Alternatively, if the economy is initially at $Y_1$ and $i_1$, as defined by the intersection of $IS$ with $LM_1$, the combination implies a balance of payments deficit. Balance of payments disequilibrium tends again, however, to be self-correcting. The deficit causes the money supply to shrink as the monetary authority sells foreign exchange. This shifts the $LM$ curve to the left, so that equilibrium once again tends to be established at income level $Y_2$ and interest rate $i_2$.

These considerations show that the balance of payments tends to equilibrate automatically even when the competitive position of one country vis-à-vis others is not permitted to change either because of rigidities in the wage-price structure or because exchange rates remain pegged. Under the circumstances, the variables that have to give way are the levels of income and employment. Thus this simple model shows quite clearly why many economists believe that constant rates of international currency exchange are bought at a potentially heavy cost.

Equilibrium in the balance of payments in Figure 11–3 is at $Y_2$ and $i_2$, but full employment may imply income level $Y_1$. The tendency for the LM curve always to be shifted to the left by the balance of payments deficit could be counteracted by expansionary monetary policy in such a way that the opposing forces keep the LM curve at $LM_1$. But this would perpetuate the deficit, and the country would soon find its reserves of foreign exchange and gold running out.

The IS curve could be made to intersect BOP at $Y_1$ by an expansionary fiscal policy. If the LM curve adjusts to intersect the two functions at the same point, balance of payments equilibrium and full employment would then be attained simultaneously. This advantage of fiscal policy derives from the fact (emphasized in Chapter 8) that expansionary fiscal policy tends to raise the rate of interest as it raises the level of income. While the rise in the level of income reduces net exports, the rise in the rate of interest produces an inflow of capital. It is therefore possible, by means of expansionary fiscal policy, to effect a higher level of income and balance of payments equilibrium simultaneously. Expansionary monetary policy could not accomplish this. The trouble is that expansionary monetary policy lowers the rate of interest and raises the level of income; it therefore causes both net exports and the net inflow of capital to decline.

Although we have not drawn the new functions into Figure 11–3, the reader can easily imagine a new IS curve cutting BOP at income $Y_1$. If the initial LM curve is $LM_1$, it can be shifted up to where it cuts the new IS and BOP curves at $Y_1$, either automatically because at $i_1$ and $Y_1$ the deficit shrinks the money supply, or by conscious restrictive monetary policy which can shift the LM curve to the left and eliminate the deficit immediately. Evidently, then, expansionary fiscal policy, combined with a reduction in the money supply, seems to be an appropriate way to deal with an initial situation in which the full-employment level of income is associated with a deficit in the balance of payments (as at $Y_1$, $i_1$).

The foregoing is one example, of which there are more to come, of how the mix of policy can be changed in a way that helps to reconcile different economic targets. We will pursue this fascinating subject of optimal policy mix in Part 4. Meanwhile, we must complete the analysis of automatic balance of payments adjustment. Accordingly, we now adopt the classical assumption of competitive markets and wage-price flexibility. As shown in the previous chapter, these assumptions imply equilibrium at full employment and a vertical aggregate supply function.

Consider Figure 11–4. The $IS_0$, $LM_0$, and $BOP_0$ curves all intersect at $i_0$, $Y_0$ so that the goods and money markets and the balance of payments are all momentarily in equilibrium. The trouble with the situation is that, at the existing price level $p_0$, aggregate demand falls short of aggregate supply, and income level $Y_0$ is therefore below the full-employment level $Y^*$. The situation quite clearly implies that the labor market is in a state of excess supply. Under present assumptions this means that the money wage rate will fall and that, via the argument of the previous chapter, the price level must also fall.

The fall in the price level now affects all three functions in the upper half of Figure 11–4. Whereas the $IS$ curve was independent of the price level in our previous example, this is no longer the case because of the dependence of exports and imports on the price level. A fall in the price level raises net exports, and this shifts the $IS$ curve to the right.

Similarly, the BOP curve, which was stationary in the example of Figure 11–3 because the price level was held constant, now also shifts to the right. Note from the BOP equation (11–5) that at any arbitrary level of income the fall in the price level tends to increase net exports. If balance of payments equilibrium is to be maintained, this increase in net exports must be offset by a reduction in the net capital inflow; this implies that the rate of interest must decline. Or, to look at it another way, at any arbitrarily fixed rate of interest, there will be a fixed net inflow of capital. Equilibrium in the overall balance of payments therefore would require net exports to remain constant despite the fall in the price level. Therefore, since the fall in the price level tends to increase net exports, this would have to be offset by a higher level of income since that will raise the level of imports. No matter how one looks at it, therefore, the BOP curve shifts to the right when the price level falls, and it would, of course, shift to the left if the price level rises.

Finally, we know that a fall in the price level will increase the real value of the money supply, and this will shift the $LM$ curve to the right. As a consequence of these shifts, equilibrium will be established at the full-employment level of income $Y^*$. This is shown in the upper part of Figure 11–4, where $IS_1$, $LM_1$, and $BOP_1$ all intersect at income level $Y^*$ and interest rate $i_1$. Meanwhile, the lower part shows aggregate demand equaling aggregate supply at the new equilibrium price level $p_1$. In the new situation all markets are in equilibrium and there is no balance of payments deficit. The movement from $Y_0$ to $Y^*$ is accompanied by an increase in imports due to income expansion, but the fall in the price level tends to offset this by raising exports and lowering imports.

In comparing the two examples that we have discussed so far, we should note that automatic forces tend always to bring the balance of payments into equilibrium. However, rigidities in the wage-price structure may force this result to be obtained at the cost of fluctuations in income and employment. Wage-price flexibility, on the other hand, makes for compatibility between balance of payments equilibrium and full employment in the domestic economy.

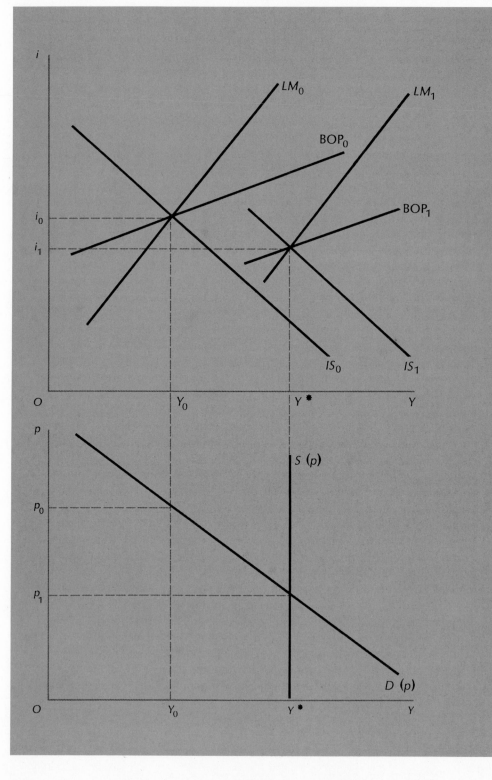

To make sure we understand these relationships, let us quickly consider another example. Consider Figure 11–5. The $IS_0$ and $LM_0$ curves intersect at the full-employment level of income, and aggregate demand intersects the vertical classical aggregate supply curve at price level $p_0$. The only problem, as indicated by the location of the $BOP_0$ curve, is that this situation is associated with a surplus in the balance of payments. The first consequence of this is that the nominal stock of money increases as the monetary authority purchases foreign exchange. This shifts both the $LM$ curve and the aggregate demand function to the right; since this implies excess demand at the existing price level, the money wage rate and the price level both rise. As this happens, the BOP curve shifts up while the $IS$ curve shifts down. The $LM$ curve, meanwhile, is torn between opposing forces, the surplus in the balance of payments tending to shift it to the right, and the rise in the price level tending to move it to the left. As a result of these several forces, the triangle labeled $abc$ formed by the original intersection of the three functions tends to collapse into a single point such as $d$, while the rise in the price level from $p_0$ to $p_1$ compensates for the upward shift in aggregate demand.

The new equilibrium implies the same level of real income as before, but the surplus in the balance of payments has been eliminated. This is because the higher price level has caused net exports to decline and because the decline in the rate of interest (compare the interest rate at point $b$ with $d$) lowers the net inflow of capital. The lower rate of interest also raises investment, and this offsets the domestic expenditure effect of the reduction in net exports.

To complete our discussion, let us consider how a change in the exchange rate might serve as a substitute for wage-price flexibility. The assumptions that underlie Figure 11–6 are similar to those of Figure 11–3. Wages and prices are rigid in the downward direction. The full-employment level of income is $Y^*$. However, at the intersection of $IS_0$ with $LM_1$, there is a deficit in the balance of payments. The BOP curve intersects $IS_0$ at $Y_0$. However, this income level is below full employment. This economy is therefore in somewhat of a quandary; if it favors a policy for full employment it will have a balance of payments deficit, whereas if it chooses balance of payments equilibrium it will have unemployment.

Earlier we saw that one way out of this dilemma was to change the monetary-fiscal mix. Another way out might be to devalue, that is, to raise the official price of foreign exchange. The rise in the price of foreign exchange will tend to raise net exports, for reasons explained earlier, and it will therefore shift the $IS$ curve to the right. Similarly, the BOP curve will shift to

**FIGURE 11–4**

Automatic movement to full employment in the open economy with wage-price flexibility (all values in real terms)

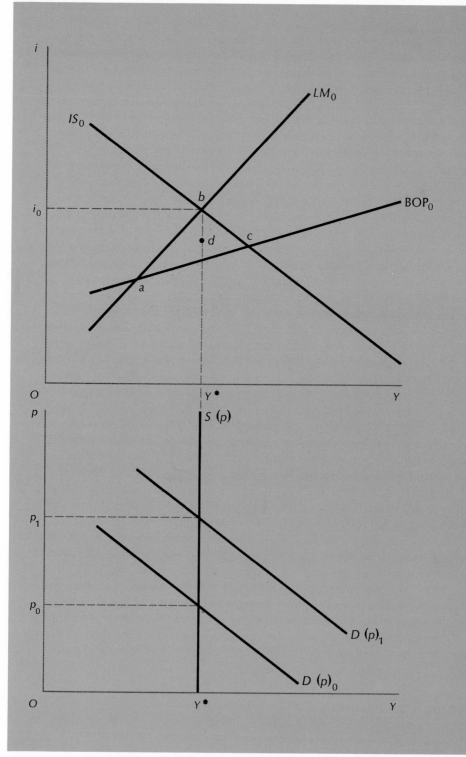

the right, so that in combination the new intersection of the *IS* and BOP functions will be closer to the income target of *Y*\*. Notice, therefore, that devaluation serves two ends. It makes the economy more competitive, thereby raising net exports, and by doing this adds to aggregate expenditure and raises the level of income. Note, however, that if the devaluation occurs when the economy is already at full employment, the increase in aggregate demand implied by the devaluation will raise the price level, and this will tend to counteract the effect of the devaluation on net exports.

## 11–4
## SUMMARY AND PROSPECTUS

In this chapter we opened the economy to international trade and examined the process of income transmission and balance of payments adjustment under fixed exchange rates. Exchange rates are pegged by governments through their policy of purchasing and selling foreign currencies in exchange for their own currency at a fixed "official" price. The consequence is that deficits in the balance of payments cause shrinkage of domestic money supplies, whereas surpluses cause expansion. These monetary movements produce effects that tend automatically to bring the balance of payments into equilibrium because a reduction in the money supply will tend to raise the rate of interest and to lower the level of income and the level of prices. These changes tend both to raise net exports and to raise the net inflow of capital, and they will therefore tend to eliminate a deficit in the balance of payments. If wages and prices are flexible, adjustment can be accomplished by movements in the price level without causing fluctuations in real income and employment. Rigidities in the cost-price structure, on the other hand, cause the adjustment in the balance of payments to be at the expense of the levels of income and employment. Between these extremes would be an aggregate supply function with a positive slope, such as the Keynesian case discussed in the previous chapter, and under these circumstances the adjustment process would involve some movement in both income and in the level of prices.

Modern governments are committed to full employment and, in theory at least, to price stability. They are, therefore, reluctant to permit the automatic adjustment mechanisms to operate. As a consequence of this reluctance, deficits and surpluses tend to continue. Often the policy responses that are designed to improve the balance of payments are destructive, as when countries raise tariffs and place quotas on imports, impose restrictions on who can and who cannot obtain foreign exchange, subsidize exports, and place discriminatory taxes on foreign investments. These policies are designed to

**FIGURE 11–5**
Elimination of a balance of payments surplus
by a rise in the price level (all values in real
terms)

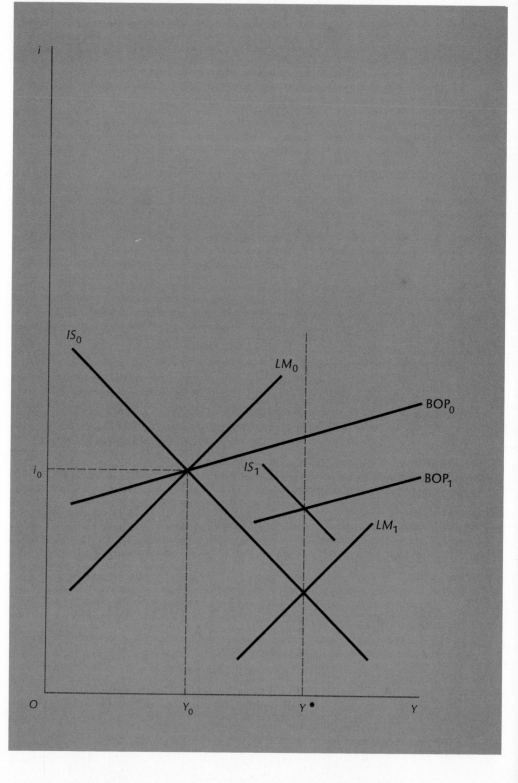

produce a surplus in the balance of payments. However, they misallocate resources and since they invite retaliation, they tend to be self-defeating.

Reconciling the internal goal of full employment at stable prices with the external goal of balance of payments equilibrium is a tall order—so tall, in fact, that we will devote another chapter to it in Part 4. Among the questions that we will raise are the following: When is it appropriate to use monetary and fiscal policies to deal with a balance of payments problem and when is it not? What is the appropriate monetary-fiscal mix for the simultaneous achievement of external and internal equilibrium? When is it appropriate to vary the exchange rate and when is it inappropriate? Under what circumstances must some change in the mix of policy be employed? How would flexible exchange rates alter the process of income transmission; and how would monetary and fiscal policies affect the variables of the system under flexible exchange rates as compared with fixed exchange rates? How, finally, would these results change by varying the responsiveness of capital movements to changes in the rate of interest?

FIGURE 11–6
Devaluation of the exchange rate raises net
exports and increases the level of income
(all values in real terms)

# 3

# GROWTH AND FLUCTUATIONS IN ECONOMIC ACTIVITY

# 12

# INTRODUCTION TO MACROECONOMIC DYNAMICS

## INTRODUCTION

In this part of the book we will take up various so-called dynamic problems, including such topics as economic growth, systematic fluctuations in business activity, and the problem of steady inflation of the price level. The conventional understanding of a dynamic problem is that it explicitly involves the behavior of economic variables over time. However, as a method of analysis, economic dynamics is the study of how the economic system behaves when it is out of equilibrium. The present chapter introduces the subject of economic dynamics by focusing on the very important methodology of "stability analysis."

Except for the multiplier process of Chapter 4, the models of Part 2 are "comparative static" models. The solutions to the equation systems of such models define equilibrium values for the variables. Beginning with a point of equilibrium, a shift in one of the functions due to a change in the money supply or government expenditures causes the equations to give a new equilibrium point as a solution. The models did not make explicit the process by which the variables of the system move to the new equilibrium. We did, to be sure, discuss the process of adjustment from one equilibrium to the next, but the various adjustment processes were in no way implied by the equations themselves. The models would have been truly dynamic only if the equations had specified explicitly how the variables would behave when the system is out of equilibrium.

If we were reasonably sure that an increase in the money supply would lower the rate of interest and raise the level of income to a new equilibrium level, as implied by the models of Part 2, and if we were not particularly concerned about how long it took to get to the new equilibrium point, there would be no pressing reason to complicate our comparative static models by specifying exactly how adjustments to disequilibrium take place. Unfortunately, however, we cannot always be sure that the equilibrium solutions predicted by comparative static models will be correct. The equilibria may be "unstable"; i.e., if the variables of the system happen to be at the equilibrium point, they will tend to stay there. But should the equilibrium be disrupted by some disturbance, a progressive divergence from, rather than a movement toward, the equilibrium point will occur. Thus the comparative static solutions may be erroneous. For example, although an increase in the money supply leads our models of Part 2 to predict a rise in income and a fall in the rate of interest, this may not occur. The changes may, in fact, move in a direction opposite to that predicted by the static model.

As a starting point for our discussion of dynamics, let us set forth the following fundamental proposition: It is frequently impossible to determine the effect of a shift of the *IS*, the *LM*, or any other function for that matter, in a comparative static model without examining the underlying dynamic process of adjustment. This proposition, developed by P. A. Samuelson[1] and called the "correspondence principle," is the subject of the analysis of this chapter.

## 12-2
### DYNAMIC ADJUSTMENT AND THE *IS-LM* MODEL
Throughout Part 2 we assumed that the investment demand equation was $I = I(i)$. However, in Chapter 6 we took note of the fact that it might be reasonable to write

$$I = I(i,Y)$$

The inclusion of the level of income as an independent variable in the investment demand equation does not at first seem like much of a change. But, as

[1] P. A. Samuelson, *Foundations of Economic Analysis*, Chap. 9, Harvard University Press, Cambridge, Mass., 1947, especially pp. 276–283.

**FIGURE 12-1**
Product market equilibrium with investment
a function of the level of income (all values
in real terms)

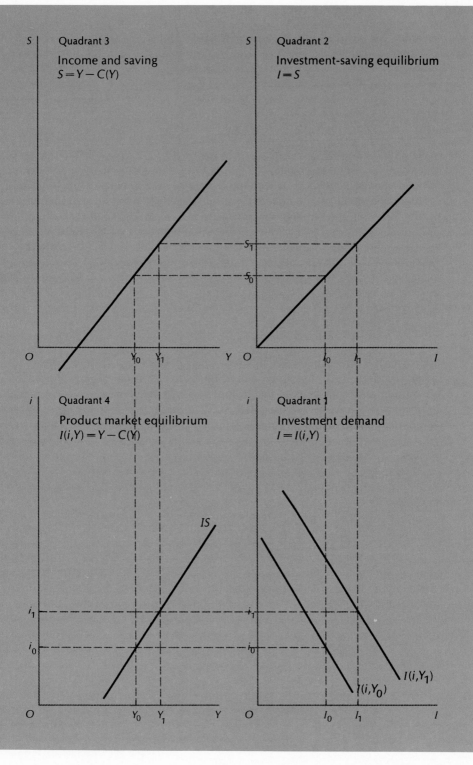

we shall see, it introduces some formidable and intriguing new problems.

With the new investment demand function the equation for the *IS* schedule becomes

$$I(i,Y) = Y - C(Y) \tag{12-1}$$

The first thing we must notice is that the *IS* schedule is no longer necessarily negatively sloped. Recall from Chapter 6 that with the new investment demand equation there will be a whole family of investment demand curves in quadrant 1. Thus in Figure 12–1 income $Y_0$ is associated with investment demand schedule $I(i,Y_0)$. Consequently, interest rate $i_0$ equates intended investment and saving at income level $Y_0$. Similarly, when the level of income is $Y_1$, the relevant investment demand schedule is $I(i,Y_1)$, so that by tracing around the four quadrants, we observe that interest rate $i_1$ gives product market equilibrium.

In the present example the *IS* schedule has a positive slope, although the slope may also be negative. If we define $h$ as the "marginal propensity to invest," i.e., the increase in investment that is induced by a $1 increase in income, the *IS* curve will have a positive slope if $h$ is greater than the marginal propensity to save and a negative slope if the reverse is the case. Let us see why this is so.

When investment increases to a new level, the level of income rises until saving has risen by an amount equal to the increase in investment. But given our present assumption about investment demand, the increase in income induces further increases in investment. If the marginal propensity to invest is greater than the marginal propensity to save, saving cannot rise fast enough to balance intended investment with saving. The level of income would therefore tend to keep rising indefinitely, and product market equilibrium would never be attained. However, equilibrium can be restored if the rate of interest rises and reduces intended investment. Consequently, when the marginal propensity to invest exceeds the marginal propensity to save, product market equilibrium implies that as the level of income rises, the rate of interest must also rise.

Let us now consider how the system adjusts to disequilibrium in this more general model. In Figure 12–2 the *IS-LM* curves are represented with their conventional shapes. We assume that the initial equilibrium is at $i_0$ and $Y_0$ and that the equilibrium is disturbed by a shift to the right of the *LM* curve.

We wish now to trace the process of adjustment to the new equilibrium point $(Y_1,i_1)$. To do this, we need to introduce some dynamic assumptions about how the system behaves when it is out of equilibrium. Accordingly, let us assume that the rate of interest adjusts instantaneously to monetary distur-

**FIGURE 12–2**
Dynamic adjustment: case 1, stable equilibrium (all values in real terms)

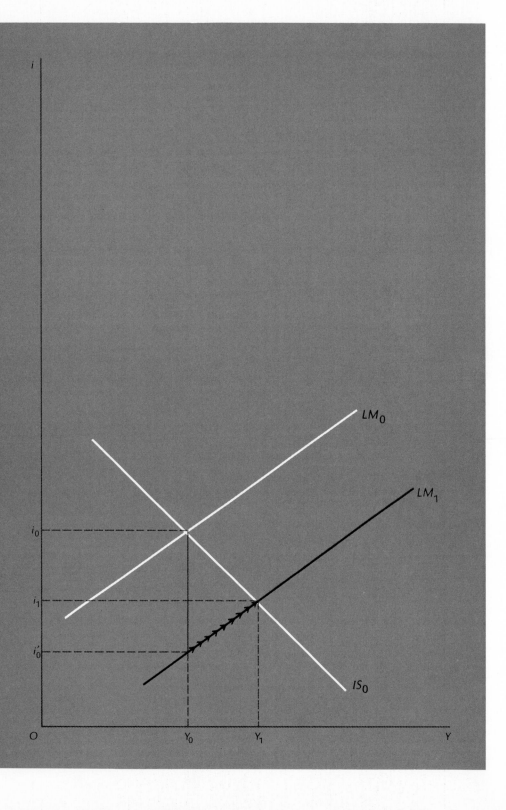

bances and that the speed of adjustment in the product market is equal to the difference between investment and saving (that is to say, the difference between aggregate demand and what is currently being produced). The assumption of instantaneous money market adjustment allows us to trace the path of income and the interest rate along the *LM* curve from which, by our assumption, we can never depart.

Referring again to Figure 12–2, we see that the shift in the *LM* curve together with our assumption about interest rate adjustments implies that the interest rate falls immediately to $i'_0$. But at $i'_0$ with income level $Y_0$ intended investment exceeds saving. Consequently, income begins to rise. As the level of income rises, the quantity of money demanded for transactions purposes increases so that the interest rate also begins to rise. The adjustment now continues upward (following the arrows) along the *LM* curve until $Y_1$ and $i_1$ are reached. At this point intended investment again equals saving, and equilibrium is restored.

Suppose next that the *IS* curve has a positive slope, as shown in Figure 12–3. The shift in the *LM* curve causes the interest rate to fall immediately to $i'_0$. This again means that intended investment exceeds saving and that income must therefore rise. But the rise in income stimulates further investment because of our assumption that investment is a function of the level of profits and income. Consequently, the original monetary disturbance causes income to rise; this causes additional investment to be induced, and this, in turn, causes income to rise still further.

Will income continue to rise indefinitely, or will a new equilibrium point be found? In the present case the rise in income causes the interest rate to rise and to dampen investment more rapidly than the rise in income stimulates further investment. In other words the rate of interest that keeps the money market in equilibrium rises more rapidly than the rate of interest that keeps the product market in equilibrium. Consequently, a new stable equilibrium point will be reached at $Y_1$ and $i_1$. The path of adjustment again follows the arrows upward along the *LM* curve.

Finally, consider the third case shown in Figure 12–4. This differs from the second case in that the *IS* curve is now assumed to have a steeper slope than the *LM* curve. If we knew nothing about the adjustment process, we would assume that the shift in the *LM* curve to $LM_1$ would cause the equilibrium level of income to fall to $Y_1$ and the rate of interest to fall to $i_1$. A fall in income in response to an increase in the money supply does not seem to be a very sensible result; yet that is what the comparative static model predicts. It is the dynamics that will disclose what the problem is.

As before, the shift in the *LM* curve causes the interest rate to fall immedi-

**FIGURE 12–3**
Dynamic adjustment: case 2, stable
equilibrium (all values in real terms)

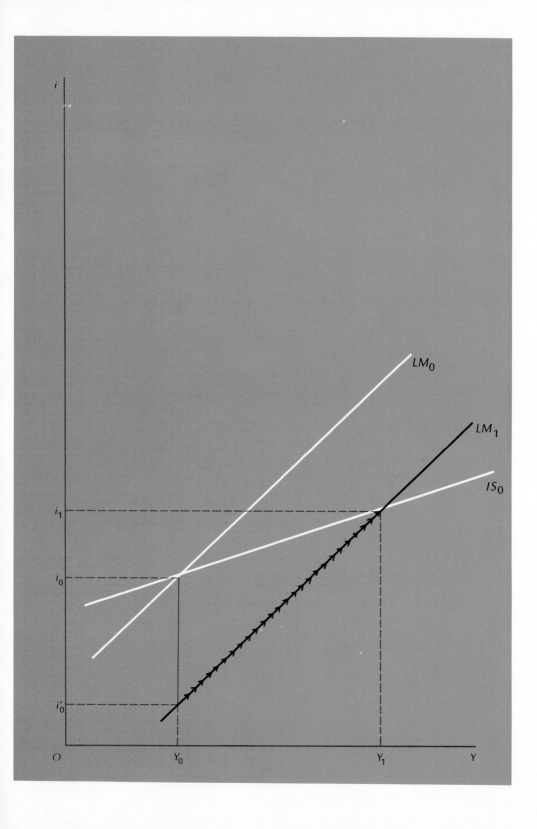

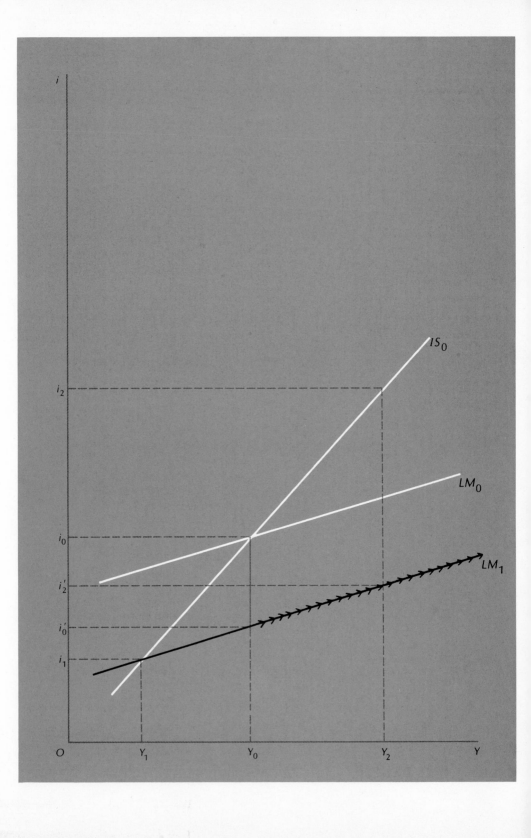

ately to $i_0'$. Consequently, investment exceeds saving, and, contrary to what the static model predicts, income, instead of moving down to $Y_1$, rises. The rise in income causes additional investment to be induced. In the previous case the rise in income eventually caused the transactions demand and therefore the interest rate to rise fast enough to keep income from expanding indefinitely. But in this case the actual interest rate (along the *LM* curve) rises less rapidly than it would have to rise (along the *IS* curve) in order to bring intended investment into equilibrium with saving. Thus at $Y_2$, for example, the interest rate that equates saving and investment $i_2$ is in excess of the rate of interest that gives monetary equilibrium $i_2'$ by more than at lower income levels. Income therefore continues to rise and at an increasingly rapid rate.

In the case just considered the system is said to be "unstable," and the intersection points of the *IS* and *LM* curves are said to be "unstable equilibrium" points. As long as we assumed that the *IS* curve was negatively sloped, we did not have to worry about this problem. Indeed, even a positively sloped *IS* curve produced an unstable system only when the slope of the *IS* curve was greater than the slope of the *LM* curve.

## 12–3
## IMPLICATIONS OF THE ANALYSIS
In this chapter we have attempted to introduce the reader to stability analysis. Such analysis is conducted by introducing explicit assumptions about how the system behaves when it is out of equilibrium. This permits stable equilibrium solutions to be distinguished from unstable solutions and thereby provides a means of verifying the correctness of comparative static results. Stability analysis ruled out the comparative static result of Figure 12–4, where the *IS* curve has a larger positive slope than the *LM* curve, and this provided the important result that if an increase in the money supply changes income at all, the change in income must be positive. Thus, by permitting the analyst to rule out unstable cases, the direction in which a change in a policy variable changes other variables in the system can be ascertained. Unfortunately this does not hold true for all variables. Thus, in the example of this chapter the equilibrium rate of interest could either rise or fall under stable conditions.

The reader should attempt to verify similar propositions by repeating the analysis, using other policy changes. This should show, for example, that in a stable system a rise in government purchases cannot lower the rate of interest or the level of income. However, it could raise the level of investment if the expansionary effect on investment of higher income is not overcome by the crowding-out effect of the higher rate of interest.

**FIGURE 12–4**
Dynamic adjustment: case 3, unstable
equilibrium (all values in real terms)

# 13
# FUNDAMENTALS OF GROWTH ECONOMICS

## INTRODUCTION

During the discussion of the targets of economic activity in Chapter 1 we referred to the concept of "potential" or "full-employment" output, and we noted that potential output grows over time. In the models of Part 2 we abstracted from the concept of potential output, but we did make progress in pinning the concept down by relating it to labor market equilibrium in the classical sense. Abstracting from growth seems reasonable enough when dealing with short-run problems. It is not, for example, too damaging to short-run analysis to assume that the increase in the productive capacity of the economy that results from net investment in one year is so small that it can safely be ignored. But the cumulative effects of continued net investment over a longer period of time cannot be ignored, nor can the growth of productivity. The labor demand function will shift to the right over time for both of these reasons. Similarly, population growth produces an excess of entrants into the labor market over those who retire from it, and the supply curve of labor therefore also shifts to the right. If the demand curve shifts to the right faster than the supply curve, the real wage rate and per capita income will tend to rise. It is fair to say that growth economics mainly concerns itself with ensuring that the demand for labor grows more rapidly than its supply.

The static models of Part 2 failed to bring out the fact that investment has a dual character. Although investment expenditures are a component of aggregate demand, they are made for the purpose of increasing productive capacity. This means that they expand the potential supply of output at the same time as they increase current income from the demand side. Thus a positive level of net investment means that the supply of output is capable of continued increase over time, and full utilization of this capacity will necessitate continued increases in aggregate expenditure in the future. In addition, if, as seems to be the case, the absolute volume of full-employment saving increases over time, increasing absolute amounts of investment must be forthcoming in every year if full-employment saving is to be balanced by an equivalent amount of investment expenditure. But as the absolute flow of investment increases every year, the capital stock of the economy increases by larger and larger amounts; this means that income must increase by larger and larger amounts to maintain full employment.

Productive capacity not only grows as a result of net investment expenditure but also becomes more efficient as the result of technical progress. By technical progress we mean improvements in the efficiency of the stock of capital that result from technological and organizational changes, and improvements in the quality of the labor force that result from improved education, training, and health. As a consequence of technical progress the productivity of capital and labor has been increasing, and this, to a large extent, is what has permitted citizens of those countries that have not suffered from excessive population growth to enjoy a rising standard of living.

The purpose of this chapter is to explore the consequences of the dual character of investment and the effects of technical progress and population growth. We begin our study of this topic with an extension of the simple Keynesian model in which the dual character of investment is highlighted but in which there is assumed to be no technical progress and in which the labor force is assumed to grow at the same rate as the capital stock. Given these assumptions, the rate of growth of income that utilizes existing capacity will also provide full employment for the growing labor force.

## 13–2
## CAPITAL EXPANSION AND THE MAINTENANCE OF FULL-CAPACITY OUTPUT[1]

For the purpose of illustrating the ingredients of the growth process, we assume in this section that the level of output which the economy is capable of producing is proportional to the stock of capital. We therefore postulate the production function

$$Y = \sigma K$$

---

[1] The simple model presented here follows the approach of E. Domar, "Capital Expansion, Rate of Growth and Employment," *Econometrica*, 14:137–147, 1946. A similar earlier approach is that of R. F. Harrod, "An Essay in Dynamic Theory," *Economic Journal*, 49:14–33, 1939. See also W. J. Baumol, *Economic Dynamics*, The Macmillan Company, New York, 1951.

where the term $\sigma$ is known as the "capital coefficient." If $\sigma$ had a value of 0.25, $4 worth of capital stock would be required to produce an annual flow of output of $1.

To simplify matters, we also assume that there is no government economic activity and that there is no foreign trade. Finally, we assume as a long-run matter that consumption is proportional to the level of income. These assumptions imply that equilibrium income obtains when

$$I = S$$

and that the consumption function may be represented by

$$C = bY$$

Now let us consider a numerical example in which the value of the capital coefficient is assumed to be 1.0, and the value of the marginal propensity to consume is 0.5. The situation is illustrated in Figure 13–1 where it is assumed that the initial full-employment level of income is $100 billion. At this income level the level of consumption is $50 billion. Consequently, if full employment is to be achieved, the level of intended investment must be $50 billion.

Assuming that this required $50 billion of investment spending is actually forthcoming, there will be a net addition to the stock of capital of $50 billion. If our assumption that the capital coefficient has a value of 1.0 holds, it implies that in the next year the full-employment level of output will be $150 billion. Thus, as can be seen in Figure 13–1, the level of consumption will be $75 billion, and therefore investment must now rise to $75 billion if full employment is to be maintained. Assuming again that the required amount of investment is actually forthcoming, the full-employment output potential of the economy rises by $75 billion to $225 billion. At this income level, consumption is $112.5 billion, and the required level of investment is $112.5 billion.

In this example the level of investment that maintains full employment rises in successive periods from $50 billion, to $75 billion, to $112.5 billion. The period-by-period rate of growth is therefore 50 percent. This rate of growth exactly equals the product of the capital coefficient and the marginal propensity to save; that is,

$$\sigma(1 - b) = 1.0(0.5) = 0.5$$

That this should be the case is no accident. Let us see why.

If full employment is to be maintained over successive periods, the increase in total spending from one period to the next must exactly equal the increase in the full-employment supply of output. The increase in total spending is the increase in investment times the multiplier. Consequently, from the demand side we have

$$\Delta Y = \frac{\Delta I}{1 - b}$$

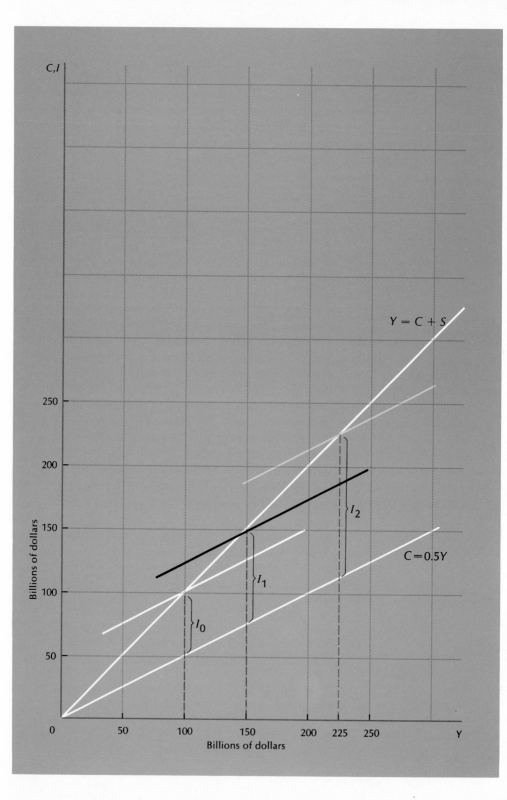

as the increase in total spending. From the production function we see that the increase in the supply of output will be

$$\Delta Y = \sigma \, \Delta K$$

However, the change in the stock of capital is the level of net investment. Consequently, we may replace the foregoing expression by

$$\Delta Y = \sigma I$$

When we equate this increment to supply with the increment to demand, we obtain

$$\frac{\Delta I}{1 - b} = \sigma I$$

and when we rearrange this expression, we find that the percentage rate of growth that keeps the growth in demand and supply in balance is

$$\frac{\Delta I}{I} = \sigma(1 - b)$$

This model, which economists call the "Domar model," suggests that if we want the economy to grow more rapidly, we can attempt to make capital more productive (raise the value of $\sigma$) and/or increase the proportion of income that is saved. An increase in the productivity of capital implies that the output of the economy must increase at a faster rate than before because each dollar that is invested increases the full-employment level of output by more output than before. Consequently, the rate of growth of aggregate expenditure that is necessary to maintain full employment must rise. Similarly, if at every level of income more is saved than previously, more will have to be invested. Therefore in each period more is added to the capital stock than before, so that total spending must rise more rapidly if full employment is to be maintained.

This simple model teaches an important lesson. It is not sufficient if we wish to maintain full employment for the level of investment to remain constant. A constant level of investment implies a constant period-by-period level of total spending. However, as long as there is any net investment at all, the capital stock and therefore full-employment output will be growing. And this fact implies, finally, that investment must grow if total spending is to keep up with the ability of the system to produce. A constant level of investment would therefore imply a progressive divergence between the actual level of income and the full-employment level. The economy must, as the Red Queen in *Through the Looking Glass* would say, run faster all the time just to remain standing still.

**FIGURE 13–1**
The growth process (all values in real terms)

## 13–3
## THE RAZOR'S EDGE

The type of model that we considered in the preceding section has been called a "razor-edge" model because of its precarious balance and volatile behavior when there is a slight deviation from the required rate of growth. The economy appears to teeter, as if prepared to shoot off either into hyperinflation or into deep depression at any moment. While this circumstance suggests less about the real world than about the oversimplified nature of the model, it nevertheless brings to our attention the important fact that overinvestment will lead to capital scarcity, whereas underinvestment will lead to excess capacity. Apparently, if entrepreneurs invest too much, it will look as if they have invested too little; if they invest too little, it will appear as if they have invested too much.

Figure 13–1 helps to clear up these paradoxes. Initially, full-employment income is $100 billion, and the level of investment that is required for full employment is therefore $50 billion. Now suppose that businesses underinvest in period 0; that is, instead of investing $50 billion, they invest only $40 billion. As a result of this insufficient investment, the equilibrium level of income will be $80 billion instead of $100 billion. Thus there will be excess capacity of $20 billion because income is below the potential of period 0. In addition, the positive net investment of $40 billion in period 0 adds another $40 billion to potential output. Consequently, at the start of period 1 entrepreneurs will discover that there is substantial excess capacity, so that investment will be further reduced, if indeed it does not collapse entirely. Underinvestment therefore leads to excess capacity. Had businesses invested $50 billion instead of only $40 billion, they would have found that the demand for goods and services was just sufficient to employ all productive resources.

Suppose, on the other hand, that the rate of growth of expenditures exceeds the required rate. In this case the volume of investment goods demanded by business will exceed the supply of such goods released by saving. In the face of underproduction in the previous period, businesses will attempt to produce more in the current period. But the increased output of the current period will induce larger investment plans in the next period, causing further underproduction. Thus the attempt to increase output too rapidly leads to renewed attempts to expand more rapidly and to continued underproduction. In Figure 13–1, if the level of intended investment in period 0 is $60 billion, aggregate demand is in excess of what can be supplied. Prices are thus bid up, and businesses are moved to increase their investment spending even further in day 1, that is, far in excess of the required amount of $75 billion, in order to attempt to make up the gap between the demand for goods and their productive capacity. It is, however, these very attempts to catch up that widen the gap.

## 13–4
## NEOCLASSICAL GROWTH ECONOMICS

Given its preoccupation with unemployment, economic thinking of the 1930s concentrated almost exclusively on labor as a factor of production. Conversely, the early post–World War II growth theorists pushed the pendulum to the opposite extreme and concentrated on the role of capital in the growth process. More recently economists have tried to develop an integrated view that combines the effects of labor force growth, capital growth, and improved technology in explaining economic growth. Many very interesting questions have been raised. If output per capita tends to grow at a particular rate in a full-employment economy, what is the magnitude of that growth rate, and what are its determinants? What fraction of growth is due to the fact that each worker has more capital with which to work? What fraction is due to the fact that the capital is improved? And, finally, what fraction is due to the fact that labor itself might be becoming more productive as standards of health, education, and training improve?

The body of analysis that attempts to answer these questions is known as "neoclassical growth economics."[1] Typically, the neoclassical theorist assumes that full-employment saving is automatically invested. He then attempts to analyze the properties of the full-employment growth path by making various assumptions about the rate of technical change, the rate of growth of the labor supply, and the possibility of technical substitution between the factors of production. Neoclassical theory has destroyed the simple elegance of the Domar model because it suggests that the capital coefficient cannot be treated as a parameter and that it is, instead, a variable that depends upon such factors as the rate of technical change and the relative supplies of capital and labor inputs.

Much of the analysis of neoclassical theory is quite complicated, and it relies heavily on mathematics. Its essential ingredients can, however, be illustrated if we follow the early literature and assume that the production potential of the economy can be represented by what is called the "Cobb-Douglas" production function

$$Y = AK^a N^{1-a} \tag{13–1}$$

where the exponent $a$ is a positive fraction. The full-employment level of output in this formulation is a function of the quantity of capital $K$, the supply

[1] We cannot cite all the relevant literature on the subject here. The interested reader should, however, take a look at some of the fundamental contributions of Robert M. Solow, "A Contribution to the Theory of Economic Growth," *Quarterly Journal of Economics*, 70:65–94, 1956, and "Technical Change and the Aggregate Production Function," *Review of Economics and Statistics*, 39:312–320, 1957; and Edmund Phelps, "The Golden Rule of Accumulation: A Fable for Growthmen," *American Economic Review*, 51:638–643, 1961, and "The New View of Investment: A Neo-classical Analysis," *Quarterly Journal of Economics*, 76:548–567, 1962. A simple outline of neoclassical theory that, however, relies heavily on mathematics is provided in T. F. Dernburg and J. Dernburg, *Macroeconomic Analysis*, Chaps. 10–11, Addison-Wesley Publishing Company, Inc., Reading, Mass., 1969.

of labor $N$, and of a scale factor $A$ which we can assume grows at a steady rate and at any one time represents the level of technology. The following assumptions are implied by the Cobb-Douglas formulation:

**1**   The production function is homogeneous of degree one. This means that if both $K$ and $N$ increase by some proportion, output will increase in the same proportion.

**2**   Production is subject to diminishing returns. This means that if the quantity of one factor is held constant, increases in the quantity of the other factor will yield positive, though successively smaller, increments to output.

**3**   The exponent $a$ is the fraction of income that accrues to capital, and it also equals the elasticity of output with respect to changes in the capital stock. Similarly, $1 - a$ is labor's relative share of the national income, and it also equals the elasticity of output with respect to changes in labor input.

**4**   Technical change is "neutral." This means that technical change (growth in the index $A$) will raise the marginal product of both factors in the same proportion and that the marginal rate of substitution (the ratio of the marginal products) will therefore be constant.[1]

---

[1] A little bit of mathematics permits all these propositions to be confirmed. First, multiply $K$ and $N$ by a constant $u$. Thus, we have

$$A(uK)^a(uN)^{1-a} = AK^aN^{1-a}u = uY$$

which shows that the production function is homogeneous of degree one. To calculate the marginal products of capital and labor we take the partial derivatives of $Y$ with respect to $K$ and $N$, respectively. This gives

$$\frac{\partial Y}{\partial K} = a\frac{Y}{K} \qquad \frac{\partial Y}{\partial N} = (1-a)\frac{Y}{N}$$

and shows that the marginal products decline as the ratios of output to capital and output to labor diminish. In competitive equilibrium the marginal product of labor equals the real wage, and the marginal product of capital equals the rate of interest. Thus if we wish to calculate the absolute shares of income that accrue to the respective factors of production, we need merely multiply both sides of the preceding expressions by $K$ and $N$, respectively, to obtain

$$K\frac{\partial Y}{\partial K} = aY \qquad N\frac{\partial Y}{\partial N} = (1-a)Y$$

Next, if we wish to calculate the fraction of income accruing to the respective factors, we divide both sides of the expressions by $Y$ to obtain

$$\frac{K}{Y}\frac{\partial Y}{\partial K} = a \qquad \frac{N}{Y}\frac{\partial Y}{\partial N} = 1-a$$

and we therefore say that $a$ and $1 - a$ represent the "relative shares" of capital and labor, respectively. Note that the left side of each equation is an elasticity, that is, a ratio of two percentage changes. Thus $a$ is the capital elasticity of output, and $1 - a$ is the labor elasticity of output.
    Calculating the ratios of the marginal products we obtain

$$\frac{\partial Y/\partial K}{\partial Y/\partial N} = \frac{a}{1-a}\frac{N}{K}$$

which shows that the marginal rate of substitution is a function of the ratio of labor to capital and is independent of technical change. Thus in the Cobb-Douglas case technical change raises the marginal product of both factors proportionately.

When we rearrange the production function to read

$$Y = A \left(\frac{N}{K}\right)^{1-a} K$$

and compare this with Domar's

$$Y = \sigma K$$

we see that the capital coefficient may be expressed as

$$\sigma = A \left(\frac{N}{K}\right)^{1-a} \tag{13-2}$$

and it is therefore immediately evident that the capital coefficient will rise with an improvement in technology and with a rise in the labor-capital ratio.

Let us now use the production function to calculate the rate of growth of potential output. The calculation involves some simple mathematics that is shown in the accompanying footnote.[1] The result is

$$G_y = G_t + aG_k + (1 - a)G_n \tag{13-3}$$

where $G_y$, $G_t$, $G_k$, and $G_n$ are the percentage rates of growth of output, technical change, the stock of capital, and the supply of labor, respectively. Thus the rate of growth of potential output increases as the rate of technical progress, the rate of capital growth, and the rate of growth of the labor force increase.

Now consider the requirements for steady growth at a constant percentage rate in the very long run. Such an equilibrium or "golden age" growth path requires that output, investment, and the stock of capital all grow at the same rate. Since investment is a component of income, it would have to grow at exactly the same rate as income so as not to become an ever-increasing or decreasing fraction of income. Moreover, since investment represents the growth of the capital stock, it follows that the capital stock must also grow at

---

[1] Differentiation of the Cobb-Douglas function with respect to time yields

$$\frac{dY}{dt} = K^a N^{1-a} \frac{dA}{dt} + aAK^{a-1}N^{1-a} \frac{dK}{dt} + (1 - a)AK^a N^{-a} \frac{dN}{dt}$$

When both sides of this expression are divided by Y, we get the percentage rate of growth

$$\frac{1}{Y}\frac{dY}{dt} = \frac{1}{A}\frac{dA}{dt} + a\frac{1}{K}\frac{dK}{dt} + (1 - a)\frac{1}{N}\frac{dN}{dt}$$

The shorthand notation of the text results from letting

$$G_y = \frac{1}{Y}\frac{dY}{dt}$$

$$G_t = \frac{1}{A}\frac{dA}{dt}$$

$$G_k = \frac{1}{K}\frac{dK}{dt}$$

$$G_n = \frac{1}{N}\frac{dN}{dt}$$

this very same rate.[1] Consequently, if there is a constant long-run equilibrium rate of growth, it must be such that $G_y = G_k$. If this is the case, Eq. (13–3) reduces to

$$G_y = \frac{G_t}{1 - a} + G_n \qquad (13\text{–}4)$$

and we therefore see that the long-run equilibrium rate of growth is a function of the rate of technical progress and of the rate of growth of the labor supply.

Several important conclusions emerge from this result. First, growth in per capita output is not possible in the absence of technical progress. Notice that if $G_t = 0$, Eq. (13–4) reduces to

$$G_y = G_n$$

and since the rate of growth of per capita output is $G_y - G_n$, per capita output will not grow at all. In this case, aggregate output grows at a rate that is equal to, and determined by, the rate of growth of labor supply.

Second, observe that the long-run rate of growth is not a function of the fraction of income that is saved. This surprising result, which is in conflict with the Domar model, arises from the presence of diminishing returns in the neoclassical model. If the fraction of income saved increases, the required amount of investment increases, and the stock of capital and the level of income initially grow more rapidly. However, as can be seen from Eq. (13–2), this implies that the labor-capital ratio falls, and therefore the increased relative supply of capital causes the capital coefficient to fall. Therefore, each dollar of investment adds less to potential output, so that the growth rate tends to diminish and to return to its initial level. We see from Eq. (13–2) that in the extreme case where $G_t$ is assumed to be zero any decrease in the ratio of $N/K$ brought about by an increase in saving immediately reduces the capital coefficient and the rate of growth. Consequently, although the Domar result that the rate of growth is $\sigma(1 - b)$ may be correct, it is not very interesting since any increase in the saving rate is eventually offset by an equivalent decline in the capital coefficient.

---

[1] If output, capital, and investment all grow at constant rates in the long run, their time paths can be described by the equations

$$Y = Y_0 e^{yt} \qquad I = I_0 e^{it} \qquad K = K_0 e^{kt}$$

where $y$, $i$, and $k$ are the respective growth rates. Since investment equals the growth of capital, we have

$$\frac{dK}{dt} = k K_0 e^{kt} = I_0 e^{it} = I$$

which holds for all values of $t$ only if $k = i$. Similarly, since saving equals investment, we may write

$$S = (1 - b)Y = (1 - b)Y_0 e^{yt} = I_0 e^{it} = I$$

where $1 - b$ is the saving rate. Again, this equation holds for all values of $t$ only if $y = i$. Thus the growth of investment, capital, and output must all proceed at the same rate.

Theories of growth such as the Domar model suggest that the well-being of the future is limited only by the willingness of the present generation to save. By forgoing present consumption, society can raise the growth rate and thereby enjoy a higher level of both consumption and saving in the future. Neoclassical theory, however, suggests that this proposition is false. The growth rate cannot be permanently raised by an increase in the fraction of income that is saved and invested because of the presence of diminishing returns to capital.

Although the equilibrium rate of growth cannot be affected by a change in the fraction of income saved, the saving rate is an important determinant of the level of per capita consumption that society may enjoy. This fact can be illustrated by considering the effect of some extreme assumptions about saving behavior. A society that saves and invests nothing at all will have no capital stock and therefore no output or consumption. At the opposite extreme, a society that is so frugal that it saves all its output will have a large stock of capital and a large level of output, and yet it too will have no consumption. These extreme examples suggest that somewhere in the middle there must be some optimum saving rate that maximizes per capita consumption. As is shown in the appendix, the optimum saving rate is that rate which causes society to save and invest its competitive profits and to consume its labor income. Thus per capita consumption is maximized over time if

$$a = 1 - b$$

where again $1 - b$ is the fraction of income saved.

Let us make sure that we understand the nature of this "golden rule of accumulation." If we could raise the growth rate by saving more, per capita consumption would eventually be higher even though a higher fraction of income is saved. However, neoclassical theory shows that it is the level of output for all time rather than its rate of growth that is associated with a particular saving rate. The optimum saving rate is that rate at which the reduction in per capita consumption due to the next dollar of saving is exactly offset by the increase in per capita consumption which the higher output makes possible.

The model of growth that we have discussed here has been criticized on the ground that it assumes that technical change is entirely "organizational" or "disembodied." In other words, technical change proceeds at a uniform rate and is not affected by the quantity of investment that takes place. It ought to be recognized, however, that most technological improvements enter the productive process by being embodied in new machinery and equipment. As Phelps has shown,[1] the assumption of embodied technical change does not affect the fundamental conclusions of neoclassical growth economics. If society A saves and invests a larger fraction of its output than society B, its stock of capital will be younger and more productive. However, this does not mean

[1] Phelps, "The New View of Investment: A Neo-classical Analysis," op. cit.

that the stock of capital is growing more rapidly. Society A will enjoy a higher level of output than B, but the economy will not grow any more rapidly unless its rates of embodied and disembodied technical change are greater.

Although the treatment of technical change does not affect the basic conclusions of neoclassical analysis, there are important issues for which this question is critical. One such issue involves the empirical measurement of the relative contributions to the growth process of the various sources of growth. In conjunction with this issue is the question of the relationship between alternative economic policies and the growth rate in both the short and the long run. It is to some of these questions that we now turn.

## 13–5
## THE SOURCES OF ECONOMIC GROWTH

The theoretical investigations of the growth paths of developed economies have been accompanied by a series of studies of the statistical record of past economic growth. These studies have attempted to identify the sources of economic growth by disentangling the observed interrelationships between such variables as output, labor force, the stock of capital, and the rate of technical progress. The purpose of the effort is to assign relative weights to the importance of the various factors that serve as inputs to the growth process. For example, in our growth rate equation of the preceding section, Eq. (13–2), we need to obtain empirical estimates of the values of the capital elasticity of output and the rate of technical change if we are to assess the relative importance of capital, labor, and technical change in determining the rate of growth of output.

One approach to the empirical testing of hypotheses about the process of growth has been through the fitting of aggregate production functions, such as the Cobb-Douglas function, to historical data. This approach is most closely associated with the name of Robert Solow.[1] Unfortunately, the results obtained through this "production function" approach are extremely sensitive to changes in the assumptions regarding the nature of technical change in the economy. The issue is whether technical change should be assumed to be organizational (disembodied) and therefore independent of the quantity of capital or whether it should be assumed to be embodied in new capital. What this amounts to is attempting to decide whether the index A in Eq. (13–1) should be allowed to grow independently of the growth of the capital stock or whether it should be thought of as being associated with (embodied in) the growth of the capital stock.

When technical change is assumed to be disembodied, as in the simple Cobb-Douglas case of the preceding section, fitting a production function to American data for the period 1929–1961 yields an estimate of the rate of

[1] R. M. Solow, "Technical Change and the Aggregate Production Function," op. cit., and "Technical Progress, Capital, Formation, and Economic Growth," *American Economic Review*, 52:76–86, 1962. The latter article serves as the basis for much of the present discussion.

technical change of 2.5 percent per year, an elasticity of output with respect to capital of 0.11, and an elasticity of output with respect to labor of 0.89.[1] Using these values in the growth rate equation, Eq. (13–3), gives

$$G_y = 2.5 + 0.11G_k + 0.89G_n$$

This is a very peculiar looking result. It suggests that a 1 percent increase in the rate of growth of capital will lead to only a 0.1 percent increase in the rate of growth of output in the short run,[2] but that a 1 percent increase in the rate of labor force growth will raise the growth rate of output by 0.9 percent. Thus this formulation assigns very little weight to capital accumulation, and it suggests that policies which affect saving and investment are of very little importance in influencing the rate of growth.

The foregoing conclusion is suspect. What appears to be wrong is that this formulation of the problem fails to allow for the fact that an acceleration in the rate of investment brings with it an acceleration in the rate at which the efficiency of the capital stock increases. Thus technical change should be assumed to be embodied in new investment.

In an alternative model Solow examines the effect of assuming that all technical change is embodied in new capital. To reconstruct his model in this manner, the capital stock data are adjusted to make present additions to the capital stock more productive than earlier additions. This is done by adjusting each "vintage" of capital for depreciation and by multiplying the surviving capital of each vintage by an improvement factor that grows steadily over time. The resulting sum of the adjusted vintages of capital then represents a measure of the "effective" stock of capital. When a production function was fitted to these adjusted data for the period 1929–1961, Solow obtained an elasticity of output with respect to the stock of capital of 0.51. Thus this "new view of investment" suggests a much more important role for capital in the growth process. Evidently, if technical change is disembodied, an increase in the rate of capital growth will have little effect on the growth of output. But if the benefits of advancing technology accrue to the system by being embodied in new capital, a larger contribution of the rate of growth of output can be realized by raising the rate of capital accumulation.

Even though the results of the second hypothesis seem more plausible on both intuitive and empirical grounds, Solow's tests of statistical significance failed to yield a clear-cut choice between them. Since the theories assume full employment and that factors of production are paid their marginal products, but actual data are derived from historical experience that does not conform to these conditions, it is hardly surprising that statistical tests often fail to be conclusive.

---

[1] By the assumption of constant returns to scale, the sum of the elasticities is constrained to equal 1.0.

[2] Although $G_y$ and $G_k$ must be equal under conditions of long-run equilibrium growth, an acceleration of capital growth will nevertheless raise the rate of growth of output in the short run.

Solow's assumptions were extreme: In one case all technical change is disembodied; in the other it is entirely embodied. Some of each is not only possible but likely. Subsequent investigations have therefore varied assumptions in an effort to find the right combination. Thurow and Taylor, after testing a number of alternatives, came to the conclusion that the period 1929–1965 could best be represented by a model that allowed for a combination of disembodied technical change, embodied technical change, and successive improvements embodied in the quality of the labor force.[1] This latter factor represents an attempt to allow for improvements in the level of education and training and in the health of the labor force. As is perhaps not surprising, Thurow and Taylor arrived at results that were intermediate to Solow's extremes. Both forms of technical change were found to be important, and the elasticities of output with respect to the two inputs were found to lie between the values derived by Solow. Thurow and Taylor attempted 36 alternative formulations. However, their "preferred" model cannot be identified by means of the normal statistical tests of significance. The fitting of aggregate production functions of the type described above to historical statistics has unfortunately not yielded conclusive results.

A somewhat different approach to the problem of quantifying the sources of growth has been taken by Denison.[2] His procedure can be illustrated by means of a simple example. Assume as always that there are two factor inputs — labor and capital. Then consider a base period, preferably one of full employment, and construct an index of the stock of inputs by taking the number of the respective inputs and multiplying these by their relative contributions to production as measured by their relative share of income in the base period. If each factor is paid the value of its marginal product, the input index that uses income shares as weights will be an appropriate base since the number of inputs times the output per unit of input will exhaust the total product in the base period. As time passes, both output and inputs will grow; but if there is any improvement in the productivity of the inputs, output will grow more rapidly from the base year than the quantity of inputs. Moreover, whatever growth of total output is not accounted for by growth in inputs can be attributed to a growth in output per unit of input. Thus, if total real output rises 3 percent in one year and if the supply of inputs weighted in terms of their contribution to total product in the base year increases by 1 percent, then output per unit of input must have increased by 2 percent.

Denison's approach is actually quite similar to the production function approach. All inputs are lumped into one basket, and all output growth that is not accounted for by the growth of inputs is attributed to a residual term

---

[1] L. C. Thurow and L. D. Taylor, "The Interaction between the Actual and Potential Rate of Growth," *Review of Economics and Statistics*, 48:351–360, 1966.

[2] E. F. Denison, *The Sources of Economic Growth in the United States,* Supplementary Paper No. 13, Committee for Economic Development, New York, 1962.

**TABLE 13-1**
Allocation of the growth rate of total real national income among the sources of growth,
United States, 1929–1957 (percentage points in the growth rate)

| | | | |
|---|---|---|---|
| Real national income | | | 2.93 |
| Increase in total inputs | | | 2.00 |
| Labor, adjusted for quality | | 1.57 | |
| Employment and hours | 0.80 | | |
| Education | 0.67 | | |
| Other | 0.10 | | |
| Capital | | 0.43 | |
| Increases in output per unit of input | | | 0.93 |
| Advances in knowledge | | 0.58 | |
| Economies of scale | | 0.34 | |
| Other | | 0.01 | |

*Source:* E. F. Denison, *The Sources of Economic Growth in the United States,* Supplementary
Paper No. 13, Table 32, p. 266, Committee for Economic Development, New York, 1962.

called "productivity," which in Solow's terms would be the index of technical change. However, Denison's method makes it possible in principle to
break down the relative contributions to economic growth of the various
factors of production and, in particular, to separate out various components of
the residual.[1] Table 13–1 presents a summary of Denison's estimates. They
are derived from data for the American economy for the period 1929–1957.
The table apportions total growth of real national income among the various
contributors to that growth. These contributors are divided into two major
headings: growth in the quantity of inputs and growth in output per unit of
input.

The table shows that between 1929 and 1957 real national income of the
United States grew at an average annual rate of 2.93 percent. Of this total
2.00 percentage points were attributable to the growth of the labor force
(including changes in its quality) and to the growth of the capital stock. The
remaining 0.93 percentage point was attributable to increases in output per
unit of input. The table also shows that the labor component of total input
contributed 1.57 percentage points to the total growth rate. Within this component, contributions were made by expanding employment, while a reduction was due to declining hours of work per employee. Other contributions to
growth resulted from the expanding educational level of the work force and
from changes in its age/sex composition. Notice, finally, that Denison's table
distinguishes between "education" and "advances in knowledge." The contribution of education under the heading of labor refers only to the improve-

---

[1] This assumes that the inputs can be adequately measured. However, a measure of standard
labor input for the period 1929–1957 would have to be adjusted for changes in the proportion of
females in the work force, for changes in average hours worked, and for changes in the level of
education of the labor force.

ment in the labor input which resulted from increases in the quantity of formal education received by members of the labor force. The contribution of overall advances in knowledge, which may be thought of as technical change, is entered in the form of gains in output per unit of input.

One of the purposes of attempts to assign quantitative weights to the sources of growth is to provide a basis for prescribing policy alternatives designed to affect the growth rate. Denison's work, which separates out the contributions of a large number of variables, can be used to illustrate what he calls a "menu of choices available to increase the growth rate." The kinds of choices available can be broken down into two general categories: those that would provide a one-shot increase in growth and those that would permanently raise the rate of growth. Examples of the former are removal of barriers to resource mobility and, as we saw in the preceding section, a once-for-all increase in the fraction of income saved and invested. An example of the latter type of change is an increase in the rate of improvement of the quality of education.

In presenting his menu, Denison provided a series of measures that would have raised the average annual growth rate over the period 1960–1980 by 0.1 percentage point over what it would have been in the absence of the change. It was assumed that the changes were to be instituted in 1960, and the effects on the output of 1980 were then estimated. The incremental output was then translated into an average annual growth rate over the entire period. For example, the average annual growth rate would have been 0.1 percentage point higher if time lost from production as a result of sickness could have been reduced one-half. Similarly, Denison estimated that if no time were lost in labor-management disputes starting in 1960, the effect would have been to raise the growth rate by 0.1 percentage point per year.

Other examples of changes that would raise the growth rate by 0.1 percentage point per year are a work week one hour longer than otherwise and an increase in private net investment by about one-fourth. Policies that would raise the growth rate by less than 0.1 percentage point per year are elimination of barriers to free international trade (0.07 percentage point) and elimination of inefficiencies attributable to monopoly in private labor markets (0.03 percentage point). In all, Denison notes 31 components to his menu of policy alternatives that would have either a temporary or a permanent impact on the growth rate.

One of the most striking aspects of Denison's estimates is the relatively small impact that the various policies would have on the growth rate. Of the 31 possibilities on Denison's list, only 13 showed a maximum impact of 0.1 percentage point per year. Thus, influencing the growth rate by means of public policy is apt to be difficult. Possibly the most important contribution that macroeconomic policy can make toward rapid economic growth is to ensure that the economy does not suffer the retardation in its growth rate that occurs each time it sustains a recession.

**13–6**

## THE ROLE OF POPULATION

Population and labor force growth have played a passive role in the discussion thus far. This, indeed, is a characteristic of neoclassical theory. Denison, for example, begins his book with the sentence: "By 'economic growth' I shall refer to the increase in the national product, measured in constant dollars."[1] No mention is made of population growth presumably because it is assumed that the rate of growth of American real product will always exceed the rate of growth of population.

Most neoclassical models assume that population growth is exogenous and that it tends to grow at a constant percentage rate. Moreover, although the rate of population growth is a determinant of the rate of growth of total output in the long run, it has no influence on the rate of growth of per capita output. This can be seen from the long-run growth rate equation that we introduced earlier,

$$G_y = \frac{G_t}{1 - a} + G_n$$

If the rate of labor force growth increases by one percentage point, the rate of output growth increases by the same amount. However, the rate of growth of per capita output $G_y - G_n$ equals $G_t/(1 - a)$ and therefore depends only on the rate of technical change and on the capital elasticity of output.

Neoclassical theory is obviously deficient in a number of ways. It implicitly assumes that natural resources are unlimited in supply; it ignores the effect of growth on the environment; and it is irrelevant to large parts of the world where the size of the population is itself a function of the level of income. In view of these circumstances, it seems appropriate to supplement our discussion with some notes on the role of population. We do this with considerable reluctance since the subject is as controversial as it is vast. However, some of the major ideas that economists have had about the interrelationship between population growth and economic growth should be reviewed.

Attitudes concerning the desirability of rapid population growth have fluctuated with almost as much regularity as the ocean tides. The founder of modern economics, Adam Smith, viewed a growing population as a major and beneficial variable in the growth process.[2] A growing population makes possible through widening markets an increasing "division of labor" as each worker becomes more and more of a specialist. Further increases in labor productivity result from the fact that increasing specialization fosters increasing inventiveness and the finding of more efficient ways of doing jobs. Rising labor productivity and per capita income then induce further population

---

[1] Denison, op. cit., p. 3.

[2] Adam Smith, *An Enquiry into the Nature and Causes of the Wealth of Nations*, Modern Library, Inc., New York, 1937.

growth, and further specialization then induces additional gains in labor productivity.

Smith's theory assumed ever-increasing returns to labor. It contained little reference to capital in the growth process, and like the theories of most economists before Marx, it concentrated exclusively on the supply side of the process. Because he was unaware of the concept of diminishing returns, Smith was optimistic about the possibility that economic growth could become a cumulative process characterized by ever-rising per capita income.

Smith's optimism gave way to the pessimism of Robert Malthus and David Ricardo who regarded population growth as the evil that caused a steady decline in per capita income, leading ultimately to a "stationary state" in which no economic progress takes place.[1] According to Malthus, population tends to grow at a geometric rate, doubling every generation, as long as there is an available supply of food. Because of limitations on the supply of land, the food supply cannot, however, be increased at the same rate. Although capital accumulation could affect the race between the expanding population and the "means of subsistence" by increasing the rate at which output increases, the rate of capital accumulation tends to decline. This is because capital accumulation depends on profits, and these profits are in turn adversely affected by the growth of population. If a growing population is to be fed, argued Ricardo, progressively less fertile land must be taken into cultivation. If landowners are to be persuaded to bring this less efficient land into use, food prices must rise. As food prices rise, landowners who are fortunate enough to own fertile land earn a surplus called "rent," while the capitalist is obliged to pay higher wages. Thus as time passes the shares of the national income going to rent and wages rise, but the share of profits drops to zero. When profits disappear, net investment falls to zero, and economic growth ceases. Wages in this stationary state are at a subsistence level, and population growth comes to an end. The available food supply cannot sustain additional life.

In the Western world the gloomy prognosis of Malthus and Ricardo has not been realized. Despite the growth of population, advances in technology have held the specter of diminishing returns at bay. Nevertheless, there are vast areas in the world today where, unhappily, the Malthusian model is appropriate. Increases in output are matched by population growth, so that no headway is made in raising per capita income, and population is held in check by disease and famine. The fundamental distinction between the neoclassical and the Malthusian models is that in the former population growth is exogenous, whereas in the various examples of the latter, population is itself a function of the growth of output. This distinction may, in fact, be the most fundamental difference between the study of growth in industri-

---

[1] The writings of Malthus and Ricardo are summarized in any number of standard texts on the history of economic thought. Examples are F. A. Neff, *Economic Doctrines*, 2d ed., McGraw-Hill Book Company, New York, 1950; and R. Heilbroner, *The Worldly Philosophers*, Simon & Schuster, Inc., New York, 1953.

ally advanced countries and the study of the economic development of the poor countries.

The main concern of growth economics is to ensure that output grows faster than population. It should be added, however, that the rate of population growth may be important in determining the level of aggregate demand. This can be seen most clearly by considering the demand for housing. With a stationary population it would not be necessary to make any new additions to the stock of housing. Worn-out houses would have to be replaced, but the total number of houses would remain the same. It is only if population grows that net additions to the stock of housing become necessary.

The interrelation between population growth and aggregate demand was most strongly stressed in the writings of Alvin H. Hansen.[1] Writing during the depressed 1930s Hansen asked whether the depression was merely an unusual conjunction of cyclical troughs, or whether it signaled a period of secular stagnation for the American economy.

In the nineteenth and early part of the twentieth centuries the United States developed at an impressive rate. Population grew rapidly, while real output grew at an even faster rate, so that per capita product grew constantly. But as the twentieth century proceeded, the pace of development began to tail off. Looking for the cause of this slowdown, Hansen delineated four principal factors: a declining rate of population growth, the disappearance of the geographic frontier, the growth of the absolute volume of saving, and a tendency for new techniques of production to be capital-saving.

Hansen saw the expanding population of nineteenth-century America as one of the mainsprings of its growth. Expanding population and the settlement of new territory required tremendous investment expenditures for everything from houses and schools to railroads and utilities. However, as the rate of population growth declined because of a declining birth rate and rigid immigration restrictions and as the geographic frontier vanished, the investment outlets for America's ever-growing volume of saving declined. As we have seen, a slowly growing population does not need many new homes, and once the railroads and utilities are in place, the demand for investment goods is apt to decline. If, moreover, a capital-saving invention such as the airplane comes on the scene, distant points can be connected with far less capital outlay than would be necessary if the points were to be connected by a railroad.

The solution to the problem of economic stagnation resulting from deficient aggregate private demand was as Hansen saw it the expansion of public demand. During World War II the expansion of the public sector eliminated in eighteen months an unemployment problem that had plagued the economy for ten years. War and defense in the subsequent period have maintained a large role for the government sector, and increasing pressure for alleviation of social problems has perhaps ensured that the long-run expectation is for demand pressure upon available resources.

[1] A. H. Hansen, "Economic Progress and Declining Population Growth," *American Economic Review*, 21:1–15, 1939.

In the poor countries of Asia where population constantly presses against resources there is little hope for growth in living standards except through rigid population control.[1] Limiting population growth has not until recently come to be viewed as desirable or important in the United States. However, as evidence of resource depletion and ecological damage grows, an increasing number of critics has appeared who condemn economic growth and who call for rigid control of population growth in the United States. Economists, these critics argue, have grabbed the wrong end of the problem. Instead of worrying about how to maintain or increase the rate of growth of the supply of output, the real problem is how to reduce the rate of population growth so that the rate of growth of output can be lowered without lowering per capita income.

The United States is, to be sure, facing environmental problems of massive proportions. Moreover, although it has only 6 percent of the world's population, it uses up 50 percent of the natural resources consumed in the world each year. Thus there are those who feel we must stop ravaging the world's resources and fouling its environment and that this requires us to live with less growth of population and output. The recent evidence that population growth in the United States is slowing drastically is taken as a hopeful sign by those who subscribe to this view.

Economists are likely to be less optimistic. They will note that as long as productivity continues to grow, zero population growth (ZPG) will not bring with it zero economic growth (ZEG). They will note also that as the growth of population slows, the median age of the population will tend to increase, and more women will wish to work because they have fewer children to care for. Both factors make for a higher labor force participation rate. For a time, therefore, labor force growth may continue at a rate in excess of the rate of population growth.

Unfortunately, even if ZPG and ZEG do come to pass, there is no guarantee that they will solve the depletion and pollution problems. These developments would merely slow the rate at which our resources and environment are destroyed. They do nothing to avert or to reverse the process. The annual damage to the environment caused by economic activity depends primarily on the level of activity and only marginally upon its rate of growth. Constant population and output would merely mean that there will be no more abuse heaped on the environment this year than last. It will not reduce or eliminate pollution, nor will it eliminate depletion of natural resources. In the long run slower population growth will help to stretch out scarce resources, but in the short run it can have very little impact.

Elimination of pollution requires an active program of resource realloca-

---

[1] It is a great deal easier to talk about population control than to achieve it. The only old-age insurance available to poor peasants in Bangladesh is their own children, many of whom will not survive to adulthood. Exhortation will not convince these peasants not to procreate. The tragedy is that the behavior which is rational for the individual is so devastatingly suicidal for the nation as a whole.

tion and massive investments in new technology. Similarly, massive investments and newly developed technology will be necessary if resources are to
be conserved through the recycling of waste and used products and if the
resource base is to be expanded by finding ways of utilizing hitherto useless or
inaccessible materials. This being the case, one can argue that it is more
promising to foster economic growth so that society will feel rich enough to
devote some of its income to cleaning the environment. It seems, unfortunately, to be the case that pollution is a concern mainly to those who can afford to be concerned about it.

# 14

# FLUCTUATIONS IN ECONOMIC ACTIVITY

In this chapter we shall take a look at some of the factors that jolt the economy off its path of balanced growth. In the past it was thought that the ups and downs in economic activity were inevitable and that they occurred with a fair degree of regularity. Economists talked of business cycles, and they delineated waves of activity of different duration. There were long swings of twenty-five-year duration known as "Kondratieff waves," eight- to ten-year swings known as "Juglar cycles," and short fluctuations of four years known as "Kitchin cycles." Popular mythology held that what goes up must come down. And there was an important corollary which insisted that recession, like a hangover, was the price the economy had to pay for past excesses.

Little credence is placed in these notions nowadays. What goes up does not need to come down because monetary and fiscal policy can provide the necessary lift. There were three recessions during the 1950s but none at all between 1961 and late 1969 because public policy prevented their occurrence. When recession did again arrive in late 1969, it was induced not by the "natural" forces that impart cycles to economic activity but by a deliberate application of monetary and fiscal restraint.

In the past, economists constructed elaborate theories of the business cycle. These would include an explanation of the process of expansion, the cause of the upper turning point, the nature of the subsequent contraction, and, finally, the character of the lower turning point and revival. With the massive intrusion of government into economic life such theorizing is perhaps less relevant than it once was. Nevertheless the sources of the disturbances that tend to generate fluctuations in economic activity are still very much with us, and it is important that we familiarize ourselves with some of the more important of these.[1]

## 14–2
## THE ACCELERATION PRINCIPLE

An extremely important potential source of instability arises from the fact that the *level* of certain expenditure components depends on *changes* in the values of some other variable. In Chapter 13 we saw that a constant population requires no additions to its stock of housing. Consequently, the level of new housing net of replacement must be a function of changes in the size of the population. Similarly, in Chapter 6 we saw that if the desired stock of capital is proportional to the level of output, the *level* of investment will be proportional to *changes* in the level of output. To recall the argument again, this fact is true because investment is the change in the stock of capital, and there would be no point in changing the size of the capital stock if output were not growing. Similar kinds of considerations apply to investment in inventories. Inventory investment represents the addition to stocks of materials, work in process, and finished goods. If sales were not increasing or expected to increase, there would be no point in making such additions to inventory.

The idea that a portion of investment depends on changes in demand is known as the "acceleration principle."[2] It represents an important source of instability that we can illustrate by resort to a numerical example. Imagine an economy in which only one consumer good is produced and that the price per unit of this good is $1. Assume next that the production of one unit per day of the consumer good necessitates the use of one machine. Suppose that each new machine has a value of $3, so that the desired capital-output ratio in this economy is 3 : 1. Finally, assume that there is a one-day lag between

---

[1] There are many excellent surveys of the literature of business cycles. Among the most useful are J. A. Estey, *Business Cycles*, 3d ed., Prentice-Hall, Inc., Englewood Cliffs, N.J., 1956; A. H. Hansen, *Business Cycles and National Income*, W. W. Norton & Company, Inc., New York, 1951; R. A. Gordon, *Business Fluctuations*, Harper & Row, Publishers, Incorporated, New York, 1952.

[2] The most famous early exposition of the acceleration principle is by J. M. Clark, "Business Acceleration and the Law of Demand," *Journal of Political Economy*, 25:217–235, 1917. Interest in the principle was revived when it was found that the Keynesian consumption function and the acceleration principle could be combined into a self-generating cyclical mechanism. One such attempt was P. A. Samuelson, "Interactions between the Multiplier Analysis and the Principle of Acceleration," *Review of Economics and Statistics*, 21:78–88, 1939. R. F. Harrod, *The Trade Cycle*, Oxford University Press, London, 1936, developed a theory along similar lines. More recent works on the principle include J. R. Hicks, *A Contribution to the Theory of the Trade Cycle*, Oxford University Press, London, 1950; and R. M. Goodwin, "The Non-Linear Accelerator and the Persistence of Business Cycles," *Econometrica*, 19:1–17, 1951.

**TABLE 14–1**

| Time (1) | Consumption ($) (2) | Required Machines (3) | Available at Start of Day (4) | Gross Investment | |
|---|---|---|---|---|---|
| | | | | Number (5) | Value ($) (6) |
| 1 | 20 | 20 | 18 | 2 | 6 |
| 2 | 20 | 20 | 18 | 2 | 6 |
| 3 | 21 | 21 | 18 | 3 | 9 |
| 4 | 23 | 23 | 19 | 4 | 12 |
| 5 | 25 | 25 | 21 | 4 | 12 |
| 6 | 25 | 25 | 23 | 2 | 6 |
| 7 | 21 | 21 | 23 | 0 | 0 |
| 8 | 17 | 17 | 21 | 0 | 0 |
| 9 | 17 | 17 | 19 | 0 | 0 |
| 10 | 17 | 17 | 17 | 0 | 0 |
| 11 | 17 | 17 | 15 | 2 | 6 |
| 12 | 21 | 21 | 15 | 6 | 18 |
| 13 | 29 | 29 | 18 | 11 | 33 |

the receipt of income and its expenditure by consumers, that the marginal propensity to consume is ⅔, that the life of one machine is 10 days, and that machines can be produced instantaneously.

Let us trace out the day-by-day changes in this economy in Table 14–1. In column 2 we enter the level of current consumption. Column 3 shows the number of machines required to produce the day's output of consumer goods. Column 4 gives the number of machines that are available for use at the start of each day. Column 5 shows the number of machines that must be added during the day and therefore represents the difference between columns 3 and 4. Column 6, finally, shows the dollar value of these new machines and therefore represents the value of gross investment.

During days 1 and 2 the economy is in equilibrium. Consumption is valued at $20, and since two machines need to be replaced, gross investment is $6, while net investment is zero. Evidently, NNP in this economy is $20, and GNP equals $26. Now let this equilibrium be disrupted in day 3. Suppose, for example, that there is a change in consumer tastes that causes consumption to rise by 5 percent to $21. Since only 18 machines are available at the start of day 3, gross investment must now rise to 3 machines, an increase of 50 percent. The increase in investment creates $3 of additional income, and since the marginal propensity to consume is ⅔, consumption in day 4 rises by $2 to a new level of $23. Consequently, 23 machines are now needed, so that 4 machines must be built in day 4. Income therefore again rises by $3 and consumption by $2, so that 4 new machines must be installed in day 5. Now notice that this implies exactly the same level of gross investment as took place in day 4 ($12) and that because of this constancy of the level of investment no further increase in income develops. Consumption therefore remains at $25, and investment falls to $6 since it is necessary to replace only the 2 machines that are worn out. Since 2 fewer machines are produced, income drops by $6 and consumption by $4. This means that in day 7 only 21 machines are needed. But since 23 are available, gross investment drops to zero. At this stage it is not even necessary to engage in replacement investment because there is plentiful excess capacity.

The fall in gross investment to zero produces a further fall in consumption of $4 to a depression low of $17. At this level of consumption 17 machines are required. But since 21 are available, gross investment remains at zero. Since there is no change in gross investment (it cannot be negative), no further drop in income takes place. Consumption remains at $17 in day 9, and since there are 19 available machines, there will again be no gross investment, so that consumption in day 10 again remains at $17. With just 17 machines available, gross investment still stays at zero. But in day 11 the wearing out of 2 more machines means that a situation has finally been reached where the required number of machines (17) exceeds the available number (15). Since 2 new machines are needed, gross investment rises to $6, and the level of consumption therefore subsequently rises to $21. This then means that 6 machines must be produced in day 12, and the cycle is therefore once again on its upward course.

It is apparent from this illustration that the durability of capital equipment introduces a strong element of instability into the economy. An increase in consumption of 5 percent at the beginning of day 3 caused gross investment to rise by 50 percent. If machines were assumed to have a life of five days rather than ten, the first two days of equilibrium would have involved the replacement of 4 machines, so that the initial increase in machine production in day 3 would have been only 25 percent (from 4 machines to 5). If machines lasted only one day, a 5 percent increase in consumption would require a 5 percent increase in gross investment. Clearly, the more durable the units of capital, the larger will be the percentage fluctuations in investment. Furthermore, because the economy will languish in depression until excess capacity is eliminated, an economy with extremely durable capital will tend to remain depressed longer than an economy in which capital wears out more rapidly.

In Table 14–1 it can be seen that there are two influences on gross investment at the start of the second upswing. Two machines wear out each day up to the beginning of day 12. In day 13, however, 3 machines wear out because that is the number that was installed 10 days before. Since 4 machines were bought on day 4, they will wear out and have to be replaced on day 14. As is obvious from the table, the backwash of the first boom serves to intensify the second boom. Once the purchase of durable goods proceeds at an uneven rate, there will be a tendency for it to continue doing so. "Replacement waves," as such echo effects are called, tend to become diffused over time. All equipment does not have the same life, and new sources of disturbance soon predominate. Nevertheless in countries where there are only a few

large industries, a serious disruption such as a major war can lead to a significant succession of replacement waves.

Returning to our discussion of the acceleration principle, we should observe that since induced investment results from increases in output, an
increase in investment requires consumption not only to increase but to do so
at an increasing rate. It was the failure of consumption to meet this requirement that caused the downturn in our previous example. The upturn, on the
other hand, resulted from the fact that net investment cannot remain negative
indefinitely. When the capital stock wears down to the point where some
replacement is required, gross investment rises, income and consumption expand, and revival gets under way.

The foregoing outline of a possible cyclical process presents a very crude
and oversimplified picture. Nevertheless the acceleration principle can be
made the driving force in sophisticated theories of the business cycle provided
a few amendments are made. One such theory is that of J. R. Hicks.[1] He
proposes the following changes:

**1**  Hicks points out that investment should depend not on changes in consumption alone but on changes in output in general. In our earlier example
we ignored the fact that when it was necessary to produce more capital
goods, it would also be necessary to have more plant capacity to produce
these investment goods. Thus any increase in demand, whether it be consumption or investment, tends to induce investment.

**2**  In our earlier example the upper turning point resulted from the failure of
consumption to grow at a fast enough rate. Hicks would call such an occurrence a "free cycle." However, for the most part Hicks thought that the values of the acceleration coefficient[2] and the marginal propensity to consume
were such that expansion would tend to boom ahead indefinitely in the absence of some external interfering factor. The interfering factor is full employment which Hicks called the "ceiling of real resources," and a cycle that runs
up against this ceiling he called a "constrained" cycle.

**3**  Hicks separated investment into two components: induced and autonomous. Induced investment is associated with immediate needs for new
capacity in line with the acceleration principle. Autonomous investment, on
the other hand, is geared to long-run trend factors such as the growth of population and advances in technology.

Hicks's model of the cycle is illustrated in Figure 14–1, where time is
measured horizontally and the logarithms of real income and investment are

---

[1] Hicks, op. cit.

[2] The acceleration coefficient is defined as the amount of extra capacity required to produce an
additional unit of output. In our example the value of the acceleration coefficient was 3 since we
needed $3 of extra capacity (one machine) to produce $1 of additional consumption goods. For
obvious reasons, the acceleration coefficient is sometimes referred to as the marginal capital-
output ratio.

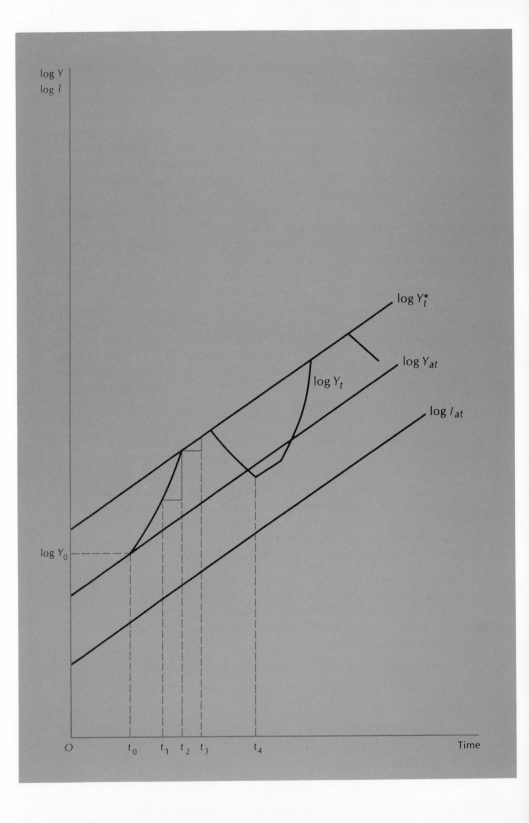

measured vertically. The lowest line describes the course of autonomous investment (log $I_{at}$). The middle line describes the log of the time path of output when only autonomous investment materializes (log $Y_{at}$). The highest line is the "ceiling" beyond which output cannot expand (log $Y_t^*$). Since the full-employment level of output presumably depends on the growth of population and the rate at which advances in technology are made, Hicks assumes the ceiling rate of growth to be the same as the rate of growth of autonomous investment.

Suppose that the economy is in the midst of depression at time $t_0$ with output $Y_0$. Since long-run growth factors cause autonomous investment to rise, there results an automatic increase in the level of output which, if excess capacity has been substantially reduced by depreciation and obsolescence, induces investment. But the induced investment raises the level of output still further, so that more investment is induced through additional capacity requirements. Expansion, driven by the accelerator, continues to push output upward until the ceiling is reached at time $t_2$. At this point output can expand only at the ceiling rate of growth. But this means that the change in output that is possible between periods $t_2$ and $t_3$ must be less than the change in the preceding period. This, however, means that an absolute fall in investment must take place. Consequently output shrinks, gross induced investment falls to zero, and the economy enters a slump. In period $t_4$ the bottom of recession is reached. A new expansion must now await the wearing out of the excess equipment. When growth factors again produce a positive change in output or when gross investment rises because of the necessity of replacement, expansion proceeds once more.

The Hicks model, although presented here in a highly simplified form, serves as a useful framework for the analysis of cyclical fluctuations within a context of long-run growth. It serves especially to emphasize that in a capital intensive economy with no compensatory monetary or fiscal policy, a period of contraction is quite likely to follow a period of expansion. Since the rate of expansion of output is greater than the rate at which full-employment output grows (this must be the case or full employment would never be reached), the ceiling imposes an enforced period of slowdown; because induced investment depends on changes in output, this implies that there will be an absolute fall in the level of investment.

Hicks's model also suggests that the duration of depression depends upon the rate of technical progress. There are two reasons for this: First, without technical progress, autonomous investment may not rise over time, and thus a positive change in output, needed to set the accelerator in motion, will not take place until equipment has worn out to the point where some replace-

**FIGURE 14–1**
The Hicksian theory of the cycle (all values
in real terms)

ment investment is necessary. Second, if there is no technical progress, the time at which this replacement is necessary will be deferred because no help is obtained from the obsolescence of existing equipment. The whole burden of starting the accelerator is thus placed on the wearing out (depreciation) of equipment. Small wonder that depressions are more severe and long-lasting during periods when long-run growth factors seem to be in abeyance.

Although the Hicks model provides a framework within which to analyze fluctuations in a context of growth, it does not really deal with the interaction of trend and cycle. The full-employment ceiling that Hicks defines is independent of the path of output. It depends rather on the growth of population, advances in technology, and the like; it is therefore assumed to grow at the same rate as autonomous investment. But the full-employment level of output depends on the magnitude of the resources that are available to the economy. The capital stock is one such resource. This implies that the ceiling is raised in any period during which the capital stock is increasing. Since the rate at which output increases determines the rate at which the capital stock changes, the ceiling level of output will differ depending on the time path of output. One cannot therefore separate the long-run full-employment trend from what happens during a cycle.

In the United States many past ups and downs in economic activity, especially since World War II, have been primarily due to fluctuations in inventory investment. These fluctuations, too, can perhaps be interpreted as reflecting a form of the acceleration principle. The amount of inventory that merchants keep on hand depends upon such factors as the rate of interest, price expectations, obsolescence, perishability, and the advantages of bulk purchasing. However, undoubtedly the most important variable which determines the size of desired stocks is the level of sales. In fact, if we assume that the desired level of stock is proportional to the level of sales,[1] additions to inventory will be proportional to changes in the level of sales. This puts us right back into the world of the acceleration principle.

To illustrate the inventory accelerator, consider the numerical example shown in Table 14–2.[2] Here it is assumed that the desired ratio of stocks to sales is 2 : 1 and that the marginal propensity to consume is 0.5. Assume that the level of sales in day 1 is $100. The desired level of inventory will therefore be $200. If sales in day 2 are also $100, the desired level of inventory will remain at $200, so that orders in day 2 will be the $100 needed to replace the sales of the day. Inventory investment, that is, net changes in the stock of inventory, is zero under these conditions.

[1] This is similar to the assumption of classical monetary theory that the transactions demand for money is proportional to the volume of transactions.

[2] The discussion is based on the well-known work of L. A. Metzler. See his "The Nature and Stability of Inventory Cycles," *Review of Economic Statistics*, 23:113–129, 1941; and "Business Cycles and the Modern Theory of Employment," *American Economic Review*, 36:278–291, 1946.

**TABLE 14–2**

| Time (1) | Sales (Consumption) (2) | Desired Stocks (2) × 2 (3) | Orders to Adjust Inventory (4) | Total Orders (Income) (2) + (4) (5) |
|---|---|---|---|---|
| 1 | 100.00 | 200.00 | 0.00 | 100.00 |
| 2 | 100.00 | 200.00 | 0.00 | 100.00 |
| 3 | 112.00 | 224.00 | 24.00 | 136.00 |
| 4 | 130.00 | 260.00 | 36.00 | 166.00 |
| 5 | 145.00 | 290.00 | 30.00 | 175.00 |
| 6 | 149.50 | 299.00 | 9.00 | 158.50 |
| 7 | 141.25 | 282.50 | −16.50 | 124.75 |
| 8 | 124.38 | 248.75 | −33.75 | 90.62 |
| 9 | 107.31 | 214.62 | −34.12 | 73.19 |
| 10 | 98.59 | 197.19 | −17.44 | 81.16 |
| 11 | 102.58 | 205.16 | 7.97 | 110.55 |
| 12 | 117.27 | 234.55 | 29.39 | 146.66 |

*Note:* Detail may not add to total because of rounding.

Now suppose that in day 3 consumers decide to increase their consumption by $12. Orders in day 3 must rise by $12 to replace stocks that were sold, plus an additional $24 because the desired level of stocks has risen to $224. Total orders in day 3 therefore amount to $136. Since this represents a change in income of $36 over the previous level and since the marginal propensity to consume is 0.5 in this example, sales in day 4 rise by $18 to a new level of $130. The desired level of stocks now rises to $260, so that orders in day 4 must be $130 + ($260 − $224) = $166. Since this represents an income increase, consumption once again rises.

The cyclical upswing advances until day 6 when, despite an increase in consumption (from $145 to $149.50), orders nevertheless fall from $175 to $158.50. Since orders fall, income and consumption subsequently fall, and the cycle starts its downward course. Eventually, it reaches a point (day 10) where, despite a fall in consumption, orders nonetheless rise, so that expansion begins again.

What brings about these turning points? Orders consist of two components: the amount needed to replace the day's sales and the amount needed to adjust inventory to the desired level of stocks. The first component equals the level of sales, and the second depends on the change in the level of sales. Even though the absolute level of sales rises, thereby increasing the first component of orders, overall orders may fall if the change in sales is less than it previously was. In day 5 sales are $145; since the change in sales between days 4 and 5 is $15, desired stocks rise by $30. But between days 5 and 6 sales rise by only $4.50, so that desired stocks rise by only $9. Orders to build up inventories therefore fall by $21. Since this is not overcome by the positive change in sales of $4.50, there results an absolute decline in orders of $16.50.

In the present model the desired level of stocks is able to catch up to sales because the marginal propensity to consume is less than unity. Once this catch-up occurs, there is no further need for upward inventory adjustment; the absolute volume of orders therefore falls, and contraction sets in. Similarly, and again because the marginal propensity to consume is less than unity, sales do not fall as rapidly as orders, and a time therefore comes (day 10) when, despite a fall in sales, there is an absolute increase in orders because sales have fallen by less than in the preceding day. If the marginal propensity to consume had been equal to one, there would have been no turning point because actual stocks could never catch up to desired stocks. Consumption would always rise by exactly the amount of the change in orders, and a downturn would therefore never occur in the absence of a "nonlinearity," that is, an external factor, such as Hicks's ceiling.

In conclusion: If investment is a function of changes in demand, a small percentage increase in demand can induce a huge magnification in the demand for investment goods. Similarly, if output fails to grow fast enough, investment may fall even though final demand is increasing. The acceleration principle clearly is a strong source of instability.

## 14–3
## MONETARY FACTORS

The acceleration principle is one source of systematic shift in the *IS* curve, and it is therefore known as a "real" theory of the business cycle. On the other hand, monetary changes that affect the *LM* curve may also be quite important. In fact, there is a whole group of monetary theories of the business cycle. In this section we shall take a very brief look at some of these theories. Our purpose is to understand how monetary factors can generate instability and how monetary policy may offset or accentuate these forces.

The well-known Austrian economist F. A. von Hayek argued that in the absence of monetary disturbances there would be no fluctuations in economic activity at all.[1] Suppose that the economy is in equilibrium at full employment, and suppose that banks are required to maintain a ratio of reserves to deposits of 100 percent. Assume also that no change takes place in the money supply or in the velocity of circulation. Under such conditions all borrowing for investment must originate with funds released through current saving. In this situation the saving habits of the community will determine the amount of current output that can be devoted to expanding the future income stream. If the community decides to consume less today in order that future consumption might be increased, saving rises, resources are released from

[1] F. A. von Hayek, *Prices and Production*, 2d ed., Routledge & Kegan Paul, Ltd., London, 1951.

consumption, and, because this prompts the interest rate to fall, the resources are absorbed into investment.

Those resources that are devoted to the production of current consumption goods are said to be utilized in the "higher" stages of production, that is, those closest to the consumer, while those devoted to investment goods production are said to be devoted to the "lower" stages of production. At full employment an increase in investment involves a shifting of resources from the higher to the lower stages of production. This shift is known as a lengthening of the structure of production or an increase in the "roundaboutness" of production.

As long as such a change in roundaboutness occurs as a result of the voluntary behavior of savers, no harm can come of it. The difficulty arises when easy credit creates the temporary illusion that it is profitable to lengthen the structure of production. Since the illusion disappears when credit gets tighter, more resources may be devoted to the production of capital goods than can profitably be employed. In Hayek's terms a "vertical maladjustment" takes place, and a subsequent recession then occurs during which the structure of production is shortened.

Under a fractional reserve banking system it is possible for entrepreneurs to obtain resources for investment in excess of those that are voluntarily released by saving even at full employment. The process whereby this is accomplished is called "forced saving." Since banks are profit-making institutions, they will attempt to expand their loan-making operations when excess reserves appear. In so doing, they lower the market rate of interest below the natural rate, and entrepreneurs are therefore induced to use the artificially created bank credit to bid resources away from consumers. The resultant increase in consumer goods prices reduces real income and consumption and thus "forces" the community to save.

The inflationary boom that could be created by this process can be sustained as long as the artificially low market rate of interest prevails. But as money income rises as a result of the investment expenditures, consumers use this added income to purchase consumption goods. Consumer goods prices therefore rise beyond the initial increase, and a tendency develops for resources to be bid back into consumption goods lines. As long as ample bank credit is available, this tendency can be thwarted. But as reserves grow smaller relative to deposits, lending operations are curtailed, and the market rate of interest rises. This means that many of the new investment projects now become unprofitable; a vertical maladjustment develops; and recession, viewed as the period during which the appropriate equilibrium structure of production is restored, sets in.

Hayek attempted to explain the extraordinary cyclical variation in capital goods production without relaxing the assumption of full employment and constant real income. The typical recession is, of course, marked by unemployed resources, and this makes possible the simultaneous expansion of consumption and investment goods. The fact that in the short run the percentage of income consumed falls as income rises is all that need be said to explain why investment goods production rises in greater proportion than consumption.

Despite its rather severe limitations, Hayek's analysis serves to illustrate that a boom could be sustained by the action of the banking system and that an artificially sustained boom may make the subsequent recession all the more serious if investment has been undertaken in areas where no true long-run profit opportunities exist.

Monetary factors undoubtedly also influence inventory fluctuations since the desired ratio of stocks to sales tends to rise as the rate of interest falls. As we saw in Chapter 7, this is true for the transactions demand for money, and standard inventory theory suggests it should be true for all types of stocks. Weighted against the desirability of holding inventories is the cost of holding these stocks—a cost that is partly dependent on the rate of interest. A high rate of interest raises carrying costs and therefore prompts merchants to try to get by on a smaller margin of inventory, while a low interest rate will have the opposite effect.

The eminent British economist R. G. Hawtrey[1] believed that inventory cycles are the consequence of fluctuations in the desired ratio of stocks to sales in response to interest rate changes. If banks acquire excess reserves and attempt to put these reserves to work, the resulting fall in the rate of interest will raise the desired ratio of stocks to sales. This leads entrepreneurs to borrow funds to increase inventory and therefore to promote expansion. The added income results in added consumption, which then leads to further increases in orders and a continued expansion in the familiar pattern of the inventory cycle.

With a given volume of bank reserves, the time must come when the increased transactions demand impinges on the money supply. This process is aggravated in Hawtrey's view by the fact that during the later stages of expansion, the increased volume of transactions leads to a drain of cash from the banks. As the ratio of reserves to deposits reaches a critically low level, banks restrict credit, interest rates rise, the ratio of desired stocks to sales falls, orders decline, and contraction gets under way. As orders decline, income and consumption shrink; orders decline still further, and so on in a cumulative contraction. If the banks realized that this process of contraction ultimately causes cash to move back to the banks, they would not contract to a significant degree. But since they show no such awareness, the contraction continues until the flow of cash back into the banks again produces excess reserves. This causes a lowering of the interest rate, at which point the process starts over again.

Unfortunately, none of this provides much guidance for monetary policy. Prosperity is associated with high credit demands and high interest rates, and

---

[1] R. G. Hawtrey, *Good and Bad Trade,* Constable & Co., Ltd., London, 1913.

recession reduces the demand for credit and tends to lower interest rates. Common sense suggests that stabilizing monetary policy ought to accentuate these swings, making credit less costly and easier to obtain during recession and more costly and difficult to obtain during prosperity. On the other hand, if the source of the fluctuation in economic activity is itself traceable to fluctuating interest rates, the exact opposite policy prescription will then be appropriate. Monetary policy in such cases should strive for constant interest rates. This issue, which we raise here only in passing, has been the central dilemma for monetary policy in the United States. In Part 4 we shall consider this problem in detail.

## 14-4
## INNOVATION AND TECHNICAL CHANGE

Hicks divided investment into an induced and an autonomous component, with the former playing the driving role in generating fluctuations. A considerable body of opinion, however, thinks that it is fluctuations in autonomous investment that represent the chief source of disturbance and that the acceleration principle is less important than it appears.

The most famous exponent of the view that business cycles are a natural outgrowth of economic progress was J. A. Schumpeter.[1] Schumpeter drew a sharp distinction between invention (the discovery and development of new processes, new goods, and new methods by engineers and scientists) and innovation (the process whereby entrepreneurs put the invention to commercial use). The importance of the distinction between invention and innovation lies in the fact that invention may proceed quite smoothly but innovation tends to move in fits and starts. It is this discontinuity in the rate of innovation that in Schumpeter's view causes fluctuations in economic activity.

Innovation does not proceed smoothly because people are by nature conservative. They tend to stick to proven methods and to avoid the adoption of new ones until the value of the new methods has been demonstrated by others or until their deteriorating competitive position forces them to take action. There are, however, a few bold innovators who under favorable conditions will lead the way. Once such an innovator starts the process, others begin to follow until ultimately there is a deluge of investment spending and a full-scale boom.

Why do the others imitate? For one thing, competitors cannot afford to let themselves be outstripped by an aggressive rival. The more firms that follow the lead, the greater is the pressure on the remainder. In addition, the innovation, especially if it takes place in a situation of full or near full employment, causes prices to rise because bidding for the available supply of resources is intensified. Profit opportunities appear rosier, and investment is stimulated. If there is increased investment, prices again rise, and investment is once more stimulated.

[1] J. A. Schumpeter, *The Theory of Economic Development,* Harvard University Press, Cambridge, Mass., 1934; and *Business Cycles,* McGraw-Hill Book Company, New York, 1939.

Ultimately the innovative wave weakens and the boom dies. The new factories are eventually completed, so that investment spending begins to tail off. At the same time the new factories begin turning out consumer goods. Coming at a time when investment is falling or increasing at a decreasing rate, the added supply of consumption goods will not all be bought, prices break, widespread disappointment with respect to profits results, and recession begins. From there the economy gropes toward equilibrium which is again disrupted when a new wave of innovation commences.

One of the most significant aspects of the Schumpeterian analysis is the hypothesis that the same forces that create instability are the forces that also make for economic progress. Economic progress is impossible in the absence of innovation. But since innovation does not proceed smoothly, periodic ups and downs are the inevitable consequence.

The view of Schumpeter could be challenged on the grounds that it is innovation and technical change that perhaps save the economy from the ravages of the acceleration principle.[1] In Chapter 6 we considered two industries. In the first it was assumed that no new technology is developed that would lead to a reduction in costs, improved products, or the introduction of new products. In such a stagnant industry there would never be any reason to invest except if demand were expected to increase. The size of the investment expenditures in this industry would depend on the size of the expected increase in demand. All net investment would involve the installation of more equipment of a kind that duplicates existing facilities. This kind of technical situation would tend to put an economy into the violent world of the acceleration principle as discussed in Section 14–2. When the economy runs out of excess capacity, it booms upward for a short time; it then turns down the moment the rate of growth of output declines; and it then drifts into a deep and lengthy depression from which it does not emerge until the capital stock is again worn down to the amount needed to produce the depression level of output.

Now imagine an economy in which entrepreneurs propose to put cost-saving innovations into practice, to manufacture new products, or to improve existing products. Under these conditions the size of the investment expenditures that will be undertaken depends not so much on how much demand is expected to increase as upon the absolute size of expected markets. Moreover, the existence of excess capacity is not a deterrent to investment because different types of capacity are needed. Investment would be worth undertaking even if demand were expected to be stationary or even to decline slightly, although the size of the projected expenditures might be scaled down in the face of a decline in the level of economic activity.

To summarize: In a technologically stagnant economy, investment tends to be purely repetitive. It is therefore never undertaken when excess capacity

---

[1] T. F. Dernburg, "Technical Progress and the Business Cycle," *Nebraska Journal of Economics and Business*, 2:23–32, 1963.

exists, and it responds only to increases in the level of demand. In the technologically progressive economy, new facilities compete and render existing facilities obsolete, and the level of investment is geared to the level of demand rather than to changes in demand. These circumstances make for an enormous difference in the nature of cyclical fluctuations. In the first place, an upswing can take place without waiting for existing capacity to wear out, and the presence of innovation and technical change itself hastens this process of ridding the system of excess capacity. Second, since expansion of investment can proceed even while excess capacity exists in many industries, it is possible to expand output more smoothly and with fewer shortages as the boom develops. Third, even though the rate of growth of output may slow down as the boom proceeds, there is no reason why investment should collapse since it is geared to total demand rather than to the growth of demand. Thus the boom can be prolonged long beyond the time that a simple accelerator model would suggest. Similarly, the skid into recession need not be abrupt since there is no need for gross investment to fall to zero as would be the case with the accelerator model. Finally, the continued advance of new technology sustains investment during the recession and hastens the obsolescence and elimination of old capacity. It thereby speeds up the time at which the next upswing arrives.

## 14-5
## CONCLUDING NOTES

The discussion of this chapter is similar to traditional business cycle analysis in that it looks to the investment component of aggregate expenditure as the chief source of instability. Indeed a glance at the postwar recessions in the United States shows that the recession of 1957–1958 followed on the heels of a capital goods boom and that the recession of 1949 and the recessions of the 1950s were primarily attributable to inventory fluctuations similar to those described in this chapter. Similarly, the slowdown of late 1966 and early 1967 involved a combination of a slump in housing demand, a fall in inventory investment, and a dip in capital goods spending. However, something new had been added. The boom of 1966 was attributable to a rapid rise in government purchases associated with the war in Vietnam, and the subsequent slump in housing was the product of the tight monetary policy designed to slow that boom. Moreover, the dislocations that caused inventory investment to drop almost $20 billion between the fourth quarter of 1966 and the second quarter of 1967 were almost entirely attributable to erratic and unpredictable federal fiscal and monetary policies rather than to the instability of private demand. The subsequent inflation had its origin in the faulty policies that began with the escalation of the war in 1965. The recession of 1969–1970 was almost totally the product of belated restrictive monetary and fiscal policies that were designed to stop that inflation.

Policy-induced instability has characterized the United States economy, as well as the economies of the industrialized world, for the past decade. During that time inflation has become ever more rampant, the international monetary system has broken down, and policy is often in a hopeless quandary since inflation and recession keep on rearing their ugly heads simultaneously. As if that were not enough, the lags between the time a policy is undertaken and the time it affects economic activity are so variable and so imperfectly understood that policies designed to deal with today's emergency are worse than useless because they come too late to deal with the emergency but do precipitate or exacerbate tomorrow's crisis.

It is fitting, under the circumstances, that we devote the remainder of this book to the three most pressing macroeconomic problems that now confront the industrialized world. Can inflation be controlled without excessive demand restrictions and consequent unemployment? Can an international monetary system be designed that does not inflict instability on individual economies? And, finally, can policy itself learn to overcome its tendency to make bad situations worse?

# 15

# INFLATION

## INTRODUCTION

On September 20, 1974 the Bureau of Labor Statistics announced that the consumer price index in the United States had risen by 1.3 percent during the month of August. If the rate were to keep up for a year it would imply an annual rate of inflation of 16.8 percent. Inflation, in the judgment of most persons, is one of the major economic problems of our time. The problem seems to be getting worse and in 1974 gave the appearance of becoming uncontrollable. It is, moreover, a worldwide phenomenon. Despite the poor price performance of the United States in recent years, the rate of inflation in most European countries has generally been even higher.

Controlling inflation is not difficult. It is necessary only to pursue restrictive monetary and fiscal policies to such an extent that excess supply appears in the bulk of product and factor markets. Firms will not raise prices if they cannot sell their output at existing prices, nor will workers demand higher wages if they cannot find jobs at existing wages. The trouble with this remedy is that it is extremely harsh and costly, involving heavy unemployment and lost output. Indeed the old-fashioned cure of balanced budgets and tight money may well be worse than the disease and, in fact, may not even work very well since it is politically impossible to apply it long enough and drastically enough to get people to revise their inflationary expectations. The United States government used its monetary and fiscal powers to attempt to halt inflation in 1968–1969 and in so doing brought on the costly recession of 1970 without, it is fair to say, making very much headway against inflation. Restrictive policies were again applied in 1973–1974 and were largely responsible for bringing about the worst recession since the great depression of the 1930s.

Most industrial countries are committed to maintaining full employment, so that extreme deflationary policies are generally ruled out as unsuitable. However, the very fact of the full-employment commitment tends to invite inflation because it is expected that any unemployment which results from excessively rapid wage and price increases will be offset by expansionary monetary-fiscal policies. The issue, therefore, is not how to stop inflation, since that is easy, but how to do so without causing unemployment, lost output, and retardation of economic growth. This is, perhaps, the single most pressing and vexing problem of contemporary macroeconomics. It has, more-over, been greatly complicated by the fact that excessive unemployment and price inflation have recently shown an unfortunate tendency to exist side by side periodically. Such situations, which are sometimes known as "infla-tionary recession," or "stagflation," create a double dilemma for policy since it is not clear whether to expand aggregate expenditure to raise employment, or whether to restrict expenditure in order to slow inflation.

Inflationary periods of the past were most often associated with periods of war and the aftermath of war. When it is not possible to raise sufficient reve-nue by taxation, governments print and spend money, or, what amounts to the same thing, they borrow from the central bank. There are many examples of war-induced inflation. Among the more dramatic examples are the infla-tion that accompanied the Civil War in the United States when the Confeder-ate currency ultimately became worthless due to overissue and, in more recent history, the hyperinflation in Germany that followed World War I. Sim-ilar to war-induced inflation is the kind of rapid inflation that has for years beset Latin American countries. Such inflation has tended to stem from the ef-forts of governments to mobilize resources for economic development. Tax revenues are very difficult to raise in these countries, in part because the gov-ernments are weak, but the governments nevertheless are determined to acquire additional resources for public investment purposes, and they there-fore increase their expenditures in the hope that the resources needed for development can be obtained by a process known as "forced saving." The idea is to reduce the real disposable income and consumption of potential taxpayers through inflation rather than through direct payments.

Before proceeding further, we need to be clear about the meaning of the term "inflation." First, the term usually refers to a continuing rise in prices as measured by an index such as the consumer price index (CPI) or by the implicit price deflator for gross national product. A rise in prices may come about either because of changes in demand conditions or because of changes in supply, or because of interactions between demand and supply. All these possibilities need to be carefully distinguished and analyzed. When a rise in demand causes inflation, this is usually known as "buyers'" or "excess demand" inflation. When the price level rises because resources are unable to adjust smoothly to changes in the composition of demand, this is called "demand shift" inflation. "Cost push" or "sellers'" inflation occurs when groups with monopoly market power force up wages and prices, or when there are restrictions in labor supply or, as has recently happened, when the supplies of energy and of agricultural production undergo significant restriction.

The second thing to bear in mind is that there may be inflationary pressures that do not, however, manifest themselves in higher prices. The usual symptom, that inflation is under way when price indexes are rising, is suggestive only when prices are free to move in response to market forces. If price controls are imposed, as they were in the United States during World War II, a price index no longer serves as a useful measure of inflationary pressure. Price increases are suppressed artificially, but inflationary pressure still exists.

Third, it is most important to bear in mind that some increases in the price level reflect a transition from one equilibrium to another, whereas other price level increases are manifestations of a state of persistent inflationary pressure and disequilibrium. Failure to distinguish between these two circumstances has given rise to some of the most serious confusions and bizarre policy prescriptions imaginable. A prime example is the reasonable enough notion that an increase in sales taxes is passed on to consumers in the form of higher prices and is therefore inflationary. The logical extension of the argument, however, is that inflation could be eliminated by reducing sales taxes, with further logical extension that the government could continue to lower the price level by granting unlimited subsidies.

This reasoning, which we have deliberately reduced to the level of absurdity, shows the danger of confusing a rise in prices which represents a transition from one equilibrium to another, with a rise in prices that reflects persistent disequilibrium. An increase in sales taxes would, to be sure, tend to raise the equilibrium price level in an individual market. But this ignores the fact that the resulting increase in prices reduces the real value of aggregate disposable income, and that it therefore will reduce aggregate real consumption and narrow the gap between aggregate demand and aggregate supply. The policy, therefore, will tend to slow the rate of inflation even though its initial impact may be to put upward pressure on the level of prices.

In this chapter we shall begin with a formal analysis of excess demand inflation. We then move to a consideration of the cost push type of phenomena and the issue of the so-called trade-off between unemployment and inflation. We complete the chapter with some notes on the costs of inflation and on the measurement of inflation, and with some suggestions for how to live painlessly with inflation. The problem of inflationary recession, or stagflation, is deferred to the next chapter where policy mix questions are considered in detail.

## 15–2
### EXCESS DEMAND INFLATION

Inflation reflects disequilibrium. Rising prices imply that aggregate demand exceeds aggregate supply. In the classical view, aggregate supply is fixed and it must therefore follow that inflation is the consequence of demand mis-

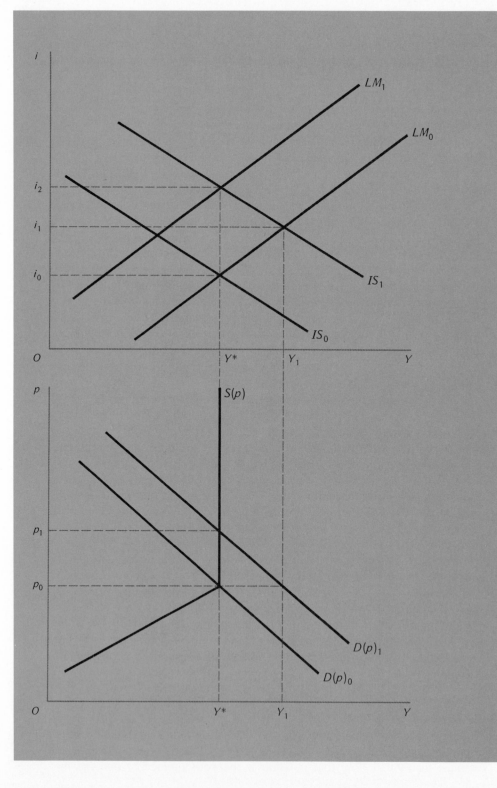

management. Figure 15–1 shows an economy in equilibrium at full employment. Wages and prices are assumed flexible in the upward direction, but below the full-employment level of income $Y^*$ it is assumed that money wages will be rigid. The aggregate supply function is therefore positively sloped below $Y^*$ and becomes vertical at $Y^*$. Initial equilibrium is at income level $Y^*$ and price level $p_0$, and the $IS_0$ and $LM_0$ curves intersect this income level at interest rate $i_0$. To avoid complications, the economy is for the moment assumed closed to international movements of goods and capital, and the Pigou effect is assumed inoperative. The $IS$ curve is, therefore, independent of the price level.

First, let government purchases increase and assume that this increase is unaccompanied by an increase in taxes. This shifts the $IS$ curve to $IS_1$ and the aggregate demand curve to $D(p)_1$. The intersection of $IS_1$ with $LM_0$ is at income level $Y_1$ and interest rate $i_1$. However, as can be seen in the lower quadrant, this situation implies excess demand at the initial price level $p_0$. The level of prices therefore tends to rise, and as this happens the real value of the money supply declines, and the $LM$ curve shifts to the left. Equilibrium is reestablished at the full-employment level of income $Y^*$, but at the higher price level $p_1$ and the higher interest rate $i_2$. The excess demand caused by the rise in government expenditure therefore eliminates itself even without any attempt to match the government expenditure increase by a rise in taxes. If taxes had been raised, the increase in the government's share of full-employment income would have come at the expense of consumption. Without the rise in taxes the resources obtained by the government come at the expense of investment, and this reduction in investment is brought about by the rise in the rate of interest.

Figure 15–1 may also be utilized to show the effect of an expansionary monetary policy. We assume again that the initial price level is $p_0$, but suppose that the $IS$ and $LM$ curves are initially $IS_1$ and $LM_1$, respectively, so that the initial rate of interest is $i_2$. An increase in the nominal stock of money which shifts the $LM$ curve from $LM_1$ to $LM_0$ lowers the rate of interest to $i_1$. This raises the aggregate demand curve from $D(p)_0$ to $D(p)_1$ and therefore creates excess demand. The price level now rises, and since this reduces the real value of the money supply, the $LM$ curve shifts back to the left. Obviously, excess demand will not be eliminated until aggregate demand cuts aggregate supply. This implies price level $p_1$ and a return of the $LM$ curve to $LM_1$. The result, then, is self-limiting, and the price level rises in exact proportion to the rise in the nominal stock of money, thereby returning the real value of the money supply to its original value.

**FIGURE 15–1**
Effect of one-time expansionary policies on
the price level at full employment (all values
in real terms)

We have seen that one-time shifts in exogenous variables will produce one-time changes in the price level. Such shifts cannot therefore account for steady inflation. Indeed it is the rise in the price level itself that restores equilibrium. The increase in the money supply temporarily increased investment spending, but the rise in the price level reversed this. Similarly, the increase in government expenditure raised total expenditure above the full-employment supply, but the economy was then again brought into equilibrium because the rise in the price level caused the rate of interest to rise.

As the reader will have noted, the tendency for inflation to come to an end automatically has, thus far in the discussion, been entirely the product of the tendency of the *LM* curve to shift automatically as the price level rises. We must note, however, that the *IS* curve may also shift as a consequence of a rise in a price level and that this will augment the equilibrating tendency of the shift in the *LM* curve. First of all, we should recall the Pigou effect that was discussed in Chapter 10. We saw there that the value of the stock of money and government bonds increased as the price level decreased and vice versa, so that a rise in the price level reduces the net wealth of the private sector of the economy. This reduces consumption at all levels of income and moves the *IS* curve to the left. Also a rise in the price level will lower net exports, and this will shift the *IS* curve to the left. Some of the inflation therefore tends to get exported. Finally, recall that the personal income tax structure in most countries is based on money income rather than real income. Consequently, a rise in money income which reflects a rise in the price level but not a rise in real income will be assumed by the tax structure to be the same as a rise in real income. The taxpayers' average effective tax rate in real terms then increases in a progressive tax system. As a consequence of this, real disposable income declines and so, therefore, does real consumption expenditure. Consequently, the money illusion in the tax structure causes the *IS* curve to shift to the left, and this again supplements the stabilizing forces.

Observe that if we repeat the analysis of the effect of an increase in the nominal money stock, while bearing in mind the effects of an increase in the price level on the *IS* curve, then the price level adjustment that tends to shift the $LM_0$ curve of Figure 15–1 back to the left will also be accompanied by some shift to the left of the *IS* curve. Consequently, the economy need not return to the original interest rate $i_2$ but will instead equilibrate at a lower rate of interest. We point this out to show that if a change in the price level can move the *IS* curve then a change in the money supply imposed in an economy that is at full employment can change the equilibrium rate of interest. This is contrary to the classical money veil theory, according to which the rate of interest cannot be affected by monetary policy, and its importance is that a one-time change in the money supply, because it can change the equilibrium rate of interest, can change the distribution of expenditure among consumption, investment, and government purchases and can therefore influence the allocation of resources and possibly also the rate of economic growth.[1]

The forces discussed thus far are equilibrating. There are, however, also some disequilibrating forces that may appear and tend to produce steady inflation. These forces are most likely to arise from the effect of inflation on expectations and from the tendency of government to persist, often inadvertently, in its policy of stimulating demand excessively. If households and businesses expect prices to rise rapidly and persistently, they will raise their expenditure levels to acquire physical commodities before these commodities become more expensive. The anticipation of inflation may therefore itself be a strong source of inflation. Businesses will build plants ahead of time in anticipation of rising construction costs, and they will tend to overstock their inventories. Consumers will reduce their savings or dissave in order to buy this year's model car rather than next year's model which will carry a higher price tag. All of this adds to aggregate demand, moves the *IS* curve to the right, and therefore tends to perpetuate disequilibrium and cause the inflation to continue.

The *LM* curve, too, may shift to the right as a result of inflationary expectations. When prices are rising, idle money balances earn a negative real rate of interest. There is, therefore, likely to be a strong aversion to liquidity, and there will be an incentive to hold as little money as possible between transactions. Monetary velocity therefore tends to speed up during inflation. Consequently, although the rise in the price level reduces the real value of the money supply and tends to shift the *LM* curve to the left, the inflation also causes the demand for money in real terms to decline; this will tend to shove the *LM* curve back to the right. Indeed, under conditions of so-called hyperinflation, people lose confidence in the currency because its value declines so rapidly, and they tend not to accept it at all in payment; if they do accept it, they will try to spend it as fast as possible. A less favorable climate for the orderly and efficient conduct of economic activity can scarcely be imagined.

The discussion thus far suggests that, if inflation is to continue, it will have to be fueled by continuous monetary and/or fiscal injections so that aggregate demand persistently remains in excess of aggregate supply. This can happen during a protracted period of national emergency when government expenditures rise continuously, and it can also happen quite inadvertently if the monetary authority focuses its attention on the rate of interest as a target for policy rather than on the level of income or the level of prices. During World War II the Fed "supported" the government bond market by standing ready to purchase a sufficient quantity of United States government securities to prevent their prices from falling and interest rates from rising. Given the magnitude of the deficit, the failure of the Fed to lend such support would soon

---

[1] This fact was noted and elaborated in a well-known paper by L. A. Metzler, "Wealth, Saving and the Rate of Interest," *Journal of Political Economy*, 59:93–116, 1951.

have caused the security prices to fall and would have made the deficit increasingly difficult to finance. There was, therefore, considerable justification for the policy under such emergency conditions. However, the policy is also costly because it fuels the inflation. The money supply increases when the Treasury borrows from the Fed, and the failure to permit interest rates to rise causes aggregate demand to be persistently excessive. The interest rate "pegging" policy may therefore have been justified during the emergency conditions of World War II, but there certainly was no justification for its continuation after the war, nor is there justification for the Fed's more or less persistent tendency to concern itself with interest rates and so-called orderly bond markets.

Let us consider the consequences of the pegging policy in some detail. The real rate of interest implied by the $IS$ curve is the rate that equates the injections into the income stream with leakages from the income stream. The particular rate of interest that equates injections with leakages at the full-employment level of income is sometimes referred to as the "natural" rate of interest. This contrasts with the rate of interest implied by the $LM$ curve, which equates the demand for real money balances with real value of the money supply, and may be called the "money" rate of interest. For equilibrium to exist at full employment, these two rates must coincide at the full-employment level of income. This is the situation shown in Figure 15-2 where the aggregate supply function is vertical and intersects $D(p)_0$ at price level $p_0$, and where $IS_0$ and $LM_0$ intersect at $Y^*$ and the natural rate of interest $i_n$.

If the monetary authority is under pressure from the Treasury to support the government bond market in order to raise bond prices and lower interest rates, then the monetary authority must engage in open market purchases of government securities. Suppose therefore that $i_t$ is set as the target rate of interest, and let the monetary authority therefore shift the $LM$ curve to $LM_1$ where this money rate of interest is established. However, the fall in the rate of interest stimulates investment as reflected in an upward shift in the aggregate demand function to $D(p)_1$. The price level therefore rises and the real value of the money supply declines, and equilibrium will tend to be restored at the natural rate of interest and at the higher price level $p_1$.

However, if the monetary authority is committed to the pegging policy, it must offset the equilibrating tendency of the leftward move of the $LM$ curve due to the rising price level, by continually shoving the $LM$ curve back to the right to maintain the interest rate at $i_t$. This means that in the next round aggregate demand shifts to $D(p)_2$, and the price level tends to rise to $p_2$; but

**FIGURE 15-2**
Pegging the interest rate below the natural
rate produces steady inflation (all values
except the price level in real terms)

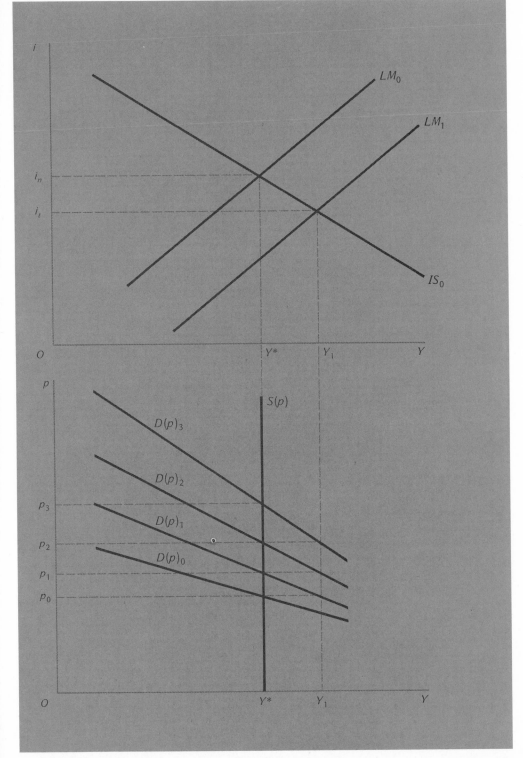

the monetary authority again increases the money supply, moving aggregate demand to $D(p)_3$, and so on in a perpetual inflationary process. The process is marked by the fact that, since the monetary authority tries to keep the real value of the money supply fixed, it must increase the nominal amount by even larger amounts as the price level increases. Under the circumstances, then, policies to peg interest rates are apt to be quite mischievous even though they appear harmless to the unwary and even beneficial when offered in such noble terms as attempting to prevent disorderly conditions in financial markets.

## 15-3
## INFLATION DUE TO MARKET IMPERFECTIONS: DEMAND SHIFT AND COST PUSH

When demand shifts rapidly from one sector to another, prices tend to rise in those sectors in which demand increases and tend to fall in those sectors in which demand decreases. If the overall level of aggregate demand remains the same, there should, in theory, be no change in the overall level of prices. However, modern industrial economies are characterized by two circumstances, sluggish resource mobility and stickiness of prices and wages in the downward direction, that combine to cause such shifts in demand to create inflation and unemployment simultaneously. When demand shifts from sector B to A, prices tend to rise in sector A, but institutional rigidities prevent prices from falling in B. Meanwhile, since resources move sluggishly or not at all in response to the shift in demand, the price increase in sector A is accentuated by scarcities, and at the same time a surplus of resources and unemployment develops in sector B. Thus we have a case of demand shift inflation.[1]

In addition to demand shift, market imperfections may produce upward pressure on wages and prices of a kind that could not exist under competitive conditions. The idea, variously known as cost push or wage push inflation, had a pervasive influence on economic thought and policy in the 1950s. It has enjoyed a revival in recent years as the recession of 1970 failed for a long time to produce any slowing in the rate of inflation and as it continues to be difficult to explain the presence of inflation under conditions in which aggregate demand does not appear to be excessive. In its crudest form the wage push argument is that the market power of unions is so great that wages are forced up steadily, and the resulting cost increase then increases the level of prices.

Wage push inflation may be illustrated by referring to Figure 15-3. Ini-

---

[1] See C. L. Schultze, *Recent Inflation in the United States,* Study Paper No. 1, *Employment, Growth and Price Levels,* U.S. Congress, Joint Economic Committee, Washington, 1959.

**FIGURE 15-3**
Effect of an exogenous rise in the money
wage rate (all values except the price level
in real terms)

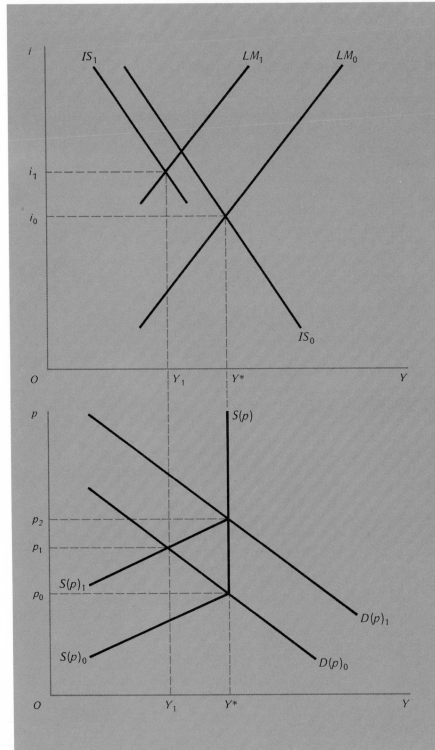

tially, equilibrium is at income $Y^*$, interest rate $i_0$, and price level $p_0$. Assume next that there is an exogenous increase in the money wage rate brought about by a change in union preferences or, perhaps, by an increase in the legal minimum wage rate. Since the real wage is increased by the rise in money wages, firms react by reducing output and employment. As a consequence of the fall in output, consumption will decline but, because the marginal propensity to consume is less than unity, by less than the fall in output. Consequently, there is excess demand in commodity markets, and the price level rises. Figure 15–3 summarizes these circumstances by noting that the rise in money wages shifts the aggregate supply curve upward; this means that there is excess demand at the existing price level $p_0$. The price level now rises, and as this happens the LM curve shifts to the left because the real value of the money supply declines, and the IS curve also shifts to the left because of such factors as the Pigou effect, the country's deteriorating international competitive position, and the rise in the real value of income tax collections due to the money illusion which is built into the tax structure.

Equilibrium may then be established at the intersection of the new aggregate supply curve with $D(p)_0$, implying the higher price level $p_1$. This would be consistent with the intersection of the new IS and LM curves ($IS_1$ and $LM_1$, respectively) at income $Y_1$ and interest rate $i_1$. The trouble with the solution is that the new equilibrium is at a lower level of income $Y_1$ and a lower level of employment than existed previously.

Considerations of this sort tend to explain why many economists doubt the efficacy of minimum wage legislation. Despite its humanitarian appeal, a rise in the legal minimum wage, although it raises the real wage of some workers, may do so only because it creates unemployment for other workers. To eliminate the unemployment, policy may now shift the IS and LM curves back to $IS_0$ and $LM_0$ so that they again intersect at $Y^*$. This shifts the aggregate demand curve up to $D(p)_1$ and implies a further rise in the price level, since the real wage must be lowered in order to restore output and employment to their original levels. Equilibrium may then be established at $Y^*$ and $p_2$, implying a net raise in the price level which is exactly proportional to the rise in the money wage rate. Thus the rise in the minimum wage accomplishes nothing as long as employers are at liberty to determine how much output to produce and how many workers to hire. Indeed, the economy may be worse off in the end since the higher levels of money wages and prices may create balance of payments difficulties.

The process we have described here does not yet qualify as a theory of inflation. However, it becomes one if policy insists on continuing to run on the wage-price treadmill. Friends of labor will note that the rise in the price level has eroded the real wage gain and they therefore suggest another rise in the minimum wage rate. If the monetary authority then responds by preventing unemployment, the inflation will keep on going in a merry wage-price chase.

The increase in the money wage rate could have been caused by the monopoly power of labor unions, and the analysis of this wage push would have been similar to the foregoing. Repetition of the analysis, moreover, would have confirmed that it is the possibility of intervention by the monetary authority that turns the situation into one of danger for price stability. If a wage increase creates unemployment and if this is offset by an expansionary monetary policy, the presumption is that since output and employment will then be the same as before, real wages will also be the same. Consequently, prices will have risen in proportion to the wage increase. Since real wages therefore return to their original level, the unions now force a new increase in money wages which is again countered by an increase in the money supply. Thus a steady inflationary process can be generated if the monetary authority "legitimizes" the wage increases by offsetting their unfavorable employment effects.

The cost push doctrine is a bleak one. First, it implies that the monetary authority is in a hopeless dilemma. It can combat inflation only if it tolerates unemployment. Second, the doctrine suggests that a guarantee of full employment such as is contained in the United States Employment Act of 1946 acts as an open invitation for irresponsible wage-price behavior since the guarantee commits the government to policies designed to maintain high levels of employment and tight labor markets. And, finally, the cost push doctrine suggests that, during periods of unemployment, increases in aggregate demand may not raise output and employment but may, rather, be frittered away in the form of wage-price increases. Readers can imagine for themselves the discouraging situation that would arise if an upward shift in the aggregate demand function were always matched by an equal upward shift in the aggregate supply function.

## 15–4
## THE PHILLIPS CURVE AND THE TRADE-OFF
## BETWEEN INFLATION AND UNEMPLOYMENT

The assumption that underlies the aggregate supply curve of Figure 15–1 is that, as aggregate demand is increased at less than full employment, money wages remain invariant and aggregate demand increases are reflected in increases in output, employment, and the price level. Then, once involuntary unemployment is eliminated and the full-employment output level $Y^*$ is reached, further increases in aggregate demand provoke proportional increases in money wages and prices. Since this means that the real wage remains unchanged, no further increases in output and employment take place.

It is often suggested that in practice no such sharp break exists. Changes in aggregate demand tend to evoke both price and quantity responses. During recession characterized by ample excess capacity and considerable involuntary unemployment the aggregate supply curve may be close to horizontal, additional output and employment being purchasable at almost no cost in terms of a higher price level. Then, as output and employment continue to

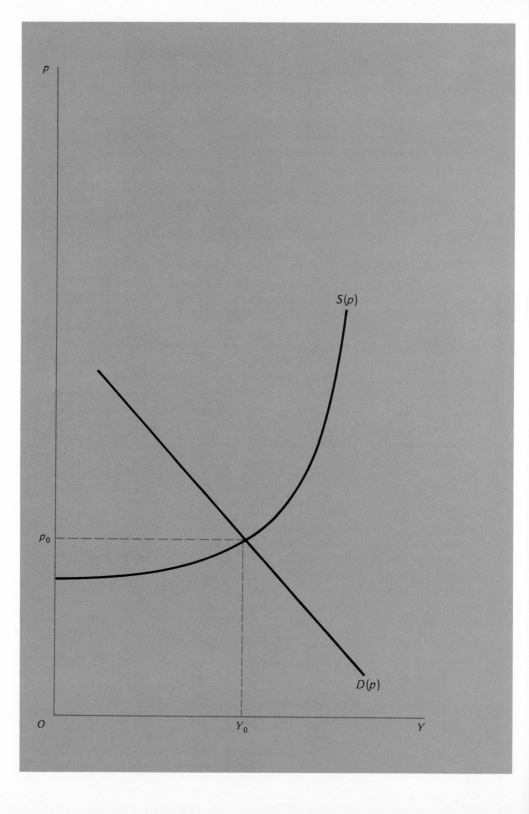

increase, shortages and labor and capacity bottlenecks begin to appear, so that an increase in demand evokes less of an output and more of a price level response. Successive additional increases in aggregate demand will continue to increase the proportion in which the demand increase is reflected in a rise in the price level, reaching, in the limit, the classical case where there is no further output change at all.

The aggregate supply curve which reflects these considerations might appear as the $Y = S(p)$ function of Figure 15–4. Unfortunately, it is no longer possible to state what the full-employment level of income is. The point at which it is desirable to have the aggregate demand function intersect is a matter of choice, some persons favoring lower output in return for a lower price level, while others prefer a more high-pressure economy with lower unemployment.

A relationship which, in spirit, is similar to the variable elasticity aggregate supply function is the "Phillips curve," which relates the rate of increase of money wage rates to the unemployment rate. Utilizing data for the United Kingdom, A. W. Phillips derived an empirical relationship which suggested that when unemployment is high the rate of wage increase is low, whereas when unemployment is low wages tend to rise rapidly.[1] An example of this inverse relation is pictured in Figure 15–5 where we assume that the initial Phillips curve is $SPC_1$. Low unemployment tends to be associated with both labor scarcities and a high relative level of aggregate demand so that competition among employers for labor causes wages to rise rapidly. Conversely, high unemployment implies labor surplus, and wage rates therefore tend to rise less rapidly.

To attempt to understand the nature of the Phillips curve we must first call attention to the fact, implicit in our analysis of the growth process, that rising wages do not necessarily imply rising prices once the effect of productivity change is allowed for. The cost of producing one more unit of output, "marginal cost" as this is known, can be calculated by dividing the money wage rate by the marginal product of labor. Thus, if a worker is paid $5 an hour and contributes an additional 2 units of output per hour to the product of the firm, the cost of producing each of the extra units is $5/2 = $2.50. An increase in productivity which increases the output of this one worker by 50 percent so that her or his marginal product rises from 2 to 3 units, would lower marginal cost to $5/3 = $1.67. However, if at the same time the wage is increased by 50 percent to $7.50, marginal cost would then be

---

[1] A. S. Phillips, "The Relation between Unemployment and the Rate of Change of Money Wage Rates in the United Kingdom, 1862–1957," *Economica*, 25:283–299, 1958.

**FIGURE 15–4**
**Illustration of an aggregate supply function with increasing slope as real output increases**

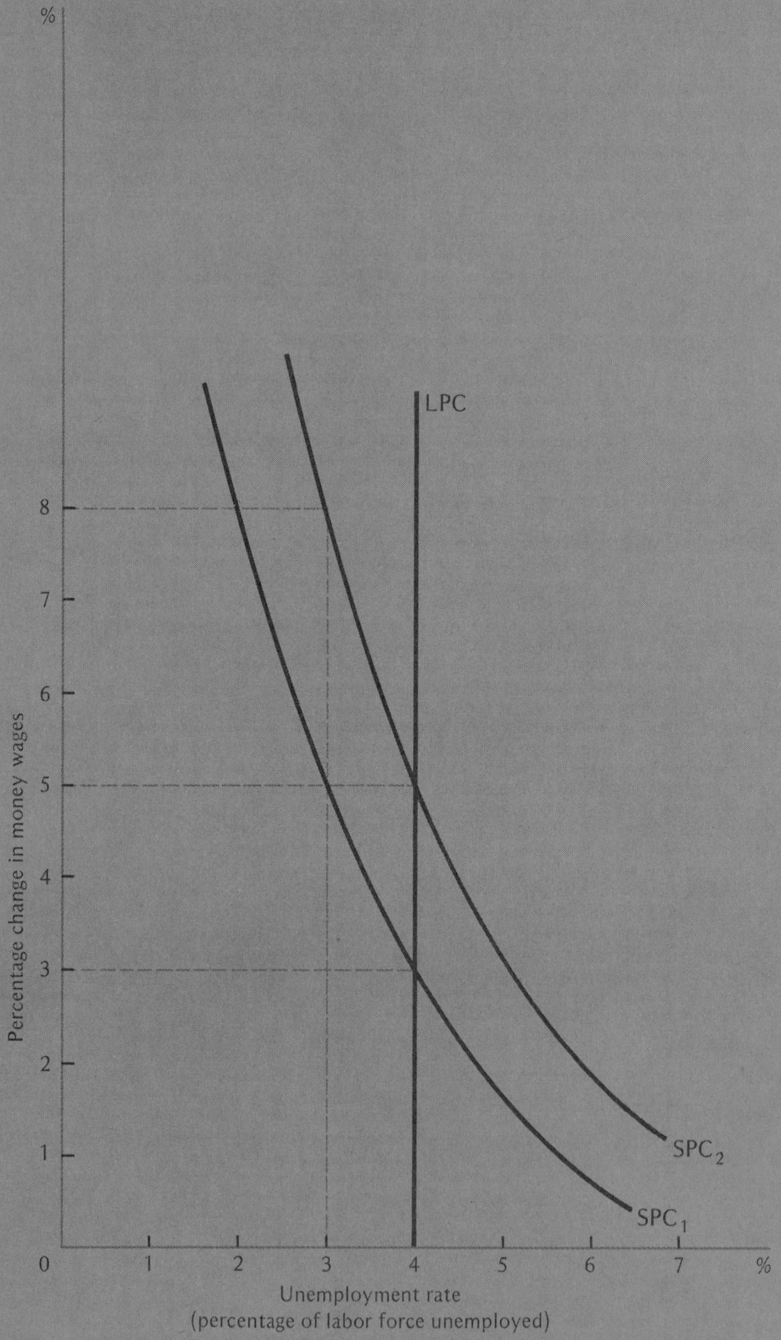
%
Percentage change in money wages
8
7
6
5
4
3
2
1
0
1
2
3
4
5
6
7
%
Unemployment rate
(percentage of labor force unemployed)
LPC
SPC$_2$
SPC$_1$

$7.50/3 = \$2.50$ and would therefore be the same as it was originally. Consequently, we see here that increases in wages increase marginal cost; that increases in marginal productivity reduce marginal cost; and that if both wages and productivity rise in the same proportion, marginal cost will remain constant. Since marginal costs increase only when wages grow more rapidly than productivity, it is only then that there is a tendency for wage increases to be translated into higher prices.

The Phillips curve suggests that there is a "trade-off" between unemployment and inflation. Stable prices can be attained only at the expense of considerable unemployment, whereas unemployment can be brought down to reasonable levels only at the cost of a rate of inflation that may be regarded as excessive. There is some presumption, moreover, that perhaps the post–World War II Phillips curves of industrial countries are farther to the right than their prewar counterparts, and the trade-off problem has therefore become more acute. Some of the reasons for this are cited below. Before we get to these reasons, we should examine the analytical basis of the Phillips curve. It is, after all, somewhat unique. The aggregate demand and supply curves relate the level of output (and therefore employment) to the *level* of prices and wages. However, the Phillips curve relates employment to the *rate of change* of wages.

Suppose the rate of growth of money wages is 3 percent so that the unemployment rate, as indicated by $SPC_1$ in Figure 15–5, is 4 percent. Suppose also that the rate of productivity growth is 3 percent and that, since marginal costs are therefore constant, the price level remains constant. Now suppose that aggregate demand is increased and that this lowers unemployment to 3 percent and raises the rate of wage increase to 5 percent per year. If productivity continues to grow at 3 percent, this will imply that marginal costs are rising at a rate of 2 percent; this suggests that the price level will also tend to rise at a rate of about 2 percent a year. However, if this is the case, real wages will still be rising at the same 3 percent as before, and it will therefore be difficult to explain why the 5 percent rate of money wage increase should bring forth any more employment than the 3 percent rate.

Considerations of this sort have led many economists to doubt the validity of the trade-off implications of the Phillips curve. Professor Friedman argued that an attempt to lower unemployment below what he called the "natural rate" (assume that to be the 4 percent rate of Figure 15–5) would have effects that are very similar to attempts to lower the rate of interest below its natural rate.[1] Both efforts would result in endless inflation. The argument can be illustrated by distinguishing between a short-run and a long-run Phillips curve. In

[1] M. Friedman, "The Role of Monetary Policy," *American Economic Review*, 58:1–17, 1968.

**FIGURE 15–5**
Illustration of the Phillips curve and the
trade-off in the short run and the long run

Figure 15–5 the initial increase in aggregate demand that lowered the unemployment rate to 3 percent and raised the rate of wage increase to 5 percent involved a movement along the short-run Phillips curve SPC$_1$. However, as the price level begins to rise, and workers begin to realize that real wages are not growing any more rapidly than before, the amount of labor offered will return to its original level so that the unemployment rate will return to 4 percent, even while the rate of wage increase remains at 5 percent. What we have, therefore, is a negatively sloped short-run Phillips curve (SPC$_1$) which, however, gives way to the vertical long-run Phillips curve (LPC) located at the natural rate of unemployment.

The situation that will exist once the rate of inflation is fully taken into account in employment and labor supply decisions is that the natural rate of unemployment will be associated with a 5 percent rate of wage increase. It is, therefore, where the long-run Phillips curve cuts the new short-run Phillips curve SPC$_2$. If policy makers continue to believe that this unemployment rate is excessive and attempt to deal with the problem by raising aggregate demand again, this may lower the unemployment rate to 3 percent in the short run but, as can be seen from the SPC$_2$ curve, it will raise the rate of wage inflation to 8 percent; this implies that the rate of price inflation will rise to 5 ($=8-3$) percent. Once people get used to this, they will again realize that real wages are not rising any faster than before, and measured unemployment then will drift back to the natural rate. Thus, to conclude, in this view the long-run Phillips curve is vertical. This means that there is no trade-off except in the short run, that the natural rate of unemployment is compatible with *any* rate of inflation, and that a lower rate of unemployment implies ever-*accelerating* inflation. The message for policy is that demand management should not be used to attempt to reduce the unemployment rate below the natural rate any more than it should attempt to lower the rate of interest below its natural rate. If unemployment at the natural rate is judged to be excessive, ways had better be found to shift the long-run Phillips curve to the left.

We have deliberately put the anti–Phillips curve argument in a somewhat extreme form. In defense of the concept, it should be said that there are, as we shall show, in Part 4, legitimate trade-off considerations.[1] Moreover, the fact that the Phillips curve is less elastic with respect to inflation in the long run than it is in the short run does not impair the usefulness of the concept as a device which assists the analyst to discuss anti-inflation policy. Finally, although the natural rate of unemployment is useful as an abstraction, its practical relevance is somewhat limited by the fact that no one knows what it is. In theory the natural rate of unemployment ought to be the level of

[1] Passive policy that contents itself with sluggish labor markets in the interest of preventing the short-run Phillips curve from rising has been attacked by a number of economists. For discussions of some of the legitimate trade-offs between the low- and high-pressure economies, see J. Tobin, "Inflation and Unemployment," *American Economic Review*, 62:1–18, 1972; and A. Okun, "Upward Mobility in a High-Pressure Economy," *Brookings Papers on Economic Activity*, 3:207–252, 1973.

measured unemployment which, given the procedures for measuring unemployment, would be observed if the labor market were in equilibrium. But since we do not know what this level of employment is, we cannot know for sure what the natural rate of unemployment is; since that is the case, the theory of the natural rate provides little guidance for policy.

## 15-5
## INCOMES POLICY AND OTHER NON-MONETARY-FISCAL APPROACHES TO THE CONTROL OF INFLATION

The kind of anti-inflation policy that is appropriate depends upon the cause of the inflation and on the way in which the economy reacts to market forces and to policy changes. In thinking about the problem it is useful to attempt first to decide if there is some point on the existing Phillips curve that is satisfactory. If a tolerable degree of price stability that is not accompanied by excessive unemployment appears feasible, then the job can be done satisfactorily by resort to general monetary and fiscal controls that regulate the level of aggregate demand. On the other hand, if an acceptable degree of price stability appears incompatible with reasonable full employment, one must conclude that the existing terms of the trade-off are unsatisfactory and that policy must be directed toward shifting the Phillips curve to the left. Some of the policies that might qualify are those that are designed to restore or intensify competition. This might involve a tougher and more comprehensive antitrust policy; it might involve labor legislation; and it might involve elimination of protective tariffs and other barriers to import competition. Second, a shift to the left of the Phillips curve might be accomplished by policies designed to make resources more adaptable to alternative employments and policies that increase their mobility. Worker training, job information services, and relocation loans would appear to be in order here. Finally, one can force the Phillips curve to the left by suppressing market forces and resorting to direct wage-price controls or to some milder form of nonmarket control such as wage-price guideposts, a wage increase moratorium, and the like.

Old-fashioned theory implied that the best defense against inflation lay in policies designed to maintain a reasonably competitive economy combined with policies to prevent erratic and excessive growth of the money supply. In combination these policies would ensure both price stability and full employment. Even after the Keynesian revolution it was thought that the maintenance of an appropriate level of aggregate demand would be sufficient to deal simultaneously with unemployment and inflation. The idea that inflation could be accompanied by unemployment was not seriously considered until well after World War II.

It became clear during the 1950s that restrictive monetary and fiscal policies were exacting an awesome cost in terms of lost output, high unemployment, and sluggish growth as a price for stopping inflation. It was at this time that economists began talking about a trade-off and about the need for policies designed to improve it. During the recession of 1957–1958 when the price level and the unemployment rate climbed simultaneously, there was considerable discussion of a new phenomenon known as "structural unemployment." It was argued that because of rapid technical change ("automation" in the jargon of the era) there were groups in the labor force whose skills had become obsolete and who therefore could no longer find employment. It followed that price stability would be associated with a higher level of unemployment than previously; and it also implied that the expansion of demand would create inflation rather than full employment because the creation of a job opportunity was no guarantee that the job could be capably filled even though unemployment was high. The Phillips curve, in this view, had shifted to the right because of accelerated technical change.

The structural unemployment thesis did not find a ready market among economists, and, indeed, little evidence could be mustered on its behalf.[1] Certainly, the smooth expansion and rapid growth of employment after 1960 proved that the unemployment problem was quite amenable to demand expansion. Nevertheless it is important to note that the quality of the labor force may itself be a function of the level and duration of unemployment. When labor is scarce and demand buoyant, business itself invests in the training of its work force. At other times the job is left to the government, or it is not done at all. Prolonged idleness brings with it the danger of deterioration and obsolescence of worker skills. Thus the trade-off may appear to be growing worse just when monetary-fiscal stimulus is most needed, and it therefore acts as a deterrent to the use of such policies.

The structural debate of the 1950s was one of the first in a continuing attempt to examine the component parts of the wage-employment determination process.[2] Recent work emphasizes that there is no such thing as a single national labor market, and that the clue to the explanation of inflation in the absence of excessive aggregate demand lies in an examination of how wage and price decisions are reached in individual markets. The important question that must be answered is: How is it possible for firms to accede to union demands for wage increases that are persistently in excess of productivity gains? Firms who do this constantly must eventually be forcing themselves out of business. Nevertheless there seems no doubt that the continued inflation of 1969–1970 in the face of sharply restrictive monetary-fiscal policy and rising unemployment was largely sustained by excessive wage increases. The wage settlements were particularly large in the highly organized craft unions in the construction industry.

The forces that may be at work can be studied by visualizing the economy as a system of interconnected submarkets. Many of these submarkets are dominated by a few powerful sellers. In such submarkets it is easy for the

---

[1] J. W. Knowles and E. D. Kalacheck, "High Unemployment Rates, 1957–1960: Structural Transformation or Inadequate Demand," U.S. Congress, Subcommittee on Economic Statistics of the Joint Economic Committee, Government Printing Office, Washington, 1961.

[2] For example E. S. Phelps et al., *Microeconomic Foundations of Employment and Inflation Theory*, W. W. Norton & Company, Inc., New York, 1970.

parties to believe that they are to a large extent isolated from and independent of the rest of the economy. Thus a craft union makes an unreasonable wage demand because it believes employers have little choice but to accede; and employers grant the request because they do not consider that the resulting price increase will bring retaliatory competitive pressure. Neither party fully realizes that its behavior is suicidal in the long run. Firms price themselves out of markets, and substitutes for union labor are eventually found.

In addition to the dilemma discussed in the preceding section, the monetary-fiscal authorities have to consider sectoral problems. If they expand the money supply to offset the unemployment created by a wage-price increase of a particular sector, they create excess demand in other sectors. On the other hand, if they stand firm against inflation, their restrictive policies may impinge on the sectors that are not generating the inflation, with the consequence that inflationary recession results. Some submarkets of the economy are vulnerable to credit restriction; others are not. Similarly, a reduction in government purchases will have disproportionate impacts on different markets. Because of resource immobility and other barriers that isolate submarkets, the labor surplus in one area may have little impact on wages and prices in another.

Various considerations such as the effective separation of labor markets, the cost push dilemma model discussed earlier, and the structural unemployment argument long ago suggested to policy makers that supplementary tools would be necessary to reconcile full employment with stable prices. The most common tool employed in industrial countries is direct government intervention in the wage-price determination process. Such policy goes under the rubric "incomes policy" because ultimately it represents an agreement as to how the national income will be split up between wages and other shares. Incomes policy encompasses a wide range of possibilities. Wages may be controlled directly by means of legal wage freezes, or by attempts to moderate wage demands by establishing objective criteria for wage determination. Sometimes only wages are controlled, and sometimes prices are controlled as well. The degree of toughness of enforcement varies from the level of exhortation all the way to control enforced by legal sanction.

Incomes policies were common in many European countries after World War II, primarily because these countries felt the need to keep their price levels in check because of their severe balance of payments problems. The United States did not adopt an incomes policy until early 1962 (although it did resort to price controls during the Korean war), at which time the Council of Economic Advisers introduced wage-price "guideposts." These guideposts reflected the Council's belief that general monetary and fiscal tools needed to be supplemented by guidelines for *specific* wage-price decisions that would be consistent with general price stability. Thus the Council's guideposts implied a clear effort to shift the Phillips curve to the left, in order to enjoy higher employment without inflation. Specifically, the Council recommended that the rate of increase of money wages be limited to the overall rate of productivity increase. With respect to prices, the Council called for price stability in those industries in which productivity was growing at the national average rate, for price declines in industries with above-average productivity growth, and for price increases where productivity was growing more slowly than the average.

The guideposts try to hold wage changes to the rate of growth of output per worker-hour. In so doing, the guideposts attempt to produce the wage-price behavior that would have occurred naturally in a competitive economy. If there were no imperfections in labor and product markets, wages paid for similar occupations would tend toward equality in all industries. The general wage level, moreover, would rise at a rate equal to the rate of increase of national average productivity. Under these competitive conditions, any industry that failed to realize the average national productivity gain would lose its relative share of the national market. This is because competition would keep wage rates at a uniform level, so that industries in which productivity did not grow at the national average would find their costs per unit of output rising, and prices would therefore rise relative to prices in other industries. Output in such industries would tend to shrink, and resources would be transferred to industries where rapid productivity growth was causing market expansion. Under such conditions, price increases in low-productivity areas would be offset by declining prices in high-productivity areas, and the overall level of prices would remain stable. It was the attempt to attain a competitive solution, where competition does not in fact exist, that constituted the essential logic of the guideposts.

The United States guideposts were not received with overwhelming enthusiasm in all quarters, although as time wears on an increasing fraction of the electorate appears to be becoming convinced that direct government interference in the wage-price-making process is appropriate. A problem with guideposts is that they are virtually unenforceable since the only sanction against offenders is bad publicity. Nevertheless, the guideposts appear to have been moderately successful in combating inflation up to 1965. They were, of necessity, abandoned in early 1968. By that time prices were rising rapidly, and it was no longer possible to ask workers to limit their wage demands to the rate of productivity growth since that was equivalent to asking them to take a cut in real wages. Guideposts, unfortunately, appear to work best during a period of stable prices when they are least needed. They are probably most useful during periods of slack demand and rising prices when their imposition might help to moderate inflationary expectations, thereby permitting increased demand to raise output and employment rather than wages and prices.

The evidence on the efficacy of incomes policies is mixed. It is very difficult to measure the impact of incomes policy on the price level, and even if this could be done it is not a fair test, since the true test is whether the policy has improved the trade-off. Experience suggests that even where unions are committed to a national incomes policy, there tends to be considerable upward "wage drift." This occurs when employers attempt to retain and reward valued employees by promoting them into higher-paying job categories, and the brisker the demand for labor the more rapid the promotions and the faster the wage drift. Also, productivity-based incomes policies usually cannot withstand rapidly changing import prices. When the cost of imported fuel rises, this will raise the domestic price level and lower real wages. Workers cannot then be expected to stick to a previously agreed money wage increase. Similarly, heavy dependence on imported foods creates a situation that constantly threatens to undermine wage agreements because of the danger that food prices will rise. The productivity arithmetic, that a rise in wages equal to the growth of productivity implies a stable price level, works only for a closed economy.

The continuance of inflationary pressure in the United States in 1969–1970 long after aggregate demand ceased to be excessive brought with it a renewal of demands for guideposts and other anti-inflationary schemes. As suggested earlier, the reintroduction of the guideposts might have been beneficial under the circumstances as a means of moderating inflationary expectations. We will never know if the policy would have worked because it was not tried, the administration seeing truth at the time only in the monetarist doctrine that inflation is caused by excessively rapid growth in the money supply. As the inflation continued in 1971 and the balance of payments situation became critical, the Administration gave up on monetarism. The direct controls that it had sworn would never be imposed, and that it had claimed would never work, were suddenly imposed and hailed as the salvation. A comprehensive temporary freeze was imposed in mid-1971; this was then followed by an endless succession of "phases" which phased out the controls but failed to phase out the inflation. In the meantime the Administration found time to freeze beef prices for three months in mid-1973, and to muddle its way through the subsequent "energy crisis" by resorting to "allocation" schemes that created shortages, waiting lines, and huge inconveniences in a futile effort allegedly designed to prevent increase in the prices of hydrocarbon fuels.

In the United States direct controls and incomes policies are viewed as temporary devices to be resorted to only in emergency. This tendency to view the policies as emergency measures introduces the role of expectations in a critical manner. If there is considerable discussion of the need for wage and price controls, the discussion may lead to the expectation that controls are about to be imposed. This would lead to attempts to increase wages and prices prior to the freeze. Thus the anticipation of the controls itself brings about a rise in prices, and those who are the most aggressive in securing increases receive the greatest benefits. Once the controls are in place, there will be constant incentives to find ways to evade them, and those who are the cleverest, the most unscrupulous, and the most favored by some arbitrary circumstance will be the principal gainers.

Since comprehensive controls require massive administrative machinery, a method of gaining compliance without establishing the enforcement apparatus is to announce that the freeze will be temporary. If people believe this, firms will then feel that they can raise prices after the freeze is over so that not much is lost by compliance. Workers, similarly, may be willing to accept a temporary wage pause if they think they can make up for it later. Unfortunately, such compliance is bought at the price of defeating one of the aims of price control, the breaking of inflationary expectations. Furthermore, during a temporary freeze it pays to attempt to hoard goods for the purpose of future sale, and firms will therefore attempt to accumulate inventories while pretending to their customers that they are out of merchandise. However, their suppliers will have similar ideas in mind and will withhold supplies. Finally, workers will not be eager to work hard if they can make up the lost hours by inflated overtime pay after the freeze. The tendency, therefore, is for a temporary freeze to accentuate shortages, and that hardly seems like the way to stop inflation.

In addition to the huge administrative difficulties associated with price controls are a number of economic dangers. In a market economy, price changes are signals that call forth the resource shifts that then produce the productivity improvements that cause real income to expand. The difficulty lies in attempting to separate the desirable relative price changes from the undesirable general price increases that represent inflation. A price stability goal that is couched in terms of some general price index makes room for the kind of relative price changes that serve as economic signals. The guideposts, for example, recognized explicitly that changing relative prices are essential to the efficient operation of the economy. But what about selective or general wage and price controls? If prices and wages are arbitrarily prevented from changing in response to the forces of demand and supply, the system loses the signals that direct resources into their various uses. Rising and falling stocks of goods, long waiting lines, and empty seats will indicate whether output should be raised or lowered and whether price should be changed. But prices cannot be changed. If entrepreneurs attempt to react by varying output, they will find it difficult to do this legally since it would be illegal to pay a premium to attract additional labor and other inputs.

The fact that it appears to be market imperfections that make full employment and stable prices so difficult to attain simultaneously has rekindled interest in restoring competition to the economy. Experience suggests that very little can be accomplished by antitrust policy. However, it does seem feasible to break down some of the barriers that surround submarkets by improving the mobility of resources. This idea applies particularly to labor, and it includes business executives and professional persons as well as unskilled and semiskilled workers. A modest number of programs designed to retrain those displaced by mechanization or demand shift have already been initiated. There are also limited programs of assistance for those workers and their families who must move to find employment. Other programs exist that subsidize industries to relocate in pockets of high unemployment. It would certainly be helpful if the federal government embarked on a program of making relocation loans since the absence of credit is often a serious deterrent to mobility.

To reduce the cost of the trade-off, any barriers to entry into any profession or occupation that is unrelated to the ability and skill of the applicant should be eliminated. Obviously, we have just begun to scratch the surface. Recently the barriers to entry into the craft unions in the construction industries have come under attack. But what about other crafts? And what about restricted entry in such professions as medicine? Racial barriers to employment remain formidable, and discrimination against women continues to be widespread even in such unlikely places as universities. The artificial barriers to labor mobility that exist in the United States are too numerous and pervasive to warrant relating.

Despite the great importance of structural reform, there is one point that the macroeconomist must continually emphasize. Even though monetary-fiscal controls may be incapable of maintaining full employment without inflation, it is important to realize that full employment cannot be maintained without an adequate level of aggregate demand. There is, after all, little point in retraining or relocating a person if there is no job available to him or her anywhere or on any terms.

## 15–6
### SOME PERSPECTIVES ON THE INFLATION PROBLEM
Some people find it easy to get upset about inflation but they find it difficult to be specific about what is bothering them once it is pointed out to them that their incomes are probably rising about as fast or faster than prices. They hardly ever seem aware of the severe costs of stopping inflation, and they are not often very clear about why inflation is injurious, and if it is, who the in-jured parties are. In this section we shall deal, rather briefly, with such ques-tions as who is hurt by inflation, how well do we measure inflation, and are there simple methods of easing the pain of inflation without resorting to poli-cies that create unemployment.

Let us take up these questions in order. First, why is inflation bad, and who is hurt by it? In answering this question it is perhaps useful to consider the ex-treme—hyperinflation. Hyperinflation, as indicated earlier, has usually been the product of war and its aftermath. More recently very rapid rates of infla-tion have occurred where governments, impatient to get on with development plans, have consistently spent in excess of tax revenues. In any case, the cause of hyperinflation is invariably a prolonged period during which govern-ment expenditures exceed tax yield, and during which the resultant deficit causes the money supply to be increased rapidly. The combination of expan-sionary policies with inflationary expectations continually shifts the *IS* and *LM* curves to the right and keeps aggregate demand and the price level moving upward. The climax of hyperinflation appears when the flight from money is such that the velocity of circulation approaches infinity, and price increases become calibrated in daily rather than in annual rates.[1]

The government cannot indefinitely acquire resources by means of cur-

---

[1] See the paper by Phillip Cagan, "The Monetary Dynamics of Hyperinflation," in Milton Friedman, ed., *Studies in the Quantity Theory of Money*, The University of Chicago Press, Chicago, 1956, for a discussion of the effect of price expectations on transactions velocity.

rency issue. When the price level rises at such a rapid rate that the public loses faith in the stability of the monetary unit, trade will no longer be carried on with money. Such a flight from currency implies that exchanges will be made on a purely barter basis. Since the government has nothing to barter, it must resort to outright requisition.

We may well imagine how demoralizing hyperinflation would be. Merchants will not sell goods for money in the morning if they expect prices to double by the afternoon. Unless they are given a physical unit of some commodity, they will prefer to hoard their stocks of goods rather than make the exchange. Exchange during hyperinflation inevitably degenerates into primitive bartering.

Production is also impaired by hyperinflation. The workers in an automobile plant cannot be paid in anything other than money. It would not do to divide a car into parts and pay workers with fenders, heaters, and radiators. Because they must be paid in money, the workers have no incentive to work, so that production breaks down except in a few areas where it is possible to make compensation in kind. If, as seems unlikely, the car actually gets produced, it is difficult to see how it can be sold because the car producer is not likely to want a car's worth of groceries or a car's worth of paperclips in return.

The social consequences of hyperinflation are no less terrifying than the economic effects. Debtors pursue creditors in order to pay back past obligations with worthless currency. The earnings of fixed-income groups are wiped out. The value of accumulated liquid saving disappears. Some groups in society are able to defend themselves against inflation, but others are not. The end result can only be one in which society is set against itself and in which political institutions are placed under strain. Hyperinflation replaces industry and thrift with hoarding and speculation. Normal economic activity simply cannot function under such conditions.

To some extent there is danger that even creeping inflation may have similar, though less drastic, consequences. If the long-run outlook is for a rising price level, the inducement to save may be impaired. Interest rates will rise because of the decline in the supply of real saving and because of expected price increases. Investment and growth may therefore be retarded. Creeping inflation may injure small savers. Government bonds, insurance policies, saving deposits, pension rights, and other forms of fixed-interest-bearing assets all decline in real value.

The evidence that economic efficiency and saving-investment decisions have been seriously distorted as a result of the sort of inflation that the industrial nations have experienced in the last several decades is mixed. Those who are hysterical about inflation tend to emphasize its arbitrary redistributive consequences, the fact that a relaxed view of inflation may cause a slow rate to accelerate into a more rapid and perhaps uncontrollable rate, and the fact that inflation creates balance of payments problems as long as fixed exchange rates are maintained.

The evil distributional effects of creeping inflation have undoubtedly been exaggerated. Persons can learn that they ought not to invest their savings in assets that earn 8 percent a year when the expectation is that prices will rise at a rate of 10 percent. Moreover, it is only myopia and obsolete usury laws that make it possible for anyone to borrow at such a low rate as 8 percent during a period of rapid inflation. A competitive market in which correct price level expectations are held would cause the nominal rate of interest to equal the real rate plus the rate of inflation. Persons on a "fixed income," over whom the anti-inflationists constantly wring their hands, undoubtedly exist, although they are somewhat difficult to identify. Many private pension plans pay in fixed nominal amounts, but this is deceiving. Many take inflation into account by paying benefits based on the most recent level of earnings of the employee before retirement. Moreover, the federal government's social security system keeps up with inflation because benefit increases in the United States are now geared to the cost of living.

Despite what was said above, it would be wrong to dismiss lightly the difficulties that the average family encounters in attempting to protect itself against inflation. If savings are put into time deposits, the interest paid may be below the rate of inflation and so the real interest received is negative. To add insult to injury, the nominal interest which is earned is taxable income. In addition, under the progressive income tax structure as it exists in most countries, the family will find that its average tax rate is rising as nominal earnings increase, even though real wages may be declining if prices are rising faster than wages.

It is certainly important to be concerned about inflation, especially when it reaches the "double digit" rate experienced in 1974, but it is also important not to lose sight of the trade-off. People tend to think, quite erroneously, that inflation can be halted at no cost in terms of increased unemployment. Similarly, they think that prosperity and rising living standards could be accompanied by price stability if only the government stopped spending, if unions would suddenly disappear, and if businesses stopped trying to make money. The homemaker who pickets her food store because the cost of meat is going up probably does not realize that it is only through the grace of prosperity (and its inflationary by-products) that her husband is employed and enjoying wage increases. Meanwhile, the husband believes that he is entitled to a 20 percent wage increase and at the same time complains that the government is doing nothing about inflation.

Surely it must be better to have one's income eroded by rising prices than not to have any income to begin with? It is axiomatic that it is not possible for society to enrich itself by restricting output and creating unemployment. Yet that is what we do every time we attempt to combat inflation by inducing recession through applications of the "old-time religion" as tight money and restrictive budgets have recently come to be called. Each such episode brings us face to face with the inescapable conclusion that the costs incurred by inducing recession for the purpose of slowing inflation easily outweigh the cost of the inflation itself. A less destructive way of dealing with the problem is urgently needed.

A second area of economic misunderstanding lies in a widespread failure, even among sophisticated people, to appreciate the benefits of productivity gains and high employment and how these benefits are transmitted throughout the economic system. Why, for example, would it make any difference to a professor at a midwestern college whether employment was high and stable in Pittsburgh and whether productivity and real wages were rising in the steel industry? The reason is that steady employment and a rapid rise in steelworkers' real wages enable them to send their children to college, so that the demand for the professor's service increases. It is this that pulls up the professor's real income and that causes national productivity gains to be transmitted to areas, such as college education, where little or no change in productivity is generally discernible. If the professor, or any other citizen for that matter, is unduly concerned about inflation and indifferent to unemployment in Pittsburgh, he may inadvertently be denying himself the possibility of a gain in real income.

Another matter that we must be cautious about is the interpretation of our measures of inflation. We use various kinds of price indexes to measure inflation, and we should be aware of the fact that these indexes have a tendency to be upwardly biased and therefore to exaggerate the rate of inflation. The relative biases between actual indexes and bias-corrected indexes tends to diminish as the rate of inflation rises because the absolute difference is apt to remain the same. Therefore, when the "true" rate of inflation is 15 percent, the price index may record it as 17 percent; when the true rate of inflation is 3 percent, the 2 percentage point bias may continue, and the measured rate of inflation will then be 5 percent. The difference between 15 and 17 percent will be of little importance, but the difference between 3 and 5 percent most certainly is important. When, as was the case in the United States during the late 1950s, a rise in the consumer price index creates the erroneous impression that the economy is suffering from excess demand, and when this impression imposes a deflationary bias on economic policy, the situation becomes serious indeed. Thus while today's rapid inflation perhaps makes concern over biases in price indexes somewhat untimely, it is nevertheless an important problem that should be discussed.

The most commonly used measure of the rate of inflation in the United States is the consumer price index (CPI). The CPI attempts to measure changes in the prices of a standard bundle of commodities purchased by a typical urban blue-collar or clerical worker. As such, it is not an index of prices but rather a measure of the cost of living for a particular representative group. Excluded from the CPI are luxury items such as Cadillacs and included are items such as mortgage interest that ought not be included at all in a price index. Interest, properly treated, is a factor payment and not a commodity. Nevertheless, it is part of the "cost of living" and therefore included in the CPI. The inclusion has the unfortunate consequence that a rise in interest rates which reflect an attempt to restrain inflation by means of restrictive monetary policy is then reflected as an inflationary increase in the CPI.

Usually indexes such as the CPI are constructed by taking a weighted sum of quantities multiplied by their prices in a base year. This base is then divided into a figure that takes the same quantity weights but multiplies these by current prices. If the resultant ratio is 1.4, we then say that there has been a 40 percent increase in prices over the base period.

The biases that such procedures invite are enormous. First, what happens when the composition of demand shifts, so that the base-year weights bear no resemblance to the present composition of output? Second, how do we introduce entirely new commodities into an index of prices, and what happens when some existing commodity falls into total disuse? Third, how does one deal with the problem that associated with the life cycle of each commodity there tends to be a life cycle of price behavior?[1] Fourth, how does one deal with noncomparability due to changes in the quality of commodities? And, finally, how does one deal with the problem that the cost increases of various services ought to be offset by the fact that the quality of these services has improved greatly?

All these areas of difficulty tend to bias our indexes. The last two, however, are of particular concern to our present problem since the biases they introduce tend to be systematically in the inflationary direction.

When a worker produces twice as many units of a given commodity or performs the same service in one-half the time, we say that his or her productivity has doubled. Unfortunately, the measurement of productivity improvement in many areas is not possible because output itself is not measurable. Most of us have been appalled at the enormous increase in the cost of medical services over the last decade. The cost of a hospital room has skyrocketed, and physicians' fees have become astronomical. However, medical technology has advanced, so that while it may cost twice as much per day to rent a hospital room, the average patient may have to spend only half as much time there. Similarly, doctors' fees may have doubled, but if they are able to cure their patients twice as fast, with half as many office calls, and with less pain, discomfort, and anxiety, are we then entitled to regard the increase in their fees as inflation? An ideal price index would assess the cost of a unit of medical service, that is, the cost of curing a disease, and it would ignore the cost per day of hospital rooms or the physician's hourly fee. The index, in other words, would take productivity improvements into account. Since in practice it is not possible to do this, we tend to underestimate the productivity gains and thereby overestimate the pure price increases. We need hardly belabor the point that this is a very serious source of inflationary bias in our price indexes.

Quite similar problems arise because of quality improvements in different products. Autos cost many times more than they did in 1940; however, it is not clear that all the price difference reflects inflation. The modern version is

---

[1] New products tend to be expensive. Thereafter economies of mass production and mass marketing cause prices to drop. Finally, the commodity becomes obsolete and is of interest only to eccentrics and collectors, and at this point it again becomes expensive.

heavier, longer, faster, more powerful, more comfortable, and more reliable, it has better brakes and easier steering, and it may, possibly, even be safer. The two cars are obviously not the same product, and comparison of prices must therefore be undertaken with care. Our price indexes are asked to deal with such problems when obviously they cannot.

A number of attempts have been made to estimate the biases in price indexes that are due to failure to take quality change into account. One such study is the attempt by Griliches to compute the effect on automobile prices of differences in length, weight, horsepower, and other characteristics.[1] Over the period 1954–1960 list prices of cars rose steadily. The CPI's "new automobile component" index rose from a value of 129.7 in 1954 to a value of 144.3 in 1960. However, Griliches' method of computing the index yielded a fall from 129.8 to 111.3. Consequently, when quality change was taken into account, it appeared that car prices actually fell during the period.

If we are concerned about the general level of prices rather than just consumer prices, we might properly be concerned with an index such as the "deflator" for total gross national product. However, the GNP deflator suffers from many of the drawbacks of the CPI and some additional ones as well. To cite one problem, the GNP deflator includes government, and the price of government services is measured at cost. It is, moreover, arbitrarily assumed that productivity in the government sector never changes. Thus any time government employees receive a pay increase, the GNP deflator immediately records this as a price increase.

If full employment cannot be maintained without some inflation, it behooves us to ask how the evils of inflation can be mitigated. An attractive approach, which has been advocated for a long time and which is now being taken seriously, is to introduce cost-of-living escalation into various contracts. Such a procedure, sometimes referred to as "indexing" or inflation "correction," would eliminate many of the distributional effects of inflation. The government should take the initiative in indexing by issuing purchasing-power bonds that would provide small savers with the opportunity to inflation-proof their savings. The government should also automatically raise the pay of public employees in accordance with the rate of inflation. A third, and most important, step would be to abolish the obsolete usury laws and interest rate ceilings that prevent interest rates from responding to market forces, therefore distorting saving and investment decisions and producing periodic financial "crunches." Finally, governments should follow the example of countries such as Canada and index their personal income tax systems in such a way as to prevent the progressivity of the system from increasing the real value of the tax burden merely as a result of inflation. This can be done by raising exemptions and widening brackets at the rate of inflation.

Opponents of indexing argue that such schemes provide the basis for run-

---

[1] Z. Griliches, "Hedonic Price Indexes for Automobiles: An Econometric Analysis of Quality Change," *The Price Statistics of the Federal Government,* No. 73, National Bureau of Economic Research, Inc., New York, 1961.

away inflation. Purchasing-power bonds suggest that the government has given up in its fight against inflation. And indexing of the income tax implies that taxes are being reduced during inflation when, if anything, they ought to be raised. However, perfect indexing would make the rate of inflation irrelevant as a legitimate policy target; but even so it is not clear that indexing would raise the rate of inflation. If no one had to be concerned about the erosion of his or her real income through inflation, there would be no temptation to engage in such activities as anticipatory buying, hoarding, and aggressive wage bargaining, all of which exacerbate inflation. In short, generalized indexing would permit economic decisions to be made without consideration of the expected rate of inflation. It might, then, be much easier to slow the rate of inflation because indexing would create the kind of climate in which stabilization policies could operate on output and employment, rather than on the levels of wages and prices.

The argument that indexing of the income tax is undesirable because taxes should be raised during inflation is valid only if the inflation is a reflection of excess demand. Even then, raising taxes may not be the most efficient way to remove the excess demand. This brings us, then, to the subject of the next chapter where problems of policy mix and efficient use of policy instruments are discussed.

# 4

# PROBLEMS IN THE CONTROL OF ECONOMIC ACTIVITY

# 16

# THE THEORY OF MACROECONOMIC POLICY AND THE PROBLEM OF INFLATIONARY RECESSION

## 16–1
## INTRODUCTION TO PART 4

Although we have certainly not shied away from policy discussion in past chapters, we have not as yet addressed ourselves to policy questions in a manner that attempts to account for the various trade-offs between targets and that takes account of some of the practical difficulties of implementing particular policies. These are the tasks of Part 4. We begin with an attempt to introduce the so-called theory of economic policy which, to put it as simply as possible, prescribes rules for the cooperation of different policy instruments in such a way as to achieve a multiplicity of economic targets simultaneously. After introducing the ideas, we will attempt to apply them to various important problems. One such problem is how to combat recession and inflation that exist simultaneously. Another is how to reconcile equilibrium in the balance of payments with high domestic employment and price stability. Chapter 18 then focuses on the specific instrument of fiscal policy, tracing the evolution of fiscal policy and of fiscal thinking in the United States, and continuing with a discussion of the practical problems of implementing fiscal policy. Chapter 19 then deals, in a similar manner, with monetary policy and the national debt.

## 16–2
## THE THEORY OF ECONOMIC POLICY[1]

The theory of economic policy attempts to look at policy making as a process of varying a number of policy *instruments* in such a way as to achieve a set of predetermined *targets*. Instead of focusing on a single objective such as full employment, or price stability, or rapid growth, or balance of payments equilibrium, and so on, the theory of economic policy recognizes that there are trade-offs between all these objectives, and it attempts, by asking if the mix of policy can be changed, to ascertain whether the various targets can be reconciled. Policy economics is in the realm of "normative" economics and should be distinguished from the "positive" economics with which much of this book has been concerned. Positive economics deals with analytical matters of cause and effect. For example, the question of how much the level of income will be raised by an increase in government purchases, without at the same time inquiring if the change is, in some sense, good or desirable, is a question of positive economics. Policy economics turns the question around. Beginning with some predetermined target level of income that society judges to be desirable, it asks how much of a change in government purchases will be needed to attain this target.

To develop the principles of economic policy, let us keep the discussion as simple as possible by resorting to the familiar *IS-LM* model. Let us simplify the example by assuming a Keynesian demand model were the aggregate supply curve is horizontal, so that variations in aggregate demand change the level of real income but do not change the price level. Finally, since we want to do some simple algebraic manipulations, we will assume that the several functions of the model are linear. The model, then, is as follows:

$$Y = C + I + G \qquad (16-1)$$

is the definition of equilibrium income in a closed economy. The linear consumption function is

$$C = C_0 + b(Y - T) \qquad (16-2)$$

---

[1] The well-known Dutch economist Jan Tinbergen is generally credited with being the father of the theory of economic policy. See his *Economic Policy: Principles and Design*, North-Holland Publishing Company, Amsterdam, 1956. Additional important references are Leif Johansen, *Public Economics*, Rand McNally & Company, Chicago, 1965, and Bent Hansen, *The Economic Theory of Fiscal Policy*, Harvard University Press, Cambridge, Mass., 1958.

where $b$ is the marginal propensity to consume. The linear investment function is

$$I = I_0 + ai \tag{16-3}$$

where the slope $a$ is negative in accordance with the usual hypothesis that investment falls as the rate of interest rises. We assume government purchases and taxes to be exogenous. Therefore, on combining the three expressions, we obtain an explicit equation for the $IS$ curve:

$$(1 - b)Y - ai = C_0 - bT + I_0 + G \tag{16-4}$$

The two endogenous variables, as before, are the level of income $Y$ and the rate of interest $i$. The exogenous policy variables $G$ and $T$ appear on the right side along with the intercept terms of the functions, and it is evident that changes in these variables will shift the entire $IS$ curve.

A linear $LM$ curve can be written

$$M = M_0 + kY + ci \tag{16-5}$$

where, because the price level is assumed fixed in this example, it is not necessary to distinguish between the real and the nominal stock of money. Once again there are two endogenous variables $Y$ and $i$, and the exogenous policy variable is the supply of money.

Now let us rearrange the $LM$ curve slightly and write the two equations together as

$$(1 - b)Y - ai = C_0 - bT + I_0 + G \tag{16-4}$$

$$kY + ci = M - M_0 \tag{16-5'}$$

which shows them as a system of two simultaneous equations in two variables, $Y$ and $i$. In past chapters the solutions were obtained implicitly by noting where the functions cut each other on an $IS$-$LM$ diagram. Now, however, let us derive an explicit solution. A bit of simple algebra shows that the equilibrium solutions for $Y$ and $i$, respectively, are

$$Y = \frac{c}{\Delta} (C_0 - bT + I_0 + G) + \frac{a}{\Delta} (M - M_0) \tag{16-6}$$

$$i = \frac{-k}{\Delta} (C_0 - bT + I_0 + G) + \frac{1 - b}{\Delta} (M - M_0) \tag{16-7}$$

The term $\Delta$ that appears in the denominator of all these expressions is the quantity

$$\Delta = c(1 - b) + ak$$

which is negative since $a$ and $c$ are both negative, and $1 - b$ and $k$ are both positive.

These expressions yield the usual results that an increase in government purchases raises the equilibrium level of income and the equilibrium rate of interest, that an increase in taxes does the opposite, and that an increase in the money supply raises the level of income and lowers the rate of interest. Note, also that the various coefficients in the equations, such as $c/\Delta$, $a/\Delta$, are the multipliers inclusive of monetary repercussions. For example,

$$\frac{c}{\Delta} = \frac{c}{c(1 - b) + ak}$$

is the increase in income that results from an increase in government purchases of $1. To see how this relates to earlier discussion, we divide both numerator and denominator by $c$. This gives

$$\frac{1}{(1 - b) + ak/c}$$

Now recall that in the Keynesian liquidity trap case, $c$ becomes infinitely large, in which event the term $ak/c$ disappears and the expression then reduces to the familiar multiplier

$$\frac{1}{1 - b}$$

Similarly, in the classical case there is no liquidity preference, so that $c = 0$, and the multiplier then also equals zero.

Up to here we have merely put past analysis, such as that of Chapter 8, into explicit algebraic form. What Eqs. (16–6) and (16–7) are designed to do is to answer positive multiplier questions: What will be the effect on income and the rate of interest of arbitrary changes in the values of the policy variables? To move the discussion to the normative level, we begin by asking if there are particular values of the target variables $Y$ and $i$ that we desire. We may think that there is a certain level of income $Y^*$ that will yield full employment without inflation; and we may think that a certain rate of interest $i^*$ yields a desirable allocation of resources as between investment and other uses. Thus we impose these values on the system, we therefore add two new equations,

$$Y = Y^*$$

$$i = i^*$$

and we substitute these into Eqs. (16–6) and (16–7). As a result of this, the level of income and rate of interest are no longer the endogenous variables of the system but become, instead, the exogenously determined constants. The policy variables, on the other hand, now become the endogenous variables. If we write the equations again we have

$$Y^* = \frac{c}{\Delta} (C_0 - bT - I_0 + G) + \frac{a}{\Delta} (M - M_0) \qquad (16\text{–}6')$$

$$i^* = \frac{-k}{\Delta} (C_0 - bT + I_0 + G) + \frac{1 - b}{\Delta} (M - M_0) \qquad (16\text{–}7')$$

where it is now evident that, with fixed $Y^*$ and $i^*$, satisfying the equations requires that the policy variables $G$, $T$, and $M$ be permitted to vary. In particular, the equations now serve to specify the combinations of the policy variables that satisfy the condition that $Y$ and $i$ be equal to their target values. Thus we are now in a position to ask, for a given level of taxes, how must $M$ be made to change when $G$ varies in order to maintain $Y$ at $Y^*$. Or, again for a given level of taxes, how must $M$ be made to vary when $G$ varies in order to maintain $i$ at $i^*$? And, finally, what combination of $G$ and $M$ will attain both targets simultaneously?

The idea, therefore, is to substitute in the multiplier equations (16–6) and (16–7) the target values of the variables $Y^*$ and $i^*$, and then solve the equations again, this time treating the policy instruments as the variables for which a solution is sought. Rather than doing this algebraically, it may be instructive to pursue the idea by means of a diagram that illustrates the nature of the problem and that represents one of a family that will be as useful to our further discussion, as was the *IS-LM* diagram of past chapters.

Figure 16–1 shows the new orientation of policy economics by measuring the values of the policy instruments on the respective axes, rather than the target variables $Y$ and $i$. The money supply is measured on the vertical axis, and the level of government purchases is measured horizontally. The curve YY' is the iso-income target function which specifies the combination of $G$ and $M$ that keeps $Y$ at its target level $Y^*$; it therefore amounts to a graph of Eq. (16–6') with $T$ held constant at some arbitrary level. YY' must have a negative slope. A reduction in the money supply would lower $Y$ below $Y^*$, but this could be offset by a rise in $G$. Similarly, the ii' function is the iso-interest rate target function specifying the combination of $G$ and $M$ that keeps the interest rate at its target level $i^*$. Its slope must be positive; an increase in government purchases would raise the rate of interest and therefore the money supply would have to be decreased to offset this.

The combination of $G$ and $M$ that satisfies both targets is at the point of intersection of the two functions. The policy problem is therefore solved when the level of government purchases, as shown in Figure 16–1, is set equal to $\overline{G}$, and the money supply is set equal to $\overline{M}$. Both targets are then achieved simultaneously; that is, for a given level of $T$, Eqs. (16–6') and (16–7') have been solved for the equilibrium values of $G$ and $M$.

An important principle of economic policy, which should now have become obvious, is that there must, as a general rule, be at least as many variable policy instruments as there are targets if all the targets are to be attained. This can be seen with reference either to the equations or to Figure 16–1. If, for some reason, it is not possible to vary $T$ and $G$, then variation in $M$ could still achieve the target income level $Y^*$, or it could achieve the target interest rate $i^*$, but it could *not* achieve both targets simultaneously except by accident. With the two targets we clearly need at least two variable instruments.

In the present example we actually have three instruments $G$, $T$, and $M$, but only two targets $Y^*$ and $i^*$; since this means we only have two equations in our system with three variables to solve for, we lack a unique solution for the policy variables unless one of them is arbitrarily fixed. This means that we

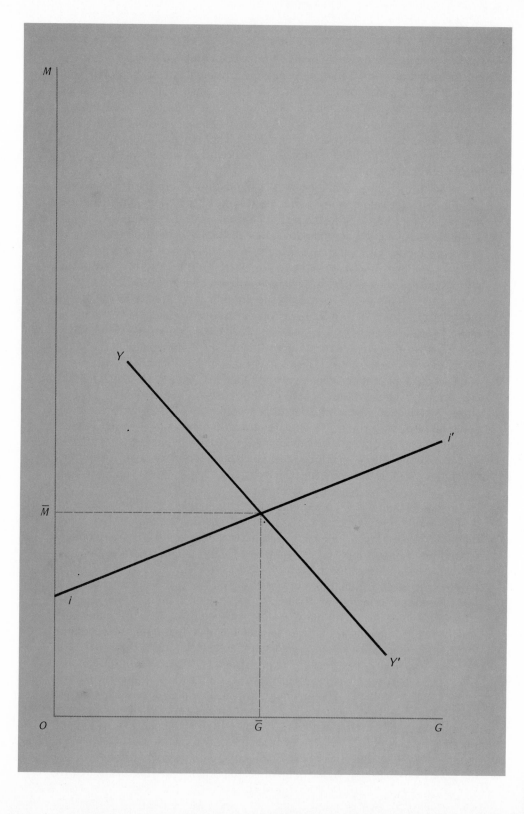

have the luxury of a surplus instrument in our system that may be freed to seek a third target. Most of the time, unfortunately, the problem is the reverse. We tend to be shooting for more goals than we have means to deal with them, and that is one of the facts that complicates economic policy making.

Equality of instruments and targets is a general principle required to achieve a solution to policy problems, but it is neither a necessary nor a sufficient condition. Consider the foregoing example, but imagine that the liquidity trap conditions prevail. The rate of interest cannot be changed by monetary or fiscal policy, and the level of income can be changed only by fiscal policy. Since the rate of interest will be the liquidity trap rate, irrespective of the values of the policy variables, the presence of monetary policy as an additional instrument is of no benefit in achieving a target rate of interest different from the liquidity trap rate.[1]

Targets, obviously, have to be realistic. Some are out of reach under any circumstances, whereas others, although perhaps individually attainable, are incompatible with each other. If we set a 10 percent growth rate as our target, we shall have to invest such a large fraction of our output in raising the rate of technical change and capital formation that it will be impossible to maintain a satisfactory level of per capita consumption. Or, if we set a 2 percent unemployment rate as our employment target, we may find that the labor market will be so tight that it will be impossible to keep costs and prices from rising at an excessive rate. Thus some targets are not attainable or are incompatible with other targets, and the addition of more policy instruments will not help to achieve them. The mathematician would say that there are "constraints" or "boundary conditions" to the values that the target variables may take. In practical terms, the economist would say that the targets have to be realistic.

Finally, the focus of economic policy on the need to solve for the appropriate values of the instruments quite naturally draws attention to the problem of coordination of policies. This raises all the innumerable difficulties involved in getting separate decision making authorities, such as the monetary authority and the authorities over taxes and expenditures, to understand that the instrument over which they exercise control is but one in a simultaneous system. This requires them to understand that, if they move closer to one target, they may move farther away from another. And it requires them to understand that a coordinated approach to policy is essential.

We will come back to the very interesting and important subject of policy coordination in the last section of this chapter. In the meantime it seems

---

[1] The reader should attempt to work out the implications of this and other extreme cases, utilizing the multiplier equations to note how these assumptions affect the slopes of the target functions of Fig. 16–1.

**FIGURE 16–1**
Illustration of iso-target functions and derivation of equilibrium instrument values

appropriate to apply what we have learned to the very serious and timely problem of how to deal with the double dilemma of inflationary recession.

## 16-3
## INFLATIONARY RECESSION AND THE
## APPROPRIATE MIX OF POLICY

When unemployment is too high and prices are still rising, neither the employment nor the price stability target is being achieved. The theory of economic policy then naturally raises the question whether this could not be a problem of the policy mix. It has had trouble in the past inasmuch as the basic theory of income and employment which we have studied throughout this book has never encompassed a situation in which demand is excessive in commodity markets (thereby causing prices to rise), while it is deficient as far as the labor market is concerned (thereby creating unemployment). That, essentially, is the stagflation or inflationary recession riddle which we will discuss in this section.

Consider Figure 16-2 in which the real value of the money supply, $m = M/p$, is measured on the vertical axis, and the real value of taxes $T$ is measured horizontally. Since we will wish to concentrate on the tax-money mix we will assume throughout that the level of government purchases is fixed, and we also assume that the only taxes in the system are direct taxes on persons. Now imagine an iso-employment function that shows the combinations of money supply and taxes that keeps the demand for labor equal to its supply so that there will be neither involuntary unemployment nor excess demand with a tendency for money wages to rise. The iso-employment function is labeled $NN'$ in Figure 16-2. It must have a positive slope since a rise in taxes will reduce aggregate demand, tending to lower employment, so that the money supply must be raised in order to offset the deflationary effect of the tax increase. Presumably, therefore, combinations of $M/p$ and $T$ that lie below the $NN'$ curve imply excess supply of labor and unemployment, whereas points above it imply excess demand for labor and a tendency toward wage inflation.

A similar combination of money supply and taxes can be visualized that maintains equilibrium in the market for goods and services and that therefore prevents the price level from changing. Given the existing equilibrium price level, a rise in taxes will reduce consumption which tends to lower the price level, but this can be offset by an increase in the money supply because this stimulates investment spending. This curve, too, will be positively sloped with points above it, implying a combination of money supply and taxes that is too expansionary and therefore causes price inflation, whereas points below the

**FIGURE 16-2**
Iso-employment and iso-price level functions in the standard Keynesian model

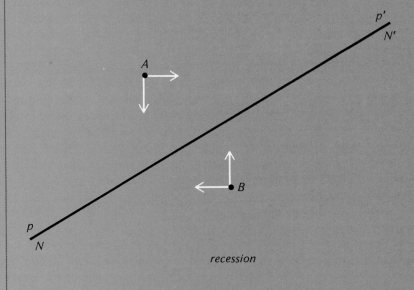

$M/p$

$O$ $T$

inflation

$p'$
$N'$

$A$

$B$

$p$
$N$

recession

curve imply a restrictive combination of policies that create excess supply in the product market and that tend, therefore, to cause the price level to fall.

An important property of the standard theory of income and employment developed in Part 2 is that the iso-employment *NN'* and iso-price level functions *pp'* are one and the same and are therefore superimposed, as shown in Figure 16–2. This means that if the goods market and the labor market are both initially in equilibrium, and if a change in the money supply disrupts that equilibrium, then the change in taxes that restores equilibrium in one of the markets automatically does so also in the other market.[1]

Under these conditions changes in the money supply and changes in the level of taxes may be thought of as perfect substitutes for each other. Either policy, or any one of an infinite number of combinations, can be used to eliminate recession or inflation. As suggested by Figure 16–2, at a point such as *A* in the inflation zone either a reduction in money supply or a rise in taxes can move the system out of inflation and onto the joint *NN'-pp'* curve, and the opposite change in either instrument can, from a point such as *B* in the recession zone, restore full employment and secure simultaneous product and labor market equilibrium. One policy may, apparently, even be used to compensate for a movement in the wrong direction by the other policy. Upward pressure on prices, finally, combined with downward pressure on wages cannot exist in the standard model, so that simultaneous inflation or deflation in both the product and the labor market is the only possibility visualized in the standard theory. It is hardly a wonder that inflationary recession poses such a dilemma for economic analysis.

As in the case of the debate between Keynes and the classicists, the clue to the puzzle may once again lie in the assumption governing the behavior of labor supply. In the classical theory a rise in taxes creates excess supply of labor and a fall in money wages. In the Keynesian theory the money wage rate simply remains constant in the face of a tax increase. But what if the classical theory were turned completely on its head and that it could be shown that a rise in taxes would cause wages to increase?

There is a good deal of recent evidence that suggests that this is, in fact, what happens. In the age of heavy direct taxation, workers have come to realize that what is important to them is their net wage *after* taxes rather than their *gross* wage before taxes. A rise in direct taxes will therefore cause them to demand higher money wages in order to maintain their real income after tax. In the aggregate this means that workers attempt to bargain for wages in a manner that maintains real disposable income even in the face of a rise in taxes. The evidence that wages behave in this manner, though not conclusive, is nevertheless considerable. Econometric wage equations developed for individual countries often exhibit positive correlation between money wage rates and wage taxes, and considerable concern has been exhibited by various

---

[1] The reader should consult the appendix to this chapter for a proof of this proposition. It is, unfortunately, one that is difficult to establish without resort to a bit of mathematics.

governments over what they perceive as a threat of wage retaliation against higher personal taxation.[1] Indeed, it has been suggested that in some European countries wage bargaining is less a negotiation between unions and employers than a negotiation between unions and government. So-called stabilization agreements and social contracts involve a promise on the part of government to hold down taxes and government expenditure in return for which labor promises to exercise wage restraint. Surprisingly perhaps, there is evidence that positive wage adjustment occurs in response to tax increases even in such countries as the United States where unions are comparatively weak, and where only a fraction of the labor force is organized.[2] Indeed, as shown in the next section, many of the successes and failures of United States tax policy during the 1960s are quite reasonably interpreted by a model that incorporates the kind of labor supply behavior here suggested. It is notable, finally, that during President Ford's "economic summit" of the summer of 1974 one of the suggestions that was being taken seriously was tax relief for lower-income groups in the interest of moderating the upward wage pressures that were expected in the near future.

In order to develop the analysis of inflationary recession, we take the basic Keynesian model of Chapter 10 and merely change the labor supply assumption. We will, moreover, simplify the analysis by ignoring the Pigou effect and the other factors that might cause the *IS* curve to shift when the price level changes. We will call the resulting system the "wage-adjustment" model, and we will begin our analysis with the comparative statics of the model.[3] We have studied how an increase in taxes affects the equilibrium values of the variables of the system, and how a rise in the money wage affects these variables. What we need to do, therefore, is to combine the effects of the two exogenous changes.

In the Keynesian case with fixed money wages, a tax increase reduces consumption expenditure and creates excess supply in the product market. Profit-maximizing behavior on the part of individual producers then implies readjustments which lead to lower equilibrium levels of output, employment, and

---

[1] The tax-wage interactions in various countries are discussed in a wide variety of sources, many of them government documents. The Swedish experience is discussed in A. Lindbeck, "Theories and Problems in Swedish Economic Policy in the Post War Period," *American Economic Review*, (Supplement), 58:1–87, 1968. The impact of heavy wage taxation on wage behavior in the United Kingdom is analyzed by D. Jackson, H. A. Turner, and F. Wilkinson, *Do Trade Unions Cause Inflation?*, Chap. 3, Cambridge University Press, New York, 1972. Some econometric evidence for the United States is provided by R. J. Gordon, "Inflation in Recession and Recovery," *Brookings Papers on Economic Activity*, 1:105–166, 1971.

[2] Gordon, ibid., provides such empirical evidence.

[3] The analysis is abstracted from T. F. Dernburg, "Personal Taxation, Wage Retaliation, and the Control of Inflation," *International Monetary Fund Staff Papers*, 21:758–788 1974. Some other attempts to analyze the effects of the wage push phenomenon are A. S. Blinder, "Can Income Tax Increases Be Inflationary? An Expository Note," *National Tax Journal*, 16:295–301, 1973; and J. H. Hotson, "Neo-Orthodox Keynesianism and the 45° Heresy," *Nebraska Journal of Economics and Business*, 6:34–49, 1967.

prices. The tax increase may be thought to be deflationary in the sense that it reduces the equilibrium level of prices.

If business firms maximize profits by equating the marginal product of labor with the real wage rate, an exogenous rise in the money wage rate will initially cause output and employment to fall. The consequent reduction in real income is accompanied by a fall in aggregate consumption; but as long as the marginal propensity to consume is less than unity, this reduction will be less than the fall in real output. Consequently, excess demand appears in the product market, and this will cause the price level to rise. This, in turn, reduces the real value of the money supply, raises the rate of interest, and lowers the level of planned investment. This, finally, causes the equilibrium levels of output and employment to fall permanently. Had there been no fall in investment, either because of a liquidity trap or because investment is not responsive to changes in the rate of interest, or because the monetary authority raises the nominal money supply in such a way as to keep the real value of the money supply from changing, there would be no change in employment. The price level would then rise in the same proportion as the increase in the money wage rate.

By combining the analysis of the effect of the tax increase with the analysis of the effect of the increase in the money wage, we can conclude that the wage adjustment in response to a tax increase would accentuate the fall in output and employment because both the tax and the wage effect work in that direction. On the other hand, the wage adjustment reduces the extent to which the price level falls because the tax and the wage push effect work in the opposite direction with respect to the price level. Indeed, if the wage adjustment is pronounced enough, the upward thrust of the wage push may overcome the downward pressure caused by the tax increase, and the equilibrium price level could therefore quite possibly rise.

The picture painted by the wage-adjustment model appears pretty gloomy, inasmuch as it suggests that a rise in taxes may merely reduce output and employment without materially lowering the price level. We cannot, however, jump to the conclusion that tax increases are of no use in combating inflation because we have compared only equilibrium points. Before we can come to reasonable conclusions about the appropriate way to control inflation, we will have to examine the dynamic implications of the wage-adjustment model. This can be done with the aid of Figure 16–3 which again shows the iso-employment and iso-price level functions and measures the real value of the money supply $M/p$ on the vertical axis, and the real value of personal

**FIGURE 16–3**
Divergence of iso-employment and iso-price level functions due to wage adjustments as a possible explanation for inflationary recession

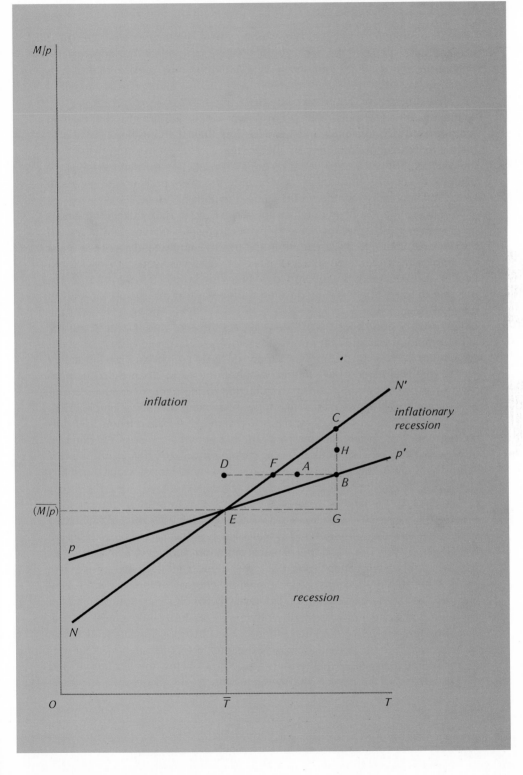

taxes $T$ on the horizontal axis. The difference between Figures 16–2 and 16–3 is that the iso-employment and iso-price level functions are no longer super-imposed in the wage-adjustment model. While the $NN'$ curve remains in its initial position, the $pp'$ curve rotates in a clockwise manner as the result of the wage adjustment. Let us see why this is the case.

If a tax increase is accompanied by upward wage adjustment, the resultant fall in the equilibrium price level will be less than without the wage adjust-ment. It will therefore require a smaller increase in the money supply to main-tain the equilibrium price level at its original level. This means that the slope of the $pp'$ curve is reduced by a tendency for taxes and money wages to move systematically together in the same direction.[1]

Turning to the $NN'$ curve, when upward wage adjustment accompanies a tax increase, the reduction in employment is accentuated, and it would therefore require a greater increase in the money supply than before to offset the employment reduction due to the tax increase. We would, therefore, ex-pect a counterclockwise rotation of $NN'$. This would be the case if the nominal money supply were measured on the vertical axis since, for a given nominal money supply, wage adjustment would lower the real value of the money supply and, because this reduces investment, would accentuate the fall in employment resulting from the tax increase. However, since we mea-sure the real value of the money supply on the vertical axis, we implicitly prevent the real value of the money supply from rising when a tax increase moves the policy combination in the diagram to the right. Consequently our way of labeling the axes means that there will be no additional employment effect due to wage adjustment, and the $NN'$ curve therefore remains in its ini-tial position. Put slightly differently, a strictly rightward move in the diagram implies that the monetary authority is keeping the real value of the money supply constant in the face of an increase in taxes and money wages, and this eliminates the employment effect of the wage increase.

The result of the flattening out of the $pp'$ curve is to produce the situation depicted in Figure 16–3. There are now four possible zones instead of the two of the standard analysis shown in Figure 16–2. Above and below both the $NN'$ and $pp'$ functions are the classical inflation and recession zones, re-spectively. In the inflation zone both the labor and the product markets are in states of simultaneous excess demand, whereas in the recession zone both markets are in excess supply. However, between the zones, one market exhibits excess demand whereas the other is characterized by excess supply. The zone to the right of the intersection of the functions appears to describe what is understood to be inflationary recession. At a point such as $A$ there is excess supply in the labor market since point $A$ lies below the $NN'$ curve, and excess demand in the product market since point $A$ lies above $pp'$. The wage-

[1] The greater the degree of wage adjustment, the greater is the clockwise rotation. It is conceiv-able that the rotation might be so extensive that the $pp'$ curve could become negatively sloped, a possibility that we do not, however, wish to explore further here.

adjustment model therefore provides one possible explanation of how unemployment and inflation may exist simultaneously.

Let us make sure we understand the nature of the inflationary recession zone. Consider Figure 16–3 and begin at point *E* with both markets in equilibrium. Now let taxes be raised by an amount *EG*. If the tax increase is accompanied by upward wage adjustment, the increase in the money supply needed to prevent the price level from falling may be only *BG*, whereas the amount needed to prevent employment from falling must be a larger amount, such as *CG*. Some intermediate response such as *GH* implies that since the monetary response exceeds *BG* it must produce excess demand in the goods market. However, since it is less than *CG* it is not sufficient to prevent the tax increase from causing excess supply in the labor market. The result then is inflationary recession: The market for goods and services is in a state of excess demand while excess supply exists simultaneously in the labor market.

Each of the four separate zones requires different policy responses. However, for the present let us concern ourselves with inflationary recession. As can be seen in Figure 16–3, a situation of inflationary recession such as is represented by point *A* implies, given the values of other policy instruments such as the level of government purchases, that taxes and the money supply are both too high. To eliminate inflationary recession and to achieve equilibrium at point *E*, it would be efficacious to lower taxes. This would secure a pause in wage demands since lower taxes substitute for higher wages, and since this provides a favorable cost-price relationship, it causes output and employment to be expanded. The inflationary pressures may then be relieved by a modest reduction in the money supply. According to the present hypothesis, therefore, equilibrium may be secured by a tighter money–easier tax mix of policy.

The policy prescription follows from the fact that the wage adjustment causes a tax change to have a relatively more powerful effect on the level of employment than it does on the price level, whereas the opposite is the case for a change in the money supply. Consequently, although a tax reduction does have an inflationary effect, this can be neutralized by a reduction in the money supply, with the net additional benefit that the level of employment and output will be higher after the two policy changes. Conversely, a reversal in this policy mix would be wholly inappropriate. Consider point *A* in Figure 16–3 and imagine raising taxes to eliminate inflation (moving from *A* to *B*). This would eliminate inflation but it would also provoke upward wage adjustment and produce a drop in employment (point *B* is farther away from *NN'* than point *A*). Monetary expansion could then restore full employment (reach *NN'* at point *C*), but the inflation would then be much worse than ever.

As we have seen, the interpretation of inflationary recession provided by the wage-adjustment model is that the malady is the product of a situation in which both the real value of the money supply and the level of personal taxes are too high. Such a situation may arise as the result of an attempt to combat inflation by raising taxes, combined with a well-intentioned effort by the monetary authority to avert fiscal "overkill" by expanding the money supply. Or it may arise as the consequence of an attempt to raise the economy's growth rate by changing the policy mix in favor of easier money and higher personal taxes, in an effort to shift resources from consumption to investment. The trouble with such a change in the policy mix is that if the tax increase provokes wage adjustment, it will cause employment to drop sharply. Meanwhile the easier monetary policy produces excess product demand, with inflationary recession being the net result of the change in the policy mix.

Finally, inflationary recession may be brought about through the purely automatic response of the progressive income tax. This is an important consideration that we should examine with care. Throughout the discussion we have been assuming that the real value of direct taxes is exogenous and remains unchanged except through the action of discretionary policy. We must now, however, take into account the fact that direct personal taxes tend to be income taxes. When the economy is in the classical inflation zone, real income will be fixed, but the price level will be rising and money income will therefore be increasing. In the normal progressive income tax system the rise in money income will raise tax rates for the average taxpayer so that the real value of the aggregate tax burden rises automatically. Consequently, imagine that the economy is at point *D* in Figure 16–3 and assume the monetary authority holds the real value of the money supply constant. The rise in the price level, however, raises the real value of taxes so the policy combination is automatically pulled to the right from point *D* toward point *F*. As the real value of taxes rises, the wage-adjustment process comes into play, with the consequence that excess demand in the labor market is eliminated more rapidly than excess product demand. Consequently, when point *F* is reached, the price inflation continues, the real value of taxes keeps rising, and the economy is dragged into the inflationary recession zone where unemployment emerges, while inflation continues.

These considerations supply considerable support for the policy of inflation indexing of the personal income tax which was discussed briefly in the preceding chapter. If this were done, the economy would remain at point *D* in Figure 16–3 because an indexed tax system would keep the average tax rate of taxpayers constant unless their real income changes, or until a discretionary tax change is introduced. Such indexing would, of course, perpetuate inflation since the economy would tend to remain at point *D*, but it would also avert inflationary recession. Indexing of the tax system would prevent the rightward drift into the inflationary recession zone, and restrictive monetary policy could eliminate the inflation. That, it appears, is the correct policy combination.

## 16–4
## PROBLEMS OF POLICY ADJUSTMENT AND THE
## APPROPRIATE PAIRING OF INSTRUMENTS
## AND TARGETS

The wage-adjustment model shows that a "comparative advantage" develops between the two policy instruments with respect to their relative effectiveness in changing employment as opposed to the price level. In the standard theory, when a rise in taxes disrupts equilibrium in the two markets, the rise in money supply which restores equilibrium in one of the markets does so as well in the other. However, wage adjustment destroys this proportionality, as reflected in the different values of the slopes of the $NN'$ and $pp'$ curves. When the slopes of the iso-target functions diverge, one instrument becomes more efficient in affecting one target relative to another target. In the present case, tax changes become a relatively inefficient way to change the equilibrium price level. The opposite is the case for changes in the money supply. This can be seen in Figure 16–4. Suppose that taxes are raised from point $E$ to $G$. The increase in the money supply needed to stop the price level from falling is $BG$; but the increase in the money supply needed to restore full employment is $CG$. Clearly, then, monetary policy has an easier time getting the price level under control after a given tax change than it does in attempting to restore full employment. The opposite is, of course, true for tax policy.

The theory of economic policy teaches that when such comparative advantage develops, the usual one-on-one instrument-target prescriptions can no longer be relied upon. For example, the standard notion that it is appropriate to raise taxes during inflation is correct if the superimposed $NN'$-$pp'$ curves of Figure 16–2 are descriptive of the situation. However, it is not at all clear that this is appropriate in the comparative-advantage situation described by Figure 16–4. At point $H$ the securing of equilibrium does, to be sure, suggest the conventional medicine that taxes be raised and the money supply lowered. However, consider point $I$ which is also in the inflation zone. Getting to $E$ suggests that if the money supply is lowered to its appropriate level ($\overline{M/p}$) then the appropriate tax change is a reduction rather than an increase. The trouble is that taxes appear too low at $I$ only because the money supply is chronically too high. Following the conventional prescription of raising taxes because of the existence of inflation would, under the circumstances, just get the economy farther away from equilibrium.

If the present diagnosis of inflationary recession is correct, it provides at least one source of comfort. That is, the policy directives during inflationary recession are at least unambiguous; lower taxes, and pursue a tighter monetary policy. No such clear directive emerges in the classical inflation zone above both functions. As we have already seen, the attainment of equilibrium might (once an appropriate monetary policy response is assured) imply a rise in taxes, and it might imply a fall. The same, unfortunately, could be true for monetary policy. From Figure 16–4 it appears that there is a fair presumption that inflation is normally associated with excessive money supply. However, inflation also exists at point $J$ where taxes are chronically low in relation to equilibrium. In this case the attainment of equilibrium implies increasing the money supply and combining this with a tax increase. Policy coordination, therefore, appears clearly to be necessary under conditions of comparative advantage.

Let us consider some of the problems of coordination. Consider Figure 16–5 which once again shows the iso-employment and iso-price level functions. If the equilibrium money supply $\overline{M/p}$ and tax $\overline{T}$ values are known, the

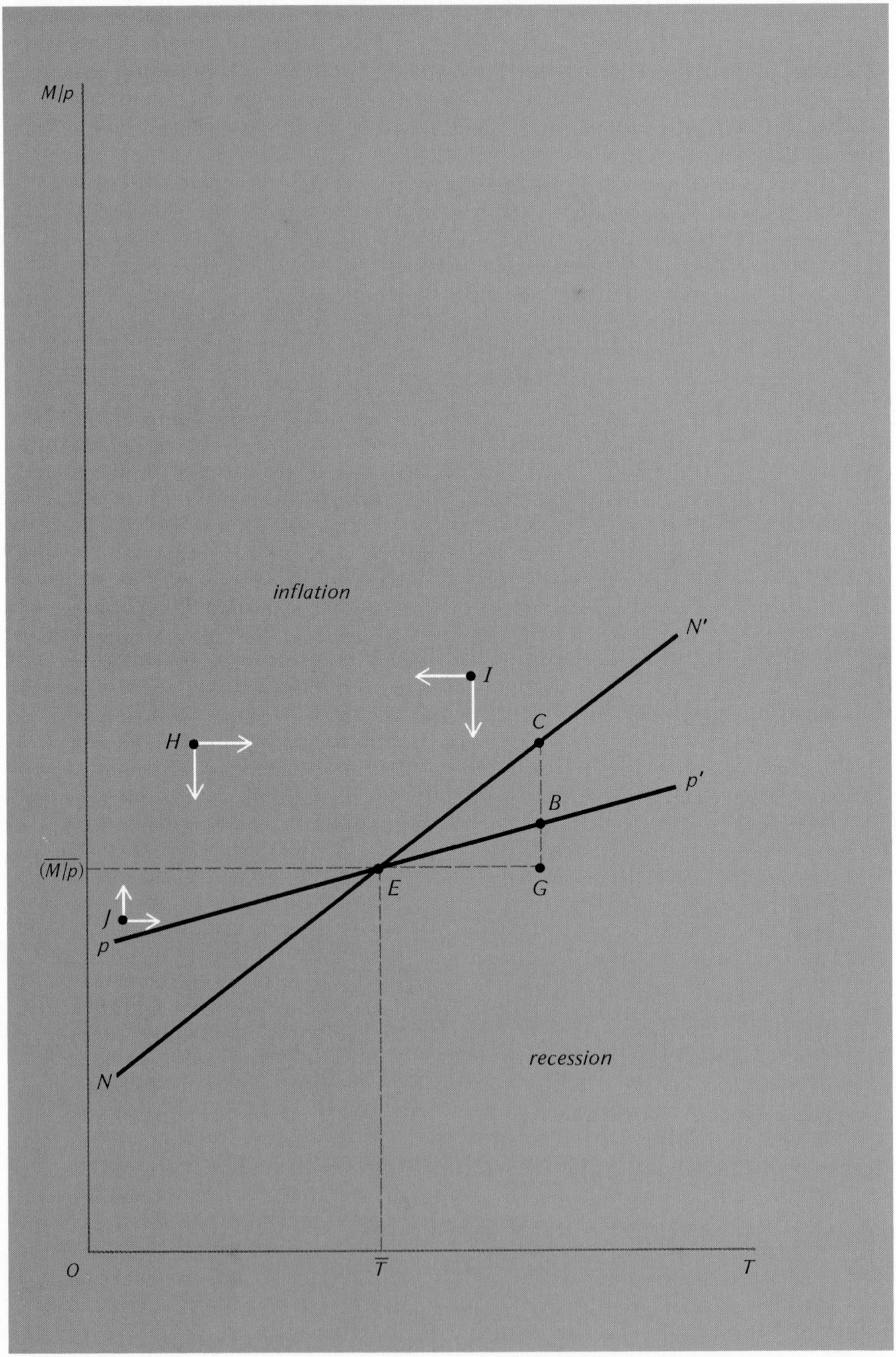

M/p
inflation
N'
I
C
H
p'
B
$(\overline{M/p})$
E
G
J
p
recession
N
O
$\overline{T}$
T

policy problem becomes simple inasmuch as the instruments could immediately be set at these values. In practice, however, exact information upon which to base policy decisions may not be available. The authorities may know that they are in one zone or another, but they probably do not know the exact shape or location of the respective iso-target functions, and therefore they will not know the magnitude of the required levels of the instrument variables. Furthermore, a particular policy-making authority may not be willing or able to coordinate its activities with the authority that controls other policy instruments, or to be fully aware of the fact that its own policy actions may prove to be either inadequate or excessive because of the unanticipated response of another instrument.

A solution to the problem of absent or faulty policy coordination and missing information was proposed by Robert Mundell.[1] He suggested that each policy instrument could ignore the fact that it is part of a simultaneous system and therefore influences all targets, and that it should instead concentrate its attention exclusively on the attainment of the target over which it has the greatest relative influence, or comparative advantage as we used that term earlier in this section.

The wage-adjustment model suggests that monetary policy's comparative advantage lies in influencing the product market, whereas the comparative advantage of tax changes lies in influencing the labor market. Therefore, according to Mundell's principle, monetary policy should be "assigned" to the price stability target and aim itself for the $pp'$ functions, whereas tax policy should pair itself with the full-employment objective and aim for the $NN'$ function. If this assignment of instruments to targets is followed, the policies will eventually approach their equilibrium values despite the absence of coordination. If the assignment is reversed, with monetary policy concerning itself about full employment while taxes are changed to maintain price stability, there will be a progressive divergence of the instrument values from their equilibrium values.

The principle of correct assignment can be illustrated with reference to Figure 16–5. Starting at point $A$ in the inflationary recession zone, monetary policy may attempt to secure full employment by expanding the money supply to $G$. This raises the rate of inflation and may prompt a tax increase which places the system at $H$. However, this creates even more unemployment than initially. The assignment of instruments to targets is therefore incorrect and destabilizing.

Alternatively, begin again at point $A$ and suppose that taxes are reduced

[1] R. A. Mundell, "The Appropriate Use of Monetary and Fiscal Policy for Internal and External Stability," *International Monetary Fund Staff Papers*, 9:70–79, 1962.

**FIGURE 16–4**
**Appropriate policy response**
**under general inflation**

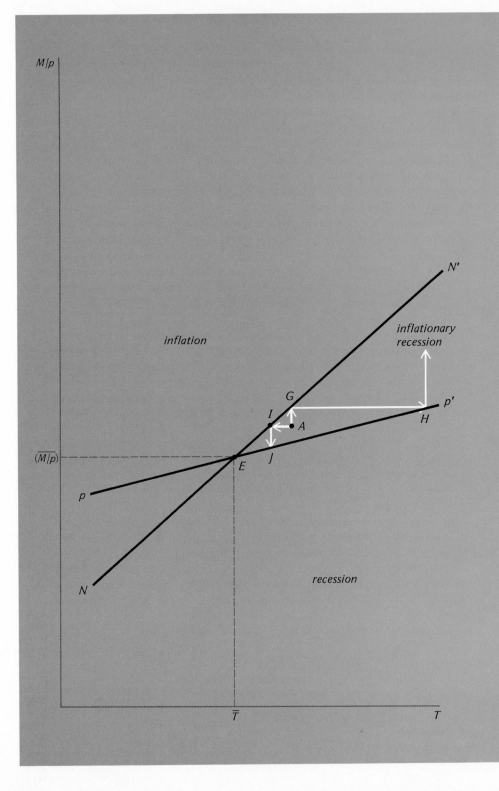

so as to place the system at point *I*. The resultant wage pause secures a large employment gain at the cost of relatively little additional inflation. Monetary restriction then moves to point *J* to eliminate the inflation, and the resultant small increase in unemployment is then eliminated by a smaller than previous tax reduction. It is evident that if this sequence is carried forward, equilibrium will eventually be secured. The instruments have, therefore, been correctly assigned to their respective targets.

It is instructive to apply the wage-adjustment model and the principle of correct policy assignment to particular actual cases. Consider, for example, the effort by the United States to raise employment by reduction of direct taxes in 1964, and the effort, in mid-1968, to slow inflation by a surtax on personal and corporate income. The 1964 tax reduction was generally credited with being successful in raising output and employment without increasing inflationary pressure. On the other hand, the 1968 surtax failed to slow inflation and seems merely to have contributed to the advent and depth of a costly recession. An important factor in each case was the behavior of monetary policy. Although the economic expansion of the early 1960s was accommodated by monetary growth, this was not excessive, as indicated by the fact that interest rates drifted upward during the period. On the other hand, the 1968 tax increase, which took effect at midyear, was accompanied by a very rapid rate of monetary growth that continued until the end of the year.

The wage-adjustment model and the principles of correct assignment provide the following interpretation of these episodes. In 1964 policies were properly assigned, taxes being lowered to raise output and employment, with monetary restraint helping to hold down growth in the price level. The tax cut provided disposable income relief. Upward wage pressure was therefore reduced, unit labor costs fell, and the result was a large gain in employment and output combined with excellent price performance.

The interpretation of the 1968 experience is as follows: The rise in taxes was followed by upward wage pressure. Unit labor costs therefore rose and caused output and employment to fall, while price inflation continued unabated due to the impact of continuing monetary expansion. Had monetary restriction been employed in the first instance, the result might have been considerably less costly and traumatic. The wage adjustment would not have occurred, and the rate of inflation would have been slowed with far less loss in output and employment.

As readers can easily convince themselves, the assignment rule works regardless of the zone in which the initial combination of instrument values places the system. Although Mundell's ingenious solution ensures convergence to equilibrium, it does not completely bypass the problem of policy

**FIGURE 16–5**
Illustration of correct and incorrect
assignments of instruments to targets

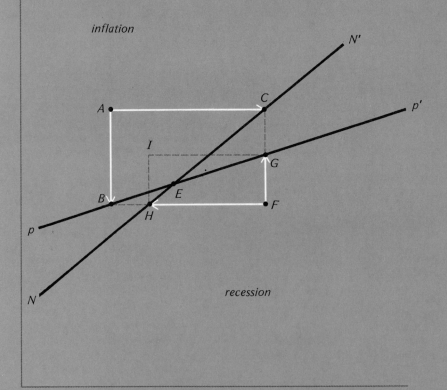

coordination because blind pursuit of a single target may produce extremely messy adjustments. By this we mean that the change in a policy variable may be discovered to have gone too far, once the effect of the change in the other policy variable is felt, and the direction of change of the policy variable may then have to be reversed. This is not only embarrassing but has harmful economic and political consequences as well.

To illustrate the problem, consider Figure 16–6 where we assume the economy to be in the inflation zone at point *A*. If taxes are raised to reach *NN'* at point *C*, and the money supply is simultaneously reduced to reach *pp'* at point *B*, the net effect of this monetary-fiscal overkill is to shove the system into recession at point *F*. If taxes are then lowered to point *H* to correct the initial error, and the money supply is raised to point *G* to correct the initial error of monetary policy, the combined effect of the two policies is to restore inflation at point *I*. Since point *I* is a better place to be than point *A*, the adjustment sequence is stabilizing because correct assignment has been followed. But this will be cold comfort to the citizens who have to endure recurring bouts of inflation and recession as the consequence of a sequence of stop-go policies.

To conclude: We have attempted in this chapter to introduce some of the principles of economic policy and to intertwine the development of these principles with analysis of a substantive contemporary policy problem. In the next chapter we will carry this procedure forward, this time considering policy issues raised by international monetary problems. Additional principles of economic policy will be introduced at that time, and it is therefore appropriate to delay a summary of the various principles until we reach the end of the next chapter.

**FIGURE 16–6**
Illustration of overshooting due to lack
of policy coordination

# 17

# INTERNATIONAL ADJUSTMENT PROBLEMS AND ECONOMIC POLICY

## 17-1
## INTRODUCTION

We left off in our earlier chapter on the macroeconomic analysis of an open economy with the comment that reconciling the internal goal of full employment at stable prices with the external goal of balance of payments equilibrium was a tall order. However, now that we know how to approach multiple-target problems we can, perhaps, make some headway with this timely, important, and most fascinating subject.

In Chapter 11 we attempted a formal extension of the closed economy model to the open economy, and we examined the automatic mechanisms of adjustment under fixed exchange rates. In this chapter our focus shifts to conscious policy. The objective is to achieve the target of full employment without inflation (internal balance) along with equilibrium in the balance of payments (external balance). Some of the questions that will be asked are the following: When is it appropriate to vary the exchange rate, and when is it inappropriate? When is it appropriate to use monetary and fiscal policies to deal with a balance of payments problem, and when is it not? What is the appropriate monetary-fiscal mix for the simultaneous achievement of external and internal balance, and what is the appropriate assignment of policies to the targets? How would flexible exchange rates alter the process of income transmission, and how would monetary and fiscal policies affect the variables of the system under flexible exchange rates as opposed to fixed exchange rates? How, finally, are these results affected by varying the responsiveness of capital movements to changes in the rate of interest?

## 17-2
## THE FOREIGN EXCHANGE MARKET
## AND THE OPTION FOR POLICY

Analysis of balance of payments adjustment policy is facilitated by focusing the discussion on the behavior of the foreign exchange market. Imagine, therefore, a world of two countries A and B, where A is the "home" country and B is the "rest of the world," and suppose that the respective national currencies are alphas ($\alpha$) and betas ($\beta$). Country A will receive a certain quantity of betas from exports to B, from interest and dividends on its overseas investments in B, government grants and loans, and from interest-sensitive capital inflows. The sum of all such foreign exchange receipts is the supply of foreign exchange to country A.

Similarly, A's imports from B, its investments in B, the transmission of dividends and interest to B, and its grants to B, all necessitate foreign exchange, and these requirements therefore constitute A's demand for foreign exchange.

In Chapter 11 we considered the effect of a change in the exchange rate, that is, the price of betas in terms of alphas, on the real value of A's exports and imports. However, balance of payments policy must concern itself with attempting to improve net foreign exchange earnings, and this may or may not be equivalent to an improvement in the balance of payments denominated in terms of domestic currency deflated for changes in the overall price level. Thus the discussion of devaluation, as we previously called raising the official price of foreign exchange, has some additional dimensions that need to be amplified.

As before, let the symbol $\pi$ denote the price of foreign exchange from A's point of view, and consider the demand side of the foreign exchange market. If A devalues (so that $\pi$ is increased) citizens of A will have to give up a larger number of alphas in order to acquire a given quantity of betas, and the effect of this will be to make B's goods more expensive to the citizens of A. The result is likely to be that the physical volume of goods imported will decline, and since producers in B will observe this as a reduction in the demand for their goods, prices of exported goods will decline in country B. Consequently, country A will end up buying fewer units of B's goods, and it will also get each unit more cheaply in terms of betas (but not alphas); it therefore must follow that, by devaluing, A will economize on its expenditures of foreign exchange. This means, finally, that if we were to draw a demand curve for foreign exchange, this demand curve would have a negative slope.

Such a demand curve is drawn in Figure 17–1. The exchange rate is measured on the vertical axis, and the quantity of betas demanded is measured on the horizontal axis. The higher the price of betas, the lower is A's expenditure of foreign exchange.

On the supply side the case is not as clear-cut. If A devalues, importers in B will notice that they need to give up fewer betas to purchase the alphas needed to acquire A's goods. They therefore lower the beta price of the imports to their domestic customers. Although this will increase the number of physical units of A's exports, A will earn less per unit because of the fall in the beta price and therefore may or may not earn more foreign exchange. If B's demand for A's goods has a price elasticity greater than unity, the proportional fall in price will be less than the proportional rise in quantity, and total beta earnings will therefore increase. If the elasticity is less than unity, the price effect will dominate the quantity effect, and B will then earn less foreign exchange for its exports even though it sends a larger volume of goods abroad.[1]

These considerations suggest that the supply curve of foreign exchange will be positively sloped in the manner of most supply curves if the demand for A's exports is elastic with respect to price, but negatively sloped if it is inelastic. The negatively sloped case has been much discussed in the literature and provides one reason why countries have often been reluctant to permit their exchange rates to be devaluated. If the demand for a country's exports is price-inelastic, devaluation will not only cause the country to earn less foreign exchange but will also cause it to sacrifice a larger physical volume of goods in the process.

In Figure 17–1 the supply curve of foreign exchange is drawn with a positive slope, implying price-elastic demand for A's exports. The functions intersect at exchange rate $\bar{\pi}$, with $\bar{\beta}$ units of foreign exchange being demanded and supplied. This is the result that would obtain in a stable, freely fluctuating market for foreign exchange. Under such conditions there would be no deficits or surpluses in the balance of payments, nor would there be any changes in domestic money supplies since the alphas (and betas) that are paid out are received back through the equilibrating action of the exchange rate.

Let us suppose, however, that the government of country A undertakes to maintain a fixed exchange rate at $\pi_0$. At this exchange rate the demand for betas exceeds the supply so that it is clear that betas are undervalued and

---

[1] The literature analyzing the effect of devaluation on the trade balance, and the relation of the changes to the underlying demand and supply price elasticities is extensive. Among the more well-known contributions to the "elasticity approach" of the effect of devaluation are A. P. Lerner, *The Economics of Control*, Chap. 28, The Macmillan Company, New York, 1944; and J. Robinson, "The Foreign Exchanges," *Essays in the Theory of Employment*, Part III, Chap. 5, Basil, Blackwell & Mott, Ltd., Oxford, 1947; reprinted in H. S. Ellis and L. A. Metzler, *Readings in the Theory of International Trade*, Chap. 4, McGraw-Hill Book Company, New York, for the American Economic Association, 1950.

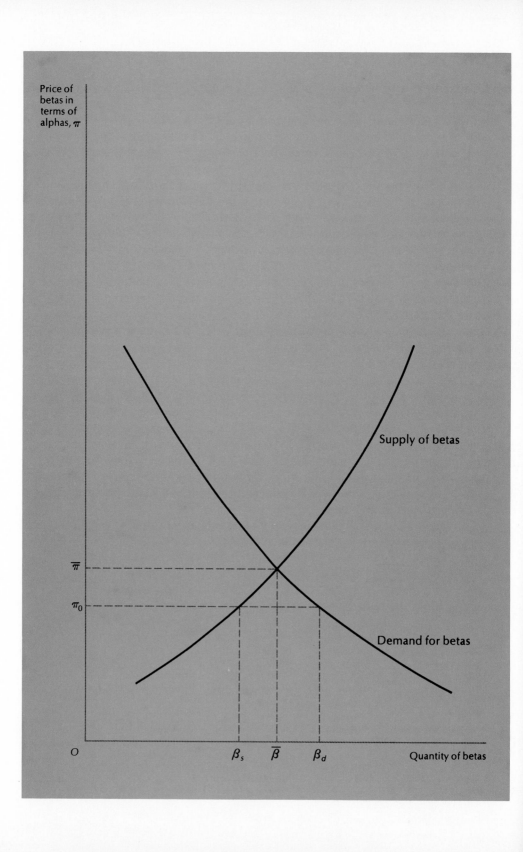

alphas are overvalued. A deficit appears in country A's balance of payments valued at $\beta_d - \beta_s$, and a corresponding surplus appears in the balance of payments of country B.

Normal market forces would tend to raise the price of betas relative to alphas in the foreign exchange market. To prevent this, A's central bank must intervene; this means it must supply the excess demand for betas from its own accumulation of foreign exchange and gold and in so doing accumulate alpha balances, thereby causing the domestic money supply to shrink. We therefore emphasize again that it is the intervention of central banks and national treasuries that prevents exchange rates from fluctuating. If the central bank of country A is willing and able to sell betas at a fixed price in exchange for alphas, the tendency for the price of betas to rise will be eliminated because holders of alphas can always convert them into betas at A's central bank at the official exchange rate.

Although A's central bank may wish to sell betas at the official rate, this may not be permanently possible. If official policy persists in undervaluing betas, the need to accommodate a continuing excess demand for betas would eventually exhaust A's accumulated supplies of gold and foreign exchange. What then are the options available to country A in combating the outflow of betas?

Inspection of Figure 17–1 shows quite clearly that if country A is committed to maintaining a rigid and overvalued exchange rate, the discrepancy between the demand for and the supply of betas can be removed only by finding ways of shifting the curves since the fixed exchange rate precludes movements along them. One way to shift the curves is to do nothing, since, as discussed in Chapter 11, the continuation of a deficit in the balance of payments will reduce the domestic money supply, raise the rate of interest, and cause shrinkage in domestic income and the level of prices. This will reduce the demand for imports, increase export earnings, and promote an inflow of capital. Indeed, country A may even augment these forces by pursuing restrictive fiscal and monetary policies; this, in fact, is what was expected under the "rules of the game" of the nineteenth-century gold standard. These policies would, to be sure, eliminate the deficit in the balance of payments, but they would do so at the cost of domestic income shrinkage. Consequently, hardly anyone except an arch deflationist would advocate such bitter medicine nowadays, and it is wholly inappropriate medicine except when a deficit is caused by excessive internal demand. Governments, utilizing common sense, have tended to move in the other direction. Instead of augmenting the natural forces that make for balance of payments adjustment by permitting the curves to shift through fluctuations in income and the price level, the tendency has been to offset these forces in order to maintain

**FIGURE 17–1**
The demand and supply of foreign exchange

domestic stability. The cost of this, however, is that the deficit in the balance of payments continues and reserves of gold and foreign exchange continue to flow abroad.

One way to avert deflation and to eliminate a balance of payments problem is to pursue restrictive trade policies. Country A may impose a tariff on B's goods; it may set import quotas; it may subsidize exports; it may impose discriminatory taxes on the overseas earnings of its residents; it may impose restrictions on the uses to which foreign exchange may be put; and it may allow the deficit to affect its foreign policy by causing it to reduce or discontinue foreign aid and to affect its military commitments. Economists generally oppose the resort to restrictive policies because such policies inhibit the free flow of resources, of goods and services, and of capital, and they therefore produce inefficient resource allocation and reduce real income throughout the world. These policies, moreover, are really hidden forms of devaluation; since they are selective and discriminatory, they distort the allocation of resources and impair economic efficiency. Domestic producers are sheltered from foreign competition, capital fails to flow into areas of maximum productive use, and consumers are denied access to foreign goods even though those goods may be less expensive and of better quality than domestic goods. The policies tend, finally, to invite retaliation, and they are, therefore, likely to be self-defeating.

If all the policies thus far discussed that shift the demand and supply curves of foreign exchange are ruled out as unacceptable, we must recognize that there is no alternative but to permit price adjustments that allow the foreign exchange market to equilibrate at the intersection of the existing demand and supply functions. This can be done either by allowing the exchange rate to fluctuate freely or by changing the official price of foreign exchange. The latter policy, which we may describe as controlled devaluation, will occupy us throughout the remainder of this section; the alternative of freely fluctuating exchange rates is the subject of the subsequent section.

Given the drawbacks of allowing the demand and supply curves of foreign exchange to shift, one naturally is inclined to inquire why countries have often exhibited such reluctance to devalue their exchange rates. One source of worry is the elasticity pessimism that we discussed earlier. A related worry is that the foreign exchange market may be unstable as the result of the activity of foreign exchange speculators. It has often been noted that when a country suffers a deficit and continuing loss of reserves, speculators begin to bet that the country cannot hold on, and they therefore begin to sell the beleaguered currency, anticipating that they can buy it back more cheaply after the country is forced to devalue. This, of course, exacerbates the country's balance of payments problem because it accelerates the rate at which foreign exchange reserves are depleted. The fear of so-called speculative raids has often caused countries to cling to an overvalued exchange rate for dear life. The hope is that if speculators can be convinced that the par value of the currency will never be changed, they will refrain from "attacking" the currency. If, on the other hand, it becomes known that devaluation is contemplated, the floodgates will swing wide open.

Indeed, to digress for a moment, one of the most serious defects of a system of fixed, but occasionally adjustable, exchange rates is the tendency for such a system to give rise to destabilizing speculative forces. For the speculator it is a "heads I win; tails you lose" proposition where the sure loser is the monetary authority. Speculators who sell alphas if they think the official price of betas is going to rise will gain if this subsequently happens. On the other hand, if country A withstands the attack and maintains the parity of the currency, speculators lose no more than their brokerage costs. It is, therefore, little wonder that the "adjustable peg" system is dangerously unstable and that periodic international currency crises ascend to the status of a way of life under it.

A third problem with attempting to eliminate a balance of payments deficit by means of devaluation is that countries that suffer deficits in their balance of payments also often tend to be suffering from inflation, and in that case devaluation may not work very well. The difficulty is that if country A devalues and if, as a consequence of this, its exports increase and its imports decrease, its income level will rise while B's income level will fall. Because these income changes increase A's demand for imports while they reduce B's, A's demand curve for foreign exchange will shift to the right while the supply curve of foreign exchange shifts to the left. Thus an attempt to eliminate excess demand by a price adjustment along *existing* demand and supply functions may be thwarted by a *shift* in these functions that results from the price adjustment itself. Conceivably, a sizable deficit could then continue to exist after the devaluation.[1]

This difficulty can be studied with the aid of some ideas suggested by S. S. Alexander.[2] The level of real income (or output) is given by

$$Y = C + I + G + (X - Z)$$

Alexander consolidates $C + I + G$ into a single term $A$ which he calls domestic "absorption." Income can then be written as the sum of absorption and the level of net exports, namely,

$$Y = A + (X - Z)$$

Evidently, if net exports are to be raised to improve the balance of payments, a country must either increase its total level of output $Y$, or it must reduce its level of absorption. Devaluation provides a price incentive to increase exports

[1] Attempts to analyze the effect of devaluation that take income changes into account are A. C. Harberger, "Currency Depreciation, Income and the Balance of Trade," *Journal of Political Economy*, 63:47–60, 1950; and S. C. Tsiang, "The Role of Money in Trade Balance Stability: A Synthesis of the Elasticity and Absorption Approaches," *American Economic Review*, 51:912–936, 1961. Both papers are reprinted in R. E. Caves and H. G. Johnson, *Readings in International Economics*, Vol. XI, Richard D. Irwin, Inc., Homewood, Ill., 1968, for the American Economic Association. These studies suggest that the simple "elasticity" approach correctly predicts the direction in which devaluation will affect net exports. However, since the elasticity approach ignores income effects, it tends to exaggerate the extent to which a given devaluation will change the trade balance.

[2] S. S. Alexander, "Effects of a Devaluation on a Trade Balance," *International Monetary Fund Staff Papers*, 2:263–278, 1952; reprinted in Caves and Johnson, op. cit., Chap. 22.

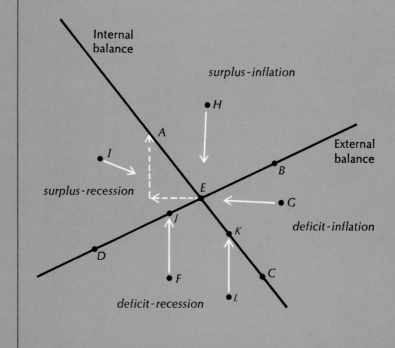

Exchange rate, $\pi$

Internal
balance

*surplus-inflation*

● H

A

External
balance

● I

● B

*surplus-recession*

E

J

● G

K

*deficit-inflation*

D

● F

C

● L

*deficit-recession*

O

Domestic absorption $(C + I + G)$

and reduce imports. If the economy is at less than full employment, the increase in $X - Z$ may be accommodated by an increase in output provided that domestic absorption rises by less than the increase in output. Normally this will happen provided the marginal propensity to consume is less than unity. However, if the economy is at full employment, $Y$ cannot be changed, and the only way in which net exports can be increased is to reduce domestic absorption, which, of course, implies that domestic demand must be suppressed by monetary and/or fiscal policies. Failing such demand suppression, the price incentives provided by the devaluation will be frittered away because the level of domestic prices will rise in such a way as to leave exports and imports in the identical competitive position as they were before. To use the terms popularized by H. G. Johnson, an "expenditure switching" policy such as devaluation must be accompanied by an "expenditure reducing" policy such as a tighter fiscal or monetary policy if devaluation is to have its intended effects.[1] To view the matter another way, we can say that at full employment, resources must first be released from domestic absorption by reducing internal spending. The relative price changes that result from the devaluation then provide the price incentives that guide these resources into the export sector and that shift spending from imports to domestic goods.

In Chapter 11 we noted that when the economic situation is characterized by both a deficit in the balance of payments and income below the full-employment level, devaluation might be appropriate since such a policy both improves the balance of payments and raises domestic income. However, we have also noted that if the economy is already at full employment a policy of devaluation may be inappropriate since that may cause inflation. Thus the initial combination of internal and external conditions is important in attempting to decide how to conduct policy; when that is the case it is best to attempt to organize further discussion along lines suggested by the theory of economic policy.

Consider Figure 17–2. The level of domestic absorption as previously defined is measured on the horizontal axis, and the exchange rate is measured on the vertical axis. Domestic absorption measures the level of internal demand, and the exchange rate measures the country's competitive position vis-à-vis other countries. A movement to the left along the horizontal axis implies that an expenditure reducing policy, to use Johnson's terminology, has been put into effect; a movement upward along the vertical axis implies

[1] H. G. Johnson, "Towards a General Theory of the Balance of Payments," *International Trade and Economic Growth: Studies in Pure Theory,* Harvard University Press, Cambridge, Mass., 1961, pp. 153–168; reprinted in Caves and Johnson, op. cit., Chap. 23.

**FIGURE 17–2**
Appropriate policy responses under
different combinations of external
and internal imbalance

competitive expenditure switching due to changes in domestic relative to international prices.[1]

Now define internal balance as a situation of full employment and stable prices, and imagine that point E in Figure 17–2 is such a point. A restrictive monetary-fiscal policy would reduce absorption and create unemployment, but this could be offset by an expenditure switching policy that raises net exports, since such an improvement in the balance of trade will stimulate the economy. Consequently, a point such as A might also imply internal balance. The locus of all such combinations of exchange rates and internal spending levels that yield full employment is the "internal balance curve." It must have a negative slope because a reduction in internal demand would increase unemployment unless this were accompanied by a sufficient rise in net exports. It is obvious that points to the left of the internal balance curve imply recession, and points to the right imply inflation.

Similarly, let us for present purposes ignore capital movements and let us define external balance as occurring when net exports equal zero. If E is such a point, an increase in absorption will raise income and imports and create a deficit. But this could be offset by expenditure switching that improves the country's competitive position. In combination, these two policies might restore external balance at a point such as B. Clearly, then, the "external balance curve" has a positive slope; points to the right of it imply a deficit, and points to the left imply a surplus.

We can now consider the various possibilities. If the economy is on neither the external nor the internal balance functions, it can find itself in one of four zones: deficit-recession, deficit-inflation, surplus-inflation, or surplus-recession. If it is on one of the balance functions but not on the other, it may have full employment combined with a deficit or a surplus; or if it enjoys external balance, this may be combined with a recession or an inflation. There are, in fact, eight possible states, not counting overall equilibrium, and the search for that equilibrium will require different combinations of policy response.

A country at point A that enjoys full employment and has a surplus should appreciate. Since this will create unemployment, the appreciation should be accompanied by expansionary monetary-fiscal policies. In other words, an increase in absorption is required to offset the unfavorable employment effects that a deterioration of the trade balance would bring about. If the economy is at point C, combining full employment with a deficit, it should pursue the opposite set of policies. If the balance of payments is in equilibrium but inflation is a problem, as at point B, the economy should pursue restrictive fiscal policies and appreciate the exchange rate. Or, finally, if external balance is combined with recession, as at D, the domestic economy should be expanded and, recognizing that this will reduce net exports, com-

---

[1] The model represented by Figure 17–2 is adapted from T. Swan, "Longer-Run Problems in the Balance of Payments," in H. W. Arndt and M. W. Corden, eds., *The Australian Economy: A Volume of Readings,* The Cheshire Press, Melbourne, 1963, pp. 384–395; reprinted in Caves and Johnson, op. cit., Chap. 27.

bine this with devaluation. Notice that all of these cases, in which we start with either internal or external balance, require a combination of policy response.

If both a deficit and a recession exist simultaneously, as at *F*, it is obvious that there is no recourse but to become more competitive. Expansionary policies that raise internal demand would increase domestic employment, but they would cause the deficit to widen. This was the unfortunate situation in which the United States economy found itself during the early 1960s and again in 1970–1971. It is, perhaps, the worst of all possible states and has often been described as the dilemma zone, even though all the zones give rise to one dilemma or another.

If a surplus is combined with inflation, as at point *H*, the conclusion is inescapable that appreciation of the exchange rate must sooner or later be undertaken. To combat the inflation by expenditure reduction would merely increase the surplus, to the considerable alarm and consternation of the deficit countries.

A surplus combined with recession, as at point *I*, should be combated by monetary-fiscal expansion. This will raise employment and at the same time reduce the size of the surplus. If, finally, a deficit is combined with inflation, as at point *G*, the inflation should be combated by restrictive domestic policies which, at the same time, would reduce the size of the deficit. This is really the only case in which the harsh remedy of deflationary stabilization policy is appropriate for dealing with a balance of payments problem.

This discussion suggests an important additional principle of economic policy. Active leadership in policy adjustment should be assigned to the instrument of policy that brings the economy nearer to both targets as it aims for a single target. The other instrument will be in a conflict role in the sense that if it moves toward one target, it will tend to move the economy further away from the other target. The principle, therefore, is that leadership in policy adjustment should always be assigned to the instrument that is not in conflict since that will avert the necessity to reverse the direction of policy and will make for a direct approach to equilibrium.

To make sure we understand this principle it will be sufficient to consider the situation in any one of the zones. In the deficit-recession zone policies that change domestic absorption are in conflict since a change that moves toward external balance moves away from internal balance. On the other hand, exchange rate policy has a clear directive to raise the price of foreign exchange since this moves the system closer to both targets. Exchange rate policy should, therefore, be the primary-active instrument, while internal stabilization policies should take a secondary-passive role until the appropriate direction of change becomes clear. If the initial situation is at point *F* in Figure 17–2, then upward movement of the exchange rate will tend to secure external balance (at point *J*) sooner than it will secure internal balance. In that event it becomes evident that a further increase in the exchange rate would produce a surplus while recession continues, and it is then evident that internal demand should be expanded. Alternatively, if the initial position is at point *L*, the rise in the exchange rate will eliminate recession (at point *K*) before it eliminates the deficit. Since a further rise in the exchange rate would then cause inflation, the appropriate subsequent internal policy is to reduce domestic absorption.

Before we move ahead, we should note that we have been assuming throughout this discussion that balance of payments equilibrium is equivalent to a zero level of net exports. Consequently, equilibrium here has meant that equilibrium in the balance of trade and capital movements have been ignored. However, as we saw in Chapter 11, there appears to be some scope for achieving simultaneous internal and external balance by changing the monetary-fiscal mix. We point this out here in order to indicate that the scope for policy may not be as limited as we have painted it in this section. We will return to this question of mix in the last section of this chapter.

To conclude: We have now considered some of the balance of payments problems of countries under the adjustable peg system which persisted during the 1950s and 1960s. Under the system, fixed exchange rates were the general rule although changes in official exchange rates were, from time to time, permissible in response to "fundamental disequilibrium." Given all the drawbacks of this system, one wonders why governments and central banks did not long ago stop selling gold and foreign exchange at fixed prices and, instead, simply permit their exchange rates to fluctuate in accordance with variations in supply and demand in free markets. In the next section we shall examine some of the characteristics of the flexible exchange rate alternative.

## 17–3
## STABILIZATION POLICY UNDER FIXED
## AND FLEXIBLE EXCHANGE RATES

Countries A and B could abandon the whole idea of maintaining an official exchange rate, and they could effect such a decision simply by refraining from any further sales of gold and foreign exchange at fixed prices. It would have to be a mutual decision since a pegging operation by either of the countries would fix the price of the currencies with respect to each other. If they decided upon flexible exchange rates as a permanent policy, they would find, first of all, that there would be no further balance of payments deficits or surpluses and that there would therefore be no need to destabilize their respective economies in order to stabilize the exchange rate. As an added set of advantages, they would find that there would be no further need to use valuable resources for the purpose of mining, refining, storing, guarding, and transporting such an inherently worthless commodity as gold. The gain in real income from these economies alone would be substantial.

The list of considerations that bear on the issue of fixed versus flexible exchange rates is virtually inexhaustible. Since this is a book on macroeconomics and not exchange rate policy, we will not attempt to discuss the entire list; instead we shall direct our attention to macro problems. One of the major macroeconomic issues is the question of whether it would be easier to stabilize the domestic economy with fiscal and monetary policies under flexible exchange rates than it would be under fixed rates. The importance of this question is such that it is appropriate to consider it with extreme care.

Let us recall that expansionary fiscal policy tends to raise the rate of interest and to attract foreign capital. Thus, even though income expansion may cause the trade balance to deteriorate, this may be offset by an inflow of capital. Monetary expansion, on the other hand, depresses interest rates and may therefore aggravate a balance of payments problem. This circumstance stands as an abiding irritation to economists who prefer to use monetary policy as the primary instrument of stabilization policy. It is a commonplace to say that under fixed exchange rates monetary policy must be directed to balance of payments considerations and that flexible exchange rates would free monetary policy to perform its role in domestic income stabilization. Let us now see how monetary and fiscal policies would work under the alternatives of fixed and flexible exchange rates.

The initial portion of the discussion is based on a well-known paper by Robert Mundell and begins with a number of simplifying assumptions.[1] First, it is assumed that capital mobility is *perfect*. This means that funds always flow to the country in which interest rates are highest and that such flows continue until interest rates are everywhere equal. Second, it is assumed that country A is so small relative to the rest of the world (country B) that changes in the domestic money supply in A have no effect on interest rates elsewhere. The equilibrium interest rate is therefore exogenously determined. Third, to provide relevance to the discussion, it is assumed that the level of income is below the full-employment level. Finally, and to further simplify the analysis, it is assumed that the aggregate supply curve is perfectly elastic, so that the price level does not vary. By fixing the price level arbitrarily we can eliminate it from the *IS* and balance of payments equations of Chapter 11 and write the *IS* equation as

$$I(i) + G + X(\pi) = Y - C(Y - T) + Z(Y,\pi)$$

while the balance of payments function is

$$BOP = X(\pi) - Z(Y,\pi) + K(i)$$

An *IS-LM* diagram combined with a BOP function will be of enormous assistance in this discussion, and let us therefore consider Figure 17–3. The initial *IS* and *LM* functions are $IS_0$ and $LM_0$. Their intersection is at income level $Y_0$, and at the exogenously determined rate of interest $i_w$. Whenever the domestic interest rate is above $i_w$, capital floods into the country, and when-

[1] R. A. Mundell, "Capital Mobility and Stabilization Policy under Fixed and Flexible Exchange Rates," *Canadian Journal of Economics and Political Science,* 29:475–485, 1963; reprinted in Mundell, *International Economics,* Chap. 18, The Macmillan Company, New York, 1968; and in Caves and Johnson, op. cit., Chap. 30.

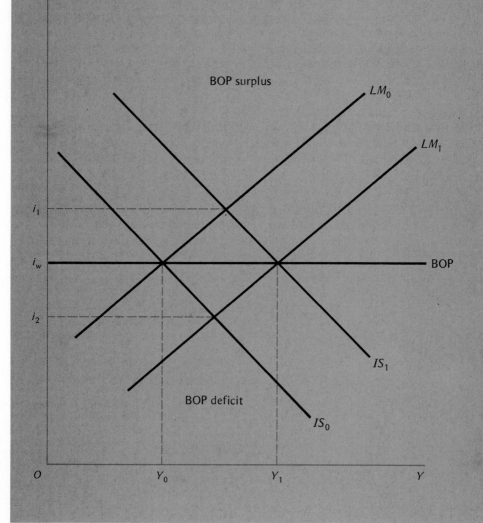

ever it is below $i_w$, the flood tide is reversed. Consequently, in the case of perfect capital mobility the BOP function, which had a positive slope under the *imperfect* capital mobility assumption of Chapter 11, is a horizontal line coincident with $i_w$.

We begin with the case of fixed exchange rates and suppose that country A's monetary authority assumes responsibility for maintaining the fixed rate. If government purchases are raised (or taxes reduced) in an effort to raise the level of income, the *IS* curve shifts to the right, for example, to $IS_1$. However, with a fixed money supply this drives up the domestic interest rate to $i_1$, and this, in turn, produces an inflow of capital. Because the demand for A's currency is thereby increased, the monetary authority must supply the excess demand and in the process accumulate foreign exchange. However, the foreign exchange is purchased by the sale of domestic money, so that the money supply in A increases; this means that the *LM* curve shifts to the right. Since equilibrium cannot be reestablished until the interest rate differential is eliminated, the money supply must continue to increase until the *LM* curve intersects $IS_1$ at $i_w$. It follows that at the new equilibrium the *LM* curve will be $LM_1$ and will cut $IS_1$ at income level $Y_1$.

If this argument is correct, it suggests that fiscal policy will have a fully multiplied effect on the level of income under fixed exchange rates. This is because official foreign exchange operations have the effect of offsetting the crowding out of investment that rising interest rates would otherwise have had.

If country A increases its domestic money supply by purchasing domestic securities on the open market, the *LM* curve will initially shift to $LM_1$. However, this has the effect of depressing the domestic rate of interest to $i_2$, and it therefore leads to an outflow of capital. The monetary authority must now support the exchange rate by selling foreign exchange. In so doing the authority buys back domestic money and contracts the domestic money supply. Equilibrium cannot be reestablished until the interest rate differential is eliminated. This means that the *LM* curve must shift back to its original position. Thus the level of income fails to rise, and the lone effect of the open market operation is to replace a portion of the foreign exchange assets of the monetary authority with domestic securities. This confirms our earlier finding that monetary policy under fixed exchange rates represents an effective means of controlling the level of foreign exchange reserves, but a wholly ineffective way of affecting the domestic money supply or the level of economic activity.

These conclusions are radically altered when the exchange rate is permitted to fluctuate freely. A monetary policy that shifts the *LM* curve to $LM_1$

**FIGURE 17–3**
The effect of alternative stabilization policies
under fixed and flexible exchange rates
under conditions of perfect capital mobility
(all values in real terms)

lowers the domestic rate of interest to $i_2$, and it therefore causes capital to flow abroad. This capital outflow increases the demand for foreign exchange, and the price of foreign exchange therefore rises. However, this has the effect of making imports more expensive and of providing exports with a competitive advantage. Consequently, net exports increase, the *IS* curve shifts to the right, and the level of income therefore expands. The increase in the money supply evidently not only shifts the *LM* curve to the right but causes the *IS* curve to be shifted to the right as well. In the new equilibrium, income will have risen by a proportion equal to the ratio of the increase in the money supply to the initial level of transactions balances. However, because the income increase is bought solely as the result of an increase in net exports, it follows that it is accomplished at the expense of a corresponding reduction in income abroad. For this reason monetary expansion under flexible exchange rates is often classified as a "beggar-my-neighbor" policy by those who are concerned about the impact of domestic policies on other countries.[1]

Finally, consider the effect of an expansionary fiscal policy under flexible exchange rates. An increase in government purchases shifts the *IS* curve to $IS_1$, and this tends to raise the level of income. However, this shift in the *IS* curve raises the domestic interest rate to $i_1$. This causes capital to flow into country A and raises the supply of betas. Consequently, the price of betas falls relative to the price of alphas. Imports now become less expensive to country A, and exports become more expensive to the potential buyers of country B. Country A's net exports therefore decline; this means that the *IS* curve is in the process of shifting back to the left. Since equilibrium cannot be restored until the interest rate differential is eliminated, we must conclude that the *IS* curve will shift all the way back to $IS_0$. Consequently, the expansionary effect of the increase in government purchases is exactly offset by the depressing effect of the fall in net exports. Note, however, that country B's net exports increase, and that its income level will therefore rise. Evidently, then, the entire effect of the fiscal policy is transmitted abroad.

Some important footnotes to this analysis are now in order. The idea that monetary policy acquires magic potency under flexible exchange rates is based on a dangerous illusion. This illusion stems from the unfortunate tendency to ignore the effects of domestic policy actions upon foreign economies. As we have seen, A's income expanded in response to monetary expansion because its net exports increased. Since this meant that B's net exports declined by an equal amount, A's income gain was bought at the expense of country B which must have suffered income shrinkage. Thus A

---

[1] Beggar-my-neighbor policies are those policies that attempt to raise domestic employment by stealing aggregate demand from abroad rather than by generating it at home. Tariffs, quotas, export subsidies, as well as exchange depreciation and a host of similar devices, all have beggar-my-neighbor effects. Unhappily there is a strong temptation to resort to such measures because they simultaneously raise the level of income and improve the balance of payments. Domestically generated demand expansion, on the other hand, carries with it the risk that the nation's balance of payments problem will worsen.

merely exported its unemployment to B. Country B could have neutralized the effect of A's monetary policy by matching it with monetary expansion of its own. Had this happened, and B would very likely have pursued such a course, the effect of the combined policies on their joint income levels would have been no more and no less than expansionary monetary policy in a closed economy. World income might rise if combined monetary expansion lowered $i_w$, but it would rise for no other reason. Thus the idea that flexible exchange rates provide monetary policy with a degree of "punch" that it would not otherwise have is plainly erroneous.

Similar considerations apply to fiscal policy. Under flexible exchange rates the entire effect of expansionary fiscal policy is transmitted abroad. A's trade balance deteriorates to the point where its fiscal expansion is completely neutralized, and country B receives the entire expansionary impact. In view of this, it hardly seems correct to say that fiscal policy is ineffective under flexible exchange rates. It should, rather, be said that it may be effective in the wrong place. If country B is already at full employment, A's expansionary policies will certainly be unwelcome in country B. Thus, if we adopt as the criterion for judging between fixed and flexible exchange rates the rule that it is better to localize the bulk of the impact of monetary and fiscal policies upon the domestic economy, then the verdict would appear to favor fixed exchange rates. As we shall see, however, this conclusion is valid only when there is considerable mobility of capital.

The preceding analysis is somewhat distorted since it has considered fiscal and monetary policy in isolation. In practice both policies are often pursued simultaneously. Bearing this in mind, suppose again that country A wishes to expand its economy. Fiscal expansion raises domestic interest rates and attracts a capital inflow. Monetary expansion does the opposite. Consequently, it should be possible to combine fiscal expansion with monetary expansion in such a way as to prevent the domestic interest rate from differing from the foreign rate of interest. This would prevent capital flows that respond to interest rate differentials and would therefore avert the pressures on the exchange rate. The resulting income change will then be the same regardless of whether the exchange rate is free to fluctuate or is fixed.[1]

The argument can be illustrated with reference to Figure 17–3. Assume that the initial level of income is $Y_0$ and that the target income level is $Y_1$. In the small-country case perfect international capital mobility makes it impossible to change the equilibrium rate of interest by country A's own policies. Consequently, rational policy would suggest simultaneous fiscal and monetary expansion in a way that moves the IS and the LM curves both to the right and that keeps them intersecting at $i_w$. In this manner any tendency for equilibrium in the foreign exchange market to be disrupted can be avoided, and there would therefore be no tendency for fiscal expansion to be offset by a fall in net exports (under flexible rates), or for the monetary expansion to be offset

---

[1] This proposition is demonstrated in T. F. Dernburg, "Exchange Rates and Co-ordinated Stabilization Policy," *Canadian Journal of Economics*, 3:1–13, 1970.

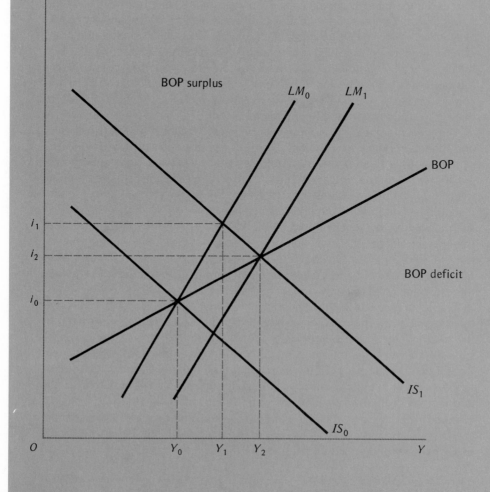

by the need to sell foreign exchange (under fixed rates). The income change, $Y_1 - Y_0$, is then attained with the identical combination of fiscal and monetary expansion under flexible rates as would have been the case under fixed rates.

The discussion thus far has been greatly simplified by the assumptions of a small country exposed to perfect international capital mobility. These assumptions permitted us to hold the equilibrium rate of interest fixed, and this led to the conclusion that under fixed exchange rates monetary policy is powerless to change the level of income but does provide an efficient means of controlling a country's foreign exchange reserves. Before concluding our discussion, we should ask how removal of the perfect capital mobility assumption alters the conclusions. Accordingly, let us first assume that capital mobility is "imperfect," which is to say that, although a change in domestic-foreign interest rate differentials will give rise to some movement of capital, this movement need not continue until interest rates are again equal. For the moment we restrict ourselves to fixed exchange rates.

Imperfect capital mobility implies positively sloped BOP functions such as those of Chapter 11, and as shown in Figures 17-4 and 17-5. For each differential between the domestic and foreign rate of interest there is some finite flow of capital per unit of time. A rise in the differential increases the net inflow, but this can be offset by a rise in income which raises the demand for imports.

In Figure 17-4 the BOP function is fairly flat, with the LM curve having a steeper slope, and we may define this as a case in which capital is "relatively mobile." This contrasts with Figure 17-5 in which the BOP curve is steeper than the LM curve. In this case we will say that capital is "relatively immobile." Now imagine an initial equilibrium at $Y_0$ and $i_0$ with all three functions, $IS_0$, $LM_0$, and BOP, intersecting at that point, and consider an expansionary fiscal policy which shifts IS to $IS_1$. At the point of intersection of $IS_1$ with $LM_0$ there will be a surplus in the balance of payments in the relatively high capital mobility case of Figure 17-4, whereas in the relatively immobile case shown in Figure 17-5 there will be a deficit. The dominant factor in the relatively mobile case is the inflow of capital which swamps the fall in net exports caused by income expansion. In the relatively immobile case, it is the fall in net exports which dominates over the sluggish capital inflow. The consequence of these balance of payments developments is that the surplus (deficit) causes an increase (decrease) in the money supply as the monetary authority is obliged to purchase (sell) foreign exchange. The change in the money supply must continue until equilibrium in the balance of payments is restored. This means that the LM curve must shift to $LM_1$ where it intersects $IS_1$

FIGURE 17-4
Effect of fiscal policy with relatively mobile capital under fixed exchange rates (all values in real terms)

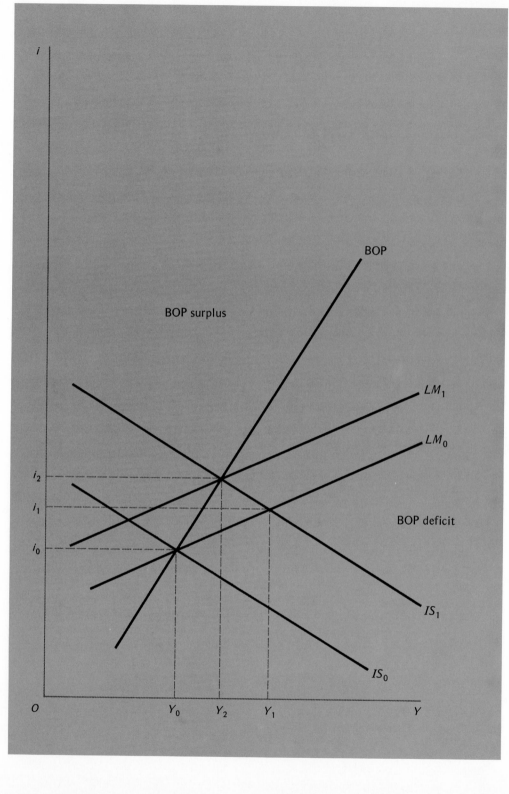

and BOP, and the final solution is therefore at income level $Y_2$ and interest rate $i_2$.

In a closed economy, income would rise to $Y_1$ where $IS_1$ intersects $LM_0$. The income change would therefore be $Y_1 - Y_0$. When capital is relatively mobile, as in Figure 17–4, the income change exceeds this amount because the balance of payments development causes the effect of the fiscal expansion to be augmented by monetary expansion. On the other hand, when capital is immobile, as in Figure 17–5, the income change is less than $Y_1 - Y_0$ because in this case the balance of payments development causes the effect of the fiscal expansion to be reduced by monetary contraction. It is clear, therefore, that a reduction in the degree of capital mobility (as reflected in a counterclockwise rotation of the BOP function) tends to reduce the effectiveness of fiscal policy in raising the level of income under fixed exchange rates.

It is evident that the dividing line occurs when the $LM$ and the BOP curves have equal slopes. We will define this as "neutral mobile" capital and note that in this event the income change is the same as in the closed economy. This dividing line serves also as the dividing line under flexible exchange rates. It is important, however, to note that the BOP curve under flexible exchange rates must be interpreted as specifying the combination of interest rates and income levels that prevents the exchange rate from changing. It is important also to note that although the dividing line is the same, the direction of fiscal policy effectiveness is opposite to that under fixed exchange rates. When capital is relatively mobile, fiscal expansion attracts capital and tends to lower the price of foreign exchange. This reduces exports, raises imports, and thereby retards the income expansion. When capital is relatively immobile, the dominant factor is the tendency for the rise in income initially to worsen the trade balance. This raises the price of foreign exchange, thereby preventing further deterioration, and causes the expansion of income to be augmented beyond the increase that would have occurred in a closed economy.

Under fixed exchange rates a single expansionary monetary policy action cannot raise the equilibrium level of income despite relaxation of the perfect capital mobility assumption. The only way in which monetary policy can raise the level of income permanently is to keep increasing the money supply indefinitely. The result, however, will be a continuous loss of foreign exchange. To verify this, note that expansionary monetary policy must always lead to a deficit in the balance of payments, regardless of the value of the slope of the BOP curve. Since the monetary authority must sell foreign exchange (and therefore purchase its own money) as long as the deficit per-

**FIGURE 17–5**
Effect of fiscal policy with relatively immobile capital under fixed exchange rates (all values in real terms)

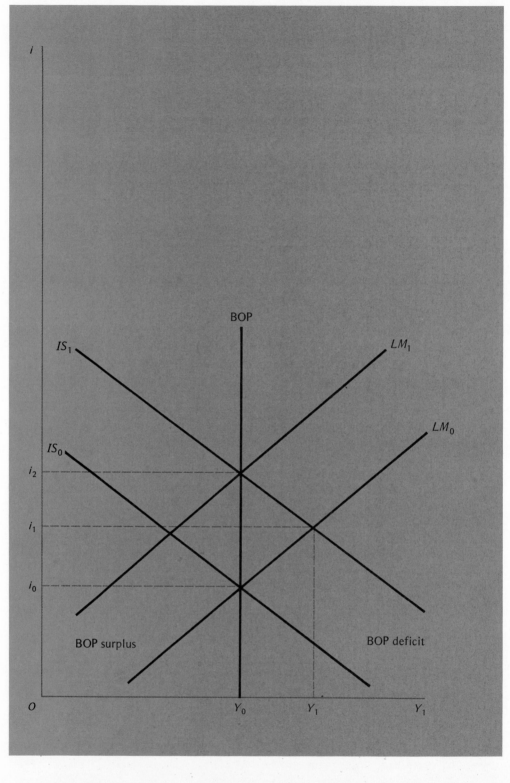

sists, any initial expansion of the money supply brought about by an action such as a central bank purchase of government securities will be offset by subsequent monetary contraction. The reader can easily verify the inevitability of this result by examining Figures 17–4 and 17–5. Starting again with equilibrium at $Y_0$ and $i_0$, a shift to the right of the $LM$ curve must create a deficit in the balance of payments, so that the $LM$ curve will automatically tend to shift back to the left. By the same token, a restrictive monetary policy which shifts the $LM$ curve to the left must produce a surplus in the balance of payments and lead to an accumulation of foreign exchange. Clearly, then, the earlier result that fiscal policy is more potent in changing the level of income, while monetary policy can more effectively be used to control the balance of payments, remains correct as long as fixed exchange rates are maintained.

It is evident that the different effects of the fiscal and monetary policies are attributable to the capital movements that flow in response to changes in the rate of interest. Therefore, to complete the discussion, let us assume that capital mobility is entirely absent, so that the term $K(i)$ vanishes from the balance of payments equation. Equilibrium in the balance of payments now requires

$$\text{BOP} = X(\pi) - Z(Y,\pi) = 0$$

When there is no capital mobility, balance of payments equilibrium cannot exist unless exports equal imports. Under fixed exchange rates exports become fixed and exogenous, and there can therefore be only one level of imports consistent with equilibrium. It follows that there is only one level of income that is consistent with equilibrium. The balance of payments equation, in other words, reduces to

$$X - Z(Y) = 0$$

The result is that neither fiscal nor monetary policy will be able to affect the equilibrium level of income under fixed exchange rates. Consider Figure 17–6 which illustrates the problem. In the absence of capital mobility, the BOP function is vertical because, with exports exogenously determined, there is only one level of income at which imports will equal exports. Assume that that level of income is $Y_0$ and that all the functions $IS_0$, $LM_0$, and BOP intersect at that income level. Next assume that expansionary fiscal policy shifts the $IS$ curve to $IS_1$. The immediate effect is to raise the level of income to $Y_1$ and the rate of interest to $i_1$. In the absence of capital mobility, the higher rate of interest has no balance of payments effect. However, the higher level of income raises imports, which means that the economy will have a deficit in its balance of payments. The central bank must therefore sell foreign exchange to support the exchange rate, and in so doing it reduces the domestic money

**FIGURE 17–6**
Ineffectiveness of stabilization policy under fixed exchange rates in the absence of capital mobility (all values in real terms)

supply. Equilibrium, then, is restored when the automatic shift in the *LM* curve moves the curve to $LM_1$ where it intersects $IS_1$ and BOP at income level $Y_0$ and interest rate $i_2$.

Expansionary monetary policy will be similarly thwarted. Any expansion of the money supply that raises income and imports produces a deficit and a subsequent reduction in the money supply. In the new equilibrium, income, the rate of interest, and the money supply will have returned to their original levels, and the expansionary policy will have had only a loss in foreign exchange and a temporary rise in income to show for it.

The absence of capital mobility clearly creates a very bad situation for stabilization policy under fixed exchange rates and makes the case for flexible exchange rates virtually decisive. When flexible exchange rates are adopted, the balance of payments equation automatically becomes

$$X(\pi) = Z(Y,\pi)$$

and since the exchange rate is now free to adjust until the balance of payments is in equilibrium, the level of income is once again free to vary. The economies, under these conditions, achieve virtual macroeconomic isolation. The balance of payments tends always to equilibrium, and the money supplies of the two economies are no longer linked. Since, moreover, the absence of capital mobility means that balance of payments equilibrium results in a zero level of net exports, domestic income must always equal domestic absorption. A change in absorption will therefore bring with it a corresponding increase in income.

To make sure we understand this, let government purchases rise. This raises the level of income and the level of imports. However, this causes the exchange rate to rise, dampens the rise in imports, and stimulates exports. Since the trade balance maintains its equilibrium, none of the domestic expansionary impact spills over into foreign economies, and the multiplier effects are then as they would be in a closed economy. Similarly, an increase in the money supply lowers the rate of interest and raises the level of income. The tendency for this to produce a deficit is again negated by a rise in the exchange rate, reducing imports, increasing exports, and thus again preventing the impact from spilling over into other countries.

In conclusion, two facts seem particularly pertinent in attempting to assess the macroeconomic case for flexible exchange rates. First, flexible exchange rates will probably result in more pronounced fluctuations in the value of a country's exports and imports. Second, flexible exchange rates are necessary if a degree of national macroeconomic autonomy is to be maintained when capital is immobile. The instability of exports and imports and the absence of capital mobility are both apt to be particularly troublesome for small countries. The smaller the country, the larger is the relative size of the foreign sector and the greater the impact of export-import fluctuations on the national income. Similarly, the absence of capital mobility means that barriers exist between potential lenders (surplus savers) and potential borrowers (investors), so that the smaller the country, the less scope there is likely to be for efficient allocation of investable funds.

These considerations suggest that small countries might be well advised to attempt to reduce barriers to capital mobility, and that if they do this they will be able to maintain fixed exchange rates vis-à-vis their major trading partners and thereby avoid export-import instability. For a large country such as the United States, flexible exchange rates would appear to be an attractive alternative to the fixed rate system where the tail often wags the dog. International capital mobility is not particularly vital for the efficient operation of the domestic capital market, and the export-import sector is small relative to the domestic sector of most economies.

Size and other considerations have caused economists to look for "optimum currency areas" in the hope of thereby acquiring the benefits, while minimizing the drawbacks, of both the fixed and flexible exchange rate systems. The idea is for small countries to band together into currency unions within which there would be either fixed exchange rates or a single monetary unit, and within which capital mobility would be encouraged. Between the areas, on the other hand, exchange rates would be free to fluctuate.

## 17-4
### EXPERIENCE WITH FLUCTUATING EXCHANGE RATES

Unfortunately, it cannot be said that the adoption of floating rates by the United States and other major industrial countries has been an unequivocal success, at least as this is measured by the fact that the period of floating rates has witnessed first a worldwide inflationary boom, and subsequently a very nasty recession. After the United States closed the gold window in the summer of 1971, the central banks of such countries as West Germany continued to purchase dollars at an overvalued price because they were concerned to maintain the international competitive position of their exporters. However, the United States deficit was so massive that continuing purchases of dollars caused the domestic money supplies of many European countries to rise substantially. It is this, in part, that touched off the inflationary worldwide boom of 1972-1973.

Realizing the domestic monetary consequences of continued support of the dollar, country after country changed its policy, and a system of floating currencies between the major industrial countries came into being. As this happened, the dollar, which had been greatly overvalued, declined in value vis-à-vis other currencies. This caused the competitive position of the United States to improve dramatically, as is shown by the increase in 1973 in merchandise exports of $22 billion, or 44 percent. In 1974, exports again increased by a huge amount, the rise of $27 billion practically paying for the increase in imports of $33 billion caused largely by increased oil costs. By 1974, of course, the economy was sagging badly, and the export increase of 38 percent was one of the few sources of strength.

There is general agreement that the downward float of the dollar has gone too far and that the dollar was undervalued throughout 1974. It was, however, the low international value of the dollar that provided United States exporters with a competitive advantage, that has made imports progressively less attractive relative to domestically produced goods, and that has kept vacationers going to Disneyland rather than to Paris. In part the dollar was weak because the stock market was weak, which caused long-term capital to drift abroad. It was also weak because short-term interest rates fell near the end of 1974 and it therefore paid to place petro dollars and other short-term funds in money markets such as London where interest rates were higher than in the United States.

As the economy attempts to climb out of the great recession of 1974–1975 it might very well expect to find recovery impeded by international developments under the floating exchange rate system. Stimulative fiscal policy undertaken in the spring of 1975 might cause the stock market to revive and this could cause long-term capital to be repatriated. If economic expansion in the United States causes short-term interest rates to rise relative to rates elsewhere, an inflow of short-term capital might result. Such an inflow might be massive since quixotic Arab oil producers were holding large balances on short-term deposits in European banks. These balances might be moved to the United States if interest rates rise.

All these fears suggested in the spring of 1975 that there could easily be a large increase in the demand for the dollar on international money markets, and that the dollar would therefore easily rise in value relative to other currencies. If this happened it would create difficulties for United States export industries, while Americans would begin traveling abroad again and would increase their purchases of foreign rather than domestic goods. These developments could, therefore, abort the recovery that stimulative fiscal policy was attempting to bring about.

As discussed earlier in this chapter, monetary policy appeared to hold the key in the floating rate system with high capital mobility. If interest rates could be held down as the economy expanded, capital inflows could be prevented and the economy would then enjoy the full impact of the fiscal policies.

Only time will tell how it will work out. We discuss these issues here not because we are brash enough to venture a forecast that is more than likely to come back to haunt us, but because we want the reader to share our uncertainties as they appeared to us at a particular critical time.

Let us complete the discussion of flexible exchange rates and the issue of policy mix by considering the question of the adequacy of the number of policy tools. The most compelling reason for adopting flexible exchange rates may well be that there are simply too few macroeconomic instruments available to secure all the targets of policy. The wage-adjustment model suggested that labor market equilibrium and product market equilibrium are distinct targets in need of two instruments to attain them. The implication of the analysis was that tax policy should direct itself toward full employment, while monetary policy should direct itself toward the price level. The price level target could, perhaps, be made the responsibility of the government purchase instrument inasmuch as neither government purchases nor money supply changes are likely to provoke wage adjustment, and neither policy will therefore enjoy any employment–price level comparative advantage.

However, monetary policy does enjoy a very distinct comparative advantage over government purchase policy in combating a balance of payments problem under fixed exchange rates since both its current and its capital account effects work in the same direction. Thus correct assignment of instruments to targets would imply the use of tax policy to stabilize employment; the use of monetary policy to secure equilibrium in the balance of payments; and the manipulation of government purchases to control the price level.

Except for the final clause of the preceding sentence, the statement sounds plausible. Common sense, however, suggests that government purchases cannot be continuously varied in the interest of maintaining stability of the price level. It has, in fact, long been recognized that speedy variations in G are very difficult to effect since the bulk of government purchases are tied to ongoing projects that cannot, and probably ought not, be varied in response to fluctuations in business activity. It is fair to say that most countries have abandoned the idea of using government purchases as a short-run macroeconomic stabilization tool and that if this instrument were to be paired with any target, that target would be the securing of a socially desirable share of national output for use by the public sector.

This, then, leaves the price level unattended to, not to mention that some macroeconomic tool ought perhaps to concern itself with society's growth target. There are, apparently, too many goals combined with too few tools. The emergence of incomes policy is, perhaps, a reflection of the attempt to provide a supplementary tool that attempts to deal with the price level; and the gradual acceptance by one country after another of exchange rate flexibility reflects an attempt to reduce the number of targets with which policy has to deal.

# 18

# FISCAL POLICY IN PRACTICE

## THE EVOLUTION OF FISCAL THINKING

In our final two chapters we move away from the theoretical aspects of macroeconomics and toward the practical problems of monetary and fiscal policy making. To a considerable extent we will be concerned with how economists have tried to simplify and sell their message to politicians and to the people. Much of the time the educational effort appears to be getting nowhere. During the 1950s economists tried very hard to educate the Eisenhower Administration. Yet after a decade of effort and of economic stagnation, the Administration could still favor a policy of attempting to balance the budget. Sometimes the educational effort is rewarded with success, as it was during the early 1960s when intelligent monetary and fiscal policies restored vigor and full employment to the economy. Sometimes, unhappily, economic advice is too avidly accepted, as is borne out by the sad record of the 1970s when deliberate applications of restrictive anti-inflation policies brought about first the recession of 1970–1971 and then, in 1974–1975, the worst economic debacle since the great depression of the 1930s.

In this section we will trace briefly some of the highlights of practical fiscal thinking, or fiscal "gimmickry," as one might call it. No matter how sophisticated economics becomes, there will always be people who look at the budget as a means of estimating the impact of fiscal policy on the economy. Consequently, economists might as well take the view that, as long as people are going to insist on simple budget concepts, they may as well help them to interpret the concepts correctly and attempt to provide them with gimmicks that at least make sense.

Modern fiscal thinking began with the erosion of the orthodox view that the federal budget should be balanced each year. It continued with the important idea of replacing annual budgetary balance with cyclical balance in an effort to take advantage of the automatic stabilizers, while at the same time preserving the principle of budgetary balance. It went on from there to the recognition that automatic stabilizers are essentially passive shock absorbers that may, however, inhibit a return to full employment and that may impede growth. It followed from there that a more aggressive "fully compensatory" fiscal policy is required in a growing economy.

The traditional principle of annual budgetary balance, if put into practice, would destabilize the economy. When income shrinks during recession, tax receipts fall and transfer expenditures on such things as unemployment compensation rise. This produces an automatic deficit in the budget, helps to cushion the fall in disposable income, and prevents national income from falling by as much as would otherwise be the case. However, if policy is directed toward budgetary balance, discretionary policies have to be introduced that raise taxes and/or reduce government expenditures. These policies tend to magnify the fall in national income, and they are, therefore, destabilizing. During inflation, similarly, the rise in nominal national income tends to produce a budget surplus. Then, if the principle of budget balance is followed, either expenditures will be raised and/or taxes will be lowered. Aggregate demand will increase and the rate of inflation will rise.

Given the obvious folly of the principle of annual budgetary balance, it is perhaps useful to begin by asking why the principle has given way so grudgingly. The traditional academic rationale for balanced budgets is the crowding-out argument that deficit spending puts governments in competition with private investors for funds, so that little can be accomplished by fiscal policy. As our previous discussion showed, the crowding-out argument is valid when the *LM* curve is completely inelastic with respect to the rate of interest, and it would also be valid if the economy were at full employment.[1] Under conditions of recession, marked by excess capacity and unemployed labor, the crowding-out objections are not valid, and few economists take the argument very seriously. This is not to say that some crowding out might not take place. It certainly would do so if expansionary fiscal policies were not accommodated by cooperative monetary policies.

Popular mythology regarding the evils of deficit spending is astonishingly rich and colorful. Since deficits occur automatically as income shrinks and tax yields drop, some people naively blame the recession on the deficit, rather than the other way around. Others associate deficits with inflation.

[1] The reader who has forgotten why this is the case or is still fuzzy about it should go back to Chap. 9 and study the classical case once more. A modern expression of this view can be found in Federal Reserve Bank of St. Louis, "A Historical Analysis of the 'Crowding Out' of Private Expenditures by Fiscal Policy Actions," *Research Department Working Paper*, St. Louis, Mo., January 1971.

Indeed, past wartime periods, when deficits were particularly pronounced, were certainly periods of rapid inflation. Conservatives have always feared the expansion of the government sector. Consequently, they have been at pains to insist that government spending should be limited to what is available through current revenue.

Much of the opposition by business executives to deficit spending stems, according to Herbert Stein, not from any inherent fear of deficits but rather from a fear of higher taxation.[1] This argument, perhaps, is the most fundamental of all. If government spending is raised to combat a recession, the expenditures will be beneficial in the short run. However, this may involve the creation of new government programs and the entrenchment of a new bureaucracy. If then the economy recovers from the recession and the need for increased expenditure no longer exists, the new programs will nevertheless have supporters who will insist on their continuation, and the new bureaucracy cannot be expected to dismantle itself voluntarily. The outcome then may be that either taxes will have to be raised, or inflation will have to be tolerated, and, in any case, the size of the government sector will have expanded permanently.[2]

Finally, there are those who fear the consequences of a growing national debt. These persons mistakenly confuse private with public debt, and they conjure up images of enormous tax burdens being levied on themselves to pay off the debt at some date in the future. Suffice it, for the moment, to indicate that there is little intellectual substance to this view. Nevertheless there is much to be said about the national debt, and we will earmark the national debt for later consideration.

Among practical people, especially politicians, annual budgetary balance has always been a doctrine more to be preached for the consumption of gullible constituents than to be practiced in reality. Even President Hoover, whom we nowadays think of as a model of fiscal respectability and conservatism, appears, in the light of a careful study, to have had fewer hang-ups on the subject than is commonly supposed.[3] Hoover evidently believed that public works projects would stimulate employment. His problem, however, was finding a means of financing these expenditures. He favored taxation over borrowing on the then very respectable academic grounds that borrowing would compete with private investment for funds and therefore be deflationary. Thus Hoover was victimized by the fact that traditional economic theory regarded borrowing, dollar for dollar, as deflationary as taxation.

---

[1] H. Stein, *The Fiscal Revolution in America,* The University of Chicago Press, Chicago, 1969.

[2] Fears of the sort described above do not apply to tax reduction. Thus it is not surprising that tax reduction is a far more popular way of stimulating the economy than expenditure expansion. It should be borne in mind that prior to World War II federal taxes were extremely low, so that there was little leverage on the tax side. One cannot cut what does not exist. Consequently, most discussions of fiscal policy during the 1930s emphasized public works and other expenditure programs.

[3] Stein, op. cit., Chap. 2.

Sophistication in matters of stabilization policy can hardly be said to have been acute during the New Deal days of the 1930s. Few New Dealers gave evidence that they had read Keynes or that they were influenced by his ideas. President Roosevelt was no exception. When told about the multiplier, he said he simply did not believe in it. New Deal economists, moreover, had a fatal habit of confusing recovery with reform. The President was able to advocate expanded public works programs as a means to recovery, while promising to balance the budget and making the tax system more equitable by taxing the rich. Public works would stimulate employment; and since the rich paid their taxes out of saving anyway, no deflationary impact would result. The formula clearly had its political advantages, but it made no sense to the macroeconomist, and it is hardly surprising that the economy continued to languish in depression throughout the 1930s.

The present federal fiscal structure of the United States is largely the outgrowth of World War II. Taxation through payroll withholding was introduced at that time, as were the high marginal tax rates on personal income and the high rate of tax on corporate income. The effect of this fiscal structure has long been recognized as having beneficial aspects because these high income tax rates and other "automatic" or "built-in" stabilizers serve as a cushion that prevents fluctuations in GNP from becoming transmitted into fluctuations in disposable income. Such stabilizers therefore flatten the consumption and investment functions and reduce the value of the multiplier. When GNP drops, personal income tax liabilities decline, social security taxes decline, and government transfer payments in the form of unemployment compensation increase. As a result, disposable income falls by less than would otherwise have been the case. Consumption spending can thereby be sustained, and the second- and third-round cumulative effects of a fall in GNP can be minimized. Although the corporate income tax is a flat rate, the yield from the tax varies greatly because the elasticity of corporate profits with respect to GNP is very high. Consequently, when GNP and corporate profits decline, corporate income tax accruals fall, so that profits after tax fall by less than would otherwise have been the case. This, then, enables corporations to maintain dividend payments and capital outlays.

These stabilizers are clearly beneficial to the economy. They operate automatically and immediately to moderate fluctuations in GNP, and they work to prevent both recession and inflationary situations from getting out of hand. However, they can also respond perversely and cause considerable damage, as happened in the case of the personal income tax during 1974 and as is detailed in a later section of this chapter.

To take advantage of the built-in stabilizers, one has to abandon a policy of annual budgetary balance. However, the principle of a balanced budget as a device for keeping federal expenditures in check is not one that conservatives can be persuaded to abandon cheerfully. Thus it came as a major and important breakthrough when, in 1947, the Committee for Economic Development (CED), a business organization, came forth with a proposal designed both to preserve the principle of budgetary balance and to retain the beneficial effects of the automatic stabilizers.[1]

To accomplish both aims, the CED pointed out that there was a fundamental difference between budgetary deficits which resulted passively from the falling revenues associated with recession and those deficits and surpluses that might exist at full employment. Passive deficits should never be offset by fiscal policies since such policies would exacerbate recessions and inflation. Thus the principle was suggested that the actual deficit or surplus was of no fundamental relevance and that it was only the "implicit" deficit or surplus that was of importance in measuring the federal government's fiscal impact upon the economy. The implicit surplus is that surplus or deficit that we would realize if we calculated revenues and expenditures by using the full-employment level of income rather than the actual level of income.

In the CED's program there was no role for so-called discretionary fiscal policies, policies designed on an ad hoc basis to deal with recession or inflation. Instead, taxes and expenditures were to be so arranged as to yield a balanced budget at full employment. The automatic stabilizers would then be permitted to operate to yield a surplus during inflation and a deficit in recession. Overall "cyclical" balance would, it was hoped, be achieved in this manner, and the implicit surplus would then remain at zero.[2]

It was on this last point, that a zero implicit surplus could be attained by a once-for-all adjustment of tax rates, that the CED's proposal exhibited its critical flaw. During the 1950s fiscal policy did operate passively, and it was clear that the stabilizers had beneficial effects in moderating the three recessions of that decade.[3] However, as we saw in Chapter 1, where actual GNP was compared with potential GNP, the economy performed poorly. Overall real growth of output plodded along at an anemic rate. The recovery from each recession left the economy farther from full employment than in the preceding recovery, and unemployment exhibited an upward trend during the decade.

The automatic stabilizers serve to cushion shocks. However, they do not help to lift the economy back to full employment. Indeed they may impede recovery. The fiscal system of the federal government has a short-run elasticity of revenues with respect to GNP that is greater than one because of the progressive nature of the personal income tax and because of the extremely high elasticity of corporate profits with respect to GNP. This tendency to gen-

[1] *Taxes and the Budget,* Committee for Economic Development, Research and Policy Committee, 1947.

[2] The idea of cyclical budgetary balance was not the invention of the CED. The principle was developed in Sweden during the 1930s and is therefore sometimes called the "Swedish budget." In this connection see G. Myrdal, "Fiscal Policy in the Business Cycle," *American Economic Review* (Supplement), 29:183–193, 1939.

[3] On this point see the splendid study by W. Lewis, Jr., *Federal Fiscal Policy in the Postwar Recessions,* The Brookings Institution, Washington, 1962.

erate large marginal leakages from the income stream reduces the value of the multiplier, and it therefore impedes recovery.

The fiscal system may also retard desirable economic growth. If the long-run elasticity of tax yield with respect to GNP exceeds unity, federal revenues will increase over time more rapidly than GNP, so that, even if expenditures increased as rapidly as GNP, an increasing deflationary burden would be placed on the economy in the form of ever-rising implicit surpluses. Thus the budget imposes a restraint on desirable economic expansion, and this is the phenomenon that has come to be called "fiscal drag." What was missing in the CED's budget was recognition of the fact that economic growth automatically generates an increase in the implicit surplus and that something must therefore be done more or less continuously to offset fiscal drag. This could involve increased government expenditures, a tax reduction, or a combination of both. In this way full employment could be maintained, and the drag of the budget could then be converted into a "fiscal dividend" which could take the form of new or enlarged government programs or of reduced tax burdens.

The implicit surplus, which subsequently came to be known as the "full-employment surplus," is an important concept of fiscal policy. It was employed by the Council of Economic Advisers (CEA) to justify an expansionary fiscal policy in the early 1960s; it was resurrected by the Nixon Administration to call attention to the fact that its actual budgetary deficits were the consequence of recession rather than of extravagant expenditure programs; and it was again used for this purpose during the recession of 1974–1975, this time by Congressional Budget Committees whose members were understandably terrified by a deficit that might exceed $70 billion in fiscal year 1976. In view of the importance that the concept has had and continues to have, it is important to take a careful look at it.

Figure 18–1 is an amended leakage-injection diagram of the kind that we have utilized in several places in this book. The idea here is to take the equilibrium condition for a closed economy

$$I + G = S + T$$

and to turn it around to read

$$I - S = T - G$$

where $T - G$ is the government surplus. In equilibrium this must equal the excess of planned investment over saving. Thus a deficit in the private sector must be offset by an equal surplus in the government sector and vice versa. Let the existing tax and other fiscal legislation be such that the budget surplus is the curve $(T - G)_1$. It has a positive slope since a rise in income raises taxes

**FIGURE 18–1**
Illustration of full-employment surplus (all
values in real terms)

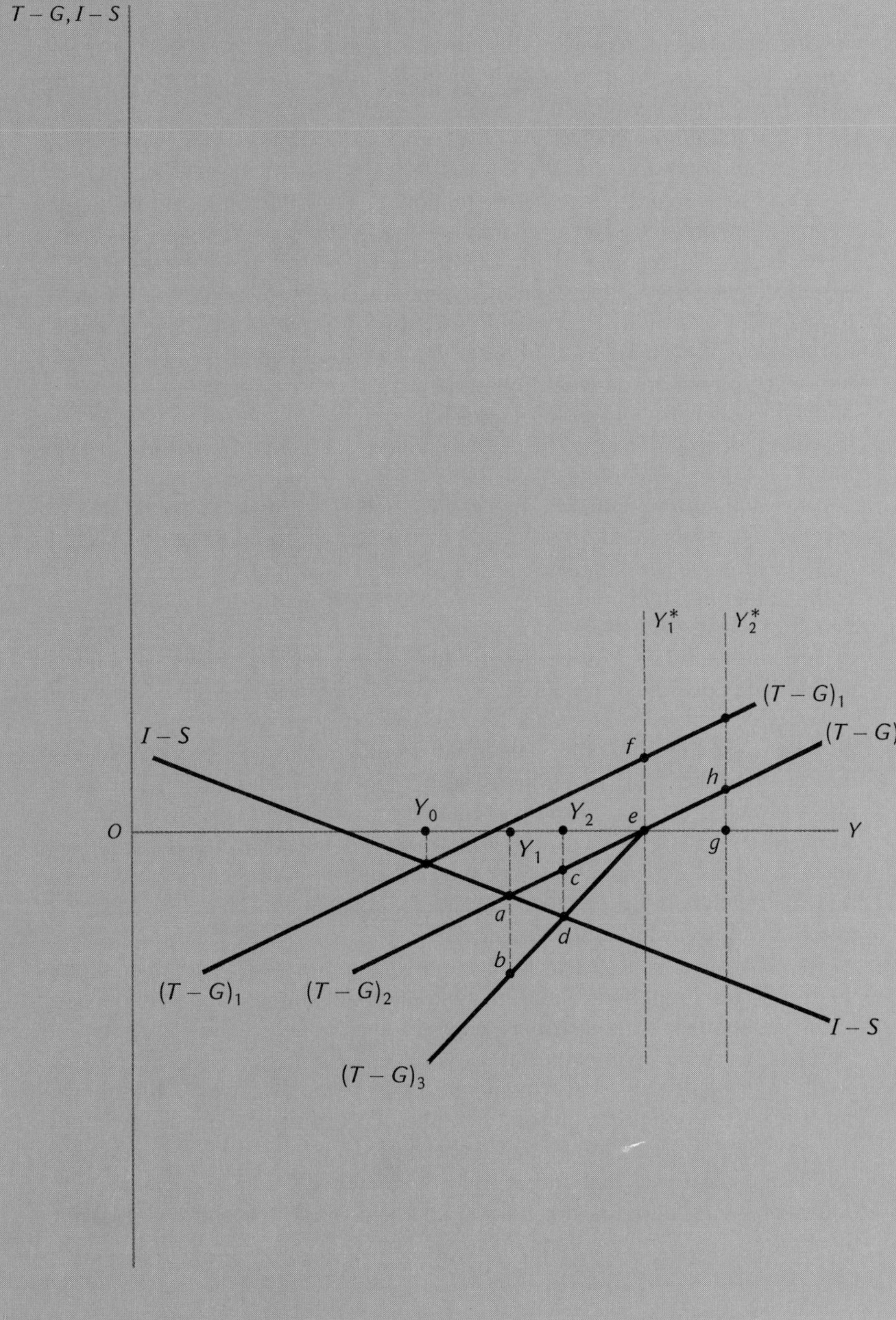

T − G, I − S
O
Y
I − S
I − S
Y_0
Y_1
Y_2
Y_1^*
Y_2^*
(T − G)_1
(T − G)_1
(T − G)_2
(T − G)_2
(T − G)_3
a
b
c
d
e
f
g
h

and reduces certain transfer expenditures and tends therefore to move the budget in the direction of surplus. Similarly, the $I - S$ curve plots the investment-saving discrepancy. This curve has a negative slope because it is assumed that a rise in income will generate an excess of incremental saving over incremental investment.

Let the full-employment level of income be $Y_f^*$. This income level is, however, not attained since the $I - S$ and $(T - G)_1$ curves intersect at income level $Y_0$. This is the typical recession situation in which intended investment is depressed relative to saving, and where the government budget is in deficit. Note, however, that the fiscal structure is such that a surplus equal to *ef* would be generated if the economy were at full employment. The budget is, in fact, highly restrictive because intended investment would have to exceed full-employment saving by *ef* in order to attain and maintain full employment.

The combination of weak investment relative to full-employment saving and a full-employment surplus causes the equilibrium level of income to be at less than full employment. This, in turn, causes the actual budget to be in deficit. The budget, therefore, is in deficit because income is depressed, not because active discretionary policies have been instituted to raise the level of income. The magnitude of the actual deficit should not therefore be taken as an indication that fiscal policy is expansionary. It is much more useful to look at the full-employment deficit or surplus since that eliminates the effect on the deficit of the state of the economy.

Suppose next that taxes are lowered or government purchases are raised in a way that causes the budget surplus function to shift to $(T - G)_2$. This expansionary fiscal policy eliminates the full-employment surplus but is not sufficient to raise the level of income to full employment since the intersection of the $(T - G)_2$ and $I - S$ functions is at income $Y_1$. The reason for this inadequacy is that in this example intended investment is less than full-employment saving so that a full-employment deficit is necessary in order to attain full employment. At another time, intended investment might be quite buoyant relative to full-employment saving, and it would then be appropriate to run a surplus at full employment.

The foregoing suggests that we must be careful not to assume that elimination of the full-employment surplus will automatically also imply elimination of the inflationary or deflationary gap as long as there is no guarantee that planned investment will equal saving at full employment. From the analytical point of view the full-employment surplus is a step backward. The relevant target for fiscal policy should be the elimination of the deflationary (or inflationary) gap. The deflationary gap is the difference between full-employment output and aggregate demand at full employment. This is equivalent to the excess of saving and taxes at full employment over investment and government purchases. We can therefore write

$$\text{Gap} = S^* + T^* - (I^* + G)$$

where the asterisks indicate magnitudes associated with the full-employment level of income. Rearranging this expression, we have

$$Gap = (T^* - G) + (S^* - I^*)$$

Clearly, when we set the full-employment surplus $T^* - G$ equal to zero, we will eliminate the gap only when the savings generated at full employment equal intended investment.[1]

Despite the inadequacy of the normative rule that fiscal policy should be such as to yield a full-employment surplus of zero, this rule has often been propounded by sophisticated economists.[2] One consideration in support of it is the idea that a discrepancy between intended investment and full-employment saving implies a sectoral imbalance that ought to be corrected by monetary policy rather than offset by a corresponding budgetary deficit or surplus. In other words, if investment falls short of full-employment saving, this should be corrected by a change in the mix of policy, with lower interest rates raising intended investment so that full employment can be maintained with a balanced budget.

This view is open to criticism. It is not clear why intended investment should be manipulated so as to equal the saving that the private sector happens to generate at full employment. To follow this rule would implicitly assign monetary policy to the maintenance of longer-run budgetary balance. This seems like a great waste, given all the important objectives to which monetary policy might more sensibly address itself.

A second notion is the idea which was often propounded by President Nixon, and used by him as a justification for vetoing spending bills and for impounding funds, that federal government expenditures should be limited to the revenues that the economy would generate at full employment. Thus Nixon used the full-employment budget as a device for limiting spending to levels that were regarded as "noninflationary."

Subject to the reservations stated above, it is appropriate to limit expenditures to full-employment revenues when private demand is strong. On the other hand, it is desirable to maintain expenditure flexibility so as to be able to run a full-employment deficit under conditions of extreme weakness of private demand. These two aims are in conflict. Much has been made of the fact that antirecession spending programs, although designed to be temporary, have often taken a long time to become geared up. As a result they have not yielded significant added expenditures at the time they were most needed. Then, after recovery is well under way, their effects become felt at a time when they result in excessive spending. They therefore contribute to

[1] As the foregoing suggests, fiscal policy rules of a simple kind have a tendency to become dogmas that inhibit clear thinking. The full-employment surplus is no exception. On this point see F. M. Bator, "Budgetary Reform: Notes on Principles and Strategy," *Review of Economics and Statistics,* 45:115–120, 1963.

[2] See, for example, Arthur M. Okun and Nancy H. Teeters, "The Full Employment Surplus Revisited," *Brookings Papers on Economic Activity* 1:77–110, 1970, for an interpretation of the normative aspects of the full-employment surplus concept.

inflation and tend to magnify rather than to reduce the amplitude of fluctuations in economic activity.[1]

Economists have suggested the introduction of expenditure programs that automatically phase themselves out as full employment is approached in order to avert the problem of having the budget become excessively expansionary when private demand revives. The first step in this approach is to divide the budget into expenditures for ongoing permanent programs—the so-called fiscal base—and expenditures for temporary antirecession programs. The permanent programs—national defense, social security, general government, support for education, general revenue sharing, etc.—would be planned without reference to the state of the economy. They would, moreover, be set equal to full-employment revenues, and if they tend to be higher than full-employment revenues this should signal the need for a tax increase.

The antirecession programs would be treated separately. These might include improvements in existing unemployment compensation and food stamp programs, or they might include new programs such as temporary public employment, or countercyclical emergency revenue sharing with state and local governments, or countercyclical public works projects. The important thing is that these programs should be speedily activated by some "triggering" mechanism and that they should quickly turn off when they are no longer needed. For example, when the unemployment rate goes above some predetermined level, funds would automatically be released for these programs, and the higher the level of unemployment the greater the amount of the expenditure would be. As recovery proceeds, the expenditures would gradually be reduced as unemployment declines, and they would be cut off entirely when full employment is reached.

The effect of such temporary antirecession programs is to raise total expenditure above full-employment receipts during periods of slack economic activity. However, since the expenditures decline as full employment is approached, and since the permanent expenditures are geared to full-employment receipts, the budget cannot become overly stimulative.

The effect of introducing a countercyclical expenditure program can be illustrated with reference to Figure 18–1. Let the initial budget be $(T - G)_2$ and let a temporary public employment program be introduced that raises the deficit by the amount $ab$ at income level $Y_1$. Since there would be no expenditures at all on this program if the economy were at the full-employment level of income $Y_1^*$, it follows that the effect of the new program is to rotate the budget surplus function about point $e$ to something resembling $(T - G)_3$.

Note that if the effect of the program is to create an addition to the deficit of $ab$ at income $Y_1$, this will cause a rise in national income to $Y_2$. The increase in the actual deficit will therefore be only $cd$, while no change at all takes place in the full-employment deficit (surplus). The change in the actual

---

[1] See Nancy H. Teeters, "Built-In Flexibility of Federal Expenditures," *Brookings Papers on Economic Activity*, 3:615–59, 1971, for an analysis of the tendency of the expenditure effects of countercyclical public works programs to be mistimed.

deficit is less than $ab$ because the rise in income raises tax yield while lowering transfer expenditures on unemployment compensation and food stamps. The full-employment deficit is not affected at all because of the automatic phase-out aspect of the program.

While looking at Figure 18–1, we should note also that the introduction of a countercyclical spending program is the practical equivalent of tax legislation that lowers tax collections at $Y_1$ in a way that adds $ab$ to the deficit but that simultaneously makes the tax more progressive so that full-employment revenues remain unchanged. This too would rotate $(T - G)_2$ so that the new budget surplus function becomes $(T - G)_3$.

Finally, note that automatic anticyclical programs can never be sufficient to restore full employment. As can be seen in Figure 18–1, there is no way that a rotation of the budget surplus function about point $e$ can cause the function to intersect a given $I - S$ function at the full-employment level of income. Those who are willing to put exclusive reliance on automatic programs are either not aiming for full employment, or they are hoping that the programs will help to stimulate investment demand and in this way cause the $I - S$ function to shift up.

Before proceeding with other matters, it is useful to remind ourselves about the concept of fiscal drag. Suppose for a moment that the $I - S$ function cuts $(T - G)_2$ at $Y_1^*$. In this case there would be full employment with a zero actual and full-employment surplus. Now imagine that time passes and that growth factors cause full-employment income to increase to $Y_2^*$. As can be seen in Figure 18–1, with budget function $(T - G)_2$ the budget now automatically becomes restrictive and generates a full-employment surplus of $gh$. Consequently, the diagram illustrates the concept of fiscal drag. It shows that the budget surplus function depicted in the diagram needs to be shifted to the right at a rate which approximates the growth of potential output. Such a shift to the right, of course, implies that expenditures should be raised, or that tax rates should be reduced, or that an appropriate combination of the two policies should be found.

The full-employment surplus concept has been extremely useful in practice. When President Kennedy entered the White House in 1961, he and his advisers were faced with the task of improving the performance of an economy whose actual output was more than $50 billion (in 1958 prices) below full employment and in which unemployment averaged 6.8 percent in the first quarter of 1961. One of the problems faced by the Administration was how to sell the idea that it was, in large measure, the drag of the federal budget that was causing the economy to perform so poorly. Matters were complicated by the fact that in 1961 there was a deficit in the actual budget. It was in this context that President Kennedy's Council of Economic Advisers resurrected the CED's implicit surplus idea, this time dubbing it the "full-employment surplus." The Council attempted to show that if the economy could somehow be moved to full employment, the additional revenues this would yield would cause the deficit to be converted into a substantial surplus.

Changes in the full-employment surplus are frequently used as a measure of the effect of discretionary fiscal policies. An increase in the full-employment surplus implies restrictive policy, whereas a decrease implies the opposite. An increase in the actual surplus does not provide grounds for making a similar inference since it could come about automatically because of a rise in income. Because the full-employment surplus measures budget changes relative to a fixed income level, it isolates the discretionary changes in the budget from the induced changes.

Figure 18–2 shows estimates by the Council of Economic Advisers of the full-employment budget surplus for the years 1956–1964, along with the actual budget results. The most striking thing to note is that in each of the nine years the achievement of full employment would have resulted in a substantial surplus, but that there was actually a deficit in six of the years.[1]

Space does not permit a full examination of the discretionary policy changes, or lack thereof, that accounted for the movements in the full-employment surplus. However, 1960 and 1963 are of interest because of the sharp increase in the full-employment surplus in those years. In his budget message of 1960 President Eisenhower stated that appropriate budget policy would be one that "not merely balances expenditures with revenues but achieves a significant surplus for debt retirement."[2] There followed a policy of strict expenditure control together with increases in social security and excise taxes. The policies resulted in a substantial increase in the full-employment surplus and, in view of their deflationary impact at a time of excessive unemployment, indicated that the Administration was out of tune with modern fiscal thinking. In the subsequent two years, increasing expenditures for defense and the space program, as well as the more liberal depreciation allowances and the 7 percent investment tax credit on machinery and equipment instituted in 1962, more than offset the normal increase in revenues that results from growth, so that the full-employment surplus was reduced. How-

---

[1] We should make clear that full employment in these calculations is implicitly achieved by an imaginary expansion of private demand and not by an increase in government purchases or a reduction in tax rates, because the full-employment surplus is calculated on the basis of an existing fiscal structure. The full-employment surplus is not the surplus that would be recorded if full employment were attained by a changed fiscal program. The naive idea that an expansion of government purchases could convert a deficit into a surplus, because of the revenue growth that income expansion would produce, is clearly erroneous. This could happen only if the expansion were accompanied by an extraordinarily strong increase in investment.

[2] *Economic Report of the President,* Government Printing Office, Washington, January 1960, p. 54.

**FIGURE 18–2**
**Federal surplus or deficit: actual and full-employment estimates** (*Source: Economic Report of the President,* Government Printing Office, Washington, 1964, p. 43, and 1965, p. 64)

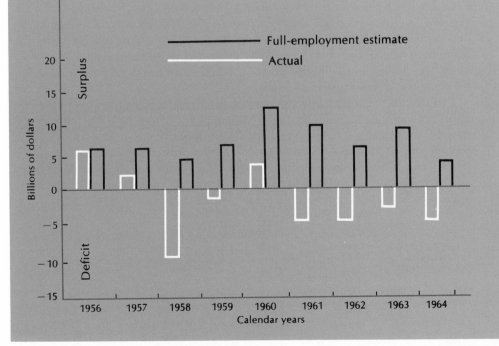

ever, the surplus remained substantial, and it eventually became clear to President Kennedy that further stimulation was required if the GNP gap was to be eliminated.

The President called for a substantial tax reduction in his budget of 1963. Congress did not enact the reduction that year, and the full-employment surplus increased. The tax reduction was finally enacted in early 1964. The CEA in its annual report of 1965 estimated that through 1965 the Revenue Act of 1964 would reduce tax liabilities by $11 billion for individuals and by $3 billion for corporations. It was estimated that in combination with multiplier effects consumption expenditures would rise by a total of $22 billion. In addition, it was anticipated that investment spending would rise as corporate cash flows increased and as the increase in consumer spending placed strain on existing productive facilities.[1] These forecasts proved to be remarkably accurate. The economy, in the wake of the tax cut and the monetary expansion that this made possible, succeeded in shaking off the pall of stagnation.[2] Unemployment in the fourth quarter of 1965 finally dropped to 4.1 percent.

A dramatic illustration of the need, persistently and continuously, to pursue discretionary policies to offset fiscal drag is provided by the CEA in its annual report of 1967.[3] Between the fourth quarter of 1960 and the second quarter of 1965 federal expenditures were increased by $25.5 billion. Over the same period total federal tax reduction was estimated to amount to $12.5 billion. Thus total federal expansionary actions came to $38 billion. Although this appears massive, it must be remembered that economic growth automatically yields added revenue. The CEA estimated this "normal revenue growth at full employment" to have been $30.5 billion. Consequently, the expansionary action of $38 billion exceeded the normal revenue growth by only $7.5 billion, and the full-employment surplus therefore fell by only that amount. Remarkably, the renewed vigor of the economy converted an actual budgetary deficit of $0.6 billion in the fourth quarter of 1960 to an actual surplus of $4.4 billion in the second quarter of 1965.

Changes in the full-employment surplus are often used as a measure of the impact of the budget on the economy. Although this is a much more reliable measure than changes in the actual surplus or deficit, there are a number of problems associated with the use of the full-employment surplus concept in this context. Changes in the actual deficit reflect both the effect of discretionary policy on the budget and the effect of changes in income. An alleged advantage of the full-employment budget is that it standardizes about a given

---

[1] For a quarter-by-quarter quantitative estimate of the impact of the tax reduction on the various expenditure components and upon GNP, see A. M. Okun, "Measuring the Impact of the 1964 Tax Reduction," in W. W. Heller, ed., Perspectives on Economic Growth, Random House, Inc., New York, 1968, pp. 27–49.

[2] This is merely to remind the reader that monetary expansion by itself would not have been possible because of the balance of payments drain this would have created.

[3] Economic Report of the President, Government Printing Office, Washington, February 1968, p. 67.

level of income and therefore eliminates the effect of the economy on the budget. However, a difficulty is that the full-employment level of income changes from year to year because of growth factors. As we saw earlier, when the full-employment level of income rises from $Y_1^*$ to $Y_2^*$ this raises the full-employment surplus, but this does not mean that discretionary policy has been restrictive.

A second problem is that it is quite possible for discretionary policies not to affect the full-employment surplus at all, or to affect it in a direction opposite to that which is expected. Figure 18–1 in fact illustrates one such case. The triggered antirecession expenditure program rotated the budget line about point e. This program had no effect upon the full-employment surplus but was clearly expansionary inasmuch as it added an amount $ab$ to the deficit at existing income level $Y_1$. Similarly, it would be quite possible to introduce a new tax structure that would collect less revenue at $Y_1$ relative to the existing structure but would collect more at the full-employment level of income $Y_1^*$. In this event, an expansionary fiscal policy would actually raise the full-employment surplus.

These considerations suggest that while the fiscal impact of discretionary policy should be measured by asking how the deficit would change if the policies had no effect on the level of income, the choice of the level of income at which the standardization is made is also important. As the example of the temporary recession spending program showed, it would clearly be more sensible to measure this by the distance $ab$ at income level $Y_1$, rather than by the zero effect at full employment. This recommendation, which is gaining acceptance, merely measures the effect of discretionary changes in the budget that would occur if these changes had no effect on income, and therefore no feedback effects on the budget.[1]

## 18–2
## ALLOCATING THE FISCAL DIVIDEND

As long as the fiscal system is so designed that economic growth increases revenues, the failure to offset fiscal drag will slow the growth of output and produce stagnation and unemployment. However, the pursuit of appropriate fiscal policies will maintain full employment, so that more output will be available for *both* private and public use than would have been the case had fiscal drag not been offset. Economic growth therefore produces a potential fiscal dividend that we may think of as equaling the normal federal revenue growth at full employment.

As emphasized before, realizing this dividend requires expansionary policies. The question that must now be answered is what is the appropriate way to do this. The debate that led to the 1964 tax cut illustrates some of the issues involved.

[1] See Alan S. Blinder and Robert M. Solow, "Analytical Foundations of Fiscal Policy," *The Economics of Public Finance*, The Brookings Institution, Washington, pp. 3–118, for a comprehensive survey and analysis of alternative measures of fiscal impact.

The fact that federal revenues tend to increase more rapidly than GNP as GNP grows at full employment is regarded by many citizens as a golden opportunity to expand badly needed social services. Probably the best-known exponent of this view is J. K. Galbraith who, along with like-minded individuals, argued that the expansionary action that was needed in the early 1960s should have taken the form of federal expenditure increases rather than tax reduction. Our contemporary concern with urban problems and the environment is old hat to the Galbraithians who long ago began to argue that the major problem confronting the American economy is a chronic imbalance between the resources that are devoted to the private and to the public sector. In his famous book *The Affluent Society*,[1] Galbraith argued that society was benefiting less from the last dollar spent on private consumption than it was from the last dollar spent in the public sector. Galbraith therefore felt that it would be in the social interest to increase government's share of GNP. In his view the solution to the problem of fiscal drag would be to increase expenditures on slum clearance, education, medical care, transportation and communication, and the control of air and water pollution.

Another idea involving the expenditure route, an idea that appealed to many of those who were reluctant to expand federal government activities, was for the federal government to maintain the long-run tightness in its fiscal system and that it then transfer, with or without strings, increasing amounts of its revenues to the state governments.[2] The division of taxing power and expenditure responsibilities is a perennial source of friction in a federal state. Canada, Australia, and Switzerland, to name but three examples, have the same problem in this respect as the United States. Even in a nonfederal system there are inevitable conflicts between the central government and the various county and city governments.

In the United States, as in other industrial countries, many of the major expansions in expenditure demands have arisen in areas that either constitutionally or traditionally lie within the jurisdiction of the states. However, the fiscal systems of the states rely heavily on property and sales taxes whose long-run yield elasticity with respect to GNP is at best one and probably considerably less than one. State and local fiscal units, moreover, find themselves under great pressure to keep taxes low because of the threat that higher taxes will cause population and industry to move to less heavily taxed jurisdictions.

When the concept of revenue sharing was first popularized during the early 1960s, it seemed to be a felicitous solution to a combination of problems. Revenue sharing would prevent the burgeoning federal surplus from becoming a fiscal drag; it would make it possible to retain the automatic stabilizing components of the fiscal system that were the cause of the surplus;

---

[1] J. K. Galbraith, *The Affluent Society*, Houghton Mifflin Company, Boston, 1960.

[2] This idea, known as "revenue sharing," has been advocated by, among others, Walter W. Heller who served as chairman of the CEA under President Kennedy. See his *New Dimensions of Political Economy*, Chap. 3, Harvard University Press, Cambridge, Mass., 1966.

and it would solve the financial plight of the state and local governments. Unhappily, the surplus quickly disappeared into the Vietnam war. Meanwhile, the plight of the states and cities worsened considerably. The inflationary recession of 1969–1970 brought a crisis to many parts of the country as costs continued to rise without commensurate increases in revenues. The state of California faced a deficit of $500 million in 1970. Pennsylvania and New York faced deficits of $400 million. At least one city, Hamtramck, Michigan, was officially declared insolvent and its affairs placed in the hands of receivers.

Responding to this crisis, the Nixon Administration in early 1971 proposed a system of revenue sharing that would turn over to the states sums proportional to their population on a no-strings-attached basis. The proposal has given rise to much controversy and opposition. The per capita formula is one source of difficulty. The states in deepest trouble are the most populous states, and their difficulty stems from the fact that they also have the largest cities. It is the cost of operating the modern megalopolis that is at the root of the problem. To give a rural state the same per capita grant as an urban state would therefore be exceedingly inefficient. A second source of difficulty concerns the no-strings aspect of the proposal. There is a basic principle, which may or may not be sound, which holds that the public authority that spends money should be responsible for raising it. Members of Congress, in particular, tend to be unenthusiastic about raising taxes to finance someone else's expenditure program. In addition, there is the concern that a state might use its grant from the federal government to reduce its own taxes by an equal amount, with the result that the level of services would fail to improve. Although some argue that a state ought to be able to decide for itself what level of services it wishes to provide, this view seems shortsighted since, for one thing, it ignores spillover effects. For example, the poorly educated of one state often end up on the welfare rolls of another. The level of services provided in one state is clearly everybody's business.

Because increases in welfare expenditures have been at the heart of the financial troubles of the cities and populous states, it may be preferable to replace revenue sharing by a federal government takeover of complete responsibility for the entire welfare field. This would relieve the fiscal burden on local governments, and it would permit a consolidation and rationalization of the jungle of programs that has come to be called the "welfare maze."

Inevitably there will be opposition to proposals that place control in the hands of Washington "bureaucrats" and therefore to continuing interest in types of proposals that help the states finance their responsibilities. A feasible scheme that avoids some of the pitfalls discussed above is to develop a measure of minimum social needs that should be met everywhere in the country, to calculate the tax base in each state, and from that to calculate the revenue that could be raised from within each state by an average tax effort. The difference between calculated expenditures and revenues could then be made up by transfers from the federal government. If a state did not tax itself as heavily as the average, it would not be able to provide for the minimum social needs of its citizens. This is because the transfers from the federal government would be based, not on the difference between actual revenues and desired expenditures, but on the revenues that would be raised by an average tax effort. A further advantage of this procedure is that it might reduce the wasteful competition involved in having states and localities attempting to attract industries from each other. This is because, by attracting industry from other states, a state's tax base would rise and its transfers from the federal government would fall proportionately. The state from which the industry was attracted would find its tax base falling and its transfers rising proportionately.

Despite the efforts of the Galbraithians in the early 1960s, the conservative tone of the pre-1965 Congress made it clear to the Administration that offsetting fiscal drag by expenditure expansion was sufficiently unpopular to warrant rejection of this route in favor of tax reduction. This would turn over the fiscal dividend to private citizens and businesses for increased consumption and investment. It would mean continued starvation of the public sector, but it was felt that would be preferable to continued stagnation and unemployment. After much debate, it was decided by the Administration that a tax reduction was the only expansionary policy that stood a chance of approval by the Congress.

If fiscal drag is to be offset by tax reduction, there remains the question of the way in which the tax reduction should be undertaken. Should the corporate income tax be reduced in order to increase the cash flow of corporations and thereby the rate of capital formation? This move might raise the rate of growth of output, and it would also have the effect of benefiting corporate shareholders and producing a regressive effect on the distribution of income. Should the tax reduction be in the personal income tax? If this is the preferred alternative, should the incidence of the tax lie more heavily on the low-income groups in order to increase the saving and investment of the high-income groups, or should the low-income groups receive the bulk of the tax relief in order to stimulate consumption and produce a more equitable distribution of income?

The tendency to mix recovery and reform measures, so prominent during the New Deal, continues to be a problem for fiscal policy. The tax structure in the United States is a nightmare. It is so replete with exemptions, exceptions, and loopholes that it encourages evasion and avoidance. It is wildly inequitable, and it has given rise to a whole profession of tax accountants and lawyers who earn lucrative livings by showing clients how to avoid taxation. Such a situation is demoralizing for a nation, and it is economically wasteful. No one is more acutely aware of this deplorable state of affairs than the United States Treasury. During the debate of the early 1960s the Treasury proposed that the tax bill contain a comprehensive package of reform. Aware that members of Congress cannot be interested in reforms that penalize wealthy constituents and potential campaign contributors, the Treasury attempted to tack the reform package onto the tax reduction proposed by the President. The hope was that the tasty carrot of a tax reduction might be strong enough to drag along the refractory donkey of reform.

Tax reform got nowhere in Congress. Realizing that the entire bill was in jeopardy, the Administration eventually gave up on reform, and the final bill represented rate reduction and not much else. Undoubtedly, the attempt to gain reform was one factor making for delay in obtaining passage of the tax bill.[1]

The political thicket in which tax reform usually finds itself has led to the quest for ways of increasing and reducing taxes that bypass all the complications that would be involved in the creation and legal interpretation of a new revenue code. In an effort to avoid these complications, and to obtain speedier congressional action, the Johnson Administration in 1967 asked the Congress for an income tax "surcharge." The idea was for taxpayers to compute their tax liability in the ordinary manner. Thereafter, they would tack on a percentage of their computed tax liability as an additional charge. The idea is a simple one that involves no change in the basic tax structure. Since the tax is a percent of the basic tax liability, it is exactly as progressive or regressive as the underlying tax structure. It is a useful device that will, no doubt, be resorted to again in the future.

Finally, it is possible to allocate portions of the fiscal dividend by indirect means. If it is judged that too small a fraction of the national product is going into capital formation, investment spending can be stimulated by easier monetary policies, by more liberal depreciation guidelines, and by increases in the size of the allowable investment tax credit. Similarly, home construction can be stimulated by easier money and has traditionally been subsidized by a "tax expenditure" in the form of tax-deductible mortgage interest.

## 18–3
## THE FAILURE OF FINE TUNING

The return to full employment by the end of 1965 was a heartening development for those who called for an expansionary fiscal policy along modern principles. The episode was widely hailed as the triumph of the "new economics." Hope was widespread that henceforth fiscal policy could be conducted along rational lines and that the federal budget could be employed to ensure full employment and rapid growth. These hopes were shattered very quickly. Indeed, the record since mid-1965 is one of a seemingly endless series of fiscal blunders. Although our purpose is not to write a history, it is worth our while to review recent experience since such a survey illustrates many of the problems that arise in attempting to conduct fiscal policy in a full-employment economy.

---

[1] An additional complicating factor was the United States Treasury. The Treasury, like any normal business, likes its income to exceed its outgo. As a result of this inclination, the original proposal presented an overzealous tax reform package that would have gained revenues through loophole closing roughly equivalent to the loss in yield due to rate reduction. With the economy in need of stimulation, it was evident that the Treasury was in need of education.

In mid-1965 President Johnson began a policy of rapid escalation of the war in Vietnam. Federal defense purchases increased dramatically, rising by $22.7 billion between the second quarter of 1965 and the second quarter of 1967. At first there was hope that increases in defense spending would be limited to no more than would bring the economy all the way to full employment. The President and his Pentagon advisers, hoping that the war would soon be terminated, failed to disclose the true picture of the extent of the expenditure increase. The Council of Economic Advisers, momentarily caught off balance, was initially unable to caution the President to seek an offset to these expenditures. However, once it realized what was happening, the CEA began a systematic campaign to convince the President that a tax increase would be necessary to offset the increases in expenditure that were being piled on top of an economy that was already very close to full employment. The President resisted this advice. Taxes had just been reduced (in early 1964), and he would look foolish to ask for an increase so quickly. If, moreover, the war could be rapidly terminated, taxes would only have to be reduced once more. If the need for higher taxes were called to the attention of Congress, it would inevitably have told him to seek the needed fiscal offset by reducing Great Society expenditures.

The consequence of inaction to offset the rising war expenditure was a booming economy in late 1965 and most of 1966 and a resumption of inflation. As this developed and as it became clear that the war would drag on, the President became persuaded of the need for a tax increase. In his message of January 1967, he proposed the enactment of a surcharge on personal and corporate income. However, because his advisers had predicted temporary sluggishness in the economy for the first half of 1967, he asked the Congress to take the issue under advisement and to remain ready to act on the surcharge when the sluggishness subsided and the need for fiscal tightness reappeared.

The CEA was correct about its forecast of a slow economy in the first half of 1967. However, the decision to postpone the request for the surcharge may have been a fundamental mistake. The poor performance of the economy in the first half of 1967 was attributable almost entirely to an inventory adjustment. Sales expectations had not been realized during the fourth quarter of 1966, with the consequence that inventories piled up at an annual rate of $19.9 billion. This rate was about double a normal rate of accumulation, and it therefore signaled that sales would subsequently be made from the overloaded shelves, that new orders would be postponed, and that production would therefore slow down until the excess inventories were worked off.[1]

Between the fourth quarter of 1966 and the second quarter of 1967 GNP increased only $12.8 billion, compared with a normal gain of about $30 billion. But the underlying demands, fueled by rapidly rising defense expenditures, grew rapidly. This is clear from the fact that the total of all components of GNP except for inventory investment—"final sales" as this is called—grew

---

[1] Under normal conditions inventory investment tends to run at about 1 percent of GNP.

by $29.3 billion during this half-year period. However, inventory investment fell from $19.9 billion to $3.4 billion in the second quarter. The GNP gain therefore came to a meager $12.8 billion.

The expansion of final sales of $29.3 billion in the first half of 1967 had been exceeded in only one other half-year period in our history.[1] Under the circumstances, it is difficult to see how an increase in taxes which would have yielded less than $10 billion could have had serious adverse consequences. At all events, it was decided to wait until the inventory adjustment was over before asking Congress to raise taxes.

When the request for the tax increase did come in mid-1967, Congress found itself being asked to raise taxes after a half year of subpar economic performance. Prices, moreover, had been relatively stable during the first half of 1967, and there appeared to be little danger of renewed inflation. The prospects for stability, finally, appeared favorable since increases in defense spending were expected to taper off.[2]

Administration economists presented charts and arguments that showed the inventory adjustment to be over, and they pointed out that when inventory investment again began to increase, GNP growth would snap back, and an inflationary boom would be under way. Despite the accuracy of this forecast, it was, of course, only a forecast. Moreover, it was on the basis of such a forecast that Congress was being asked to raise taxes. It is fair to say that members of Congress in general do not trust economists, and they trust the forecasts that economists make even less. Had they raised taxes only to find the forecast to be wrong, they would have been in a very awkward position. In view of this, it hardly came as a surprise to find the House Ways and Means Committee, which initiates revenue measures, cool to the Administration's request.

One lesson of late 1967 is that Congress will not pass a tax bill purely on the basis of a forecast. Evidence must be at hand that the direction of economic movement is clear.[3] In 1961, with a GNP gap in excess of $50 billion, and again in 1975, it took little wisdom, let alone a precise forecast, to point the direction in which fiscal policy should move, However, with an economy at full employment the problem of keeping it there without permitting it to drift off into inflation or recession depends critically on accurate forecasting. Even if economic forecasting were to become considerably more reliable than

[1] This was the second half of 1965 when final sales increased $33.5 billion.

[2] This proved to be the case. Federal defense purchases increased $6.3 billion in the first half of 1967 but only $2.7 billion in the second half.

[3] Matters were further complicated in late 1967 because the economic indicators were giving conflicting signals. On that occasion the trouble was caused by a strike against the Ford Motor Company. Striking workers are not counted as unemployed. However, strikes cause workers in supplier industries to be laid off, and this increases measured unemployment. Similarly, a major strike reduces industrial production. Thus the economic indicators may turn sour even though there is no shortage of aggregate demand. In October 1967, the unemployment rate jumped to 4.3 percent, and industrial production, as measured by the Federal Reserve Board's index, gained a puny one-tenth of a point, rising from 156.8 to 156.9, for the month.

it now is, it is doubtful if Congress could be persuaded to engage in the perennial "fine tuning" that would be required to keep the economy within the narrow band that exists between excessive unemployment and inflation.

Having been asked to raise taxes, Congress countered by asking the Administration to do its share by limiting expenditures.[1] Chairman Mills of the House Ways and Means Committee insisted on holding out for such an Administration concession. Twice during the last half of 1967 he held hearings on the tax bill, and twice he suspended the hearings, each time saying that the Administration had provided insufficient assurance that expenditures would be cut. The result of this insistence on expenditure reduction was to introduce further delay, and it also created the fear that the final product might represent fiscal overkill. It had originally been estimated that the 10 percent surcharge would be sufficient to keep the coming boom at bay. If an expenditure reduction were added to the tax increase, the total package might be excessively deflationary.

The tax bill was finally passed in the middle of 1968, three years after it appeared to have been necessary, and a year and a half after the President had finally become convinced of this fact.[2] As it happened, the surtax came into effect just as the boom of 1967–1968 had begun to die of its own weight. However, by this time the persistence and acceleration of inflation and the expectation of further inflation had created an environment in which inflation would be difficult to control without resort to abrupt and drastic measures of a sort likely to produce recession.

The problem of controlling the situation in 1968 was vastly complicated by extraordinarily reckless monetary policy that saw the money supply grow at an annual rate of 7.4 percent in the first half of 1968, and to continue at a rate of 6.9 percent throughout the second half of the year. Meanwhile, the need for a tax increase, which had been so clear earlier, was beginning to ebb somewhat as the growth of defense purchases slowed and as normal growth of revenues moved the budget closer to balance. With forecasts suggesting that a slowdown in real output was imminent, and with fiscal policy primarily concerned with control of inflation, it is reasonable to conclude that policy in 1968 was, along the lines suggested in Chapter 16, misassigned. Taxes were assigned to the price level, and monetary policy assigned itself to the maintenance of output growth. The result was destabilizing. Restrictive monetary policy with no rise in taxes would have produced a far better result. The rise in unit labor costs which was so pronounced after the middle of 1968 would

---

[1] A standard joke in Washington is that regardless of whether the Administration wants taxes raised or lowered, Congress will insist on federal expenditure reduction in return. In 1963 the full-employment surplus increased as President Kennedy held down expenditures in an attempt to bargain for the tax cut. In 1967–1968 President Johnson had to promise to hold down expenditures in return for a tax increase.

[2] The method of passage was characteristically bizarre. Having battled the President for almost a year, Congressman Mills could no longer publicly reverse himself by sponsoring the surcharge. He therefore reported out a fairly innocuous bill that extended some federal excise taxes, and the Senate then attached the surcharge to this bill as a rider.

have been held down, output and employment would have shown less of a slowdown, and the rate of inflation might not have accelerated.

One can hardly give fiscal policy very high marks for its performance since mid-1965. Most of the expenditure and tax changes could not have been more ill-timed and perverse. It was a period during which the erratic course of government expenditure and revenue policies, rather than instability of private demand, were responsible for the resultant instability and inflation.

Most economists believed that with the expiration of the boom and the imposition of the surcharge in mid-1968, together with a jump in social security taxes scheduled for the end of the year, the economy would enter a period of sluggishness and slow growth. It was assumed also that these circumstances would moderate the rate of inflation. The slower real growth did, in fact, begin immediately.[1] However, unemployment surprisingly continued to remain low, and the rate of inflation continued to increase. With the slowing down of the expansionary pressure attributable to the federal budget came an increase in business fixed investment that would sustain a semblance of boom throughout the first half of 1969. This was clearly a phenomenon attributable to high profits, inflationary expectations, and excessive monetary expansion. Although capacity utilization indexes showed that ample capacity existed in most areas, capital goods orders remained abnormally high. Given the rapid rise in capital goods prices, it apparently seemed desirable to businesses to expand capacity before the cost of capital goods mounted even further.

Meanwhile the Nixon Administration began a policy of expenditure restraint, and the Fed reversed its easy money policies of 1967–1968. For a while during 1969 the overheated economy kept pushing ahead, and large budgetary surpluses were generated. However, as the restrictive measures took hold and as the investment boom expired, the economy slowed, and the surpluses once again became deficits. Real growth continued to rise slowly until the third quarter of 1969. Thereafter it paused, and unemployment began once again to mount. The inflation that continued to roll despite these restrictive policies showed no signs of abating. The Administration's "game plan," which had been ballyhooed as a means of slowing inflation without creating recession, was an obvious flop. By the fourth quarter of 1970 unemployment had risen to 5.8 percent, only a year and a half after the 3.6 percent of the second quarter of 1969.

As pointless and costly as it was, the recession of 1970–1971 was but a quiet prelude to the disaster which befell the United States economy in 1974–1975. Following the resumption of expansionary policies in time for the 1972 election, the economy moved out of the recession and into boom conditions in 1973. The strength of the expansion had been underestimated since very few forecasters realized the powerful effect that the devaluation of

[1] The growth of real GNP zipped along at an astonishing annual rate of 6.6 percent in the first half of 1968. It then tapered off to a more normal rate of 3.6 percent in the second half of the year, dropped to 2.3 percent in the first half of 1969, and then fell to an anemic 0.9 percent in the last half of the year.

the dollar would have on our international competitive position. The consequence was that exports boomed, rising by $28 billion in 1973, and almost $40 billion in 1974, providing a powerful stimulus to the economy.

The recession of 1974–1975 began in the late months of 1973 and produced the deepest and most prolonged economic slide since the great depression of the 1930s. By April 1975 unemployment rose to over 8 million workers, representing 8.9 percent of the labor force, and it appeared as if the rate would go higher. The gap between actual and potential GNP was a massive $230 billion in current prices. With the exception of exports, which continued to show strength, the various sectors of the economy were verging on collapse and panic. In the first quarter of 1975 fixed investment was declining rapidly as desired capacity levels shrank, and state and local governments were busy laying off employees and cutting services in response to the revenue losses that the recession had inflicted on them.

The recession of 1974–1975 was again the product of economic mismanagement except that this time the mismanagement was of mammoth proportions. Once again these economic policy crimes were committed in the name of inflation control. The seeds were sown in the third quarter of 1973 when, panicking over rising prices, the Federal Reserve abruptly slowed the rate of monetary growth to an annual rate of less than 1 percent. The result was a new credit crunch and marked the beginning of a slide in residential construction that, by the first quarter of 1975, had seen the number of new housing unit starts fall by more than one-half and the value of construction activity by 40 percent. There was, moreover, no relief in sight at that time.

The second major shock was the combination of the quadrupling of oil prices in late 1973 and the poor harvests throughout the world in that year. Both had the effect of raising the domestic price level for reasons having little to do with excessive domestic demand. Since crop prices are essentially determined by world demand conditions, it is ridiculous to resort to restrictive monetary-fiscal policies to prevent the domestic price level from rising when world food prices rise. Such a policy merely deflates the rest of the economy, creating unemployment and lost production for no good reason whatsoever.

Similarly, the oil price increase added enormously to our import bill and gave a huge upward shove to our price level. Policy makers in the Administration did not show an awareness that the inflation this produced was comparable to what would have occurred had the rise in oil prices been brought about by an enormous excise tax on oil. Such a tax would raise the price of oil and in this sense be inflationary, but since it would severely restrict consumer real income, it would in fact be massively deflationary.

The appropriate job for policy in the circumstances is to finance these non-domestic supply-induced price increases. The Administration did the opposite. Having its eye only on the rate of inflation without understanding its cause, it chose restriction. It encouraged tight money, permitted the full-employment surplus to ride up unmercifully, and added insult to injury by proposing, as late as October 1974, that taxes be raised.

The third catastrophe, which followed in part from the second, was that during 1974 the federal budget very rapidly and automatically became restrictive at a time when real GNP was plummeting downward. The main source of this was the personal income tax which, rather than acting as a benign automatic stabilizer, suddenly became an automatic destabilizer. The explanation for this lies in the facts. Between the fourth quarter of 1973 and the third quarter of 1974 real GNP declined at an annual rate of 3.6 percent. However, prices, as measured by the GNP deflator, rose at a rate of 11.1 percent. The consequence of this was that nominal GNP increased at a rate of 7.2 percent. Along with this came a rise in nominal personal income at a rate of 8.4 percent. Because our income tax system is geared to nominal (rather than real) income, and because it is progressive, this rise in nominal personal income caused personal income taxes to rise at a rate of 12.9 percent. The consequence was that the ratio of taxes to personal income rose from 14.5 percent to 15.0 percent, in the space of only three quarters, and at a time when real GNP was falling.

This was disastrous. It meant that real disposable income fell even faster than real GNP, even though an automatic stabilizer is supposed to ensure the opposite, and it inflicted tremendous punishment on the consumption sector. During the first three quarters of 1974 the effect of the lost income was, to an extent, absorbed by reduced personal saving. But by the fourth quarter consumers had had enough, and that is when the auto and many other industries virtually collapsed.

The same attitudes that produced the policies that caused the recession produced a subsequent paralysis that precluded action to end the slide. It is a fact that from the beginning of the downturn in late 1973 to the time a tax reduction was finally enacted 15 months later, absolutely nothing was done to moderate the economic deterioration. The budget was permitted to become increasingly restrictive, and the rate of monetary growth was held to 4.5 percent in 1974. When the tax reduction finally came, it barely made up for the automatic inflation-induced tax increase that took place in 1974. As a result of this drift, the economy became so deeply mired below its potential that it will take many years to restore a semblance of full employment. Projections of feasible recovery paths suggest that we will be very fortunate if unemployment falls below 5 percent by the time we prepare a new edition of this book.

## 18–4
## IMPROVING FISCAL PERFORMANCE

What can be done to prevent the recurrence of 1974–1975 style debacles in the future? Within the narrow province of fiscal policy reform one obvious problem is crying for attention. As we suggested above, the real value of personal income taxes kept rising in 1974 even while real GNP was falling, with the consequence that an automatic stabilizer became a destabilizer. This happened because income tax exemptions and brackets are defined in nominal terms. Consequently, rising nominal wages caused some poor people to be dragged over the level of their exemptions and into the tax net, and it caused other persons to be pulled into higher tax brackets. In the aggregate, this meant that the ratio of personal taxes to personal income increased at a time when this was most harmful to the economy.

If income tax exemptions and bracket limits were widened at the rate of inflation in a way that keeps their real values constant, the tax burdens of individuals would not change merely as a consequence of inflation, and the perverse macroeconomic effects of the kind experienced in 1974 could not recur. Taxes would have been geared to real income, and since real income fell in 1974, the ratio of taxes to personal income would also have fallen, providing a cushion to consumer spending and averting a deep recession.

In Chapter 16 we showed how the progressive income tax geared to nominal income could cause stagflation, and the experience of 1974 shows how it could become an automatic destabilizer. It is surely time to follow the lead of Canada and other countries and, at the very least, consider reform of this very damaging aspect of our tax system. Inflation indexing of the income tax would not eliminate progressivity of the tax with respect to real income, and it would not preclude the use of tax policy to slow inflation since marginal rates can always be increased even as the brackets to which they apply are widened. Indexing would, however, eliminate the possibility that the government would automatically gain a larger share of claim over resources as the result of an inflation that the government itself had brought about. And it would eliminate the disruptive macroeconomic effects of the tax as it is presently constituted.

A problem that nearly always arises when improvement in the performance of fiscal policy is under consideration is the problem of lags. When the economy is well below full employment, expansionary fiscal policy is the salvation that offsets fiscal drag and helps to power the economy toward full employment. Under such conditions the need for accurate forecasting is not vital, timing mistakes are less critical and noticeable, and policy is essentially free to pursue its objectives without fear of serious error. However, at or near full employment the situation is quite different. As the events of the past decade have shown, fiscal policy in such a situation becomes a clumsy device that seems very likely to produced ill-timed and destabilizing effects. The time patterns involved in making discretionary fiscal policy changes and in waiting for these changes to affect the economy have been discussed by economists in terms of two time lags known as the "inside" and the "outside" lags. The inside lag refers to the time between a change in the economic situation and the enactment of the policy intended to offset the change; the outside lag refers to the time between the policy change and its actual impact on the economy.[1]

The inside lag is easily the most troublesome. After waiting three years for taxes to be reduced in the early 1960s, and three years for them to be raised

---

[1] For a discussion of lags in fiscal policy see A. Ando and E. C. Brown, "Lags in Fiscal Policy: A Summary," in *Stabilization Policies*, Research Studies Prepared for the Commission on Money and Credit, Prentice-Hall, Englewood Cliffs, N.J., 1963, pp. 7–13.

in the late 1960s, we need hardly say any more about this lag. The outside lag, by comparison, palls into insignificance. Perhaps a month is required to change an increase in personal tax rates into increased tax withholding and therefore a reduction in disposable income. It then takes some time for the reduction in disposable income to reduce expenditures, still longer for this to slow down the rate of production, and far longer still to have any impact on the rate of inflation. Nevertheless, the bulk of the initial spending effects seems to take place quite quickly. Tax changes, certainly, can be expected to have an immediate impact on spending.[1]

As noted in our discussion of the full-employment budget, experience suggests that countercyclical expenditure programs are very likely to be mistimed. An increase in federal purchases implies either the expansion of existing projects or the development of new programs. All of this takes time so that the bulk of the expenditures tend to come not during the recession when they are needed but after recovery is well under way. Also, it appears to be the case that the impact of increased federal transfers to state and local governments operates only after a considerable lag.[2] Nevertheless, the recent revival of interest in temporary antirecession spending programs to be triggered by movements in the unemployment rate has considerable promise.

Automatic triggering linked to some index of economic activity is certainly not a novel idea. It used to be known as "formula flexibility," and it can be applied to the tax as well as to the expenditure side. Its effect would be to convert the automatic stabilizers from passive damping mechanisms into somewhat more aggressive stimulators. Under our existing income tax system, a fall in income produces a reduction in tax revenues because there is less income available to tax and because taxpayers shift into lower brackets. A much more powerful effect could be obtained if tax rates on all brackets were automatically reduced at the same time as taxpayers were sliding into lower brackets. Thus, under formula flexibility, tax rates would vary automatically in response to changing economic conditions. Tax rates might, for example, automatically fall in proportion to the rise in the unemployment rate.

In a very illuminating simulation study, Howard Pack has shown that properly designed formula flexibility would have greatly moderated and shortened the recessions of the 1950s.[3] Even though formula flexibility is an attractive device that would go well beyond the automatic stabilizers and that would greatly ease problems of timing, there are two critical difficulties. First, the

---

[1] In his paper, "Measuring the Impact of the 1964 Tax Reduction," op. cit., Arthur M. Okun estimates that a permanent $1 increase in disposable income will eventually result in an increase in consumption of 95 cents. Consumption rises by 37 cents during the quarter in which disposable income is increased; by the third quarter it is up to 75 cents; and by the sixth quarter it is up to 90 cents.

[2] See Ando and Brown, op. cit.

[3] H. Pack, "Formula Flexibility: A Quantitative Appraisal," in A. Ando, E. C. Brown, and A. F. Friedlander, *Studies in Economic Stabilization*, Chap. 1, The Brookings Institution, Washington. A simulation study involves the construction of a dynamic model of the economy in which the values of the parameters are either assumed or estimated empirically. Different assumed policies are then imposed on the model, and the time paths of output and other variables are then simulated.

automatic changes have to be based on the movement of some economic index. Most such indexes are subject to influence from strikes, crop failures, and other factors that may have little or nothing to do with whether aggregate demand is excessive or inadequate. Moreover, the differential lags that cause output and employment to respond more rapidly than the rate of inflation sometimes produce a situation in which the different alarm clocks might ring at the same time. In the last half of 1970 unemployment slipped to over 5 percent. At the same time prices kept rising rapidly. What kind of formula would cover such a situation of "inflationary recession"?

A second way of streamlining fiscal policy that has been suggested is to persuade Congress to turn over to the President a certain amount of discretionary power. Imagine the impact that might be achieved if the President had the authority to suspend or reduce tax collections for a month or for a quarter. Or imagine that Congress controls the overall tax structure, but that it empowers the President to impose a discretionary surcharge between zero and 10 percent. In this way the longest, most arduous, and least predictable part of the inside lag could be partially eliminated. Fiscal policy could be turned into a speedy, and responsive, stabilizing device. Even if Congress refused to go this far, it ought, at the very least, to agree to act on the Administration's tax proposals within a reasonable, previously specified, period of time.

An extremely important step in reducing the inside lag was taken in 1974 when the United States Congress passed the Congressional Budget and Impoundment Control Act. This act created budget committees in the House and the Senate and also created a joint staff known as the Congressional Budget Office. More importantly, the new machinery provides for a formal procedure for reviewing annually the federal budget in the light of the overall fiscal needs of the economy.

Such a procedure has been entirely lacking in the past. Budget authority is in the hands of numerous separate appropriations subcommittees that determine the appropriations of the different federal agencies and programs. The individual decisions of these subcommittees have tended to produce a total of budget authority and outlay that is largely uncontrolled and uncoordinated. The overall fiscal needs of the economy were generally not considered at all. The outlays for individual programs did not add up to a total that achieved a socially desirable allocation between federal programs and the other sectors of the economy, and the allocation within the federal sector did not yield a rational division among federal expenditure programs.

Solving all these problems is, perhaps, too much to ask of the new approach. The important thing is that the individual appropriations committees will be pressured to live within the overall guidelines of the budget resolutions, and that a mandatory annual review of the overall fiscal needs of the economy must be undertaken by the Congress. Congress is now forcing itself to think about fiscal policy and has finally hired a staff to help it do so. Preliminary indications are that the process is viable and that the Congress will henceforth be better able to deal with fiscal policy problems than in the past.

# 19 MONETARY POLICY

## INTRODUCTION

The Federal Reserve System was established in 1913. Prior to that time the United States had no monetary policy in the modern sense since machinery for influencing monetary and credit conditions was absent. The creation of the Fed gave rise to the hope that the periodic financial crises that had marked our previous history would henceforth be averted. It was also hoped that the supply of money and credit could be expanded in accordance with the needs of the economy rather than determined by such accidental events as gold discoveries.

During its initial years the Fed was concerned almost exclusively with the international monetary and domestic financial problems associated with World War I. The war produced a sharp inflation which was followed by a short but severe recession in 1921. Subsequently, the economy embarked on the expansion of the "roaring twenties." The Fed's first real test came in 1929. Unhappily, it failed this test miserably. In retrospect it is clear that the Fed's sharp restriction of credit at the end of 1929 was one of the prime factors in precipitating the monetary crisis that eventually led to a wave of bank failures and to the worst depression in American history.

Confidence in the efficacy of monetary policy was seriously damaged by the great depression. Although bank reserves increased enormously during the early 1930s, these increases were not translated into increased loans. After a wave of bank failures bankers became exceedingly cautious, while borrowers with sufficiently good credit standing were scarce. There was, in Keynesian terms, a strong preference for liquidity. One could supply reserves to the banking system, but one could not guarantee that this action would stimulate economic activity. Discouraged by this experience, many economists gave up on monetary policy altogether. It was said that expansionary monetary policy was like pushing on a string and that the only hope for escaping from depression lay in expansionary fiscal policy.

During World War II the Fed abandoned its function of stabilizing the economy in favor of a policy of enabling the Treasury to borrow huge sums at low and stable interest rates. This interest rate pegging policy was effected by the Fed's guarantee to purchase treasury bonds at a fixed price. In the process the Fed bought large quantities of government debt and therefore added large sums to the money supply. Despite the fact that such a policy contributed to inflationary pressure, there may have been no alternative given the size of the wartime federal deficit. Unfortunately, the Fed continued the pegging policy long after the termination of the war. And there can therefore be little doubt that the Fed was a prime contributor to the postwar inflation.

The Fed officially suspended its interest rate pegging policy in an accord reached with the Treasury in March 1951. Thereafter, the Fed attempted to use its power to promote stability. However, critics affirm that the Fed was excessively concerned with the problem of inflation and that it showed little concern for the problem of unemployment that grew progressively more serious throughout the decade. Between 1952 and 1960, real GNP groped along at an anemic average annual rate of 2.6 percent. Although much of this poor performance was the consequence of fiscal drag, the situation was undoubtedly aggravated by a monetary policy that limited the rate of growth of the money supply to an average of 1.3 percent per year. The Fed's excessive anti-inflationary biases clearly found expression during this period.

The power of the Fed to foster expansion in the early 1960s was limited by our worsening balance of payments position. International currency convertibility was reestablished in the late 1950s, and capital was free to flow abroad. Had the Fed pursued a vigorous expansionary policy, interest rates would have fallen, capital would have sought higher yields abroad, and the balance of payments deficit would have widened. Thus the Fed was forced to take a back seat to fiscal policy in promoting expansion. As fiscal policy pushed the *IS* curve to the right, the Fed responded by permitting the money supply to expand in such a way as to accommodate the growth of GNP without, at the same time, causing interest rates to fall. Indeed, most interest rates drifted upward gradually between 1960 and 1965, a clear indication that expansion originated from the real rather than from the monetary sector.

The smooth expansion that marked that period was rudely disrupted by the escalation of the Vietnam war. In the absence of a fiscal offset to sharply rising defense expenditures, the Fed took it upon itself to prevent inflation. Monetary policy accordingly moved sharply toward restriction near the end of 1965. Although this policy did slow down the economy, the impact of monetary restriction was so uneven that it threw the normal balance between the sectors of the economy out of line and created severe and unnecessary hardships in many areas. Residential building was particularly hard hit as sources of mortgage financing dried up. Nevertheless, the episode did prove that a sufficiently restrictive monetary policy could slow down an overheated economy. Whether it can speed up a sluggish economy remains open to debate.

Since the 1930s when many felt monetary policy to be powerless, there has been a gradual shift in the opinion of economists toward greater confidence in the effectiveness of monetary policy. Some admire its potential flexibility in contrast to fiscal policy. Others believe, as did the pre-Keynesians, that money ultimately controls the level of total spending and that the money supply is a more important determinant of money GNP than the federal budget. The vast majority of economists today believe that the issue is not monetary versus fiscal policy, but rather monetary and fiscal policy correctly timed and in the right proportions. Nevertheless there are extremists on both sides of the issue.

Our first task in this chapter is to look at these extremes. This will provide an opportunity to review contemporary monetary thinking and to introduce some considerations not yet discussed in this book. In subsequent sections we shall take up practical problems of monetary policy. First, we shall look at the individual instruments of monetary policy, assess their virtues and their failings, and ask whether the operation of these instruments can be improved and whether their combined operation can be better coordinated. Second, we shall consider the issue of whether it is best to have an independent or a politically responsive monetary authority, and the related issue of whether it is best to conduct monetary policy according to previously legislated rules or whether it is best to improvise with discretionary policy changes as the economic situation seems to require. Finally, we must pay some attention to the matter of the national debt. Is it a burden, as many people claim? What are its economic effects? And how does its existence complicate stabilization policy?

## 19–2
### RECENT ISSUES IN MONETARY POLICY

Keynesian theory, as well as some of the more sophisticated classical theories, views monetary policy as operating upon the level of aggregate spending indirectly through its effect on interest rates and credit availability. An increase in the money supply lowers the relative supply of alternative financial assets; this then reduces interest rates; and this in turn increases expenditures on newly produced goods and services. In this view the effectiveness of monetary policy depends upon the considerations set forth in Chapter 9. The critical questions are how elastic are the demand for and the supply of money with respect to the rate of interest, and how responsive are spending on consumption and various categories of investment to changes in the rate of interest.

Modern monetary thinking has produced two schools of thought that have in common the idea that the interest elasticities of the various functions are of little importance. But here they part company. One view, known as the "monetarist," or "modern quantity theory," holds that monetary policy will be effective even without interest rate changes. The other, known as the "Radcliffe" or "Gurley-Shaw" view, maintains that the demand for money will shift under the impact of monetary tightness, so that the effect of tightness may be negligible even though the values of the elasticities of given demand and supply functions may lead one to believe otherwise.

For many years monetarism gained increasing influence under the able leadership of Professor Milton Friedman of the University of Chicago.[1] Unfortunately, the theory is difficult to pinpoint since its proponents have been reluctant to clarify their views and since monetarists have a tendency to insist that their position has been correctly interpreted only by those who demonstrate the proper degree of evangelical fervor. The doctrine became the official line of the Nixon Administration in 1970–1971. It was unfortunate for the economy that the policies it prescribed failed to achieve their intent. On the other hand, it is comforting to note that this failure has caused monetarists to become somewhat less strident and self-assured.

The monetarist idea seems to be that an increase in the money supply changes asset holdings and that this produces portfolio adjustment just as in the Keynesian way. However, in Keynesian theory the initial impact is to produce portfolio adjustment purely in financial assets. Subsequent spending effects then occur because the interest rate changes. In the monetarist view an increase in the money supply produces a direct change in spending. This is because spending on goods and services — recall the permanent income hypothesis — is but one form in which portfolios are adjusted in response to a change in the relative supply of some asset.

A fall in interest rates raises capital values and increases the wealth of the private sector of the economy. If this were the source of the predicted spending increase, one could accept the argument as a modern generalization of the Pigou effect.[2] Extreme monetarists, however, seem prepared to argue that the spending effect would occur even in the absence of interest rate changes. This very strange doctrine bears some examination.

If wealth were increased by expansionary monetary policy, one could eas-

[1] Professor Friedman's views have been expressed in a wide variety of publications. An outline of the modern quantity theory is in "The Quantity Theory of Money — A Restatement," in Milton Friedman, ed., *Studies in the Quantity Theory of Money*, The University of Chicago Press, Chicago, 1956, pp. 3–21. His empirical conclusions concerning the interest elasticity of the demand for money are reported in Milton Friedman, "The Demand for Money; Some Theoretical and Empirical Results," *Journal of Political Economy*, 67:327–351, 1959. A most useful brief review of Federal Reserve policy together with Friedman's views on monetary policy is contained in Milton Friedman, *A Program for Monetary Stability*, Fordham University Press, New York, 1959. Monetarism has also invaded the Federal Reserve Bank of St. Louis. To Fed watchers their particular kind of monetary analysis is known as "Brand X."

[2] Such a generalization has been undertaken by Don Patinkin in *Money, Interest, and Prices*, 2d ed., Harper & Row, Publishers, Incorporated, New York, 1965.

ily believe that spending would increase. However, monetary policy effected through the purchase and sale of securities on the open market has no effect on wealth except insofar as the policy changes the interest rate. If a bond is purchased by the Fed and if this has no effect on interest rates, the result is a simple one-for-one swap of assets with no change whatever occurring in the value of private wealth. Thus it is very difficult to see why an individual who sold the bond would increase his or her consumption spending. If the Fed's purchases have no effect on the rate of interest, one may presume that bonds and money are perfect substitutes, so that portfolio adjustment is complete at the moment of the purchase. Thus, the quantity theory makes little sense if it claims the interest rate is irrelevant.

On the other hand, if the interest rate does fall when the money supply is increased, there will be an increase in private wealth as the result of a capital gain. This may, indeed, stimulate spending both via the conventional interest-investment mechanism and also because of the wealth effect of falling interest rates. Recognition of the latter is an important advance over simple Keynesian theory. Nevertheless, it is difficult to see how this addition alone can do much to improve the case for monetary policy, and it certainly does not get around the problem that the demand for money may, under certain circumstances, be highly elastic with respect to the rate of interest. If the interest rate does not change, none of these effects will be operative.

The analysis of wealth effects is extremely tricky. For example, the forego-ing has ignored the role of multiple credit expansion.[1] If bank reserves are increased through expansionary monetary policy and if this leads to sub-sequent multiple credit expansion, the total supply of money will increase by a multiple of the initial increase in reserves. Consequently, the total value of the money supply and the value of government securities held by the private sector increase even though initially there was a one-for-one swap of se-curities for money. In conventional analysis this expansion is assumed not to involve a wealth change because it has no effect on the net worth of the private sector of the economy, each subsequent increase in bank loans and investments being matched by a corresponding increase in deposit liabilities. However, recently it has been argued that the strict accounting identity which leaves net worth unaffected is misleading. Monetary expansion increases the profitability of banks. Since this raises the market value of bank stocks, a sub-stantial wealth effect emerges which then increases the spending of the owners of these stocks. Thus the monopoly position of commercial banks — the position that enables them to create money — may in fact provide a means for the creation of wealth which then gets transmitted into the expan-sion of spending on goods and services.

Although monetary policy may get some added punch through this route, it is nevertheless difficult to see how it can acquire the magic potency that its supporters claim for it. One possible way is to alter the assumptions with

[1] B. Pesek and T. Saving, *Money, Wealth and Economic Theory,* The Macmillan Company, New York, 1967.

respect to how the money supply is increased. Imagine that instead of an expansion of the money supply via open market purchases, the money supply is increased by dropping newly printed dollar bills out of airplanes. Such a policy of "money rain" would increase the money holdings of individuals without, at the same time, requiring them to give up other assets in return. Such a change is very likely to have powerful spending effects. First of all, the recipients enjoy a temporary increase in disposable income. Second, the money supply is increased, and interest rates may therefore fall. Third, the private sector will be wealthier because the value of its holdings of claims against the government will have increased. However, a moment's reflection shows that this is not a pure monetary policy at all. It is, in fact, identical to the combination of monetary and fiscal effects that would result from a government transfer payment such as a veterans' bonus financed by the sale of treasury bonds to the Fed. Thus, if this is typically the way the money supply is increased, the monetarist may, inadvertently, be establishing the case for fiscal policy.

Monetarists might now agree that the foregoing policy involves both monetary and fiscal elements. However, they would probably argue that it is the money and wealth transfer, rather than the disposable income change, that affects spending. In making this claim they tend to ignore the fact that the wealth effect of the policy is primarily attributable to the direct transfer (fiscal) element of the policy. Pure monetary policy, defined as a purchase by the Fed of government securities, lacks power because it does not involve the transfer of wealth that monetary expansion via fiscal means entails. Consequently, to make their position convincing, monetarists ought to be made to show that expansion of the money supply has identical spending effects no matter how this expansion is brought about.

Monetarists avoid many of the hard issues by resorting to a "positive" methodology that shows no interest in the mechanism by which cause is translated into effect.[1] The methodology asks only that the final result be predictable. The winning trump card is that there appears to be a closer statistical correlation between GNP and the money supply than there is between GNP and such expenditure components as government purchases and investment. To put it differently, monetary velocity is more stable and predictable than the expenditure multiplier.[2]

Crude empirical tests are often misleading in an environment of multiple causality, interaction, and feedback. There are good reasons for supposing that statistical correlation between money and GNP ought to be perfect even though there is no causality between changes in the money supply and GNP.

---

[1] See Milton Friedman, "The Methodology of Positive Economics," in his *Essays in Positive Economics,* The University of Chicago Press, Chicago, 1953.

[2] A number of empirical tests designed to verify this proposition are presented by Milton Friedman and David Meiselman, "The Relative Stability of Monetary Velocity and the Investment Multiplier in the United States, 1897–1958," in *Stabilization Policies: A Series of Research Studies Prepared for the Commission on Money and Credit,* Prentice-Hall, Inc., Englewood Cliffs, N.J., 1963.

Moreover, there are good reasons why changes in exogenous spending are poorly correlated with GNP even though they may be the primary driving force in expansion and contraction.

Consider first the relationship between the money supply and the growth of GNP. As GNP expands because, for example, of an increase in investment, interest rates tend to rise, and this causes banks to economize excess reserves so that the money supply expands. Statistically, GNP and money will be closely correlated. Worse still, if, as Friedman himself argues, the Fed's policy has historically been falsely directed at the target of maintaining stable interest rates, any shift in the *IS* curve will be matched by an equivalent shift in the *LM* curve. Thus the data will record a near-perfect correlation between the money supply and the level of GNP, and they will show no influence of the rate of interest on GNP.[1] Thus we have the very peculiar result that past perverse Fed policies of the kind Friedman deplores are used as evidence to support the view that it is only money that matters, when, in fact, it is the extreme passivity of the money supply in the past that provides the close statistical fit. Conversely, had the Fed pursued appropriate monetary policies, the historical correlation between money and GNP would quite probably have been extremely loose, and the data might have revealed the importance of the interest rate. The cart, here, is clearly before the horse.

Now consider the effect of an expansionary fiscal policy. The *IS* curve can shift for all sorts of reasons—changes in federal government purchases, taxes, and transfer payments; changes in state and local budgets; exogenous shifts in consumption, in investment, and in the trade balance. Usually, some or all these factors will be at work simultaneously. Thus during any arbitrary period of time there will be some variation between an increase in federal government purchases and the magnitude of the shift in the *IS* curve that occurs over the same period of time. However, the Fed, in pursuing a policy of stabilizing interest rates, makes this shift in *IS* correlate perfectly with changes in the money supply. It is then hardly surprising that statistical analysis should yield a much higher correlation between GNP and the supply of money than between GNP and the various "real" variables.

We have seen that expansion in the real sector (any shift in *IS*) tends to be accompanied by monetary expansion and that this tendency is accentuated by the propensity of the Fed to focus on stable interest rates as a target of policy. Fiscal expansion, in particular, tends to be accompanied by monetary expansion. In the past such joint expansion would have been likely to occur even if the Fed had not attempted to stabilize interest rates. One factor tending to bring about this result is the balance of payments effect under fixed exchange rates. Had monetary policy alone attempted to restore full employ-

---

[1] For a discussion of this point see Lyle E. Gramley, "Guidelines for Monetary Policy: The Case Against Simple Rules," paper delivered at the Financial Conference of the National Industrial Conference Board, New York, February 1969; reprinted in W. L. Smith and R. L. Teigen, *Readings in Money, National Income, and Stabilization Policy*, 2d ed., Richard D. Irwin, Inc., Homewood, Ill., 1970, pp. 488–495.

ment in the early 1960s, interest rates would have fallen, short-term capital would have flowed abroad, and our balance of payments position would have deteriorated. Our official foreign exchange holdings would have been depleted, and these sales of foreign exchange would have directly reduced the domestic money supply. Expansionary fiscal policy, on the other hand, raises interest rates, produces a capital inflow, and the money supply then expands as foreign exchange is accumulated. Restrictive monetary policy could undoubtedly have thwarted the expansionary effects of the fiscal actions taken during 1961–1965. However, it is inconceivable that the expansion of GNP could have been accomplished exclusively by monetary policy. The balance of payments alone would have ensured the failure of such an effort.

Second, even if the Fed has no particular desire to maintain stable interest rates, there nevertheless is considerable pressure in this direction from the United States Treasury. An expansionary fiscal policy implies that the amount of new federal debt which the Treasury must sell will increase. However, the sale of an increasing quantity of securities by the Treasury will tend to depress bond prices and raise interest rates. This, in turn, increases the difficulty of selling new treasury securities, and it raises the interest cost of such securities.[1] As a consequence, the Treasury has frequently put pressure on the Fed to purchase part of its bond offerings in an attempt to prevent the prices of government bonds from falling. If the Fed succumbs to this pressure, the money supply is increased. Here again, expansionary fiscal and expansionary monetary policies tend to go hand in hand.

In conclusion, monetarism has been an attempt at a counterrevolution to Keynesian ideas. Although it enjoyed a certain vogue in recent years, its star is on the wane. Few serious analysts believe that full employment can be maintained purely by appropriate Fed policy, with no attention paid to the budget and to such recurrent problems as fiscal drag. The ascendance of monetarism seems to us to have been due more to the fervor of the faithful than to its substantive theoretical and empirical foundations.

In completing this section we now turn to a brief consideration of another recent development in monetary thinking. This development casts a certain amount of doubt upon the ability of the Fed to exercise an adequate degree of influence over economic activity. It argues that the private sector of the financial system has become so adaptable and efficient at finding money substitutes that it can largely negate the effect of the Fed's attempts to control the money supply, interest rates, and economic activity. The names most

---

[1] When United States government securities reach maturity, the Treasury redeems them at their face value but then issues new securities to replace them. Such an operation is known as "refinancing." If a bond with a face value of $1,000 pays $50 per year in interest, the effective rate paid by the Treasury is 5 percent. However, if at the time of maturity interest rates have doubled, the Treasury can raise $1,000 only if it either offers a 10 percent yield on a new $1,000 bond or if it offers 5 percent and permits the value of the bond to drop by one-half. In the latter case it will have to sell twice as many bonds. Thus in either case the interest cost per dollar of borrowing doubles.

frequently associated with this development are Gurley and Shaw, and the British Radcliffe Committee.[1]

Economic development in the United States has been accompanied by a perennial search for money substitutes and for more efficient ways to use the existing money supply. Pay-as-you-go taxation, splitting the monthly paycheck into weekly installments, and charge accounts that permit concentration of bill paying at the time of income receipt, all reduce the demand for money because they help to synchronize receipts and expenditures. More recently the growth of credit cards has been a powerful money substitute.

Central to developments designed to make each dollar support more activities has been the growth of so-called financial intermediaries. Commercial banks are financial intermediaries that channel funds from net savers to those who desire to spend in excess of their current income. Commercial banks are not the only institutions that perform this intermediation role. An increasingly important place has been assumed by such nonbank intermediaries as saving and loan associations, life insurance companies, mutual savings banks, and pension funds. The function of intermediaries is to pool funds from small savers and to lend these funds to finance expenditures. In so doing they purchase I.O.U.s that usually are known as "primary securities." These primary securities include government securities, common and preferred stocks, mortgages, and consumer and other short-term debt. To obtain the funds, the intermediaries issue and sell "indirect securities" such as time deposits, saving and loan shares, and insurance policies. Thus the financial system brings net savers (lenders) and investors (borrowers) together by channeling funds from one to the other. The gain to borrowers from intermediation is that they can obtain a larger quantity of funds from an intermediary than they can from an individual saver, and they can borrow the funds for a longer period of time. Primary lenders, in turn, automatically have their risk diversified and by placing funds in a saving account or similar indirect security are not required to make a long-term sacrifice of their liquidity position. The profits of the intermediaries result from the fact that the yield on primary securities exceeds the interest they must pay on indirect securities.

The rapid growth of nonbank financial intermediaries has provided a pow-

---

[1] The principal references are J. G. Gurley, *Liquidity and Financial Institutions in the Postwar Economy*, Study Paper No. 14, U.S. Congress, Joint Economic Committee, 1960; J. G. Gurley and E. S. Shaw, "Financial Aspects of Economic Development," *American Economic Review*, 45:515–538, 1955; J. G. Gurley and E. S. Shaw, *Money in a Theory of Finance*, The Brookings Institution, Washington, 1960. The British counterpart to Gurley-Shaw thinking centers about the "Radcliffe Report." See Great Britain, Committee on the Workings of the Monetary System, *Report*, HMSO, London, 1959. For summary views see R. S. Sayers, "Monetary Thought and Monetary Policy in England," *Economic Journal*, 70:710–724, 1960; and J. G. Gurley, "The Radcliffe Report and Evidence," *American Economic Review*, 50:672–700, 1960. Valuable reviews of contemporary monetary thinking are innumerable. In our opinion two of the best are L. S. Ritter, "The Role of Money in Keynesian Theory," in Dean Carson, ed., *Banking and Monetary Studies*, Richard D. Irwin, Inc., Homewood, Ill., 1963, pp. 134–150; and H. G. Johnson, "Monetary Theory and Policy," *American Economic Review*, 52:335–384, 1962.

erful means of economizing money balances. Small savers have no need to hold money balances when they can readily convert such balances into interest-earning indirect securities which can be liquidated without difficulty whenever cash is needed. Thus the volume of transactions that a given money supply can support at a given level of interest rates depends not only upon the money supply but also upon the total liquidity of the economy. Financial intermediaries provide this liquidity when they issue indirect securities.

This circumstance is said to create difficulties for monetary policy. Abstracting from the effect on velocity of a change in interest rates, it has traditionally been thought that the frequency of turnover of the average dollar (its "velocity") could change only slowly as institutional payments practices change. However, the new view suggests that nonbank financial intermediaries have it in their power to expand liquidity quickly, thereby speeding up velocity on short notice. In some interpretations it is implied that financial intermediation increases the interest elasticity of the *LM* function, whereas other writers view the growth of money substitutes as causing the entire *LM* function to shift.[1]

Consider the difficulty of attempting to restrain inflation. If the Fed tightens credit by means of an open market sale, interest rates will tend to rise. Nonbank intermediaries as a group, finding the yields on primary securities rising, now raise the rates they are willing to pay on indirect securities. This increase encourages individual savers to shift from demand deposits into time deposits, saving and loan shares, and other indirect securities. Nonbank intermediaries are thus able to purchase additional primary assets which will finance further investment expenditure. The money will most likely then flow back into the commercial banks who will end with an unchanged quantity of deposits. Thus, if the individual savers who have traded demand deposits for indirect securities do not change their expenditures, there will be a net increase in total spending.

To put the argument differently, if the required ratio of transactions balances to income falls as income rises because of the availability of money substitutes, the rise in income will not lead to a proportional increase in the demand for money. Restricting the money supply may not then produce any substantial excess demand for money. Upward pressure on interest rates will be less than anticipated, spending will continue unchecked, and the monetary policy will have little or no effect on the inflation. A shift in the supply of money may, in this view, induce a corresponding shift in the demand for money, with the effect that the *LM* curve, after some initial perturbations, may settle down at or near its original position.

---

[1] The elasticity view is implied in the writings of W. L. Smith. See his "Financial Intermediaries and Monetary Control," *Quarterly Journal of Economics,* 73:533–553, 1959; and W. L. Smith, "The Effects of Financial Intermediaries on Velocity," in *Employment, Growth, and Price Levels: Staff Report,* U.S. Congress, Joint Economic Committee, Government Printing Office, Washington, pp. 351–356. On the other hand, Ritter, op. cit., suggests that it is the entire *LM* function that shifts.

This way of putting the matter seems extreme. The incentive to create money substitutes arises from upward pressure on interest rates. It would be a strange world in which the reactions are so extensive that ultimately interest rates would settle down at their original levels or even below these levels. Ruling out such cases, it seems clear that, despite intermediation, tight money will tend to raise interest rates and therefore tend to reduce spending. As long as this is the case, monetary policy can be effective. Intermediaries may increase the elasticity of the *LM* curve, or they may partially offset shifts in it, but as long as the elasticity is not infinite or the shift complete, there is no basis for claiming that monetary policy is powerless. Certainly, the more extreme view that changes in velocity promptly and completely offset changes in the money supply finds little support in evidence.[1]

On the other hand, it is undoubtedly true that the presence of large-scale intermediation makes the quantitative impact of monetary policy difficult to predict. A period of tight money induces new means of finding money substitutes. Such changes involve institutional adjustments that often become permanent, persisting beyond the period of tight money that induced them. Thus the monetary history of a particular attempt to control inflation may provide no clue whatever regarding the magnitude of monetary restriction required at some future time. The important contribution of the economists who have emphasized financial intermediation is their insistence that it is the total volume of liquidity in the economy that supports economic activity. Money is only a fraction of this total stock of finance. In emphasizing liquidity, these economists have clearly pointed up the inadequacy of a monetary policy which, as Friedman and others would have it conducted, is directed only at controlling the total quantity of money.

## 19–3
## THE INSTRUMENTS OF MONETARY POLICY

When the Federal Reserve System was established in 1913, it was supposed that its principal role would be that of a "lender of last resort." The Fed was empowered to supply reserves to the banking system by making loans to its member banks at interest. This lending process is known as "rediscounting" because it is secured by commercial paper already discounted by the member bank. The interest rate charged by the Fed on these loans is known as the "rediscount rate." By varying the rediscount rate, the Fed can influence the terms upon which credit is available. A high rediscount rate would discourage member bank borrowing and reduce the amount of bank lending. On the other hand, the ability to borrow from the Fed could, in a pinch, avert financial crisis.

In the 1920s the Fed discovered that purchases of securities on the open market had a powerful effect on money market conditions. In attempting to change the composition of its portfolio to include more earning assets, the

[1] See Smith, "The Effects of Financial Intermediaries on Velocity," op. cit.

Fed inadvertently discovered what has come to be its most important, powerful, and flexible tool.

In addition, the Fed is empowered, within limits set by Congress, to vary legal minimum reserve requirements. This power establishes the maximum amount of deposit creation that it is possible to effect with a given reserve base. In addition, the Fed from time to time receives authority to regulate credit selectively. For example, the Fed has been empowered to regulate the terms on which consumer installment loans may be made, while "Regulation Q" imposes ceilings on the interest that banks may pay on time deposits. Finally, the Fed resorts to exhortation and admonition in efforts to create the expectations and the financial climate it deems desirable. Thus, in summary, the Fed has at its disposal several policy instruments. It may make loans to member banks and may vary the rediscount rate charged. It may engage in the open market purchase and sale of securities, vary legal minimum reserve requirements, utilize selective credit controls, and, finally, exercise "moral suasion," which is the official term used to classify attempts to influence financial conditions by resort to what some have called "open-mouth policy."

The theory of economic policy teaches that there must be at least as many instruments as there are targets. Nevertheless there is danger that a multiplicity of instruments that are redundant, in the sense that they are all essentially directed to the same proximate target, may be less efficient than a single instrument. The multiplicity of instruments available to the Fed for varying the money supply has been attacked on several grounds. First, some instruments have critical technical deficiencies that make it desirable to accomplish a desired end by an alternative route. Second, it is possible to offset the intended effect of a policy if the various instruments have not been coordinated. An example of the latter is when an open market sale which is intended to lower bank reserves is offset by increased borrowing from the Fed. Another example is when the Fed accompanies open market sales by simultaneously reducing reserve requirements.

Rediscounting was an important instrument of the Fed's policy during the 1920s. However, the presence of excess reserves in the 1930s reduced member bank borrowing to negligible proportions. Although borrowing grew somewhat in the 1950s and 1960s, its quantitative importance has remained small in comparison with the 1920s. Nevertheless, rediscount policy has come under considerable fire from economists. Most knowledgeable monetary economists advocate some form of reform, while some would go so far as to abolish the privilege of member bank borrowing entirely.[1]

---

[1] Among the contributions to the literature are Friedman, *A Program for Monetary Stability,* op. cit; W. L. Smith, "The Instruments of General Monetary Control," *National Banking Review,* 1:47–76, 1963, reprinted in Smith and Teigen, op. cit., pp. 253–282; W. L. Smith, "The Discount Rate as a Credit-Control Weapon," *Journal of Political Economy,* 66:171–177, 1958; J. Tobin, "Towards Improving the Efficiency of the Monetary Mechanism," *Review of Economics and Statistics,* 42:276–279, 1960.

Rediscounting played a central role before it was realized that reserves could be supplied to the banking system by open market operations. However, once open market operations became a standard tool of monetary policy, the question arose as to whether rediscounting was not only redundant but perhaps harmful to the economy as well. The effect of the Fed's sales of securities could be offset by member bank borrowing from the Fed. To prevent this, the Fed would have to be clever enough to combine its restrictive open market policy with an appropriate increase in the rediscount rate. Thus the rediscounting privilege requires a degree of coordination between instruments that the Fed has not always been capable of effecting satisfactorily.

Worse still, changes in the rediscount rate are newsworthy and taken to be indicative of changes in the Fed's policy. Economists call such changes "announcement effects." They affect expectations regarding the course of the Fed's policy and the trend of economic activity. Unfortunately, changes in the rediscount rate frequently do not provide accurate signals. They tend, instead, to give signals that are erroneous and that could more easily and correctly be supplied by simple and candid announcements of policy intentions.

The destabilizing possibilities inherent in rediscount policy can be illustrated by reference to Figure 19–1. The continuous sine-like curve in the figure traces an imaginary path of short-term interest rates over a hypothetical business cycle. Interest rates tend to move up and down with the business cycle. A cyclical upswing raises credit demands, produces excess demand for money, and thereby causes interest rates to rise. Conversely, a decline in economic activity reduces credit demands, creates an excess supply of money, and causes interest rates to fall. Now imagine that the rediscount rate is at $d_0$ and that the rate is held at the same value as the upswing commences. Initially, the rediscount rate is above free market rates, so that this is essentially a tight money policy, it being less costly to borrow at market rates than at the Fed. At $t_1$ the fixed rediscount rate $d_0$ suddenly implies an expansionary policy since it has now become cheaper to borrow at the Fed than on competitive market terms. Nevertheless, this crucial turn in monetary policy is hardly ever recognized, and it has come about without the Fed's doing anything at all. Clearly, the fact that the Fed has not changed the rediscount rate does not mean it is pursuing a "neutral" monetary policy even though it might claim that this is the case.

Now let the expansion proceed to time $t_2$, and suppose the Fed decides it is now time to raise the rediscount rate to dampen the boom. If the rediscount rate is raised to $d_1$, the newspapers will hail this as a restrictive policy. But since $d_1$ is less than market rates, it is still cheaper to borrow at the Fed, so the situation has to be regarded as an expansionary monetary policy, even though it is less expansionary than previously.

Next we pass the upper turning point and reach time $t_3$. At this time the expansionary policy automatically becomes restrictive, but at a time when monetary policy ought to be eased in order to prevent the impending recession. Assume finally that the rediscount rate is then belatedly lowered to $d_2$. This reduction creates the final misleading signal that monetary policy is becoming expansionary when, in fact, it is only becoming less restrictive.

The foregoing example illustrates how very easily well-intentioned monetary policy may become destabilizing. Although the Fed may raise the rediscount rate in prosperity and lower it in recession, these changes are destabilizing unless they are of such a magnitude as to guarantee cheaper borrowing at the Fed than elsewhere during recession and more costly borrowing at the Fed than elsewhere during inflation. This would imply rediscount rates at $d_4$ and $d_3$, respectively. However, historically the pattern has often been more nearly in line with the $d_0$, $d_1$, $d_2$ pattern of the hypothetical example, and we must therefore conclude that rediscount policy may have helped to accentuate cyclical swings in economic activity.

What is to be done about this situation? Some economists have proposed that the rediscount rate be changed continuously to reflect free market rates. For example, the rates determined at the weekly treasury bill auction could automatically set the rediscount rate. At the very least this would prevent rediscount policy from having destabilizing announcement effects. On the other hand, such a policy would not eliminate the problem that borrowing from the Fed can be used to offset or to postpone the impact of open market operations. If banks are able to postpone contraction and expansion of their reserves through borrowing and repayment at the Fed, the lag between the initiation of monetary policy and its ultimate effect on the economy is lengthened, and this of course creates further danger of instability. Thus in the view of many economists the rediscounting privilege is an obsolete nuisance that ought to be abolished. Reserves can be supplied to the banking system by open market purchases, and individual banks that suffer a reserve shortage ought to be required to compete for funds on a free market.

Changes in legal minimum reserve requirements can have potentially powerful monetary effects. If the banking system is fully loaned up, a rise in reserve requirements which is not offset by borrowing at the Fed produces an immediate reserve deficiency, it forces banks to call in loans and sell securities, and it shrinks the supply of money and credit. Conversely, a reduction in reserve requirements may have the opposite effects although these are less certain since contraction can be forced while expansion can only be encouraged. Moreover, a reduction in reserve requirements supplies excess reserves without creating a corresponding liability on bank balance sheets. Consequently, a fall in reserve requirements may carry with it a powerful wealth effect.

A change in reserve requirements as an instrument of monetary policy is

**FIGURE 19–1**
Rediscount policy and the cyclical movement
of short-term interest rates

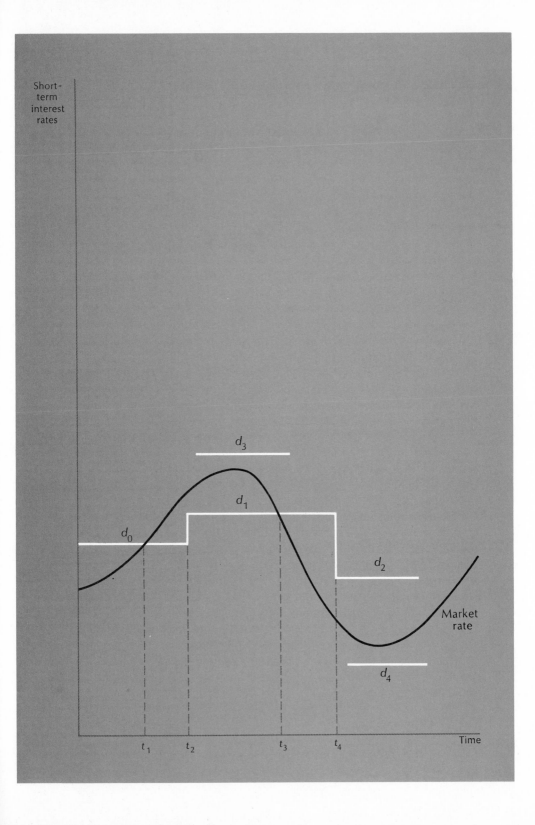

subject to many of the same defects as rediscount policy. Changes tend to be abrupt and newsworthy, and they tend therefore to produce potentially undesirable announcement effects. Although it might be possible to make minute day-to-day changes, such changes would be opposed by bankers. Finally, reserve requirement changes can, and have, been used to offset the intended effects of other instruments. For example, open market sales were used during the 1950s to reduce bank reserves, but reserve requirements were lowered several times, thereby replacing the excess reserves that were lost through open market policy.

Most economists now feel that there is little role for changing reserve requirements. A suitable requirement should be established and retained permanently. Reserves can be varied by other means if the aim is short-run stabilization, and open market purchases can provide for secular growth of the money supply.[1] Correct, rather than misleading, announcement of Fed policy and intentions can be effected by straightforward policy statements. Finally, most economists would like to see the imposition of uniform reserve requirements on all commercial banks. This would prevent the creation and destruction of money and credit merely as a result of shifts in deposits between banks with differing reserve requirements.

There is general agreement that open market policy is the single most useful instrument of the Fed's policy. The initiative in conducting open market operations is firmly in the hands of the Fed. In contrast, the effect of a change in the rediscount rate depends on the unpredictable response of commercial banks. Open market operations are flexible with respect to timing and magnitude. Since they are carried on continuously, they do not create announcement effects that accompany changes in the rediscount rate or in reserve requirements.

Another aspect of open market policy should perhaps be mentioned. The Fed may deal in government securities of different maturities. It may sell short-term securities, and it may simultaneously purchase long-term securities. Such operations raise the yields on short-term securities relative to the yields on long-term securities. Thus by altering the relative supplies of securities of different maturities, the Fed is able to affect the so-called term structure of interest rates. In the early 1960s it was desirable to stimulate investment. However, lower interest rates would have worsened the balance of payments problem. As a consequence the Fed attempted to "twist" the yield structure by selling short-term securities in the hope that this would attract short-term capital from abroad, and at the same time it purchased long-term securities in the hope that a reduction in the cost of long-term credit would stimulate investment.

The instruments we have been discussing thus far are known as "general" instruments of monetary control in contrast to such "selective" instruments as

---

[1] One advantage of providing for monetary growth through open market purchases is that the volume of federal debt held by the public will decline, and the Treasury's interest costs will therefore be reduced.

consumer credit control. The impact of general monetary controls falls indiscriminately and unevenly on the various sectors of the economy. Some sectors, especially where expenditures are heavily financed by borrowing, are more sharply affected by monetary policy than are other sectors. It may therefore happen that a restrictive monetary policy designed to slow inflation may have little effect on the sector whose rapid expansion caused the inflation. Its main impact, then, may be to create unemployment in other sectors. The economy experienced a case of this sort during the 1955–1957 period. Automobile demand increased sharply in 1955, gross auto product rising 45 percent over its 1954 level. The effect of this was to set the accelerator in motion and to induce a capital goods boom. Thus between 1955 and 1956 business fixed investment increased almost 15 percent even though automobile demand now receded by about 20 percent. The capital goods boom brought with it a sharp increase in capital goods prices of 5.6 percent in 1956, and this generated an overall rate of price increase of 3.4 percent as measured by the GNP deflator.

In this environment the Fed attempted to control the inflation by a sharp restriction of money and credit. However, the resultant increase in interest rate appears to have had very little effect in dampening the capital goods boom which was generating the inflation. But, at the same time, the tight monetary and credit conditions were having an impact on consumer credit, and this, in turn, had a depressing effect on automobile demand. Consequently, the policy was not slowing inflation; it was, instead, creating unemployment in an industry in which sales had already fallen and in which there was no danger that inflation would be generated.

Some economists feel that the only way to avoid a repetition of episodes such as that of 1955–1957 is through selective credit controls and other measures designed to affect the level of activity in specific sectors of the economy.[1] While it is not clear how a poll of economists would come out on the issue of selective credit controls, it is clear that selective controls have often created more trouble than they are worth. This is especially the case where our old bugaboo interest rate fixing is involved.

Much of the instability of the home-building industry is directly attributable to well-meaning but misplaced attempts to assist veterans, small savers, and other worthy persons to own homes. Fixing interest rates on FHA-insured and VA-guaranteed mortgages means that funds for such mortgages are available when uncontrolled interest rates are below the fixed level. However, when other rates rise to where it is profitable to move funds elsewhere, the mortgages suddenly become unavailable, and the construction industry is dealt a very abrupt and violent blow.

The credit "crunch" of 1966 serves as a prime example of the uneven im-

---

[1] For a description of the 1955–1957 period together with a favorable appraisal of selective credit controls, see W. L. Smith, "Possibilities of Making Monetary Policy More Effective," in *Employment, Growth, and Price Levels: Staff Report,* U.S. Congress, Joint Economic Committee, Government Printing Office, Washington, 1959, pp. 349–495.

pact of monetary policy and of the way this may be accentuated rather than reduced by selective controls. Mortgage lending involves a long-term commitment at a fixed interest rate. Institutions such as saving and loan associations are obliged by law to confine their lending to mortgages. Thus, during periods of rising interest rates they cannot raise their earnings as rapidly as commercial banks whose portfolios are subject to much more rapid turnover. The saving and loan institutions cannot therefore increase the interest that they, in turn, pay to obtain funds. This circumstance, in itself, accounts for a great deal of the variability in the supply of mortgage financing and therefore in the instability of the home-building industry. When credit gets tight and interest rates rise, there is a tendency for the yield on primary securities to rise faster than the yield on indirect securities. Holders of time deposits and saving and loan shares now tend to sell such assets (withdraw their deposits) and convert them into bonds, common stocks, and the like. The net savers in the economy move into a position of greater direct contact with primary borrowers, while a smaller fraction of saving is channeled through financial intermediaries. This process, which is known as financial "disintermediation," tends to occur during periods of tight money. Moreover, it is accentuated by regulations that attempt to fix the yields on indirect securities. Obviously, those industries that are heavily dependent on intermediaries for credit are the industries that will tend to be the most susceptible to influence by monetary policy.

The home-building industry is clearly the most vulnerable. Its troubles during the tight money period of 1966 may have been accentuated by the Fed's well-intentioned Regulation Q which sets ceilings on the interest that may be paid on time deposits. As part of its effort to offset the effects of the rising defense spending that began in 1965, the Fed increased the rate that it permitted commercial banks to pay on time deposits. Since commercial banks were able to increase earnings more rapidly than the saving and loan associations with their long-term mortgage commitments, the commercial banks raised the rates they paid on time deposits, whereas saving and loan associations were unable to do this. The saving and loan institutions were therefore unable to compete for deposits, and a drastic shrinkage in the supply of mortgage finance followed.

The effects of the credit crunch of 1966 were staggering. Lending by saving and loan associations dropped about 70 percent between the fourth quarter of 1965 and the fourth quarter of 1966. During the same period expenditures for residential construction dropped $5.9 billion, a percentage decline of 22 percent in a single year. The business of controlling interest rates by law and by administrative fiat, instead of by free market forces, seems to have been responsible for much of this violent instability.

The philosophy of fairness that underlies well-intentioned attempts to fix interest rates administratively fails to take into account the fact that attempts to fix prices are generally bought at the cost of increasing the amplitude of fluctuations in quantity. In the case of a specific effort such as Regulation Q, price fixing continues even though the original rationale for it has long since passed. The purpose of placing a ceiling on the amount of interest that banks may pay on time deposits is to prevent banks from competing with each other for deposits in the hope that this would protect depositors against the risk of bank failure. However, with the advent of federal deposit insurance in the early 1930s, this rationale has long since become irrelevant. Clearly, the business of fixing interest rates, selectively or generally, does a great deal of harm and very little good.

The uneven impact of monetary policy was again illustrated by events after 1966. The boom that got under way in mid-1967 and reached its peak in early 1968 was sustained for an additional year by abnormally high business investment spending. Much of the inflation of the period was being generated in the capital goods sector. The Fed's attempt to slow the capital goods boom by means of another period of tight money failed miserably as it had in 1966. Investment spending appears to have been hardly affected at all, while the brunt of the impact once more fell on housing, state and local governments, and small business. Finally, and as noted in the preceding chapter, the seeds of the recession of 1974–1975 were sown by a new monetary crunch in late 1973 that inflicted even worse havoc on the home-building industry than the crunch of 1966.

One way to influence the sectoral impact of monetary policy might be to impose reserve requirements that vary according to the composition of a bank's loan portfolio. For example, a bank might be required to hold one dollar in reserve for every dollar loaned for the purchase of a capital good, whereas the reserve requirement for a mortgage loan might amount to no more than 10 percent.

Variable reserve requirements would certainly create a hassle. The Fed would be charged with favoritism, and it would be a hopeless task to police the uses to which borrowed funds are put. Nevertheless, it is an intriguing idea that deserves consideration. It is certainly likely to appeal to those who are concerned with sharpening the sectoral impact of monetary policy.

## 19–4
### INDEPENDENCE VERSUS RESPONSIBILITY, RULES VERSUS AUTHORITY

The Federal Reserve System was created by Congress as an agency separate from the three major branches of the federal government. Thus the Fed is an independent agency that, in theory, is free from political influence. Primary responsibility for Fed policy is in the hands of a seven-man board of governors who serve for overlapping terms of fourteen years. Although appointed by the President, board members cannot be dismissed, and they are not responsible to the President in the same way as the heads of the departments within the executive branch of the government. In principle, the Fed is free to make monetary policy as it pleases.

Considerable controversy has arisen over the issue of whether the Fed should be independent or whether monetary policy ought to be subject to the same political forces and processes that determine other economic policies.

Conservatives maintain that politicians invariably want to spend more than they tax, so that an independent monetary authority is needed to prevent inflation and to maintain the international competitiveness of the economy. A less extreme view suggests that politics and sound economic policies simply do not mix. There are, indeed, many who in the interest of efficiency would prefer to see both fiscal and monetary policy in the hands of nonpolitical bodies of experts. Others take the view that such attitudes are authoritarian and that the potential inefficiency of competing checks and balances is one of the prices that must be paid for democracy.

There are many reasons for regarding an independent monetary authority as undesirable. Perhaps the most important reason is to eliminate the bias which causes the Fed to focus on proximate targets. The Fed has very little control over many of the factors that determine the overall economic climate. Because of an inability to control or influence such variables as the federal budget, the Fed has exhibited a tendency to draw back from such primary targets as full employment, rapid growth, and price stability in favor of such proximate targets as interest rates and the money supply. The Fed can control these variables; perhaps this explains why it treats them as targets.

If the Fed were a partner in the overall economic strategy of the federal government, it would be forced to concern itself with the overall needs of the economy and with the overall objectives of policy. Some critics believe that the only way to establish such partnerships is to change the legal status of the Fed. They would make the Fed an agency of the executive branch with a status similar to that of the Treasury or of the Office of Management and Budget, in the hope that such a change would have the dual advantage of integrating monetary policy with overall economic policy and of removing monetary policy from a position where it can be blamed for other policy failures.

Other critics, especially the Chicago monetarist school, feel that reforms designed to make the monetary authority more politically responsible do not get at the basic problem. The issue, in the view of these economists, is not a question of political responsibility; it is, rather, a question of whether discretionary monetary policy can do a better job than a set of fixed rules. Professor Friedman, for example, argues that the lag between the initiation of a monetary policy and the time at which the policy is effective is so long and so variable that discretionary policy stands a strong chance of being destabilizing.[1] Friedman therefore proposes to increase the money supply by a fixed percent

[1] Milton Friedman, "The Demand for Money: Some Theoretical and Empirical Results," *Journal of Political Economy*, 67:327–351, 1959; "The Effect of a Full-Employment Policy on Economic Stability: A Formal Analysis," in *Essays in Positive Economics*, The University of Chicago Press, Chicago, 1953, pp. 117–132; and "The Lag in the Effect of Monetary Policy," *Journal of Political Economy*, 69:447–466, 1961. See also M. Bronfenbrenner, "Statistical Tests of Rival Monetary Rules," *Journal of Political Economy*, 69:1–14, 1961; J. M. Culbertson, "Friedman on the Lag in the Effect of Monetary Policy," *Journal of Political Economy*, 68:617–621, 1960; T. Mayer, "The Inflexibility of Monetary Policy," *Review of Economics and Statistics*, 40:358–374, 1958; and W. H. White, "The Flexibility of Anticyclical Monetary Policy," *Review of Economics and Statistics*, 43:142–147, 1961.

per year. There should, moveover, be no deviation from this rule under any circumstance. The alleged advantage is that this would provide the monetary basis for long-term growth; it would eliminate the potential destabilizing effects of discretionary policy; and it would create an environment of confidence within which smooth growth could proceed without danger of monetary disruption. Obviously, if such a rule were adopted, it would make little difference whether the Fed continued in its present role or whether it became an executive department. Its functions, in either case, would be purely mechanical.

Many of the critics of a rigid rule for monetary policy acknowledge that adherence to such a rule in the past would probably have produced better results than were actually attained by the Fed's discretionary policies. Nevertheless, these critics argue that it would be unwise to put monetary policy into a self-imposed straitjacket. In the first place, improvements in analysis, forecasting, and economic sophistication may make it possible to rely on discretionary policy in the future. In the second place, the existence of large quantities of money substitutes means that orderly growth of the money supply may not imply orderly growth of the total supply of finance. Third, one might as well recognize that a rule that seems oppressive will be violated the moment it seems important to do so.

The main trouble with rules is that they impose rigidity upon the behavior of instrument variables at the risk of the destabilization of target variables, whereas what is wanted is flexibility of the instruments in the interest of stability of the targets. The money supply is an instrument that affects the relevant targets of economic activity: employment, output, and prices. Nevertheless, the money supply is treated as a target by monetarists just as fixed interest rates have been treated as a target by the Fed.

The fixed rate of monetary growth target is an improvement over a fixed interest rate target, albeit not much of one. If we abstract from economic growth, the quantity of money target implies a fixed money supply. The fixed interest rate target would imply shifting the LM curve to restore the original rate of interest following a disturbance. Finally, an income stabilization target would shift LM by whatever amount was needed to restore income to its original level.

Now consider Figure 19–2(a). Full-employment equilibrium prevails at $Y^*$ and $i^*$. Assume that some bad news raises liquidity preference and that this causes the LM curve to shift to $LM_1$. If the Fed observes the quantity-of-money rule, it will do nothing, so that income drops to $Y_1$. On the other hand, if it adopts either a fixed interest rate or an income stabilization target, it will expand the money supply, thereby shifting the LM curve back to $LM_0$, and in the process restore full employment. In this case the quantity-of-money rule is the worst rule for policy makers to follow.

Imagine instead that the IS curve, as depicted in Figure 19–2(b), shifts to the left because of an exogenous decline in some component of spending. A quantity-of-money policy would do nothing, and income would therefore

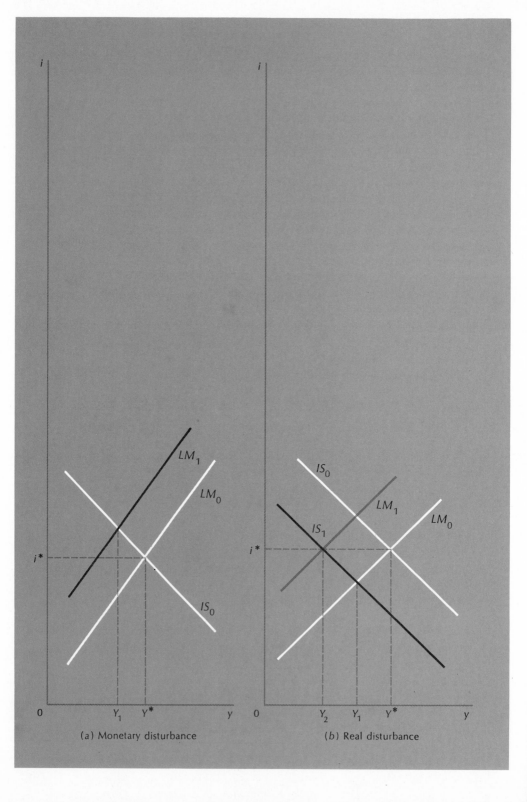

(a) Monetary disturbance

(b) Real disturbance

shrink to $Y_1$. A fixed interest rate monetary policy would exacerbate the situation by moving $LM$ to $LM_1$, thereby causing income to drop all the way to $Y_2$. Monetary policy oriented to full employment, finally, would expand the money supply in an attempt to make $LM$ cut $IS_1$ at $Y^*$.

There are a large number of different circumstances that could be illustrated. In general, rules directed at proximate targets such as the rate of interest and the quantity of money are distinctly second best, and they may even widen the amplitude of cyclical fluctuations. When the source of the original disturbance is real in origin, the fixed money supply target is less harmful than the fixed interest rate target. When the disturbance is monetary in origin, the fixed interest rate target is superior. In practice, the money supply target appears superior to the fixed interest rate target in two respects. First, it is potentially less destabilizing. Second, the preponderance of disturbances that cause income to change seems to originate in the real sector of the economy. No rule, however, is a substitute for appropriate policy designed to maintain output at the full-employment level.

Attempts to bring the Fed off its pedestal and to make it accept responsibility for national economic objectives have not been successful. Under a recent law, the Chairman of the Fed must report to Congress on a quarterly basis and set forth his objectives for monetary policy. Chairman Arthur Burns' response to this has consisted largely of deliberate attempts to confuse the issues and to befuddle the Congress. It has become accepted to define the money stock, as we have defined it in this book, as $M_1$. When time deposits at commercial banks are added, the result is called $M_2$. Chairman Burns created also $M_3$, $M_4$, $M_5$, and $M_6$, claiming that it is all very complicated and uncontrollable and that it is therefore not reasonable to ask the Fed to spell out its targets for all these monetary indicators.

Worse still, in early 1975, and with unemployment close to 9 percent, Chairman Burns was threatening to kill off the expansionary effects of fiscal policies by maintaining tight reins on the money supply. His preferred position on the Phillips curve was clearly different from that of the Congress. As a consequence of this failure there could be no policy coordination or coherent national economic policy. Tight money would thwart the employment objectives of fiscal policy; but since it does this by inhibiting investment, it would also interfere with growth objectives. Appropriate policy mix is not possible as long as there is disagreement over fundamental aims.

The new posture of the Fed that monetary policy cannot be held accountable because it is too difficult to control monetary aggregates is not supported by evidence or by experience elsewhere. In recent years economic performance in West Germany has been considerably better than in other industrial

**FIGURE 19–2**
Illustration of alternative monetary rules
(all values in real terms)

countries including the United States. One reason for this has been the intelligent use of monetary policy in a simple and comprehensible way. The German authorities control what they know they can control, namely high-powered money, and they pay no attention to interest rates or other irrelevancies. Moreover, at the beginning of the year they announce what their target rate of growth of the money stock will be. In this way business and labor will both know what to expect and will be able to plan accordingly. For example, given the target rate of monetary growth, labor will know at the outset what rate of wage increase is compatible with the prevention of increases in unemployment.

In contrast to this, our Fed continues to resort to secrecy, obfuscation, and stratagems that maximize confusion and uncertainty. In doing so, it comes very close to admitting inadvertently that it is incompetent to play the role that central banks were long ago invented to perform.

## 19–5
## MONETARY POLICY AND THE NATIONAL DEBT

One of the most important facts we have stressed is that a fully managed compensatory fiscal policy—one that sets its sights on the objectives of full employment, price stability, and rapid growth—is incompatible with the notion that budgetary balance should also be viewed as a target of economic policy. To go into problems of debt management in detail would carry us far afield. Our purpose here is to note the somewhat paradoxical circumstance that while much federal debt has resulted from attempts to combat past recessions, the existence of such past debt may complicate the problem of combating future recession. The difficulty is especially acute with respect to the operation of monetary policy. This, indeed, is why we feel it appropriate to complete this chapter with a brief discussion of the problems associated with national debt.

The national debt, which stood at a level of nearly $500 billion at the end of 1974, is viewed by fiscal conservatives as an unmitigated horror which betrays our puritan heritage.[1] Projected increases in the debt, even under Republican administrations, are regarded as living proof that the government of the United States has become the captive of sinister and subversive forces bent on sapping our national life of its vital bodily fluids. It is said that future generations are mortgaged by the follies of the past by an amount that now exceeds all of $2,000 per person.

It is often not pointed out that these follies, in part, represent efforts to combat depression, that they were incurred as the consequence of wars, and that they also represent the consequences of raising capital to make productive public investments in roads, schools, and other areas where private en-

---

[1] This $500 billion is technically called the "total gross public debt" and includes nonmarketable issues (e.g., savings bonds) and special issues held only by various United States government agencies.

terprise cannot be counted upon to perform adequately. If the future is burdened by the follies of the past, it would have to be shown that the failure of the past to "live within its means" has caused the potential per capita consumption of the future to be impaired. Finally, public investments are harmful only if the alternative private use of the resources would have yielded a greater marginal social benefit. However, since nearly all non-war-induced federal debt is recession-induced, the resources which the government mobilizes would otherwise have been idle (i.e., their rate of return in private use is zero), and their mobilization by the government could therefore not possibly be harmful either to the present or to the future.

Public debt and private debt are fundamentally different although this fact is avidly denied by those who make budget balancing a fetish. When individuals and corporations go into debt, they receive in return a claim over real resources that they otherwise would not have had. When the time for repayment comes, real resources must be transferred back to the creditor. Hence if productive use is not made of the borrowed resources, the individual will not be able to make repayment, and he or she will go bankrupt. The nation as a whole, however, obviously cannot borrow resources from itself in one year and pay them back in some subsequent year. Thus the idea that present debt creation comes out of the hide of future generations is pure nonsense. If some government of the future were to undertake to repay the debt, it would raise taxes and use the resultant proceeds to purchase the outstanding debt. The net effect would be to redistribute wealth. There would, however, be no net change in the real productive resources that are available to the economy and therefore in its consumption potential. It should be remembered that for all taxpayers who feel they are "mortgaged" by national debt, there are also bondholders who find themselves wealthier by virtue of their ownership of such debt.

The national debt must be serviced. This means that each year taxes must be collected in order to pay the interest that accrues to bondholders. If federal debt is mainly held by the higher-income groups while taxes are imposed upon the public at large, growth of debt might imply that income is being continually more regressively redistributed. Thus the national debt may impose a "redistributive burden" upon the economy. Following an analysis by Domar, we may derive a tax rate which when applied to taxable income just suffices to pay the interest on the debt.[1] If the value of the debt is $D$ and the service charge on each dollar of debt is $i$, then the total service charge must be $iD$. Taxable income is the sum of net national product plus the interest income from the debt. The tax rate is the ratio of debt service to taxable income. Consequently, we may write the tax rate or "burden" of the debt as

$$\gamma = \frac{iD}{iD + Y}$$

[1] E. D. Domar, "The Burden of the Debt and the National Income," *American Economic Review*, 34:798–827, 1944.

If we divide numerator and denominator by $D$ we get

$$\gamma = \frac{i}{i + Y/D}$$

which shows that the tax burden depends, not on the absolute size of the debt, but rather upon the ratio of income to debt. The higher this ratio, the lower will be the burden. Notice that the tax rate can never exceed 100 percent. Those who get panicky about the debt often forget that the interest on the debt is itself taxable income. Consequently, it would not be possible for the debt to be so large that there is insufficient income available for debt service.

In the United States the ratio of debt to income, and therefore the tax burden of the debt, has fallen from the all-time high reached in 1945. Although deficits have exceeded surpluses and the debt has therefore grown, it has not grown as rapidly as GNP and the ratio of debt to GNP has therefore declined.

The presence of a sizable national debt may in some respects complicate stabilization policy. In particular, the effective pursuit of anti-inflationary monetary policy may conflict with the attempts of the Treasury to manage the debt. During the inflationary era of the 1940s and the early 1950s no subject occupied economists more intensively than the problem of debt management and monetary policy. Today the issues that were raised at that time are less pressing. There is, however, the possibility that the future will bring about a similar era and that we may then look back to our past experience with profit.

On balance, the debt probably has an inflationary impact in that it constitutes a stock of liquid wealth for its owners, and liquid asset holdings are positively correlated with consumption expenditures. One of the fears held by economists during the late 1940s was that the public might at a moment's notice attempt to convert its large stock of liquid assets into physical assets, thereby creating inflationary pressure. Without a large accumulation of debt, it is doubtful whether consumers would have been able to increase their spending by as much as they did at the start of the Korean war.

There may also be stabilizing benefits to be derived from the existence of the national debt. When prices and incomes shrink, the Pigou effect is strengthened by the existence of a large stock of government obligations. When the price level rises, it is possible that the reverse effect may take place. These effects may be reversed by price expectations that are likely in an inflationary period to lead to attempted conversion of liquid into physical assets, while the reverse can be expected to occur during a period of falling prices. Both of these destabilizing movements are facilitated by the existence of public debt.

One of the more unfortunate aspects of having to live with the national debt was that an inflationary bias became built into policy during the 1940s. There was an ever-present temptation to lower interest rates below the natural rate in order to make debt management easier.[1] As we have suggested before, this can be accomplished by forcing the Fed to peg the market rate of interest by buying up such quantities of bonds as are necessary to maintain their prices. The effect of such an operation is inflationary and therefore serves the added purpose of reducing the real value of the government debt.

This last point is worthy of special emphasis because it was rarely mentioned during the days, prior to 1951, when the Secretary of the Treasury proclaimed himself the champion of an "orderly" bond market and the defender of widows, orphans, educational institutions, and other holders of the federal debt. Whether widows and orphans are protected by pegging operations is open to doubt. At any one time there will be some natural rate of interest that equates the demand for goods and services with the full-employment supply. At full employment, any attempt to lower the market rate below the natural rate by monetary expansion will produce increases in the price level. Bondholders thus have two unpleasant alternatives: (1) policy makers may allow the market rate to rise to the natural rate, in which case bondholders take an immediate capital loss; (2) policy makers may peg the rate, so that bondholders take their capital loss in the form of a reduction in the real value of their bonds caused by a rising price level. In practice, the latter alternative is likely to be chosen since it creates the illusion of easing the day-to-day problem of Treasury financing and because wealth holders are apt to be more conscious of a quick and sharp capital loss than of the long-term attrition that results from a rising price level. Although there is no net benefit for bondholders inherent in this process, except in the short run, the pegged interest rate gospel was preached with a high degree of success during the years following World War II.

The pegging policy of the postwar years went considerably beyond such bond purchases by the Fed as were required to maintain stable interest rates. On several occasions the Fed lowered member bank reserve requirements. Such action during an inflationary period might have been taken as prima facie evidence of insanity had it not been for the pressing need to find a resting place for federal debt. A reduction in reserve requirements makes it possible for banks to substitute part of the public debt in place of the required reserves otherwise held idle in their reserve accounts. While this policy of subsidizing commercial banks helped to place the debt, it also presented banks with "secondary reserves" that they could convert into other forms of earning assets by simply allowing their short-term government obligations to mature. A reduction in reserve requirements at a time of full employment is

---

[1] Recalling the discussion of Chap 6, if a long-term bond issued for a par value of $1,000 pays 5 percent interest on the par value, a rise in the market rate of interest to 10 percent will reduce the market value of the bond to approximately $500. At the maturity date the Treasury must pay the par value on the old issue, and if it refinances (i.e., issues new long-term bonds to replace the old ones), it must offer 10 percent per $1,000 if it is to sell the issue. The service charge therefore doubles from $50 to $100 per $1,000 borrowed.

obviously inflationary and can have no justification in terms of economic stability.

What can be done to reduce the conflict of interest between credit control and Treasury financing?[1] Most of the suggestions that were made were in the form of gimmicks designed either to isolate portions of the debt from market fluctuations or to lengthen the average maturity of the debt so as to reduce the number of refunding operations in which the Treasury would have to engage. Proposals of the former sort involved recommendations that the commercial banking system be forced to hold a certain portion of required reserves in the form of short-term government debt and that part of the debt be converted into nonmarketable bonds such as the familiar Series E bond, which could only be sold back to the Treasury. The proposal to freeze part of the debt in the hands of the banks was critized on the ground that it would not affect the marginal holdings that banks switch into alternative uses when the opportunity arises. However, if such a freeze had involved an addition to required reserves rather than a mere substitution of debt for required money reserves, the policy would clearly have had a deflationary impact and would have served to quarantine a portion of the debt.

The proposal to convert marketable debt into nonmarketable bonds of the Series E variety appears to have some merit. But if interest rates were to rise significantly under the impact of a Fed policy of restraint, these bonds would be sold back to the Treasury, and a drain of cash from the Treasury would take place. The tight money policy would thus be thwarted, and the Treasury would lose funds at the very time when added borrowing would prove to be most expensive. It is, moreover, unlikely that large investors in government obligations could be persuaded to hold nonmarketable bonds without an extremely high yield inducement. This is not to say that some progress might not be made with nonmarketable debt. It is possible, for example, to program a redemption schedule that puts a high penalty on early redemption and makes it more and more attractive to hold the bonds as maturity is approached. The fact remains, however, that as long as the debt is marketable at the Treasury, a rise in interest rates will lead to redemption and a drain in the Treasury's cash at a time when its borrowing prospects from the public are the poorest. The Treasury may then be driven to borrow from the Fed and thereby negate the Fed's attempts at credit restraint.

The second type of proposal called for a concerted attempt on the part of the Treasury to lengthen the maturity of the debt. This was recommended in the hope that the number of times the debt had to be refinanced would be reduced and that more time would be left between funding operations during which credit restraint might be applied. The ideal situation would be achieved if all the debt were funded into consols since this would remove the necessity, once and for all, of refinancing maturing debt. On the other hand,

---

[1] R. V. Roosa, "Integrating Debt Management and Open Market Operations," *American Economic Review* (Supplement), 42:214–235, 1952, provides a comprehensive survey of the issues.

there is some advantage in debt of varying maturities. Long-term debt presumably competes with other long-term uses of funds, whereas short-term debt competes with other short-term uses. Thus some economists argue that during recession the debt should be funded into short-term debt in the hope that the long-term funds thus released will be driven into capital formation. During an inflationary period, on the other hand, the debt should be lengthened so that holding long-term debt becomes an attractive alternative to capital formation.[1]

If the great society is ever to become the fair society it will have to do something to prevent small savers from being "ripped off" whenever there is inflation. These small savers do not have the time or the expertise to invest carefully, and the size of the transactions they are able to make are too small, and the transactions costs too large, to enable them to do much with their savings other than to put them into time deposits. Half the time, however, the nominal interest which is earned, and which is fixed by federal regulation and state usury laws, is so meager that the small saver ends up with a negative real return.

Quite possible the most important change in our approach to national debt would be to convert a portion of it into purchasing-power bonds of small denomination. This would enable the small saver to protect himself from inflation, and it would go a long way toward eliminating the inequities that inflation causes. With this kind of competition, saving and loan institutions could no longer pay negative real interest, and it would therefore be essential to combine the issuance of such purchasing-power bonds with an end to the regulation of interest rates through nonmarket forces.

[1] For an excellent discussion of principles of debt management, see W. E. Laird, "The Changing Views on Debt Management," *Quarterly Review of Economics and Business,* 3:7–17, 1963; reprinted in Smith and Teigen, op. cit., pp. 508–518.

# MATHEMATICAL APPENDIXES

These appendixes are presented for the benefit of readers who have an interest in the quantification and mathematical analysis of economic theories, and who may find it interesting and useful to have the verbal and diagrammatic exposition of the text supplemented by mathematical methods. The attempt here is not to provide a comprehensive mathematical backup to the text, but rather to provide illustrations of the kind of analysis that readers will encounter if they continue their study of economic theory at the advanced level.

## APPENDIX TO CHAPTER 5: ALGEBRAIC ANALYSIS OF TAX AND EXPENDITURE POLICIES

### 1 Lump-Sum Taxation

In linear form the basic model from which the conclusions of Chapter 5 were derived is

$$Y = C + I + G \tag{5-1}$$

$$C = a + bY_d = a + b(Y - T) \tag{5-2}$$

where the levels of intended investment and government purchases are assumed to be autonomous. Combining (5-1) and (5-2) and solving for $Y$ yields

$$Y = \frac{a + I + G - bT}{1 - b} \tag{5-3}$$

as the equilibrium level of income. When Eq. (5–3) is differentiated with respect to $I$, $G$, and $T$, respectively, we obtain the multipliers

$$\frac{dY}{dI} = \frac{1}{1-b} \qquad \frac{dY}{dG} = \frac{1}{1-b} \qquad \frac{dY}{dT} = \frac{-b}{1-b} \tag{5–4}$$

When the government purchase and tax multipliers are added together, the result is the balanced budget multiplier,

$$\frac{dY}{dG} + \frac{dY}{dT} = \frac{1}{1-b} - \frac{b}{1-b} = \frac{1-b}{1-b} = 1$$

## 2 Income Taxation

Assume that taxes are a linear function of the level of income, and let the tax function be

$$T = u + tY \tag{5–5}$$

where $T$ is the level of net tax yield and $t$ is the marginal tax rate. Substitution of the tax function into Eq. (5–2) gives the consumption function

$$C = a - bu + b(1 - t)Y \tag{5–6}$$

where the slope of the function $b(1 - t)$ is the marginal propensity to consume real NNP ($Y$) and $b$ is the marginal propensity to consume disposable income. When Eq. (5–6) is substituted into Eq. (5–1) and we solve for $Y$, we have

$$Y = \frac{a - bu + I + G}{1 - b(1 - t)} \tag{5–7}$$

The multipliers for $I$ and $G$ are obtained by differentiating Eq. (5–7) with respect to these variables. The result is

$$\frac{dY}{dI} = \frac{dY}{dG} = \frac{1}{1 - b(1 - t)} \tag{5–8}$$

and since $1 - b(1 - t) > 1 - b$, we see immediately that income taxation reduces the value of the multiplier and therefore provides the system with "automatic" or "built-in" stability.

The effects of a change in tax legislation depend upon whether the entire tax structure is shifted, as when the value of $u$ is changed, or whether the changes are at the margin and therefore involve a change in $t$. In the former case,

$$\frac{dY}{du} = \frac{-b}{1 - b(1 - t)} \tag{5–9}$$

and in the latter case,

$$\frac{dY}{dt} = \frac{-bY}{1 - b(1 - t)} \tag{5–10}$$

From Eq. (5–10) we see that the effect of a change in $t$ depends upon the value of $Y$ prior to the change in the marginal tax rate. The lower the level of income, the less the effect a given change in $t$ will have on tax yield and disposable income, and therefore on consumption and on the equilibrium level of income.

When the government purchase multiplier and the multiplier that results from a shift in the tax structure are added together, the result is

$$\frac{dY}{dG} + \frac{dY}{du} = \frac{1 - b}{1 - b(1 - t)} \tag{5–11}$$

which does not equal unity and suggests that the balanced budget multiplier does not hold under income taxation. However, this conclusion is incorrect. From the tax function it can be seen that

$$dT = du + t(dY) \tag{5–12}$$

and this implies that if there is some induced income change that results from the change in the tax structure, the shift in the structure will differ from the change in total tax yield. To put it differently: $du$ is the change in tax yield that would occur if the level of income did not change.

Let us now see if we can find some $du$ (shift in the tax function) that will satisfy the unit multiplier condition. From the tax function we have $dT = du + t(dY)$. However, if government purchases rise by the same amount as tax yield, then $dG = dT$, so that

$$du = dG - t(dY) \tag{5–13}$$

Differentiating Eq. (5–7) with respect to both $G$ and $u$ gives

$$dY = \frac{-b(du) + dG}{1 - b(1 - t)}$$

from which it follows that upon substitution of Eq. (5–13)

$$dY = dG = dT$$

We conclude that the balanced budget multiplier holds provided that the tax change is defined, not as the shift in the tax structure or change in the tax rate at a given level of income, but rather as the change in tax yield taking induced effects into account. This means that it is always possible to find some change in the tax structure or in the marginal tax rate that will yield additional revenue equal to a change in government purchases and that, if this budget-balancing change is effected, the result will be to change the level of income by an amount equal to the change in the balanced budget.

Readers may now wish to amuse themselves by using this model to illustrate the danger of pursuing a balanced budget policy. Let investment fall by $dI$. Income, as a consequence, falls by

$$dY = \frac{dI}{1 - b(1 - t)}$$

From the tax function we see that tax yield falls by

$$dT = t(dY) = \frac{t(dI)}{1 - b(1 - t)}$$

Now assume that government purchases are lowered by exactly enough to balance the budget, and bear in mind that any reduction in $G$ will further lower $Y$ and therefore $T$. You should find that the required change in $G$ is

$$dG = \frac{t(dI)}{(1 - b)(1 - t)}$$

which of course is negative. Finally, you should be able to show that the total income change due to the drop in investment and the drop in government purchases is

$$dY = \left[\frac{dI}{1 - b(1 - t)}\right]\left[1 + \frac{t}{(1 - b)(1 - t)}\right]$$

which, because the bracketed term on the right is greater than one, implies that income falls by more than would have been the case had fiscal policy done nothing at all.

## APPENDIX TO CHAPTER 9: EFFECTIVENESS OF MONETARY AND FISCAL POLICY

The question of the relative effectiveness of monetary and fiscal policy in changing the level of income readily lends itself to mathematical analysis. At the outset we ignore taxes and we assume that fiscal policy consists of variations in the level of government purchases. In contrast with the explicit linear model of the preceding appendix, we use the present opportunity to show how multiplier analysis can be conducted with an implicit model.

Product market equilibrium obtains when intended investment plus government purchases equals saving. Accordingly, we write

$$I(i) + G = Y - C(Y)$$

which for convenience may be rewritten as

$$G = Y - C(Y) - I(i) \qquad (9-1)$$

Monetary equilibrium is given by

$$m = kY + L(i) \qquad (9-2)$$

The effect of an increase in the money supply can be observed by differentiating the equations totally with respect to $m$. This yields

$$0 = (1 - C_y)\left(\frac{dY}{dm}\right) - I_i\left(\frac{di}{dm}\right) \qquad (9-3)$$

$$1 = k\left(\frac{dY}{dm}\right) + L_i\left(\frac{di}{dm}\right) \qquad (9-4)$$

where $C_y$ is the partial derivative of consumption with respect to income (the marginal propensity to consume); $I_i$ is the partial derivative of investment with respect to the interest rate (the reciprocal of the slope of the investment demand schedule); and $L_i$ is the partial derivative of the speculative demand for money with respect to the interest rate (the reciprocal of the slope for the speculative demand function). Solving simultaneously we get

$$\frac{dY}{dm} = \frac{I_i}{L_i(1 - C_y) + kI_i}$$

and

$$\frac{di}{dm} = \frac{(1 - C_y)}{L_i(1 - C_y) + kI_i}$$

In the Keynesian case, $L_i$ is infinite, so that

$$\frac{dY}{dm} = 0$$

and

$$\frac{di}{dm} = 0$$

In the classical case $L_i = 0$, so that

$$\frac{dY}{dm} = \frac{1}{k}$$

and

$$\frac{di}{dm} = \frac{1 - C_y}{kI_i}$$

The change in the rate of interest therefore depends on the slope of the saving function, the transactions demand for money function, and the investment demand schedule.

The effect of an increase in government purchases can be observed by differentiating Eqs. (9–1) and (9–2) totally with respect to $G$. This gives

$$1 = (1 - C_y)\left(\frac{dY}{dG}\right) - I_i\left(\frac{di}{dG}\right) \tag{9–5}$$

$$0 = k\left(\frac{dY}{dG}\right) + L_i\left(\frac{di}{dG}\right) \tag{9–6}$$

so that

$$\frac{dY}{dG} = \frac{L_i}{L_i(1 - C_y) + kI_i}$$

and

$$\frac{di}{dG} = \frac{-k}{L_i(1 - C_y) + kI_i}$$

In the Keynesian case $L_i$ is infinite so that

$$\frac{dY}{dG} = \frac{L_i}{L_i(1 - C_y) + kI_i} = \frac{1}{(1 - C_y) + (kI_i/L_i)} = \frac{1}{(1 - C_y)}$$

i.e., the ratio of the change in income to the change in $G$ equals one divided by the marginal propensity to save. Again, since $L_i$ is infinite,

$$\frac{di}{dG} = 0$$

In the classical case $L_i = 0$, so that

$$\frac{dY}{dG} = 0$$

and

$$\frac{di}{dG} = \frac{-1}{I_i}$$

which implies that the change in the interest rate depends on the slope of the investment demand schedule. As was seen in the text, the rate of interest must rise by enough to crowd out investment in an amount equal to the change in government purchases.

In the last section of Chapter 9 we developed the consequences of a possible link between the budget deficit and the money supply. We leave it to interested readers to develop the mathematical analysis of such a link. One might begin by introducing a tax function $T = T(Y)$ and might then use the equation

$$m_t - m_{t-1} = a(G - T)$$

where $m_t - m_{t-1}$ is the change in money supply between two arbitrarily defined periods of time, to link a budget deficit to changes in the money supply. Readers should attempt to show that equilibrium income can exist only when $G = T$ and that the long-run (steady-state) multiplier must equal the reciprocal of the marginal tax rate.

## APPENDIX TO CHAPTER 10:
## AGGREGATE DEMAND AND SUPPLY

It is much easier to work with an explicit model. Therefore let

$$Y = C + I + G \tag{10-1}$$

$$C = \bar{C} + b(Y - T) \qquad 0 < b < 1 \tag{10-2}$$

$$I = \bar{I} + ai \qquad\qquad a < 0 \tag{10-3}$$

$$\frac{M}{p} = \bar{m} + kY + ci \qquad k > 0 \qquad c < 0 \tag{10-4}$$

Equations (10–1) to (10–3) may be combined to yield the *IS* curve. Treating *Y* as the dependent variable we can write

$$Y = \frac{\overline{C} - bT + G + \overline{I}}{1 - b} + \frac{ai}{1 - b} \qquad (10-5)$$

which can be seen to yield the standard multiplier results, provided that $i$ is held constant.

Equation (10-4) is the *LM* curve which equates the demand for money with the supply of money. Upon rearranging this equation to solve for $i$, we get

$$i = \frac{M}{cp} - \frac{\overline{m}}{c} - \frac{k}{c} Y$$

This expression can now be used to eliminate $i$ from Eq. (10-5). The result is the aggregate demand function,

$$Y_d = \frac{1}{\Delta} \left( \overline{I} - \frac{a\overline{m}}{c} + \overline{C} + G - bT + \frac{aM}{c} \frac{1}{p} \right) \qquad (10-6)$$

where

$$\Delta = 1 - b + \frac{ak}{c} > 0$$

and where it is evident that, with fixed $G$, $T$, and $M$, the aggregate demand for output is a decreasing function of the price level.

When we differentiate Eq. (10-6) with respect to $p$ we obtain

$$\frac{dy}{dp} = \frac{1}{\Delta} \left( -\frac{aM}{cp^2} \right) < 0 \qquad (10-7)$$

which shows that the aggregate demand curve must have a negative slope. However, in the liquidity trap case, $c \to -\infty$, and if investment is unresponsive to changes in the interest rate, $a = 0$. In either case the slope of the aggregate demand function as defined by Eq. (10-7) is zero. Consequently, the aggregate demand function is vertical when output is plotted on the horizontal axis and the price level is plotted on the vertical axis as was done in the text.

If the price level is held fixed, it is evident from Eq. (10-6) that aggregate demand will increase when $G$ and $M$ increase and when $T$ decreases.

In order to derive the aggregate supply function it is necessary to add to the model a production function and a profit-maximizing condition. An explicit form of short-run production function that captures the notion of positive but diminishing returns is

$$Y = uN^\lambda \qquad 0 < \lambda < 1 \qquad (10-8)$$

where $\lambda$ is the elasticity of output with respect to employment and is assumed to be a positive fraction. Since

$$\frac{\partial Y}{\partial N} = \lambda u N^{\lambda-1} = \lambda \frac{Y}{N}$$

the marginal product of labor is positive but diminishing with respect to increases in $N$. The profit-maximizing condition is that the real wage equals the marginal product of labor. Accordingly, we have

$$\frac{w}{p} = \lambda u N^{\lambda-1} = \lambda \frac{Y}{N} \tag{10-9}$$

To derive the aggregate supply function we first rearrange Eq. (10–9) to solve for $N$. This gives

$$N = \lambda Y \left(\frac{p}{w}\right)$$

which we then insert into the production function in order to eliminate $N$. This gives the function

$$Y_s = \alpha p^\theta w^{-\theta} = \alpha \left(\frac{w}{p}\right)^{-\theta} \tag{10-10}$$

where $\alpha$ is a combination of constants and $\theta = \lambda/(1 - \lambda)$. This formulation expresses aggregate supply as a function of the real wage rate and implies that aggregate supply will increase when the real wage rate falls.

Differentiating Eq. (10–10) with respect to $p$ and $w$ gives

$$dY_s = \theta Y_s \left(\frac{dp}{p} - \frac{dw}{w}\right) \tag{10-11}$$

which shows that aggregate supply will increase if the proportionate rise in the price level exceeds the proportionate rise in the money wage rate. In the classical case labor market equilibrium necessitates that any proportionate change in the money wage, $dw/w$, be matched by an exactly equal proportionate change in the price level, $dp/p$. As a result, Eq. (10–11) implies that $dY_s = 0$, and the aggregate supply curve is therefore vertical when plotted with $Y$ on the horizontal axis and $p$ on the vertical axis, as in the text.

In the Keynesian case the money wage rate remains fixed as the price level changes so that the slope of the aggregate supply curve is

$$\frac{dY_s}{dp} = \frac{\theta Y_s}{p} = \frac{\lambda}{1 - \lambda} \frac{Y_s}{p} > 0 \tag{10-12}$$

Since the slope of the aggregate supply function is positive, a rise in the price level increases aggregate supply in the Keynesian case. Equation (10–12) also shows that the elasticity of the aggregate supply curve is directly related to the elasticity of output with respect to labor input, and that the elasticity of aggregate output with respect to the price level increases as the latter increases. The higher the value of $\lambda$, the less important is the problem of diminishing returns to labor as a barrier to the expansion of output.

## APPENDIX TO CHAPTER 11:
## THE STANDARD TWO-COUNTRY FOREIGN
## TRADE MULTIPLIER

Consider two countries I and II, and let the respective equilibrium income levels be

$$Y_1 = C_1 + I_1 + G_1 + (Z_2 - Z_1)$$
$$Y_2 = C_2 + I_2 + G_2 + (Z_1 - Z_2)$$

(11–1)

where $Z_1$ and $Z_2$ are the imports of the respective countries. Let the consumption and import functions be

$$C_1 = a_1 + b_1 Y_1 \qquad C_2 = a_2 + b_2 Y_2$$
$$Z_1 = u_1 + v_1 Y_1 \qquad Z_2 = u_2 + v_2 Y_2$$

When we substitute these functions into Eqs. (11–1), we obtain the simultaneous linear equations

$$(1 - b_1 + v_1)Y_1 \qquad - v_2 Y_2 = I_1 + G_1 + a_1 + u_2 - u_1 = E_1$$
$$-v_1 Y_1 + (1 - b_2 + v_2)Y_2 = I_2 + G_2 + a_2 + u_1 - u_2 = E_2$$

(11–2)

The right-hand terms represent all the exogenous components: investment, government purchases, and the consumption and import intercepts. For convenience, we consolidate all these into the terms $E_1$ and $E_2$. Thus a change in any exogenous component, such as $dG_1$, is reflected in an equivalent $dE_1$. Notice that, if country I's import function shifts up, we would have $du_1 = -dE_1 = dE_2$ because in this event exogenous expenditures in both countries would be affected simultaneously.

Applying Cramer's rule to these simultaneous equations we get the equilibrium solutions

$$Y_1 = \frac{1 - b_2 + v_2}{\Delta} E_1 \qquad + \frac{v_2}{\Delta} E_2$$
$$Y_2 = \qquad \frac{v_1}{\Delta} E_1 + \frac{1 - b_1 + v_1}{\Delta} E_2$$

(11–3)

where

$$\Delta = (1 - b_1 + v_1)(1 - b_2 + v_2) - v_1 v_2$$

(11–4)

If we assume that all marginal propensities to save are no less than zero, $\Delta$ will clearly be positive. Notice also that in the form of Eqs. (11–3) the equilibrium solutions are functions of the level of exogenous spending in the two countries. The coefficients of the equations are the multipliers. Upon differentiating the two equations with respect to $E_1$ we can calculate the effect on the income levels of the two countries. The results are

$$\frac{dY_1}{dE_1} = \frac{1 - b_2 + v_2}{(1 - b_1 + v_1)(1 - b_2 + v_2) - v_1 v_2}$$

(11–5)

$$\frac{dY_2}{dE_1} = \frac{v_1}{(1 - b_1 + v_1)(1 - b_2 + v_2) - v_1 v_2}$$

The second of these expressions is the effect on country II's income of an increase in exogenous spending in country I. As the term in the numerator makes clear, such an effect occurs because a rise in I's income causes it to increase its imports from II.

The first of the expressions in Eqs. (11–5) is usually termed the "foreign trade multiplier." It shows the effect on I's own income level of a domestic increase in exogenous expenditures, taking foreign repercussions into account.

If country II's marginal propensity to import is zero, the foreign trade multiplier reduces to

$$\frac{1}{1 - b_1 + v_1} \tag{11–6}$$

which the reader will recognize as the "small-country" multiplier of Chapter 11. If country I's marginal propensity to import is zero as well, the economies function in isolation, and we then have the familiar "isolated-country" multiplier

$$\frac{1}{1 - b_1} \tag{11–7}$$

We can arrange the foreign trade multiplier as

$$\frac{dY_1}{dE_1} = \frac{1}{(1 - b_1 + v_1) - v_1 v_2/(1 - b_2 + v_2)}$$

which shows that the denominator must be less than $1 - b_1 + v_1$, and it therefore follows that the foreign trade multiplier can be no smaller than the small-country multiplier. Similarly, we can rearrange the expression as

$$\frac{dY_1}{dE_1} = \frac{1}{(1 - b_1) + v_1(1 - b_2)/(1 - b_2 + v_2)}$$

which shows that the denominator is greater than $1 - b_1$, so that the foreign trade multiplier can be no larger than the isolated-country multiplier. In combination, then, these results imply

$$\frac{1}{1 - b_1 + v_1} \leqslant \frac{dY_1}{dE_1} \leqslant \frac{1}{1 - b_1}$$

As shown above, the minimum value of the foreign trade multiplier is the small-country multiplier. Since consumption includes imports, the marginal propensity to import can be no greater than the marginal propensity to consume. In this extreme case the small-country multiplier formula gives a multiplier value of one. Consequently, we have proved that a $1 increase in aggregate demand must raise domestic income by at least $1.

We now consider the combined effect of the change in exogenous expenditures on both economies. Adding together the multipliers we get

$$\frac{dY_1 + dY_2}{dE_1} = \frac{1 - b_2 + v_2 + v_1}{(1 - b_1 + v_1)(1 - b_2 + v_2) - v_1 v_2}$$

If the marginal propensities to consume in the two countries are equal, $b_1 = b_2$, and this expression reduces to

$$\frac{dY_1 + dY_2}{dE_1} = \frac{1}{1 - b}$$

which shows that the total effect on world income equals the ordinary multiplier and that in this case different values of the marginal import propensities do not affect the result.

It is time now to examine the effect of the changes in exogenous spending on the level of net exports of the respective countries. For country I the level of net exports is

$$B_1 = Z_2 - Z_1$$

Consequently,

$$\frac{dB_1}{dE_1} = \frac{dZ_2}{dE_1} - \frac{dZ_1}{dE_1} \tag{11-8}$$

However, from the import functions we know that

$$\frac{dZ_1}{dE_1} = v_1 \frac{dY_1}{dE_1} \qquad \frac{dZ_2}{dE_1} = v_2 \frac{dY_2}{dE_1}$$

so that, on using these results together with the multiplier equations, Eqs. (11–5), we obtain the change in country I's net exports:

$$\frac{dB_1}{dE_1} = \frac{-v_1(1 - b_2)}{\Delta} < 0$$

Since this expression is negative, it is evident that country I's net exports decline, while country II's increase.

Notice that if country II's marginal propensity to save is zero, the offset on the trade balance will be complete. Moreover, as can be seen from inspecting Eqs. (11–5), country I's foreign trade multiplier will reduce to the isolated-country multiplier. On the other hand, if I's marginal propensity to save is zero, we have

$$\frac{dY_1}{dE_1} = \frac{1 - b_2 + v_2}{v_1(1 - b_2)}$$

$$\frac{dY_2}{dE_1} = \frac{1}{1 - b_2}$$

$$\frac{dB_1}{dE_1} = -1$$

Next, let us assume that there is a shift in tastes which causes the intercept of country II's import function to shift up. Differentiating Eqs. (11–3) with respect to $u_2$ gives

$$dY_1 = \frac{1 - b_2 + v_2}{\Delta} du_2 + \frac{v_2}{\Delta} (-du_2)$$

$$dY_2 = \frac{v_1}{\Delta} du_2 + \frac{1 - b_1 + v_1}{\Delta} (-du_2)$$

which simplify to

$$\frac{dY_1}{du_2} = \frac{1 - b_2}{\Delta} \qquad \frac{dY_2}{du_2} = \frac{-(1 - b_1)}{\Delta} \qquad\qquad (11\text{–}9)$$

The shift in tastes has the effect of raising income in country I and lowering it in country II. If the marginal propensities to save are the same, the income gain of I exactly equals II's loss, and there will be no change in total world income.

The change in I's net exports is given by

$$\frac{dB_1}{du_2} = \frac{dZ_2}{du_2} - \frac{dZ_1}{du_2} \qquad\qquad (11\text{–}10)$$

and from the import functions we have

$$\frac{dZ_2}{du_2} = 1 + v_2 \frac{dY_2}{du_2} \qquad \frac{dZ_1}{du_2} = v_1 \frac{dY_1}{du_2}$$

Substituting these results into Eq. (11–10) and using Eqs. (11–9) gives

$$\frac{dB_1}{du_2} = \frac{(1 - b_1)(1 - b_2)}{\Delta} > 0$$

It is evident from this result that country I's net exports increase as a result of the transfer of expenditures and that II's net exports decline. However, if either country has a marginal propensity to save of zero, the induced changes completely offset the exogenous shift. If $1 - b_1 = 0$, we get

$$\frac{dY_1}{du_2} = \frac{1}{v_1} \qquad \frac{dY_2}{du_2} = 0$$

Hence country II's income does not change, while I's rises by exactly enough to increase imports by as much as the initial exogenous increase in exports.

If $1 - b_2 = 0$, we get

$$\frac{dY_1}{du_2} = 0 \qquad \frac{dY_2}{du_2} = \frac{-1}{v_2}$$

so that in this case country I's income fails to change, while II's falls by exactly enough to reduce imports by the amount of the initial exogenous increase.

Our analysis in this appendix is restricted to a two-country world. However, multicountry models can easily be constructed and analyzed in similar fashion.[1] As it happens, the propositions that emerge from the two-country model are barely changed by such complications. Interested readers should attempt to construct such a multicountry model. They should be able to show that for any country an increase in exogenous expenditures that results from internally generated demand will tend to raise income in all countries, and it will cause the country's net exports to decline. On the other hand, when the increase in demand is externally generated, it will tend to raise income while it raises net exports. It can also be proved that the small-country and the isolated-country multipliers serve as lower and upper bounds, respectively, for the foreign trade multiplier. And, finally, it can be shown that if all countries have equal marginal propensities to consume, the total change in world income that results from an increase in exogenous spending will equal the simple multiplier.

## APPENDIX TO CHAPTER 12:
## STABILITY ANALYSIS

Stability analysis employs a large number of extremely useful mathematical concepts and techniques. Consequently, this appendix should be of particular interest to those readers who wish to note how a wide range of mathematical topics can be applied to a problem of economic analysis. The first example of this appendix utilizes the concept of a differential equation and its solution, and the concept of Taylor's expansion. The second example utilizes the idea of a matrix and its inverse, a vector, and a characteristic equation.

The static model that underlies the analysis of Chapter 12 consists of the two equations

$$I(i,Y) = Y - C(Y) \tag{12-1}$$

$$m = L(i,Y) \tag{12-2}$$

It will be useful for future reference to know the equations for the slopes of these functions. Differentiation with respect to $i$ and $Y$ gives

$$\left(\frac{di}{dY}\right)_{IS} = \frac{1 - C_y - I_y}{I_i} \tag{12-3}$$

$$\left(\frac{di}{dY}\right)_{LM} = \frac{-L_y}{L_i} \tag{12-4}$$

All the symbols except $I_y$, the marginal propensity to invest, are familiar. We assume that $I_y > 0$, although beyond this we know very little about it. Since $L_i < 0$ and $L_y > 0$, the slope of the $LM$ function is definitely positive. Since $I_i < 0$, the slope of $IS$ will be negative if $(1 - C_y) > I_y$, that is, if the marginal propensity to save is greater than the marginal propensity to invest, and it will be positive if the reverse is the case.

[1] For examples of such multicountry models the reader is urged to consult L. A. Metzler, "A Multiple-Region Theory of Income and Trade," *Econometrica*, 18:329–354, 1950; and J. S. Chipman, "The Multi-Sector Multiplier," *Econometrica*, 18:355–373, 1950.

If we increase the money supply, we obtain the familiar set of simultaneous linear equations

$$0 = (1 - C_y - I_y)\left(\frac{dY}{dm}\right) - I_i\left(\frac{di}{dm}\right)$$

$$1 = L_y\left(\frac{dY}{dm}\right) + L_i\left(\frac{di}{dm}\right)$$

From these equations it follows that

$$\frac{dY}{dm} = \frac{\begin{vmatrix} 0 & -I_i \\ 1 & L_i \end{vmatrix}}{\Delta} = \frac{I_i}{\Delta}$$

and

$$\frac{di}{dm} = \frac{\begin{vmatrix} (1 - C_y - I_y) & 0 \\ L_y & 1 \end{vmatrix}}{\Delta} = \frac{(1 - C_y - I_y)}{\Delta}$$

where

$$\Delta = \begin{vmatrix} (1 - C_y - I_y) & -I_i \\ L_y & L_i \end{vmatrix} = L_i(1 - C_y - I_y) + I_iL_y \tag{12-5}$$

Observe that the sign of $\Delta$ is ambiguous. $L_i < 0$, but $(1 - C_y - I_y)$ may be either positive or negative, depending upon whether the marginal propensity to invest is greater or less than the marginal propensity to save. Consequently, we cannot tell whether the increase in the money supply will raise or lower the level of income and the rate of interest. Notice also that if we had retained our assumption of Part 2 that investment is not a function of the level of income, $I_y = 0$, we would have

$$\Delta' = L_i(1 - C_y) + I_iL_y \tag{12-6}$$

which is definitely negative. Thus an increase in the money supply would unambiguously raise the level of income and lower the rate of interest. But when $I_y > 0$, our comparative static analysis no longer gives unambiguous results, especially since we know very little about the value of $I_y$.

In this situation dynamic analysis can help us out. Let us assume, as we did in the text, that the rate of change of income is equal to the difference between intended investment and saving and that money market adjustments are instantaneous. This permits us to write the dynamic model

$$\frac{dY}{dt} = I(i,Y) + C(Y) - Y \tag{12-7}$$

$$0 = L(i,Y) - m \tag{12-8}$$

where $dY/dt$ is the rate of change of income.

To make further headway, we need to find linear approximations to these equations. What we can do is to assume that in the neighborhood of equilibrium the functions are linear. Accordingly, we apply Taylor's expansion and retain only linear terms. Equations (12–7) and (12–8) are therefore rewritten as

$$\frac{dY}{dt} = -(1 - C_y - I_y)(Y - \overline{Y}) + I_i(i - \overline{i})$$ (12–9)

$$0 = L_y(Y - \overline{Y}) + L_i(i - \overline{i})$$ (12–10)

where $Y - \overline{Y}$ and $i - \overline{i}$ are the deviations of income and the rate of interest from the equilibrium values $\overline{Y}$ and $\overline{i}$, respectively.

By substituting Eq. (12–10) into (12–9), we can reduce Eq. (12–9) to a linear first-order differential equation in $Y$. Such an equation has a solution of the form

$$Y = \overline{Y} + ae^{qt}$$ (12–11)

where $a$ and $q$ are constants and $e$ is the base of the natural logarithmic system. If the term $ae^{qt}$ is to disappear and $Y$ is to return to $\overline{Y}$, the root $q$ must be negative.

By differentiating Eq. (12–11) with respect to time, we obtain

$$\frac{dY}{dt} = q(Y - \overline{Y})$$ (12–12)

Using this expression to replace $dY/dt$ in Eq. (12–9) allows us to rewrite Eqs. (12–9) and (12–10) as

$$0 = -(1 - C_y - I_y + q)(Y - \overline{Y}) + I_i(i - \overline{i})$$ (12–13)

$$0 = L_y(Y - \overline{Y}) + L_i(i - \overline{i})$$ (12–14)

If these equations are to be valid for all values of the variables, the determinant formed by the coefficients must be zero. Accordingly,

$$0 = \begin{vmatrix} -(1 - C_y - I_y + q) & I_i \\ L_y & L_i \end{vmatrix} = [L_i(1 - C_y - I_y) + I_iL_y] + L_iq$$

Now observe that the term in square brackets is nothing other than $\Delta$. Hence

$$\Delta + L_iq = 0$$

or

$$q = \frac{-\Delta}{L_i}$$

Since stability, i.e., a return of $Y$ to $\overline{Y}$ after a disturbance, requires that $q < 0$ and since we know definitely that $L_i < 0$, it follows that $\Delta$ must be negative.

Since we now know definitely that $\Delta$ must be negative if the system is stable, the logical step is to examine the properties of $\Delta$ and see what the stability condition implies. We know that

$$\Delta = L_i(1 - C_y - I_y) + I_iL_y < 0$$ (12–15)

This expression can easily be rearranged to read

$$\frac{(1 - C_y - I_y)}{I_i} + \frac{L_y}{L_i} < 0$$

From Eqs. (12–3) and (12–4) it is apparent that this is equivalent to

$$\left(\frac{di}{dY}\right)_{IS} - \left(\frac{di}{dY}\right)_{LM} < 0$$

In other words, the slope of the *IS* curve plus the slope of the *LM* curve with its sign changed must be negative. Recalling the three cases of the text, the first case, in which *IS* had a negative slope, clearly meets the stability condition. *IS* has a negative slope and *LM* has a positive slope. When we add the slope of the *IS* curve to the slope of the *LM* curve with its sign changed, the sum must be negative.

In the second case *IS* had a positive slope, but we still found the equilibrium to be stable. According to our condition for stability, this would imply that the positive value of the slope of *IS* must be absolutely less than the value of the slope of the *LM* curve. If we check back again to Figure 12–3, we can see that this is indeed the case.

In the third case the slope of the *IS* curve was greater than the slope of the *LM* curve. We found this situation to be unstable, a result that is confirmed by the mathematical analysis. In this case the sum of the slope of the *IS* curve and the slope of the *LM* curve with its sign changed will be positive. This means that $\Delta$ is positive; $q$ will therefore also be positive; and the term $ae^{qt}$ of Eq. (12–11) will grow progressively larger. The static equilibrium values $\bar{Y}$ and $\bar{i}$ are therefore irrelevant. Although the system may lodge at this point for a time, any disturbance will make the variables of the system deviate progressively from the equilibrium levels.

In summary: Stability analysis makes it possible to identify cases in which the results of comparative static analysis are erroneous. The present analysis, for example, has shown that if an increase in the money supply changes income at all, the change in income must be positive. This conclusion could not have been derived from comparative static analysis, and it is therefore evident that an examination of the underlying dynamics of the system is an important step which the careful analyst must take.

Readers who are satisfied to get some idea of what stability analysis is about and what it accomplishes may feel free to skip the remainder of this appendix. However, if they wish to probe the subject a bit more deeply and consider another example, they are invited to read on. The additional mathematics we will need for our next example involves the concepts of a matrix and its inverse, a vector, and a characteristic equation.

Let us consider the two-country foreign trade multiplier model which was discussed in the appendix to Chapter 11. There we simply assumed that the denominator in the multiplier formula, namely

$$\Delta = (1 - b_1 + v_1)(1 - b_2 + v_2) - v_1 v_2$$

was positive. Stability analysis will prove that this must be the case.

The usual assumption that economists make in stability analysis is that the rate of income change is proportional to the difference between expenditure and output. Using the two-country symbols of the appendix to Chapter 11, this implies

$$\frac{dY_1}{dt} = \lambda_1 [C_1 + I_1 + G_1 + (Z_2 - Z_1) - Y_1]$$

$$\frac{dY_2}{dt} = \lambda_2 [C_2 + I_2 + G_2 + (Z_1 - Z_2) - Y_2]$$

(12–16)

where the $\lambda$'s are positive "reaction coefficients" that allow for differences in the speed of adjustment of the income levels in the two countries.

When we make substitutions using the consumption and import functions of the appendix to Chapter 11 and when we consolidate the exogenous expenditure terms into the $E_1$ and $E_2$ terms of that appendix, we get the dynamic counterpart of the static equations of that appendix, namely

$$\frac{dY_1}{dt} = \lambda_1 [(b_1 - v_1)Y_1 + v_2 Y_2 + E_1 - Y_1]$$

$$\frac{dY_2}{dt} = \lambda_2 [v_1 Y_1 + (b_2 - v_2)Y_2 + E_2 - Y_2]$$

We can now put this into a form identical to the form of the dynamic Keynesian model considered above by replacing the income levels by the sum of their equilibrium levels and their displacements from equilibrium. In other words let $Y_1 = \overline{Y}_1 + (Y_1 - \overline{Y}_1)$ and $Y_2 = \overline{Y}_2 + (Y_2 - \overline{Y}_2)$, where $\overline{Y}_1$ and $\overline{Y}_2$ are the respective equilibrium levels; and substitute these definitions into the dynamic equations. For country I the result is

$$\frac{dY_1}{dt} = \lambda_1 [(b_1 - v_1)(Y_1 - \overline{Y}_1) + v_2(Y_2 - \overline{Y}_2) - (Y_1 - \overline{Y}_1)]$$
$$+ \lambda_1 [(b_1 - v_1)\overline{Y}_1 + v_2 \overline{Y}_2 + E_2 - \overline{Y}_1]$$

Although we did not put bars over the variables to indicate equilibrium values in the appendix to Chapter 11, it is obvious that in equilibrium, expenditures equal income, so that the term

$$[(b_1 - v_1)\overline{Y}_1 + v_2 \overline{Y}_2 + E_2 - \overline{Y}_1]$$

equals zero. As a result our dynamic equations reduce to the "homogeneous" form

$$\frac{dY_1}{dt} = \lambda_1 [(b_1 - v_1)(Y_1 - \overline{Y}_1) + v_2(Y_2 - \overline{Y}_2) - (Y_1 - \overline{Y}_1)]$$

$$\frac{dY_2}{dt} = \lambda_2[v_1(Y_1 - \overline{Y}_1) + (b_2 - v_2)(Y_2 - \overline{Y}_2) - (Y_2 - \overline{Y}_2)]$$

The variables are now expressed as deviations from their equilibrium values, and it is in this form that we can now conduct our analysis of the stability of equilibrium.

As before, we assume solutions of the form

$$Y_1 = \overline{Y}_1 + e^{qt} \qquad Y_2 = \overline{Y}_2 + e^{qt}$$

so that

$$\frac{dY_1}{dt} = q(Y_1 - \overline{Y}_1) \qquad \frac{dY_2}{dt} = q(Y_2 - \overline{Y}_2)$$

Substituting these results into Eqs. (12–16) and rearranging terms, we get

$$[q + \lambda_1(1 - b_1 + v_1)](Y_1 - \overline{Y}_1) - \lambda_1 v_2(Y_2 - \overline{Y}_2) = 0$$

$$-\lambda_2 v_1(Y_1 - \overline{Y}_1) + [q + \lambda_2(1 - b_2 + v_2)](Y_2 - \overline{Y}_2) = 0$$

In matrix form this set of simultaneous equations could be written

$$\begin{bmatrix} q + \lambda_1(1 - b_1 + v_1) & -\lambda_1 v_2 \\ -\lambda_2 v_1 & q + \lambda_2(1 - b_2 + v_2) \end{bmatrix} \begin{bmatrix} Y_1 - \overline{Y}_1 \\ Y_2 - \overline{Y}_2 \end{bmatrix} = 0$$

where the $2 \times 2$ matrix on the left is known as the "characteristic matrix," and the $2 \times 1$ vector to the right is known as the "characteristic vector." In compact matrix notation we could write

$$\mathbf{BY} = 0$$

where $\mathbf{B}$ is the characteristic matrix, and $\mathbf{Y}$ is the characteristic vector. If this matrix equation is to hold for all values of the displacements of the actual income levels from their equilibrium values, the characteristic matrix cannot have an inverse. If it did have an inverse, it would then follow that

$$\mathbf{B}^{-1}\mathbf{BY} = 0$$

so that

$$\mathbf{Y} = 0$$

This result, of course, is trivial since it implies that the equation holds only when all income levels are in equilibrium. As a consequence of this, the characteristic matrix must be "singular," and this means that it does not have an inverse and that its determinant must therefore equal zero. Consequently, we can write the "characteristic determinant"

$$\begin{vmatrix} q + \lambda_1(1 - b_1 + v_1) & -\lambda_1 v_2 \\ -\lambda_2 v_1 & q + \lambda_2(1 - b_2 + v_2) \end{vmatrix} = 0$$

and when we evaluate this determinant, we get the "characteristic equation"

$$q^2 + [\lambda_1(1 - b_1 + v_1) + \lambda_2(1 - b_2 + v_2)]q + \lambda_1\lambda_2\Delta = 0$$

where $\Delta$ is the "determinant of coefficients." The value of this determinant is already familiar from the appendix to Chapter 11, namely

$$\Delta = \begin{vmatrix} 1 - b_1 + v_1 & -v_2 \\ -v_1 & 1 - b_2 + v_2 \end{vmatrix} = (1 - b_1 + v_1)(1 - b_2 + v_2) - v_1 v_2$$

Stability of equilibrium requires the characteristic roots to be negative. This condition would obtain if all the coefficients of the characteristic equation were positive since if this were the case, no positive value of $q$ could possibly satisfy the equation. Consequently the system would be stable if both

$$\lambda_1(1 - b_1 + v_1) + \lambda_2(1 - b_2 + v_2)$$

and

$$(1 - b_1 + v_1)(1 - b_2 + v_2) - v_1 v_2$$

were positive.

In the appendix to Chapter 11 we merely assumed that $\Delta$ was positive. Stability analysis now proves that this is a necessary condition for a system that is dynamically stable.

## APPENDIX TO CHAPTER 13:
## NEOCLASSICAL GROWTH ECONOMICS

Neoclassical growth theory has three building blocks. First, there is a saving function that usually makes saving proportional to income. Accordingly, we can write

$$S = (1 - b)Y \tag{13-1}$$

where $1 - b$ is the fraction of income saved. Second, there is a labor supply function that incorporates the assumption that the labor supply is exogenous and grows at a constant rate over time. Therefore

$$N = N_0 e^{nt} \tag{13-2}$$

where $N_0$ is the supply of labor in some arbitrarily chosen initial period ($t = 0$ in this case), and $n$ is the rate of growth. Finally, there is a production function which in the simpler models is of the Cobb-Douglas form

$$Y = AK^a N^{1-a} \tag{13-3}$$

The term $A$ is the index of technical change and is assumed to grow at a constant rate. Consequently, the production function may be written more explicitly as

$$Y = A_0 e^{rt} K^a N^{1-a} \tag{13-4}$$

Full employment is assumed to exist at all times, so that investment is assumed automatically to equal full-employment saving.

Before we proceed further, readers should remind themselves from the discussion of the text that the parameters $a$ and $1 - a$ represent the respective relative shares of capital and labor in the national product and that their respective marginal products are

$$\frac{\partial Y}{\partial K} = aA \left(\frac{K}{N}\right)^{a-1} = a \frac{Y}{K}$$

$$\frac{\partial Y}{\partial N} = (1 - a)A \left(\frac{K}{N}\right)^{a} = (1 - a) \frac{Y}{N}$$

By differentiating Eq. (13–4) with respect to time we get

$$\frac{dY}{dt} = rY + \frac{aAK^aN^{1-a}}{K} \frac{dK}{dt} + (1 - a) \frac{AK^aN^{1-a}}{N} \frac{dN}{dt}$$

and when we divide both sides of this expression by $Y$, we obtain

$$y = r + ak + (1 - a)n \tag{13–5}$$

where $y$, $r$, $k$, and $n$ are the rates of growth of output, technical change, capital, and labor, respectively.

Long-run equilibrium (golden age) growth is a situation in which all variables grow at a constant exponential rate or they do not grow at all. Thus in addition to the labor supply function we must have

$$Y = Y_0 e^{yt} \tag{13–6}$$

$$K = K_0 e^{kt} \tag{13–7}$$

$$I = I_0 e^{it} \tag{13–8}$$

where, again, lower case letters represent growth rates. As we have seen, the rates of growth of the labor force and of technical change are assumed to be determined exogenously. The other growth rates remain to be calculated.

Net investment is the growth in capital stock. Therefore the derivative with respect to time of Eq. (13–7) must be equivalent to Eq. (13–8), and we therefore must have

$$I_0 e^{it} = kK_0 e^{kt}$$

Similarly, since saving equals investment, we can use Eq. (13–6) in combination with the saving function, Eq. (13–1), to write

$$(1 - b)Y_0 e^{yt} = I_0 e^{it} = kK_0 e^{kt} \tag{13–9}$$

If Eq. (13–9) is to hold for all values of $t$, it must be the case that $y$, $i$, and $k$ are all equal. Thus output, investment, and capital all grow at the same rate under conditions of long-run equilibrium growth. Using this result to replace $k$ by $y$ in Eq. (13–5), we get

$$y = \frac{r}{1 - a} + n \tag{13–10}$$

which specifies the value of the equilibrium growth rate and shows that it is an increasing function of the rate of technical progress and the rate of population growth.

Let us now derive the golden rule, namely, the condition under which per capita consumption is maximized. Dividing both sides of the production function by $N$ gives per capita output

$$\frac{Y}{N} = A \left(\frac{K}{N}\right)^a \tag{13-11}$$

Since investment is the growth of capital and since capital and output grow at the same rate, we can write per capita investment as

$$\frac{I}{N} = y \frac{K}{N} \tag{13-12}$$

Using Eqs. (13–11) and (13–12) we can write per capita consumption as the difference between per capita output and per capita investment. Consequently, we have

$$\frac{C}{N} = A \left(\frac{K}{N}\right)^a - y \frac{K}{N} \tag{13-13}$$

When we differentiate this equation with respect to $K/N$ and set the resulting derivative equal to zero, we obtain

$$aA \left(\frac{K}{N}\right)^{a-1} = y \tag{13-14}$$

Now the term on the left side of the equality is the marginal product of capital $\partial Y / \partial K$; and since this must equal the rate of interest in equilibrium, we see that per capita consumption is maximized when the capital-labor ratio is selected so as to make the rate of interest equal to the equilibrium growth rate.

Although the foregoing is one way of expressing the golden rule, there is an alternative way that is perhaps more useful for the purpose of guiding saving and investment policy. To derive this alternative, note that since $A(K/N)^a = Y/N$, Eq. (13–14) can be written

$$a \frac{Y/N}{K/N} = y$$

or

$$a \frac{Y}{N} = y \frac{K}{N}$$

However, $y(K/N)$ is per capita investment. Since this must equal per capita saving, we can use the saving function to write

$$a \frac{Y}{N} = y \frac{K}{N} = (1 - b) \frac{Y}{N}$$

from which it follows that

$$a = 1 - b$$

This last result represents the fundamental golden rule. Per capita consumption is maximized for all time when society saves and invests an amount equal to capital's share of output and consumes the remainder.

This discussion merely scratches the surface. Among other interesting questions are the following: Is the golden age attainable? That is, will an economic system that is off the equilibrium path tend to get back on it, and how long will this take? What is the nature of technical change, and how can its rate of improvement be affected? How should depreciation of capital and embodied technical change be handled? What happens if factor substitution possibilities are severely limited? Interested readers may explore these topics by consulting a very excellent collection of papers edited by Stiglitz and Uzawa.[1] This collection has brought together the main strands of contemporary thinking about economic growth.

## APPENDIX TO CHAPTER 16:
## THE WAGE-ADJUSTMENT MODEL

The model which underlies the analysis of inflationary recession of Chapter 16 is the basic Keynesian model which was presented in Chapter 10 and in the appendix to that chapter. For convenience of reference we write the model again here:

$$Y = C + I + G \tag{16-1}$$

$$C = \bar{C} + b(Y - T) \qquad 0 < b < 1 \tag{16-2}$$

$$I = \bar{I} + ai \qquad a < 0 \tag{16-3}$$

$$m = \bar{m} + kY + ci \qquad k > 0 \qquad c < 0 \tag{16-4}$$

$$Y = uN^\lambda \qquad 0 < \lambda < 1 \tag{16-5}$$

$$\frac{w}{p} = \lambda u N^{\lambda-1} = \lambda \frac{Y}{N} \tag{16-6}$$

Equations (16–1) to (16–3) require no comment except to note that all variables are expressed in real terms. It should be noted that in the monetary equilibrium, Eq. (16–4), the real value of the money supply $m$ replaces the $M/p$ of Chapter 10. Implicit in this formulation is that the monetary authority adjusts the nominal quantity of money when the price level changes in a way that maintains a constant real value of money supply. This is, to be sure, a gratuitous assumption and is made here both because it simplifies the mathematics and because it provides a mathematical treatment that is consistent with the diagrams of the text. Equation (16–5), finally, is the short-run production function, and Eq. (16–6) is the profit-maximizing relation which equates the real wage rate with the marginal product of labor.

It is possible to reduce the number of equations and variables by a process of successive substitution. The variables of primary concern in Chapter 16 are

---

[1] J. L. Stiglitz and H. Uzawa, *Readings in the Modern Theory of Economic Growth,* Massachusetts Institute of Technology Press, Cambridge, Mass., 1969.

the levels of employment and the level of prices. The substitution procedure therefore preserves these as endogenous variables, together with the rate of interest, while eliminating the others. The equations may therefore be compressed into the three equations

$$(1 - b)uN^\lambda \qquad\qquad - ai = \bar{C} + \bar{I} + G - bT \qquad\qquad (16\text{--}7)$$

$$p\lambda u N^{\lambda-1} \qquad\qquad = w \qquad\qquad (16\text{--}8)$$

$$+ ci = m - \bar{m} \qquad\qquad (16\text{--}9)$$

In inspecting these equations, note that care has been taken to place all the endogenous variables, $N$, $i$, and $p$, on the left side of the equations and all the exogenous variables, $G$, $T$, $m$, and the money wage $w$ on the right side. Equation (16–7) was obtained by combining Eqs. (16–1) to (16–3) and then using the production function (16–5) to eliminate $Y$. Equation (16–8) is the profit-maximizing condition, and Eq. (16–9) is the monetary equilibrium relation with $Y$ again replaced by use of the production function.

As a consequence of the production function which incorporates the property of positive, but diminishing, returns, the model is not linear, and an explicit solution is therefore difficult to obtain. However, the model will be linear in the derivatives, and we therefore proceed by differentiating the three equations totally with respect to all variables. The result, written as a matrix equation, is

$$\begin{bmatrix} (1-b)(w_0/p_0) & 0 & -a \\ (\lambda-1)(w_0/p_0) & \lambda Y_0/p_0 & 0 \\ k(w_0/p_0) & 0 & c \end{bmatrix} \begin{bmatrix} dN \\ dp \\ di \end{bmatrix} = \begin{bmatrix} dG - b\,dT \\ (N_0/p_0)\,dw \\ dm \end{bmatrix} \qquad (16\text{--}10)$$

where the subscript 0 denotes the preexisting equilibrium values.

In order to obtain a solution for the vector of endogenous variables, $dN$, $dp$, and $di$, it is necessary to invert the left-hand matrix of coefficients. The result is

$$\begin{bmatrix} dN \\ dp \\ di \end{bmatrix} = \frac{1}{\Delta} \begin{bmatrix} \lambda c Y_0/p_0 & 0 & a\lambda Y_0/p_0 \\ c(1-\lambda)(w_0/p_0) & [c(1-b)+ak](w_0/p_0) & a(1-\lambda)(w_0/p_0) \\ -\lambda k w_0 Y_0/p_0^2 & 0 & (1-b)\lambda w_0 Y_0/p_0^2 \end{bmatrix}$$

$$\times \begin{bmatrix} dG - b\,dT \\ (w_0/p_0)\,dw \\ dm \end{bmatrix} \qquad\qquad (16\text{--}11)$$

where $\Delta$ is the determinant of the coefficient matrix and is equal to

$$\Delta = \frac{w_0 Y_0 \lambda}{p_0^2} [c(1-b)+ak] < 0 \qquad\qquad (16\text{--}12)$$

It is evident from inspecting the inverse matrix that a rise in government purchases raises employment, the price level, and the rate of interest. A rise in taxes does the opposite. An increase in the real value of the money supply raises employment and the price level but lowers the rate of interest. An increase in the money wage rate, finally, raises the price level but does not affect the rate of interest or the level of employment. This curious result follows from the restriction which we arbitrarily built into the model that the change in the price level is not permitted to affect the real value of the money supply. If, instead, the nominal money supply had been held constant when the wage rate rises, the result would have been to raise the price level, to reduce the real value of the money supply, to raise the rate of interest, and to reduce the levels of output and employment.

The wage-adjustment model of Chapter 16 was constructed on the assumption that a rise in taxes would cause the money wage rate to increase. Therefore, we now add the wage-adjustment equation

$$dw = \epsilon \left( \frac{p_0}{N_0} \right) dT \tag{16-13}$$

where $\epsilon$ is the "wage-adjustment coefficient" which may vary between 0 and $+1$, depending upon the degree to which a wage increase offsets a tax increase. This wage-adjustment relation may now be used to replace $dw$ in the vector of exogenous changes, which therefore becomes

$$\begin{bmatrix} dG - b\, dT \\ \epsilon\, dT \\ dm \end{bmatrix} \tag{16-14}$$

To derive the slope of the iso-employment function of Chapter 16 we permit $m$ and $T$ to vary and use Eq. (16–11) combined with the new vector of exogenous changes (16–14) to calculate the change in employment. The result is

$$\Delta dN = -\lambda bc \left( \frac{Y_0}{p_0} \right) dT + a\lambda \left( \frac{Y_0}{p_0} \right) dm$$

To get the slope of the iso-employment curve it is now only necessary to set $dN = 0$ and to solve the foregoing expression for $dm/dT$. The result is

$$\left( \frac{dm}{dT} \right)_n = \frac{bc}{a} > 0 \tag{16-15}$$

which is positive and independent of the wage-adjustment coefficient because, as discussed in the text, a rise in wages affects employment through its effects on the real value of the money supply.

The slope of the iso-price level function may similarly be calculated by use of Eqs. (16–11) and (16–14). The result in this case is

$$\left( \frac{dm}{dT} \right)_p = \frac{bc(\lambda - 1) + [c(1 - b) + ak]\epsilon}{a(\lambda - 1)} \gtrless 0 \tag{16-16}$$

which may be greater or less than zero. It is important to note that the slope of the iso-price level curve diminishes as the wage-adjustment coefficient increases. It is important to note also that if wage adjustment is absent Eq.

(16–16) reduces to

$$\left(\frac{dm}{dT}\right)_p = \frac{bc}{a}$$

which is the same as the slope of the iso-employment function as shown by Eq. (16–15). Consequently, in the standard model where tax changes are assumed to be unaccompanied by wage changes, tax changes and money supply changes are perfect substitutes in terms of their relative effects on employment and the price level. In the wage-adjustment model, on the other hand, wage adjustment means that for a given tax increase the increase in the money supply needed to prevent the price level from rising is less than the increase needed to prevent unemployment.

As suggested in Chapter 16, this circumstance provides tax policy with a comparative advantage in securing full employment and monetary policy with a comparative advantage in securing price stability. It was suggested also that this implied a pairing of the instruments to the targets in accordance with their comparative advantage. Readers may now wish to use the tools which were developed in the appendix to Chapter 12 to show that the pairing rule is nothing more than a stability condition.

# INDEX